From the painting by Sir Joshua Reynolds

SAMUEL JOHNSON

The Lake Library Edition

LIFE OF SAMUEL JOHNSON

BY

JAMES BOSWELL

ABRIDGED AND EDITED

BY

HERBERT VAUGHAN ABBOTT

PROFESSOR OF ENGLISH LITERATURE, SMITH COLLEGE

SCOTT, FORESMAN AND COMPANY

CHICAGO   ATLANTA   NEW YORK

Printed in the United States of America

PREFACE

No abridgment can hope to do full justice to its original. In the pages of Boswell's *Life of Johnson* there is a desultory and leisurely gravity, a quaint turn for speculation, a mingling of complacency and sociability, smacking of the times, of which perhaps this volume gives no hint. The truth is, it has a different aim. Its almost sole purpose has been to bring out what is distinctive and of force in Dr. Johnson's own intellectual powers and moral character.

A close observer and an industrious recorder of what he himself saw and heard, Boswell was sometimes, where verification was impossible, invitingly credulous, and could easily be fooled with hearsay. There are passages in which he seems to have been the ready victim of witty friends, and certainly into the early life of Johnson he has introduced old wives' tales, which have made what must have been a crude and harsh childhood into one puerile and inane. These opportunities for misleading I have been willing pretty largely to omit. A reader unquestionably can make due allowance for them, but just as surely, a busy reader, curious only to know what manner of man Johnson really was, can reasonably be spared them.

Boswell is perhaps as unjust to himself in his *Life of Johnson* as he is to his subject. He was a preposterous mimic of other men's manners; he was a sedulous seeker of their advice; but he was not essentially servile. He persisted in his own course, regardless of advice, though it was often the course of folly. He reminds one of William Blake's apothegm: "If a fool would persist in his folly, he would become wise." Boswell was not wise; but at least he retained to the end of his life the force of his own individuality. This fact, hardly discernible in his masterpiece, but evident enough in his lesser writings, I hope I have illustrated clearly in the notes.

I have used them also to gather what I have found most significant of Johnson from the anecdotes of his various con-

temporaries as well as from his own public writings and private
letters. They serve, too, a third purpose. Johnson apparently
in boyhood was little more than a bookworm. It was by sheer
will power and with manly conviction that he forced himself to
grapple with the hard facts of his experience and get their
intrinsic worth without evasion and with as little self-delusion as
can perhaps be hoped for by fallible man. When he had pretty
much found himself in his struggle, fortune sent him a number
of new friends and acquaintances whose sheltered lives and
superficial habits of thinking had given them an easy, if not
glib, optimism, some vanity over their own liberalism, and a
somewhat callous complacency over what they thought their
sympathy with the rights of man. They dined him, flattered
him, cross-questioned him, and aired their views, somewhat
tentatively, before him. He was pleased, diverted, and at the
same time frequently incensed beyond endurance. These companions and annoyers I have tried to describe faithfully, though
briefly, in the notes. None of the easy generalizations with
which they were satisfied contented Johnson. If he seems often
to contradict himself in contradicting them, it is well to bear
in mind that to deny one superficial proposition is not necessarily
to accept its equally glib opposite.

No one can concern himself long with Johnson without recog-
nizing one's debt to the labors of Birkbeck Hill, the most delightful and illuminating of annotators. This volume, I hope, will
turn some readers to the thirteen volumes in which he has so
fully and sympathetically edited the Life, the Letters, the Lives
of the Poets, and what he has well called *Johnsonian Miscellanies*. For, after all, the most flattering as well as the best use
that one can make of an abridgment is to use it not as substitute
for the original but as an introduction to it.

                                        HERBERT VAUGHAN ABBOTT

Northampton, Massachusetts,
      November 15, 1923.

CONTENTS

A BRIEF BIBLIOGRAPHY

To list all the works which have been consulted in the preparation of this volume would require more space than is either possible or desirable. I have, therefore, noted only those books on which a Johnsonian recruit might wisely make a beginning. They will suggest many others, and those still others; and so will open the door for indefinite research:

BOSWELL, JAMES: An Account of Corsica, the Journal of a Tour to That Island, and Memoirs of Pascal Paoli. *1 vol.*

BOSWELL, JAMES: Letters Addressed to the Rev. W. J. Temple. *1 vol.*

BOSWELL, JAMES: Life of Johnson (including Boswell's Journal of a Tour to the Hebrides), ed. by George Birkbeck Hill. *6 vols.*

D'ARBLAY, FANNY BURNEY, MME.: Diary and Letters, ed. by her niece, Charlotte Barrett, with Preface and Notes by Austin Dobson. *6 vols.*

JOHNSON, SAMUEL: Lives of the Poets, ed. by George Birkbeck Hill. *3 vols.*

JOHNSON, SAMUEL: Letters, ed. by George Birkbeck Hill. *2 vols.*

JOHNSON, SAMUEL: [In his works] Lives of Boerhaave, Sir Thomas Browne, Edward Cave, Sir Francis Drake, the King of Prussia; Plan of the English Dictionary, Preface to the English Dictionary, Preface to Shakespeare; Prologue on the Opening of the Drury Lane Theater; London; the Vanity of Human Wishes; Journey to the Western Islands of Scotland; Review of a Free Beginning into the Nature and Origin of Evil; The Rambler.

JOHNSONIAN MISCELLANIES: ed. by George Birkbeck Hill. *2 vols.*

PIOZZI, HESTER LYNCH SALUSBURY, MRS.: Autobiography, Letters, and Literary Remains, ed. by A. Hayward. *1 vol.*

RALEIGH, SIR WALTER ALEXANDER: Six Essays on Johnson. Oxford. 1910. *1 vol.*

TINKER, CHAUNCEY BREWSTER: Young Boswell. 1922. The Atlantic Monthly Press. *1 vol.*

INTRODUCTION

I

JAMES BOSWELL

Milton's famous remark that "a good book is the precious lifeblood of a master spirit" seems, of course, a violent exaggeration when we think of the many excellent books of information that come out every year, serve their purpose, and then give way to later knowledge. But perhaps it tells us more clearly than any other phrase what it is which makes us set some books apart from these and treasure them as pure literature, as preserving for posterity the "seasoned life of man."

It is evidently of this personal element, this "lifeblood," that Goethe is thinking when he urges us "to seek out for what is internal and peculiar in a book which particularly interests us, and to weigh in what relation it stands to our own inner nature and how far by that vitality our own is excited and rendered faithful."

This search is preëminently the true, the ideal work of the critic and the biographer. Boswell, alas! was not the stuff of which fidelity is made, nor was he capable of a scrupulous weighing of his own inner nature, but in other respects he continually tried to do with living men, with Voltaire, with Rousseau, with Dr. Johnson, with Paoli, what Goethe would have us do with books. He was eager to get at what was "internal and peculiar in them."

Apart from this, though brisk and bustling enough to be always interesting, he was not so important as to be famous. The son and heir of a Scotch gentleman, Lord Auchinleck, with a great estate and six hundred tenants on his future domains, he could look forward, if he chose, to becoming, sooner or later, a country magnate of first importance in his neighborhood; where, with the help of a little imagination, he could play Scottish chieftain, but he was restive, he was eager for the capitals of Europe; for a little while he thought of being a soldier, dropped the idea, made the Grand Tour, as far as Rome, studied law and later practiced it, ventured into the wilds of Corsica for a few months, advertised himself as the "Corsican Boswell," flirted outrageously, married a cousin, made a rather trying husband, a somewhat better father, was good to his tenants, wrote one entertaining book besides his life of Johnson, drank too hard, and died in 1795, at the age of fifty-five.

His only claim to distinction is that he was the most ardent and persistent of biographers. He would engage in any maneuver to gain a little more insight into the prejudices, the point of view, the passions of any man he accounted great. He poured out confidences in order to win confidences in return, was often adulatory, often impudent, made himself an object of advice, or a butt for wit. He was pleased with being "a man of feeling," as the phrase ran then, and would do anything to observe the feelings of others and record them in his notebooks.

II

Johnson and Boswell in Contrast

"And yet" . . . . Dr. Johnson once made the remark—the reader will run across it somewhere in this volume—"a fallible being will fail somewhere." It is as true of biographers as of any other race of mortals, of Boswell, perhaps the greatest of them, as of any other biographer. An eager listener, a vivid reporter, he could pare down a conversation to what really counted and yet leave it lifelike, but he was never close enough, never resolute enough in his thinking to follow with complete understanding Dr. Johnson's way of reasoning. Emotions he could always understand far better than principles, he had nothing of Johnson's sturdiness of character, his own point of view toward life was altogether different—more different than he knew. Some of these differences it is worth our while to investigate a little further.

Today so many people believe that the human race is continually on the upward trend, is slowly but surely advancing toward perfection, that it is difficult to imagine a state of civilization when such a notion was so rare as not to be worth noting.

Yet such seems to have been the case.   In the sixteenth century, for instance, most educated men saw the history of the race as the rise and fall of kingdoms, the gradual development and then the sudden ruin of one great civilization after another; and the object of the most far-sighted was, not to share in the general progress of the race, for to their thinking there was no such progress, but to gain what little stability they could for themselves and their descendants from an uncertain and unstable world.   Such a man if he were conscientious would try to make a true man of himself, establish a character for his family, and add what he could to the welfare of his country or community. But he never argued on the assumption that there is a universal good time coming.

In the eighteenth century, in the days of Johnson and Boswell, we see something of a transition from these views I have just described to something more like our modern fashion of thinking.   Already there were a good many men, of a sort of liberality of view, who were beginning first to wish, then to hope, then to entertain the idea, which sometimes ripened into a conviction, that with a little more knowledge, a few changes in government and social customs, a reasonable increase in general prosperity, the world might become a very perfect world.   James Boswell liked to "live pleasant," and this was a pleasant doctrine to pick up or to drop, according to convenience.   Buoyant, rather easily captivated by novelties and popular vogues, full of notions that flattered him rather than of convictions, he floated along on a general current of optimism.

Dr. Johnson was of a different temper.   He had to judge what the mass of men were likely to do by the sort of things they had done.   He did not think society unimprovable, but neither did he think it perfectible.   Civilization, men's habits of living in the mass, he thought pretty well rooted in human nature.   "No, sir," he once said, "let fanciful men do as they will, depend upon it, it is difficult to disturb the system of life." With his fellow-men he was companionable; he aimed to understand them with the same sincerity with which he aimed to understand himself; he was accustomed to make liberal allowance for them, but it was not his practice to idealize them or to imagine that they belonged to a race capable of perfection. Johnson had what Walter Bagehot and William Hazlitt, before him, have called an experiencing nature. He took things to heart. He scrutinized and sifted, he weighed and considered; he went through the processes of observation and reflection. So he was schooled into a point of view, as consistent as experience and a solid, though tumultuous, character could make it, toward the inconsistencies of human nature, its prejudices, its pretexts, its way of making its reasons fit its wishes. Many times he seems to be contradicting himself when he is simply reminding some abstract reasoner of the contradictions that honest observers will always find in life.

No doubt Boswell took to life as a duck to water. But not much of it soaked in. He shook off one experience to plunge more easily into the next. He sought out famous men, one after another, asked their advice to draw them out, and put it all down in his notebooks as an interesting record of the way their minds worked. For this reason he was gay with the wicked John Wilkes, melancholy and "romantic" with the sentimental Rousseau, pious and serious with the doggedly honest Dr. Johnson. He loved crowded taverns, rushing streets, and theaters, lighted by torches at night. He took to the fashionable habit of praising the innocent Indian and his simple life in the forest. He thought himself respectable and substantial in defending such great vested interests as the slave trade. He grew eloquent over the charms of universal liberty. Qualification, too often, seemed to him to be contradiction; chasing one enthusiasm, and then another, to be the same thing as leading a consistent life.

Modern publishers have a habit of covering a book with a jacket of paper, on which they print such glowing praise of the book within that it sometimes turns modest readers against it. Boswell was a little like such a jacket. In this fashion, he grows superlative over Dr. Johnson's *Dictionary of the English Language*. But Johnson, himself, was not superlative. Whatever his thought when he first undertook his task, as he toiled over it, he realized that "everything in life is set either above or below our faculties," that a free people are, fortunately, too big to endure a final authority, even though he be only a dictionary maker, that words must perpetually change their meanings with the circumstances which they describe, so that dictionaries are as imperfect as watches; if the worst is better than none, the best cannot be expected to go quite true; that "definition," indeed, "is not the province of man." A lexicographer he whimsically defines in his own dictionary as a "harmless drudge." And yet with it all, he had learned to like such "muddling work." So, pretty skeptical as to the exact worth of what he accomplishes, he plays his part as best he can and, as he calls it, drives on the "system of life."

How Boswell preferred to drive is pretty well symbolized by a little incident in his career. He was coaching with two companions, as exuberant as himself, from the Hague to Rotterdam. One of them, says Mr. Tinker in his delightful volume on "Young Boswell," seized the reins from a Dutch blockhead who held them and showed him how a party of young Britons expected to travel. Boswell said he drove so hard "that the very moles came above ground to look at him." And Boswell liked it.

Johnson used sometimes to refer to himself as an old struggler. He fought not only against hard circumstances and his own physical infirmities but against his own doubts and passions. There is no finer passage in Boswell than the last pages of this volume, where he describes these contending passions, unless it be where he compares the struggle against them to that of a gladiator with the mad beasts of the arena. Out of this tumult grew Dr. Johnson's philosophy of life. It was very like the old philosophy of Sir Roger de Coverley, "Much may be said on both sides," but reasserted with the most zealous intensity. It included a great desire for the right, and a recognition that the exact right was difficult to find, a passionate dislike of slipping into extremes and a contempt for wabbling and evasion. It was often suspense of judgment without peace of mind. It was compromise with others without disloyalty to oneself. It was keeping an even keel in a tempestuous sea. This was the sort of unstable equilibrium that Johnson constantly maintained through more than half a century. Only by trying to live and relive it with him can we fully understand it.

There are, no doubt, inconsistencies in Dr. Johnson. Passions will sometimes break out, friendship or compassion will color his views on occasion, and indolence will have its day. Men grow, too; they sometimes mellow and ripen into a fuller recognition of their own philosophy and its practical demands upon them. At thirty-nine, a man, eager for stimulating social conversation, may lose all patience with anyone who will "shuffle cards and rattle dice from noon to midnight without tracing any new idea in his mind." At sixty, he may realize that a great many people have not much capacity for new ideas; he may grow tolerant of the little knots grouped in partnerships and drawn together in rivalries over something, not very important, but which, at least, they can understand. He may find that card playing after all "generates kindness and consolidates society." A man may hold that giving employment is better than giving charity and yet when passing a shilling to a beggar and asked why, may respond with sturdy frankness, "to enable him to beg on." A man may wax indignant over an attempt to influence Parliament through petitions signed by all sorts of people under all sorts of pressure, and yet when a criminal's life is at stake, be moved into thinking that a petition in his behalf of twenty thousand signatures should have some weight. He may even be excused for the lack of all patience when he exclaims to a gentleman who, he thought, made little allowance for the temptations of life, "Sir, you are so grossly ignorant of human nature as not to know that a man may be very sincere in good principles without having good practice."

But most of Johnson's apparent inconsistencies, or what Boswell guesses to be such, prove on a little investigation to be among his most thorough and consistent views of men and society. One day, for example, in the Harwich stage coach, Johnson fell in with, and then fell out with, a fat, elderly gentlewoman, who, being an uncompromising Protestant, bitterly attacked the inquisition. Johnson defended it. And Boswell's only comment is that the Doctor could talk on any side of any subject. Of course he could; and equally, of course, it was his very sincerity which prompted him to see that every side should have its due. Here was a question the old lady had raised, without being aware of it, between the right to freedom and the right of protection against the freedoms of others. Johnson often pondered on it. "The danger of unbounded liberty," he was later to write in his life of Milton, "and the danger of bounding it, have produced a problem in the science of government, which human understanding seems hitherto unable to solve. If nothing may be published but what civil authority shall have previously approved, power must always be the standard of truth; if every dreamer of innovations may propagate his projects, there can be no settlement; if every murmurer at government may diffuse discontent, there can be no peace; and if every skeptic in theology may teach his follies, there can be no religion."

This same problem he has recognized more pithily, more wittily in the words: "Sir, I have got no further than this: Every man has a right to utter what he thinks truth and every other man has a right to knock him down for it." Of course, a man who can sympathize with both sides of a controversy to this degree can hardly have convictions so one-sided that he can pound a face or use a thumb-screw in their defense. The most he can claim for himself is to say, as Johnson, indeed, has said: "Sir, I considered myself as entrusted with a certain portion of truth. I have given my opinion sincerely; let them show me where they think me wrong." And this in almost every case is where Johnson personally stands.

Again, on the duel, Boswell thinks he detects Dr. Johnson in an inconsistency. But here, too, he misses the true ground of Dr. Johnson's opinion. It is the business of society, Johnson thinks, either by law or custom, to prescribe the tests by which men may settle their quarrels and yet remain civilized. Its tests are none of them perfect, none of them ideal. It has tried, not very successfully, to draw up mutual understandings for the decent prosecution of war; it has established a long line of rather complicated precedents for determining when a man may use fatal weapons in the defense of his life. It has invented a method, by no means infallible, of trial by jury. In Johnson's day, through public opinion it offered to men of a certain station in society still another method, more imperfect even

than trial by jury, the punctilious code of the duel, by which
a man, if insulted, might vindicate his courage and so his honor.
A man who refused this test was looked upon with a certain
degree of ignominy. If, to be a consistent Christian, a man
must interpret every text of the Bible literally, if he must hate
his father and mother, if he must give to everyone that asketh
of him, if he must never go to law with a fellow-Christian, if he
must never kill, either in war or peace, he must regard most of
the tests that secular society offers him as evils. But Johnson
was not a literalist. With the great mass of stanch Christians
he believed that the follower of the gospel could consistently
defend his own life, and what should be still more precious to
him, his wife, his family, his country, his honor. Civilized
communities tried to offer such a man a civilized means of
doing so. A man of character and responsibility would abide
by its terms. No doubt these principles are no longer applicable
to the duel, for it is no longer an accepted test. Nor is there
any evidence that Dr. Johnson would revive it. But if the
reader discovers that he wavered more than once on the general principle I have outlined above, he will have discovered
more than I have.

A more thoughtful man than Boswell has accused Johnson
of "loose talk" on another subject. It regards the way eighteenth
century England treated its criminals. A great number of
crimes besides that of murder were punishable by death. The
forger of a note, the thief of some shillings, like the assassin
of a whole family, was led in a procession through the streets, a
disorderly crowd of curiosity-seekers tagging after him, to the
public gallows, and there hanged before the mob. Dr. Johnson
was a humane man, but he wished for a reasonably stable state
of society and was willing to see it maintained by the punishment
and, if necessary, even by the death of the offender. But the
execution of a petty criminal, surely, was not necessary. The
poor fellow did not need to die. Such disproportionate penalties
still further hardened the callous and led the weak, by sympathy
with the victim of injustice, into sympathy with his crime.
Unfortunately, English laws did not grow more merciful in
Johnson's day. But the administration of the law took a new

turn. The procession was given up and the gallows removed from its commanding position in the public street to the comparative quiet of the prison yard. Again, let us remember that Dr. Johnson was, in his own way, an honest as well as a humane man. To remedy the injustice of disproportionate punishments by hiding them away was not to his mind. As for just ones, he had an understanding above that of most men, of the dullness, the daily grind of the hopelessly poor. He would not deprive them of any relief or pleasure, however distasteful to more fortunate men, until he could furnish them with better. And he had not much hope for better. He did not begrudge them in their hunger the smell of their ill-ventilated kitchens; himself, a total abstainer for most of his life, he did not begrudge them their gin. He would not take from even the most sordid murderer perhaps the only gleam of prominence and importance he would ever have; nor, if a man must be hanged, rob the dull multitude of their brutal holiday. He would make life as congenial as possible to the grossest of men. "The public," he exclaimed peevishly, "was gratified by a procession, the criminal was supported by it. Why is all this to be swept away?" Many things may be wrong about this reasoning; it may be based on false assumptions; it may leave some important matters wholly out of account; but could anything be more consistent with itself?

There are a few other points on which we need to guard ourselves against forming too hasty impressions of Johnson from Boswell's lively and picturesque representation of him. What man really is at all like his mimics? And Boswell was, often consciously, sometimes in spite of himself, a mimic. Even in the manner of expression he and Johnson bore no real resemblance. Boswell assumed an air of seriousness to which he was not entitled and for its sake often suppressed a relish of life that was in him. Johnson was serious, but the stress of his feeling sharpened his seriousness into something keen and penetrating. He was intense, and he was a wit. Very rare are the times when Johnson was merely facetious. When a man is lively, wit is an irresistible plaything to cut with. When he is angry, indignant, passionate with moral principle, teased into uneasiness, as Johnson often was, wit is his readiest, keenest weapon. But whether in sport or in earnest, wit is always too sharp, too pointed, to be confounded with mere chatter. It always has something to say.

In some few matters, Johnson was dictatorial and dogmatic, but that is far from meaning that he was altogether pleased with himself or confident of his opinion. Cardinal Newman has somewhere suggested that we seldom take the trouble to say, "I am sure of anything, if no doubt of it has ever crossed our minds." And, we may add, the more positive we are in our words, the more evidence we give of our own uncertainty. Johnson's doubts were many. He had faith that God was infinitely good, but what could so imperfect a being as man know about the nature of infinite goodness? So, Johnson wearied himself trying to comprehend the incomprehensible. The differences of opinion among Christians unsettled him. Even the differences among different world religions did not leave him in peace. "You do not know," he once said, "what a Brahmin has to say for himself." He relished honest men, thinking men, the free exchange of genuine opinions, and yet there was no more than the simple truth in his confession: "Every man who attacks my belief diminishes in some degree my confidence in it, and therefore makes me uneasy; and I am angry with him who makes me uneasy."

There was one belief of which Dr. Johnson was so sure that he could afford to be complacent about it: "All rebellion," he once said with a smile, "is natural to man." But he himself had gradually learned not to be rebellious. He had fought his own way as much as any man. But how impossible that way would have been, had there been no laws, no constituted authorities, no money and no right to earn it and retain it, no mutual respect and deference, no feeling that a wife and children had any share in the respect due to the husband and father! Johnson had no great illusions about any particular wisdom in law-makers, about any inborn superiority in men of rank. He never courted them. He was sometimes intolerably vexed with them. But the man who climbs a peg in a social scale should respect the scale; the man who accepts support from civilized society should give it his support in return. Johnson's whole theory of society, his theory of *subordination* as he calls it, amounts pretty much to this: As long as men mean to enjoy all the conveniences of laws and kings and parliaments, of customs and social distinctions, let them pay for what they get by a square and manly loyalty. After all, this is not the theory to gratify a George III. It seems to make very honest company with the doctrine that all government depends on the consent of the governed.

There were an astonishing number of people in the London of Johnson's day, who, to quote his own phrase, "hung loose upon society." To the vices of these—the dissipated, the vagrant, the hand-to-mouth poor—Dr. Johnson was always lenient. How lenient appears best in Mrs. Thrale's anecdotes of him. It was another and very different class which caused him all his exasperation and made him sometimes harsh in speech. They were the men and women so comfortably off in mind and body that they never understood, they never tried, they only pretended, to understand the struggles of life, the temptations of poverty, the conflict with one's own doubts and passions, the stuff of which character and heroism are made. They considered themselves virtuous whenever they "felt good." They lazily trusted to impressions rather than to honest facts and hard-earned experience. Their very sentimentality prevented them from making true allowance for other men, because they never entered with intelligence into other men's minds and circumstances. They said to themselves, "I cannot bear to think such and so," and then thought as they pleased. This habit of mind Dr. Johnson denounced as *cant*, and yet some of his dearest friends, such as Boswell and Mrs. Thrale, were full of it.

There was another class of men, always few in number, and fewer than ever in the eighteenth century, of whose force and strength Dr. Johnson had no inkling; men so full of imagination and their own sense of beauty, and so eager to express it in sound or picture or words, that they could not if they would see the mere circumstances about them at all clearly and justly. The music of such men meant nothing to him; their pictures next to

nothing; he was too much of a reader not to be interested in verse
as well as prose, but what we usually think of today as a poetic
imagination meant very little.   When he wrote of poets, as he
often did, he brought to his task uprightness of character and
much practical good sense.   He described them as husbands,
fathers, neighbors, citizens, engagers in the transactions of life;
he tested their logic and consistency; he noted in their verse
those passages that chanced to fit helpfully into the collected
practical wisdom of the world.   But, after all, he was but a
lame critic.   Like them, perhaps like all great men, he was
astonishingly limited on some sides.   Like them, he had an
overpowering inner impulse.   But his impulse, unlike theirs,
drove him steadily on toward an understanding, an allowance,
an acceptance of the actual workaday world, with its com-
petitions, its discussions, its misunderstandings and reconcilia-
tions, its unforeseen good luck and bad.   In that sort of world
he made a place for himself.   There he preserved his sense of
obligation, his generosity, and his independence.   There "he
dogmatized and was contradicted and in this conflict of opinions
and sentiments he found delight."

Let us beware of trying to run off with the fruit of another
man's experience, second-hand.   Eighteenth century London
is not our problem, nor Dr. Johnson's temperament, the temperament we have to adjust to life.   Every new situation makes
its own challenge and the essence of every virtue consists in
our earning it for ourselves.   But another great buffeter with
life, Sir Walter Raleigh, has said: *"For conversation of particular greatness and dignity, there is nothing more noble and
glorious than to have felt the force of every fortune."*   Perhaps
some of that greatness and dignity we may find in the conversations of this volume.

BOSWELL'S LIFE OF JOHNSON

Samuel Johnson was born at Lichfield, in Staffordshire, on the 18th of September, N. S.* 1709. His father was Michael Johnson, of obscure extraction, who settled in Lichfield as a bookseller and stationer. His mother was Sarah Ford, descended of an ancient race of substantial yeomanry* in Warwickshire. They were well advanced in years when they married, and never had more than two children, both sons: Samuel, their first-born, and Nathanael,[1] who died in his twenty-fifth year.

Mr. Michael Johnson was a man of large and robust body, and of a strong and active mind; yet, as in the most solid rocks veins of unsound substance are often discovered, there was in him a mixture of that disease, the nature of which eludes the most minute inquiry, though the effects are well known to be a weariness of life, an unconcern about those things which agitate the greater part of mankind, and a general sensation of gloomy wretchedness. From him, then, his son inherited, with some other qualities, "a vile melancholy," which, in his too strong expression of any disturbance of mind, "made him mad all his life, at least not sober." Michael was, however, forced by the narrowness of his circumstances[2] to be very diligent in business, not only in his shop, but by occasionally resorting to several towns in the neighborhood. At that time booksellers' shops in the provincial towns of England

---

*See Glossary for all asterisks.

1. *Nathanael.* Exposed in some dishonesty, when twenty-four or thereabouts, he wrote to his mother: "I know not nor do I much care in what way of life I shall hereafter live, but this I know, it shall be an honest one, and that it can't be more unpleasant than some part of my life past." The letter is given in full by Aleyn Lyell Reade.

2. *Narrowness of his circumstances.* "My father could not bear to talk of his affairs, and my mother, being unacquainted with books, cared not to talk of anything else. Of business she had no distinct conception; and therefore her discourse was composed only of complaint, fear, and suspicion." *Johnson.*

were very rare, so that there was not one even in Birmingham, in which town old Mr. Johnson used to open a shop every market day. He was a pretty good Latin scholar,[1] and a citizen so creditable as to be made one of the magistrates of Lichfield; and, being a man of good sense, and skill in his trade, he acquired a reasonable share of wealth, of which however he afterwards lost the greatest part, by engaging unsuccessfully in a manufacture of parchment. He was a zealous high-church* man and royalist, and retained his attachment to the unfortunate house of Stuart, though he reconciled himself, by arguments of expediency and necessity, to take the oaths imposed by the prevailing power.

Young Johnson had the misfortune to be much afflicted[2] with the scrofula, or king's evil, which disfigured a countenance naturally well formed, and hurt his visual nerves so much that he did not see at all with one of his eyes, though its appearance was little different from that of the other. His mother, yielding to the superstitious notion, which, it is wonderful to think, prevailed so long in this country, as to the virtue of the regal touch, carried him to London, where he was actually touched by Queen Anne. Being asked if he could remember Queen Anne—he had, he said, "a confused, but somehow a sort of solemn recollection of a lady in diamonds, and a long black hood." I ventured to say to him, in allusion to the political principles in which he was educated, and of which he ever retained some odor, that "his mother had not carried him far enough; she should have taken him to Rome."[3]

He began to learn Latin with Mr. Hawkins, undermaster of Lichfield school, "a man," said he, "very skillful in his little way."

1. *Latin scholar.* A clergyman, writing from Trentham in 1716, says half-humorously of Michael: "Johnson, the Lichfield librarian, is now here; he propagates learning all over this diocese; and advanceth knowledge to its just height; all the clergy here are his pupils, and suck all they have from him."

2. *Much afflicted.* "I remember my Aunt Nath. Ford told me when I was about . . . years old that she would not have picked such a poor creature up in the street." *Johnson: Annals.*

3. *Rome.* For some time the home of the exiled Stuart court, which maintained, of course, that the "royal touch" inhered only in the Stuarts and not in the sovereigns who had displaced them on the throne.

He then rose to be under the care of Mr. Hunter, the head-master, who, according to his account, "was very severe."[1] "He used," said he, "to beat us unmercifully; and he did not distinguish between ignorance and negligence. He would ask a boy a question, and if he did not answer it, he would beat him, without considering whether he had an opportunity of knowing how to answer it."

Dr. Percy,[2] the Bishop of Dromore, who was long intimately acquainted with Dr. Johnson, and has preserved a few anecdotes concerning him, informs me, that "when a boy he was im-moderately fond of reading romances of chivalry,[3] and he retained his fondness for them through life; "so that," adds his Lordship, "spending part of a summer at my parsonage house in the country, he chose for his regular reading the old Spanish ro-mance of *Felixmarte of Hyrcania*, in folio, which he read quite through. Yet I have heard him attribute to these extravagant fictions that unsettled turn of mind which prevented his ever fixing in any profession." [Johnson] used to mention one curious instance of his casual reading, when but a boy. Having imagined that his brother had hid some apples behind a large folio upon an upper shelf in his father's shop, he climbed up to search for them. There were no apples; but the large folio proved to be *Petrarch*, whom he had seen mentioned, in some preface, as one of the restorers of learning. His curiosity having been thus excited, he sat down with avidity, and read a great part

1. *Very severe.* "Abating his brutality, he was a very good master." *Johnson, 1772.* "No science can be communicated by mortal creatures without attention from the scholar; no attention can be obtained from children without the infliction of pain; and pain is never remembered without resentment." *Johnson, quoted by Mrs. Piozzi.* "I would rather have the rod to be the general terror to all than tell a child if you do thus or thus you will be more esteemed than your brothers and sisters." *Johnson, 1773.*

2. *Dr. Percy.* Thomas Percy (1729-1811), collector of ballads. "These barbarous productions of unpolished ages," as he called them, he refined and civilized to suit the fastidious taste of his day, and pub-lished in 1765 as the *Reliques of Ancient Poetry.* Hannah More called him "quite a sprightly modern instead of a rusty antique."

3. *Romances of chivalry.* Of Don Quixote, he writes, "When we laugh, our hearts inform us that he is not more ridiculous than our-selves, except that he tells what we have only thought."

of the book. What he read during these two years, he told me, was not works of mere amusement, "but all literature, sir, all ancient writers, all manly."

He went to Oxford and was entered a commoner* of Pembroke College on the 31st of October, 1728, being then in his nineteenth year. While he was at Lichfield in the college vacation of the year 1729, he felt himself overwhelmed with a gloom and despair which made existence misery. He told Mr. Paradise that he was sometimes so languid and inefficient that he could not distinguish the hour upon the town clock. Johnson, upon the first violent attack of this disorder, strove to overcome it by forcible exertions. He frequently walked to Birmingham and back again, and tried many other expedients, but all in vain. His distress became so intolerable that he applied to Dr. Swinfen, physician in Lichfield, his godfather, and put into his hands a state of his case, written in Latin. Dr. Swinfen was so much struck with this paper that he showed it to several people. His daughter, Mrs. Desmoulins, who was many years humanely supported in Dr. Johnson's house in London, told me, that upon his discovering that Dr. Swinfen had communicated his case, he was so much offended that he was never afterwards fully reconciled to him. He indeed had reason to be offended; for though Dr. Swinfen's motive was good, he inconsiderately exposed a complaint of his young friend and patient, which, in the superficial opinion of the generality of mankind, is attended with contempt and disgrace.

I am aware that Johnson himself was too ready to call such a complaint by the name of *madness*. But there is surely a clear distinction between a disorder which affects only the imagination and spirits, while the judgment is sound, and a disorder by which the judgment itself is impaired. This distinction was made to me by the late Professor Gaubius of Leyden, in a conversation which I had with him several years ago. "If," said he, "a man tells me that he is grievously disturbed, for that he *imagines* he sees a ruffian coming against him with a drawn sword, though at the same time he is *conscious* it is a delusion, I pronounce him to have a disordered imagination; but if a man tells me that he *sees* this, and in consternation calls to me to look at it, I pronounce him to be *mad*."

The history of Johnson's mind as to religion is an important article. "Sunday," said he, "was a heavy day with me when I was a boy. My mother confined me on that day and made me read *The Whole Duty of Man,* from a great part of which I could derive no instruction. I fell into an inattention to religion in my ninth year. The church at Lichfield, in which we had a seat, wanted reparation, so I was to go and find a seat in other churches; and having bad eyes, and being awkward about this, I used to go and read in the fields on Sunday. This habit continued till my fourteenth year; and still I find a great reluctance to go to church. I then became a sort of lax *talker* against religion, for I did not much *think* against it; and this lasted till I went to Oxford, where it would not be *suffered.* When at Oxford, I took up Law's *Serious Call to a Holy Life,*[1] expecting to find it a dull book, as such books generally are, and perhaps to laugh at it. But I found Law quite an overmatch for me; and this was the first occasion of my thinking in earnest of religion, after I became capable of rational inquiry." From this time forward religion was the predominant object of his thoughts; though he lamented that his practice of its duties fell far short of what it ought to be.

His apartment in Pembroke College was that upon the second floor over the gateway. One day, while he was sitting in it quite alone, Dr. Panting, then master of the College, whom he called "a fine Jacobite fellow," overheard him uttering this soliloquy in his strong, emphatic voice: "Well, I have a mind to see what is done in other places of learning. I'll go and visit the Universities abroad. I'll go to France and Italy. I'll go to Padua.—And I'll mind my business. For an *Athenian* blockhead[2] is the worst of all blockheads."

---

1. *Serious Call to a Holy Life* (1728) by the English clergyman William Law. "The best way," he says, "for anyone to know how much he ought to aspire after holiness is to consider, not how much will make his present life easy, but to ask himself how much will make him easy at the hour of death." His book develops this idea logically in regard to the minutest details of life.

2. *An Athenian blockhead.* When one John Gilbert Cooper was praised one day in Johnson's presence as a good scholar, Johnson retorted: "Yes, it cannot be denied that he has good materials for playing the fool and makes abundant use of them."

Dr. Adams told me that Johnson, while he was at Pembroke College, "was caressed and loved by all about him, was a gay and frolicsome fellow, and passed there the happiest part of his life." When I mentioned to him this account as given me by Dr. Adams, he said, "Ah, sir, I was mad and violent. It was bitterness which they mistook for frolic. I was miserably poor, and I thought to fight my way by my literature and my wit; so I disregarded all power and all authority."

The Bishop of Dromore observes in a letter to me, "The pleasure he took in vexing the tutors and fellows* has been often mentioned. But I have heard him say—what ought to be recorded to the honor of the present venerable master of that College, the Reverend William Adams, D.D., who was then very young, and one of the junior fellows—that the mild but judicious expostulations of this worthy man made him really ashamed of himself, 'though I fear,' said he, 'I was too proud to own it.'

"I have heard from some of his contemporaries that he was generally seen lounging at the College gate, with a circle of young students round him, whom he was entertaining with wit and keeping from their studies, if not spiriting them up to rebellion against the College discipline, which in his maturer years he so much extolled."

I do not find that he formed any close intimacies with his fellow collegians. But Dr. Adams told me that he contracted a love and regard for Pembroke College, which he retained to the last. He took a pleasure in boasting of the many eminent men who had been educated at Pembroke. Johnson was peculiarly happy in mentioning how many of the sons of Pembroke were poets; adding with a smile of sportive triumph, "Sir, we are a nest of singing birds."

He was not, however, blind to what he thought the defects of his own college; and I have, from the information of Dr. Taylor, a very strong instance of that rigid honesty which he ever inflexibly preserved. Taylor had obtained his father's consent to be entered of Pembroke, that he might be with his schoolfellow Johnson, with whom, though some years older than himself, he was very intimate. This would have been a great comfort to Johnson. But he fairly told Taylor that he could not, in conscience, suffer him to enter where he knew he could not have an able tutor. He then made inquiry all round the University, and having found that Mr. Bateman, of Christ Church, was the tutor of highest reputation, Taylor was entered of that College. Mr. Bateman's lectures were so excellent that Johnson used to come and get them at secondhand from Taylor, till his poverty being so extreme that his shoes were worn out, and his feet appeared through them, he came no more. He was too proud to accept of money, and somebody having set a pair of new shoes at his door, he threw them away with indignation.

His debts in College, though not great, were increasing; and his scanty remittances from Lichfield, which had all along been made with great difficulty, could be supplied no longer, his father having fallen into a state of insolvency. Compelled, therefore, by irresistible necessity, he left the College in autumn, 1731, without a degree, having been a member of it little more than three years.

In the December of this year his father died. The state of poverty[1] in which he died appears from a note in one of Johnson's little diaries of the following year, which strongly displays his spirit and virtuous dignity of mind. "1732, *Julii* 15. *Undecim aureos deposui, quo die quicquid ante matris funus (quod serum sit precor) de paternis bonis sperari licet, viginti scilicet libras, accepi. Usque adeo mihi fortuna fingenda est. Interea, ne paupertate vires animi languescant, nec in flagitia egestas abigat, cavendum.*—I laid by eleven guineas on this day, when I received twenty pounds, being all that I have reason to hope for out of my father's effects, previous to the death of my mother; an event which I pray God may be very remote. I now therefore see that I must make my own fortune. Meanwhile, let me take care that the powers of my mind be not debilitated by poverty, and that indigence do not force me into any criminal act."

---

1. *Poverty.* "Poverty . . . . makes some virtues impracticable, and others extremely difficult." *Johnson to Boswell, 1782.* See also the second footnote, page 19.

In the forlorn state of his circumstances, he accepted of an offer to be employed as usher* in the school of Market-Bosworth, in Leicestershire, to which it appears, from one of his little fragments of a diary, that he went on foot, on the 16th of July. This employment was very irksome to him in every respect, and he complained grievously of it in his letters to his friend, Mr. Hector, who was now settled as a surgeon at Birmingham. Mr. Hector recollects his writing that it was unvaried as the note of the cuckoo; and that he did not know whether it was more disagreeable for him to teach, or the boys to learn, the grammar rules. His general aversion to this painful drudgery was greatly enhanced by a disagreement between him and Sir Wolstan Dixie, the patron of the school, in whose house, I have been told, he officiated as a kind of domestic chaplain, so far, at least, as to say grace at table, but was treated with what he represented as intolerable harshness; and, after suffering for a few months such complicated misery, he relinquished a situation which all his life afterwards he recollected with the strongest aversion, and even a degree of horror.

Being now again totally unoccupied, he was invited by Mr. Hector to pass some time with him at Birmingham, at the house of Mr. Warren, with whom Mr. Hector lodged and boarded. Mr. Warren was the first established bookseller at Birmingham and was very attentive to Johnson who, he soon found, could be of much service to him in his trade, by his knowledge of literature. He continued to live as Mr. Hector's guest[1] for about six months, and then hired lodgings in another part of the town, finding himself as well situated at Birmingham as he supposed he could be anywhere, while he had no settled plan of life, and very scanty means of subsistence. He made some valuable acquaintances there, amongst whom was Mr. Porter, a mercer, whose widow he afterwards married.

---

1. *Guest.* Here Mr. Hector got him a piece of translation to do. "The work," says Boswell, "was at a stand. Mr. Hector . . . represented to him that the printer could have no other employment till this undertaking was finished, and that the poor man and his family were suffering. Johnson, upon this, exerted the powers of his mind. He lay in bed with the book before him, and dictated while Hector wrote."

Miss Porter told me that when he was first introduced to her mother he was lean and lank, so that his immense structure of bones was hideously striking to the eye, and the scars of the scrofula were deeply visible. He also wore his hair,[1] which was straight and stiff, and separated behind; and he often had, seemingly, convulsive starts and odd gesticulations, which tended to excite at once surprise and ridicule. Mrs. Porter was so much engaged by his conversation that she overlooked all these external disadvantages, and said to her daughter, "This is the most sensible man that I ever saw in my life."

Though Mrs. Porter was double the age of Johnson, and her person and manner, as described to me by the late Mr. Garrick,[2] were by no means pleasing to others, she certainly inspired him with a more than ordinary passion; and she having signified her willingness to accept of his hand, he went to Lichfield to ask his mother's consent to the marriage. Mrs. Johnson knew too well the ardor of her son's temper, and was too tender a parent to oppose his inclinations.

I know not for what reason the marriage ceremony was not performed at Birmingham; but a resolution was taken that it should be at Derby, for which place the bride and bridegroom set out on horseback. Though Mr. Topham Beauclerk used archly to mention Johnson's having told him with much gravity, "Sir, it was a love marriage on both sides," I have had from my illustrious friend the following curious account of their journey to church upon the nuptial morn: "Sir, she had read the old romances, and had got into her head the fantastical notion that a woman of spirit should use her lover like a dog. So, sir, at first she told me that I rode too fast, and she could not keep up with me; and when I rode a little slower, she passed me, and complained that I lagged behind. I was not to be made the slave of caprice; and I resolved to begin as I meant

---

1. *Wore his hair.* During most of his life Dr. Johnson followed the general custom of the time and wore a wig. "The great bushy wig, which throughout his life he affected to wear, was ever nearly as impenetrable by a comb as a quickset hedge." *Sir John Hawkins: Life of Johnson.*

2. *Mr. Garrick.* He knew her from the time of his school days.

to end. I therefore pushed on briskly, till I was fairly out of
her sight. The road lay between two hedges, so I was sure
she could not miss it; and I contrived that she should soon
come up with me. When she did, I observed her to be in tears."

He now set up a private academy,[1] for which purpose he
hired a large house, well situated near his native city. But the
only pupils that were put under his care were the celebrated
David Garrick and his brother George, and a Mr. Offely, a
young gentleman of good fortune, who died early. His own
acquisitions had been made by fits and starts, by violent irrup-
tions into the regions of knowledge; and it could not be expected
that his impatience would be subdued, and his impetuosity
restrained, so as to fit him for a quiet guide to novices. We
need not wonder, therefore, that he did not keep his academy
above a year and a half. From Mr. Garrick's account he did
not appear to have been profoundly reverenced by his pupils.
His oddities of manner, and uncouth gesticulations, could not
but be the subject of merriment to them.

While Johnson kept his academy, there can be no doubt that
he was insensibly furnishing his mind with various knowledge;
but I have not discovered that he wrote anything except a
great part of his tragedy of *Irene*. When he had finished some
part of it, he read what he had done to Mr. Walmsley, who
objected to his having already brought his heroine into great
distress, and asked him, "How can you possibly contrive to
plunge her into deeper calamity?" Johnson, in sly allusion to
the supposed oppressive proceedings of the court of which Mr.
Walmsley was registrar, replied, "Sir, I can put her into the
Spiritual Court!"

Mr. Walmsley, however, was well pleased with this proof of
Johnson's abilities as a dramatic writer, and advised him to
finish the tragedy, and produce it on the stage.

Johnson now thought of trying his fortune in London. It is

---

1. *Private academy.* "Every man that has ever undertaken to
instruct others can tell what slow advances he has been able to make,
and how much patience it requires to recall vagrant inattention, to
stimulate sluggish indifference, and to rectify absurd misapprehension."
Johnson: Life of Milton.

a memorable circumstance that his pupil David Garrick went
thither at the same time, with intent to complete his education,
and follow the profession of the law, from which he was soon
diverted by his decided preference for the stage.

Johnson had a little money when he came to town,[1] and he
knew how he could live in the cheapest manner. His first
lodgings were at the house of Mr. Norris, a staymaker, in
Exeter Street, adjoining Catharine Street, in the Strand. "I
dined," said he, "very well for eight pence, with very good
company, at the Pine Apple in New Street, just by. Several
of them had traveled. They expected to meet every day; but
did not know one another's names. It used to cost the rest a
shilling, for they drank wine; but I had a cut of meat for six
pence, and bread for a penny, and gave the waiter a penny; so
that I was quite well served, nay, better than the rest, for they
gave the waiter nothing."

He at this time, I believe, abstained entirely from fermented
liquors; a practice to which he rigidly conformed for many
years together, at different periods of his life.

His Ofellus in the *Art of Living in London,* I have heard him
relate, was an Irish painter, whom he knew at Birmingham,
and who had practiced his own precepts of economy for several
years in the British capital. He assured Johnson, who, I suppose, was then meditating to try his fortune in London, that
thirty pounds a year was enough to enable a man to live there
without being contemptible. He allowed ten pounds for clothes
and linen. He said a man might live in a garret at eighteen
pence a week; few people would inquire where he lodged; and
if they did, it was easy to say, "Sir, I am to be found at such a
place." By spending three pence in a coffee house, he might
be for some hours every day in very good company; he might
dine for six pence, breakfast on bread and milk for a penny,

---

1. *When he came to town.* "One curious anecdote was communicated
by himself to Mr. John Nichols. Mr. Wilcox, the bookseller, on being
informed by him that his intention was to get his livelihood as an
author, eyed his robust frame attentively, and with a significant look,
said, 'You had better buy a porter's knot.' He, however, added
'Wilcox was one of my best friends.' " *Boswell.*

and do without supper. On "clean-shirt-day" he went abroad
and paid visits. "This man," said he [Johnson], gravely, "was a
very sensible man, who perfectly understood common affairs;
a man of a great deal of knowledge of the world, fresh from
life, not strained through books."

Amidst this cold obscurity, there was one brilliant circumstance to cheer him. He was well acquainted with Mr. Henry
Hervey, one of the branches of the noble family of that name,
who had been quartered at Lichfield as an officer of the army,
and had at this time a house in London, where Johnson was
frequently entertained, and had an opportunity of meeting
genteel company. Not very long before his death, he described
this early friend thus, "He was a vicious man, but very kind
to me. If you call a dog Hervey, I shall love him."

In the course of the summer he returned to Lichfield,[1] where
he had left Mrs. Johnson. His residence at Lichfield at this
time was only for three months. He removed to London with
Mrs. Johnson; but her daughter, who had lived with them, was
left with her relations in the country.

His tragedy, being by this time, as he thought, fit for the
stage, he solicited Mr. Fleetwood, the patentee of Drury Lane
Theater, to have it acted, but Mr. Fleetwood would not accept
it, and it was not acted till 1749, when his friend David Garrick
was manager of that theater.

The *Gentleman's Magazine*, begun and carried on by
Mr. Edward Cave,[2] under the name of Sylvanus Urban, had
attracted the notice and esteem of Johnson before he came to
London as an adventurer in literature. He told me that when
he first saw St. John's Gate, the place where that miscellany
was originally printed, he "beheld it with reverence." He

---

1. *Lichfield.* A two days' journey from London. "Johnson let
more than twenty years go by without visiting his native town, being
hindered, no doubt, mainly by poverty. In the last seventeen years
of his life, he visited it a dozen times." *Birkbeck Hill.*

2. *Mr. Edward Cave.* A somewhat close-fisted taskmaster, not
altogether reputable in some of the things he published. Johnson,
however, has said of him: "He saw little at a time, but that little he
saw with great exactness. He was long in finding the right, but seldom
failed to find it at last."

was now enlisted by Mr. Cave as a regular coadjutor in his magazine, by which he probably obtained a tolerable livelihood.[1] That part of his labor which consisted in the improvement of the productions of other contributors can be perceived only by those who had an opportunity of comparing the original with the altered copy. What we certainly know to have been done by him in this way was the debates in both houses of Parliament, under the name of the "Senate of Lilliput." Parliament then kept the press in a kind of mysterious awe, which made it necessary to have recourse to such devices.

The debates, which were brought home by Guthrie,[2] whose memory was very quick and tenacious, were sent by Cave to Johnson for his revision; and, after some time, when Guthrie had attained to greater variety of employment, and the speeches were more and more enriched by the accession of Johnson's genius, it was resolved that he should do the whole himself, from the scanty notes furnished by persons employed to attend in both houses of Parliament. Sometimes, however, as he himself told me, he had nothing more communicated to him than the names of the several speakers,[3] and the part which they had taken in the debate.

But what first displayed his transcendent powers, and "gave the world assurance of the *man*," was his "London, a Poem, in Imitation of the Third Satire of Juvenal."

---

1. *Tolerable livelihood.* "The authors of London were formerly computed by Swift at several thousands . . . Of these, only a few can be said to produce, or endeavor to produce, new ideas; the rest, however arrogant . . . perceive no particular summons to composition except the sound of the clock." *Johnson: The Rambler.*

2. *Guthrie.* "Guthrie arrived, dressed in loud clothes, and talking loud to everybody, and soon fell a-wrangling with a gentleman about tragedy and comedy and the unities, etc., and laid down the law of the drama in a peremptory manner, supporting his arguments with cursing and swearing." *A. Carlyle: Autobiography.*

3. *Names of the several speakers.* Later in the Life, Boswell says: "Johnson told me that as soon as he found that the speeches were thought genuine, he determined that he would write no more of them; for he 'would not be accessary to the propagation of falsehood.' And such was the tenderness of his conscience that a short time before his death he expressed his regret for his having been the author of fictions, which had passed for realities."

It has been generally said, I know not with what truth, that Johnson offered his "London" to several booksellers, none of whom would purchase it. To this circumstance Mr. Derrick alludes in the following lines of his "Fortune, a Rhapsody":

> Will no kind patron Johnson own?
> Shall Johnson friendless range the town?
> And every publisher refuse
> The offspring of his happy Muse?

But Mr. Robert Dodsley[1] had taste enough to perceive its uncommon merit, and bargained for the whole property of it, for which he gave Johnson ten guineas; who told me, "I might perhaps have accepted of less, but that Paul Whitehead had a little before got ten guineas for a poem; and I would not take less than Paul Whitehead." The Reverend Dr. Douglas, now Bishop of Salisbury, was then a student at Oxford, and remembers well the effect which "London" produced. Everybody was delighted with it; and there being no name to it, the first buzz of the literary circle was, "Here is an unknown poet, greater even than Pope."

The nation was then in that ferment against the Court and the Ministry, which some years after ended in the downfall of Sir Robert Walpole;[2] and as it has been said that Tories are Whigs when out of place, and Whigs Tories when in place— so, as a Whig Administration ruled with what force it could,

---

1. *Robert Dodsley.* Bookseller (and publisher) since 1735. "You know how decent, humble, inoffensive a creature Dodsley is; how little apt to forget or disguise his having been a footman." *Horace Walpole, 1758.*

2. *Sir Robert Walpole.* The greatest Whig of his day, and chief minister of the Crown from 1721 to 1742, during which time he corruptly manipulated Parliament in order to preserve peace abroad, and "the reign of common sense at home." Toward the close of his administration the Spanish government tried to stop all English trade with Spanish-American ports and brutally treated some of the English traders they caught. Like most of the wits of his day, who, like himself, were Tories, Johnson smarted under Walpole's peace policy. He smarted too, as many did, at Walpole's invention of new internal taxes, particularly at his invention of taxes on paper, which had almost ruined old Michael Johnson's business.

beat him.   But it was not in his shop; it was in my own chamber."

[In 1744], he produced *The Life of Richard Savage;*[1] a man of whom it is difficult to speak impartially, without wondering that he was for some time the intimate companion of Johnson; for his character was marked by profligacy, insolence, and ingratitude; yet, as he undoubtedly had a warm and vigorous, though unregulated, mind, had seen life in all its varieties, and been much in the company of the statesmen and wits of his time, he could communicate to Johnson an abundant supply of such materials as his philosophical curiosity most eagerly desired; and as Savage's misfortunes and misconduct had reduced him to the lowest state of wretchedness as a writer for bread, his visits to St. John's Gate naturally brought Johnson and him together.

It is melancholy to reflect that Johnson and Savage were sometimes in such extreme indigence that they could not pay for a lodging; so that they have wandered together whole nights in the streets.   Yet in these almost incredible scenes of distress, we may suppose that Savage mentioned many of the anecdotes with which Johnson afterwards enriched the life of his unhappy companion, and those of other poets.

He told Sir Joshua Reynolds that one night in particular, when Savage and he walked round St. James's Square for want of a lodging, they were not at all depressed by their situation; but, in high spirits and brimful of patriotism, traversed the square for several hours, inveighed against the Minister, and "resolved they would *stand by their country.*"

In Johnson's *Life of Savage* the various incidents are related in so clear and animated a manner, and illuminated throughout with so much philosophy, that it is one of the most interesting narratives in the English language.   Sir Joshua Reynolds told me that upon his return from Italy he met with it in Devonshire, knowing nothing of its author, and began to read it while he was standing with his arm leaning against a chimney-piece.   It seized his attention so strongly that, not being able

---

1. *Savage.* See Appendix A, page 545.

to lay down the book till he had finished it, when he attempted
to move, he found his arm totally benumbed.

[1747]. This year [Johnson's] old pupil and friend, David
Garrick, having become joint patentee and manager of Drury
Lane Theater, Johnson honored his opening of it with a prologue, which for just and manly dramatic criticism on the
whole range of the English stage is unrivaled. It was during
the season often called for by the audience. The most striking
and brilliant passages of it have been so often repeated that it
would be superfluous to point them out. But the year 1747 is
distinguished as the epoch when Johnson's arduous and important
work, his *Dictionary of the English Language*, was announced
to the world by the publication of its "Plan," or prospectus.

How long this immense undertaking had been the object
of his contemplation, I do not know. I have been informed by
Mr. James Dodsley that several years before this period,
sitting in his brother Robert's shop, he heard his brother suggest to him that a Dictionary of the English Language would
be well received by the public; that Johnson seemed at first
to catch at the proposition, but, after a pause, said in his abrupt,
decisive manner, "I believe I shall not undertake it."

The "Plan" was addressed to Philip Dormer, Earl of Chesterfield, then one of his Majesty's principal Secretaries of State,
a nobleman who was very ambitious of literary distinction and
who, upon being informed of the design, had expressed himself
in terms very favorable to its success. Johnson told me,
"Sir, the way in which the 'Plan' of my *Dictionary* came to be
inscribed to Lord Chesterfield was this: I had neglected to
write it by the time appointed. Dodsley suggested a desire
to have it addressed to Lord Chesterfield. I laid hold of this
as a pretext for delay, that it might be better done, and let
Dodsley have his desire. I said to my friend Dr. Bathurst,
'Now if any good comes of my addressing to Lord Chesterfield,
it will be ascribed to deep policy, when, in fact, it was only a
casual excuse for laziness.' " Dr. Taylor told me that Johnson
sent his "Plan" to him in manuscript, for his perusal; and that
when it was lying upon his table, Mr. William Whitehead
happened to pay him a visit, and being shown it, was highly

pleased with such parts of it as he had time to read and begged to take it home with him, which he was allowed to do; that from him it got into the hands of a noble lord, who carried it to Lord Chesterfield. When Taylor observed this might be of an advantage, Johnson replied, "No, sir; it would have come out with more bloom, if it had not been seen before by anybody."

Dr. Adams found him one day busy at his *Dictionary*, when the following dialogue ensued. ADAMS: "This is a great work, sir. How are you to get all the etymologies?" JOHNSON: "Why, sir, here is a shelf with Junius, and Skinner, and others; and here is a Welsh gentleman who has published a collection of Welsh proverbs, who will help me with the Welsh." ADAMS: "But, sir, how can you do this in three years?" JOHNSON: "Sir, I have no doubt that I can do it in three years." ADAMS: "But the French Academy,[1] which consists of forty members, took forty years to compile their Dictionary." JOHNSON: "Let me see; forty times forty is sixteen hundred. As three is to sixteen hundred so is the proportion of an Englishman to a Frenchman." With so much ease and pleasantry could he talk of that prodigious labor he had undertaken.

For the mechanical part he employed, as he told me, six amanuenses; and let it be remembered by the natives of North Britain, to whom he is supposed to have been so hostile, that five of them were of that country. To all these painful laborers Johnson showed a never-ceasing kindness, so far as they stood in need of it. Mr. Macbean[2] had afterwards the honor of being librarian to Archibald, Duke of Argyle, for many years,

---

1. *French Academy.* Established in 1635 to purify and fix French usage by the publication of an authoritative dictionary, grammar, etc. It is a self-perpetuating body of forty distinguished authors and scholars popularly called the "Immortals." The first edition of its dictionary appeared in 1694. In 1780 we find Dr. Johnson ridiculing the notion that England had ever needed such an academy, "the decrees of which every man would have been willing and many would have been proud to disobey."

2. *Macbean.* "He is a man of great learning, and for his learning I respect him . . . but he knows nothing of life. I advised him to write a geographical dictionary; but I have lost all hopes of his ever doing anything properly, since I found he gave as much labor to Capua as to Rome." *Johnson, quoted by Mme. D'Arblay.*

but was left without a shilling. Johnson, by the favor of
Lord Thurlow, got him admitted a poor brother of the Charterhouse.[1] For Shiels, who died of a consumption, he had much
tenderness. Peyton, when reduced to penury, had frequent
aid from the bounty of Johnson, who at last was at the expense
of burying both him and his wife.

While the *Dictionary* was going forward, Johnson lived part
of the time in Holborn, part in Gough Square, Fleet Street,
and he had an upper room fitted up like a counting-house,
in which he gave to the copyists their several tasks.

The necessary expense of preparing a work of such magnitude for the press must have been a considerable deduction
from the price stipulated to be paid for the copyright. I
understand that nothing was allowed by the booksellers[2] on
that account; and I remember his telling me that a large portion of it having, by mistake, been written upon both sides
of the paper, so as to be inconvenient for the compositor, it
cost him £20 to have it transcribed upon one side only.

He is now to be considered as "tugging at his oar." But
his mind could not be satisfied without more diversity of employment, and the pleasure of animated relaxation. He,
therefore, not only exerted his talents in occasional composition very different from lexicography, but formed a club in
Ivy Lane,[3] Paternoster Row, with a view to enjoy literary
discussion and amuse his evening hours.

In January, 1749, he published *The Vanity of Human Wishes,
being the Tenth Satire of Juvenal imitated.* Mrs. Johnson,

---

1. *Charterhouse.* An ancient monastery in London which passed
into private hands in the reign of Henry VIII, and in the reign of James I
became a home for "decayed gentlemen" and a school for boys. "Yon-
der sit some threescore old gentlemen pensioners of the hospital, listen-
ing to the prayers and the psalms. You hear them coughing feebly
in the twilight—the old reverend black gowns." *Thackeray: Pendennis.*

2. *Booksellers.* Seven prominent booksellers, among them Robert
Dodsley, had induced Dr. Johnson to undertake the work by the offer
of £1575.

3. *Ivy Lane.* At a tavern there. "I have heard [Johnson] assert
that a tavern chair was the throne of human felicity. 'Wine there,'
he said, 'exhilarates my spirits, and prompts me to free conversation,
and an interchange of discourse with those whom I most love. I

for the sake of country air, had lodgings at Hampstead, to which he resorted occasionally, and there the greatest part, if not the whole, of this Imitation was written. The fervid rapidity with which it was produced is scarcely credible. I have heard him say that he composed seventy lines of it in one day, without putting one of them upon paper till they were finished.

Garrick being now vested with theatrical power by being manager of Drury Lane Theater, he generously made use of it to bring out Johnson's tragedy, which had been long kept back for want of encouragement. But in this benevolent purpose he met with no small difficulty from the temper of Johnson, which could not brook that a drama which he had formed with much study, and had been obliged to keep more than the nine years of Horace, should be revised and altered at the pleasure of an actor. Yet Garrick knew well that without some alterations it would not be fit for the stage. A violent dispute having ensued between them, Garrick applied to the Reverend Dr. Taylor[1] to interpose. Johnson was at first very obstinate. "Sir," said he, "the fellow wants me to make Mahomet run mad, that he may have an opportunity of tossing his hands and kicking his heels." He was, however, at last, with difficulty, prevailed on to comply with Garrick's wishes, so as to allow of some changes; but still there were not enough.

---

dogmatize and am contradicted, and in this conflict of opinions and sentiments I find delight.' " *Hawkins: Life of Johnson.*

"Mrs. Lenox . . . had written a novel, which in the spring of 1751 was ready for publication. One evening at the club Johnson proposed to us the celebrating the birth of Mrs. Lenox's first literary child, as he called her book, by a whole night spent in festivity. The place appointed was the Devil Tavern, and there, about the hour of eight, Mrs. Lenox and her husband, as also the Club, and friends to the number of near twenty assembled. Their supper was elegant, and Johnson had directed that a magnificent hot apple pie should make a part of it, and this he would have stuck with bay leaves; and further, he had prepared for her a crown of laurel, with which, but not till he had invoked the Muses by some ceremonies of his own invention, he encircled her brows. About five, Johnson's face shone with meridian splendor, though his drink had been only lemonade." *Hawkins: Life of Johnson.*

1. *Taylor.* Burly and vehement. Not noted for diplomacy.

Dr. Adams was present the first night of the representation of *Irene*, and gave me the following account: "Before the curtain drew up, there were catcalls whistling, which alarmed Johnson's friends. The 'Prologue,' which was written by himself in a manly strain, soothed the audience, and the play went off tolerably, till it came to the conclusion, when Mrs. Pritchard, the heroine of the piece, was to be strangled upon the stage, and was to speak two lines with the bow-string round her neck. The audience cried out *'Murder! Murder!'* She several times attempted to speak; but in vain. At last she was obliged to go off the stage alive."[1] This passage was afterwards struck out, and she was carried off to be put to death behind the scenes, as the play now has it.

When asked how he felt upon the ill success of his tragedy, [Johnson] replied, "Like the Monument."[2] Instead of peevishly complaining of the bad taste of the town [he] submitted to its decision without a murmur. He had, indeed, upon all occasions a great deference for the general opinion: "A man," said he, "who writes a book thinks himself wiser or wittier than the rest of mankind; he supposes that he can instruct or amuse them, and the public to whom he appeals, must, after all, be the judges of his pretensions."

On occasion of his play being brought upon the stage, Johnson had a fancy that his dress should be more gay than what he ordinarily wore; he therefore appeared behind the scenes, and even in one of the side boxes, in a scarlet waistcoat, with rich gold lace, and a gold-laced hat. He humorously

1. *Off the stage alive.* By the loyal efforts of Garrick, the play was made to run nine nights. By this means, in accordance with a current custom, Johnson received the receipts of the third, sixth, and ninth nights, less certain charges. This, together with his copyright on the play, brought him about three hundred pounds.

2. *Monument.* A shaft two hundred feet high erected in the heart of London to assert that Roman Catholics were responsible for the great fire of London in 1666.

> " .   .   . London's column pointing to the skies,
> Like a tall bully, lifts its head and lies." *Pope.*

"What is good only because it pleases cannot be pronounced good, till it has been found to please." *Johnson: Life of Dryden.*

observed to Mr. Langton that when in that dress he could not treat people with the same ease as when in his usual plain clothes. Dress indeed, we must allow, has more effect even upon strong minds than one should suppose, without having had the experience of it. His necessary attendance while his play was in rehearsal, and during its performance, brought him acquainted with many of the performers of both sexes, which produced a more favorable opinion of their profession than he had harshly expressed in his *Life of Savage*. With some of them he kept up an acquaintance as long as he and they lived, and was ever ready to show them acts of kindness.

In 1750 he came forth in the character for which he was eminently qualified—a teacher of moral and religious wisdom. The vehicle which he chose was that of a periodical paper which he knew had been, upon former occasions, employed with great success. [He] was, I think, not very happy in the choice of his title—*The Rambler*, which certainly is not suited to a series of grave and moral discourses; which the Italians have literally, but ludicrously, translated by *Il Vagabondo*. He gave Sir Joshua Reynolds the following account of its getting this name: "What *must* be done, sir, *will* be done. When I was to begin publishing that paper, I was at a loss how to name it. I sat down at night upon my bedside, and resolved that I would not go to sleep till I had fixed its title. *The Rambler* seemed the best that occurred, and I took it."

With what sentiments this paper was undertaken is evidenced by the following prayer, which he composed and offered up on the occasion: "Almighty God, the giver of all good things, without whose help all labor is ineffectual, and without whose grace all wisdom is folly, grant, I beseech Thee, that in this undertaking Thy Holy Spirit may not be withheld from me, but that I may promote Thy glory, and the salvation of myself and others; grant this, O Lord, for the sake of Thy son, Jesus Christ. Amen."

The first paper of *The Rambler* was published on Tuesday, the 20th of March, 1749-50; and its author was enabled to continue it, without interruption, every Tuesday and Saturday, till Saturday the 17th of March, 1752, on which day it closed.

This is a strong confirmation of the truth of a remark of his, that "a man may write at any time, if he will set himself doggedly[1] to it."

Sir Joshua Reynolds once asked him by what means he had attained his extraordinary accuracy and flow of language. He told him that he had early laid it down as a fixed rule to do his best on every occasion, and in every company; to impart whatever he knew in the most forcible language he could put it in; and that by constant practice, and never suffering any careless expressions to escape him, or attempting to deliver his thoughts without arranging them in the clearest manner, it became habitual to him.

As *The Rambler* was entirely the work of one man, there was, of course, such a uniformity in its texture as very much to exclude the charm of variety; and the grave and often solemn cast of thinking, which distinguished it from other periodical papers, made it, for some time, not generally liked. So slowly did this excellent work, of which twelve editions have now issued from the press, gain upon the world at large, that even in the closing number the author says, "I have never been much a favorite of the public."

Johnson told me, with an amiable fondness, a little pleasing circumstance relative to this work. Mrs. Johnson, in whose judgment and taste he had great confidence, said to him, after a few numbers of *The Rambler* had come out, "I thought very well of you before; but I did not imagine you could have written anything equal to this."

[1751]. The Reverend Dr. Douglas having detected a gross forgery and imposition upon the public by William Lauder, a Scotch schoolmaster, who had with equal impudence and ingenuity represented Milton as a plagiary from certain modern

---

1. *Doggedly.* "[Gray] had a notion, not very peculiar, that he could not write but at certain times or at happy moments; a fantastic foppery to which my kindness for a man of learning and of virtue wishes him to have been superior." *Johnson: Life of Gray.* "The mechanic cannot handle his hammer and his file at all times with equal dexterity; there are hours, he knows not why, when his hand is out." *Johnson: Life of Milton.*

I find no inconsistency in these three statements.—EDITOR.

Latin poets, Johnson, who had been so far imposed upon as to furnish a preface and postscript to his work, now dictated a letter for Lauder, addressed to Dr. Douglas, acknowledging his fraud in terms of suitable contrition.[1]

This extraordinary attempt of Lauder was no sudden effort. He had brooded over it for many years; and to this hour it is uncertain what his principal motive[2] was, unless it were a vain notion of his superiority[3] in being able, by whatever means, to deceive mankind.[4] To effect this, he produced certain passages from Grotius, Masenius, and others which had a faint resemblance to some parts of the *Paradise Lost*. In these he interpolated some fragments of Hogg's Latin translation of that poem, alleging that the mass thus fabricated was the archetype from which Milton copied. These fabrications he published from time to time in the *Gentleman's Magazine;* and, exulting in his fancied success, he in 1750 ventured to collect them into a pamphlet. To this pamphlet Johnson wrote a preface, in full persuasion[5] of Lauder's honesty, and a postscript, recommending, in the most persuasive terms, a subscription for the relief of a granddaughter of Milton.

That there should be a suspension of his literary labors during a part of the year 1752 will not seem strange when it

---

1. *Suitable contrition.* Long after he had signed this letter, Lauder returned to the charge, which clearly exercised a morbid fascination over him.

2. *His principal motive.* Lauder had become involved in a bitter quarrel over the comparative merits of two modern Latin poets when his eye chanced to light on a couplet by Alexander Pope in which his favorite was sneeringly contrasted with Milton. It angered him and, with a perversity more natural to insanity than to a man in his senses, he turned his malice, not against Pope, but against Milton. He brooded on the matter till he almost persuaded himself that Milton was a scoundrel. At least he determined to prove him one.

3. *Superiority.* "Every man wishes to be wise, and they who cannot be wise are almost always cunning." *Johnson: The Idler.*

4. *To deceive mankind.* "Cunning has effect from the credulity of others rather than from the abilities of those who are cunning. It requires no extraordinary talents to lie and deceive." *Johnson, 1773.*

5. *In full persuasion.* On being reminded of this episode in 1780, Johnson remarked: "I was deceived by thinking the man too frantic [insane] to be fraudulent."

is considered that soon after closing his *Rambler* he suffered a loss which, there can be no doubt, affected him with the deepest distress.[1] On the 17th of March, O. S.,* his wife died.

Her wedding ring, when she became his wife, was, after her death, preserved by him, as long as he lived, with an affectionate care, in a little round wooden box, in the inside of which he pasted a slip of paper, thus inscribed by him in fair characters, as follows:

Eheu!
Eliz. Johnson,
Nupta Jul. 9° 1736,
Mortua, eheu!
Mart. 17° 1752.

After his death, Mr. Francis Barber,[2] his faithful servant, and residuary legatee, offered this memorial of tenderness to Mrs. Lucy Porter, Mrs. Johnson's daughter; but she having declined to accept of it, he had it enameled as a mourning ring for his old master, and presented it to his wife, Mrs. Barber, who now has it.

I have, indeed, been told by Mrs. Desmoulins, who, before her marriage, lived for some time with Mrs. Johnson at Hampstead, that she indulged herself in country air and nice living at an unsuitable expense, while her husband was drudging in the smoke of London, and that she by no means treated him with that complacency which is the most engaging quality in a wife. But all this is perfectly compatible with his fondness

---

1. *Deepest distress.* See Appendix B, page 545, for more notes on Dr. Johnson's married life.

2. *Francis Barber.* Originally a negro slave in the West Indies. His master, the father of Johnson's dear friend, Dr. Bathurst, took him to England, sent him to school there, and in his will left him his freedom. In 1752 Barber entered Dr. Johnson's service, who for some time continued his schooling, and always protected him, leaving him a comfortable annuity by will. A clergyman by the name of Turner describes how he once called at No. 1 Inner Temple Lane to see Johnson. Francis opened the door and a group of his African countrymen sitting round a fire in the gloomy anteroom all turned their sooty faces at once to stare at him.

for her, especially when it is remembered that he had a high opinion of her understanding, and that the impressions which her beauty, real or imaginary, had originally made upon his fancy, being continued by habit, had not been effaced, though she herself was doubtless much altered for the worse.

From Mr. Francis Barber I have had the following account of the situation in which he found him after his wife's death: "He was in great affliction. Mrs. Williams[1] was then living in his house, which was in Gough Square. He was busy with the *Dictionary*. Mr. Shiels and some others of the gentlemen who had formerly written for him used to come about him. He had then little for himself, but frequently sent money to Mr. Shiels when in distress. The friends who visited him at that time were chiefly Dr. Bathurst,[2] and Mr. Diamond,

---

1. *Mrs. Williams.* Unmarried, the term *Mrs.* in the eighteenth century being often applied to spinsters. "Mrs. Anna Williams, daughter of a very ingenious Welsh physician, having come to London in hopes of being cured of a cataract in both her eyes, which afterwards ended in total blindness, was kindly received as a constant visitor at his house while Mrs. Johnson lived; and after her death, having come under his roof in order to have an operation upon her eyes performed with more comfort to her than in lodgings, she had an apartment from him during the rest of her life, at all times when he had a house." *Boswell: Life of Johnson.*

"Her acquisitions were many and her curiosity universal; so that she partook of every conversation." *Johnson, 1783.* "Age and sickness and pride have made her so peevish that I was forced to bribe the maid to stay with her by a secret stipulation of half a crown a week over her wages." *Johnson, 1777.*

2. *Dr. Bathurst.* A London physician without much practice. He became a ship's doctor and died in the West Indies in 1757. "A physician in a great city seems to be the mere plaything of fortune; his degree of reputation is for the most part totally casual; they that employ him know not his excellence; they that reject him know not his deficience." *Johnson.*

" 'Dear Bathurst,' said [Johnson] to me one day, 'was a man to my very heart's content; he hated a fool, and he hated a rogue, and he hated a Whig; he was a very good hater.' " *Mrs. Piozzi: Anecdotes of Johnson.* " 'My dear friend Dr. Bathurst,' said he with a warmth of approbation, 'declared he was glad that his father, who was a West Indian planter, had left his affairs in total ruin because, having no estate, he was not under the temptation of having slaves.' " *Boswell: Life of Johnson.*

an apothecary in Cork Street, Burlington Gardens, with whom he and Mrs. Williams generally dined every Sunday. There was also Mr. Cave, Dr. Hawkesworth,[1] Mr. Ryland,[2] merchant on Tower Hill, Mrs. Masters, the poetess, who lived with Mr. Cave, Mrs. Carter,[3] and sometimes Mrs. Macaulay;[4] also, Mrs. Gardiner,[5] wife of a tallow-chandler on Snow Hill, not in the learned way, but a worthy, good woman; Mr. (now Sir Joshua) Reynolds; Mr. Millar, Mr. Dodsley, Mr. Bouquet, Mr. Payne, of Paternoster Row, booksellers; Mr. Strahan, the printer; the Earl of Orrery,[6] Lord Southwell, Mr. Garrick."

Many are, no doubt, omitted in this catalogue of his friends, and in particular, Mr. Robert Levet,[7] an obscure practicer in physic amongst the lower people, his fees being sometimes very small sums, sometimes whatever provisions his patients could afford him; but of such extensive practice in that way

---

1. *Dr. Hawkesworth.* For a time so successful as an essayist and compiler that he grew "foppish." He became very unpopular before his death, possibly because of his frankness in religious matters.

2. *Ryland,* John. Hawkesworth's brother-in-law. A merchant, dissenter, Old School Whig, and sound scholar; Johnson's lifelong friend.

3. *Mrs. Carter.* The learned Mrs. Carter (unmarried) who, according to Johnson, "could make a pudding as well as translate Epictetus." "Her whole face seems to beam with goodness, piety, and philanthropy." *Mme. D'Arblay: Diary.*

4. *Mrs. Macaulay.* (1731-1791) Still Miss Catherine Sawbridge. Later, as Mrs. Macaulay, she became literary, a giver of good dinners, and a patroness of republicanism and democratic equality. Horace Walpole called her the brood hen of fashion, and a shallow fanatic.

5. *Mrs. Gardiner.* "Mrs. Gardiner was very zealous for the support of the charity-school in the parish of St. Sepulcher." *Boswell.*

6. *Orrery.* "That man spent his life in catching at an object [literary eminence] which he had not power to grasp." *Johnson, 1770.*

7. *Levet.* At one time a waiter in a coffee-house in Paris. He picked up some knowledge of medicine, chiefly through free lectures. "When *in deshabille,* he might have been taken for an alchemist." *Gentleman's Magazine, LV: 110.*

"Levet is a brutal fellow, but I have a good regard for him; for his brutality is in his manners, not his mind." *Johnson, 1778.* "Mr. Levet, who thinks his ancient rights invaded [by the introduction of another guest into the household], stands at bay, *fierce as ten furies.* Mrs. Williams growls and scolds." *Johnson, 1778.* "Here is Mr. Levet, just come in at fourscore from a walk to Hampstead, eight miles in August." *Johnson, 1780.*

that, Mrs. Williams has told me, his walk was from Houndsditch to Marylebone. It appears from Johnson's diary that their acquaintance commenced about the year 1746; and such was Johnson's predilection for him, and fanciful estimation of his moderate abilities, that I have heard him say he should not be satisfied, though attended by all the College of Physicians, unless he had Mr. Levet with him. Ever since I was acquainted with Dr. Johnson, and many years before, as I have been assured by those who knew him earlier, Mr. Levet had an apartment in his house, or his chambers, and waited upon him every morning, through the whole course of his late and tedious breakfast. He was of a strange, grotesque appearance, stiff and formal in his manner, and seldom said a word while any company was present.

When Johnson lived in Castle Street, Cavendish Square, he used frequently to visit two ladies who lived opposite him, Miss Cotterells, daughters of Admiral Cotterell. Reynolds[1] used also to visit there, and thus they met. The ladies were regretting the death of a friend, to whom they owed great obligations; upon which Reynolds observed, "You have, however, the comfort of being relieved from a burthen of gratitude." They were shocked a little at this suggestion, as too selfish; but Johnson defended it in his clear and forcible manner, and was much pleased with the *mind*, the fair view of human nature, which it exhibited, like some of the reflections of Rochefaucault. The consequence was that he went home with Reynolds, and supped with him.

Sir Joshua told me [an] anecdote of Johnson about the time

---

1. *Reynolds*, Sir Joshua (1723-1792).

"To coxcombs averse, yet most civilly steering,
When they judged without skill, he was still hard of hearing;
When they talked of their Raphaels, Correggios, and stuff,
He shifted his trumpet and only took snuff." *Goldsmith.*

Sir James Northcote, the painter, is reported to have said of him: "I never heard the words, 'Your lordship' or 'Your ladyship' come from his mouth, nor did he ever say 'sir' in speaking to anyone but Dr. Johnson." "[Johnson] may be said to have formed my mind, and to have brushed from it a great deal of rubbish." *Sir Joshua Reynolds.*

of their first acquaintance. When they were one evening together at the Miss Cotterells', the then Duchess of Argyle and another lady of high rank came in. Johnson, thinking that the Miss Cotterells were too much engrossed by them, and that he and his friend were neglected, grew angry; and resolving to shock[1] their supposed pride, addressed himself in a low tone to Mr. Reynolds, saying, "How much do you think you and I could get in a week, if we were to *work as hard* as we could?"—as if they had been common mechanics.

His acquaintance with Bennet Langton,[2] Esq. of Langton, in Lincolnshire, commenced soon after the conclusion of his *Rambler,* which that gentleman, then a youth, had read with so much admiration that he came to London chiefly with a view of endeavoring to be introduced to its author. By chance he happened to take lodgings in a house where Mr. Levet frequently visited; and having mentioned his wish to his landlady, she introduced him to Mr. Levet, who readily obtained Johnson's permission to bring Mr. Langton to him. Mr. Langton was exceedingly surprised when the sage first appeared. From perusing his writings, he fancied he should see a decent, well-dressed, in short, a remarkably decorous philosopher. Instead of which, down from his bed chamber, about noon, came, as newly risen, a huge, uncouth figure, with a little dark wig which scarcely covered his head, and his clothes hanging loose about him. But his conversation was so rich, so animated, and so forcible, and his religious and

---

1. *Resolving to shock.* "Men whose consciousness of their own merit sets them above the compliances of servility are apt enough in their association with superiors to watch their own dignity with troublesome and punctilious jealousy, and in the fervor of independence, to exact that attention which they refuse to pay." *Johnson: Life of Gray, 1780.*

2. *Langton.* Langton was only seventeen when he first met Johnson. He later went to Oxford, married, was negligent regarding his estate, sedulous regarding the happiness and moral welfare of his friends, and devoted to his children, whom Johnson thought he had too much about him. He saw all things through a pleasant atmosphere of learning. But he was rather too ready to give moral advice where it was not welcome. In the pages of this book he is often alluded to as a *worthy friend.*

political notions so congenial with those in which Langton had been educated, that he conceived for him that veneration and attachment which he ever preserved. Johnson was not the less ready to love Mr. Langton for his being of a very ancient family; for I have heard him say, with pleasure, "Langton, sir, has a grant of free warren* from Henry the Second; and Cardinal Stephen Langton, in King John's reign, was of this family."

Mr. Langton afterwards went to pursue his studies at Trinity College, Oxford, where he formed an acquaintance with his fellow student, Mr. Topham Beauclerk,[1] who, though their opinions and modes of life were so different that it seemed utterly improbable that they should at all agree, had so ardent a love of literature, so acute an understanding, such elegance of manners, and so well discerned the excellent qualities of Mr. Langton, that they became intimate friends.

Johnson, soon after this acquaintance began, passed a considerable time at Oxford. He at first thought it strange that Langton should associate so much with one who had the character of being loose, both in his principles and practice; but by degrees he himself was fascinated. Mr. Beauclerk's being of the St. Alban's family, and, having, in some particulars, a resemblance to Charles the Second, contributed, in Johnson's imagination, to throw a luster upon his other qualities; and in a short time the moral, pious Johnson and the gay, dissipated Beauclerk were companions. Beauclerk could take more liberty with him than anybody with whom I ever saw him; but, on the other hand, Beauclerk was not spared by his respectable companion when reproof was proper. Beauclerk had such a propensity to satire that at one time Johnson said to him,

---

1. *Beauclerk.* Four years Langton's junior. He was great-grandson of the witty, profligate Charles II and the brazen orange girl, Nell Gwynne. Their eldest son was created Duke of St. Albans. "He was eccentric; often querulous; entertaining a contempt for the generality of the world, which the politeness of his manners could not always conceal; but to those whom he liked, most generous and friendly." *Lord Charlemont.* "Topham Beauclerk (wicked and profligate as he wished to be accounted) was yet a man of very strict veracity. O Lord! how I did hate that horrid Beauclerk." *Mrs. Piozzi.*

"You never open your mouth but with intention to give pain; and you have often given me pain, not from the power of what you said, but from seeing your intention." At another time applying to him, with a slight alteration, a line of Pope, he said,

Thy love of folly, and thy scorn of fools—

"Everything thou dost shows the one, and everything thou say'st, the other." At another time he said to him, "Thy body is all vice, and thy mind all virtue." Beauclerk not seeming to relish the compliment, Johnson said, "Nay, sir, Alexander the Great, marching in triumph into Babylon, could not have desired to have had more said to him."

Johnson was some time with Beauclerk at his house at Windsor, where he was entertained with experiments in natural* philosophy. One Sunday, when the weather was very fine, Beauclerk enticed him, insensibly, to saunter about all the morning. They went into a churchyard, in the time of divine service, and Johnson laid himself down at his ease upon one of the tombstones. "Now, sir," said Beauclerk, "you are like Hogarth's 'Idle Apprentice.'" When Johnson got his pension, Beauclerk said to him in the humorous phrase of Falstaff, "I hope you'll now purge and live cleanly, like a gentleman."

One night, when Beauclerk and Langton had supped at a tavern in London, and sat till about three in the morning, it came into their heads to go and knock up Johnson, and see if they could prevail on him to join them in a ramble. They rapped violently at the door of his chambers in the Temple,[1] till at last he appeared in his shirt, with his little black wig on the top of his head, instead of a nightcap, and a poker in his hand, imagining, probably, that some ruffians were coming to attack him. When he discovered who they were, and was told their errand, he smiled, and with great good humor agreed to their proposal: "What, is it you, you dogs! I'll have a

---

1. *The Temple.* A quiet garden, or small park, together with the law buildings and old church which were attached to it. On one side it was open to the River Thames. On the opposite side, it was accessible to busy Fleet Street through a lane and archway.

frisk with you." He was soon dressed, and they sallied forth together into Covent Garden,[1] where the greengrocers and fruiterers were beginning to arrange their hampers, just come in from the country. Johnson made some attempts to help them; but the honest gardeners stared so at his figure and manner, and odd interference, that he soon saw his services were not relished. They then repaired to one of the neighboring taverns, and made a bowl of that liquor called "Bishop," which Johnson had always liked; while in joyous contempt of sleep, from which he had been roused, he repeated the festive lines,

> Short, O short then be thy reign,
> And give us to the world again!

They did not stay long, but walked down to the Thames, took a boat, and rowed to Billingsgate.[2] Beauclerk and Johnson were so well pleased with their amusement that they resolved to persevere in dissipation for the rest of the day; but Langton deserted them, being engaged to breakfast with some young ladies. Johnson scolded him for "leaving his social friends to go and sit with a set of wretched *un-ideaed* girls." Garrick, being told of this ramble, said to him smartly, "I heard of your frolic[3] t'other night. You'll be in the Chronicle." Upon which Johnson afterwards observed, "*He* durst not do such a thing. His *wife* would not *let* him!"

---

1. *Covent Garden.* "The two great national theaters on one side, a churchyard full of moldy but undying celebrities on the other; a fringe of houses studded in every part with anecdote and history; a place where the very latest suppers and the earliest breakfasts jostle each other on the footways—such is Covent Garden Market, with some of its surrounding features." *William Makepeace Thackeray.*

2. *Billingsgate.* "Billingsgate is at this present a large water-gate, port, or harborough, for ships and boats commonly arriving there with fish, both fresh and salt, shellfishes, oranges, onions, and other fruits and roots, wheat, rye, and grain of divers sorts." *John Stow: A Survey of London, 1598.*

3. *Frolic.* Of another frolic of Johnson's—this time on a country walk—Langton is quoted as saying: "Taking out of his lesser pockets whatever might be in them—keys, pencil, purse, or penknife, and laying himself parallel with the edge of the hill, he actually descended, turning himself over and over till he came to the bottom."

[1754]. Lord Chesterfield,[1] to whom Johnson had paid the compliment of addressing to his Lordship[2] the "Plan" of his *Dictionary*, had behaved to him in such a manner as to excite his contempt and indignation. The world has been for many years amused with a story confidently told, and as confidently repeated with additional circumstances, that a sudden disgust was taken by Johnson upon his having been one day kept long in waiting in his Lordship's antechamber; that at last, when the door opened, out walked Colley Cibber;[3] and that

---

1. *Lord Chesterfield.* A retired diplomatist and statesman, fifteen years older than Johnson. He devoted himself without let or scruple to being diplomatic, cultivating equally a vice or a virtue in order to gain his ends. As Lord Lieutenant of Ireland, he conducted the affairs of that kingdom without friction by means of his pleasant wit and air of good nature. As a member of the House of Peers, he advocated liberal measures, for he believed in preparing as gracefully as possible for the coming days of more popular rule. He had no real respect for energetic feelings which must express themselves honestly at all costs; what he liked was graceful, temperate art and literature. But his suavity he carried so far that it made him ridiculous in some sophisticated quarters and an object of fear or suspicion in those less practiced. "There are many avenues to every man, and when you cannot get at him through the great one, try the serpentine ones and you will arrive at last." *Chesterfield: Letters to His Son.*

2. *Addressing to his Lordship.* In the eighteenth century men who wrote for a living were growing more and more to depend on what they could get from their rather hard taskmasters, the booksellers, but it was still not unusual for an author to dedicate a volume to some man of wealth and position whom he wanted for his "patron." From this patron he hoped for a private pension, an easy berth in his household, a snug political appointment, or at least a generous sum of money in the lump. Dr. Johnson was persuaded to dedicate the "Plan," or "Prospectus," of his *Dictionary* to Lord Chesterfield against his own natural inclinations. He was, therefore, probably all the more angry that his effort brought no real attention and only a sum of money so small (£10) as to be a mark of contempt. In the *Dictionary* itself he defined *patron* as "Commonly, a wretch who supports with insolence and is paid with flattery."

3. *Cibber.* Colley Cibber (1671-1757), comedian, dramatist, and theater-manager, thirty-eight years Johnson's senior. "That good-humored and honest veteran so unworthily aspersed by Pope." *Horace Walpole.* "That old irreclaimable sinner of 79 . . . Vice in youth is not excusable, but in old age it is unpardonable." *Lady Bradshaigh, 1751.*

Johnson was so violently provoked when he found for whom he had been so long excluded that he went away in a passion, and never would return. I remember having mentioned this story to George Lord Lyttelton, who told me he was very intimate with Lord Chesterfield; and, holding it as a well-known truth, defended Lord Chesterfield by saying that "Cibber, who had been introduced familiarly by the back-stairs, had probably not been there above ten minutes." It may seem strange even to entertain a doubt concerning a story so long and so widely current; but Johnson himself assured me that there was not the least foundation for it. He told me that there never was any particular incident which produced a quarrel between Lord Chesterfield and him; but that his Lordship's continued neglect was the reason why he resolved to have no connection with him. When the *Dictionary* was upon the eve of publication, Lord Chesterfield attempted, in a courtly manner, to soothe and insinuate himself with the Sage, conscious, as it should seem, of the cold indifference with which he had treated its learned author; and further attempted to conciliate him by writing two papers in *The World*,[1] in recommendation of the work; and it must be confessed that they contain some studied compliments, so finely turned that if there had been no previous offense, it is probable that Johnson would have been highly delighted.

His Lordship says, "I think the public in general, and the republic of letters in particular, are greatly obliged to Mr. Johnson for having undertaken and executed so great and desirable a work. Perfection is not to be expected from man; but if we are to judge by the various works of Johnson already published, we have good reason to believe that he will bring this as near to perfection as any man could do. The plan of it, which he published some years ago, seems to me to be a

---

1. *Two papers in The World*. In one of them Chesterfield describes how an intrigue had been spoiled because a "lady" had blundered in spelling the address on a letter and he advises all *such* persons "to conform to Mr. Johnson's rules of true orthography" if they wish to succeed in their purposes. The coarseness and indignity of this jest made no impression on Boswell.

proof of it. Nothing can be more rationally imagined, or more accurately and elegantly expressed. I therefore recommend the previous perusal of it to all those who intend to buy the *Dictionary*, and who, I suppose, are all those who can afford it.

"It must be owned that our language is, at present, in a state of anarchy, and hitherto, perhaps, it may not have been the worse for it. During our free and open trade, many words and expressions have been imported, adopted, and naturalized from other languages, which have greatly enriched our own. Let it still preserve what real strength and beauty it may have borrowed from others; but let it not, like the Tarpeian maid,[1] be overwhelmed and crushed by unnecessary ornaments. The time for discrimination seems to be now come. Toleration, adoption, and naturalization have run their lengths. Good order and authority are now necessary. But where shall we find them, and at the same time, the obedience due to them? We must have recourse to the old Roman expedient in times of confusion, and choose a dictator. Upon this principle I give my vote for Mr. Johnson to fill that great and arduous post, and I hereby declare that I make a total surrender of all my rights and privileges in the English language, as a free-born British subject, to the said Mr. Johnson, during the term of his dictatorship.[2] Nay, more, I will not only obey him like an old Roman, as my dictator, but, like a modern Roman, I will implicitly believe in him as my pope, and hold him to be infallible while in the chair, but no longer. More than this he cannot well require; for, I presume that obedience can never be expected where there is neither terror to enforce, nor interest to invite it."

---

1. *Tarpeian maid.* According to legend, a Roman maiden who was tempted by the gold ornaments of a hostile army to open the citadel of Rome. As the invaders entered they contemptuously threw their shields on her and crushed her to death.

2. *Dictatorship.* "Things modified by human understandings . . . and changeable as experience advances knowledge or accident modifies caprice are scarcely to be included in any standing form of expression because they are always suffering some alteration of their state. Definition is, indeed, not the province of man." *Johnson: The Rambler.*

This courtly device[1] failed of its effect. Johnson despised the honeyed words, and was even indignant that Lord Chesterfield should, for a moment, imagine that he could be the dupe of such an artifice. His expression to me concerning Lord Chesterfield upon this occasion was, "Sir, after making great professions, he had, for many years, taken no notice of me; but when my *Dictionary* was coming out, he fell a scribbling in *The World* about it. Upon which, I wrote him a letter expressed in civil terms, but such as might show him that I did not mind what he said or wrote, and that I had done with him." This is that celebrated letter of which so much has been said, and about which curiosity has been so long excited, without being gratified. I for many years solicited Johnson to favor me with a copy of it. He delayed from time to time to give it me; till at last in 1781, when we were on a visit at Mr. Dilly's, at Southill in Bedfordshire, he was pleased to dictate it to me from memory. He afterwards found among his papers a copy of it, which he had dictated to Mr. Baretti, with its title and corrections, in his own handwriting. This he gave to Mr. Langton; adding that if it were to come into print, he wished it to be from that copy. By Mr. Langton's kindness, I am enabled to enrich my work with a perfect transcript of what the world has so eagerly desired to see.

"February 7, 1755.

"To the Right Honorable the Earl of Chesterfield.

"MY LORD: I have been lately informed by the proprietor of *The World* that two papers, in which my *Dictionary* is recommended to the public, were written by your Lordship. To be so distinguished is an honor which, being very little accustomed to favors from the great, I know not well how to receive, or in what terms to acknowledge.

---

1. *This courtly device.* "Johnson said to Garrick and others, 'I have sailed a long and painful voyage round the world of the English language; and does he now send out two cock-boats to tow me into harbor?'" *Murphy: An Essay on the Life and Genius of Samuel Johnson.*

"When, upon some slight encouragement, I first visited your Lordship, I was overpowered, like the rest of mankind, by the enchantment of your address, and could not forbear to wish that I might boast myself *Le[1] vainqueur du vainqueur de la terre;* —that I might obtain that regard for which I saw the world contending; but I found my attendance so little encouraged that neither pride nor modesty would suffer me to continue it. When I had once addressed your Lordship in public, I had exhausted all the art of pleasing which a retired and uncourtly scholar can possess. I had done all that I could; and no man is well pleased to have his all neglected, be it ever so little.

"Seven years, my Lord, have now passed, since I waited in your outward rooms, or was repulsed from your door; during which time I have been pushing on my work through difficulties, of which it is useless to complain, and have brought it, at last, to the verge of publication, without one act of assistance,[2] one word of encouragement, or one smile of favor. Such treatment I did not expect, for I never had a patron before.

"The shepherd in Virgil grew at last acquainted with Love, and found him a native of the rocks.

"Is not a patron, my Lord, one who looks with unconcern on a man struggling for life in the water, and, when he has reached ground, encumbers him with help? The notice which you have been pleased to take of my labors, had it been early, had been kind; but it has been delayed till I am indifferent, and cannot enjoy it; till I am solitary, and cannot impart it; till I am known, and do not want it. I hope it is no very cynical asperity not to confess obligations where no benefit has been received, or to be unwilling that the public should consider me as owing that to a patron, which Providence has enabled me to do for myself.

---

1. Translations will be found in the Glossary.
2. *One act of assistance.* "Dr. Johnson when he gave me this copy of his letter desired that I would annex to it his information to me that whereas it is said in the letter that 'no assistance had been received,' he did once receive from Lord Chesterfield the sum of ten pounds; but as that was so inconsiderable a sum, he thought the mention of it could not properly find place in a letter of the kind that this was." *Langton.*

"Having carried on my work thus far with so little obligation to any favorer of learning, I shall not be disappointed though I should conclude it, if less be possible, with less; for I have been long wakened from that dream of hope, in which I once boasted myself with so much exultation,

"My Lord,
"Your Lordship's most humble,
"Most obedient servant,
"SAM. JOHNSON."

There is a curious minute circumstance which struck me in comparing the various editions of Johnson's *Imitations of Juvenal*. In the tenth Satire one of the couplets upon the vanity of wishes even for literary distinction stood thus:

> Yet think what ills the scholar's life assail,
> Toil, envy, want, the garret, and the jail.

But after experiencing the uneasiness which Lord Chesterfield's fallacious patronage made him feel, he dismissed the word *garret* from the sad group, and in all the subsequent editions the line stands,

> Toil, envy, want, the *Patron*, and the jail.

Dr. Adams mentioned to Mr. Robert Dodsley that he was sorry Johnson had written his letter to Lord Chesterfield. Dodsley, with the true feelings of trade, said he was very sorry, too; for that he had a property in the *Dictionary*, to which his Lordship's patronage might have been of consequence. He then told Dr. Adams that Lord Chesterfield had shown him the letter. "I should have imagined," replied Dr. Adams, "that Lord Chesterfield would have concealed it." "Poh!" said Dodsley, "do you think a letter from Johnson could hurt Lord Chesterfield? Not at all, sir. It lay upon his table, where anybody might see it. He read it to me; said, 'this man has great powers,' pointed out the severest passages, and observed how well they were expressed." This air of indifference[1] was certainly nothing but a specimen of that dissimulation which Lord Chesterfield inculcated as one of the most essential lessons for the conduct of life. His Lordship excused his neglect of Johnson by saying that he had heard he had changed his lodgings, and did not know where he lived; as if there could have been the smallest difficulty to inform himself of that circumstance, by inquiring in the literary circle with which his Lordship was well acquainted, and was, indeed, himself one of its ornaments.

Dr. Adams expostulated with Johnson, and suggested that his not being admitted when he called on him was probably not to be imputed to Lord Chesterfield; for his Lordship had declared to Dodsley that he would have turned off the best servant he ever had if he had known that he denied him to a man who would have been always more than welcome; and in confirmation of this he insisted on Lord Chesterfield's general affability and easiness of access, especially to literary men. "Sir," said Johnson, "that is not Lord Chesterfield; he is the proudest man this day existing." "No," said Dr. Adams, "there is one person, at least, as proud; I think, by your own account, you are the prouder man of the two." "But mine," replied Johnson instantly, "was *defensive* pride."

Johnson, having now explicitly avowed his opinion of Lord Chesterfield, did not refrain from expressing himself concerning that nobleman with pointed freedom: "This man," said he, "I thought had been a lord among wits; but, I find, he is only a wit among lords!"

Mr. Andrew Millar,[2] bookseller in the Strand, took the

1. *This air of indifference.* "When things happen to be said of you, the most prudent way is to seem not to suppose they are meant at you; and, should they be so plain that you cannot be supposed ignorant of their meaning, to join in the laugh of the company against yourself; acknowledge the hit to be a fair one and the jest a good one, and play off the whole thing in seeming good humor." *Chesterfield: Letters to His Son.*

2. *Mr. Andrew Millar.* "I respect Millar, sir; he has raised the price of literature." *Johnson.*

principal charge of conducting the publication of Johnson's *Dictionary;* and as the patience of the proprietors was repeatedly tried and almost exhausted by their expecting that the work would be completed within the time which Johnson had sanguinely supposed, the learned author was often goaded to dispatch, more especially as he had received all the copy money, by different drafts, a considerable time before he had finished his task. When the messenger who carried the last sheet to Millar returned, Johnson asked him, "Well, what did he say?"—"Sir," answered the messenger, "he said, 'Thank God I have done with him.'" "I am glad," replied Johnson, with a smile, "that he thanks God for anything."

The definitions have always appeared to me such astonishing proofs of acuteness of intellect and precision of language as indicate a genius of the highest rank. This is what marks the superior excellence of Johnson's *Dictionary* over others equally or even more voluminous, and must have made it a work of much greater mental labor than mere lexicons, or word-books, as the Dutch call them. They who will make the experiment of trying how they can define a few words of whatever nature will soon be satisfied of the justice of this observation, which I can assure my readers is founded upon much study and upon communication with more minds than my own.

A few of his definitions must be admitted to be erroneous. Thus *windward* and *leeward*, though directly of opposite meaning, are defined the same way; nor was he at all disconcerted when an instance was pointed out to him. A lady once asked him how he came to define *pastern*, "the knee of a horse"; instead of making an elaborate defense, as she expected, he at once answered, "Ignorance, madam, pure ignorance."[1] His definition of *network*[2] has often been quoted, with sportive

---

1. *Ignorance, madam, pure ignorance.* Of one error in the *Dictionary*, Sir Joshua Reynolds says: "I asked him how he came not to correct it in the second edition. 'No,' says he, 'they made so much of it that I would not flatter them by altering it.'"

2. *Network.* "Anything reticulated or decussated, at equal distances, with interstices between the intersections."

malignity, as obscuring a thing in itself very plain. But to these frivolous censures no other answer is necessary than that with which we are furnished by his own preface:

"To explain requires the use of terms less abstruse than that which is to be explained, and such terms cannot always be found."

His introducing his own opinions, and even prejudices, under general definitions of words, while at the same time the original meaning of the words is not explained, as his *tory*,[1] *whig*,[2] *pension*, *oats*, *excise*, and a few more cannot be fully defended, and must be placed to the account of capricious and humorous indulgence. Talking to me upon this subject when we were at Ashbourne in 1777, he mentioned a still stronger instance of the predominance of his private feelings in the composition of this work than any now to be found in it. "You know, sir, Lord Gower forsook the old Jacobite interest. When I came to the word *renegado*, after telling that it meant 'one who deserts to the enemy, a revolter,' I added, 'Sometimes we say a Gower.' Thus it went to the press, but the printer had more wit than I, and struck it out."

---

1. *Tory.* "One who adheres to the ancient constitution of the state and the apostolical hierarchy of the Church of England; opposed to a Whig."

2. *Whig.* "The name of a faction."

Elsewhere, Johnson makes a fairer distinction between the two. He says: "A wise Tory and a wise Whig, I believe, will agree. Their principles are the same, though their modes of thinking are different. A high Tory makes government unintelligible; it is lost in the clouds. A violent Whig makes it impracticable; he is for allowing so much liberty to every man that there is not power enough to govern any man. The prejudice of the Tory is for establishment; the prejudice of the Whig is for innovation. A Tory does not wish to give more real power to Government; but that Government should have more reverence. Then they differ as to the Church. The Tory is not for giving more legal power to the clergy, but wishes they should have a considerable influence, founded on the opinion of mankind; the Whig is for limiting and watching them with a narrow jealousy." What the poet Shenstone has said of Whigs helps explain Johnson's dislike of them: "Abstract reasoners, of no manner of attachment to persons . . . but prodigiously devoted to the ideas of virtue, liberty, and so forth, are generally Whigs."

Let it, however, be remembered that this indulgence does not display itself only in sarcasm toward others, but sometimes in playful allusion to the notions commonly entertained of his own laborious task. Thus: *"Grub Street,* the name of a street in London, much inhabited by writers of small histories, dictionaries, and temporary poems; whence any mean production is called *Grub Street."—"Lexicographer,* a writer of dictionaries, *a harmless drudge."*

At the time when he was concluding his Preface, Johnson's mind appears to have been in a state of depression. "I," says he, "may surely be contented without the praise of perfection, which if I could obtain in this gloom of solitude, what would it avail me? I have protracted my work till most of those whom I wished to please have sunk into the grave, and success and miscarriage are empty sounds. I therefore dismiss it with frigid tranquillity, having little to fear or hope from censure or from praise."

It must undoubtedly seem strange that the conclusion of his Preface should be expressed in terms so desponding, when it is considered that the author was then only in his forty-sixth year. But we must ascribe its gloom to that miserable dejection of spirits to which he was constitutionally subject, and which was aggravated by the death of his wife two years before. It pleased God to grant him almost thirty years of life after this time; and once when he was in a placid frame of mind, he was obliged to own to me that he had enjoyed happier days and had many more friends since that gloomy hour than before.

It is a sad saying that "most of those whom he wished to please had sunk into the grave"; and his case at forty-five was singularly unhappy, unless the circle of his friends was very narrow. I have often thought that as longevity is generally desired, and I believe, generally expected, it would be wise to be continually adding to the number of our friends, that the loss of some may be supplied by others.

The proposition which I have now endeavored to illustrate was, at a subsequent period of his life, the opinion of Johnson himself. He said to Sir Joshua Reynolds, "If a man does not make new acquaintance[1] as he advances through life, he will soon find himself left alone. A man, sir, should keep his friendship *in constant repair*."

The celebrated Mr. Wilkes, whose notions and habits of life were very opposite to his, but who was ever eminent for literature and vivacity, sallied forth with a little *Jeu d'Esprit* upon the following passage in his "Grammar of the English Tongue," prefixed to the *Dictionary:* "*H* seldom, perhaps never, begins any but the first syllable." In an essay printed in the *Public Advertiser*, this lively writer enumerated many instances in opposition to this remark; for example, "The author of this observation must be a man of a quick *appre-hension*, and of a most *compre-hensive* genius." The position is undoubtedly expressed with too much latitude.

In 1756 Johnson found that the great fame of his *Dictionary* had not set him above the necessity of "making provision for the day that was passing over him." He had spent, during the progress of the work, the money for which he had contracted to write his *Dictionary*. We have seen that the reward of his labor was only fifteen hundred and seventy-five pounds; and when the expense of amanuenses and paper, and other articles, are deducted, his clear profit was very inconsiderable. I once said to him, "I am sorry, sir, you did not get more for your *Dictionary*." His answer was, "I am sorry, too. But it was very well. The booksellers are generous, liberal-minded men."[2]

---

1. *New acquaintance.* This is one of the few instances in which Dr. Johnson's principles and Boswell's practice tally exactly. "I am writing in a great English parlor, to have my letter ready for the post at nine. I have thought of making a good acquaintance in each town on the road. No man has been more successful in making acquaintance easily than I have been; I even bring people quickly on to a degree of cordiality." *Boswell to Mr. Temple, 1775.*

2. *Liberal-minded men.* On March 16th of this year, Dr. Johnson wrote to the famous novelist, Samuel Richardson: "Sir, I am obliged to entreat your assistance. I am now under an arrest for five pounds, eighteen shillings. If you will be so good as to send me this sum, I will very gratefully repay you, and add it to all former obligations."

[He] engaged to contribute largely to the *Literary Magazine, or Universal Review*, the first number of which came out in May this year. In his review of the *Memoirs of the Court of Augustus* he has the resolution to speak from his own mind, regardless of the cant[1] transmitted from age to age in praise of the ancient Romans. Thus: "The Romans, like others, as soon as they grew rich, grew corrupt; and in their corruption sold the lives and freedoms of themselves, and of one another." Again, "A people, who while they were poor robbed mankind; and as soon as they became rich robbed one another."

This year Mr. William Payne published *An Introduction to the Game of Draughts,* to which Johnson contributed a "Dedication to the Earl of Rochford." There is a composure and gravity in draughts which insensibly tranquillizes the mind; and, accordingly, the Dutch are fond of it, as they are of smoking, of the sedative influence of which, though he himself never smoked, he had a high opinion. Besides, there is in draughts some exercise of the faculties; and, accordingly, Johnson wishing to dignify the subject in his "Dedication" with what is most estimable in it, observes, "Triflers may find or make anything a trifle; but since it is the great characteristic of a wise man to see events in their causes, to obviate consequences, and ascertain contingencies, your Lordship will think nothing a trifle by which the mind is inured to caution, foresight, and circumspection."

He this year resumed his scheme of giving an edition of Shakespeare with notes. It is remarkable that at this time his fancied activity was for a moment so vigorous that he promised his work should be published before Christmas, 1757. Yet nine years elapsed before it saw the light. His throes in bringing it forth had been severe and remittent, and at last we may conclude that the Cesarian operation was performed

---

1. *Cant.* Particularly among men of Boswell's way of thinking, who were taking Plutarch's idealized pictures of Greeks and Romans as if they were true to life and significant of the capacities of human nature. Nor did Dr. Johnson's manly protest produce any noticeable effect. Plutarch's vogue increased through the century.

by the knife of Churchill,[1] whose upbraiding satire, I dare say, made Johnson's friends urge him to dispatch—

> He for subscribers[2] baits his hook,
> And takes your cash; but where's the book?
> No matter where; wise fear, you know,
> Forbids the robbing of a foe;
> But what, to serve our private ends,
> Forbids the cheating of our friends?

On the fifteenth of April [1758] he began a new periodical paper, entitled *The Idler*, which came out every Saturday. Mr. Langton remembers Johnson, when on a visit at Oxford, asking him one evening how long it was till the post went out, and on being told about half an hour, he exclaimed, "Then we shall do very well." He upon this instantly sat down and finished an *Idler*. Mr. Langton having signified a wish to read it, "Sir," said he, "you shall not do more than I have done myself." He then folded it up and sent it off.

"To Bennet Langton, Esq., of Trinity College, Oxford.

"DEAR SIR: Though I might have expected to hear from you upon your entrance into a new state of life at a new place, yet recollecting, not without some degree of shame, that I owe you a letter upon an old account, I think it my part to write first.

"I know not anything more pleasant or more instructive[3] than to compare experience with expectation, or to register from time to time the difference between idea and reality. It is by this kind of observation that we grow daily less liable to be disappointed. You, who are very capable of anticipating futurity, and raising phantoms before your own eyes, must often have imagined to yourself an academical life, and have

---

1. *Churchill.* Charles Churchill (1731-64), a biting satirist and fast fellow about town.

2. *Subscribers.* In the eighteenth century authors often got the names and at least part of the money of some buyers beforehand. The names of these "subscribers" were published in the book when it came out, to give it prestige.

3. *More pleasant or more instructive.* Johnson thinks differently on page 71.

conceived what would be the manners, the views, and the conversation of men devoted to letters; how they would choose their companions, how they would direct their studies, and how they would regulate their lives. Let me know what you expected, and what you have found.

"Your very humble servant,
"SAM. JOHNSON.

"June 28, 1758."

"To Bennet Langton, Esq., at Langton, near Spilsby, Lincolnshire.

"DEAR SIR: I should be sorry to think that what engrosses the attention of my friend should have no part of mine. Your mind is now full of the fate of Dury.[1] A violent death is never very painful; the only danger is lest it should be unprovided. But if a man can be supposed to make no provision for death in war, what can be the state that would have awakened him to the care of futurity? When would that man have prepared himself to die, who went to seek death without preparation? Let us endeavor to see things as they are, and then inquire whether we ought to complain. Whether to see life as it is will give us much consolation, I know not; but the consolation which is drawn from truth, if any there be, is solid and durable; that which may be derived from error, must be, like its original, fallacious and fugitive.

"I am, dear, dear sir,
"Your most humble servant,
"SAM. JOHNSON.

"Sept. 21, 1758."

In 1759, in the month of January, his mother died at the great age of ninety, an event which deeply affected him.[2] I have been told that he regretted much his not having gone to visit his mother for several years previous to her death.

---

1. *Dury.* "Major General Alexander Dury, who fell in the gallant discharge of his duty, near St. Cas, in the well-known, unfortunate expedition against France in 1758." *Boswell.* He was Langton's uncle by marriage.

2. *Affected him.* "Whose death," he had written ten years before, "is one of the few calamities on which I think with terror."

But he was constantly engaged in literary labors which confined him to London, and though he had not the comfort of seeing his aged parent, he contributed liberally to her support. Soon after this event he wrote his *Rasselas, Prince of Abyssinia,* that with the profits he might defray the expense of his mother's funeral, and pay some little debts which she had left. He told Sir Joshua Reynolds that he composed it in the evenings of one week, sent it to the press in portions as it was written, and had never since read it over.

Voltaire's *Candide,* written to refute the system of Optimism, which it has accomplished with brilliant success, is wonderfully similar in its plan and conduct[1] to Johnson's *Rasselas;* insomuch, that I have heard Johnson say that if they had not been published so closely one after the other that there was not time for imitation, it would have been in vain to deny that the scheme of that which came latest was taken from the other. Though the proposition illustrated by both these works was the same, namely, that in our present state there is more evil than good, the intention of the writers was very different. Voltaire, I am afraid, meant only by wanton profaneness to obtain a sportive victory over religion, and to discredit the belief of a superintending Providence. Johnson meant, by showing the unsatisfactory nature of things temporal, to direct the hopes of man to things eternal.

Notwithstanding my high admiration of *Rasselas,* I will not maintain that the "morbid melancholy" in Johnson's constitution may not, perhaps, have made life appear to him more insipid and unhappy than it generally is, for I am sure that he had less enjoyment from it than I have. The truth, however, is that we judge of the happiness and misery of life differently at different times, according to the state of our changeable frame. I always remember a remark made to me by a Turkish lady, educated in France, *"Ma foi, Monsieur, notre bonheur dépend de la façon que notre sang circule."* After much speculation and various reasonings, I acknowledge myself convinced of

---

1. *Wonderfully similar in its plan and conduct.* See Appendix C, page 546.

the truth of Voltaire's conclusion, *"Après tout c'est un monde passable."* But we must not think too deeply:

> —— where ignorance is bliss,
> 'Tis folly to be wise,

is, in many respects, more than poetically just. Let us cultivate, under the command of good principles, *"la théorie des sensations agréables"*; and, as Mr. Burke once admirably counseled a grave and anxious gentleman, "Live pleasant."

I would ascribe to this year the following letter to a son of one of his early friends at Lichfield, Mr. Joseph Simpson.

"To Joseph Simpson, Esq.

"DEAR SIR: Your father's inexorability not only grieves but amazes me; he is your father; he was always accounted a wise man; nor do I remember anything to the disadvantage of his good nature; but in his refusal to assist you there is neither good nature, fatherhood, nor wisdom.

"If you married imprudently, you miscarried at your own hazard, at an age when you had a right of choice. It would be hard if the man might not choose his own wife, who has a right to plead before the Judges of his country.

"If your imprudence has ended in difficulties and inconveniences, you are yourself to support them; and with the help of a little better health you would support them and conquer them. Surely, that want which accident and sickness produces is to be supported in every region of humanity, though there were neither friends nor fathers in the world. You have certainly from your father the highest claim of charity, though none of right; and therefore I would counsel you to omit no decent nor manly degree of importunity. Your debts in the whole are not large, and of the whole but a small part is troublesome. Small debts are like small shot: they are rattling on every side, and can scarcely be escaped without a wound. Great debts are like cannon; of loud noise, but little danger. You must, therefore, be enabled to discharge petty debts, that you may have leisure, with security, to struggle with the rest. Neither the great nor little debts disgrace you. I am

sure you have my esteem for the courage with which you contracted them, and the spirit with which you endure them. I
wish my esteem could be of more use. I have been invited,
or have invited myself, to several parts of the kingdom. Whither
I shall fly is matter of no importance. A man unconnected is
at home everywhere; unless he may be said to be at home
nowhere. I am sorry, dear sir, that where you have parents,
a man of your merits should not have a home. I wish I could
give it you. I am, my dear sir,

"Affectionately yours,

"SAM. JOHNSON."

[1760].[1] Johnson was now very idle or very busy with his
Shakespeare; for I can find no other public composition by
him except an "Introduction to the proceedings of the Committee
for clothing the French Prisoners,"[2] one of the many proofs
that he was ever awake to the calls of humanity.

On Easter eve [1761] he laments that his life, since the communion of the preceding Easter, had been "dissipated* and
useless." He, however, contributed this year the Preface to
Rolt's *Dictionary of Trade and Commerce.* I asked him whether
he knew much of Rolt, and of his work. "Sir," said he, "I
never saw the man, and never read the book. The booksellers wanted a preface to a *Dictionary of Trade and Commerce.*
I knew very well what such a dictionary should be, and I wrote
a preface accordingly." Rolt, who wrote a great deal for the

---

1. [*1760*]. "He had removed about the beginning of the year 1760,
to chambers two doors down the Inner Temple Lane; and I have been
told by his neighbor at the corner that during the time he dwelt there,
more inquiries were made at his shop for Mr. Johnson than for all the
inhabitants put together of both the Inner and Middle Temple." *Sir
John Hawkins.*

"In Dodsley's *London,* published in 1761, the side of the Temple
fronting the Thames is described as 'lying open and airy, and enjoying
a delightful prospect into Surrey.'" *Birkbeck Hill.*

2. *French Prisoners.* England was now at war with France. Of
them, Johnson wrote: "We know that for prisoners of war there is no
legal provision; we see their distress, and we are certain of its cause;
we know that they are poor and naked; and poor and naked without a
crime."

booksellers, was, as Johnson told me, a singular character.
When Akenside's *Pleasure of the Imagination* first came out,
he did not put his name to the poem. Rolt went over to
Dublin, published an edition of it, and put his own name to
it. Upon the fame of this he lived for several months, being
entertained at the best tables as "the ingenious Mr. Rolt."
His conversation, indeed, did not discover much of the fire of
a poet; but it was recollected that both Addison and Thomson
were equally dull till excited by wine. Several instances of
such literary fraud have been detected. Some years ago a
little novel, entitled *The Man of Feeling*, was assumed by
Mr. Eccles, a young Irish clergyman, who was afterwards
drowned near Bath.[1] He had been at the pains to transcribe
the whole book, with blottings, interlineations, and corrections that it might be shown to several people as an original.
It was, in truth, the production of Mr. Henry Mackenzie, an
attorney in the Exchequer at Edinburgh; but the belief with
regard to Mr. Eccles became so general that it was thought
necessary to publish an advertisement in the newspapers, contradicting the report. I can conceive this kind of fraud to be
very easily practiced with successful effrontery. The *filiation*
of a literary performance is difficult of proof; seldom is there
any witness present at its birth. A man, either in confidence
or by improper means, obtains possession of a copy of it
in manuscript, and boldly publishes it as his own. The true
author, in many cases, may not be able to make his title clear.

[1762]. A lady having at this time solicited [Johnson] to obtain
the Archbishop of Canterbury's patronage to have her son sent
to the University, he wrote to her the following answer:

"MADAM: When you made your request to me, you should
have considered, madam, what you were asking. You ask me
to solicit a great man, to whom I never spoke, for a young
person whom I had never seen, upon a supposition which I
had no means of knowing to be true. There is no reason why,
amongst all the great, I should choose to supplicate the Archbishop, nor why, among all the possible objects of his bounty,

---

1. *Drowned near Bath.* In attempting to save a boy's life.

the Archbishop should choose your son. I know, madam, how unwillingly conviction is admitted when interest opposes it; but surely, madam, you must allow that there is no reason why that should be done by me which every other man may do with equal reason, and which, indeed, no man can do properly without some very particular relation both to the Archbishop and to you. If I could help you in this exigence by any proper means, it would give me pleasure; but this proposal is so very remote from usual methods that I cannot comply with it but at the risk of such answer and suspicions as I believe you do not wish me to undergo.

"I have seen your son this morning; he seems a pretty youth, and will, perhaps, find some better friend than I can procure him; but though he should at last miss the University, he may still be wise, useful, and happy.

"I am, madam,

"Your most humble servant,

"Sam. Johnson.

"June 8, 1762."

"To Mr. Joseph Baretti,[1] at Milan.

"London, July 20, 1762

"Sir: As you have now been long away, I suppose your curiosity may pant for some news of your old friends. Miss Williams and I live much as we did. Mr. Reynolds gets six thousands a year. Levet is lately married, not without much suspicion that he has been wretchedly cheated in his match.[2] Mr. Richardson is dead of an apoplexy, and his second daughter has married a merchant.

---

1. *Baretti.* An Italian writer ardently devoted to London life and English literature. He has described himself as a fiery fellow who turns savage and whose hand turns to his sword. One night in London, attacked by three bullies, he mortally stabbed one in self-defense, and had difficulty in being acquitted of murder. Edmund Burke, Garrick, Beauclerk, and Dr. Johnson testified in his behalf.

2. *Cheated in his match.* He was not long married before his wife ran away. Soon after, apparently much to his gratification, she was arrested for picking pockets.

"My vanity, or my kindness, makes me flatter myself that you would rather hear of me than of those whom I have mentioned; but of myself I have very little which I care to tell. Last winter I went down to my native town, where I found the streets much narrower and shorter than I thought I had left them, inhabited by a new race of people, to whom I was very little known. My playfellows were grown old, and forced me to suspect that I was no longer young. My only remaining friend has changed his principles, and was become the tool of the predominant faction. My daughter-in-law[1] has lost the beauty and gayety of youth, without having gained much of the wisdom of age. I wandered about for five days and took the first convenient opportunity of returning to a place where, if there is not much happiness, there is, at least, such a diversity of good and evil that slight vexations do not fix upon the heart.

> "Sir,
>
> "Your most affectionate, humble servant,
> "SAM. JOHNSON."

The accession of George the Third to the throne of these kingdoms opened a new and brighter prospect to men of literary merit. His present Majesty's education in this country, as well as his taste and beneficence, prompted him to be the patron of science and the arts; and early this year Johnson, having been represented to him as a very learned and good man, without any certain provision, his Majesty was pleased to grant him a pension[2] of three hundred pounds a year.

---

1. *Daughter-in-law.* In other words, step-daughter; Lucy Porter. Five years later Johnson speaks jocosely of her "hoary virginity." "Lucy is a philosopher; and considers me as one of the external and accidental things that are to be taken and left without emotion." *Johnson, 1771.* "When you complained for want of oysters, I ordered you a barrel weekly for a month; you sent me word sooner that you had enough, but I did not countermand the rest. If you could not eat them, could you not give them away?" *Johnson in 1778 to Miss Porter.*

2. *Pension.* Johnson's definition of pension in his *Dictionary* had included the following sentence: "In England it is generally understood to mean pay given to a state hireling for treason to his country."

The Earl of Bute,[1] who was then Prime Minister, had the honor to announce this instance of his Sovereign's bounty, concerning which various stories have been propagated, maliciously representing it as a political bribe to Johnson to desert his avowed principles and become the tool of a government which he held to be founded in usurpation. I have taken care to have it in my power to refute them from the most authentic information. Lord Bute told me that Mr. Wedderburne,[2] now Lord Loughborough, was the person who first mentioned this subject to him.

Mr. Thomas Sheridan and Mr. Murphy,[3] who then lived a good deal both with [Johnson] and Mr. Wedderburne, told me that it was perfectly understood by all parties that the pension was merely honorary. Sir Joshua Reynolds told me that Johnson called on him and said that he wished to consult his friends as to the propriety of his accepting this mark of the royal favor. Sir Joshua answered that there could be no objection to his receiving from the King a reward for literary merit. Johnson did not call again till he had accepted the pension and had waited on Lord Bute to thank him. He then told Sir Joshua that Lord Bute said to him expressly, "It is not given you for anything you are to do, but for what you have done." His Lordship, he said, behaved in the handsomest manner. He repeated the words twice, that he might be sure Johnson heard them, and thus set his mind perfectly at ease.

---

1. *Earl of Bute.* So frightened by hostile mobs that he resigned in his first year.

2. *Wedderburne.* Very competent but unscrupulous. "He . . . hears himself despised, execrated, detested without fear and without anger." *Junius.*

3. *Murphy.* Arthur Murphy, a retired actor, author, and lawyer. Gentlemanly and quiet, he was well adapted to act as an intermediary on matters which required tact. At Lord Loughborough's request he first tendered the suggestion of a pension to Johnson. It was in the lexicographer's "wretched" rooms in Inner Temple Lane. Johnson made a long pause, fell into a deep meditation, recalled his definition of *pensioner*, and only on the following day "gave up all his scruples." For Murphy's biographical essay on Dr. Johnson, see Birkbeck Hill's *Johnsonian Miscellanies.*

Mr. Murphy and the late Mr. Sheridan severally contended for the distinction of having been the first who mentioned to Mr. Wedderburne that Johnson ought to have a pension. When I spoke of this to Lord Loughborough, he said, "All his friends assisted"; and when I told him that Mr. Sheridan strenuously asserted his claim to it, his Lordship said, "He rang the bell."

But I shall not detain my readers longer by any words of my own, on a subject on which I am happily enabled to present them with the following letter:

"To the Right Honorable the Earl of Bute.

"MY LORD: When the bills* were yesterday delivered to me by Mr. Wedderburne, I was informed by him of the future favors which his Majesty has, by your Lordship's recommendation, been induced to intend for me.

"Bounty always receives part of its value from the manner in which it is bestowed; your Lordship's kindness includes every circumstance that can gratify delicacy or enforce obligation. You have conferred your favors on a man who has neither alliance nor interest, who has not merited them by services nor courted them by officiousness; you have spared him the shame of solicitation, and the anxiety of suspense.

"What has been thus elegantly given, will, I hope, not be reproachfully enjoyed; I shall endeavor to give your Lordship the only recompense which generosity desires—the gratification of finding that your benefits are not improperly bestowed. I am, my Lord,

> "Your Lordship's most obliged,
> "Most obedient, and most humble servant,
> "SAM. JOHNSON.

"July 20, 1762."

This year his friend Sir Joshua Reynolds paid a visit of some weeks to his native country, Devonshire, in which he was accompanied by Johnson, who was much pleased with this jaunt.

Sir Joshua mentions a very characteristical anecdote of

Johnson while at Plymouth. Having observed that in consequence of the dock-yard a new town had arisen about two miles off as a rival to the old; and knowing from his just observation of human nature that it is certain if a man hates at all, he will hate his next neighbor, he concluded that this new and rising town could not but excite the envy and jealousy of the old, in which conjecture he was very soon confirmed; he therefore set himself resolutely on the side of the old town, the *established* town, in which his lot was cast, considering it as a kind of duty to *stand by* it. He accordingly entered warmly into its interests, and upon every occasion talked of the *dockers*, as the inhabitants of the new town were called, as upstarts and aliens. Plymouth is very plentifully supplied with water by a river brought into it from a great distance, which is so abundant that it runs to waste in the town. The Dock, or New-town, being totally destitute of water, petitioned Plymouth that a small portion of the conduit might be permitted to go to them, and this was now under consideration. Johnson, affecting to entertain the passions of the place, was violent in opposition; and half laughing at himself for his pretended zeal, where he had no concern, exclaimed, "No, no! I am against the *dockers;* I am a Plymouth man. Rogues! let them die of thirst. They shall not have a drop!"

Lord Macartney obligingly favored me with a copy of the following letter, in his own handwriting, from the original, which was found by the present Earl of Bute among his father's papers.

"To the Right Honorable the Earl of Bute.

"MY LORD: That generosity by which I was recommended to the favor of his Majesty will not be offended at a solicitation necessary to make that favor permanent and effectual.

"The pension appointed to be paid me at Michaelmas I have not received, and know not where or from whom I am to ask it. I beg, therefore, that your Lordship will be pleased to supply Mr. Wedderburne with such directions as may be necessary, which, I believe, his friendship will make him think it no trouble to convey to me.

"To interrupt your Lordship, at a time like this, with such petty difficulties, is improper and unseasonable; but your knowledge of the world has long since taught you that every man's affairs, however little, are important to himself. Every man hopes that he shall escape neglect; and with reason may every man whose vices do not preclude his claim expect favor from that beneficence which has been extended to,

    "My Lord,

        "Your Lordship's

            "Most obliged, and most humble servant,

                        "SAM. JOHNSON.

"Temple Lane,
   "Nov. 3, 1762."

[1763]. This is to me a memorable year; for in it I had the happiness to obtain the acquaintance of that extraordinary man whose memoirs I am now writing, an acquaintance which I shall ever esteem as one of the most fortunate circumstances in my life. Though then but two-and-twenty,[1] I had for several years read his works with delight and instruction,

---

1. *But two-and-twenty.*

      "Boswell is pleasant and gay,
      For frolic by nature designed;
      He heedlessly rattles away
      When the company is to his mind.
      This maxim he says you may see,
      We can never have corn without chaff;
      So not a bent sixpence cares he
      Whether with him or at him you laugh."

                    Boswell on Himself.

"He is of an ancient family in the west of Scotland, upon which he values himself not a little. At his nativity there appeared omens of his future greatness; his parts are bright, and his education has been good; he has traveled in post chaises miles without number; he is fond of seeing much of the world; he eats of every good dish, especially apple pie; he drinks old hock; he has a very fine temper; he is somewhat of a humorist [whimsical fellow] and a little tinctured with pride; he has a good manly countenance, and he owns himself to be amorous; he has infinite vivacity, yet is observed at times to have a melancholy cast; he is rather fat than lean, rather short than tall, rather young than old; his shoes are neatly made, and he never wears spectacles." *Boswell on Himself.*

and had the highest reverence for their author, which had grown up in my fancy into a kind of mysterious veneration by figuring to myself a state of solemn, elevated abstraction, in which I supposed him to live in the immense metropolis of London. Mr. Gentleman, a native of Ireland, who passed some years in Scotland as a player, and as an instructor in the English language, a man whose talents and worth were depressed by misfortunes, had given me a representation of the figure and manner of "Dictionary Johnson!" as he was then generally called; and during my first visit to London, which was for three months in 1760, Mr. Derrick, the poet, who was Gentleman's friend and countryman, flattered me with hopes that he would introduce me to Johnson. But he never found an opportunity, which made me doubt that he had promised to do what was not in his power; till Johnson some years afterwards told me, "Derrick, sir, might very well have introduced you. I had a kindness for Derrick, and am sorry he is dead."

In the summer of 1761 Mr. Thomas Sheridan[1] was at Edinburgh, and delivered lectures upon the English Language and Public Speaking. I was often in his company, and heard him frequently expatiate upon Johnson's knowledge, talents, and virtues, repeat his pointed sayings, describe his particularities, and boast of his being his guest sometimes till two or three in the morning. At his house I hoped to have many opportunities of seeing the sage.

When I returned to London in the end of 1762, to my surprise and regret I found an irreconcilable difference[2] had taken place between Johnson and Sheridan. A pension of two hundred pounds a year had been given to Sheridan. Johnson, who thought slightingly of Sheridan's art, upon hearing that he was also pensioned, exclaimed, "What! have they given *him* a pension? Then it is time for me to give up mine."

---

1. *Sheridan.* "A wrong-headed, whimsical man." *Dr. Parr.*
2. *Irreconcilable difference.* "We talked of one of our friends' taking ill, for a length of time, a hasty expression of Dr. Johnson's to him. *Johnson:* 'What is to become of society if a friendship of twenty years is to be broken off for such a cause?' " *Boswell: Journal of a Tour to the Hebrides.*

Johnson complained that a man who disliked him repeated his sarcasm to Mr. Sheridan without telling him what followed, which was that after a pause he added, "However, I am glad that Mr. Sheridan has a pension, for he is a very good man." Sheridan could never forgive this hasty, contemptuous expression. It rankled in his mind, and though I informed him of all that Johnson said, and that he would be very glad to meet him amicably, he positively declined repeated offers which I made, and once went off abruptly from a house where he and I were engaged to dine, because he was told that Dr. Johnson was to be there. I could not but smile, at the same time that I was offended, to observe Sheridan in the *Life of Swift*, which he afterwards published, attempting, in his resentment, to depreciate Johnson by characterizing him as "A writer of gigantic fame, in these days of little men"; that very Johnson whom he once so highly admired and venerated.

This rupture with Sheridan deprived Johnson of one of his most agreeable resources for amusement in his lonely evenings; for Sheridan's well-informed and bustling mind never suffered conversation to stagnate, and Mrs. Sheridan was a most agreeable companion to an intellectual man.

Mr. Thomas Davies the actor, who then kept a bookseller's shop in Russell Street, Covent Garden, told me that Johnson came frequently to his house, where he more than once invited me to meet him; but by some unlucky accident or other he was prevented from coming to us.

Mr. Thomas Davies was a man of good understanding and talents, with the advantage of a liberal education. Though somewhat pompous, he was an entertaining companion, and his literary performances have no inconsiderable share of merit. He was a friendly and very hospitable man. Both he and his wife, who has been celebrated for her beauty, though upon the stage for many years, maintained an uniform decency of character; and Johnson esteemed them, and lived in as easy an intimacy with them as with any family which he used to visit. Mr. Davies recollected several of Johnson's remarkable sayings, and was one of the best of the many imitators of his voice and manner, while relating them. He increased my impatience more and more to see the extraordinary man whose works I highly valued, and whose conversation was reported to be so excellent.

At last, on Monday the 16th of May, when I was sitting in Mr. Davies's back parlor, after having drunk tea with him and Mrs. Davies, Johnson unexpectedly came into the shop; and Mr. Davies having perceived him through the glass door in the room in which we were sitting, advancing toward us— he announced his awful approach to me, somewhat in the manner of an actor in the part of Horatio when he addresses Hamlet on the appearance of his father's ghost, "Look, my Lord, it comes." I found that I had a very perfect idea of Johnson's figure, from the portrait of him painted by Sir Joshua Reynolds soon after he had published his *Dictionary*, in the attitude of sitting in his easy chair in deep meditation. Mr. Davies mentioned my name, and respectfully introduced me to him. I was much agitated and recollecting his prejudice against the Scotch, of which I had heard much, I said to Davies, "Don't tell where I come from."—"From Scotland," cried Davies, roguishly. "Mr. Johnson," said I, "I do indeed come from Scotland, but I cannot help it." I am willing to flatter myself that I meant this as light pleasantry to soothe and conciliate him, and not as an humiliating abasement at the expense of my country. But however that might be, this speech was somewhat unlucky for he seized the expression "come from Scotland," and retorted, "That, sir, I find, is what a very great many of your countrymen cannot help." This stroke stunned me a good deal and when we had sat down, I felt myself not a little embarrassed, and apprehensive of what might come next. He then addressed himself to Davies: "What do you think of Garrick? He has refused me an order for the play for Miss Williams, because he knows the house will be full, and that an order would be worth three shillings." Eager to take any opening to get into conversation with him, I ventured to say, "Oh, sir, I cannot think Mr. Garrick would grudge such a trifle to you." "Sir," said he, with a stern look, "I have known David Garrick longer than you have done, and I know no right you have to talk to me on the subject." Perhaps I deserved this check, for it was rather presumptuous in me, an entire stranger, to express any doubt of the justice of his animadversion upon his old acquaintance and pupil. I now felt myself much mortified, and began to think that the hope which I had long indulged of obtaining his acquaintance was blasted. And, in truth, had not my ardor been uncommonly strong, and my resolution uncommonly persevering, so rough a reception might have deterred me forever from making any further attempts. Fortunately, however, I remained upon the field not wholly discomfited, and was soon rewarded by hearing some of his conversation, of which I preserved the following short minute without marking the questions and observations by which it was produced.

"People," he remarked, "may be taken in once, who imagine that an author is greater in private life than other men. Uncommon parts require uncommon opportunities for their exertion.

"In barbarous society, superiority of parts is of real consequence. Great strength or great wisdom is of much value to an individual. But in more polished times there are people to do everything for money, and then there are a number of other superiorities, such as those of birth and fortune and rank, that dissipate men's attention and leave no extraordinary share of respect for personal and intellectual superiority. This is wisely ordered by Providence, to preserve some equality among mankind.

"The notion of liberty amuses the people of England and helps to keep off the *tedium vitæ*. When a butcher tells you that *his heart bleeds for his country*, he has, in fact, no uneasy feeling.

"Derrick may do very well, as long as he can outrun his character,* but the moment his character gets up with him, it is all over."

It is, however, but just to record that some years afterwards, when I reminded him of this sarcasm, he said, "Well, but

Derrick has now got a character that he need not run away from."

I was highly pleased with the extraordinary vigor of his conversation, and regretted that I was drawn away from it by an engagement at another place. I had, for a part of the evening, been left alone with him, and had ventured to make an observation now and then, which he received very civilly, so that I was satisfied that though there was a roughness in his manner, there was no ill-nature in his disposition. Davies followed me to the door, and when I complained to him a little of the hard blows which the great man had given me, he kindly took upon him to console me by saying, "Don't be uneasy. I can see he likes you very well."

A few days afterwards I called on Davies, and asked him if he thought I might take the liberty of waiting on Mr. Johnson at his chambers in the Temple. He said I certainly might, and that Mr. Johnson would take it as a compliment. So upon Tuesday the 24th of May, after having been enlivened by the witty sallies of Messieurs Thornton,[1] Wilkes, Churchill, and Lloyd, with whom I had passed the morning, I boldly repaired to Johnson. His Chambers were on the first floor of No. 1, Inner Temple Lane, and I entered them with an impression given me by the Reverend Dr. Blair,[2] of Edinburgh, who had been introduced to him not long before, and described his

---

1. *Thornton, Wilkes, Churchill, and Lloyd.* Famous for wit, and for dissipation that startled the town. Men of this sort were among Boswell's favorite companions. Yet he once wrote to Wilkes, "I do, in my conscience, believe you to be an enemy to the true old British Constitution, and to the order and happiness of society. That is to say, I believe you to be a very Whig, and a very libertine."

2. *The Reverend Dr.* [*Hugh*] *Blair* (1718-1800). Boswell's cousin; a collector of ballads and other folk literature as well as a professor of rhetoric and *belles lettres* in the University of Edinburgh. "He was as eager about a new paper to his wife's drawing-room or his own new wig as about a new tragedy or a new epic poem." *Alexander Carlyle.* His *Rhetoric* (1783), now old-fashioned and onerous, was welcomed when it was published, by those eager to rally to a new esthetics. It had a great vogue, not only in England but on the Continent.

having "found the Giant in his den."[1]   Dr. Blair had been
presented to him by Dr. James Fordyce.   At this time the
controversy concerning the pieces published by Mr. James
Macpherson,[2] as translations of *Ossian*, was at its height.
Johnson had all along denied their authenticity and, what
was still more provoking to their admirers, maintained that
they had no merit.   The subject having been introduced by
Dr. Fordyce, Dr. Blair, relying on the internal evidence of
their antiquity, asked Dr. Johnson whether he thought any
man of a modern age could have written such poems.   Johnson
replied, "Yes, sir, many men, many women, and many children."   Johnson at this time did not know that Dr. Blair
had just published a "Dissertation," not only defending their
authenticity, but seriously ranking them with the poems of
Homer and Virgil; and when he was afterwards informed of
this circumstance, he expressed some displeasure at Dr. Fordyce's
having suggested the topic, and said, "I am not sorry that they
got thus much for their pains.   Sir, it was like leading one to
talk of a book when the author is concealed behind the door."[3]

He received me very courteously, but it must be confessed
that his apartment and furniture and morning dress were
sufficiently uncouth.   His brown suit of clothes looked very
rusty; he had on a little, old, shriveled, unpowdered wig, which
was too small for his head; his shirt-neck and knees of his
breeches were loose; his black, worsted stockings ill drawn up,
and he had a pair of unbuckled shoes by way of slippers.   But

---

1. *Giant in his den.*   "Now I saw in my dream that at the end of
the Valley lay blood, bones, ashes, and mangled bodies of men, even
of pilgrims that had gone this way formerly; and, while I was musing
what should be the reason, I espied a little before me a cave, where two
giants, Pope and Pagan, dwelt in old time, by whose power and tyranny
the men, whose bones, blood, ashes, etc., lay there, were cruelly put to
death."   *Bunyan: Pilgrim's Progress, 1677.*

2. *Macpherson.*   See Appendix D, page 547.

3. *When the author is concealed behind the door.*   One day, twenty
years before, thinking himself too shabbily dressed to appear at his
publisher's table, Johnson sat hidden behind a screen, where "a plate
of victuals" was passed out to him.   In this concealed position, he
had to overhear the conversation turn to his last book.

all these slovenly particularities were forgotten the moment that he began to talk. Some gentlemen, whom I do not recollect, were sitting with him, and when they went away, I also rose, but he said to me, "Nay, don't go."—"Sir," said I, "I am afraid that I intrude upon you. It is benevolent to allow me to sit and hear you." He seemed pleased with this compliment, which I sincerely paid him, and answered, "Sir, I am obliged to any man who visits me."[1]—I have preserved the following short minute of what passed this day.

"Madness frequently discovers itself merely by unnecessary deviation from the usual modes of the world. My poor friend Smart[2] showed the disturbance of his mind by falling upon his knees and saying his prayers in the street, or in any other unusual place. Now although, rationally speaking, it is greater madness not to pray at all than to pray as Smart did, I am afraid there are so many who do not pray that their understanding is not called in question."

Concerning this unfortunate poet, Christopher Smart, who was confined in a mad-house, he had, at another time, the following conversation with Dr. Burney:[3] "I did not think he ought to be shut up. His infirmities were not noxious to society. He insisted on people praying with him; and I'd as lief pray with Kit Smart as anyone else. Another charge was that he did not love clean linen; and I have no passion for it."

---

1. *Who visits me.* "Solitude is dangerous to reason, without being favorable to virtue; pleasures of some sort are necessary to the intellectual as well as to the corporeal health; . . . the mind stagnates for want of employment, grows morbid, and is extinguished like a candle in foul air." *Johnson, quoted by Mrs. Piozzi.*

2. *Smart.* His most famous poem—his "Song to David"—he scrawled originally on the walls of his cell. Of a still more gifted victim of insanity, Johnson once wrote: "Poor dear Collins! Let me know whether you think it would give him pleasure if I should write to him. I have often been near his state [morbid melancholy], and therefore have it in great commiseration."

3. *Burney.* Charles Burney (1726-1814), a fashionable teacher of music and an agreeable seeker after talented and improving society; the father of Mme. D'Arblay.

Johnson continued, "Mankind have a great aversion to intellectual labor, but even supposing knowledge to be easily attainable, more people would be content to be ignorant than would take even a little trouble to acquire it."

Talking of Garrick, he said, "He is the first man in the world for sprightly conversation."

When I rose a second time, he again pressed me to stay, which I did.

He told me that he generally went abroad at four in the afternoon, and seldom came home till two in the morning. I took the liberty to ask if he did not think it wrong to live thus, and not make more use of his great talents. He owned it was a bad habit. On reviewing, at the distance of many years, my journal of this period, I wonder how, at my first visit, I ventured to talk to him so freely, and that he bore it with so much indulgence.

Before we parted, he was so good as to promise to favor me with his company one evening at my lodgings, and, as I took my leave, shook me cordially by the hand. It is almost needless to add that I felt no little elation at having now so happily established an acquaintance of which I had been so long ambitious.

I did not visit him again till Monday, June 13. He asked me why I did not come oftener to him. Trusting that I was now in his good graces, I answered that he had not given me much encouragement, and reminded him of the check I had received from him at our first interview. "Poh, poh!" said he, with a complacent smile, "never mind these things. Come to me as often as you can. I shall be glad to see you."

I had learned that his place of frequent resort was the Mitre Tavern in Fleet Street, where he loved to sit up late, and I begged I might be allowed to pass an evening with him there soon, which he promised I should. A few days afterwards I met him near Temple Bar, about one o'clock in the morning, and asked him if he would then go to the Mitre. "Sir," said he, "it is too late; they won't let us in. But I'll go with you another night with all my heart."

A revolution of some importance in my plan of life had just taken place; for instead of procuring a commission in the foot-guards,[1] which was my own inclination, I had, in compliance with my father's wishes, agreed to study the law, and was soon to set out for Utrecht,[2] to hear the lectures of an excellent Civilian in that University, and then to proceed on my travels. Though very desirous of obtaining Dr. Johnson's advice[3] and instructions on the mode of pursuing my studies, I was at this time so occupied—shall I call it—or so dissipated, by the amusements of London, that our next meeting was not till Saturday, June 25, when, happening to dine at Clifton's eating-house, in Butcher Row, I was surprised to perceive Johnson come in and take his seat at another table. The mode of dining, or rather being fed, at such houses in London, is well known to many to be particularly unsocial, as there is no ordinary,* or united company, but each person has his own mess, and is under no obligation to hold any intercourse with anyone. A liberal and full-minded man, however, who loves to talk will break through this churlish and unsocial restraint.

---

1. *Foot-guards.* "I am thinking of the brilliant scenes of happiness I shall enjoy as an officer of the guards. How I shall . . . become a favorite of ministers of state, and the adoration of ladies of quality, beauty, and fortune! How many parties of pleasure shall I have in town! How many fine jaunts to the noble seats of dukes, lords, and members of Parliament! I am thinking of the perfect knowledge which I shall acquire of men and manners, of the intimacies which I shall have the honor to form with the learned and ingenious in every science, and of the many amusing literary anecdotes which I shall pick up." *Boswell to Andrew Erskine, 1763.*

2. *Utrecht.* "I could almost weep to think of leaving dear London and the calm retirement of Inner Temple. . . . You may see I am somewhat melancholy; pray comfort me. This is very effeminate and very young, but I cannot help it." *Boswell to Mr. Temple.*

3. *Dr. Johnson's advice.* "You tell me gravely to follow the plan which my father prescribes, whatever it may be; and in doing so, I shall certainly act most wisely. I forgive you this, for I say just the same to young people when I advise. To enter into a detail of the little circumstances which compose the felicity of another is what a man of any genius can hardly submit to. We, therefore, give a good, wholesome, general counsel; and he who consults us thinks a little, and then endeavors to take his own way as well as he can." *Boswell to Sir Andrew Mitchell, 1764.*

Johnson and an Irish gentleman got into a dispute concerning the cause of some part of mankind being black. What the Irishman said is totally obliterated from my mind, but I remember that he became very warm and intemperate in his expressions, upon which Johnson rose and quietly walked away. When he had retired, his antagonist took his revenge, as he thought, by saying, "He has a most ungainly figure, and an affectation of pomposity, unworthy of a man of genius."

Johnson had not observed that I was in the room. I followed him, however, and he agreed to meet me in the evening at the Mitre. I called on him, and we went thither at nine. We had a good supper, and port wine, of which he then sometimes drank a bottle. The orthodox high-church sound of the *Mitre*, the figure and manner of the celebrated Samuel Johnson, the extraordinary power and precision of his conversation, and the pride arising from finding myself admitted as his companion, produced a variety of sensations, and a pleasing elevation of mind beyond what I had ever before experienced. I find in my *Journal* the following minute of our conversation, which, though it will give but a very faint notion of what passed, will be curious as showing how habitual to his mind were some opinions which appear in his works.

"Sir, I do not think Gray a first-rate poet. He has not a bold imagination,[1] nor much command of words.[2] The obscurity[3] in which he has involved himself will not persuade

---

1. *Not a bold imagination.* "He said . . . he had been used to write only lyric poetry, in which the poems being short, he was able to polish every part; that this having become a habit, he could not write otherwise." *Norton Nicholls: Reminiscences of Gray, 1805.*

2. *Nor much command of words.* "The poverty of rime, the crowd of monosyllables, the collision of harsh consonants, and the want of picturesque expression which, I will be bold to say, our language labors under *now* more than it did a hundred years ago." *Gray, 1760.*

3. *Obscurity.* "Must I plunge into metaphysics? Alas! I cannot see in the dark; nature has not furnished me with the optics of a cat. Must I pore upon mathematics? Alas! I cannot see in too much light; I am no eagle. It is very possible that two and two make four, but I would not give four farthings to demonstrate this ever so clearly; and if these be the profits of life, give me the amusements of it." *Gray, 1786.* See also Landor on Gray in the *Imaginary Conversations.*

us that he is sublime. His Elegy in a Churchyard has a happy selection of images, but I don't like what are called his great things. His ode, which begins

> Ruin seize thee, ruthless King,
> Confusion on thy banners wait!

has been celebrated for its abruptness, and plunging into the subject all at once. But such arts as these have no merit, unless when they are original. We admire them only once, and this abruptness has nothing new in it. We have had it often before. Nay, we have it in the old song of Johnny Armstrong:

> Is there ever a man in all Scotland,
> From the highest estate to the lowest degree, etc.

And then, sir,

> Yes, there is a man in Westmoreland
> And Johnny Armstrong they do him call.

There now, you plunge at once into the subject. You have no previous narration to lead you to it.—The two next lines in that ode are, I think, very good:

> Though fanned by conquest's crimson wing,
> They mock the air with idle state."

Here let it be observed, that although his opinion of Gray's poetry was widely different from mine, and I believe from that of most men of taste, by whom it is with justice highly admired, there is certainly much absurdity in the clamor which has been raised, as if he had been culpably injurious to the merit of that bard, and had been actuated by envy. That his opinion on this subject was what in private and in public he uniformly expressed, regardless of what others might think, we may wonder, and perhaps regret; but it is shallow and unjust to charge him with expressing what he did not think.

Finding him in a placid humor, I opened my mind to him ingenuously, and gave him a little sketch of my life, to which he was pleased to listen with great attention.

I acknowledged that though educated very strictly in the principles of religion, I had for some time been misled into a certain degree of infidelity, but that I was come now to a better way of thinking, and was fully satisfied of the truth of the Christian revelation, though I was not clear as to every point considered to be orthodox. Being at all times a curious examiner of the human mind, and pleased with an undisguised display of what had passed in it, he called to me with warmth, "Give me your hand; I have taken a liking to you." He then began to descant upon the force of testimony, and the little we could know of final causes,* so that the objections of, why was it so? or why was it not so? ought not to disturb us;[1] adding, that he himself had at one period been guilty of a temporary neglect of religion, but that it was not the result of argument, but mere absence of thought.

After having given credit to reports of his bigotry, I was agreeably surprised when he expressed the following very liberal sentiment, which has the additional value of obviating an objection to our holy religion, founded upon the discordant tenets of Christians themselves: "For my part, sir, I think all Christians, whether Papists or Protestants, agree in the essential articles,[2] and that their differences are trivial, and rather political than religious."

We talked of belief in ghosts. He said, "Sir, I make a distinction between what a man may experience by the mere strength of his imagination, and what imagination cannot possibly produce. Thus, suppose I should think that I saw a form, and heard a voice cry, 'Johnson, you are a very wicked fellow, and unless you repent you will certainly be punished'— my own unworthiness is so deeply impressed upon my mind

1. *Not to disturb us.* "Why, sir, the greatest concern we have in this world, the choice of our profession, must be determined without *demonstrative reasoning* [absolute proof] . . . And take the case of a man who is ill. I call two physicians; they differ in opinion. I am not to lie down and die between them. I must do something." *Johnson, quoted in Boswell's Journal of a Tour to the Hebrides.*

2. *Agree in the essential articles.* Note that Johnson says this when he is standing on the defensive regarding the Christian religion. At other times he might not be so tolerant.

that I might *imagine* I thus saw and heard, and therefore I should not believe that an external communication had been made to me. But if a form should appear, and a voice should tell me that a particular man had died at a particular place[1] and a particular hour, a fact which I had no apprehension of, nor any means of knowing, and this fact, with all its circumstances, should afterwards be unquestionably proved, I should, in that case, be persuaded that I had supernatural intelligence imparted to me."

Here it is proper, once for all, to give a true and fair statement of Johnson's way of thinking upon the question, whether departed spirits are ever permitted to appear in this world, or in any way to operate upon human life. He has been ignorantly misrepresented as weakly credulous upon that subject; and, therefore, though I feel an inclination to disdain and treat with silent contempt so foolish a notion concerning my illustrious friend, yet as I find it has gained ground, it is necessary to refute it. The real fact then is that Johnson had such a rational respect for testimony[2] as to make him submit his understanding to what was authentically proved, though he could not comprehend why it was so. Being thus disposed, he was willing to inquire into the truth of any relation of supernatural agency, a general belief of which has prevailed in all nations and ages. But so far was he from being the dupe of implicit faith that he examined the matter with a jealous

---

1. *A particular man had died at a particular place.* "Men mark when they hit and never mark when they miss." *Francis Bacon: Of Prophecies.*

2. *Respect for testimony.* The following principles Dr. Johnson sometimes follows and sometimes disregards: (1) Never accept any explanation which you cannot reconcile in some way with your general body of belief. Believing contradictions, knowing them to be contradictions, is to believe nonsense. (2) Accept an opinion only when the evidence of the facts is on the whole for it. When the evidence is on the whole against it, or when there is no evidence at all, dismiss the notion from the mind. (3) Accept the simplest and least extraordinary explanation that will account for the facts. These principles Dr. Johnson preferred to the sentimental vaporing which was almost as popular in his own generation as it is today. But he sometimes lost his hold on them and became "weakly credulous" and "fearfully superstitious."

attention, and no man was more ready to refute its falsehood when he had discovered it. Churchill, in his poem entitled "The Ghost," availed himself of the absurd credulity imputed to Johnson, and drew a caricature of him under the name of "Pomposo,"[1] representing him as one of the believers of the story of a Ghost in Cock Lane,[2] which, in the year 1762, had gained very general credit in London. Many of my readers, I am convinced, are to this hour under an impression that Johnson was thus foolishly deceived. It will therefore surprise them a good deal when they are informed upon undoubted authority that Johnson was one of those by whom the imposture was detected. The story had become so popular that he thought it should be investigated, and in this research he was assisted by the Reverend Dr. Douglas, now Bishop of Salisbury, the great detector of impostures, who informs me that after the gentlemen who went and examined into the evidence were satisfied of its falsity, Johnson wrote in their presence an account of it, which was published in the newspapers and *Gentleman's Magazine*, and undeceived the world.

Our conversation proceeded.

---

1. *Pomposo. . . .* insolent and loud.
    "Vain idol of a scribbling crowd,

    . . .

    Who, cursing flattery, is the tool
    Of every fawning, flattering fool;

    . . .

    Who scorns those common wares to trade in,
    Reasoning, convincing, and persuading,
    But makes each sentence current pass
    With puppy, coxcomb, scoundrel, ass;

    . . .

    Who, to increase his native strength,
    Draws words six syllables in length,
    With which, assisted with a frown,
    By way of club, he knocks us down."

    Charles Churchill: The Ghost.

2. *Ghost in Cock Lane.* A trick. The mysterious knockings and scratchings by which the "ghost" was supposed to make his presence felt were the work of a little girl of eleven set on and managed by her rascally father to pay off a grudge. The purpose of the "ghost" was to accuse one Kent of poisoning his sister-in-law and to get him hanged.

I mentioned Mallet's[1] tragedy of *Elvira*, which had been acted the preceding winter, and that the Honorable Andrew Erskine,[2] Mr. Dempster, and myself, had joined in writing a pamphlet against it; that the mildness of Dempster's disposition had, however, relented, and he had candidly said, "We have hardly a right to abuse this tragedy, for bad as it is, how vain should either of us be to write one not near so good." JOHNSON. "Why no, sir; this is not just reasoning. You *may* abuse a tragedy, though you cannot write one. You may scold a carpenter who has made you a bad table, though you cannot make a table. It is not your trade to make tables."

When I talked to him of the paternal estate to which I was heir, he said, "Sir, let me tell you that to be a Scotch landlord, where you have a number of families dependent upon you, and attached to you, is, perhaps as high a situation as humanity can arrive at. A merchant upon the 'Change of London, with a hundred thousand pounds, is nothing; an English Duke, with an immense fortune, is nothing; he has no tenants who consider themselves as under his patriarchal care, and who will follow him to the field upon an emergency."

His notion of the dignity of a Scotch landlord had been formed upon what he had heard of the Highland Chiefs; for it is long since a lowland landlord has been so curtailed in his feudal authority that he has little more influence over his tenants than an English landlord, and of late years most of the Highland Chiefs have destroyed, by means too well known, the princely power which they once enjoyed.

He proceeded: "Your going abroad, sir, and breaking off idle habits, may be of great importance to you. I would go where there are courts and learned men. There is a good deal of Spain that has not been perambulated. I would have you go thither. A man of inferior talents to yours may furnish us with useful observations upon that country." His supposing

---

1. *Mallet.* "The prettiest dressed puppet about town." *Johnson.*
2. *Erskine.* "Just about the time that he first met Johnson, he [Boswell] and his friend, the Hon. Andrew Erskine, had published in their own names a very impudent little volume of the correspondence that had passed between them." *Birkbeck Hill.*

me, at that period of life, capable of writing an account of my travels that would deserve to be read, elated me not a little.

I complained to him that I had not yet acquired much knowledge, and asked his advice as to my studies. He said, "Don't talk of study now. I will give you a plan, but it will require some time to consider of it." "It is very good in you," I replied, "to allow me to be with you thus. Had it been foretold to me some years ago that I should pass an evening with the author of the *Rambler*, how should I have exulted!" What I then expressed was sincerely from the heart. He was satisfied that it was, and cordially answered, "Sir, I am glad we have met. I hope we shall pass many evenings, and mornings too, together." We finished a couple of bottles of port, and sat till between one and two in the morning.

He wrote this year in *The Critical Review* the account of "Telemachus, a Mask," by the Reverend George Graham, of Eton College. The subject of this beautiful poem was particularly interesting to Johnson, who had much experience of "the conflict of opposite principles," which he describes as "The contention between pleasure and virtue, a struggle which will always be continued while the present system of nature shall subsist."

As Dr. Oliver Goldsmith will frequently appear in this narrative, I shall endeavor to make my readers in some degree acquainted with his singular character. He was a native of Ireland and a contemporary with Mr. Burke at Trinity College, Dublin, but did not then give much promise of future celebrity. He, however, observed to Mr. Malone, that "though he made no great figure in mathematics, which was a study in much repute there, he could turn an ode of Horace into English better than any of them." He afterwards studied physic at Edinburgh and upon the Continent, and, I have been informed, was enabled to pursue his travels on foot, partly by demanding at Universities to enter the lists as a disputant, by which, according to the custom of many of them, he was entitled to the premium of a crown when luckily for him his challenge was not accepted, so that, as I once observed to Dr. Johnson, he *disputed* his passage through Europe. He then came to England and was employed successively in the capacities of an usher to an academy, a corrector of the press, a reviewer, and a writer for a newspaper. He had sagacity enough to cultivate assiduously the acquaintance of Johnson. To me and many others it appeared that he studiously copied[1] the manner of Johnson, though, indeed, upon a smaller scale.

At this time I think he had published nothing with his name, though it was pretty generally known that *one* Dr. Goldsmith was the author of *An Inquiry into the Present State of Polite Learning in Europe*, and of *The Citizen of the World*, a series of letters supposed to be written from London by a Chinese. No man had the art of displaying with more advantage as a writer, whatever literary acquisitions he made. *"Nihil quod tetigit non ornavit."* His mind resembled a fertile, but thin, soil. There was a quick, but not a strong vegetation, of whatever chanced to be thrown upon it. No deep root could be struck. The oak of the forest did not grow there, but the elegant shrubbery and the fragrant parterre appeared in gay succession. It has been generally circulated and believed that he was a mere fool in conversation; but, in truth, this has been greatly exaggerated. He had, no doubt, a more than common share of that hurry of ideas which we often find in his countrymen, and which sometimes produces a laughable confusion in expressing them. He was very much what the French call *un étourdi*,[2] and from vanity and an eager desire of being conspicuous wherever he was, he frequently talked carelessly without knowl-

---

1. *Studiously copied.* Of Boswell himself Mme. D'Arblay says: "He had an odd mock solemnity of tone and manner that he had acquired imperceptibly from constantly thinking of and imitating Dr. Johnson. Every look and movement displayed either intentional or involuntary imitation. Yet certainly it was not meant as caricature." In the *Rambler*, fifteen years before meeting young Boswell, Dr. Johnson had written: "Almost all absurdity of conduct arises from imitation of those whom we cannot resemble."

2. *Un étourdi*, a stupid. "Sir, he was a fool. The right word never came to him. If you gave him a bad shilling, he'd say, 'Why, it's as good a shilling as ever was *born.*' You know he ought to have said *coined*. *Coined*, sir, never entered his head. He was a fool." *William Cooke, quoted by Samuel Rogers.*

edge of the subject, or even without thought.[1] His person was
short, his countenance coarse and vulgar, his deportment that
of a scholar awkwardly affecting the easy gentleman. Those
who were in any way distinguished excited envy in him to so
ridiculous an excess that the instances of it are hardly credible.
When accompanying two beautiful young ladies with their
mother on a tour in France, he was seriously angry that more
attention was paid to them[2] than to him, and once at the
exhibition of the *Fantoccini* in London, when those who sat
next him observed with what dexterity a puppet was made to
toss a pike, he could not bear that it should have such praise,
and exclaimed, "Pshaw! I can do it better myself."

He, I am afraid, had no settled system of any sort, so that
his conduct must not be strictly scrutinized, but his affections
were social and generous, and when he had money he gave it
away very liberally. His desire of imaginary consequence predominated over his attention to truth. He boasted to me of
the power of his pen in commanding money, which I believe
was true in a certain degree, though in the instance he gave he
was by no means correct. He told me that he had sold a novel
for four hundred pounds. This was his *Vicar of Wakefield*.
But Johnson informed me that he had made the bargain for

1. *Without thought.* "When Goldsmith entered a room, sir, people
who did not know him became for a moment silent from awe of his
literary reputation; when he came out again, they were riding upon
his back." *James Northcote, quoted by James Prior.* It was Sir
Joshua Reynolds's opinion that Goldsmith often made himself a joke
because he preferred the good-fellowship that followed to being surrounded by an atmosphere of awe or cold respect.

2. *More attention was paid to them.* "In the vicinity of the hotel
at which they put up, a part of the garrison going through some military maneuvers drew them to the windows, when the gallantry of the
officers broke forth into a variety of compliments intended for the ears
of the English ladies. Goldsmith seemed amused; but, at length,
assuming something of a severity of countenance, which was a peculiarity of his humor often displayed when most disposed to be jocular,
turned off, uttering something to the effect that elsewhere he would
also have his admirers. This, added my informant, was said in mere
playfulness, and I was shocked many years afterwards to see it adduced
in print as a proof of his envious disposition." *James Prior: Life of
Goldsmith.*

Goldsmith, and the price was sixty pounds. "And, sir," said he, "a sufficient price too, when it was sold, for then the fame of Goldsmith had not been elevated, as it afterwards was, by his *Traveller*, and the bookseller had such faint hopes of profit by his bargain that he kept the manuscript by him a long time, and did not publish it till after *The Traveller* had appeared. Then, to be sure, it was accidentally worth more money."

Mrs. Piozzi and Sir John Hawkins[1] have strangely misstated the history of Goldsmith's situation and Johnson's friendly interference when this novel was sold. I shall give it authentically from Johnson's own exact narration:

"I received one morning a message from poor Goldsmith that he was in great distress, and as it was not in his power to come to me, begging that I would come to him as soon as possible. I sent him a guinea, and promised to come to him directly. I accordingly went as soon as I was dressed, and found that his landlady had arrested him for his rent, at which he was in a violent passion. I perceived that he had already changed my guinea, and had got a bottle of Madeira and a glass before him. I put the cork into the bottle, desired he would be calm, and began to talk to him of the means by which he might be extricated. He then told me that he had a novel ready for the press, which he produced to me. I looked into it, and saw its merit; told the landlady I should soon return, and having gone to a bookseller, sold it for sixty pounds. I brought Goldsmith the money, and he discharged his rent, not without rating his landlady in a high tone for having used him so ill."

My next meeting with Johnson was on Friday the 1st of July, when he and I and Dr. Goldsmith supped at the Mitre. I was before this time pretty well acquainted with Goldsmith, who was one of the brightest ornaments of the Johnsonian school. Goldsmith's respectful attachment to Johnson was

1. *Sir John Hawkins.* According to all reports, small-minded and ponderously smug. Dr. Johnson called him "a most unclubable man." His attitude toward Goldsmith was one of vast superiority. Mrs. Piozzi, though sprightly herself, was often equally obtuse to Goldsmith's whimsical humor.

then at its height, for his own literary reputation had not yet distinguished him so much as to excite a vain desire of competition with his great master. He had increased my admiration of the goodness of Johnson's heart by incidental remarks in the course of conversation, such as, when I mentioned Mr. Levet, whom he entertained under his roof, "He is poor and honest, which is recommendation enough to Johnson"; and when I wondered that he was very kind to a man of whom I had heard a very bad character, "He is now become miserable, and that insures the protection of Johnson."

Goldsmith, attempting this evening to maintain, I suppose from an affectation of paradox, "that knowledge was not desirable on its own account, for it often was a source of unhappiness"—JOHNSON. "Why, sir, that knowledge may in some cases produce unhappiness, I allow. But, upon the whole, knowledge, *per se*, is certainly an object which every man would wish to attain, although, perhaps, he may not take the trouble necessary for attaining it."

Dr. John Campbell, the celebrated political and biographical writer, being mentioned, Johnson said, "Campbell is not always rigidly careful of truth in his conversation, but I do not believe there is anything of this carelessness in his books. Campbell is a good man, a pious man. I am afraid he has not been in the inside of a church for many years, but he never passes a church without pulling off his hat. This shows that he has good principles.[1] I used to go pretty often to Campbell's on a Sunday evening till I began to consider that the shoals of Scotchmen who flocked about him might say, when anything of mine was well done, 'Aye, aye, he has learned this of Cawmell!'"

He talked very contemptuously of Churchill's poetry, observ-

---

1. *Good principles.* At one time Johnson remarked, "Sir, you are so grossly ignorant of human nature as not to know that a man may be very sincere in good principles without having good practice." At another time he observed—and there is surely truth in both observations—"There are men who always confound the praise of goodness with the practice."

"I have now spent fifty-five years in resolving, having from the earliest times almost that I can remember been forming schemes of a better life." *Johnson: Prayers and Meditations.*

ing that "it had a temporary currency, only from its audacity of abuse, and being filled with living names, that it would sink into oblivion." I ventured to hint that he was not quite a fair judge, as Churchill had attacked him violently. JOHNSON. "Nay, sir, I am a very fair judge. He did not attack me violently till he found I did not like his poetry, and his attack on me shall not prevent me from continuing to say what I think of him. No, sir, I called the fellow a blockhead at first, and I will call him a blockhead still. However, I will acknowledge that he has shown more fertility than I expected. To be sure, he is a tree that cannot produce good fruit; he only bears crabs.* But, sir, a tree that produces a great many crabs is better than a tree which produces only a few."

Let me here apologize for the imperfect manner in which I am obliged to exhibit Johnson's conversation at this period. In the early part of my acquaintance with him I was so wrapped in admiration of his extraordinary colloquial talents, and so little accustomed to his peculiar mode of expression that I found it extremely difficult to recollect and record his conversation with its genuine vigor and vivacity. In progress of time, when my mind was, as it were, *strongly impregnated with the Johnsonian ether*, I could with much more facility and exactness carry in my memory and commit to paper[1] his wisdom and wit.

At this time *Miss* Williams, as she was then called, though she did not reside with him in the Temple under his roof, but had lodgings in Bolt Court, Fleet Street, had so much of his attention that he every night drank tea with her before he went home, however late it might be, and she always sat up for him. This, it may be fairly conjectured, was not alone a proof of his regard for *her*, but of his own unwillingness to go

---

1. *Commit to paper.* Usually from memory, as soon after the event as possible. Occasionally, it seems, he took out his notebook in public to the disgust of the company. "I try to keep a journal . . . but it is hardly credible . . . what a variety of men and manners I contemplate in a day, and all the time . . . my exuberant spirits will not let me listen enough." *Boswell.* "I have sometimes been obliged to run half over London in order to fix a date correctly." *The same.*

into solitude before that unseasonable hour at which he
had habituated himself to expect the oblivion of repose.
Dr. Goldsmith, being a privileged man, went with him this
night, strutting away, and calling to me with an air of
superiority, like that of an esoteric over an exoteric disciple
of a sage of antiquity, "I go to Miss Williams." I confess,
I then envied him this mighty privilege, of which he seemed
so proud, but it was not long before I obtained the same
mark of distinction.

On Tuesday, the 5th of July, I again visited Johnson. He
told me he had looked into the poems of a pretty voluminous
writer, Mr. (now Dr.) John Ogilvie, one of the Presbyterian
ministers of Scotland, which had lately come out, but could
find no thinking in them. BOSWELL. "Is there not imagination in them, sir?" JOHNSON. "Why, sir, there is in them
what *was* imagination, but it is no more imagination in *him*,
than sound is sound in the echo. And his diction too is not
his own. We have long ago seen *white-robed innocence*, and
flower-bespangled meads."

Talking of London, he observed, "Sir, if you wish to have
a just notion of the magnitude of this city, you must not be
satisfied with seeing its great streets and squares, but must
survey the innumerable little lanes and courts. It is not in
the showy evolutions of buildings, but in the multiplicity of
human habitations which are crowded together, that the wonderful immensity of London consists."—I have often amused
myself with thinking how different a place London is to different people. They whose narrow minds are contracted to
the consideration of some one particular pursuit view it only
through that medium. A politician thinks of it merely as the
seat of government in its different departments; a grazier, as a
vast market for cattle; a mercantile man, as a place where a
prodigious deal of business is done upon 'Change; a dramatic
enthusiast, as the grand scene of theatrical entertainments; a
man of pleasure, as an assemblage of taverns. But the intellectual man is struck with it, as comprehending the whole of
human life in all its variety, the contemplation of which is
inexhaustible.

On Wednesday, July 6, he was engaged to sup with me at my lodgings in Downing Street, Westminster.* But on the preceding night, my landlord having behaved very rudely to me and some company who were with me, I had resolved not to remain another night in his house. I was exceedingly uneasy at the awkward appearance I supposed I should make to Johnson and the other gentlemen whom I had invited, not being able to receive them at home, and being obliged to order supper at the Mitre. I went to Johnson in the morning, and talked of it as of a serious distress. He laughed, and said, "Consider, sir, how insignificant this will appear a twelve-month hence. There is nothing," continued he, "in this mighty misfortune; nay, we shall be better at the Mitre." I told him that I had been at Sir John Fielding's[1] office, complaining of my landlord, and had been informed that though I had taken my lodgings for a year, I might, upon proof of his bad behavior, quit them when I pleased, without being under an obligation to pay rent for any longer time than while I possessed them. The fertility of Johnson's mind could show itself even upon so small a matter as this. "Why, sir," said he, "I suppose this must be the law[2] since you have been told so in Bow Street.* But if your landlord could hold you to your bargain, and the lodgings should be yours for a year, you may certainly use them as you think fit. So, sir, you may quarter two life-guardsmen upon him, or you may send the greatest scoundrel you can find into your apartments, or you may say that you want to make some experiments in natural philosophy, and may burn a large quantity of asafetida in his house."

I had as my guests this evening at the Mitre Tavern, Dr. Johnson, Dr. Goldsmith, Mr. Thomas Davies, Mr. Eccles, an Irish gentleman, for whose agreeable company I was obliged to Mr. Davies, and the Reverend Mr. John Ogilvie.

Goldsmith, as usual, endeavored, with too much eagerness,

---

1. *Sir John Fielding.* A famous police magistrate of London, brother of Henry Fielding, the novelist.

2. *This must be the law.* "Let us hear, sir, no general abuse; the law is the last result of human wisdom acting upon human experience for the benefit of the public." *Johnson, quoted by Mrs. Piozzi.*

to *shine*, and disputed very warmly with Johnson against the
well-known maxim of the British constitution, "The king can
do no wrong," affirming that "what was morally false could
not be politically true; and as the king might, in the exercise
of his regal power, command and cause the doing of what was
wrong, it certainly might be said, in sense and in reason, that
he could do wrong." JOHNSON. "Sir, you are to consider
that in our constitution according to its true principles, the
king is the head, he is supreme; he is above everything, and
there is no power by which he can be tried. Therefore, it is,
sir, that we hold the king can do no wrong; that whatever
may happen to be wrong in government may not be above our
reach by being ascribed to Majesty. Redress is always to be
had against oppression by punishing the immediate agents.
The king, though he should command, cannot force a judge
to condemn a man unjustly; therefore it is the judge whom we
prosecute and punish. Political institutions are formed upon
the consideration of what will most frequently tend to the
good of the whole, although now and then exceptions may
occur. Thus it is better in general that a nation should have
a supreme legislative power, although it may at times be abused.
And then, sir, there is this consideration, that *if the abuse be
enormous, Nature will rise up, and claiming her original rights,
overturn a corrupt political system.*"

This generous sentiment, which he uttered with great fervor,
struck me exceedingly, and stirred my blood to that pitch of
fancied resistance, the possibility of which I am glad to keep
in mind, but to which I trust I never shall be forced.

"Great abilities," said he, "are not requisite[1] for a historian,
for in historical composition all the greatest powers of the
human mind are quiescent. He has facts ready to his hand;

---

1. *Not requisite.* History apparently bored Dr. Johnson. He had
little confidence in historians and their rhetorical devices for amplifying
the facts at their command. "I asked him once," says Mrs. Piozzi,
"concerning the conversation powers of a gentleman with whom I was
myself unacquainted. 'He talked to me at the Club,' replies the Doctor,
'concerning Catiline's conspiracy—so I withdrew my attention, and
thought about Tom Thumb.'"

so there is no exercise of invention. Imagination is not required in any high degree; only about as much as is used in the lower kinds of poetry. Some penetration, accuracy, and coloring will fit a man for the task, if he can give the application which is necessary.

"Bayle's *Dictionary* is a very useful work for those to consult who love the biographical part of literature, which is what I love most."

Mr. Ogilvie was unlucky enough to choose for the topic of his conversation the praises of his native country. He began with saying that there was very rich land around Edinburgh. Goldsmith, who had studied physic there, contradicted this, very untruly, with a sneering laugh. Disconcerted a little by this, Mr. Ogilvie then took a new ground, where, I suppose, he thought himself perfectly safe, for he observed that Scotland had a great many noble, wild prospects. JOHNSON. "I believe, sir, you have a great many. Norway, too, has noble, wild prospects, and Lapland is remarkable for prodigious noble, wild prospects. But, sir, let me tell you, the noblest prospect which a Scotchman ever sees is the high road that leads him to England!" This unexpected and pointed sally produced a roar of applause. After all, however, those who admire the rude grandeur of Nature cannot deny it to Caledonia.*

On Saturday, July 9, I found Johnson surrounded with a numerous levee, but have not preserved any part of his conversation. On the 14th we had another evening by ourselves at the Mitre. It happening to be a very rainy night, I made some commonplace observations on the relaxation of nerves and depression of spirits which such weather occasioned, adding, however, that it was good for the vegetable creation. Johnson, who denied that the temperature of the air had any influence on the human frame, answered, with a smile of ridicule, "Why, yes, sir, it is good for vegetables, and for the animals who eat those vegetables, and for the animals who eat those animals." This observation of his aptly enough introduced a good supper, and I soon forgot, in Johnson's company, the influence of a moist atmosphere.

Feeling myself now quite at ease as his companion, though

I had all possible reverence for him, I expressed a regret that I could not be so easy with my father,[1] though he was not much older than Johnson, and certainly, however respectable, had not more learning and greater abilities, to depress me. I asked him the reason of this. JOHNSON. "Why, sir, I am a man of the world. I live in the world, and I take, in some degree, the color of the world as it moves along. Your father is a Judge in a remote part of the island, and all his notions are taken from the old world. Besides, sir, there must always be a struggle between a father and son, while one aims at power and the other at independence." I said I was afraid my father would force me to be a lawyer. JOHNSON. "Sir, you need not be afraid of his forcing you to be a laborious practicing lawyer; that is not in his power. For as the proverb says, 'one man may lead a horse to the water, but twenty cannot make him drink.' He may be displeased that you are not what he wishes you to be, but that displeasure will not go far. If he insists only on your having as much law as is necessary for a man of property, and then endeavors to get you into Parliament, he is quite in the right."

He enlarged very convincingly upon the excellence of rime over blank verse in English poetry. I mentioned to him that Dr. Adam Smith, in his lectures upon composition, when I studied under him in the College of Glasgow, had maintained the same opinion strenuously, and I repeated some of his arguments. JOHNSON. "Sir, I was once in company with Smith,

---

1. *So easy with my father.* "I esteem and love my father and I am determined to do what is in my power to make him easy and happy; but you will allow that I may endeavor to make him happy and *at the same time not be too hard upon myself*." *Boswell to Sir Andrew Mitchell, 1754.* "My father has allowed me £60 a quarter . . . that is not a great allowance, but with economy I may live very well upon it. However, I am determined not to encourage the least narrowness of disposition as to saving money; but to draw upon my father for any sums I find necessary." *Boswell to Mr. Temple, 1763.* "I write to him with warmth, with honest pride, wishing that he should think of me as I am; but my letters shock him. . . . How galling is it in the friend of Paoli to be treated so! I have answered him in my own style. I will be myself." *Boswell, 1767.* These quotations, perhaps, throw some light on the question.

and we did not take to each other; but had I known that he loved rime as much as you tell me he does, I should have *hugged* him."

Talking of those who denied the truth of Christianity, he said, "It is always easy to be on the negative side. If a man were now to deny that there is salt upon the table, you could not reduce him to an absurdity. Come, let us try this a little further. I deny that Canada is taken,[1] and I can support my denial by pretty good arguments. The French are a much more numerous people than we, and it is not likely that they would allow us to take it. 'But the ministry have assured us, in all the formality of the *Gazette*,* that it is taken.'—Very true. But the ministry have put us to an enormous expense by the war in America, and it is their interest to persuade us that we have got something for our money.—'But the fact is confirmed by thousands of men who were at the taking of it.'— Aye, but these men have still more interest in deceiving us. They don't want that you should think the French have beat them, but that they have beat the French. Now suppose you should go over and find that it really is taken, that would only satisfy yourself, for when you come home we will not believe you. We will say you have been bribed.—Yet, sir, notwith-standing all these plausible objections, we have no doubt that Canada is really ours. Such is the weight of common testi-mony. How much stronger are the evidences of the Christian religion?"

To such a degree of unrestrained frankness had he now accustomed me that in the course of this evening I talked of the numerous reflections which had been thrown out against him on account of his having accepted a pension from his present Majesty. "Why, sir," said he, with a hearty laugh,

---

1. *Canada is taken.* In 1760 the whole of Canada surrendered to the British as a result of the French and Indian War. In 1819 Archbishop Whately wittily imitated Johnson's method of argument in his *Historic Doubts Relative to Napoleon Bonaparte*, like Johnson, making no distinction between miraculous evidence of supernatural power and merely surprising events or between reports of contemporary events and reports that have arisen in a distant past.

"it is a mighty foolish noise that they make. I have accepted of a pension as a reward which has been thought due to my literary merit; and now that I have this pension, I am the same man in every respect that I have ever been; I retain the same principles. It is true that I cannot now curse (smiling) the House of Hanover,[1] nor would it be decent for me to drink King James's health in the wine that King George gives me money to pay for. But, sir, I think that the pleasure of cursing the House of Hanover and drinking King James's health are amply overbalanced by three hundred pounds a year."

I have heard him declare that if holding up his right hand would have secured victory at Culloden[2] to Prince Charles's army, he was not sure he would have held it up; so little confidence had he in the right claimed by the House of Stuart, and so fearful was he of the consequences of another revolution on the throne of Great Britain; and Mr. Topham Beauclerk assured me he had heard him say this before he had his pension. At another time he said to Mr. Langton, "Nothing has ever offered that has made it worth my while to consider the question fully." He, however, also said to the same gentleman, talking of King James the Second, "It was become impossible for him to reign any longer in this country." He no doubt had an early attachment to the House of Stuart, but his zeal had cooled as his reason strengthened. Indeed, I heard him once say that after the death of a violent Whig,[3] with whom he used to contend with great eagerness, he felt his Toryism much abated. I suppose he meant Mr. Walmsley.

Yet there is no doubt that at earlier periods he was wont

---

1. *House of Hanover.* The heirs of Prince George of Hanover, who was crowned George I of England in 1714.

2. *Culloden.* In 1745 Prince Charles (the Young Pretender) landed in Scotland and proclaimed his father (the Old Pretender) King James III of England. In 1746, after having administered three defeats to the government troops, he was himself overwhelmingly defeated at the Battle of Culloden. The danger of his return passed forever.

3. *Whig.* The revolution which drove the last male heir of the Stuarts off the throne replaced him by a Whig. The dynasty that followed was therefore considered a Whig creation, even though some of them, as individuals, were Tories.

often to exercise both his pleasantry and ingenuity in talking Jacobitism. One day when dining at old Mr. Langton's, where Miss Roberts, his niece, was one of the company, Johnson, with his usual complacent attention to the fair sex, took her by the hand and said, "My dear, I hope you are a Jacobite."* Old Mr. Langton, who, though a high and steady Tory, was attached to the present royal family, seemed offended, and asked Johnson, with great warmth, what he could mean by putting such a question to his niece! "Why, sir," said Johnson, "I meant no offense to your niece; I meant her a great compliment. A Jacobite, sir, believes in the divine right of kings. He that believes in the divine right of kings believes in a divinity. A Jacobite believes in the divine right of bishops. He that believes in the divine right of bishops believes in the divine authority of the Christian religion. Therefore, sir, a Jacobite is neither an atheist nor a deist. That cannot be said of a Whig; for *Whiggism is a negation of all principle.*"

He advised me when abroad to be as much as I could with the professors in the Universities, and with the clergy, for from their conversation I might expect the best accounts of everything in whatever country I should be, with the additional advantage of keeping my learning alive.

It will be observed that when giving me advice as to my travels, Dr. Johnson did not dwell upon cities and palaces and pictures and shows and Arcadian scenes. He was of Lord Essex's opinion, who advises his kinsman Roger Earl of Rutland, "rather to go a hundred miles to speak with one wise man than five miles to see a fair town."

I described to him an impudent fellow from Scotland who affected to be a savage and railed at all established systems. JOHNSON. "There is nothing surprising in this, sir. He wants to make himself conspicuous. He would tumble in a hog-sty, as long as you looked at him and called to him to come out. But let him alone, never mind him, and he'll soon give it over."

I added that the same person maintained that there was no distinction between virtue and vice. JOHNSON. "Why, sir, if the fellow does not think as he speaks, he is lying, and I

see not what honor he can propose to himself from having the
character of a liar.   But if he does really think that there is no
distinction between virtue and vice, why, sir, when he leaves
our houses let us count our spoons."

He recommended to me to keep a journal of my life, full
and unreserved. He said it would be a very good exercise,
and would yield me great satisfaction when the particulars
were faded from my remembrance. I mentioned that I was
afraid I put into my journal too many little incidents. JOHNSON.
"There is nothing, sir, too little for so little a creature as man.
It is by studying little things that we attain the great art of
having as little misery and as much happiness as possible."

Next morning Mr. Dempster happened to call on me and
was so much struck even with the imperfect account which I
gave him of Dr. Johnson's conversation that to his honor be it
recorded, when I complained that drinking port and sitting up
late with him affected my nerves for some time after, he said,
"One had better be palsied at eighteen than not keep company
with such a man."

On Tuesday, July 18, I found tall Sir Thomas Robinson
sitting with Johnson. Sir Thomas said that the King of
Prussia[1] valued himself upon three things—upon being a hero,
a musician, and an author. JOHNSON. "Pretty well, sir, for
one man. As to his being an author, I have not looked at his
poetry, but his prose is poor stuff. He writes just as you may
suppose Voltaire's foot-boy to do, who has been his amanuensis.
He has such parts as the valet might have, and about as much
of the coloring of the style as might be got by transcribing his
works."   When I was at Ferney,[2] I repeated this to Voltaire in

---

1. *King of Prussia*. Frederick the Great (1712-86). Johnson has
written a manly sketch of him, in which he praises Frederick's care for
the physical development of his own subjects, but notes with indignation
his cynical violation of treaties, his mean anger against those who
defended themselves against wanton, treacherous attack, and his cruelty
to non-combatants.

2. *Ferney*. Near Geneva. Here Voltaire maintained lavish, open
house. Free-thinkers and souls proud of their "sensibility" flocked
to him. On special days he might entertain at his table from sixty
to eighty guests.

order to reconcile him somewhat to Johnson, whom he, in affecting the English mode of expression, had previously characterized as "a superstitious dog"; but after hearing such a criticism on Frederick the Great, with whom he was then on bad terms, he exclaimed, "An honest fellow!"

Mr. Levet this day showed me Dr. Johnson's library,[1] which was contained in two garrets over his chambers, where Lintot, son of the celebrated bookseller of that name, had formerly his warehouse. I found a number of good books, but very dusty and in great confusion. The floor was strewed with manuscript leaves in Johnson's own handwriting. I observed an apparatus for chemical experiments, of which Johnson was all his life very fond. The place seemed to be very favorable for retirement and meditation. Johnson told me that he went up thither without mentioning it to his servant when he wanted to study, secure from interruption; for he would not allow his servant to say he was not at home when he really was. "A servant's strict regard for truth," said he, "must be weakened by such a practice. A philosopher may know that it is merely a form of denial, but few servants are such nice distinguishers. If I accustom a servant to tell a lie for *me*, have I not reason to apprehend that he will tell many lies for *himself?*" I am, however, satisfied that every servant, of any degree of intelligence, understands saying his master is not at home, not at all as the affirmation of a fact, but as the customary words intimating that his master wishes not to be seen, so that there can be no bad effect from it.

Mr. Temple, now vicar of St. Gluvias, Cornwall, who had been my intimate friend for many years, had at this time chambers in Farrar's buildings, at the bottom of Inner Temple Lane, which he kindly lent me upon my quitting my lodgings,

---

1. *Johnson's library.* "July 19, 1763. I was with Mr. Johnson today. I was in his garret up four pair of stairs; it is very airy, commands a view of St. Paul's and many a brick roof. He has many good books, but they are all lying in confusion and dust." *Letters of Boswell.* "I hope to put my rooms in order. Disorder I have found one great cause of idleness." *Johnson: Prayers and Meditations.*

he being to return to Trinity Hall, Cambridge. I found them particularly convenient for me, as they were so near Dr. Johnson's.

On Wednesday, July 20, Dr. Johnson, Mr. Dempster, and my uncle, Dr. Boswell, who happened to be now in London, supped with me at these chambers. JOHNSON. "Pity[1] is not natural to man. Children are always cruel. Savages are always cruel. Pity is acquired and improved by the cultivation of reason. We may have uneasy sensations for seeing a creature in distress, without pity; for we have not pity unless we wish to relieve them. When I am on my way to dine with a friend, and finding it late, have bid the coachman make haste, if I happen to attend when he whips his horses, I may feel unpleasantly that the animals are put to pain, but I do not wish him to desist. No, sir, I wish him to drive on."

Mr. Alexander Donaldson, bookseller, of Edinburgh, had for some time opened a shop in London, and sold his cheap editions of the most popular English books, in defiance of the supposed common-law right of *Literary Property*. Johnson, though he concurred in the opinion which was afterwards sanctioned by a judgment of the House of Lords, that there was no such right, was at this time very angry that the booksellers of London, for whom he uniformly professed much regard, should suffer from an invasion of what they had ever considered to be secure; and he was loud and violent against Mr. Donaldson. "He is a fellow who takes advantage of the law to injure his brethren; for notwithstanding that the statute secures only fourteen years of exclusive right, it has always been understood by the *trade* that he who buys the copyright of a book from the author obtains a perpetual property; and upon that belief numberless bargains are made. Now Donaldson, I say, takes advantage here of people who have really an equitable title from usage." DEMPSTER. "Donaldson, sir, is

---

1. *Pity.* "[Johnson] said he would not sit at table where a lobster that had been roasted alive was one of the dishes." *Thomas Tyers.*

anxious for the encouragement of literature. He reduces the price of books, so that poor students may buy them." JOHNSON (laughing). "Well, sir, allowing that to be his motive, he is no better than Robin Hood, who robbed the rich[1] in order to give to the poor."

Rousseau's treatise on the inequality of mankind was at this time a fashionable topic.[2] It gave rise to an observation by Mr. Dempster that the advantages of fortune and rank were nothing to a wise man, who ought to value only merit. JOHNSON. "If man were a savage, living in the woods by himself, this might be true; but in civilized society we all depend upon each other, and our happiness is very much owing to the good opinion of mankind. Now, sir, in civilized society external advantages make us more respected. A man with a good coat upon his back meets with a better reception than he who has a bad one. Sir, you may analyze this, and say what is there in it? But that will avail you nothing, for it is a part of a general system. Pound St. Paul's church into atoms, and consider any single atom; it is, to be sure, good for nothing; but put all these atoms together and you have St. Paul's church. So it is with human felicity, which is made up of many ingredients, each of which may be shown to be very insignificant. In civilized society personal merit will not serve you so much as money will. Sir, you may make the experiment. Go into the street and give one man a lecture on morality, and another a shilling, and see which will respect you most. If you wish only to support nature, Sir William Petty[3] fixes your allowance at three pounds a year, but as times are much altered, let us call it six pounds. This sum will fill your belly, shelter you from the weather, and even get you a strong,

---

1. *Robbed the rich.* "I am just now returned from eating a most excellent pig with the most magnificent Donaldson." *Boswell: Letters, 1761.*

2. *A fashionable topic.* See Appendix E, page 548.

3. *Sir William Petty* (1623-87). "He is so exceeding nice in sifting and examining all possible contingencies that he adventures at nothing which is not demonstration." *Evelyn, 1675.*

lasting coat, supposing it to be made of good bull's hide.   Now, sir, all beyond this is artificial, and is desired in order to obtain a greater degree of respect from our fellow creatures.   And, sir, if six hundred pounds a year procure a man more consequence, and, of course, more happiness than six pounds a year, the same proportion will hold as to six thousand, and so on, as far as opulence can be carried.   Money, to be sure, of itself is of no use, for its only use is to part with it.   Rousseau and all those who deal in paradoxes are led away by a childish desire of novelty.   When I was a boy, I used always to choose the wrong side of a debate, because most ingenious things, that is to say, most new things, could be said upon it.   Sir, there is nothing for which you may not muster up more plausible arguments than those which are urged against wealth and other external advantages.   Why, now, there is stealing; why should it be thought a crime?   When we consider by what unjust methods property has been often acquired, and that what was unjustly got it must be unjust to keep, where is the harm in one man's taking the property of another from him?   Besides, sir, when we consider the bad use that many people make of their property, and how much better use the thief may make of it, it may be defended as a very allowable practice. Yet, sir, the experience of mankind has discovered stealing to be so very bad a thing that they make no scruple to hang a man for it.   When I was running about this town a very poor fellow, I was a great arguer for the advantages of poverty, but I was, at the same time, very sorry to be poor.   Sir, all the arguments which are brought to represent poverty as no evil, show it to be evidently a great evil.   You never find people laboring to convince you that you may live very happily upon a plentiful fortune.—So you hear people talking how miserable a king must be, and yet they all wish to be in his place."

It was suggested that kings must be unhappy, because they are deprived of the greatest of all satisfactions, easy and unreserved society.   JOHNSON.   "That is an ill-founded notion. Great kings have always been social.   The King of Prussia, the only great king at present, is very social.   Charles the

Second, the last King of England who was a man of parts, was social, and our Henrys and Edwards were all social."

Mr. Dempster having endeavored to maintain that intrinsic merit *ought* to make the only distinction amongst mankind. JOHNSON. "Why, sir, mankind have found that this cannot be. How shall we determine the proportion of intrinsic merit? Were that to be the only distinction amongst mankind, we should soon quarrel about the degrees of it. Were all distinctions abolished, the strongest would not long acquiesce, but would endeavor to obtain a superiority by their bodily strength. But, sir, as subordination is very necessary for society, and contentions for superiority very dangerous, mankind, that is to say, all civilized nations, have settled it upon a plain, invariable principle. A man is born to hereditary rank, or his being appointed to certain offices gives him a certain rank. Subordination tends greatly to human happiness. Were we all upon an equality, we should have no other enjoyment than mere animal pleasure."

I said I considered distinction of rank to be of so much importance in civilized society that if I were asked on the same day to dine with the first Duke in England and with the first man in Britain for genius, I should hesitate which to prefer. JOHNSON. "To be sure, sir, if you were to dine only once, and it were never to be known where you dined, you would choose rather to dine with the first man for genius, but to gain most respect, you should dine with the first Duke in England. For nine people in ten that you meet with would have a higher opinion of you for having dined with a Duke, and the great genius himself would receive you better, because you had been with the great Duke."

He took care to guard himself against any possible suspicion that his settled principles of reverence for rank and respect for wealth were at all owing to mean or interested motives, for he asserted his own independence as a literary man:

"No man," said he, "who ever lived by literature has lived more independently than I have done."

Next morning I found him alone and have preserved the following fragments of his conversation: "Everything that

Hume[1] has advanced against Christianity had passed through my mind long before he wrote. Always remember this, that after a system is well settled upon positive evidence, a few partial objections ought not to shake it. The human mind is so limited that it cannot take in all the parts of a subject, so that there may be objections raised against anything. There are objections against a *plenum* and objections against a *vacuum;* yet one of these must certainly be true."[2]

I mentioned Hume's argument[3] against the belief of miracles. JOHNSON. "Why, sir, the great difficulty of proving miracles should make us very cautious in believing them. But let us consider: although God has made Nature to operate by certain fixed laws, yet it is not unreasonable to think that He may suspend those laws in order to establish a system highly advantageous to mankind. Now, the Christian religion is a most beneficial system, as it gives us light and certainty where we were before in darkness and doubt. The miracles which prove it are attested by men[4] who had no interest in deceiving us, but who, on the contrary, were told that they should suffer persecution, and did actually lay down their lives in confirma-

---

1. *Hume.* David Hume (1711-76), a Scotch philosopher of the eighteenth century, noted for the acuteness of his analysis of philosophic questions. There is not much indication that Dr. Johnson really understood him. His boast was perhaps only a way of buttressing up his own tottering confidence in his own opinions.

2. *One of these must certainly be true.* "That is, either all space is full of matter, or there are parts of space which have no matter." *Penny Cyclopedia: Vacuum.*

3. *Hume's argument.* "When anyone tells me that he saw a dead man restored to life, I immediately consider with myself whether it be more probable that this person should either deceive or be deceived, or that the fact which he relates should really have happened." *Hume: Essay on Miracles.*

4. *Attested by men.* Dr. Johnson did not always show such respect for human testimony: "He who has not made the experiment or who is not accustomed to require rigorous accuracy from himself, will scarcely believe how much a few hours take from certainty of knowledge, and distinctness of imagery; how the succession of objects will be broken, how separate parts will be confused, and how many particular features and discriminations will be compressed and conglobated into one gross and general idea." *Johnson: A Journey to the Western Isles.*

tion of the truth of the facts which they asserted. Indeed, for some centuries the heathens did not pretend to deny the miracles, but said they were performed by the aid of evil spirits. This is a circumstance of great weight. Then, sir, when we take the proofs derived from prophecies which have been so exactly fulfilled, we have most satisfactory evidence. Supposing a miracle possible, as to which, in my opinion, there can be no doubt, we have as strong evidence for the miracles in support of Christianity as the nature of the thing admits."

At night Mr. Johnson and I supped in a private room at the Turk's Head coffee-house, in the Strand. "I encourage this house," said he, "for the mistress of it is a good civil woman, and has not much business."

"Sir, I love the acquaintance of young people;[1] because, in the first place, I don't like to think myself growing old. In the next place, young acquaintances must last longest, if they do last; and then, sir, young men have more virtue than old men; they have more generous sentiments in every respect. I love the young dogs of this age; they have more wit and humor and knowledge of life than we had; but, then, the dogs are not so good scholars. Sir, in my early years I read very hard. It is a sad reflection, but a true one, that I knew almost as much at eighteen as I do now. My judgment, to be sure, was not so good, but I had all the facts. I remember very well, when I was at Oxford, an old gentleman said to me, 'Young man, ply your book diligently now, and acquire a stock of knowledge, for when years come upon you, you will find that poring upon books will be but an irksome task.'"

He mentioned to me now, for the first time, that he had been distressed by melancholy, and for that reason had been obliged to fly from study and meditation to the dissipating variety of life. Against melancholy he recommended constant

---

1. *Acquaintance of young people.* "An old man must be a father to bear with patience those follies and absurdities which he will perpetually imagine himself to find in the schemes and expectations, the pleasures and the sorrows, of those who have not yet been hardened by time and chilled by frustration." *Johnson: The Rambler.*

occupation of mind, a great deal of exercise, moderation in eating and drinking, and especially to shun drinking at night. He said melancholy people were apt to fly to intemperance for relief, but that it sank them much deeper in misery. He observed that laboring men who work hard and live sparingly are seldom or never troubled with low spirits.

He again insisted on the duty of maintaining subordination of rank. "Sir, I would no more deprive a nobleman of his respect than of his money. I consider myself as acting a part in the great system of society, and I do to others as I would have them to do to me. I would behave to a nobleman as I should expect he would behave to me, were I a nobleman and he Sam. Johnson. Sir, there is one Mrs. Macaulay[1] in this town, a great republican. One day when I was at her house, I put on a very grave countenance and said to her, 'Madam, I am now become a convert to your way of thinking. I am convinced that all mankind are upon an equal footing, and to give you an unquestionable proof, madam, that I am in earnest, here is a very sensible, civil, well-behaved fellow-citizen, your footman; I desire that he may be allowed to sit down and dine with us.' I thus, sir, showed her the absurdity of the leveling doctrine. She has never liked me since. Sir, your levelers wish to level *down* as far as themselves, but they cannot bear leveling *up* to themselves. They would all have some people under them; why not then have some people above them?" I mentioned a certain author who disgusted me by his forwardness, and by showing no deference to noblemen into whose company he was admitted. JOHNSON. "Suppose a shoemaker should claim an equality with him, as he does with a Lord; how he would stare. 'Why, sir, do you stare?' says the shoemaker, 'I do great service to society. 'Tis true, I am paid for doing it, but so are you, sir, and I am sorry to say

---

1. *Mrs. Macaulay.* Author of a history of England in eight volumes. "She imputes everything to tyrannic views, nothing to passions, weakness, error, prejudice, and still less to what operates oftenest—accident and little motives. She seems to think men have acted from no views but those of establishing a despotism or a republic." *Horace Walpole: Memoirs of the Reign of George III.*

it, better paid than I am, for doing something not so necessary. For mankind could do better without your books than without my shoes.'"

I spoke of Sir James Macdonald as a young man of most distinguished merit, who united the highest reputation at Eton and Oxford with the patriarchal spirit of a great Highland chieftain. I mentioned that Sir James had said to me that he had never seen Mr. Johnson, but he had a great respect for him, though at the same time it was mixed with some degree of terror. JOHNSON. "Sir, if he were to be acquainted with me, it might lessen both."

The mention of this gentleman led us to talk of the Western Islands of Scotland, to visit which he expressed a wish that then appeared to be a very romantic fancy which I little thought would be afterwards realized. He told me that his father had put Martin's account of those islands into his hands when he was very young, and that he was highly pleased with it; that he was particularly struck with the St. Kilda man's notion that the high church of Glasgow had been hollowed out of a rock, a circumstance to which old Mr. Johnson had directed his attention. He said he would go to the Hebrides with me when I returned from my travels, unless some very good companion should offer when I was absent, which he did not think probable, adding, "There are few people whom I take so much to as you." And when I talked of my leaving England, he said with a very affectionate air, "My dear Boswell, I should be very unhappy at parting, did I think we were not to meet again."—I cannot too often remind my readers that although such instances of his kindness are doubtless very flattering to me, yet I hope my recording them will be ascribed to a better motive than to vanity, for they afford unquestionable evidence of his tenderness and complacency, which some, while they were forced to acknowledge his great powers, have been so strenuous to deny.

He maintained that a boy at school was the happiest of human beings. I supported a different opinion, from which I have never yet varied, that a man is happier, and I enlarged upon the anxiety and sufferings which are endured at school.

JOHNSON. "Ah! sir, a boy's being flogged is not so severe as a man's having the hiss of the world[1] against him. Men have a solicitude about fame, and the greater share they have of it, the more afraid they are of losing it."

On Tuesday, July 26, I found Mr. Johnson alone. It was a very wet day, and I again complained of the disagreeable effects of such weather. JOHNSON. "Sir, this is all imagination, which physicians encourage; for man lives in air as a fish lives in water so that if the atmosphere press heavy from above, there is an equal resistance from below. To be sure, bad weather is hard upon people who are obliged to be abroad, and men cannot labor so well in the open air in bad weather as in good; but, sir, a smith or a tailor, whose work is within doors, will surely do as much in rainy weather as in fair. Some very delicate frames, indeed, may be affected by wet weather, but not common constitutions."

We talked of the education of children,[2] and I asked him what he thought was best to teach them first. JOHNSON. "Sir, it is no matter what you teach them first, any more than what leg you shall put into your breeches first. Sir, you may stand disputing which is best to put in first, but in the meantime your breech is bare. Sir, while you are considering which of two things you should teach your child first, another boy has learned them both."

He laughed heartily when I mentioned to him a saying of his concerning Mr. Thomas Sheridan, which Foote took a wicked pleasure to circulate. "Why, sir, Sherry is dull, naturally dull, but it must have taken him a great deal of pains to become what we now see him. Such an excess of stupidity, sir, is not in Nature."

---

1. *Hiss of the world.* "There is nothing more dreadful to an author than neglect; compared with which, reproach, hatred, and opposition are names of happiness; yet this worst, this meanest, fate, everyone who dares to write has reason to fear." *Johnson: The Rambler.*

2. *Education of children.* "I advised him to let the child alone; and told him that the matter was not great whether he could read at the end of four years or of five." *Johnson to Mrs. Thrale, 1776.* "Let the people learn necessary knowledge; let them learn to count their fingers and to count their money before they are caring for the classics.' *Johnson, quoted by Mrs. Piozzi.*

He now added, "Sheridan cannot bear me. I bring his declamation to a point. Besides, sir, what influence can Mr. Sheridan have upon the language of this great country, by his narrow exertions? Sir, it is burning a farthing candle at Dover to show light at Calais."

Talking of a young man who was uneasy from thinking that he was very deficient in learning and knowledge, he said, "A man has no reason to complain who holds a middle place and has many below him, and perhaps he has not six of his years above him—perhaps not one. Though he may not know anything perfectly, the general mass of knowledge that he has acquired is considerable. Time will do for him all that is wanting."

The conversation then took a philosophical turn. JOHNSON. "Human experience, which is constantly contradicting theory, is the great test of truth. A system built upon the discoveries of a great many minds is always of more strength than what is produced by the mere workings of any one mind, which, of itself, can do little. There is not so poor a book in the world that would not be a prodigious effort were it wrought out entirely by a single mind, without the aid of prior investigators."

He this evening again recommended to me to perambulate Spain. I said it would amuse him to get a letter from me dated at Salamanca. JOHNSON. "I love the University of Salamanca, for when the Spaniards were in doubt as to the lawfulness of their conquering America,[1] the University of Salamanca gave

1. *Conquering America.* "I do not much wish well to discoveries, for I am always afraid they will end in conquest and robbery." *Johnson: Letters, 1773.* "We are openly told that [the Portuguese] had the less scruple concerning their treatment of the savage people because they scarcely considered them as distinct from beasts; and indeed the practice of all the European nations, and among others of the English barbarians that cultivate the southern islands of America, proves that this opinion, however absurd and foolish, however wicked and injurious, still continues to prevail. Interest and pride harden the heart, and it is in vain to dispute against avarice and power." *Johnson: Introduction to the World Displayed.* "What but false hope or resistless terror can prevail upon a weaker nation to invite a stranger into their country, to give their lands to strangers whom no affinity of manners or similitude of opinion can be said to recommend, to permit them to

it as their opinion that it was not lawful." He spoke this
with great emotion, and with that generous warmth which
dictated the lines in his "London," against Spanish encroach-
ment.

I expressed my opinion of my friend Derrick as but a poor
writer. JOHNSON. "To be sure, sir, he is, but you are to
consider that his being a literary man has got for him all that
he has. It has made him King of Bath.[1] Had he not been a
writer, he must have been sweeping the crossings in the streets
and asking halfpence from everybody that passed."

Johnson said once to me, "Sir, I honor Derrick for his presence
of mind. One night when Floyd, another poor author, was
wandering about the streets in the night, he found Derrick fast
asleep upon a bulk;* upon being suddenly waked, Derrick
started up, 'My dear Floyd, I am sorry to see you in this destitute
state; will you go home with me to *my lodgings?*'"

I again begged his advice as to my method of study at Utrecht.
"Come," said he, "let us make a day of it. Let us go down to
Greenwich[2] and dine, and talk of it there." The following
Saturday was fixed for this excursion.

On Saturday, July 30, Dr. Johnson and I took a sculler at

---

build towns from which the natives are excluded, to raise fortresses
by which they are intimidated, to settle themselves with such strength
that they cannot afterwards be expelled, but are forever to remain the
masters of the original inhabitants, the dictators of their conduct, and
the arbiters of their fate." *Johnson: Observations on the State of Affairs
in 1756.* "Some colonies, indeed, have been established more peaceably than others . . . but those that have settled in the new
world on the fairest terms have no other merit than that of a scrivener
[law clerk] who ruins in silence over a plunderer that seizes by force."
The same. "The first propagators of Christianity recommended their
doctrines by their sufferings and virtues; they entered no defenseless
territories with swords in their hands; they built no forts upon ground
to which they had no right, nor polluted the purity of religion with the
avarice of trade or insolence of power." *Johnson: Introduction to the
World Displayed.*

1. *Bath.* A fashionable watering place. Its public dancing and
gambling were put under the direction of a master of ceremonies, called
the King of Bath.

2. *Greenwich.* On the Thames, a few miles below London; famous
for its fish, its park, and its public buildings.

the Temple-stairs¹ and set out for Greenwich. I asked him if
he really thought a knowledge of the Greek and Latin languages an essential requisite to a good education. JOHNSON.
"Most certainly, sir, for those who know them have a very
great advantage over those who do not. Nay, sir, it is wonderful what a difference learning makes upon people even in the
common intercourse of life, which does not appear to be much
connected with it." "And yet," said I, "people go through
the world very well, and carry on the business of life to good
advantage without learning." JOHNSON. "Why, sir, that
may be true in cases where learning cannot possibly be of any
use; for instance, this boy rows us as well without learning as if
he could sing the song of Orpheus to the Argonauts, who were
the first sailors." He then called to the boy, "What would
you give, my lad, to know about the Argonauts?" "Sir,"
said the boy, "I would give what I have." Johnson was much
pleased with his answer, and we gave him a double fare. Dr.
Johnson then turning to me, "Sir," said he, "a desire of knowledge is the natural feeling of mankind; and every human being
whose mind is not debauched will be willing to give all that he
has to get knowledge."

We landed at the Old Swan and walked to Billingsgate,
where we took oars and moved smoothly along the silver Thames.
It was a very fine day. We were entertained with the immense
number and variety of ships that were lying at anchor, and
with the beautiful country on each side of the river.

I talked of preaching, and of the great success which those
called Methodists² have. JOHNSON. "Sir, it is owing to their
expressing themselves in a plain and familiar manner, which
is the only way to do good to the common people and which

---

1. *Temple-stairs.* Steps from near the Temple gardens to the
surface of the Thames.
2. *Methodists.* A term applied in the eighteenth century to those,
whatever their denomination, who gave an extraordinary amount of
their time to regular and methodical exercises of devotion. "Methodist
is considered always a term of reproach, I trust, because I never yet did
hear that any one person called himself a Methodist." *Mrs. Thrale:
Letters,* 1780. "Johnson, himself, was, in a dignified manner, a Methodist."
Boswell.

clergymen of genius and learning ought to do from a principle of duty, when it is suited to their congregations; a practice, for which they will be praised by men of sense. To insist against drunkenness as a crime because it debases reason, the noblest faculty of man, would be of no service to the common people; but to tell them that they may die in a fit of drunkenness, and show them how dreadful that would be cannot fail to make a deep impression. Sir, when your Scotch clergy give up their homely manner, religion will soon decay in that country."

Afterwards he entered upon the business of the day, which was to give me his advice as to a course of study. And here I am to mention, with much regret, that my record of what he said is miserably scanty. I recollect with admiration an animating blaze of eloquence which roused every intellectual power in me to the highest pitch, but must have dazzled me so much that my memory could not preserve the substance of his discourse for the note which I find of it is no more than this: "He ran over the grand scale of human knowledge; advised me to select some particular branch to excel in, but to acquire a little of every kind."

We walked in the evening in Greenwich Park. He asked me, I suppose by way of trying my disposition, "Is not this very fine?" Having no exquisite relish of the beauties of Nature, and being more delighted with "the busy hum of men," I answered, "Yes, sir; but not equal to Fleet Street." JOHNSON. "You are right, sir."

I am aware that many of my readers may censure my want of taste. Let me, however, shelter myself under the authority of a very fashionable Baronet in the brilliant world, who, on his attention being called to the fragrance of a May evening in the country, observed, "This may be very well, but for my part, I prefer the smell of a flambeau* at the playhouse."

We stayed so long at Greenwich that our sail up the river in our return to London was by no means so pleasant as in the morning, for the night air was so cold that it made me shiver. I was the more sensible of it from having sat up all the night before recollecting and writing in my *Journal* what I thought worthy of preservation, an exertion, which, during the first part of my acquaintance with Johnson, I frequently made. I remember having sat up four nights in one week without being much incommoded in the daytime.

Johnson, whose robust frame was not in the least affected by the cold, scolded me, as if my shivering had been a paltry effeminacy, saying, "Why do you shiver?" Sir William Scott,[1] of the Commons, told me that when he complained of a headache in the post-chaise, as they were traveling together to Scotland, Johnson treated him in the same manner: "At your age, sir, I had no headache." It is not easy to make allowance for sensations in others, which we ourselves have not at the time. We must all have experienced how very differently we are affected by the complaints of our neighbors when we are well and when we are ill. In full health, we can scarcely believe that they suffer much, so faint is the image of pain upon our imagination; when softened by sickness, we readily sympathize with the sufferings of others.

We concluded the day at the Turk's Head coffee-house very socially. He was pleased to listen to a particular account which I gave him of my family and of its hereditary estate, as to the extent and population of which he asked questions and made calculations; recommending, at the same time, a liberal kindness to the tenantry, as people over whom the proprietor was placed by Providence. He took delight in hearing my description of the romantic seat of my ancestors.[2] "I must be there, sir," said he, "and we will live in the old castle; and if there is not a room in it remaining, we will build one."

After we had again talked of my setting out for Holland, he said, "I must see thee out of England; I will accompany you to Harwich." I could not find words to express what I felt upon this unexpected and very great mark of his affectionate regard.

---

1. *Sir William Scott.* An eminent lawyer, better known under his later title, *Lord Stowell.*

2. *Romantic seat of my ancestors.* "I live here in a remote corner of an old ruinous house where my ancestors have been very jovial. What a solemn idea rushes on my mind. They are all gone. I must follow. Well, and what then?" *Boswell to Erskine.*

Next day, Sunday, July 31, I told him I had been that morning at a meeting of the people called Quakers, where I had heard a woman preach. JOHNSON. "Sir, a woman's preaching is like a dog's walking on his hind legs. It is not done well, but you are surprised to find it done at all."

On Tuesday, August 2 (the day of my departure from London having been fixed for the 5th), Dr. Johnson did me the honor to pass a part of the morning with me at my Chambers. He said that he always felt "an inclination to do nothing." I observed that it was strange to think that the most indolent man in Britain had written the most laborious work, *The English Dictionary*.

I mentioned an imprudent publication by a certain friend of his at an early period of life, and asked him if he thought it would hurt him. JOHNSON. "No, sir, not much. It may, perhaps, be mentioned at an election."

I had now made good my title to be a privileged man, and was carried by him in the evening to drink tea with Miss Williams, whom, though under the misfortune of having lost her sight, I found to be agreeable in conversation; for she had a variety of literature, and expressed herself well; but her peculiar value was the intimacy in which she had long lived with Johnson, by which she was well acquainted with his habits, and knew how to lead him on to talk.

After tea he carried me to what he called his walk, which was a long narrow paved court in the neighborhood, overshadowed by some trees. There we sauntered a considerable time, and I complained to him that my love of London and of his company was such that I shrank almost from the thought of going away even to travel, which is generally so much desired by young men. He roused me by manly and spirited conversation. He advised me, when settled in any place abroad, to study with an eagerness after knowledge, and to apply to Greek an hour every day; and when I was moving about, to read diligently the great book of mankind.

On Wednesday, August 3, we had our last social evening at the Turk's Head coffee-house, before my setting out for foreign parts. I had the misfortune, before we parted, to irritate him unintentionally. I mentioned to him how common it was in the world to tell absurd stories of him, and to ascribe to him very strange sayings. JOHNSON. "What do they make me say, sir?" BOSWELL. "Why, sir, as an instance very strange indeed (laughing heartily as I spoke), David Hume told me you said that you would stand before a battery of cannon to restore the Convocation[1] to its full powers."—Little did I apprehend that he had actually said this; but I was soon convinced of my error, for, with a determined look, he thundered out, "And would I not, sir? Shall the Presbyterian *Kirk* of Scotland have its General Assembly, and the Church of England be denied its Convocation?" He was walking up and down the room while I told him the anecdote; but when he uttered this explosion of high-church zeal, he had come close to my chair, and his eye flashed with indignation. I bowed to the storm, and diverted the force of it by leading him to expatiate on the influence which religion derived from maintaining the church with great external respectability.

On Friday, August 5, we set out early in the morning in the Harwich stagecoach. A fat elderly gentlewoman and a young Dutchman seemed the most inclined among us to conversation. At the inn where we dined, the gentlewoman said that she had done her best to educate her children, and, particularly, that she had never suffered them to be a moment idle. JOHNSON. "I wish, madam, you would educate me too, for I have been an idle fellow all my life." "I am sure, sir," said she, "you have not been idle." JOHNSON. "Nay, madam, it is very true; and that gentleman there (pointing to me) has been idle. He was idle at Edinburgh. His father sent him to Glasgow, where he continued to be idle. He then came to London, where he has been very idle; and now he is going to Utrecht, where he will be as idle as ever." I asked him privately how he could expose me so. JOHNSON. "Poh, poh!" said he, "they knew nothing about you, and will think of it no more." In the afternoon

---

1. *Convocation*. The general assembly of the Church of England. Too Whiggish for the Tory bishops, it was forced to adjourn in 1717 and did not meet again till 1852. Johnson was not the only Tory to maintain its traditional right to existence.

the gentlewoman talked violently against the Roman Catholics, and of the horrors of the Inquisition.[1] To the utter astonishment of all the passengers but myself, who knew that he could talk upon any side of a question, he defended the Inquisition, and maintained that "false doctrine should be checked on its first appearance; that the civil power should unite with the church in punishing those who dare attack the established religion, and that such only were punished by the Inquisition."

He had in his pocket *Pomponius Mela De Situ Orbis*, in which he read occasionally, and seemed very intent upon ancient geography. Though by no means niggardly, his attention to what was generally right was so minute that having observed at one of the stages that I ostentatiously gave a shilling to the coachman, when the custom was for each passenger to give only sixpence, he took me aside and scolded me, saying that what I had done would make the coachman dissatisfied with all the rest of the passengers who gave him no more than his due. This was a just reprimand; for in whatever way a man may indulge his generosity or his vanity in spending his money, for the sake of others he ought not to raise the price of any article for which there is a constant demand.

He talked of Mr. Blacklock's poetry, so far as it was descriptive of visible objects; and observed that "as its author had the misfortune to be blind, we may be absolutely sure that such passages are combinations of what he has remembered of the works of other writers who could see. That foolish fellow, Spence, has labored to explain philosophically how Blacklock may have done, by means of his own faculties, what it is impossible he should do. The solution, as I have given it, is plain. Suppose I know a man to be so lame that he is absolutely incapable to move himself, and I find him in a different room from that in which I left him—shall I puzzle myself with idle conjectures that, perhaps, his nerves have by some unknown change all at once become effective? No, sir, it is clear how he got into a different room; he was *carried*."

Having stopped a night at Colchester, Johnson talked of that

---

1. *Inquisition.* See Introduction, page 12.

town with veneration, for having stood a siege for Charles the
First. The Dutchman alone now remained with us. He spoke
English tolerably well; and thinking to recommend himself to
us by expatiating on the superiority of the criminal jurispru-
dence of this country over that of Holland, he inveighed against
the barbarity of putting an accused person to the torture, in
order to force a confession. But Johnson was as ready for this
as for the Inquisition. "Why, sir, you do not, I find, understand
the law of your own country. To torture in Holland is considered as a favor to an accused person; for no man is put to the
torture there unless there is as much evidence against him as
would amount to conviction in England. An accused person
among you, therefore, has one chance more to escape punishment than those who are tried among us."

At supper this night he talked of good eating with uncommon
satisfaction. "Some people," said he, "have a foolish way of
not minding, or pretending not to mind, what they eat. For
my part, I mind my belly very studiously, and very carefully;
for I look upon it that he who does not mind his belly will
hardly mind anything else." He now appeared to me *Jean
Bull philosophe*, and he was for the moment not only serious,
but vehement. Yet I have heard him, upon other occasions,
talk with great contempt of people who were anxious to gratify
their palates. His practice indeed, I must acknowledge, may
be considered as casting the balance of his different opinions
upon this subject; for I never knew any man who relished good
eating more than he did. When at table he was totally absorbed in the business of the moment; his looks seemed riveted
to his plate; nor would he, unless when in very high company,
say one word, or even pay the least attention to what was said
by others till he had satisfied his appetite; which was so fierce,
and indulged with such intenseness that while in the act of
eating, the veins of his forehead swelled, and generally a strong
perspiration was visible. To those whose sensations were
delicate, this could not but be disgusting; and it was doubtless
not very suitable to the character of a philosopher, who should
be distinguished by self-command. But it must be owned that

Johnson, though he could be rigidly *abstemious*, was not a *temperate* man either in eating or drinking. He could refrain, but he could not use moderately. He told me that he had fasted two days without inconvenience, and that he had never been hungry but once. They who beheld with wonder how much he eat upon all occasions when his dinner was to his taste could not easily conceive what he must have meant by hunger; and not only was he remarkable for the extraordinary quantity which he eat, but he was, or affected to be, a man of very nice discernment in the science of cookery. He used to descant critically on the dishes which had been at table where he had dined or supped, and to recollect very minutely what he had liked. I remember, when he was in Scotland, his praising "Gordon's palates" (a dish of palates at the Honorable Alexander Gordon's) with a warmth of expression which might have done honor to more important subjects. "As for Maclaurin's imitation of a *made dish*, it was a wretched attempt." He about the same time was so much displeased with the performances of a nobleman's French cook that he exclaimed with vehemence, "I'd throw such a rascal into the river." When invited to dine, even with an intimate friend, he was not pleased if something better than a plain dinner was not prepared for him. I have heard him say on such an occasion, "This was a good dinner enough, to be sure; but it was not a dinner to *ask* a man to." On the other hand, he was wont to express with great glee his satisfaction when he had been entertained quite to his mind. One day when he had dined with his neighbor and landlord, in Bolt Court, Mr. Allen, the printer, whose old housekeeper had studied his taste in everything, he pronounced this eulogy: "Sir, we could not have had a better dinner had there been a *synod of cooks*."

While we were left by ourselves, after the Dutchman had gone to bed, Dr. Johnson talked of that studied behavior which many have recommended and practiced. He disapproved of it; and said, "I never considered whether I should be a grave man or a merry man, but just let inclination, for the time, have its course."

I teased him with fanciful apprehensions of unhappiness. A moth having fluttered round the candle and burned itself, he laid hold of this little incident to admonish me, saying, with a sly look, and in a solemn but a quiet tone, "That creature was its own tormentor, and I believe its name was Boswell."

Next day we got to Harwich, to dinner; and my passage in the packet-boat to Helvoetsluys being secured, and my baggage put on board, we dined at our inn by ourselves. I happened to say it would be terrible if he should not find a speedy opportunity of returning to London, and be confined in so dull a place. JOHNSON. "Don't, sir, accustom yourself to use big words for little matters. It would *not* be *terrible*, though I *were* to be detained some time here."

We went and looked at the church, and having gone into it and walked up to the altar, Johnson, whose piety was constant and fervent, sent me to my knees, saying, "Now, that you are going to leave your native country, recommend yourself to the protection of your Creator and Redeemer."

After we came out of the church we stood talking for some time together of Bishop Berkeley's[1] ingenious sophistry to prove the non-existence of matter, and that everything in the universe is merely ideal. I observed that though we are satisfied his doctrine is not true, it is impossible to refute it. I never shall forget the alacrity with which Johnson answered, striking his foot with mighty force against a large stone, till he rebounded from it, "I refute it *thus*." To me it is not conceivable how Berkeley can be answered by pure reasoning; but I know that the nice and difficult task was to have been undertaken by one

---

1. *Bishop Berkeley.* George Berkeley (1685-1753). A famous English philosopher. He did not deny that hardness, softness, taste, color, etc., were real. He denied simply that there was a mysterious, unknowable thing called "matter," of which hardness, softness, taste, color, etc., were merely the appearances. He reduced the universe to the mind of God, the minds of his creatures, and very real impressions or ideas produced directly from the will of God. He seems, however, quite oblivious of the fact that many of these impressions he himself would hardly care to associate with the mind of God as he, an orthodox Christian bishop, conceived him to be.

of the most luminous minds of the present age,[1] had not politics "turned him from calm philosophy aside." How must we, when we reflect on the loss of such an intellectual feast, regret that he should be characterized as the man,

> Who born for the universe narrowed his mind,
> And to party gave up what was meant for mankind?

My revered friend walked down with me to the beach, where we embraced and parted with tenderness, and engaged to correspond by letters. I said, "I hope, sir, you will not forget me in my absence." JOHNSON. "Nay, sir, it is more likely you should forget me than that I should forget you." As the vessel put out to sea, I kept my eyes upon him for a considerable time, while he remained rolling his majestic frame in his usual manner; and at last I perceived him walk back into the town, and he disappeared.

In February [1764] was founded that Club which existed long without a name, but at Mr. Garrick's funeral became distinguished by the title of "The Literary Club." Sir Joshua Reynolds had the merit of being the first proposer of it, to which Johnson acceded; and the original members were Sir Joshua Reynolds, Dr. Johnson, Mr. Edmund Burke, Dr. Nugent,[2] Mr. Beauclerk, Mr. Langton, Dr. Goldsmith, Mr. Chamier, and Sir John Hawkins. They met at the Turk's Head, in Gerrard Street, Soho, one evening in every week, at seven, and generally continued their conversation till a pretty late hour. This club has been gradually increased to its present number, thirty-five.[3] After about ten years, instead of supping weekly, it was resolved to dine together once a fortnight during the meeting of Parliament.

---

1. *Of the present age.* Edmund Burke (1729-97). By 1764 known to be a brilliant young admirer of civilization as the growth of centuries of effort and experience and to be full of scorn for those who would make it over to fit a few philosophic maxims. He had already written two eloquent essays, but it was not until 1765 that he began his parliamentary career. "I not only excuse Burke for his heart, but love him for letting me warm my hands at it after a lapse of a hundred and twenty years." *Augustine Birrell*, 1887.

2. *Dr. Nugent.* Burke's father-in-law; a Roman Catholic physician.

3. *Thirty-five.* Including Boswell, Fox, Sheridan, Gibbon, Adam Smith, Bishop Percy of the *Reliques*, the Wartons.

Not very long after the institution of [the] club Sir Joshua Reynolds was speaking of it to Garrick. "I like it much," said he; "I think I shall be of you." When Sir Joshua mentioned this to Dr. Johnson, he was much displeased. *"He'll be of us,"* said Johnson; "how does he know we will *permit* him? The first Duke in England has no right to hold such language." However, when Garrick was regularly proposed some time afterwards, Johnson warmly and kindly supported him, and he was accordingly elected, was a most agreeable member, and continued to attend our meetings to the time of his death.

The ease and independence to which [Johnson] had at last attained by royal munificence increased his natural indolence. In his *Meditations* he thus accuses himself: "A kind of strange oblivion has overspread me, so that I know not what has become of last year, and perceive that incidents and intelligence pass over me without leaving any impression." He then solemnly says: "This is not the life to which heaven is promised"; and he earnestly resolves an amendment.

About this time he was afflicted with a very severe return of the hypochondriac disorder which was ever lurking about him. He was so ill, as, notwithstanding his remarkable love of company, to be entirely averse to society. Dr. Adams told me that as an old friend he was admitted to visit him, and that he found him in a deplorable state, sighing, groaning, talking to himself, and restlessly walking from room to room. He then used this emphatical expression: "I would consent to have a limb amputated to recover my spirits."

Talking to himself was, indeed, one of his singularities ever since I knew him. I was certain that he was frequently uttering pious ejaculations, for fragments of the Lord's Prayer have been distinctly overheard. He had another particularity, of which none of his friends even ventured to ask an explanation. This was his anxious care to go out or in at a door or passage by a certain number of steps from a certain point, or at least so as that either his right or his left foot (I am not certain which) should constantly make the first actual movement when he came close to the door or passage. Thus I conjecture; for I have, upon innumerable occasions, observed him suddenly stop, and then seem to count his steps with a deep earnestness;[1] and when he had neglected or gone wrong in this sort of magical movement, I have seen him go back again, put himself in a proper posture to begin the ceremony, and, having gone through it, break from his abstraction, walk briskly on, and join his companion.

[1765]. This year was distinguished by his being introduced into the family of Mr. Thrale, one of the most eminent brewers in England, and member of Parliament for the borough of Southwark. Johnson used to give this account of the rise of Mr. Thrale's father:[2] "He worked at six shillings a week for twenty years in the great brewery which afterwards was his own. The proprietor of it had an only daughter, who was married to a nobleman. It was not fit that a peer should continue the business. On the old man's death, therefore, the brewery was to be sold. To find a purchaser for so large a property was a difficult matter; and, after some time, it was suggested that it would be advisable to treat with Thrale, a sensible, active, honest man, and to transfer the whole to him for thirty thousand pounds. In eleven years Thrale paid the purchase money. He acquired a large fortune, and lived to be a member of Parliament for Southwark. He gave his son and daughters the best education. The esteem which his good conduct procured him from the nobleman who had married his master's daughter made him to be treated with much attention; and his son, both at school and at the University of Oxford, associated with young men of the first rank. His allowance from his father, after he left college, was splendid; not less than a thousand a year. This, in a man who had risen as old Thrale did, was a very extraordinary instance of generosity. He used to say, 'If this young dog does not find so much after I am gone as he expects,

---

1. *Deep earnestness.* "When melancholy notions take the form of duty, they lay hold on the faculties without opposition, because we are afraid to exclude or banish them. For this reason the superstitious are often melancholy, and the melancholy almost always superstitious." *"Imlac" in Johnson's Rasselas.*

2. *Thrale's father.* According to Mrs. Thrale, a nephew of the proprietor, though always harshly treated by his uncle. For her account see *Mrs. Piozzi's Anecdotes* in Birkbeck Hill's *Johnsonian Miscellanies.*

let him remember that he has had a great deal in my own time.'" The son, though in affluent circumstances, had good sense enough to carry on his father's trade.

There may be some who think that a new system of gentility might be established upon principles totally different from what have hitherto prevailed. Our present heraldry, it may be said, is suited to the barbarous times in which it had its origin. It is chiefly founded upon ferocious merit, upon military excellence. Why should not the knowledge, the skill, the expertness, the assiduity, and the spirited hazards of trade and commerce, when crowned with success, be entitled to give those flattering distinctions by which mankind are so universally captivated?

Such are the specious, but false, arguments for a proposition which always will find numerous advocates in a nation where men are every day starting up from obscurity to wealth. To refute them is needless. The general sense of mankind cries out with irresistible force, "*Un gentilhomme est toujours gentilhomme.*"

Mr. Thrale[1] had married Miss Hester Lynch Salusbury, a lady of lively talents,[2] improved by education. That Johnson's introduction into Mr. Thrale's family, which contributed so much to the happiness of his life, was owing to her desire for his conversation, is the general supposition; but it is not the truth. Mr. Murphy, who was intimate with Mr. Thrale, having spoken very highly of Dr. Johnson, he was requested to make them acquainted. This being mentioned to Johnson, he

1. *Mr. Thrale.* "Though entirely a man of peace, and a gentleman . . . [Thrale] had a singular amusement in hearing, instigating, and provoking a war of words where there was nothing that could inflict disgrace upon defeat." *Mme. D'Arblay.*

2. *Lively talents.* "Mrs. Thrale is a most dear creature, but never restrains her tongue, nor indeed any of her feelings. She laughs, cries, scolds, sports, reasons, makes fun—does everything she has an inclination to do, without any study of prudence or thought of blame." *Mme. D'Arblay.*

The title of one of her books, for she was an author, is worth noting: *Retrospection; or a Review of the Most Striking and Important Events, Characters, Literatures, and Their Consequences, Which the Last Eighteen Hundred Years Have Presented to the View of Mankind.*

accepted of an invitation to dinner at Thrale's, and was so much pleased with his reception, both by Mr. and Mrs. Thrale, and they so much pleased with him that his invitations to their house were more and more frequent, till at last he became one of the family, and an apartment was appropriated to him, both in their house at Southwark[1] and in their villa at Streatham.

Johnson had a very sincere esteem for Mr. Thrale, as a man of excellent principles, a good scholar, well skilled in trade, of a sound understanding, and of manners such as presented the character of a plain, independent English squire. "I know no man," said he, "who is more master of his wife and family than Thrale. If he but holds up a finger, he is obeyed. It is a great mistake to suppose that she is above him in literary attainments. She is more flippant, but he has ten times her learning. He is a regular scholar, but her learning is that of a schoolboy in one of the lower forms." Mr. Thrale was tall, well proportioned, and stately. As for *Madam*, or *my Mistress*, by which epithets Johnson used to mention Mrs. Thrale, she was short, plump, and brisk. She has herself given us a lively view of the idea which Johnson had of her person on her appearing before him in a dark-colored gown: "You little creatures should never wear those sort of clothes; they are unsuitable in every way. What! have not all insects gay colors?"

Nothing could be more fortunate for Johnson than this connection. He had at Mr. Thrale's all the comforts[2] and even

---

1. *Southwark.* A part of London, across the Thames from the "City" and like it so full of commerce, manufacture, and poor dwellings that it was not very agreeable for residence.

2. *All the comforts.* "Dined at Mr. Thrale's, where there were ten or more gentlemen, and but one lady besides Mrs. Thrale. First course, soups at head and foot, removed [for a time, accompanied] by fish and a saddle of mutton; second course, a fowl they call galena at head, and a capon larger than some of our Irish turkeys at foot; third course, four different sorts of ices, pineapple, grape, raspberry, and a fourth; in each remove [set of accompanying dishes] there were, I think, fourteen dishes." *Campbell: Diary of a Visit to England in 1775.*

"Thrale's incapacity, his extravagance, and over-indulgence in eating caused his wife much anxiety." *Dictionary of National Biography.*

luxuries of life; his melancholy was diverted, and his irregular habits lessened by association with an agreeable and well-ordered family.[1] He was treated with the utmost respect, and even affection. The vivacity of Mrs. Thrale's literary talk roused him to cheerfulness and exertion, even when they were alone. But this was not often the case, for he found here a constant succession of what gave him the highest enjoyment; the society of the learned, the witty, and the eminent in every way, who were assembled in numerous companies, called forth his wonderful powers, and gratified him with admiration to which no man could be insensible.

I returned to London[2] in February [1766] and found Dr. Johnson in a good house in Johnson's Court, Fleet Street, in which he had accommodated Miss Williams with an apartment on the ground floor, while Mr. Levet occupied his post in the garret; his faithful Francis was still attending upon him.

At night I supped with him at the Mitre tavern, that we might renew our intimacy at the original place of meeting. But there was now a considerable difference in his way of living. Having had an illness in which he was advised to leave off wine, he had, from that period, continued to abstain from it, and drank only water or lemonade.

Dr. Johnson was very kind this evening and said to me, "You have now lived five-and-twenty years, and you have employed them well." "Alas, sir," said I, "I fear not. Do I know history? Do I know mathematics? Do I know law?" JOHNSON. "Why, sir, though you may know no science so well as to be able to teach it, and no profession so well as to be able to follow it, your general mass of knowledge of books and men renders you very capable to make yourself master of any science, or fit yourself for any profession." I mentioned that a gay friend had advised me against being a lawyer, because

1. *Well-ordered family.* "When Wilkes and Liberty were at their highest tide, I was bringing or losing children every year; and my studies were confined to my nursery." *Mrs. Thrale.*

2. *Returned to London.* See Appendix F., page 549, for notes on Boswell's experiences in Corsica.

I should be excelled by plodding blockheads. JOHNSON. "Why, sir, in the formulary and statutory part of law a plodding blockhead may excel, but in the ingenious and rational part of it a plodding blockhead can never excel."

Our next meeting at the Mitre was on Saturday, the 15th of February, when I presented to him my old and most intimate friend, the Reverend Mr. Temple, then of Cambridge. I having mentioned that I had passed some time with Rousseau[1] in his wild retreat,[2] and having quoted some remark made by Mr. Wilkes, with whom I had spent many pleasant hours in Italy, Johnson said, sarcastically, "It seems, sir, you have kept very good company abroad, Rousseau and Wilkes!" Thinking it enough to defend one at a time, I said nothing as to my gay friend, but answered with a smile, "My dear sir, you don't call Rousseau bad company. Do you really think *him* a bad man?" JOHNSON. "Sir, if you are talking jestingly of this, I don't talk with you. If you mean to be serious, I think him one of the worst of men; a rascal, who ought to be hunted out of society, as he has been. Three or four nations have expelled him, and it is a shame that he is protected in this country." BOSWELL. "I don't deny, sir, but that his novel[3] may, perhaps, do harm; but I cannot think his intention was bad." JOHNSON. "Sir, that will not do. We cannot prove any man's intention to be bad. You may shoot a man through the head, and say you intended to miss him; but the Judge will order you to be hanged. Rousseau, sir, is a very bad man.

---

1. *Rousseau*, Jean Jacques Rousseau (1712-78). "He acknowledges his good qualities with a noble frankness, and his faults with a frankness more noble still. He drew tears from us by the touching picture of his misfortunes, of his weakness, of his confidence repaid with ingratitude, of all the storms of his heart, so often wounded by the treacherous caresses of hypocrites; above all, of his softer passions still dear to the soul they have made unfortunate." *Joseph Dorat, 1778.*

"Everything is base in this man, who believes that he atones for disgusting vices by confiding them to the public." *Edmond Scherer, 1887.*

2. *In his wild retreat.* He had had to flee successively from France, from Geneva, from Neufchâtel, and from Berne. At this time he was in England.

3. *Novel.* The *Nouvelle Héloïse.*

I would sooner sign a sentence for his transportation than that of any felon who has gone from the Old* Bailey these many years. Yes, I should like to have him work in the plantations." BOSWELL. "Sir, do you think him as bad a man as Voltaire?" JOHNSON. "Why, sir, it is difficult to settle the proportion of iniquity between them."

This violence seemed very strange to me, who had read many of Rousseau's animated writings with great pleasure, and even edification; had been much pleased with his society, and was just come from the Continent, where he was very generally admired. Nor can I yet allow that he deserves the very severe censure which Johnson pronounced upon him. His absurd preference of savage to civilized life, and other singularities, are proofs rather of a defect in his understanding than of any depravity in his heart. And notwithstanding the unfavorable opinion which many worthy men have expressed of his *"Profession de Foi du Vicaire Savoyard,"* I cannot help admiring it as the performance of a man full of sincere reverential submission to Divine Mystery, though beset with perplexing doubts; a state of mind to be viewed with pity rather than with anger.

On his favorite subject of subordination, Johnson said, "So far is it from being true that men are naturally equal that no two people can be half an hour together but one shall acquire an evident superiority over the other."

I mentioned the advice given us by philosophers to console ourselves, when distressed or embarrassed, by thinking of those who are in a worse situation than ourselves. This, I observed, could not apply to all, for there must be some who have nobody worse than they are. JOHNSON. "Why, to be sure, sir, there are; but they don't know it. There is no being so poor and so contemptible who does not think there is somebody still poorer, and still more contemptible."

As my stay in London at this time was very short, I had not many opportunities of being with Dr. Johnson; but I felt my veneration for him in no way lessened by my having seen *multorum hominum mores et urbes.*

The roughness, indeed, which sometimes appeared in his

manners was more striking to me now, from my having been accustomed to the studied, smooth, complying habits of the Continent;[1] and I clearly recognized in him, not without respect for his honest conscientious zeal, the same indignant and sarcastical mode of treating every attempt to unhinge or weaken good principles.

One evening, when a young gentleman[2] teased him with an account of the infidelity of his servant, who, he said, would not believe the Scriptures because he could not read them in the original tongues and be sure that they were not invented: "Why, foolish fellow," said Johnson, "has he any better authority for almost everything that he believes?" BOSWELL. "Then the vulgar, sir, never can know they are right, but must submit themselves to the learned." JOHNSON. "To be sure, sir. The vulgar are the children of the State, and must be taught like children." BOSWELL. "Then, sir, a poor Turk must be a Mahometan, just as a poor Englishman must be a Christian?" JOHNSON. "Why, yes, sir; and what then? This now is such stuff as I used to talk to my mother, when I first began to think myself a clever fellow; and she ought to have whipped me for it."

Another evening Dr. Goldsmith and I called on him with the hope of prevailing on him to sup with us at the Mitre. We found him indisposed and resolved not to go abroad.* "Come, then," said Goldsmith, "we will not go to the Mitre tonight, since we cannot have the big man with us." Johnson then called for a bottle of port, of which Goldsmith and I partook, while our friend, now a water drinker, sat by us. GOLDSMITH. "I think, Mr. Johnson, you don't go near the theaters now. You give yourself no more concern about a new play than if you had never had anything to do with the stage." JOHNSON.

---

1. *Habits of the Continent.* "I am, I flatter myself, completely a citizen of the world. In my travels through Holland, Germany, Switzerland, Italy, Corsica, France, I never felt myself from home; and I sincerely love every kindred and tongue, and people and nation." *Boswell, Journal of a Tour to the Hebrides.*

2. *A young gentleman.* "In such passages as this we may generally assume that the gentleman whose name is not given is Boswell himself." *Birkbeck Hill.*

"Why, sir, our tastes greatly alter. The lad does not care for the child's rattle. As we advance in the journey of life, we drop some of the things which have pleased us; whether it be that we are fatigued and don't choose to carry so many things any farther, or that we find other things which we like better." BOSWELL. "But, sir, why don't you give us something in some other way?" GOLDSMITH. "Aye, sir, we have a claim upon you." JOHNSON. "No, sir, I am not obliged to do any more. No man is obliged to do as much as he can do. A man is to have part of his life to himself. If a soldier has fought a good many campaigns, he is not to be blamed if he retires to ease and tranquillity. A physician who has practiced long in a great city may be excused if he retires to a small town, and takes less practice. Now, sir, the good I can do by my conversation bears the same proportion to the good I can do by my writings that the practice of a physician, retired to a small town, does to his practice in a great city." BOSWELL. "But I wonder, sir, you have not more pleasure in writing than in not writing." JOHNSON. "Sir, you *may* wonder."[1]

He wrote this year a letter, not intended for publication, which has, perhaps, as strong marks of his sentiment and style as any of his compositions. The original is in my possession. It is addressed to the late Mr. William Drummond, bookseller in Edinburgh, a gentleman of good family but small estate who took arms for the house of Stuart in 1745; and during his concealment in London till the act of general pardon came out obtained the acquaintance of Dr. Johnson. It seems some of the members of the society in Scotland for propagating Christian knowledge had opposed the scheme of translating the Holy Scriptures into the Erse, or Gaelic, language, from

---

1. *You may wonder.* "Pope had been flattered till he thought himself one of the moving powers in the system of life. When he talked of laying down his pen, those who sat round him entreated and implored, and self-love did not suffer him to suspect that they went away and laughed." *Johnson: Life of Pope.*

political considerations of the disadvantage of keeping up the distinction between the Highlanders and the other inhabitants of North* Britain. Dr. Johnson being informed of this, I suppose by Mr. Drummond, wrote with a generous indignation as follows:

"To Mr. William Drummond.

"SIR: I did not expect to hear that it could be, in an assembly convened for the propagation of Christian knowledge, a question whether any nation uninstructed in religion should receive instruction; or whether that instruction should be imparted to them by a translation of the Holy Books into their own language. If obedience to the will of God be necessary to happiness, and knowledge of His will be necessary to obedience, I know not how he that withholds this knowledge, or delays it, can be said to love his neighbor as himself. He that voluntarily continues ignorance is guilty of all the crimes which ignorance produces; as to him that should extinguish the tapers of a lighthouse might justly be imputed the calamities of shipwrecks. Christianity is the highest perfection of humanity. To omit for a year, or for a day, the most efficacious method of advancing Christianity, in compliance with any purposes that terminate on this side of the grave, is a crime of which I know not that the world has yet an example, except in the practice of the planters of America, a race of mortals whom, I suppose, no other man wishes to resemble.

"The Papists have, indeed, denied to the laity the use of the Bible; but this prohibition, in few places now very rigorously enforced, is defended by arguments which have for their foundation the care of souls. To obscure, upon motives merely political, the light of revelation,[1] is a practice reserved for the

---

1. *Light of revelation.* "We talked of Kennicot's edition of the Hebrew Bible, and hoped it would be quite faithful. JOHNSON: 'Sir, I know not any crime so great that a man could contrive to commit as poisoning the sources of eternal truth.' " *Boswell: Journal of a Tour to the Hebrides.*

reformed;* and, surely, the blackest midnight of popery is meridian sunshine to such a reformation.

"Every man's opinions, at least his desires, are a little influenced by his favorite studies. My zeal for languages may seem, perhaps, rather overheated. To those who have nothing in their thoughts but trade or policy, present power, or present money, I should not think it necessary to defend my opinions; but with men of letters I would not unwillingly compound, by wishing the continuance of every language, however narrow in its extent, till it is reposited in some version of a known book, that it may be always hereafter examined and compared with other languages. For this purpose the translation of the Bible is most to be desired. It is not certain that the same method will not preserve the Highland language for the purposes of learning, and abolish it from daily use. When the Highlanders read the Bible, they will naturally wish to have its obscurities cleared. Knowledge always desires increase; it is like fire, which must first be kindled by some external agent, but which will afterwards propagate itself. When they once desire to learn, they will naturally have recourse to the nearest language by which that desire can be gratified, and one will tell another that if he would attain knowledge, he must learn English.

"This speculation may, perhaps, be thought more subtle than the grossness of real life will easily admit. Let it, however, be remembered that the efficacy of ignorance has long been tried, and has not produced the consequence expected. Let knowledge, therefore, take its turn.

"You will be pleased, sir, to assure the worthy man who is employed in the new translation that he has my wishes for his success; and if here or at Oxford I can be of any use, that I shall think it more than honor to promote his undertaking.

"I am sorry that I delayed so long to write.

"I am, sir, your most humble servant,
                              "SAM. JOHNSON.

"Johnson's Court, Fleet Street
        Aug. 13, 1766."

The opponents of this scheme being made ashamed of their conduct, the undertaking was allowed to go on.

In February, 1767, there happened one of the most remarkable incidents of Johnson's life, which gratified his monarchical enthusiasm, and which he loved to relate with all its circumstances, when requested by his friends. This was his being honored by a private conversation with his Majesty,[1] in the library at the Queen's house. He had frequently visited those splendid rooms, and noble collection of books, which he used to say was more numerous and curious than he supposed any person could have made in the time which the King had employed.

Mr. Barnard, the librarian, took care that he should have every accommodation that could contribute to his ease and convenience; so that he had here a very agreeable resource at leisure hours.

His Majesty, having been informed of his occasional visits, was pleased to signify a desire that he should be told when Dr. Johnson came next to the library. Accordingly, the next time that Johnson did come, as soon as he was fairly engaged with a book, on which, while he sat by the fire, he seemed quite intent, Mr. Barnard stole round to the apartment where the King was, and mentioned that Dr. Johnson was then in the library.

His Majesty said he was at leisure and would go to him; upon which Mr. Barnard took one of the candles that stood on the King's table, and lighted his Majesty through a suite of rooms till they came to a private door into the library, of which his Majesty had the key. Being entered, Mr. Barnard stepped forward hastily to Dr. Johnson, who was still in a

---

1. *His Majesty.* George III; twenty-nine years Johnson's junior. He had already had his first attack of insanity, from which apparently he had recovered. "Personally he was simple in his tastes and strictly moral in his habits, but in pursuit of his political aims he employed men of the vilest character, and recklessly lavished places and gifts of money on those whose services he required." *Gardiner: Students' History of England.* For pleasant pictures of him in the privacy of his own household, see Mme. D'Arblay's *Diary and Letters.*

profound study,[1] and whispered him, "Sir, here is the King."
Johnson started up, and stood still. His Majesty approached
him, and at once was courteously easy.

His Majesty inquired if he was then writing anything. He
answered he was not, for he had pretty well told the world
what he knew, and must now read to acquire more knowledge.
The King then said, "I do not think you borrow much from
anybody." Johnson said he thought he had already done his
part as a writer. "I should have thought so, too," said the
King, "if you had not written so well."—Johnson observed to
me, upon this, that "No man could have paid a handsomer
compliment, and it was fit for a King to pay. It was decisive."
When asked by another friend, at Sir Joshua Reynolds's,
whether he made any reply to this high compliment, he answered,
"No, sir. When the King had said it, it was to be so. It was
not for me to bandy civilities with my Sovereign."

His Majesty having observed to him that he supposed he
must have read a great deal, Johnson answered that he
thought more than he read; that he had read a great deal in
the early part of his life, but having fallen into ill health, he
had not been able to read much, compared with others;
for instance, he said he had not read much compared with
Dr. Warburton.[2] Upon which the King said that he heard

---

1. *Profound study.* "A man of letters, for the most part, spends in
the privacies of study that season of life in which the manners are to be
softened into ease; and, when he has gained knowledge enough to be
respected, has neglected the minuter acts by which he might have
pleased. When he enters life, if his temper be soft and timorous, he is
diffident and bashful, from the knowledge of his defects; if he was
born with spirit and resolution, he is ferocious and arrogant, from the
consciousness of his merit, quick in opposition, and tenacious in defense,
disabled by his own violence, and confused by his haste to triumph."
Johnson: The Rambler.

"A transition from an author's book to his conversation is too often
like an entrance into a large city, after a distant prospect. Remotely,
we see nothing but spires of temples and turrets of palaces; but when we
have passed the gates, we find it perplexed with narrow passages, embarrassed with obstructions and clouded with smoke." *The same.*

2. *Warburton, William* (1698-1779). Bishop of Gloucester. "Warburton, by extending his abuse, rendered it inefficient." *Johnson.*
"The worst of Warburton is that he has a rage for saying something

Dr. Warburton was a man of such general knowledge that you could scarce talk with him on any subject on which he was not qualified to speak; and that his learning resembled Garrick's acting, in its universality. His Majesty then talked of the controversy between Warburton and Lowth,[1] which he seemed to have read, and asked Johnson what he thought of it. Johnson answered, "Warburton has most general, most scholastic, learning; Lowth is the more correct scholar. I do not know which of them calls names best." "Why, truly," said the King, "when once it comes to calling names, argument is pretty well at an end."

His Majesty then asked him what he thought of Lord Lyttelton's history,[2] which was then just published. Johnson

---

when there's nothing to be said." *The same.* "Warburton may be absurd, but he will never be weak; he flounders well." *The same.* Of an author who had proved a keen critic of Warburton, Johnson once said, "A fly, sir, may sting a stately horse and make him wince; but one is but an insect, and the other is a horse still."

"The various readings of copies, and different interpretations of a passage seem to be questions that might exercise the wit without engaging the passions. But whether it be that *small things make mean men proud* and vanity catches small occasions; or that all contrariety of opinion makes proud men angry; there is often found in commentators a spontaneous strain of invective and contempt, more eager and venomous than is vented by the most furious controvertist in politics against those whom he is hired to defame." *Johnson: Preface to Shakespeare.*

1. *Lowth,* Robert (1710-87). Professor of Poetry at Oxford; Bishop of Oxford. When forced into controversy, he appears to have been a master of polite and polished sarcasm. "To the Rev. Dr. Warburton: If you use me otherwise than I deserve, your own character will suffer and not mine. Lay aside all regard to me upon this occasion, but respect yourself and the public. I am, dear sir, your most obedient, humble servant, R. Lowth."

2. *Lord Lyttelton's history.* Of Henry the Second. "Never before have I seen Dr. Johnson speak with so much passion. 'Mr. Pepys,' he cried in a voice the most enraged, 'I understand you are offended by my *Life of Lord Lyttelton.* What is it you have to say against it? Come forth, man! Here am I, ready to answer any charge you can bring.' " *Mme. D'Arblay: Diary, 1781.*

" 'Now,' says Dr. Johnson, 'is Pepys gone home hating me, who love him better than I did before; he spoke in defense of his dead friend; but, though I hope I spoke better who spoke against him, yet all my eloquence will gain me nothing but an honest man for an enemy.' " *Mrs. Piozzi: Anecdotes.*

said he thought his style pretty good, but that he had blamed
Henry the Second rather too much. "Why," said the King,
"they seldom do these things by halves." "No, sir," answered
Johnson, "not to kings." But fearing to be misunderstood,
he immediately subjoined that for those who spoke worse
of kings than they deserved he could find no excuse; but some
might speak better of them than they deserved, without any
ill intention; for those who were favored by them would frequently, from gratitude, exaggerate their praises; and as this
proceeded from a good motive, it was certainly excusable, as
far as error could be excusable.

The King then asked him what he thought of Dr. Hill.[1]
Johnson answered that he was an ingenious man, but had no
veracity; and immediately mentioned, as an instance of it, an
assertion of that writer that he had seen objects magnified
to a much greater degree by using three or four microscopes
at a time than by using one. "Now," added Johnson, "everyone acquainted with microscopes knows that the more of
them he looks through, the less the object will appear."
"Why," replied the King, "this is not only telling an untruth,
but telling it clumsily; for, if that be the case, everyone who
can look through a microscope will be able to detect him."

"I now," said Johnson to his friends, when relating what
had passed, "began to consider that I was depreciating this
man in the estimation of his Sovereign, and thought it was
time for me to say something that might be more favorable."
He added, therefore, that Dr. Hill was, notwithstanding, a
very curious observer; and if he would have been contented to
tell the world no more than he knew, he might have been a
very considerable man, and needed not to have recourse to
such mean expedients to raise his reputation.

During the whole of this interview Johnson talked to his
Majesty with profound respect, but still in his firm, manly
manner, with a sonorous voice, and never in that subdued

---

1. *Dr. Hill.* Physician, botanist, satirist, and quack; "in a chariot
one month; in a jail, the next, for debt."
   "For physic and farces, his equal there scarce is;
      His farces are physic; his physic a farce is."—*David Garrick.*

tone which is commonly used at the levee and in the drawing room. After the King withdrew, Johnson said to Mr. Barnard, "Sir, they may talk of the King as they will, but he is the finest gentleman I have ever seen." And he afterwards observed to Mr. Langton, "Sir, his manners are those of as fine a gentleman[1] as we may suppose Louis the Fourteenth or Charles the Second."

At Sir Joshua Reynolds's, where a circle of Johnson's friends was collected round him to hear his account of this memorable conversation, Dr. Joseph Warton[2] was very active in pressing him to mention the particulars. "Come now, sir, this is an interesting matter; do favor us with it." Johnson, with great good humor, complied.

He told them, "I found his Majesty wished I should talk, and I made it my business to talk. I find it does a man good to be talked to by his Sovereign. In the first place, a man cannot be in a passion—." Here some question interrupted him.

During all the time in which Dr. Johnson was employed in relating to the circle the particulars of what passed between the King and him, Dr. Goldsmith remained unmoved upon a sofa at some distance, affecting not to join in the least in the eager curiosity of the company. He assigned as a reason for his gloom and seeming inattention that he apprehended Johnson had relinquished his purpose of furnishing him with a Prologue to his play,[3] with the hopes of which he had been flattered; but it was strongly suspected that he was fretting with chagrin and envy at the singular honor Dr. Johnson had lately enjoyed. At length the frankness and simplicity of his

---

1. *As fine a gentleman.* Johnson had ridiculed this sort of admiration in his *Rasselas.* "The emperor asked me many questions concerning my country and my travels; and though I cannot now recollect anything that he uttered above the power of a common man, he dismissed me astonished at his wisdom, and enamored of his goodness."

2. *Dr. Joseph Warton* (1722-1800). "He is what Dr. Johnson calls a rapturist." *Mme. D'Arblay: Diary.* "[Johnson] at times, when in gay spirits, would take off Dr. Warton with the strongest humor; describing almost convulsively the ecstasy with which he would seize upon the person nearest to him, to hug in his arms lest his grasp should be eluded, while he displayed some picture or some prospect." *Mme. D'Arblay: Memoirs of Dr. Burney.*

3. *His play.* The *Good-Natured Man,* which appeared in 1768.

natural character prevailed. He sprung from the sofa, advanced to Johnson, and in a kind of flutter, from imagining himself in the situation which he had just been hearing described, exclaimed, "Well, you acquitted yourself in this conversation better than I should have done; for I should have bowed and stammered through the whole of it."

[1768]. In the spring of this year, having published my *Account of Corsica*, with the *Journal of a Tour to That Island*,[1] I returned to London, very desirous to see Dr. Johnson and hear him upon the subject. I found he was at Oxford with his friend Mr. Chambers, who was now Vinerian Professor. Having been told by somebody that he was offended at my having put into my book an extract of his letter[2] to me at Paris, I was impatient to be with him, and therefore followed him to Oxford. I found that Dr. Johnson had sent a letter to me to Scotland, and that I had nothing to complain of but his being more indifferent to my anxiety than I wished him to be. Instead of giving, with the circumstances of time and place, such fragments of his conversation as I preserved during this visit to Oxford, I shall throw them together in continuation.

I asked him whether, as a moralist, he did not think that the practice of the law, in some degree, hurt the nice feeling of honesty. JOHNSON. "Why no, sir, if you act properly. You are not to deceive your clients with false representations of your opinion; you are not to tell lies to a judge." BOSWELL. "But what do you think of supporting a cause which you know to be bad?" JOHNSON. "Sir, you do not know it to be good

---

1. *Journal of a Tour to That Island.* "My book has amazing celebrity. Lord Lyttelton, Mr. Walpole, Mrs. Macaulay, Mr. Garrick, have all written me noble letters about it." *Boswell.* "The author is a strange being. . . . He forced himself upon me in Paris in spite of my teeth and my doors." *Horace Walpole.* "The pamphlet proves that any fool may write a most valuable book if he will only tell us what he heard and saw with veracity." *Thomas Gray.*

2. *Extract of his letter.* Of which the following is a part: "All that you have to fear from me is the vexation of disappointing me. No man loves to frustrate expectations which have been formed in his favor. Come home, however, and take your chance. Come home and expect such a welcome as is due to him whom a wise and noble curiosity has led where perhaps no native of this country ever was before."

or bad till the Judge determines it. I have said that you are
to state facts fairly; so that your thinking, or what you call
knowing, a cause to be bad, must be from reasoning, must be
from your supposing your arguments to be weak and incon-
clusive. But, sir, that is not enough. An argument which
does not convince yourself may convince the Judge to whom
you urge it; and if it does convince him, why, then, sir, you
are wrong, and he is right. It is his business to judge; and
you are not to be confident in your own opinion that a cause
is bad, but to say all you can for your client, and then hear the
Judge's opinion." BOSWELL. "But, sir, does not affecting a
warmth when you have no warmth, and appearing to be clearly
of one opinion when you are in reality of another opinion, does
not such dissimulation impair one's honesty? Is there not
some danger that a lawyer may put on the same mask in common life in the intercourse with his friends?" JOHNSON.
"Why no, sir. A man will no more carry the artifice of the
bar into the common intercourse of society than a man who
is paid for tumbling upon his hands will continue to tumble
upon his hands when he should walk on his feet."

It always appeared to me that he estimated the compositions
of Richardson[1] too highly and that he had an unreasonable
prejudice against Fielding.[2] In comparing those two writers

1. *Richardson, Samuel* (1689-1761). Early in life, something of
a letter-writer for those in love; in 1719, he set up as a master-printer.
His career as a novelist began in 1740 with the little, self-seeking, passionately respectable maid-servant *Pamela* as his heroine, attained its
climax in 1748 in the highly tragic *Clarissa Harlowe*, and closed in 1753
with the smug and wearisome model for gentlemen, *Sir Charles Grandison*.
His novels are very long; and his characters very introspective. "Pictures of high life as conceived by a bookseller, and romances as they
would be spiritualized by a Methodist preacher." *Sir Horace Walpole*,
1764-5. "O Richardson! Richardson!—you shall remain on the same
shelf as Moses, Euripides, and Sophocles." *Diderot, 1761*. "When
I mentioned *Clarissa Harlowe* as a perfect character, 'On the contrary,'
said Johnson, 'you may observe there is always something which she
prefers to truth.' " *Mrs. Piozzi: Anecdotes.*
2. *Fielding, Henry* (1707-54). An excellent police magistrate
as well as novelist and satirist, who could afford to take a recreative
view of human nature when off the bench. His style is distinguished
and full of high spirits.

he used this expression: "that there was as great a difference between them as between a man who knew[1] how a watch was made, and a man who could tell the hour by looking on the dial plate." This was a short and figurative state of his distinction between drawing characters of nature and characters only of manners. But I cannot help being of opinion that the neat watches of Fielding are as well constructed as the large clocks of Richardson, and that his dial plates are brighter.

[Johnson's] prejudice against Scotland appeared remarkably strong at this time. When I talked of our advancement in literature, "Sir," said he, "you have learned a little from us, and you think yourselves very great men. Hume would never have written History had not Voltaire written it before him. He is an echo of Voltaire."[2] BOSWELL. "But, sir, we have Lord Kames."[3] JOHNSON. "You *have* Lord Kames. Keep him; ha, ha, ha! We don't envy you him. Do you ever see Dr. Robertson?" BOSWELL. "Yes, sir." JOHNSON. "Does the dog talk of me?" BOSWELL. "Indeed, sir, he does, and loves you." Thinking that I now had him in a corner, and being solicitous for the literary fame of my country, I pressed him for his opinion on the merit of Dr. Robertson's *History of Scotland*. But, to my surprise, he escaped.—"Sir, I love Robertson, and I won't talk of his book."

I told him that I had several times when in Italy seen the experiment of placing a scorpion within a circle of burning coals; that it ran round and round in extreme pain; and finding no way to escape, retired to the center, and like a true Stoic philosopher darted its sting into its head, and thus at once freed itself from its woes. I said this showed deliberate suicide in a reptile. Johnson would not admit the fact. He said Maupertuis[4] was of opinion that it does not kill itself, but dies

1. *Who knew*. Richardson has complacently used the same figure.
2. *Echo of Voltaire*. Probably said merely to tease Boswell, for at this time Johnson had not read Hume's history.
3. *Lord Kames*. "When Charles Townsend read some of Lord Kames's *Elements of Criticism*, he said, 'This is the work of a dull man grown whimsical.'" *George Wallace, quoted in Boswelliana.*
4. *Maupertuis*. "That philosopher whom the Great Frederick of Prussia loved and honored." *Boswell.*

of the heat; that it gets to the center of the circle, as the coolest place; that its turning its tail in upon its head is merely a convulsion, and that it does not sting itself. He said he would be satisfied if the great anatomist Morgagni, after dissecting a scorpion on which the experiment had been tried, should certify that its sting had penetrated into its head.

I asked him whether I should read Du Halde's *Account of China*.[1] "Why yes," said he, "as one reads such a book; that is to say, consult it."

A gentleman talked to him of a lady whom he greatly admired and wished to marry, but was afraid of her superiority of talents. "Sir," said he, "you need not be afraid; marry her. Before a year goes about, you'll find that reason much weaker, and that wit not so bright."

He praised Signor Baretti. "He has not, indeed, many hooks; but with what hooks he has, he grapples very forcibly."

At this time I observed upon the dial plate of his watch a short Greek inscription, taken from the New Testament, Νὺξ γάρ ἔρχεται, being the first words of our Savior's solemn admonition to the improvement of that time which is allowed us to prepare for eternity: "The night cometh when no man can work." He some time afterwards laid aside this dial plate; and when I asked him the reason, he said, "It might do very well upon a clock which a man keeps in his closet; but to have it upon his watch which he carries about with him, and which is often looked at by others, might be censured as ostentatious."

He remained at Oxford a considerable time; I was obliged to go to London, where I received his letter, which had been returned from Scotland.

"MY DEAR BOSWELL: I have omitted a long time to write to you, without knowing very well why. I could now tell why I should not write; for who would write to men who publish the letters of their friends without their leave? Yet I write to you, in spite of my caution, to tell you that I shall be glad to see you, and that I wish you would empty your head of Corsica,

---

1. *Du Halde's Account of China.* A compend. "Du Halde never traveled ten leagues from Paris; though he appears by his writings to be familiar with Chinese scenery." *D'Israeli: Curiosities of Literature.*

which I think has filled it rather too long. But, at all events,
I shall be glad, very glad, to see you.

"I am, sir,

"Yours affectionately,

"Oxford, March 23, 1768."   "SAM. JOHNSON.

Upon his arrival in London in May, he surprised me one
morning with a visit at my lodging in Half Moon Street, and
was in the kindest and most agreeable frame of mind. As he
had objected to a part of one of his letters being published, I
thought it right to take this opportunity of asking him whether
it would be improper to publish his letters after his death. His
answer was, "When I am dead, you may do as you will."

He talked in his usual style with a rough contempt of popular
liberty. "They make a rout about *universal* liberty,[1] without
considering that all that is to be valued, or indeed can be enjoyed
by individuals, is *private* liberty. Political liberty is good only
so far as it produces private liberty. Now, sir, there is the liberty of the press, which you know is a constant topic. Suppose
you and I and two hundred more were restrained from printing
our thoughts—what then? What proportion would that restraint upon us bear to the private happiness of the nation?"

This mode of representing the inconveniences of restraint
as light and insignificant was a kind of sophistry in which he
delighted to indulge himself, in opposition to the extreme
laxity for which it has been fashionable for too many to argue,

---

1. *Rout about universal liberty.* "Dr. Franklin, in a letter dated
April 16, 1768, describes the riots in London. He had seen 'the mob
requiring ladies and gentlemen of all ranks, as they passed in their
carriages, to shout for Wilkes and Liberty, marking the same word on
all their coaches with chalk.' " *Birkbeck Hill.*

"There are some, perhaps, who would imagine that every Englishman
fights better than the subjects of absolute governments, because he
has more to defend. But what has the English more than the French
soldier? Property they are both commonly without, liberty is to the
lowest rank of every nation little more than the choice of working or
starving; and this choice is, I suppose, equally allowed in every country.
The English soldier seldom has his head very full of the constitution;
nor has there been, for more than a century, any war that put the
property or liberty of a single Englishman in danger." *Johnson, 1758.*
See Goldsmith's picturesque adaptation of this idea in *The Citizen of
the World,* Letter IV.

when it is evident upon reflection that the very essence of government is restraint; and certain it is that as government produces rational happiness, too much restraint is better than too little. But when restraint is unnecessary, and so close as to gall those who are subject to it, the people may and ought to remonstrate; and, if relief is not granted, to resist. Of this manly and spirited principle, no man was more convinced than Johnson himself.

Soon afterwards he supped at the Crown and Anchor tavern, in the Strand, with a company whom I collected to meet him. He was this evening in remarkable vigor of mind, and eager to exert himself in conversation, which he did with great readiness and fluency. When I called upon Dr. Johnson next morning, I found him highly satisfied with his colloquial prowess. "Well," said he, "we had good talk." BOSWELL. "Yes, sir, you tossed and gored several persons."

The late Alexander, Earl of Eglintoune, who loved wit more than wine, and men of genius more than sycophants, had a great admiration of Johnson; but from the elegance of his own manners was, perhaps, too sensible of the roughness which sometimes appeared in Johnson's behavior. One evening when his Lordship did me the honor to sup at my lodgings, he regretted that Johnson had not been educated with more refinement, and lived more in polished society. "No, no, my Lord," said Signor Baretti, "do with him what you would, he would always have been a bear." "True," answered the Earl, with a smile, "but he would have been a *dancing* bear."

To obviate all the reflections which have gone round the world to Johnson's prejudice, by applying to him the epithet of a *bear*, let me impress upon my readers a just and happy saying of my friend Goldsmith, who knew him well: "Johnson, to be sure, has a roughness in his manner; but no man alive has a more tender heart. *He has nothing of the bear but his skin.*"

[1769]. I came to London in the autumn, and having informed him that I was going to be married in a few months,[1]

---

1. *In a few months.* "A man who is in love is like a man who has got the toothache: he feels in most acute pain, while nobody pities him. In that situation I am at present, but well do I know that I will not be so long. So much for inconsistency." *Boswell to Erskine.*

I wished to have as much of his conversation as I could before engaging in a state of life which would probably keep me more in Scotland, and prevent me seeing him so often as when I was a single man; but I found he was at Brighthelmstone[1] with Mr. and Mrs. Thrale. I was very sorry that I had not his company at the Jubilee in honor of Shakespeare at Stratford-upon-Avon, the great poet's native town. When almost every man of eminence in the literary world was happy to partake in this festival of genius,[2] the absence of Johnson could not but be wondered at and regretted. The only trace of him there was in the whimsical advertisement of a haberdasher, who sold *Shakesperian ribbands* of various dyes; and, by way of illustrating their appropriation to the bard, introduced a line from the celebrated Prologue at the opening of Drury Lane Theater:

> Each change of *many-colored* life he drew.

From Brighthelmstone Dr. Johnson wrote me the following letter, which they who may think that I ought to have suppressed, must have less ardent feelings than I have always avowed.

"To James Boswell, Esq.

"DEAR SIR: Why do you charge me with unkindness? I have omitted nothing that could do you good or give you pleasure, unless it be that I have forborne to tell you my opinion of your *Account of Corsica*. I believe my opinion, if you think well of my judgment, might have given you pleasure; but when it is considered how much vanity is excited by praise, I am not sure that it would have done you good. Your *History* is like other histories, but your *Journal* is in a very high degree curious and delightful. There is between the history and

---

1. *Brighthelmstone.* Now Brighton; recently become a fashionable seaside resort, but still to Dr. Johnson's thinking rather desolate. "The sea is so cold and the rooms are so dull, yet I do like to hear the sea roar and my mistress talk." *Johnson to Mrs. Thrale.*

2. *Festival of genius.* Boswell appeared at this festival in the dress of an armed Corsican chief, with *Viva la liberta* in gold letters on his cap.

the journal that difference which there will always be found between notions borrowed from without, and notions generated within. Your history was copied from books; your journal rose out of your own experience and observation. You express images which operated strongly upon yourself, and you have impressed them with great force upon your readers. I know not whether I could name any narrative by which curiosity is better excited or better gratified."

On the 30th of September we dined together at the Mitre. I attempted to argue for the superior happiness of the savage life. JOHNSON. "Sir, there can be nothing more false. The savages have no bodily advantages beyond those of civilized men. They have not better health; and as to care or mental uneasiness, they are not above it, but below it, like bears. Lord Monboddo,[1] one of your Scotch judges, talked a great deal of such nonsense. I suffered *him*, but I will not suffer *you*." BOSWELL. "But, sir, does not Rousseau talk such nonsense?" JOHNSON. "True, sir, but Rousseau *knows* he is talking nonsense, and laughs at the world for staring at him." BOSWELL. "How so, sir?" JOHNSON. "Why, sir, a man who talks nonsense so well must know that he is talking nonsense. But I

---

1. *Lord Monboddo*, James Burnett (1714-99). "Monboddo is a wretched place, wild and naked with a poor old house, though, if I recollect aright, there are two turrets, which mark an old baron's residence. Lord Monboddo received us at his gate most courteously. 'In such houses,' said he, 'our ancestors lived, who were better men than we.' 'No, no, my lord,' said Dr. Johnson; 'we are as strong as they and a great deal wiser.' I was afraid there would have been a violent altercation before we got into the house. But he made no reply. After dinner as the ladies were going away, Dr. Johnson would stand up. He insisted that politeness was of great consequence in society. 'It is,' said he, 'fictitious benevolence. It supplies the place of it amongst those who see each other only in public or but little. Depend upon it, the want of it never fails to produce something disagreeable to one or other.'

"My lord's black servant was sent as our guide to conduct us to the highroad. [Dr. Johnson] observed that his lordship had talked no paradoxes today, 'and as to the savage and the London shopkeeper,' said he, 'I don't know but I might have taken the side of the savage equally had anybody else taken the side of the shopkeeper.'" *Boswell: Journal of a Tour to the Hebrides.*

am *afraid* (chuckling and laughing) Monboddo does *not* know that he is talking nonsense." BOSWELL. "Is it wrong, then, sir, to affect singularity,[1] in order to make people stare?" JOHNSON. "Yes, if you do it by propagating error; and, indeed, it is wrong in any way. There is in human nature a general inclination to make people stare; and every wise man has himself to cure of it, and does cure himself. If you wish to make people stare by doing better than others, why make them stare till they stare their eyes out. But consider how easy it is to make people stare by being absurd. I may do it by going into a drawing-room without my shoes. You remember the gentleman in *The Spectator* who had a commission of lunacy taken out against him for his extreme singularity, such as never wearing a wig, but a nightcap. Now, sir, abstractedly, the nightcap was best; but, relatively, the advantage was overbalanced by his making the boys run after him."

Although I had promised myself a great deal of instructive conversation with him on the conduct of the married state, he did not say much upon that topic. When I censured a gentleman of my acquaintance for marrying a second time, as it showed a disregard of his first wife, he said, "Not at all, sir. On the contrary, were he not to marry again, it might be concluded that his first wife had given him a disgust to marriage, but by taking a second wife he pays the highest compliment to the first, by showing that she made him so happy as a married man that he wishes to be so a second time." So ingenious a turn did he give to this delicate question. And yet, on another occasion, he owned that he once had almost asked a promise of Mrs. Johnson that she would not marry again, but had checked himself. Indeed, I cannot help thinking that in his case the request would have been unreasonable; for if Mrs. Johnson forgot, or thought it no injury to the memory of her first love—the husband of her youth and the father of her children—to make a second marriage, why should she

---

1. *To affect singularity.* "The world has always a right to be regarded." *Johnson to Dr. Taylor, quoted by Birkbeck Hill.*

be precluded from a third, should she be so inclined? In Johnson's persevering fond appropriation of his "Tetty," even after her decease, he seems totally to have overlooked the prior claims of the honest Birmingham trader. I presume that her having been married before had, at times, given him some uneasiness; for I remember his observing upon the marriage of one of our common friends: "He has done a very foolish thing, sir; he has married a widow, when he might have had a maid."

I had last year the pleasure of seeing Mrs. Thrale at Dr. Johnson's one morning, and had conversation enough with her to admire her talents, and to show her that I was as Johnsonian as herself. Dr. Johnson had probably been kind enough to speak well of me, for this evening he delivered me a very polite card from Mr. Thrale and her, inviting me to Streatham.

On the 6th of October I complied with this obliging invitation, and found, at an elegant villa six miles from town, every circumstance that can make society pleasing. Johnson seemed to be equally the care of his host and hostess. I rejoiced at seeing him so happy.

He played off his wit against Scotland with a good-humored pleasantry, which gave me an opportunity for a little contest with him. I having said that England was obliged to us for gardeners, almost all their good gardeners being Scotchmen: JOHNSON. "Why, sir, that is because gardening is much more necessary amongst you than with us. Things which grow wild here must be cultivated with great care in Scotland. Pray, now (throwing himself back in his chair, and laughing), are you ever able to bring the *sloe* to perfection?"

I boasted that we had the honor of being the first to abolish the unhospitable, troublesome, and ungracious custom of giving vails* to servants. JOHNSON. "Sir, you abolished vails because you were too poor to be able to give them."

Mrs. Thrale disputed with him on the merit of Prior. He attacked him powerfully; said he wrote of love like a man who had never felt it. Mrs. Thrale stood to her gun in defense of amorous ditties,[1] which Johnson despised, till at last he silenced her by saying, "My dear lady, talk no more of this. Nonsense can be defended but by nonsense."

Mrs. Thrale then praised Garrick's talent for light, gay poetry; and as a specimen repeated his song in *Florizel and Perdita*,[2] and dwelt with peculiar pleasure on this line:

I'd smile with the simple and feed with the poor.

JOHNSON. "Nay, my dear lady, this will never do. Poor David! Smile with the simple. What folly is that? And who would feed with the poor that can help it? No, no, let me smile with the wise and feed with the rich." I repeated this sally to Garrick, and wondered to find his sensibility as a writer not a little irritated by it.

On the evening of October 10, I presented Dr. Johnson to General Paoli.[3] They met with a manly ease, conscious of their own abilities and of the abilities of each other. The General said that "a great part of the fashionable infidelity was owing to a desire of showing courage. Men who have no opportunities of showing it as to things in this life take death and futurity as objects on which to display it." JOHNSON. "That is mighty foolish affectation. Fear is one of the passions of human nature, of which it is impossible to divest it. You

---

1. *Amorous ditties.* "The dull exercises of a skillful versifier resolved at all adventures to write something about Chloe, and trying to be amorous by dint of study." *Johnson: Life of Prior.*

2. *Florizel and Perdita.* A stage adaptation, by Garrick, of Shakespeare's *Winter's Tale.*

3. *Paoli.* In 1769, after the Corsicans had been beaten in their struggle for independence, General Paoli sought refuge in England, where the government gave him a pension of £1000 a year. Naturally, his reception in England was, for a time, the talk of society.

"It may be said of Paoli as the Cardinal de Retz said of the great Montrose: *C'est un de ces hommes qu'on ne trouve plus que dans les Vies de Plutarque* (He is one of these men who are no longer to be found but in the lives of Plutarch)." *Boswell.*

"Religion seems to sit easy upon Paoli, and notwithstanding what his historian Boswell relates, I take him to be very free in his notions that way." *From a secret report to the British government in 1768, quoted by Birkbeck Hill.*

remember that the Emperor Charles V, when he read upon the tombstone of a Spanish nobleman, 'Here lies one who never knew fear,' wittily said, 'Then he never snuffed a candle with his fingers.' "

Dr. Johnson went home with me and drank tea till late in the night. He said General Paoli had the loftiest port of any man he had ever seen. He denied that military men were always the best bred men. "Perfect good breeding," he observed, "consists in having no particular mark of any profession, but a general elegance of manners; whereas, in a military man, you can commonly distinguish the *brand* of a soldier, *l'homme d'épée.*"

Dr. Johnson shunned tonight any discussion of the perplexed question of fate and free will, which I attempted to agitate. "Sir," said he, "we *know* our will is free, and *there's* an end on't."

He honored me with his company at dinner on the 16th of October, at my lodgings in Old Bond Street, with Sir Joshua Reynolds, Mr. Garrick, Dr. Goldsmith, Mr. Murphy, Mr. Bickerstaff,[1] and Mr. Thomas Davies.. Garrick played round him with a fond vivacity, taking hold of the breasts of his coat, and, looking up in his face with a lively archness, complimented him on the good health which he seemed then to enjoy; while the sage, shaking his head, beheld him with a gentle complacency. One of the company not being come at the appointed hour, I proposed, as usual upon such occasions, to order dinner to be served, adding, "Ought six people to be kept waiting for one?" "Why, yes," answered Johnson, with a delicate humanity, "if the one will suffer more by your sitting down than the six will do by waiting." Goldsmith, to divert the tedious minutes, strutted about bragging of his dress,[2] and

---

1. *Mr. Bickerstaff.* For the past six years, a writer of popular comic operas. Within four years he was to fall into gross discredit and flee to France. There he dragged out forty years of ignominious existence.

2. *Bragging of his dress.* Not more than Boswell sometimes did. "I am dressed in green and gold. I have my chaise, in which I sit alone, and Thomas rides by me in a claret-colored suit with a silver-laced hat." *Boswell to Temple, 1767.* He was particularly set on dress and finery during these years when his first book was still the talk of the town.

I believe was seriously vain of it, for his mind was wonderfully prone to such impressions. "Come, come," said Garrick, "talk no more of that. You are perhaps the worst—eh, eh!" Goldsmith was eagerly attempting to interrupt him, when Garrick went on, laughing ironically, "Nay, you will always *look* like a gentleman; but I am talking of being well or *ill dressed.*" "Well, let me tell you," said Goldsmith, "when my tailor brought home my bloom-colored coat, he said, 'Sir, I have a favor to beg of you. When anybody asks you who made your clothes, be pleased to mention John Filby at the Harrow, in Water Lane.'"

After dinner our conversation first turned upon Pope. Johnson repeated to us, in his forcible, melodious manner, the concluding lines of *The Dunciad.*[1] While he was talking loudly in praise of these lines, one of the company[2] ventured to say, "Too fine for such a poem—a poem on what?" JOHNSON (with a disdainful look). "Why, on *dunces.* It was worth while being a dunce then. Ah, sir, hadst *thou* lived in those days! It is not worth while being a dunce now, when there are no wits."[3]

Mrs. Montagu,[4] a lady distinguished for having written an essay on Shakespeare, being mentioned: REYNOLDS. "I think that essay does her honor." JOHNSON. "Yes, sir, it does *her*

---

1. *Concluding lines of the Dunciad.*

"Lo! thy dread Empire, Chaos! is restored;
Light dies before thy uncreating word;
Thy hand, great Anarch! lets the curtain fall,
And universal Darkness buries All."

2. *One of the company.* No doubt, Boswell himself.

3. *When there are no wits.* "The great topic of his [Pope's] ridicule is poverty . . . . He seems to be of an opinion, not very uncommon in the world, that to want money is to want everything." *Johnson: Life of Pope.*

4. *Mrs. Montagu.* A somewhat affected and pretentious lady, whose drawing-rooms were one of the favorite resorts of what might be called the literary world. Her social position gave her essay an extravagant reputation, which it has since altogether lost.

honor, but it would do nobody else honor. I have, indeed, not read it all. But when I take up the end of a web and find it pack-thread, I do not expect by looking further to find embroidery."

Politics being mentioned, he said, "This petitioning is a new mode of distressing government, and a mighty easy one. I will undertake to get petitions either against quarter guineas or half guineas, with the help of a little hot wine."

On Thursday, October 19, I passed the evening with him at his house. He advised me to complete a dictionary of words peculiar to Scotland, of which I showed him a portion. "Sir," said he, "Ray has made a collection of north country words. By collecting those of your country you will do a useful thing toward the history of the language." He bade me also go on with collections which I was making upon the antiquities of Scotland. "Make a large book, a folio." BOSWELL. "But of what use will it be, sir?" JOHNSON. "Never mind the use; do it."

I mentioned to him that I had seen the execution[1] of several convicts at Tyburn two days before, and that none of them seemed to be under any concern. JOHNSON. "Most of them, sir, have never thought at all." BOSWELL. "But is not the fear of death natural to man?" JOHNSON. "So much so, sir, that the whole of life is but keeping away the thoughts of it." He then in a low and earnest tone talked of his meditating upon the awful hour of his own dissolution, and in what manner he should conduct himself upon that occasion. "I know not," said he, "whether I should wish to have a friend by me, or have it all between God and myself."

Talking of our feeling for the distresses of others: JOHNSON. "Why, sir, there is much noise made about it, but it is greatly exaggerated. No, sir, we have a certain degree of feeling to prompt us to do good; more than that, Providence does not intend. It would be misery to no purpose." BOSWELL. "But

---

1. *Execution.* "I must confess that I myself am never absent from a public execution." *Boswell, 1768.* He was also eager to become acquainted with notorious criminals under sentence of death.

suppose now, sir, that one of your intimate friends were apprehended for an offense for which he might be hanged." JOHNSON.
"I should do what I could to bail him, and give him any other
assistance; but if he were once fairly hanged, I should not
suffer." BOSWELL. "Would you eat your dinner that day,
sir?" JOHNSON. "Yes, sir; and eat it as if he were eating it
with me. Why, there's Baretti, who is to be tried for his life
tomorrow; friends have risen up for him on every side; yet if
he should be hanged, none of them will eat a slice of plum-
pudding[1] the less. Sir, that sympathetic feeling goes a very
little way in depressing the mind."

I told him that I had dined lately at Foote's, who showed
me a letter which he had received from Tom Davies, telling
him that he had not been able to sleep from the concern he felt
on account of "this sad affair of Baretti," begging of him to
try if he could suggest anything that might be of service; and,
at the same time, recommending to him an industrious young
man who kept a pickle shop. JOHNSON. "Aye, sir, here you
have a specimen of human sympathy: a friend hanged and a
cucumber pickled. We know not whether Baretti or the
pickle man has kept Davies from sleep; nor does he know
himself. And as to his not sleeping, sir; Tom Davies is a very
great man; Tom has been upon the stage and knows how to do

---

1. *Plum-pudding.* Of the Roman Catholic, Dr. Nugent, Mrs.
Piozzi writes: "I fancy Dr. Nugent ordered an omelet sometimes on a
Friday or Saturday night; for I remember Dr. Johnson felt very painful
sensations at the sight of that dish soon after his death, and cried: 'Ah!
my poor, dear friend! I shall never eat omelet with thee again.'"
"We must either outlive our friends, you know, or our friends must outlive us; and I see no man that would hesitate about the choice." *Dr.
Johnson.* "It is commonly observed that among soldiers and seamen,
though there is much kindness, there is little grief; they see their friend
fall without any of that lamentation which is indulged in security and
idleness, because they have no leisure to spare from the care of themselves." *The same.* "Poor Mrs.——— is a feeler. It is well that she
has yet power to feel. Fiction durst not have driven upon a few months
such a conflux of misery. Comfort her as you can." *Johnson to Mrs. Thrale,*
1779. "There is no wisdom in useless and hopeless sorrow; but there is
something in it so like virtue that he who is wholly without it cannot be
loved, nor will, by me at least, be thought worthy of esteem." *The
same.*

those things; I have not been upon the stage, and cannot do those things." BOSWELL. "I have often blamed myself, sir, for not feeling for others as sensibly as many say they do." JOHNSON. "Sir, don't be duped by them any more. You will find these very feeling people are not very ready to do you good. They *pay* you by *feeling*."

BOSWELL. "Is there not less religion in the nation now, sir, than there was formerly?" JOHNSON. "I don't know, sir, that there is." BOSWELL. "For instance, there used to be a chaplain in every great family, which we do not find now." JOHNSON. "Neither do you find any of the state servants which great families used formerly to have. There is a change of modes in the whole department of life."

On the 26th of October we dined together at the Mitre tavern. We went home to his house to tea. Mrs. Williams made it with sufficient dexterity, notwithstanding her blindness, though her manner of satisfying herself that the cups were full enough appeared to me a little awkward; for I fancied she put her finger down a certain way till she felt the tea[1] touch it. In my first elation at being allowed the privilege of attending Dr. Johnson at his late visits to this lady, which was like being *è secretioribus consiliis*, I willingly drank cup after cup, as if it had been the Heliconian spring. But as the charm of novelty went off, I grew more fastidious; and, besides, I discovered that she was of a peevish temper.

There was a pretty large circle this evening. Dr. Johnson was in very good humor, lively, and ready to talk upon all subjects. Mr. Fergusson, the self-taught philosopher, told him of a new invented machine which went without horses; a man who sat in it turned a handle which worked a spring that drove it forward. "Then, sir," said Johnson, "what is gained is, the man has his choice whether he will move himself alone, or himself and the machine too."

---

1. *Felt the tea.* "I have since had reason to think myself mistaken, for I have been informed by a lady that she had acquired such a niceness of touch as to know, by the feeling on the outside of the cup, how near it was to being full." *Boswell.*

I know not how so whimsical a thought[1] came into my mind, but I asked, "If, sir, you were shut up in a castle, and a new-born child with you, what would you do?" JOHNSON. "Why, sir, I should not much like my company." BOSWELL. "But would you take the trouble of rearing it?" He seemed, as may well be supposed, unwilling to pursue the subject; but upon my persevering in my question,[2] replied, "Why, yes, sir, I would; but I must have all conveniences. If I had no garden, I would make a shed on the roof, and take it there for fresh air. I should feed it, and wash it much, and with warm water to please it, not with cold water to give it pain." BOSWELL. "But, sir, does not heat relax?" JOHNSON. "Sir, you are not to imagine the water is to be very hot. I would not *coddle* the child. No, sir, the hardy method of treating children does no good. I'll take you five children from London who shall cuff five Highland children. Sir, a man bred in London will carry a burthen, or run, or wrestle, as well as a man brought up in the hardest manner in the country." BOSWELL. "Good living, I suppose, makes the Londoners strong." JOHNSON. "Why, sir, I don't know that it does. Our chairmen* from Ireland, who are as strong men as any, have been brought up upon potatoes. Quantity makes up for quality." BOSWELL. "Would you teach this child, that I have furnished you with, anything?" JOHNSON. "No, I should not be apt to teach it." BOSWELL. "Would not you have a pleasure in teaching it?" JOHNSON. "No, sir, I should *not* have a pleasure in teaching it." BOSWELL. "Have you not a pleasure in teaching men!—*There* I have you. You have the same pleasure in teaching men that I should have in teaching children." JOHNSON. "Why, something about that."

Russia being mentioned as likely to become a great empire,

---

1. *So whimsical a thought.* Quite in line with a very common fancy in the eighteenth century that children reared and educated away from all the arts and traditions of civilization, in caves or hermitages, for instance, would grow up, pure of heart, clear of brain, and reasonable and wise in conduct.

2. *In my question.* "Johnson taught me to cross-question in common life." *Boswell to Mr. Temple, 1789.*

by the rapid increase of population: JOHNSON. "Why, sir, I
see no prospect of their propagating more. It is not from
reason and prudence that people marry, but from inclination.
A man is poor; he thinks, 'I cannot be worse, and so I'll e'en
take Peggy.'" BOSWELL. "But have not nations been more
populous at one period than another?" JOHNSON. "Yes, sir;
but that has been owing to the people being less thinned at
one period than another, whether by emigrations, war, or
pestilence, not by their being more or less prolific." BOSWELL.
"But, to consider the state of our own country—does not
throwing a number of farms into one hand hurt population?"
JOHNSON. "Why, no, sir; the same quantity of food being
produced, will be consumed by the same number of mouths,
though the people may be disposed of in different ways. We
see, if corn be dear and butchers' meat cheap, the farmers all
apply themselves to the raising of corn till it becomes plentiful and cheap, and then butchers' meat becomes dear; so that
an equality is always preserved. No, sir, let fanciful men do
as they will, depend upon it, it is difficult to disturb the system
of life." BOSWELL. "But, sir, is it not a very bad thing for
landlords to oppress their tenants by raising their rents?"
JOHNSON. "Very bad. But, sir, it never can have any general influence;[1] it may distress some individuals. For, consider this: landlords cannot do without tenants. Now tenants
will not give more for land than land is worth. If they can
make more of their money by keeping a shop, or any other
way, they'll do it, and so oblige landlords to let land come back
to a reasonable rent, in order that they may get tenants. Land,
in England, is an article of commerce." BOSWELL. "But, sir,
is it not better that tenants should be dependent on landlords?" JOHNSON. "Why, sir, as there are many more
tenants than landlords, perhaps strictly speaking, we should

---

1. *Any general influence.* "That [the people of the Hebrides] may
not fly from the increase of rent, I know not whether the general good
does not require that the landlords be, for a time, restrained in their
demands, and kept quiet by pensions proportionate to their loss."
Johnson: A Journey to the Western Islands of Scotland.

wish not. But if you please, you may let your lands cheap, and so get the value, part in money and part in homage. I should agree with you in that." BOSWELL. "So, sir, you laugh at schemes of political improvement." JOHNSON. "Why, sir, most schemes of political improvement are very laughable things."

He observed: "Providence has wisely ordered that the more numerous men are, the more difficult it is for them to agree in anything, and so they are governed. There is no doubt that if the poor should reason, 'We'll be the poor no longer, we'll make the rich take their turn,' they could easily do it, were it not that they can't agree. So the common soldiers, though so much more numerous than their officers, are governed by them for the same reason."

When we were alone, I introduced the subject of death, and endeavored to maintain that the fear of it might be got over. I told him that David Hume said to me he was no more uneasy to think he should *not be* after his life than that he *had not been* before he began to exist. JOHNSON. "Sir, if he really thinks so, his perceptions are disturbed; he is mad. If he does not think so, he lies. He may tell you he holds his finger in the flame of a candle without feeling pain; would you believe him? When he dies, he at least gives up all he has." BOSWELL. "Foote, sir, told me that when he was very ill he was not afraid to die." JOHNSON. "It is not true, sir. Hold a pistol to Foote's breast, or to Hume's breast, and threaten to kill them, and you'll see how they behave." BOSWELL. "But may we not fortify our minds for the approach of death?"— Here I am sensible I was in the wrong, to bring before his view what he ever looked upon with horror; for although when in a celestial frame of mind in his *Vanity of Human Wishes*, he has supposed death to be "kind Nature's signal for retreat," from this state of being to "a happier seat," his thoughts upon this awful change were in general full of dismal apprehensions. His mind resembled the vast amphitheater, the Coliseum at Rome. In the center stood his judgment, which like a mighty gladiator combated those apprehensions that, like the wild beasts of the *Arena*,[1] were all around in cells, ready to be let out upon him. After a conflict he drives them back into their dens; but not killing them, they were still assailing him. To my question, whether we might not fortify our minds for the approach of death, he answered, in a passion, "No, sir, let it alone. It matters not how a man dies, but how he lives. The act of dying is not of importance, it lasts so short a time." He added, with an earnest look, "A man knows it must be so, and submits. It will do him no good to whine."

I attempted to continue the conversation. He was so provoked that he said, "Give us no more of this"; and was thrown into such a state of agitation that he expressed himself in a way that alarmed and distressed me; showed an impatience that I should leave him, and when I was going away, called to me sternly, "Don't let us meet tomorrow."

I went home exceedingly uneasy. All the harsh observations which I had ever heard made upon his character crowded into my mind; and I seemed to myself like the man who had put his head into the lion's mouth a great many times with perfect safety, but at last had it bit off.

Next morning I sent him a note, stating that I might have been in the wrong, but it was not intentionally; he was therefore, I could not help thinking, too severe upon me; that notwithstanding our agreement not to meet that day, I would call on him in my way to the city,* and stay five minutes by my watch. "You are," said I, "in my mind, since last night, surrounded with cloud and storm. Let me have a glimpse of sunshine, and go about my affairs in serenity and cheerfulness."

Upon entering his study, I was glad that he was not alone, which would have made our meeting more awkward. There were with him Mr. Steevens and Mr. Tyers, both of whom I now saw for the first time. My note had, on his own reflec-

---

1. *Arena.* "Were I to write the life of Dr. Johnson, I would labor this point, to separate his conduct that proceeded from his passions and what proceeded from his reason, from his natural disposition seen in his quiet hours." *Sir Joshua Reynolds.*

tion, softened him, for he received me very complacently; so that I unexpectedly found myself at ease, and joined in the conversation.

He said the critics had done too much honor to Sir Richard Blackmore[1] by writing so much against him.

[He] spoke unfavorably of a certain pretty voluminous author, saying, "He used to write anonymous books, and then other books commending those books, in which there was something of rascality."

I whispered him, "Well, sir, you are now in good humor." JOHNSON. "Yes, sir." I was going to leave him, and had got as far as the staircase. He stopped me, and smiling, said, "Get you gone *in*"; a curious mode of inviting me to stay, which I accordingly did for some time longer.

This little incidental quarrel and reconciliation must be esteemed as one of many proofs which his friends had that though he might be charged with *bad humor* at times, he was always a *good-natured* man; and I have heard Sir Joshua Reynolds, a nice and delicate observer of manners, particularly remark that when upon any occasion Johnson had been rough to any person in company, he took the first opportunity of reconciliation, by drinking to him, or addressing his discourse to him; but if he found his dignified, indirect overtures sullenly neglected, he was quite indifferent, and considered himself as having done all that he ought to do, and the other as now in the wrong.

Being to set out for Scotland on the 10th of November, I wrote to him at Streatham, begging that he would meet me in town on the 9th; but if this should be very inconvenient to him, I would go thither.

His answer was as follows:

---

1. *Blackmore, Sir Richard* (1650-1729). A butt to the wits, quite as much for his manly attacks on their immorality as for the dullness of his own respectable verse. He was included in Johnson's *Lives of the Poets* at Johnson's suggestion. "So a little for love of his Christianity, a little for love of his physic, a little for love of his courage, and a little for love of contradiction, you will save him from his malevolent critics, and perhaps do him the honor to devour him yourself." *Mrs. Thrale to Dr. Johnson, 1780.*

"*To James Boswell, Esq.*

"DEAR SIR: Upon balancing the inconveniences of both parties, I find it will less incommode you to spend your night here than me to come to town. I wish to see you, and am ordered by the lady of this house to invite you hither. Whether you can come or not, I shall not have any occasion of writing to you again before your marriage, and therefore tell you now that with great sincerity I wish you happiness. I am, dear sir,

"Your most affectionate, humble servant,

"SAM. JOHNSON.

"Nov. 9, 1769."

I was detained in town till it was too late on the ninth, so went to him early in the morning of the tenth of November. "Now," said he, "that you are going to marry, do not expect more from life than life will afford. You may often find yourself out of humor, and you may often think your wife not studious enough to please you; and yet you may have reason to consider yourself as upon the whole very happily married."

I was volatile enough to repeat to him a little epigrammatic song of mine, on matrimony, which Mr. Garrick had a few days before procured to be set to music by the very ingenious Mr. Dibden.

A MATRIMONIAL THOUGHT

In the blithe days of honeymoon,
  With Kate's allurements smitten,
I loved her late, I loved her soon,
  And called her "dearest kitten."

But now my kitten's grown a cat,
  And cross like other wives,
Oh! by my soul, my honest Mat,
  I fear she has nine lives.

My illustrious friend said, "It is very well, sir; but you should not swear." Upon which I altered "Oh! by my soul," to "Alas, alas!"

In 1770 he published a political pamphlet, entitled the *False Alarm*, intended to justify the conduct of the ministry and their majority in the House of Commons for having virtually assumed it as an axiom that the expulsion of a member of Parliament was equivalent to exclusion and thus having declared Colonel Lutterel to be duly elected for the County of Middlesex, notwithstanding Mr. Wilkes[1] had a large majority of votes. This being justly considered as a gross violation of the right of election, an alarm for the constitution extended itself all over the kingdom. To prove this alarm to be false was the purpose of Johnson's pamphlet;[2] but even his vast powers were inadequate to cope with constitutional truth and reason, and his argument failed of effect; and the House of Commons have since expunged the offensive resolution from their journals.

During this year there was a total cessation of all correspondence between Dr. Johnson and me, without any coldness on either side, but merely from procrastination, continued from day to day; and as I was not in London, I had no opportunity of enjoying his company and recording his conversation. To supply this blank, I shall present my readers with some *Collectanea*, obligingly furnished to me by the Rev. Dr. Maxwell,[3] of Falkland, in Ireland, some time assistant preacher at the Temple, and for many years the social friend of Johnson, who spoke of him with a very kind regard.

"Upon a visit to me at a country lodging near Twickenham, he asked me what sort of society I had there. I told him but indifferent; as they chiefly consisted of opulent traders, retired

1. *Wilkes.* Wilkes was four times elected and four times expelled as morally unfit. He was even declared incapacited from ever sitting in the existing parliament. Notwithstanding this act of "exclusion," he was again elected over Colonel Lutterel in April 13, 1769. This time, he was ignored and the Colonel was admitted to the House as duly chosen. A large portion of London was situated in his constituency of Middlesex.

2. *Pamphlet.* "[Milton] was fantastical enough to think that the nation, agitated as it was, might be settled by a pamphlet." *Johnson: Life of Milton, 1780.*

3. *Maxwell*, William. Maxwell was very proud of his friendship with Johnson, "copying him in wig, general appearance, and manners." *Dictionary of National Biography.*

from business. He said he never much liked that class of people; 'for,' said he, 'they have lost the civility of tradesmen without acquiring the manners of gentlemen.'

"Burton's[1] *Anatomy of Melancholy,,* he said, was the only book that ever took him out of bed two hours sooner than he wished to rise.

"He had great compassion for the miseries and distresses of the Irish nation, particularly the Papists; and severely reprobated the barbarous, debilitating policy of the British government, which, he said, was the most detestable mode of persecution. To a gentleman who hinted such policy might be necessary to support the authority of the English government he replied by saying, 'Let the authority of the English government perish rather than be maintained by iniquity. Better,' said he, 'to hang or drown people at once than by an unrelenting persecution to beggar and starve them.'

"He considered the Scotch, nationally, as a crafty, designing people, eagerly attentive to their own interest, and too apt to overlook the claims and pretensions of other people. While they confine their benevolence, in a manner, exclusively to those of their own country, they expect to share in the good offices of other people. 'Now,' said Johnson, 'this principle is either right or wrong; if right, we should do well to imitate this conduct; if wrong, we cannot too much detest it.'

"Being solicited to compose a funeral sermon for the daughter of a tradesman, he naturally inquired into the character of the deceased; and being told that she was remarkable for her humility and condescension to inferiors, he observed that those were very laudable qualities, but it might not be so easy to discover who the lady's inferiors were.

---

1. *Burton.* (1577-1640). A quaint collector of bookish and fantastic learning. "Burton was a man much assailed by deepest melancholy and at other times much given to laughing and jesting, as is the way with melancholy men." *Charles Lamb.*

"Mary bids me warn you not to read the *Anatomy of Melancholy* in your present low way. You'll fancy yourself a pipkin or a headless bear, as Burton speaks of. You'll be lost in a maze of remedies for a labyrinth of diseases." *Charles Lamb to J. B. Dibdin.*

"On my observing to him that a certain gentleman had remained silent the whole evening, in the midst of a very brilliant and learned society, 'Sir,' said he, 'the conversation overflowed, and drowned him.'

"'Law,' said he, 'fell latterly into the reveries of Jacob Behmen, whom Law alleged to have been somewhat in the same state with St. Paul, and to have seen *unutterable things*. Were it even so,' said Johnson, 'Jacob would have resembled St. Paul still more by not attempting to utter them.'

"Somebody observing that the Scotch Highlanders in the year 1745 had made surprising efforts, considering their numerous wants and disadvantages: 'Yes, sir,' said he, 'their wants were numerous, but you have not mentioned the greatest of them all—the want of law.'

"Speaking of the *inward light*,[1] to which some Methodists pretended, he said it was a principle utterly incompatible with social or civil security. 'If a man,' said he, 'pretends to a principle of action of which I can know nothing, nay, not so much as that he has it, but only that he pretends to it, how can I tell what that person may be prompted to do? When a person professes to be governed by a written ascertained law, I can then know where to find him.'

"Speaking of a dull, tiresome fellow whom he chanced to meet, he said, 'That fellow seems to me to possess but one idea, and that is a wrong one.'

"Much inquiry having been made concerning a gentleman who had quitted a company where Johnson was, and no information being obtained, at last Johnson observed that he did not care to speak ill of any man behind his back, but he believed the gentleman was an *attorney*.

"Speaking of the national debt, he said it was an idle dream to suppose that the country could sink under it. Let the public creditors be ever so clamorous, the interest of millions must ever prevail over that of thousands.

---

1. *Inward light.* Direct or immediate knowledge of God's will, without any external evidence or authority.

"A gentleman who had been very unhappy in marriage married immediately after his wife died; Johnson said it was the triumph of hope over experience.

"He observed that a man of sense and education should meet a suitable companion in a wife. It was a miserable thing when the conversation could only be such as whether the mutton should be boiled or roasted, and probably a dispute about that.

"He did not approve of late marriages, observing that more was lost in point of time than compensated for by any possible advantages. Even ill-assorted marriages were preferable to cheerless celibacy.

"He said foppery was never cured; it was the bad stamina of the mind, which, like those of the body, were never rectified; once a coxcomb, always a coxcomb.

"He said a decent provision for the poor is the true test of civilization. Gentlemen of education, he observed, were pretty much the same in all countries; the condition of the lower orders, the poor especially, was the true mark of national discrimination.

"When the corn[1] laws were in agitation in Ireland, by which that country has been enabled not only to feed itself but to export corn to a large amount, Sir Thomas Robinson observed that those laws might be prejudicial to the corn trade of England. 'Sir Thomas,' said he, 'you talk the language of a savage; what, sir, would you prevent any people from feeding themselves, if by any honest means they can do it?'

"Speaking of economy, he remarked it was hardly worth while to save anxiously twenty pounds a year.

"He observed, a principal source of erroneous judgment was viewing things partially and only on *one side*: as, for instance, *fortune-hunters*, when they contemplate the fortunes *singly* and *separately* it was a dazzling and tempting object; but when they

---

1. *Corn laws.* Laws regarding the importation and exportation of grain. In this case, a law, finally passed in 1773-4, granting bounties on the export of Irish grain. Throughout the volume, *corn* is always to be interpreted as meaning *grain*, that being its significance in Great Britain.

came to possess the wives and their fortunes *together*, they began to suspect they had not made quite so good a bargain.

"He advised me, if possible, to have a good orchard. He knew, he said, a clergyman of small income, who brought up a family very reputably, which he chiefly fed with apple dumplings.

"Speaking of a certain prelate who exerted himself very laudably in building churches and parsonage-houses: 'However,' said he, 'I do not find that he is esteemed a man of much professional learning, or a liberal patron of it; yet, it is well, where a man possesses any strong positive excellence. Few have all kinds of merit belonging to their character. We must not examine matters too deeply—no, sir, a *fallible being will fail somewhere.*' "

On the 21st of March [1772], I was happy to find myself again in my friend's study. JOHNSON. "Well, how does Lord Elibank? And how does Lord Monboddo?" BOSWELL. "Very well, sir. Lord Monboddo still maintains the superiority of the savage life." JOHNSON. "What strange narrowness of mind now is that, to think the things we have not known are better than the things we have known."

He was engaged to dine abroad,* and asked me to return to him in the evening at nine, which I accordingly did.

He had said in the morning that Macaulay's[1] *History of St. Kilda* was very well written, except some foppery about liberty and slavery. I mentioned to him that Macaulay told me he was advised to leave out of his book the wonderful story that upon the approach of a stranger all the inhabitants catch cold; but that it had been so well authenticated he determined to retain it. JOHNSON. "Sir, to leave things out of a book, merely because people tell you they will not be

---

1. *Macaulay.* Rev. Kenneth Macaulay, a Scotch clergyman. Johnson once called him a "bigot to laxness." St. Kilda is one of the Hebridean islands, off the west coast of Scotland.

"This evening [Johnson] disputed the truth of what is said as to the people of St. Kilda catching cold . . . 'How can there,' said he, 'be a physical effect without a physical cause?' He said the evidence was not adequate to the improbability of the thing." *Boswell: Journal of a Tour to the Hebrides.*

believed, is meanness. Macaulay acted with more magnanimity."

I mentioned the petition to Parliament for removing the subscription to the Thirty-nine* Articles. JOHNSON. "It was soon thrown out. Sir, they talk of not making boys at the University subscribe to what they do not understand; but they ought to consider that our Universities were founded to bring up members for the Church of England, and we must not supply our enemies with arms from our arsenal. No, sir, the meaning of subscribing is not that they fully understand all the articles, but that they will adhere to the Church of England. Now take it in this way, and suppose that they should only subscribe their adherence to the Church of England; there would be still the same difficulty, for still the young men would be subscribing to what they do not understand. For, if you should ask them, 'What do you mean by the Church of England? Do you know in what it differs from the Presbyterian Church? from the Romish Church? from the Greek Church? from the Coptic Church?' they could not tell you. So, sir, it comes to the same thing."

In the morning we had talked of old families and the respect due to them. JOHNSON. "Sir, you have a right to that kind of respect, and are arguing for yourself. I am for supporting the principle, and am disinterested in doing it, as I have no such right." BOSWELL. "Why, sir, it is one more incitement to a man to do well." JOHNSON. "Yes, sir, and it is a matter of opinion very necessary to keep society together. What is it but opinion, by which we have a respect for authority,[1] that prevents us, who are the rabble, from rising up and pulling

---

1. *Respect for authority.* On whether a young woman should promise her father to marry only with his consent, Dr. Johnson wrote to Mrs. Thrale in 1773: "If Miss ——— followed a trade, would it be said that she was bound in conscience to give or refuse credit at her father's choice? And is not marriage a thing in which she is more interested, and has, therefore, more right of choice?" "Mr. Johnson caught me reprimanding the daughter of my housekeeper for having sat down unpermitted in her mother's presence. 'Why, she gets her living, does she not,' said he, 'without her mother's help? Let the wench alone.' " *Mrs. Piozzi: Anecdotes.*

down you who are gentlemen from your places, and saying,
'We will be gentlemen in our turn'? Now, sir, that respect for
authority is much more easily granted to a man whose father
has had it than to an upstart, and so society is more easily
supported." BOSWELL. "Perhaps, sir, it might be done by
the respect belonging to office, as among the Romans, where the
dress, the *toga*, inspired reverence." JOHNSON. "Why, we
know very little about the Romans. But, surely, it is much
easier to respect a man who has always had respect than to
respect a man who we know was last year no better than ourselves, and will be no better next year. In republics there is no
respect for authority, but a fear of power." BOSWELL. "At
present, sir, I think riches seem to gain most respect." JOHNSON.
"No, sir, riches do not gain hearty respect; they only procure
external attention. A very rich man, from low beginnings, may
buy his election in a borough; but, *cæteris paribus*, a man of
family will be preferred. People will prefer a man for whose
father their fathers have voted, though they should get no
more money, or even less. If gentlemen of family would allow
the rich upstarts to spend their money profusely, which they are
ready enough to do, and not vie with them in expense, the
upstarts would soon be at an end, and the gentlemen would
remain; but if the gentlemen will vie in expense with the upstarts,
they must be ruined."

On Saturday, March 27, I introduced to him Sir Alexander
Macdonald. Sir Alexander observed that the Chancellors in
England are chosen from views much inferior to the office,
being chosen from temporary political views. JOHNSON.
"Why, sir, in such a government as ours no man is appointed
to an office because he is fitted for it, nor hardly in any other
government; because there are so many connections and de-
pendencies to be studied. A despotic prince may choose a
man to an office merely because he is the fittest for it. The
King of Prussia may do it." SIR A. "I have been correcting
several Scotch accents in my friend Boswell. I doubt, sir,
if any Scotchman ever attains to a perfect English pronunciation." JOHNSON. "Why, sir, few of them do, because they

do not persevere. But we find how near they come to it; and, certainly, a man who conquers nineteen parts of the Scottish accent may conquer the twentieth. But, sir, when a man has got the better of nine-tenths, he grows weary, he relaxes his diligence, he finds he has corrected his accent so far as not to be disagreeable, and he no longer desires his friends to tell him when he is wrong; nor does he choose to be told. Sir, when people watch me narrowly, and I do not watch myself, they will find me out to be of a particular county."

Upon another occasion, Johnson said to me, "Sir, your pronunciation is not offensive." With this concession I was pretty well satisfied; and let me give my countrymen of north Britain an advice not to aim at absolute perfection in this respect. Good English is plain, easy, and smooth in the mouth of an unaffected English gentleman. A studied and factitious pronunciation, which requires perpetual attention and imposes perpetual constraint, is exceedingly disgusting. A small inter-mixture of provincial peculiarities may, perhaps, have an agree-able effect, as the notes of different birds concur in the harmony of the grove, and please more than if they were all exactly alike.

BOSWELL. "It may be of use, sir, to have a Dictionary to ascertain the pronunciation. Sheridan, I believe, has finished such a work." JOHNSON. "Why, sir, consider how much easier it is to learn a language by the ear than by any marks. Sheridan's *Dictionary* may do very well; but when you want the word, you have not the *Dictionary*. It is like a man who has a sword that will not draw. It is an admirable sword, to be sure; but while your enemy is cutting your throat, you are unable to use it. Besides, sir, what entitles Sheridan to fix the pronunciation of English? He has, in the first place, the disadvantage of being an Irishman; and if he says he will fix it after the example of the best company, why, they differ among themselves. I remember an instance: when I published the 'Plan' for my *Dictionary*, Lord Chesterfield told me that the word *great* should be pronounced so as to rime to *state;* and Sir William Yonge sent me word that it should be pronounced so as to rime to *seat*, and that none but an Irishman would pronounce it *grait*. Now here were two men, the one, the best speaker in the House of Lords, the other, the best speaker in the House of Commons, differing entirely."

I again visited him at night. Finding him in a very good humor, I ventured to lead him to the subject of our situation in a future state, having much curiosity to know his notions on that point. BOSWELL. "One of the most pleasing thoughts is that we shall see our friends again." JOHNSON. "Yes, sir; but you must consider that when we are become purely rational, many of our friendships will be cut off. We form many friendships with bad men, because they have agreeable qualities, and they can be useful to us; but, after death, they can no longer be of use to us. We form many friendships by mistake, imagining people to be different from what they really are. After death, we shall see everyone in a true light."

"Then, sir, they talk of our meeting our relations; but then all relationship is dissolved; and we shall have no regard for one person more than another, but for their real value." BOSWELL. "As to our employment in the future state, the sacred writings say little. The *Revelation* of St. John gives us many ideas, and particularly mentions music." JOHNSON. "Why, sir, ideas must be given you by means of something which you know."

On Tuesday, March 31, he and I dined at General Paoli's. A question was started whether the state of marriage was natural to man. JOHNSON. "Sir, it is so far from being natural that we find all the motives which they have for remaining in that connection, and the restraints which civilized society imposes to prevent separation, are hardly sufficient to keep them together." The General said that in a state of nature a man and woman uniting together would form a strong and constant affection; and that the same causes of dissension would not arise between them as occur between husband and wife in a civilized state. JOHNSON. "Sir, they would have dissensions enough, though of another kind. One would choose to go a-hunting in this wood, the other in that; one would choose to go a-fishing in this lake, the other in that. Besides, sir, a savage man and a savage woman meet by chance; and when the man sees another woman that pleases him better, he will leave the first."

Dr. Johnson went home with me to my lodgings in Conduit Street and drank tea, previous to our going to the Pantheon,* which neither of us had seen before.

I asked him how far he thought wealth should be employed in hospitality. JOHNSON. "You are to consider that ancient hospitality, of which we hear so much, was in an uncommercial country, when men, being idle, were glad to be entertained at rich men's tables. But in a commercial country time becomes precious, and therefore hospitality is not so much valued. No doubt a man has a satisfaction in seeing his friends eating and drinking around him. But promiscuous hospitality is not the way to gain real influence. You must help some people at table before others; you must ask some people how they like their wine oftener than others. You therefore offend more people than you please. You are like the French statesman who said, when he granted a favor, '*J'ai fait dix mécontents et un ingrat.*' Besides, sir, being entertained ever so well at a man's table impresses no lasting regard or esteem. No, sir, the way to make sure of power and influence is by lending money confidentially to your neighbors at a small interest, or perhaps at no interest at all, and having their bonds in your possession." BOSWELL. "May not a man, sir, employ his riches to advantage in educating young men of merit?" JOHNSON. "Yes, sir, if they fall in your way; but if it be understood that you patronize young men of merit, you will be harassed with solicitations. You will have numbers forced upon you, who have no merit; some will force them upon you from mistaken partiality; and some from downright interested motives, without scruple; and you will be disgraced."

We then walked to the Pantheon. I said there was not half a guinea's worth of pleasure in seeing this place. JOHNSON. "But, sir, there is half a guinea's worth of inferiority to other people in not having seen it." BOSWELL. "I doubt, sir, whether there are many happy people here." JOHNSON. "Yes, sir, there are many happy people here. There are many people here who are watching hundreds, and who think hundreds are watching them."

Happening to meet Sir Adam Fergusson, I presented him to Dr. Johnson. Sir Adam expressed some apprehension that the Pantheon would encourage luxury. "Sir," said Johnson, "I am a great friend to public amusements; for they keep people from vice."

Sir Adam suggested that luxury corrupts a people and destroys the spirit of liberty. JOHNSON. "Sir, that is all visionary. I would not give half a guinea to live under one form of government rather than another. It is of no moment to the happiness of an individual. Sir, the danger of the abuse of power is nothing to a private man. What Frenchman is prevented from passing his life as he pleases?" SIR ADAM. "But, sir, in the British constitution it is surely of importance to keep up a spirit in the people, so as to preserve a balance against the crown." JOHNSON. "Sir, I perceive you are a vile Whig. Why all this childish jealousy of the power of the crown? The crown has not power enough. When I say that all governments are alike, I consider that in no government power can be abused long. Mankind will not bear it. If a sovereign oppresses his people to a great degree, they will rise and cut off his head. There is a remedy in human nature against tyranny, that will keep us safe under every form of government. Had not the people of France thought themselves honored in sharing in the brilliant actions of Louis XIV, they would not have endured him; and we may say the same of the King of Prussia's people." Sir Adam introduced the ancient Greeks and Romans. JOHNSON. "Sir, the mass of both of them were barbarians. The mass of every people must be barbarous where there is no printing, and consequently knowledge is not generally diffused. Knowledge is diffused among our people by the newspapers." Sir Adam mentioned the orators, poets, and artists of Greece. JOHNSON. "Sir, I am talking of the mass of the people. We see

even what the boasted Athenians were. The little effect which
Demosthenes's orations had upon them shows that they were
barbarians."

I spoke of the inequality of the livings* of the clergy in
England, and the scanty provisions of some of the curates.
JOHNSON. "Why, yes, sir; but it cannot be helped. You
must consider that the revenues of the clergy are not at the
disposal of the state, like the pay of the army. Different men
have founded different churches; and some are better endowed,
some worse. The state cannot interfere and make an equal
division of what has been particularly appropriated. Now,
when a clergyman has but a small living, or even two small
livings, he can afford very little to the curate."

On Monday, April 6, I dined with him at Sir Alexander
Macdonald's, where was a young officer in the regimentals of
the Scots Royal, who talked with a vivacity, fluency, and
precision so uncommon that he attracted particular attention.
He proved to be the Honorable Thomas Erskine,[1] youngest
brother to the Earl of Buchan, who has since risen into such
brilliant reputation at the bar in Westminster Hall.*

We talked of gaming, and animadverted on it with severity.[2]
JOHNSON. "Nay, gentlemen, let us not aggravate the matter.
It is not roguery to play with a man who is ignorant of the
game, while you are master of it, and so win his money; for he
thinks he can play better than you, as you think you can play
better than he; and the superior skill carries it." ERSKINE.
"He is a fool, but you are not a rogue." JOHNSON. "That's
much about the truth, sir. It must be considered that a
man who only does what every one of the society to which he

---

1. *Honorable Thomas Erskine* (1750-1823). Twenty-two years old.
He had already cruised for four years in the West Indies as a midship-
man in His Majesty's Navy, had bought a commission in the army, and
with his young wife had spent two years on military duty in the Mediterranean. Later, he was to become the advocate of many radical reforms.

2. *With severity.* "Some years ago I had the rage of gaming, and I
lost more money than I was able to pay. Mr. Sheridan advanced me as
much as cleared me, but took a promise from me that I should not play
at all for three years." *Boswell to Temple, 1768.*

belongs would do is not a dishonest man. In the republic of
Sparta it was agreed that stealing was not dishonorable if not
discovered. I do not commend a society where there is an agreement that what would not otherwise be fair shall be fair; but I
maintain that an individual of any society who practices what
is allowed is not a dishonest man. BOSWELL. "So, then, sir,
you do not think ill of a man who wins perhaps forty thousand
pounds in a winter?" JOHNSON. "Sir, I do not call a gamester
a dishonest man; but I call him an unsocial man, an unprofitable
man. Gaming is a mode of transferring property without producing any intermediate good. Trade gives employment to
numbers, and so produces intermediate good."

I talked of the little attachment which subsisted between
near relations in London. "Sir," said Johnson, "in a country
so commercial as ours, where every man can do for himself,
there is not so much occasion for that attachment. No man is
thought the worse of here, whose brother was hanged. In uncommercial countries many of the branches of a family must depend
on the stock; so, in order to make the head of the family take
care of them, they are represented as connected with his reputation, that, self-love being interested, he may exert himself to
promote their interest. You have, first, large circles, or clans;
as commerce increases, the connection is confined to families;
by degrees that too goes off, as having become unnecessary,
and there being few opportunities of intercourse. One brother
is a merchant in the city, and another is an officer in the guards;
how little intercourse can these two have!"

I argued warmly for the old feudal* system.[1] Sir Alexander[2]
opposed it, and talked of the pleasure of seeing all men free and
independent. JOHNSON. "I agree with Mr. Boswell that there

1. *Old feudal system.* "My fellow traveler and I were now full of the
old Highland spirit. Dr. Johnson said, 'Sir, the Highland chiefs should
not be allowed to go farther south than Aberdeen. A strong-minded
man like Sir James Macdonald may be improved by an English educa-
cation, but in general they will be tamed into insignificance.'" *Boswell:
Journal of a Tour to the Hebrides.*
2. *Sir Alexander.* Himself notoriously harsh as a landlord and
mean as a chief; finally driven off his estates by the menaces of his
tenants.

must be a high satisfaction in being a feudal lord; but we are to consider that we ought not to wish to have a number of men unhappy for the satisfaction of one."

On Thursday, April 9, I called on him to beg he would dine with me at the Mitre tavern. He had resolved not to dine at all this day, I know not for what reason; and I was so unwilling to be deprived of his company that I was content to submit to suffer a want which was at first somewhat painful, but he soon made me forget it; and a man is always pleased with himself when he finds his intellectual inclinations predominate.

I mentioned witches,[1] and asked him what they properly meant. JOHNSON. "Why, sir, they properly mean those who make use of evil spirits." BOSWELL. "There is, no doubt, sir, a general report and belief of their having existed." JOHNSON. "You have not only the general report and belief, but you have many voluntary, solemn confessions." He did not affirm anything positively upon a subject which it is the fashion of the times to laugh at as a matter of absurd credulity. He only seemed willing, as a candid inquirer after truth, however strange and inexplicable, to show that he understood what might be urged for it.

On Friday, April 10, I dined with him at General Oglethorpe's,[2] where we found Dr. Goldsmith. I started the question, whether dueling was consistent with moral duty. The brave old General

---

1. *Witches.* "At supper witchcraft was introduced. Mr. Crosbie said he thought it was the greatest blasphemy to suppose evil spirits counteracting the Deity, and raising storms, for instance, to destroy his creatures. JOHNSON. 'As to storms, we know there are such things; and it is no worse that evil spirits raise them than that they rise.' CROSBIE. 'But it is not credible that witches should have effected what they are said in stories to have done.' JOHNSON. 'I am not defending their credibility; I am only saying that your arguments are not good.'" *Boswell: Journal of a Tour to the Hebrides.*

2. *General Oglethorpe* (1696-1785). Soldier and philanthropist, now seventy-six years old. He belonged to an old Jacobite family who had stood by the Stuarts long after their cause was lost; he had served against the Turks under the Austrian general, Prince Eugene, had opposed the abuses in the prison system, and negro slavery, and had founded the colony of Georgia and defended it against the Spanish. At eighty-seven he was still "in full bloom." He was a hearty admirer of Boswell's *Corsica* and Johnson's *London*.

fired at this, and said, with a lofty air, "Undoubtedly a man has a right to defend his honor." GOLDSMITH (turning to me). "I ask you first, sir, what would you do if you were affronted?" I answered, "I should think it necessary to fight." "Why, then," replied Goldsmith, "that solves the question." JOHNSON. "No, sir, it does not solve the question. It does not follow that what a man would do is therefore right." I said I wished to have it settled whether dueling was contrary to the laws of Christianity. Johnson immediately entered on the subject: "Sir, as men become in a high degree refined, various causes of offense arise which are considered to be of such importance that life must be staked to atone for them, though in reality they are not so. A body that has received a very fine polish may be easily hurt. Before men arrive at this artificial refinement, if one tells his neighbor he lies, his neighbor tells him he lies; if one gives his neighbor a blow, his neighbor gives him a blow; but in a state of highly polished society, an affront is held to be a serious injury. It must, therefore, be resented, or rather a duel must be fought upon it; as men have agreed to banish from their society one who puts up with an affront without fighting a duel. Now, sir, it is never unlawful to fight in self-defense. He, then, who fights a duel, does not fight from passion against his antagonist, but out of self-defense, to avert the stigma of the world, and to prevent himself from being driven out of society. I could wish there was not that superfluity of refinement; but while such notions prevail, no doubt a man may lawfully fight a duel."

Let it be remembered that this justification is applicable only to the person who *receives* an affront. All mankind must condemn the aggressor.

The General told us that when he was a very young man, I think only fifteen, serving under Prince Eugene of Savoy, he was sitting in a company at table with a Prince of Wirtemberg. The Prince took up a glass of wine, and, by a fillip, made some of it fly in Oglethorpe's face. Here was a nice dilemma. To have challenged him instantly might have fixed a quarrelsome character upon the young soldier; to have taken no notice of it might have been considered as cowardice. Oglethorpe therefore, keeping his eye upon the Prince, and smiling all the time, as if he took what his Highness had done in jest, said *"Mon Prince"* (I forget the French words he used; the purport however was), "that's a good joke, but we do it much better in England"; and threw a whole glass of wine in the Prince's face. An old General who sat by said, *"Il a bien fait, mon Prince; vous l'avez commencé";* and thus all ended in good humor.

Dr. Johnson said, "Pray, General, give us an account of the siege of Belgrade." Upon which the General, pouring a little wine upon the table, described everything with a wet finger: "Here we were, here were the Turks," etc., etc. Johnson listened with the closest attention.

A question was started, how far people who disagree in a capital point can live in friendship together. Johnson said they might. Goldsmith said they could not, as they had not the *idem velle atque idem nolle*—the same likings and the same aversions. JOHNSON. "Why, sir, you must shun the subject as to which you disagree. For instance, I can live very well with Burke. I love his knowledge, his genius, his diffusion, and affluence of conversation; but I would not talk to him of the Rockingham party."[1] GOLDSMITH. "But, sir, when people live together who have something as to which they disagree, and which they want to shun, they will be in the situation mentioned in the story of Bluebeard: 'You may look into all the chambers but one.' But we should have the greatest inclination to look into that chamber, to talk of that subject." JOHNSON (with a loud voice). "Sir, I am not saying that *you* could live in friendship with a man from whom you differ as to some point; I am only saying that I could do it."

On Saturday, April 11, he appointed me to come to him

---

1. *Rockingham party.* One of the three factions into which the Whig party was divided at this time; so called from its incorruptible but mediocre leader, Lord Rockingham. He was opposed to the extension of the royal power and was decidedly liberal in his attitude to the American colonies. It was to this faction that Edmund Burke belonged.

in the evening, when he should be at leisure to give me some assistance for the defense of Hastie,[1] the schoolmaster of Campbelltown, for whom I was to appear in the House of Lords. When I came, I found him unwilling to exert himself. I pressed him to write down his thoughts upon the subject. He said, "There's no occasion for my writing. I'll talk to you." He was, however, at last prevailed on to dictate to me, while I wrote:

"The charge is that he has used immoderate and cruel correction. Correction, in itself, is not cruel; children, being not reasonable, can be governed only by fear. To impress this fear is, therefore, one of the first duties of those who have the care of children. No severity is cruel which obstinacy makes necessary; for the greatest cruelty would be to desist, and leave the scholar too careless for instruction, and too much hardened for reproof. Punishments, however severe, that produce no lasting evil may be just and reasonable, because they may be necessary. If it be supposed that the enmity of their fathers proves the justice of the charge, it must be considered how often experience shows us that men who are angry on one ground will accuse on another; with how little kindness, in a town of low trade, a man who lives by learning is regarded; and how implicitly, where the inhabitants are not very rich, a rich man is hearkened to and followed.

"This, sir," said he, "you are to turn in your mind, and make the best use of it you can in your speech."

Of our friend Goldsmith he said, "Sir, he is so much afraid of being unnoticed that he often talks merely lest you should forget that he is in the company." BOSWELL. "Yes, he stands forward." JOHNSON. "True, sir, but if a man is to stand forward, he should wish to do it not in an awkward posture, not in rags, not so as that he shall only be exposed to ridicule." BOSWELL. "For my part, I like very well to hear

---

1. *Hastie.* It was stated in his trial that "scarce a day passed without some of the scholars coming home with their heads cut and their bodies discolored." The House of Lords decided against him, on which Johnson wrote to Boswell, "Poor Hastie, I think, had but his deserts."

honest Goldsmith talk away carelessly." JOHNSON. "Why, yes, sir, but he should not like to hear himself."

On Tuesday, April 14, the decree of the Court of Session in the schoolmaster's cause was reversed in the House of Lords, after a very eloquent speech by Lord Mansfield who showed himself an adept in school discipline, but I thought was too rigorous toward my client. On the evening of the next day I supped with Dr. Johnson at the Crown and Anchor tavern, in the Strand, in company with Mr. Langton and his brother-in-law, Lord Binning. I repeated a sentence of Lord Mansfield's speech: "My Lords, severity is not the way to govern either boys or men." "Nay," said Johnson, "it is the way to *govern* them. I know not whether it be the way to *mend* them."

I talked of the recent expulsion of six students from the University of Oxford, who were Methodists,[1] and would not desist from publicly praying and exhorting. JOHNSON. "What have they to do at an University who are not willing to be taught, but will presume to teach? Sir, they were examined, and found to be mighty ignorant fellows." BOSWELL. "But, was it not hard, sir, to expel them, for I am told they were good beings?" JOHNSON. "I believe they might be good beings, but they were not fit to be in the University of Oxford. A cow is a very good animal in the field, but we turn her out of a garden."

Mr. Langton told us he was about to establish a school upon his estate, but it had been suggested to him that it might have a tendency to make the people less industrious.[2] JOHNSON. "No, sir. While learning to read and write is a distinction, the few who have that distinction may be the less inclined to work; but when everybody learns to read and write, it is no

---

1. *Methodists.* "He may be justly driven from a society by which he thinks himself too wise to be governed, and in which he is too young to teach, and too opinionative to learn." *Johnson: Life of Cheynel.* For the meaning of *Methodists,* see page 118.

2. *To make the people less industrious.* In his "Review of a Free Inquiry into the Nature and Origin of Evil," Johnson answers the argument that "those born to poverty and drudgery" should not be deprived of the "opiate of ignorance," by asking how we are to determine who are "born to poverty."

longer a distinction. A man who has a laced waistcoat is too fine a man to work; but if everybody had laced waistcoats, we should have people working in laced waistcoats. There are no people whatever more industrious, none who work more, than our manufacturers; yet they have all learned to read and write. Sir, you must not neglect doing a thing immediately good, from fear of remote evil—from fear of its being abused. A man who has candles may sit up too late, but nobody will deny that the art of making candles ought to be preserved." BOSWELL. "But, sir, would it not be better to follow Nature; and go to bed and rise just as Nature gives us light or withholds it?" JOHNSON. "No, sir; for then we should have no kind of equality in the partition of our time between sleeping and waking. It would be very different in different seasons and in different places. In some of the northern parts of Scotland how little light is there in the depth of winter!"

While I remained in London this spring, I was with him at several other times, both by himself and in company. Without specifying each particular day, I have preserved the following memorable things.

A gentleman having to some of the usual arguments for drinking added this: "You know, sir, drinking drives away care and makes us forget whatever is disagreeable. Would not you allow a man to drink for that reason?" JOHNSON. "Yes, sir, if he sat next *you*."

When one of his friends endeavored to maintain that a country gentleman might contrive to pass his life very agreeably, "Sir," said he, "you cannot give me an instance of any man who is permitted to lay out his own time, contriving not to have tedious hours."

He said, "There is no permanent national character; it varies according to circumstances. Alexander the Great swept India; now the Turks sweep Greece."

A learned gentleman, who in the course of conversation wished to inform us of this simple fact that the counsel upon the circuit at Shrewsbury were much bitten by fleas, took, I suppose, seven or eight minutes in relating it circumstantially.

He in a plenitude of phrase told us that large bales of woolen cloth were lodged in the town hall; that by reason of this fleas nestled there in prodigious numbers; that the lodgings of the counsel were near the town hall; and that those little animals moved from place to place with wonderful agility. Johnson sat in great impatience till the gentleman had finished his tedious narrative, and then burst out (playfully, however), "It is a pity, sir, that you have not seen a lion; for a flea has taken you such a time that a lion must have served you a twelvemonth."

He would not allow Scotland to derive any credit from Lord Mansfield; for he was educated in England. "Much," said he, "may be made of a Scotchman, if he be *caught* young."

He said, "I am very unwilling to read the manuscripts of authors, and give them my opinion. If the authors who apply to me have money, I bid them boldly print without a name; if they have written in order to get money, I tell them to go to the booksellers and make the best bargain they can." Boswell. "But, sir, if a bookseller should bring you a manuscript to look at?" Johnson. "Why, sir, I would desire the bookseller to take it away."

"The misfortune of Goldsmith in conversation is this: he goes on without knowing how he is to get off. His genius is great, but his knowledge is small. As they say of a generous man, it is a pity he is not rich, we may say of Goldsmith, it is a pity he is not knowing. He would not keep his knowledge to himself."

Before leaving London this year, I consulted him upon a question purely of Scotch law. It was held of old, and continued for a long period to be an established principle in that law, that whoever intermeddled with the effects of a person deceased, without the interposition of legal authority to guard against embezzlement, should be subject to pay all the debts of the deceased, as having been guilty of what was technically called *vicious intromission*. The Court of Session had gradually relaxed the strictness of this principle, where the interference proved had been inconsiderable. In a case which came before that Court the preceding winter I had labored to persuade the judge to return to the ancient law. It was my own sincere opinion that they ought to adhere to it; but I had exhausted all my powers of reasoning in vain. Johnson thought as I did; and in order to assist me in my application to the Court for a revision and alteration of the judgment, he dictated to me the following argument:

" . . . . It is the quality of reason to be invariable and constant; and of equity, to give to one man what, in the same case, is given to another. The advantage which humanity derives from law is this: that the law gives every man a rule of action, and prescribes a mode of conduct which shall entitle him to the support and protection of society. That the law may be a rule of action, it is necessary that it be known; it is necessary that it be permanent and stable. The law is the measure of civil right; but if the measure be changeable, the extent of the thing measured never can be settled.

"To permit a law to be modified at discretion is to leave the community without law.[1] It is to withdraw the direction of

---

1. *Without law.* Dr. Johnson seems to qualify these statements elsewhere, though not, indeed, to contradict them. Of "a general rule that a crime should not be punished after twenty years," he says: "If the son of a murdered man should kill the murderer who got off merely by prescription, I would help him to make his escape, though, were I upon his jury, I would not acquit him. I would bid him to submit to the determination of society, because a man is bound to submit to the inconveniences of it, as he enjoys the good; but the young man, though politically wrong, would not be morally wrong. He would have to say, 'Here I am amongst barbarians. I am therefore in a state of nature; upon the eternal and immutable law of justice, which requires that he who sheds man's blood should have his blood shed, I will stab the murderer of my father.'" Again, on capital punishment for lesser offenses, he says in the *Rambler:* "He who knows not how often rigorous laws produce total impunity, and how many crimes are concealed and forgotten for fear of hurrying the offender to that state in which there is no repentance, has conversed very little with mankind. And whatever epithets of reproach or contempt this compassion may incur from those who confound cruelty with firmness, I know not whether any wise man would wish it less powerful or less extensive."

that public wisdom, by which the deficiences of private understanding are to be supplied. It is to suffer the rash and ignorant
to act at discretion, and then to depend for the legality of that
action on the sentence of the Judge. He that is thus governed
lives not by law, but by opinion; not by a certain rule to which
he can apply his intention before he acts, but by an uncertain
and variable opinion, which he can never know but after he has
committed the act on which that opinion shall be passed. He
lives by a law (if a law it be), which he can never know before
he has offended it.

"The ferocity of our ancestors, as of all other nations, produced
not fraud, but rapine. They had not yet learned to cheat, and
attempted only to rob. As manners grew more polished, with
the knowledge of good, men attain likewise dexterity in evil.
Open rapine becomes less frequent, and violence gives way to
cunning. Those who before invaded pastures and stormed
houses now begin to enrich themselves by unequal contracts
and fraudulent intromissions. It is not against the violence of
ferocity, but the circumventions of deceit, that this law was
framed; and I am afraid the increase of commerce and the
incessant struggle for riches which commerce excites give us no
prospect of an end speedily to be expected of artifice and fraud.
It therefore seems to be no very conclusive reasoning which
connects those two propositions—the nation is become less
ferocious, and therefore the laws against fraud and covin* shall
be relaxed."

I must add that their lordships, in general, though they
were pleased to call this "a well-drawn paper," preferred the
former very inferior petition which I had written; thus con-
firming the truth of an observation made to me by one of their
number, in a merry mood:

"My dear sir, give yourself no trouble in the composition
of the papers you present to us; for, indeed, it is casting pearls
before swine."

On Saturday, April 3 [1773], the day after my arrival in London, I went to his house late in the evening, and sat with Mrs.
Williams till he came home. I found in the London *Chronicle*

Dr. Goldsmith's apology[1] to the public for beating Evans, a
bookseller, on account of a paragraph in a newspaper published
by him, which Goldsmith thought impertinent to him and to a
lady of his acquaintance. The apology was written so much in
Dr. Johnson's manner that both Mrs. Williams and I supposed it
to be his; but when he came home, he soon undeceived us. When
he said to Mrs. Williams, "Well, Dr. Goldsmith's *manifesto* has
got into your paper," I asked him if Dr. Goldsmith had written
it, with an air that made him see I suspected it was his, though
subscribed by Goldsmith. JOHNSON. "Sir, Dr. Goldsmith
would no more have asked me to write such a thing as that for
him than he would have asked me to feed him with a spoon, or to
do anything else that denoted his imbecility. I as much believe
that he wrote it as if I had seen him do it. Sir, had he shown
it to any one friend, he would not have been allowed to publish
it. He has, indeed, done it very well; but it is a foolish thing
well done. I suppose he has been so much elated with the success of his new comedy that he has thought everything that
concerned him must be of importance to the public." BOSWELL.
"I fancy, sir, this is the first time that he has been engaged in

1. *Apology.* A courageous defense, not an apology in the modern
sense of the term. Goldsmith's chivalric friendship for the charming
young girl, Mary Horneck, was naturally affronted by the following
wanton attack in Evans's paper *The London Packet:* "Would man
believe it and will woman bear it to be told that for hours the great
Goldsmith will stand surveying his grotesque orang-outang's figure
in a pier-glass? Was but the lovely H—k as much enamored, you
would not sigh, my gentle swain, in vain." Goldsmith called at Evans's
office to protest at the use of the lady's name, and, unable to contain
himself, struck him with his cane. He was drenched with oil from a
broken lamp in the ensuing scuffle, was ignominiously sent home in a
coach, and to avoid legal proceedings against him for his assault, had
to pay out fifty pounds to a charity, apparently of Evans's choosing.
His letter to the *London Chronicle* on the occurrence contained the
following sentences: "Of late, the press has turned from defending
public interest to making inroads upon private life; from combating
the strong to overwhelming the feeble. How to put a stop to this
licentiousness I am unable to tell; by treating them with silent contempt, we do not pay a sufficient deference to the opinion of the world.
By recurring to legal redress, we too often expose the weakness of the
law."

such an adventure." JOHNSON. "Why, sir, I believe it is the first time he has *beat;* he may have *been beaten* before. This, sir, is a new plume to him."

I mentioned Sir John Dalrymple's *Memoirs of Great Britain and Ireland*, and his discoveries to the prejudice of Lord Russell[1] and Algernon Sydney. JOHNSON. "Why, sir, everybody who had just notions of government thought them rascals before. It is well that all mankind now see them to be rascals." BOSWELL. "But, sir, may not those discoveries be true without their being rascals?" JOHNSON. "Consider, sir; would any of them have been willing to have had it known that they intrigued with France? Depend upon it, sir, he who does what he is afraid should be known has something rotten about him. This Dalrymple seems to be an honest fellow, for he tells equally what makes against both sides. But nothing can be poorer than his mode of writing; it is the mere bouncing of a schoolboy."[2]

At Mr. Thrale's in the evening, Lord Chesterfield being mentioned, Johnson remarked that almost all of that celebrated nobleman's witty sayings were puns. He, however, allowed the merit of good wit to his Lordship's saying of Lord Tyrawley and himself, when both were very old and infirm: "Tyrawley and I have been dead these two years, but we don't choose to have it known."

The conversation having turned on modern imitations of ancient ballads, and someone having praised their simplicity, he treated them with that ridicule which he always displayed when that subject was mentioned.

---

1. *Lord Russell.* Lord Russell, known as "the Patriot," and Sydney, in theory, at least, a republican, were so hot against Charles II's use or abuse of the royal power that they sought aid from France to overturn the English government of the time. They were both beheaded for treason in 1683.

2. *Bouncing of a schoolboy.* In 1773 Johnson and Boswell visited Sir John Dalrymple's Scotch home, where they were inexcusably late to dinner. On the way, Johnson said: "Let me try to describe his situation in his own historical style. I have as good a right to make him think and talk as he has to tell us how people thought and talked a hundred years ago, of which he has no evidence. All history, so far as it is not supported by contemporary evidence, is romance."

On Thursday, April 8, I sat a good part of the evening with him, but he was very silent. He said, "Burnet's[1] *History of His Own Times* is very entertaining. The style, indeed, is mere chit-chat. I do not believe that Burnet intentionally lied; but he was so much prejudiced that he took no pains to find out the truth. He was like a man who resolves to regulate his time by a certain watch, but will not inquire whether the watch is right or not."

Though he was not disposed to talk, he was unwilling that I should leave him; and when I looked at my watch and told him it was twelve o'clock,[2] he cried, "What's that to you and me?" and ordered Frank to tell Mrs. Williams that we were coming to drink tea with her, which we did. It was settled that we should go to church together next day.

On the 9th of April, being Good Friday, I breakfasted with him on tea and cross-buns. We went to church both in the morning and evening. In the interval between the two services we did not dine, but he read in the Greek New Testament, and I turned over several of his books. I told him that Goldsmith had said to me a few days before, "As I take my shoes from my shoemaker, and my coat from the tailor, so I take my religion from the priest." I regretted this loose way of talking. JOHNSON. "Sir, he knows nothing; he has made up his mind about nothing."

April 11, being Easter Sunday, after having attended divine service at St. Paul's, I repaired to Dr. Johnson's. I had gratified my curiosity much in dining with Jean Jaques Rousseau while he lived in the wilds of Neufchatel; I had as great a curiosity to dine with Dr. Samuel Johnson in the dusky recess of a court in Fleet Street. I supposed we should scarcely have

---

1. *Burnet.* Gilbert Burnet (1643-1715), a very busy bishop of the times of Charles II, James II, and William III. He was a partisan Whig. "I am reading Burnet's *Own Times.* Did you ever read that garrulous, pleasant history? . . . Full of scandal, which all true history is. . . . Quite the prattle of age and outlived importance. Truth and sincerity staring out upon you perpetually in *alto relievo.* Himself a party man—he makes you a party man." *Charles Lamb,* 1800.

2. *Twelve o'clock.* "Whoever thinks of going to bed before twelve o'clock," said Johnson, "is a scoundrel." *Sir John Hawkins.*

knives and forks, and only some strange, uncouth, ill-dressed dish; but I found everything in very good order. We had no other company but Mrs. Williams and a young woman whom I did not know. As a dinner here was considered as a singular phenomenon, and as I was frequently interrogated on the subject, my readers may perhaps be desirous to know our bill of fare. Foote, I remember, in allusion to Francis, the *negro*, was willing to suppose that our repast was *black broth*. But the fact was that we had a very good soup, a boiled leg of lamb and spinach, a veal pie, and a rice pudding.

On Tuesday, April 13, he and Dr. Goldsmith and I dined at General Oglethorpe's. Goldsmith expatiated on the common topic that the race of our people was degenerated, and that this was owing to luxury. JOHNSON. "Sir, in the first place, I doubt the fact. I believe there are as many tall men in England now as ever there were. But, secondly, supposing the stature of our people to be diminished, that is not owing to luxury; for, sir, consider to how very small a proportion of our people luxury can reach. Our soldiery, surely, are not luxurious, who live on sixpence a day; and the same remark will apply to almost all the other classes. Luxury, so far as it reaches the poor, will do good to the race of people; it will strengthen and multiply them. I admit that the great increase of commerce and manufactures hurts the military spirit of a people, because it produces a competition for something else than martial honors—a competition for riches. It also hurts the bodies of the people, for you will observe there is no man who works at any particular trade but you may know him from his appearance to do so. One part or the other of his body being more used than the rest, he is in some degree deformed; but, sir, that is not luxury. A tailor sits cross-legged; but that is not luxury." GOLDSMITH. "Come, you're just going to the same place by another road." JOHNSON. "Nay, sir, I say that is not *luxury*. Let us take a walk from Charing Cross to Whitechapel, through, I suppose, the greatest series of shops in the world; what is there in any of these shops if you except gin-shops, that can do any human being any harm?" GOLDSMITH. "Well, sir, I'll accept your challenge. The very next shop to Northumberland House is a pickle-shop." JOHNSON. "Well, sir, do we not know that a maid can in one afternoon make pickles sufficient to serve a whole family for a year? Nay, that five pickle-shops can serve all the kingdom? Besides, sir, there is no harm done to anybody by the making of pickles, or the eating of pickles."

Dr. Johnson in his way home stopped at my lodgings in Piccadilly, and sat with me, drinking tea a second time, till a late hour. I told him that Mrs. Macaulay said she wondered how he could reconcile his political principles with his moral; his notions of inequality and subordination with wishing well to the happiness of all mankind, who might live so agreeably had they all their portions of land and none to domineer over another. JOHNSON. "Why, sir, I reconcile my principles very well, because mankind are happier in a state of inequality and subordination. Were they to be in this pretty state of equality, they would soon degenerate into brutes—they would become Monboddo's nation[1]—their tails would grow. Sir, all would be losers, were all to work for all—they would have no intellectual improvement. All intellectual improvement arises from leisure; all leisure arises from one working for another."

On Thursday, April 15, I dined with him and Dr. Goldsmith at General Paoli's. We found here Signor Martinelli,[2] of Flor-

---

1. *Monboddo's nation.* "He has lately written a strange book about the origin of language, in which he traces monkeys up to men and says that in some countries the human species have tails like other beasts." *Mrs. Piozzi.* "The orang-outang he describes as being 'of a character mild and gentle, affectionate, too, and capable of friendship, with the sense also of what is decent and becoming.'" *Birkbeck Hill.*
"Young Col told us he could run down a greyhound; 'for,' said he, 'the dog runs himself out of breath by going too quick and then I get up with him.' Dr. Johnson said, 'He is a noble animal. He is as complete an islander as the mind can figure. He is a farmer, a sailor, a hunter, a fisher; he will run you down a dog; if any man has a *tail*, it is Col. He is hospitable; and he has an intrepidity of talk whether he understands the subject or not. I regret that he is not more intellectual.'" *Boswell: Journal of a Tour to the Hebrides.*
2. *Martinelli.* A teacher of Italian in London, who kept himself very busy getting acquainted with Englishmen of eminence. His history, it is said, was all drawn from one source, the work of the French historian Rapin. It would have been hard for him to continue it beyond the place at which Rapin stopped.

ence, author of a *History of England* in Italian, printed at London.

I spoke of Allan Ramsay's "Gentle Shepherd,"[1] in the Scottish dialect, as the best pastoral that had ever been written; not only abounding with beautiful rural imagery and just and pleasing sentiments, but being a real picture of manners; and I offered to teach Dr. Johnson to understand it. "No, sir," said he, "I won't learn it. You shall retain your superiority by my not knowing it."

An animated debate took place whether Martinelli should continue his *History of England* to the present day. GOLDSMITH. "To be sure he should." JOHNSON. "No, sir; he would give great offense. He would have to tell of almost all the living great what they do not wish told." GOLDSMITH. "It may, perhaps, be necessary for a native to be more cautious; but a foreigner who comes among us without prejudice may be considered as holding the place of a judge, and may speak his mind freely." JOHNSON. "Sir, a foreigner, when he sends a work from the press, ought to be on his guard against catching the error and mistaken enthusiasm of the people among whom he happens to be." GOLDSMITH. "Sir, he wants only to sell his history, and to tell truth; one an honest, the other a laudable, motive." JOHNSON. "Sir, they are both laudable motives. It is laudable in a man to wish to live by his labors; but he should write so as he may *live* by them, not so as he may be knocked on the head. I would advise him to be at Calais before he publishes his history of the present age. A foreigner who attaches him-

---

1. *Gentle Shepherd.* " 'The Gentle Shepherd' appeared in 1725. It abounds in character, unaffected sentiment, and vivid description." *Everyman's Dictionary of English Literature.*

"A pastoral of an hundred lines may be endured; but who will hear of sheep and goats and myrtle bowers and purling rivulets, through five acts? Such scenes please barbarians in the dawn of literature, and children in the dawn of life; but will be for the most part thrown away as men grow wise and nations grow learned." *Johnson: Life of Gay.*

"It constantly moves my indignation to be applied to, to speak well of a thing which I think contemptible." *Dr. Johnson, quoted by Mme. D'Arblay.*

self to a political party in this country is in the worst state that can be imagined; he is looked upon as a mere intermeddler. A native may do it from interest." BOSWELL. "Or principle." GOLDSMITH. "There are people who tell a hundred political lies every day, and are not hurt by it. Surely, then, one may tell truth with safety." JOHNSON. "Why, sir, in the first place, he who tells a hundred lies has disarmed the force of his lies. But, besides, a man had rather have a hundred lies told of him than one truth which he does not wish should be told." GOLDSMITH. "For my part, I'd tell truth, and shame the devil." JOHNSON. "Yes, sir; but the devil will be angry. I wish to shame the devil as much as you do, but I should choose to be out of the reach of his claws." GOLDSMITH. "His claws can do you no harm when you have the shield of truth."

We talked of the King's coming to see Goldsmith's new play. "I wish he would," said Goldsmith; adding, however, with an affected indifference, "Not that it would do me the least good." JOHNSON. "Well then, sir, let us say it would do *him* good (laughing). No, sir, this affectation will not pass; it is mighty idle. In such a state as ours, who would not wish to please the Chief Magistrate?"

On Monday, April 19, he called on me with Mrs. Williams, in Mr. Strahan's[1] coach, and carried me out to dine with Mr. Elphinston[2] at his Academy at Kensington. A printer having acquired a fortune sufficient to keep his coach was a good topic for the credit of literature. Mrs. Williams said

1. *Strahan's*. "I remember your observing once to me that no two journeymen printers within your knowledge had met with such success in the world as ourselves. You soon afterwards became a member of parliament." *Benjamin Franklin to Mr. Strahan, in 1784.*

"I mentioned two friends who were particularly fond of looking at themselves in a glass. 'They do not surprise me at all by so doing,' said Johnson; 'they see, reflected in that glass, men who have risen from almost the lowest stations in life; one to enormous riches, the other to everything this world can give—rank, fame, and fortune.'" *Mrs. Piozzi: Anecdotes of Johnson.*

2. *Elphinston*. An awkward, wrong-headed scholar, brother-in-law of Mr. Strahan. His school was "in a noble mansion opposite to the King's gardens." Elsewhere Boswell spells the name Elphinstone.

that another printer, Mr. Hamilton, had not waited so long as Mr. Strahan, but had kept his coach several years sooner. JOHNSON. "He was in the right. Life is short. The sooner that a man begins to enjoy his wealth, the better."

Mr. Elphinston talked of a new book that was much admired, and asked Dr. Johnson if he had read it. JOHNSON. "I have looked into it." "What," said Elphinston, "have you not read it through?" Johnson, offended at being thus pressed, and so obliged to own his cursory mode of reading, answered tartly, "No, sir; do *you* read books *through?*"

He this day again defended dueling,[1] and put his argument upon what I have ever thought the most solid basis: that if public war be allowed to be consistent with morality, private war must be equally so. Indeed we may observe what strained arguments are used to reconcile war with the Christian religion. But, in my opinion, it is exceedingly clear that dueling, having better reasons for its barbarous violence, is more justifiable than war in which thousands go forth without any cause of personal quarrel and massacre each other.

On Tuesday, April 27, Mr. Beauclerk and I called on him in the morning. As we walked up Johnson's Court, I said, "I have a veneration for this court"; and was glad to find that Beauclerk had the same reverential enthusiasm. We found him alone.

He said, "Goldsmith should not be forever attempting to shine in conversation; he has not temper for it, he is so much mortified when he fails. Sir, a game of jokes is composed partly of skill, partly of chance; a man may be beat at times by one who has not the tenth part of his wit. Now Goldsmith's putting himself against another is like a man laying a hundred to one who cannot spare the hundred. When he contends, if he gets the better, it is a very little addition to a man of his literary reputation; if he does not get the better, he is miserably vexed."

---

1. *Dueling.* According to Horace Walpole, dueling had lately increased greatly and much was being done in print and on the stage to curb it, but it was bound to last as long as social distinctions enabled gentlemen to restrict the practice to their own class.

Johnson's own superlative powers of wit set him above any risk of such uneasiness. Garrick had remarked to me of him a few days before, "Rabelais and all other wits are nothing compared with him. You may be diverted by them; but Johnson gives you a forcible hug, and shakes laughter out of you, whether you will or no."

Goldsmith, however, was often very fortunate in his witty contests, even when he entered the lists with Johnson himself. Sir Joshua Reynolds was in company with them one day when Goldsmith said that he thought he could write a good fable, mentioned the simplicity which that kind of composition requires, and observed that in most fables the animals introduced seldom talk in character. "For instance," said he, "the fable of the little fishes who saw birds fly over their heads, and, envying them, petitioned Jupiter to be changed into birds. The skill," continued he, "consists in making them talk like little fishes." While he indulged himself in this fanciful reverie, he observed Johnson shaking his sides, and laughing. Upon which he smartly proceeded, "Why, Dr. Johnson, this is not so easy as you seem to think; for if you were to make little fishes talk, they would talk like *whales*."

On Thursday, April 29, I dined with him at General Oglethorpe's, where were Sir Joshua Reynolds, Mr. Langton, Dr. Goldsmith, and Mr. Thrale.

The custom of eating dogs at Otaheite being mentioned, Goldsmith observed that this was also a custom in China; that a dog-butcher is as common there as any other butcher; and that when he walks abroad all the dogs fall on him. JOHNSON. "That is not owing to his killing dogs, sir. I remember a butcher at Lichfield, whom a dog that was in the house where I lived always attacked. It is the smell of carnage which provokes this, let the animals he has killed be what they may." GOLDSMITH. "Yes, there is a general abhorrence in animals at the signs of massacre. If you put a tub full of blood into a stable, the horses are like to go mad." JOHNSON. "I doubt that." GOLDSMITH. "Nay, sir, it is a fact well authenticated." THRALE. "You had better prove it before you put it into your book on natural history. You may do it in my stable if you will." JOHNSON. "Nay, sir, I would not have him prove it. If he is content to take his information from others, he may get through his book with little trouble, and without much endangering his reputation. But if he makes experiments for so comprehensive a book as his, there would be no end to them; his erroneous assertions would then fall upon himself; and he might be blamed for not having made experiments as to every particular."

Dr. Goldsmith's new play, *She Stoops to Conquer*, being mentioned: JOHNSON. "I know of no comedy for many years that has so much exhilarated an audience, that has answered so much the great end of comedy—making an audience merry."

On Friday, April 30, I dined with him at Mr. Beauclerk's, where were Lord Charlemont,[1] Sir Joshua Reynolds, and some more members of the Literary Club, whom he had obligingly invited to meet me, as I was this evening to be balloted for[2] as candidate for admission into that distinguished society. Johnson had done me the honor to propose me, and Beauclerk was very zealous for me.

Goldsmith being mentioned: JOHNSON. "It is amazing how little Goldsmith knows. He seldom comes where he is not more ignorant than anyone else." SIR JOSHUA REYNOLDS. "Yet there is no man whose company is more liked." JOHNSON.

---

1. *Lord Charlemont.* A noted Whig, of an especially liberal cast of mind.
2. *To be balloted for.* "We drove over a wild moor. It rained and the scene was somewhat dreary. As we traveled on, [Dr. Johnson] told me, 'Sir, you got into our club by doing what a man can do. [I suppose Dr. Johnson meant that I assiduously and earnestly recommended myself to some of the members, as in a canvass for an election into parliament.] Several of the members wished to keep you out. Burke told me he doubted if you were fit for it; but, now you are in, none of them are sorry. Burke says that you have so much good humor naturally, it is scarce a virtue.' BOSWELL. 'They were afraid of you, sir, as it was you who proposed me.' JOHNSON. 'Sir, they knew that if they refused you, they'd probably never have got in another. I'd have kept them all out.'" *Boswell: Journal of a Tour to the Hebrides.*

"To be sure, sir. When people find a man of the most distinguished abilities as a writer their inferior while he is with them, it must be highly gratifying to them. What Goldsmith comically says of himself is very true—he always gets the better when he argues alone; meaning that he is master of a subject in his study, and can write well upon it; but when he comes into company, grows confused, and unable to talk. Take him as a poet, his *Traveller* is a very fine performance; aye, and so is his *Deserted Village*, were it not sometimes too much the echo of his *Traveller*. Whether, indeed, we take him as a poet, as a comic writer, or as an historian, he stands in the first class." BOSWELL. "An historian! My dear sir, you surely will not rank his compilation of the Roman history with the works of other historians of this age?" JOHNSON. "Why, who are before him?" BOSWELL. "Will you not admit the superiority of Robertson, in whose history we find such penetration, such painting?" JOHNSON. "Sir, you must consider how that penetration and that painting are employed. It is not history; it is imagination. He who describes what he never saw draws from fancy. Robertson paints minds as Sir Joshua paints faces in a history-piece; he imagines an heroic countenance. You must look upon Robertson's work as romance, and try it by that standard. History it is not. Besides, sir, it is the great excellence of a writer to put into his book as much as his book will hold. Goldsmith has done this in his *History*. Now Robertson might have put twice as much into his book. Robertson is like a man who has packed gold in wool; the wool takes up more room than the gold. No, sir; I always thought Robertson would be crushed by his own weight—would be buried under his own ornaments. Goldsmith tells you shortly all you want to know; Robertson detains you a great deal too long. No man will read Robertson's cumbrous detail a second time; but Goldsmith's plain narrative will please again and again. I would say to Robertson what an old tutor of a college said to one of his pupils: 'Read over your compositions, and wherever you meet with a passage which you think is particularly fine, strike it out.'

"I remember once being with Goldsmith in Westminster Abbey. While we surveyed the Poet's Corner, I said to him,

Forsitan et nostrum nomen miscebitur istis.

When we got to Temple Bar,[1] he stopped me, pointed to the heads upon it, and slyly whispered me,

Forsitan et nostrum nomen miscebitur ISTIS."

The gentlemen went away to their club, and I was left at Beauclerk's till the fate of my election should be announced to me. I sat in a state of anxiety which even the charming conversation of Lady Di Beauclerk could not entirely dissipate. In a short time I received the agreeable intelligence that I was chosen. I hastened to the place of meeting, and was introduced to such a society as can seldom be found: Mr. Edmund Burke, whom I then saw for the first time, and whose splendid talents had long made me ardently wish for his acquaintance; Dr. Nugent, Mr. Garrick, Dr. Goldsmith, Mr. (afterwards Sir William) Jones, and the company with whom I had dined. Upon my entrance Johnson placed himself behind a chair, on which he leaned as on a desk or pulpit, and with humorous formality gave me a *Charge*, pointing out the conduct expected from me as a good member of this club.

Goldsmith produced some very absurd verses which had been publicly recited to an audience for money. JOHNSON. "I can match this nonsense. There was a poem called 'Eugenio,' which came out some years ago, and concludes thus:

> And now, ye trifling, self-assuming elves,
> Brimful of pride, of nothing, of yourselves,
> Survey Eugenio, view him o'er and o'er,
> Then sink into yourselves, and be no more."

On Saturday, May 1, we dined by ourselves at our old rendezvous, the Mitre tavern. He was placid but not much

---

1. *Temple Bar.* A famous gateway in the heart of London, dividing busy Fleet Street from the street called the Strand. The heads were those of Scotch rebels executed in 1745.

disposed to talk. He observed, "I will do you, Boswell, the justice to say that you are the most *unscottified* of your countrymen. You are almost the only instance of a Scotchman that I have known who did not at every other sentence bring in some other Scotchman."

On Friday, May 7, I breakfasted with him at Mr. Thrale's in the Borough. I dined with him this day at the house of my friends, Messieurs Edward and Charles Dilly, booksellers in the Poultry.[1]

BOSWELL. "I am well assured that the people of Otaheite who have the bread tree, the fruit of which serves them for bread, laughed heartily when they were informed of the tedious process necessary with us to have bread—plowing, sowing, harrowing, reaping, threshing, grinding, baking." JOHNSON. "Why, sir, all ignorant savages will laugh when they are told of the advantages of civilized life. Were you to tell men who live without houses, how we pile brick upon brick, and rafter upon rafter, and that after a house is raised to a certain height, a man tumbles off a scaffold, and breaks his neck, he would laugh heartily at our folly in building; but it does not follow that men are better without houses. No, sir (holding up a slice of a good loaf), this is better than the bread tree."

He repeated an argument, which is to be found in his *Rambler*, against the notion that the brute creation is endowed with the faculty of reason: "Birds build by instinct; they never improve; they build their first nest as well as any one they ever build." GOLDSMITH. "Yet we see if you take away a bird's nest with the eggs in it, she will make a slighter nest and lay again." JOHNSON. "Sir, that is because at first she has full time and makes her nest deliberately. In the case you mention she is pressed to lay, and must therefore make her nest quickly, and consequently it will be slight."

I introduced the subject of toleration. JOHNSON. "Every society has a right to preserve public peace and order, and therefore has a good right to prohibit the propagation of

---

1. *The Poultry.* A street in a crowded part of London.

opinions which have a dangerous tendency." MAYO.[1] "I am of opinion, sir, that every man is entitled to liberty of conscience[2] in religion; and that the magistrate cannot restrain that right." JOHNSON. "Sir, I agree with you. Every man has a right to liberty of conscience, and with that the magistrate cannot interfere. People confound liberty of thinking with liberty of talking; nay, with liberty of preaching. Every man has a physical right to think as he pleases; for it cannot be discovered how he thinks. He has not a moral right, for he ought to inform himself, and think justly. But, sir, no member of a society has a right to *teach* any doctrine contrary to what the society holds to be true. The magistrate may be wrong in what he thinks; but while he thinks himself right, he may and ought to enforce what he thinks." MAYO. "Then, sir, we are to remain always in error, and truth never can prevail; and the magistrate was right in persecuting the first Christians." JOHNSON. "I am afraid there is no other way of ascertaining the truth but by persecution on the one hand and enduring it on the other." GOLDSMITH. "But how is a man to act, sir? Though firmly convinced of the truth of his doctrine, may he not think it wrong to expose himself to persecution? Has he a right to do so? Is it not, as it were, committing voluntary suicide?" JOHNSON. "Sir, as to voluntary suicide, as you call it, there are twenty thousand men in an army who will go without scruple to be shot at, and mount a breach for five pence a day." GOLDSMITH. "But have they a moral right

---

1. *Mayo.* Dr. Mayo, pastor of a dissenting congregation. "Dr. Mayo's calm temper and steady perseverance rendered him an admirable subject for the exercise of Dr. Johnson's powerful abilities . . . The scintillations of Johnson's genius flashed every time he was struck, without his receiving any injury. Hence he obtained the epithet of THE LITERARY ANVIL." *Boswell.*

2. *Conscience.* "Conscience is nothing more than a conviction felt by ourselves of something to be done, or something to be avoided; and in questions of simple, unperplexed morality, conscience is very often a guide that may be trusted. But before conscience can determine, the state of the question is supposed to be completely known. In questions of law, or of fact, conscience is very often confounded with opinion." *Dr. Johnson.*

to do this?" JOHNSON. "Nay, sir, if you will not take the universal opinion of mankind,[1] I have nothing to say. If mankind cannot defend their own way of thinking, I cannot defend it. Sir, if a man is in doubt whether it would be better for him to expose himself to martyrdom or not, he should not do it. He must be convinced that he has a delegation from heaven." GOLDSMITH. "I would consider whether there is the greater chance of good or evil upon the whole. If I see a man who has fallen into a well, I would wish to help him out; but if there is a greater probability that he shall pull me in than that I shall pull him out, I would not attempt it. So were I to go to Turkey, I might wish to convert the Grand Signor to the Christian faith; but when I considered that I should probably be put to death without effectuating my purpose in any degree, I should keep myself quiet." JOHNSON. "Sir, you must consider that we have perfect and imperfect obligations. Perfect obligations, which are generally not to do something, are clear and positive: as, 'Thou shalt not kill.' But charity, for instance, is not definable by limits. It is a duty to give to the poor; but no man can say how much another should give to the poor, or when a man has given too little to save his soul. In the same manner it is a duty to instruct the ignorant, and of consequence to convert infidels to Christianity; but no man in the common course of things is obliged to carry this to such a degree as to incur the danger of martyrdom, as no man is obliged to strip himself to the shirt in order to give charity. I have said that a man must be persuaded that he has a particular delegation from heaven." GOLDSMITH. "How is this to be known? Our first reformers, who were burned for not believing bread and wine to be Christ"— JOHNSON (inter-

---

1. *Opinion of mankind.* "I have found reason to pay great regard to the voice of the people, in cases where knowledge has been forced upon them by experience, without long deductions or deep researches." *Johnson: The Rambler.*

"Among the lower classes of mankind, there will be found very little desire of any other knowledge than what may contribute immediately to the relief of some pressing uneasiness, or the attainment of some near advantage." *The same.*

rupting him). "Sir, they were not burned for not believing bread and wine to be Christ, but for insulting those who did believe it. And, sir, when the first reformers began, they did not intend to be martyred; as many of them ran away as could." BOSWELL. "But, sir, there was your countryman Elwal,[1] who you told me challenged King George with his black-guards and his red-guards." JOHNSON. "My country-man, Elwal, sir, should have been put in the stocks; a proper pulpit for him; and he'd have had a numerous audience. A man who preaches in the stocks will always have hearers enough." MAYO. "But, sir, is it not very hard that I should not be allowed to teach my children what I really believe to be the truth?" JOHNSON. "Why, sir, you might contrive to teach your children *extra scandalum*,[2] but, sir, the magistrate, if he knows it, has a right to restrain you. Suppose you teach your children to be thieves?" MAYO. "This is making a joke of the subject." JOHNSON. "Nay, sir, take it thus: that you teach them the community of goods; for which there are as many plausible arguments as for most erroneous doctrines. You teach them that all things at first were in common, and that no man had a right to anything but as he laid his hands upon it; and that this still is, or ought to be, the rule amongst mankind. Here, sir, you sap a great principle in society— property. And don't you think the magistrate would have a right to prevent you? Or, suppose you should teach your children the notion of the Adamites, and they should run naked into the streets, would not the magistrate have a right to flog 'em into their doublets?" MAYO. "I think the magistrate has no right to interfere till there is some overt act." BOSWELL. "So, sir, though he sees an enemy to the state charging a blunder-buss, he is not to interfere till it is fired off!" MAYO. "He must be sure of its direction against the state." JOHNSON.

---

1. *Elwal.* According to Johnson, Elwal was an iron monger at Wolverhampton, and he had a mind to make himself famous by being the founder of a new sect. He was of the same county as Johnson; hence was called his *countryman.*

2. *Extra scandalum.* Without public scandal.

"The magistrate is to judge of that. He has no right to restrain your thinking, because the evil centers in yourself. If a man were sitting at this table and chopping off his fingers, the magistrate, as guardian of the community, has no authority to restrain him, however he might do it from kindness as a parent.—Though, indeed, upon more consideration, I think he may; as it is probable that he who is chopping off his own fingers may soon proceed to chop off those of other people. If I think it right to steal Mr. Dilly's plate, I am a bad man; but he can say nothing to me. If I make an open declaration that I think so, he will keep me out of his house. If I put forth my hand, I shall be sent to Newgate. This is the gradation of thinking, preaching, and acting: if a man thinks erroneously, he may keep his thoughts to himself, and nobody will trouble him; if he preaches erroneous doctrine, society may expel him; if he acts in consequence of it, the law takes place, and he is hanged." MAYO. "But, sir, ought not Christians to have liberty of conscience?" JOHNSON. "I have already told you so, sir. You are coming back to where you were." BOSWELL. "Dr. Mayo is always taking a return postchaise, and going the stage over again. He has it at half-price." JOHNSON. "Dr. Mayo, like other champions for unlimited toleration, has got a set of words. Sir, it is no matter, politically, whether the magistrate be right or wrong. Suppose a club were to be formed to drink confusion to King George the Third, and a happy restoration to Charles the Third; this would be very bad with respect to the State, but every member of that club must either conform to its rules or be turned out of it."

During this argument, Goldsmith sat in restless agitation, from a wish to get in and *shine*. Finding himself excluded, he had taken his hat to go away, but remained for some time with it in his hand, like a gamester, who, at the close of a long night, lingers for a little while to see if he can have a favorable opening to finish with success. Once when he was beginning to speak, he found himself overpowered by the loud voice of Johnson, who was at the opposite end of the table and did not perceive Goldsmith's attempt. Thus disappointed of his wish to obtain

the attention of the company, Goldsmith in a passion threw
down his hat, looking angrily at Johnson, and exclaimed in a
bitter tone, *"Take it."* When Toplady[1] was going to speak,
Johnson uttered some sound which led Goldsmith to think
that he was beginning again and taking the words from Toplady.
Upon which, he seized this opportunity of venting his own envy
and spleen, under the pretext of supporting another person:
"Sir," said he to Johnson, "the gentleman has heard you
patiently for an hour; pray allow us now to hear him."
Johnson (sternly). "Sir, I was not interrupting the gentleman.
I was only giving him a signal of my attention. Sir, you are
impertinent." Goldsmith made no reply, but continued in the
company for some time.

A gentleman present ventured to ask Dr. Johnson if there
was not a material difference as to toleration of opinions which
lead to action, and opinions merely speculative; for instance,
would it be wrong in the magistrate to tolerate those who
preach against the doctrine of the Trinity? Johnson was
highly offended, and said, "I wonder, sir, how a gentleman of
your piety can introduce this subject in a mixed company." He
told me afterwards that the impropriety was, that perhaps some
of the company might have talked on the subject in such terms
as might have shocked him; or he might have been forced to
appear in their eyes a narrow-minded man. The gentleman,
with submissive deference, said he had only hinted at the
question from a desire to hear Dr. Johnson's opinion upon it.
Johnson. "Why, then, sir, I think that permitting men to
preach any opinion contrary to the doctrine of the established
church tends, in a certain degree, to lessen the authority of
the church, and, consequently, to lessen the influence of religion." "It may be considered," said the gentleman, "whether
it would not be politic to tolerate in such a case." Johnson.
"Sir, we have been talking of *right;* this is another question.
I think it is *not* politic to tolerate in such a case."

---

1. *Toplady.* Rev. Augustus Toplady, a controversialist who was
known to have a sharp tongue and was well able to take care of himself
in a theological argument. Now best known as the author of "Rock
of Ages."

BOSWELL. "Pray, Mr. Dilly, how does Dr. Leland's[1] *History of Ireland* sell?" JOHNSON (bursting forth with a generous indignation): "The Irish are in a most unnatural state, for we see there the minority prevailing over the majority. There is no instance even in the ten persecutions[2] of such severity as that which the protestants of Ireland have exercised against the Catholics. Did we tell them we had conquered them, it would be above board; to punish them by confiscation and other penalties, as rebels, was monstrous injustice. King William[3] was not their lawful sovereign; he had not been acknowledged by the Parliament of Ireland when they appeared in arms against him."

He and Mr. Langton and I went together to the Club, where we found Mr. Burke, Mr. Garrick, and some other members, and amongst them our friend Goldsmith, who sat silently brooding over Johnson's reprimand to him after dinner. Johnson perceived this, and said aside to some of us, "I'll make Goldsmith forgive me"; and then called to him in a loud voice, "Dr. Goldsmith—something passed today where you and I dined; I ask your pardon." Goldsmith answered placidly, "It must be much from you, sir, that I take ill." And so at once the difference was over, and they were on as easy terms as ever, and Goldsmith rattled away as usual.

Goldsmith's incessant desire of being conspicuous in company was the occasion of his sometimes appearing to such disadvantage

---

1. *Leland.* Dr. Thomas Leland. Here Boswell adroitly introduces the name of a believer in religious toleration to whom Johnson was warmly predisposed by ties of gratitude. He had once recommended Dr. Johnson for an honorary degree from the University of Dublin, when Dr. Johnson was in great need of recognition.

2. *Ten persecutions.* According to fifth century tradition, the number of persecutions from which the Church had suffered up to that time. "The ingenious parallels of the *ten* plagues of Egypt, and of the *ten* horns of the Apocalypse first suggested this calculation to their minds." *Gibbon: Decline and Fall of the Roman Empire.*

3. *King William.* William III conquered Ireland in 1690-91. At first, he promised a certain degree of religious freedom to the Irish Catholics, but the Protestant minority insisted on the breaking of the promise. To this, English popular feeling made no objection.

as one should hardly have supposed possible in a man of his genius. One evening, in a circle of wits, he found fault with me for talking of Johnson as entitled to the honor of unquestionable superiority. "Sir," said he, "you are for making a monarchy of what should be a republic." He was still more mortified when, talking in a company with fluent vivacity, a German who sat next to him and perceived Johnson rolling himself as if about to speak, suddenly stopped him, saying, "Stay, stay— Toctor Shonson is going to say something." This was, no doubt, very provoking, especially to one so irritable as Goldsmith, who frequently mentioned it with strong expressions of indignation.

It may also be observed that Goldsmith was sometimes content to be treated with an easy familiarity, but, upon occasions, would be consequential and important. An instance of this occurred in a small particular. Johnson had a way of contracting the names of his friends; as Beauclerk, Beau; Boswell, Bozzy; Langton, Lanky; Murphy, Mur; Sheridan, Sherry. I remember one day, when Tom Davies was telling that Dr. Johnson said, "We are all in labor for a name to Goldy's play," Goldsmith seemed displeased that such a liberty should be taken with his name, and said, "I have often desired him not to call me 'Goldy.'" Tom was remarkably attentive to the most minute circumstance about Johnson. I recollect his telling me once, on my arrival in London, "Sir, our great friend has made an improvement on his appellation of old Mr. Sheridan. He calls him now "Sherry derry.'"

On Monday, May 9, as I was to set out on my return to Scotland next morning, I was desirous to see as much of Dr. Johnson as I could. But I first called on Goldsmith to take leave of him. He seemed very angry that Johnson was going to be a traveler; said he would be a dead weight for me to carry, and that I should never be able to lug him along through the Highlands and Hebrides. Nor would he patiently allow me to enlarge upon Johnson's wonderful abilities, but exclaimed, "Is he like Burke, who winds into a subject like a serpent?" "But," said I, "Johnson is the Hercules who strangled serpents in his cradle."

I dined with Dr. Johnson at General Paoli's. He was obliged, by indisposition, to leave the company early; he appointed me, however, to meet him in the evening at Mr. (now Sir Robert) Chambers's in the Temple, where he accordingly came, though he continued to be very ill. Chambers, as is common on such occasions, prescribed various remedies to him. JOHNSON (fretted by pain). "Prythee don't tease me.[1] Stay till I am well, and then you shall tell me how to cure myself." He grew better, and talked with a noble enthusiasm of keeping up the representation of respectable families. His zeal on this subject was a circumstance in his character exceedingly remarkable, when it is considered that he himself had no pretensions to blood. I heard him once say, "I have great merit in being zealous for subordination and the honors of birth, for I can hardly tell who was my grandfather." He maintained the dignity and propriety of male succession, in opposition to the opinion of one of our friends,[2] who had that day employed Mr. Chambers to draw his will, devising his estate to his three sisters, in preference to a remote heir male. Johnson called them "three *dowdies*," and said, with as high a spirit as the boldest Baron in the most perfect days of the feudal system, "An ancient estate should always go to males. It is mighty foolish to let a stranger have it because he marries your daughter, and takes your name. As for an estate newly acquired by trade, you may give it, if you will, to the dog *Towser*, and let him keep his *own* name."

I have known him at times exceedingly diverted at what seemed to others a very small sport. He now laughed immoderately, without any reason that we could perceive, at our friend's making his will; called him the *testator*, and added, "I dare say he thinks he has done a mighty thing. He won't stay till he gets home to his seat in the country, to produce this wonderful deed; he'll call up the landlord of the first inn

---

1. *Prythee, don't tease me.* In 1768, Johnson had written when ill in Chambers's residence: "He has been neither negligent nor troublesome; nor do I love him less for having been ill in his house. This is no small degree of praise."

2. *One of our friends.* Langton.

on the road; and, after a suitable preface upon mortality and the uncertainty of life, will tell him that he should not delay making his will; and here, sir, will he say, is my will, which I have just made, with the assistance of one of the ablest lawyers in the kingdom; and he will read it to him, (laughing all the time). He believes he has made this will; but he did not make it; you, Chambers, made it for him. I trust you have had more conscience than to make him say, 'being of sound understanding'; ha, ha, ha! I hope he has left me a legacy. I'd have his will turned into verse, like a ballad."

Mr. Chambers did not by any means relish this jocularity upon a matter of which *pars magna fuit*, and seemed impatient till he got rid of us. Johnson could not stop his merriment, but continued it all the way till he got without the Temple Gate. He then burst into such a fit of laughter that he appeared to be almost in a convulsion; and, in order to support himself, laid hold of one of the posts at the side of the foot pavement, and sent forth peals so loud that in the silence of the night his voice seemed to resound from Temple Bar to Fleet Ditch.[1]

In a letter from Edinburgh, dated the 29th of May, I pressed him to persevere in his resolution to make this year the projected visit to the Hebrides.

"*To James Boswell, Esq.*

"DEAR SIR: When your letter came to me, I was so darkened by an inflammation in my eye that I could not for some time read it. I can now write without trouble, and can read large prints. My eye is gradually growing stronger, and I hope will be able to take some delight in the survey of a Caledonian loch.

"Chambers is going a Judge, with six thousand a year, to Bengal. He and I shall come down together as far as Newcastle, and thence I shall easily get to Edinburgh. Let me know the exact time when your Courts intermit. I must conform a little to Chambers's occasions, and he must conform a little to

---

1. *Temple Bar to Fleet Ditch.* The most crowded part of London.

mine. The time which you shall fix must be the common point to which we will come as near as we can. Except this eye, I am very well.

"Beattie is so caressed, and invited, and treated, and liked, and flattered, by the great,[1] that I can see nothing of him. I am in great hope that he will be well provided for, and then we will live upon him at the Marischal College, without pity or modesty.

"——[2] left the town without taking leave of me, and is gone in deep dudgeon to ——. Is not this very childish? Where is now my legacy?

"I hope your dear lady and her dear baby are both well. I shall see them too when I come; and I have that opinion of your choice as to suspect that when I have seen Mrs. Boswell, I shall be less willing to go away.

"I am, dear sir,
"Your affectionate, humble servant,
"SAM. JOHNSON.

"Johnson's Court, Fleet Street,
"July 5, 1773.

"Write to me as soon as you can. Chambers is now at Oxford."

---

1. *Flattered by the great.* For his shallow *Essay on Truth*, then recently published, which was seized upon by timid believers as a convincing reply to Voltaire, Hume, and other skeptics. It contains no stronger argument than the following: "Happiness is desirable for its own sake; truth is desirable only as a means of producing happiness; for who would not prefer an agreeable delusion to a melancholy truth?" Goldsmith, though he often falls back on such sentimental lines of defense, despised Beattie and asserted that his books would be entirely forgotten in ten years. Johnson, who usually protested against sentimentality, asserted that Beattie had written "like a man conscious of the truth, and feeling his own strength." Beattie was Professor of Moral Philosophy at Marischal College, in the University of Aberdeen, and was now promised a pension of £200 a year in addition to his professional income. On hearing of this, Dr. Johnson clapped his hands, and cried "O brave we."

2. ——. Langton, gone to his native village Langton, and no doubt annoyed at Johnson's boisterous ridicule of his will.

I again wrote to him informing him that the Court of Session rose* on the twelfth of August, hoping to see him before that time, and expressing, perhaps in too extravagant terms, my admiration of him and my expectation of pleasure from our intended tour.

"To James Boswell, Esq.

"DEAR SIR: I shall set out from London on Friday, the sixth of this month, and purpose not to loiter much by the way. Which day I shall be at Edinburgh, I cannot exactly tell. I suppose I must drive to an inn, and send a porter to find you.

"I am afraid Beattie will not be at his College soon enough for us, and I shall be sorry to miss him; but there is no staying for the concurrence of all conveniences. We will do as well as we can. I am, sir,

"Your most humble servant,
"August 3, 1773."   "SAM. JOHNSON.

To the Same.

"DEAR SIR: Not being at Mr. Thrale's when your letter came, I had written the enclosed paper and sealed it; bringing it hither for a frank,* I found yours. If anything could repress my ardor, it would be such a letter as yours. To disappoint a friend is unpleasing; and he that forms expectations like yours must be disappointed. Think only when you see me that you see a man who loves you, and is proud and glad that you love him. I am, sir,

"Your most affectionate,
"SAM. JOHNSON.
"August 3, 1773."

His stay in Scotland[1] was from the 18th of August, on which day he arrived, till the 22d of November, when he set out on his return to London; and I believe ninety-four days were never passed by any man in a more vigorous exertion. His various adventures and the force and vivacity of his mind, as exercised during this peregrination, upon innumerable topics, have been

---

1. *Stay in Scotland.* See Appendix G, page 550.

faithfully, and to the best of my abilities, displayed in my *Journal of a Tour to the Hebrides*, to which, as the public has been pleased to honor it by a very extensive circulation, I beg leave to refer.

[1774].   He was now seriously engaged in writing an account of our travels in the Hebrides, in consequence of which I had the pleasure of a more frequent correspondence with him.

"To James Boswell, Esq.

"Streatham, June 21, 1774.

"DEAR SIR: Yesterday I put the first sheets of the *Journey to the Hebrides* to the press.   I have endeavored to do you some justice in the first paragraph.[1]   It will be one volume in octavo, not thick.

"I am, sir, your, &C.,
"SAM. JOHNSON."

"To James Boswell, Esq.

"DEAR SIR: I wish you could have looked over my book before the printer, but it could not easily be.   I suspect some mistakes; but, as I deal, perhaps, more in notions than in facts, the matter is not great, and the second edition will be mended, if any such there be.

"Of poor dear Dr. Goldsmith[2] there is little to be told, more than the papers have made public.   He died of a fever, made, I am afraid, more violent by uneasiness of mind.   His debts began to be heavy, and all his resources were exhausted.

* * *

"I am, dear sir,
"Your most affectionate servant,
"July 4, 1774."   "SAM. JOHNSON."

----

1. *First paragraph.*   "I was induced," says Dr. Johnson, "to undertake the journey by finding in Mr. Boswell a companion whose acuteness would help my inquiry, and whose gayety of conversation and civility of manners are sufficient to counteract the inconveniences of travel in countries less hospitable than we have passed."
2. *Goldsmith.*   In a letter to Bennet Langton, Johnson writes of Goldsmith: "But let not his frailties be remembered; he was a very great man."

[1775].   MR. BOSWELL TO DR. JOHNSON

"Edinburgh, Jan. 19, 1775.

"Be pleased to accept of my best thanks for your *Journey to the Hebrides*, which came to me by last night's post. Though ill of a bad cold, you kept me up the greatest part of the last night; for I did not stop till I had read every word of your book. I looked back to our first talking of a visit to the Hebrides, which was many years ago when sitting by ourselves in the Mitre tavern, in London, I think about witching time o'night; and then exulted in contemplating our scheme fulfilled."

MR. BOSWELL TO DR. JOHNSON

"Edinburgh, Feb. 2, 1775.

"As to Macpherson[1], I am anxious to have from yourself a full and pointed account of what has passed between you and him. It is confidently told here that before your book came out he sent to you, to let you know that he understood you meant to deny the authenticity of Ossian's poems; that the originals were in his possession; that you might have inspection of them, and might take the evidence of people skilled in the Erse language; and that he hoped after this fair offer you would not be so uncandid as to assert that he had refused reasonable proof. That you paid no regard to his message, but published your strong attack upon him; and then he wrote a letter to you in such terms as he thought suited to one who had not acted as a man of veracity. You may believe it gives me pain to hear your conduct represented as unfavorable, while I can only deny what is said, on the ground that your character refutes it, without having any information to oppose. Let me, I beg of you, be furnished with a sufficient answer to any calumny upon this occasion."

"MY DEAR BOSWELL: Macpherson never in his life offered me a sight of any original or of any evidence of any kind; but

---

1. *Macpherson.* See Appendix D, page 547.

thought only of intimidating me by noise and threats, till my last answer put an end to our correspondence.

"The state of the question is this. He, and Dr. Blair, whom I consider as deceived, say that he copied the poem from old manuscripts. His copies, if he had them, and I believe him to have none, are nothing. Where are the manuscripts? They can be shown if they exist, but they were never shown. *De non existentibus et non apparentibus*, says our law, *eadem est ratio*. No man has a claim to credit upon his own word, when better evidence, if he had it, may be easily produced. But so far as we can find, the Erse language was never written till very lately for the purposes of religion. A nation that cannot write, or a language that was never written, has no manuscripts.

"But whatever he has, he never offered to show."

What words were used by Mr. Macpherson in his letter to the Venerable Sage, I have never heard, but they are generally said to have been of a nature very different from the language of literary contest. Dr. Johnson's answer appeared in the newspapers of the day, but not with perfect accuracy. I give it as dictated to me by himself, and authenticated by a note in his own handwriting, *"This, I think, is a true copy."*

"MR. JAMES MACPHERSON: I received your foolish and impudent letter. Any violence offered me I shall do my best to repel; and what I cannot do for myself, the law shall do for me. I hope I shall never be deterred from detecting what I think a cheat, by the menaces of a ruffian.

"What would you have me retract? I thought your book an imposture; I think it an imposture still. For this opinion I have given my reasons to the public, which I here dare you to refute. Your rage I defy. Your abilities, since your *Homer*,[1] are not so formidable; and what I hear of your morals inclines me to pay regard not to what you shall say, but to what you shall prove. You may print this if you will. "SAM. JOHNSON."

---

1. *Your Homer.* Macpherson's translation of the *Iliad*.

Mr. Macpherson little knew the character of Dr. Johnson if he supposed that he could be easily intimidated, for no man was ever more remarkable for personal courage. He had, indeed, an awful dread of death, or rather, "of something after death"; but he feared nothing else. Foote,[1] who so successfully revived the old comedy by exhibiting living characters, had resolved to imitate Johnson on the stage, expecting great profits from his ridicule of so celebrated a man. Johnson being informed of his intention, and being at dinner at Mr. Thomas Davies's the bookseller, from whom I had the story, he asked Mr. Davies "what was the common price of an oak stick"; and being answered sixpence, "Why then, sir," said he, "give me leave to send your servant to purchase me a shilling one. I'll have a double quantity; for I am told Foote means to 'take me off,' as he calls it, and I am determined the fellow shall not do it with impunity." Davies took care to acquaint Foote of this, which effectually checked the wantonness of the mimic. Mr. Macpherson's menaces made Johnson provide himself with the same implement of defense; and had he been attacked, I have no doubt that, old as he was, he would have made his corporal prowess be felt as much as his intellectual.

On Tuesday, March 21, I arrived in London, and on repairing to Dr. Johnson's before dinner, found him in his study, sitting with Mr. Peter Garrick, the elder brother of David, strongly resembling him in countenance and voice, but of more sedate and placid manners. Both at this interview and in the evening at Mr. Thrale's, where he and Mr. Peter Garrick

---

1. *Foote.* "I found fault with Foote for indulging his talent of ridicule at the expense of his visitors, which I colloquially termed making fools of his company. JOHNSON. 'Why, sir, when you go to see Foote, you do not go to see a saint; you go to see a man who will be entertained at your house, and then bring you on a public stage; who will entertain you at his house for the very purpose of bringing you on a public stage. Sir, he does not make fools of his company; they whom he exposes are fools already; he only brings them into action.' " *Boswell: Life of Johnson.* After Foote's death in 1777, Johnson wrote to Mrs. Thrale: "Did you think [Foote] would so soon be gone? 'Life,' says Falstaff, 'is a shuttle.' He was a fine fellow in his way; and the world is really impoverished by his sinking glories."

and I met again, he was vehement on the subject of the Ossian controversy. He also was outrageous upon his supposition that my countrymen "loved Scotland[1] better than truth," saying, "All of them—nay not all—but *droves* of them, would come up and attest anything for the honor of Scotland." He also persevered in his wild allegation that he questioned if there was a tree[2] between Edinburgh and the English border older than himself. I assured him he was mistaken, and suggested that the proper punishment would be that he should receive a stripe at every tree above a hundred years old that was found within that space. He laughed, and said, "I believe I might submit to it for a *baubee!*"

On Friday, March 24, I met him at the Literary Club. Before he came in, we talked of his journey to the Western Islands, and of his coming away, "willing to believe the second sight,"[3] which seemed to excite some ridicule. I was then so impressed with the truth of many of the stories of it which I had been told that I avowed my conviction, saying, "He is only *willing* to believe; I *do* believe. The evidence is enough for me, though not for his great mind. What will not fill a quart bottle will fill a pint bottle. I am filled with belief." "Are you?" said Colman; "then cork it up."

On Monday, March 27, I breakfasted with him at Mr. Strahan's. He told us that he was engaged to go that evening to Mrs. Abington's[4] benefit. "She was visiting some

---

1. *Loved Scotland.* "A Scotchman must be a very sturdy moralist who does not love Scotland better than truth; he will always love it better than inquiry." *Johnson: A Journey to the Western Islands of Scotland.*

2. *A tree.* "It is well known that commerce is carried on by ships, and that ships are built out of trees; and therefore when I travel over naked plains, to which tradition has preserved the name of forests, or see hills arising on either hand, barren and useless, I cannot forbear to wonder how that commerce, of which we promise ourselves the perpetuity, shall be continued by our descendants." *Johnson: Thoughts on Agriculture.*

3. *The Second Sight.* See Appendix H, page 551.

4. *Mrs. Abington.* In childhood, a flower girl; later, a cookmaid; at seventeen, an actress; now, in her thirties. Though not forgetting some disreputable episodes in her past, society made much of her.

ladies whom I was visiting, and begged that I would come to her benefit. I told her I could not hear, but she insisted so much on my coming that it would have been brutal to have refused her." This was a speech quite characteristical. He loved to bring forward his having been in the gay circles of life, and he was, perhaps, a little vain of the solicitations of this elegant and fashionable actress.

Mr. Strahan talked of launching into the great ocean of London, in order to have a chance for rising into eminence; and, observing that many men were kept back from trying their fortunes there, because they were born to a competency, said, "Small certainties are the bane of men of talents"; which Johnson confirmed. Mr. Strahan put Johnson in mind of a remark which he had made to him: "There are few ways in which a man can be more innocently employed than in getting money." "The more one thinks of this," said Strahan, "the juster it will appear."

I met [Johnson] at Drury Lane playhouse in the evening. Sir Joshua Reynolds, at Mrs. Abington's request, had promised to bring a body of wits to her benefit; and having secured forty places in the front boxes, had done me the honor to put me in the group. Johnson sat on the seat directly behind me, and as he could neither see nor hear at such a distance from the stage, he was wrapped up in grave abstraction, and seemed quite a cloud, amidst all the sunshine of glitter and gayety. I wondered at his patience in sitting out a play of five acts, and a farce of two.

At Mr. Beauclerk's, where I supped, was Mr. Garrick, whom I made happy with Johnson's praise of his prologues; and I suppose, in gratitude to him, he took up one of his favorite topics, the nationality of the Scotch, which he maintained in a pleasant manner, with the aid of a little poetical fiction. He imitated the manner of his old master with ludicrous exaggeration, repeating, with pauses and half-whistlings interjected,

Os homini sublime dedit—cælumque tueri
Jussit—et erectos ad sidera—tollere vultus;

looking downwards all the time and, while pronouncing the four last words, absolutely touching the ground with a kind of contorted gesticulation.

Garrick, however, when he pleased, could imitate Johnson very exactly. I recollect his exhibiting him to me one day as if saying, "Davy has some convivial pleasantry about him, but 'tis a futile fellow"; which he uttered perfectly with the tone and air of Johnson.

I cannot too frequently request of my readers, while they peruse my account of Johnson's conversation, to endeavor to keep in mind his deliberate and strong utterance. His mode of speaking was indeed very impressive; and I wish it could be preserved as music is written, according to the very ingenious method of Mr. Steele,[1] who has shown how the recitation of Mr. Garrick and other eminent speakers might be transmitted to posterity *in score*.

Next day I dined with Johnson at Mr. Thrale's. He attacked Gray, calling him "a dull[2] fellow." BOSWELL. "I understand he was reserved,[3] and might appear dull in company; but surely he was not dull in poetry." JOHNSON. "Sir, he was dull in company, dull in his closet,* dull everywhere. He was dull in a new way, and that made many people think him *great*. He was a mechanical[4] poet."

Mrs. Thrale maintained that his Odes were melodious; upon which he exclaimed,

> Weave the warp, and weave the woof;

I added, in a solemn tone,

> The winding sheet of Edward's race.

---

1. *Steele.* Joshua Steele.
2. *Dull.* "When you have seen one of my days, you have seen a whole year of my life; they go round and round like the blind horse in the mill." *Gray, 1735.*
3. *Reserved.* "I hate a fellow whom pride, or cowardice, or laziness drives into a corner, and [who] does nothing when he is there but sit and *growl*; let him come out as I do, and *bark*." *Johnson, quoted by Mrs. Piozzi.*
4. *Mechanical.* "He wrote English verses as his brother Eton schoolboys wrote Latin, filching a phrase now from one author, and now from another." *William Wordsworth.*

"*There* is a good line."—"Aye," said he, "and the next line is a good one" (pronouncing it contemptuously),

> Give ample verge and room enough.

"No, sir, there are but two good stanzas in Gray's poetry, which are in his 'Elegy in a Country Churchyard.' " He then repeated the stanza,

> For who to dumb forgetfulness a prey, etc.

mistaking one word; for instead of *precincts* he said *confines*. He added, "The other stanza I forget."

On Friday, March 31, I supped with him and some friends at a tavern. One of the company[1] attempted, with too much forwardness, to rally him on his late appearance at the theater; but had reason to repent of his temerity. "Why, sir, did you go to Mrs. Abington's benefit? Did you see?" JOHNSON. "No, sir." "Did you hear?" JOHNSON. "No, sir." "Why then, sir, did you go?" JOHNSON. "Because, sir, she is a favorite of the public; and when the public cares the thousandth part for you that it does for her, I will go to your benefit too."

Next morning I won a small bet from Lady Diana Beauclerk, by asking him as to one of his particularities, which her Ladyship laid I durst not do. It seems he had been frequently observed at the club to put into his pocket the Seville oranges, after he had squeezed the juice of them into the drink which he made for himself. Beauclerk and Garrick talked of it to me, and seemed to think that he had a strange unwillingness to be discovered. We could not divine what he did with them; and this was the bold question to be put. I saw on his table the spoils of the preceding night, some fresh peels nicely scraped and cut into pieces. "Oh, sir," said I, "I now partly see what you do with the squeezed oranges which you put into your pocket at the Club." JOHNSON. "I have a great love for them." BOSWELL. "And, pray, sir, what do you do with them? You scrape them it seems, very neatly, and what next?" JOHNSON. "Let them dry, sir." BOSWELL. "And

---

1. *One of the company.* "Very likely, Boswell." *Birkbeck Hill.*

what next?" JOHNSON. "Nay, sir, you shall know their fate no further." BOSWELL. "Then the world must be left in the dark. It must be said (assuming a mock solemnity) he scraped them and let them dry, but what he did with them next, he never could be prevailed upon to tell." JOHNSON. "Nay, sir, you should say it more emphatically—he could not be prevailed upon, even by his dearest friends, to tell."

I visited him by appointment in the evening, and we drank tea with Mrs. Williams. He told me that he had been in the company of a gentleman whose extraordinary travels[1] had been much the subject of conversation. But I found he had not listened to him with that full confidence, without which there is little satisfaction in the society of travelers. I asked if he was not a man of sense. JOHNSON. "Why, sir, he is not a distinct relater; and I should say he is neither abounding nor deficient in sense. I did not perceive any superiority of understanding." BOSWELL. "But will you not allow him a nobleness of resolution, in penetrating into distant regions?" JOHNSON. "That, sir, is not to the present purpose; we are talking of sense; a fighting cock has a nobleness of resolution."

Next day, Sunday, April 2, I dined with him at Mr. Hoole's.[2] We talked of Pope. JOHNSON. "He wrote his *Dunciad* for fame. That was his primary motive. Had it not been for that, the dunces might have railed against him till they were weary, without his troubling himself about them. He delighted to vex them, no doubt; but he had more delight in seeing how well he could vex them."

I talked of the cheerfulness of Fleet Street, owing to the constant, quick succession of people which we perceive passing

1. *A gentleman whose extraordinary travels.* James Bruce, the explorer of Abyssinia. "His notorious vanity, the singular adventures he related, and the generally embellished character which he imparted to his narrative, excited some degree of skepticism, and he was subject to a good deal of satire, to which, though much annoyed, he did not reply. It is, however, generally allowed that he had shown great daring, perseverance, and zeal in his explorations, and that he made a real addition to the geographical knowledge of his day." *Everyman's Dictionary of English Literature.*

2. *Hoole.* A fantastic, old-fashioned clerk; translator of Tasso.

through it. JOHNSON. "Why, sir, Fleet Street has a very animated appearance; but I think the full tide of human existence is at Charing Cross."

He made the common remark on the unhappiness which men who have led a busy life experience when they retire in expectation of enjoying themselves at ease. He mentioned as strong an instance of this as can well be imagined. "An eminent tallow chandler in London, who had acquired a considerable fortune, gave up the trade in favor of his foreman, and went to live at a country house near town. He soon grew weary, and paid frequent visits to his old shop, where he desired they might let him know their *melting-days*, and he would come and assist them; which he accordingly did. Here, sir, was a man to whom the most disgusting circumstances in the business to which he had been used was a relief from idleness."

On Thursday, April 6, I dined with him at Mr. Thomas Davies's, with Mr. Hicky, the painter, and my old acquaintance, Mr. Moody, the player.

Dr. Johnson, as usual, spoke contemptuously of Colley Cibber. "It is wonderful that a man, who for forty years had lived with the great and the witty, should have acquired so ill the talents of conversation; and he had but half to furnish, for one half of what he said was oaths." Davies said he was the first dramatic writer who introduced genteel ladies upon the stage. Johnson refuted his observation by instancing several such characters in comedies before his time. DAVIES (trying to defend himself from a charge of ignorance). "I mean genteel moral characters." "I think," said Hicky, "gentility and morality are inseparable." BOSWELL. "By no means, sir. The genteelest characters are often the most immoral. Does not Lord Chesterfield[1] give precepts for uniting wickedness and the graces?" JOHNSON. "It is certain that a man may be very immoral with exterior grace. Lovelace, in *Clarissa*, is a very genteel and a very wicked character. Tom

---

1. *Chesterfield*. "A real man of fashion and pleasure observes decency; at least neither borrows nor affects vices; and if he unfortunately has any, he gratifies them with choice, delicacy, and secrecy." *Chesterfield: Letters to His Son.*

Hervey,[1] who died t'other day, though a vicious man, was one of the genteelest men that ever lived." Tom Davies instanced Charles the Second.[2] JOHNSON (taking fire at any attack upon that Prince, for whom he had an extraordinary partiality). "Charles the Second was licentious in his practice; but he always had a reverence for what was good. Charles the Second knew his people, and rewarded merit. The Church was at no time better filled than in his reign. He was the best King we have had from his time till the reign of his present Majesty, except James the Second, who was a very good King, but unhappily believed that it was necessary for the salvation of his subjects that they should be Roman Catholics. *He* had the merit of endeavoring to do what he thought was for the salvation of the souls of his subjects, till he lost a great Empire. *We*, who thought that we should *not* be saved if we were Roman Catholics, had the merit of maintaining our religion, at the expense of submitting ourselves to the government of King William (for it could not be done otherwise)—to the government of one of the most worthless scoundrels that ever existed. No; Charles the Second was not such a man as —— (naming another king).[3] He did not destroy his father's will.

"He took money, indeed, from France; but he did not betray those over whom he ruled. He did not let the French fleet pass* ours. George the First[4] knew nothing, and desired to know nothing; did nothing, and desired to do nothing; and the only good thing that is told of him[5] is that he wished to

---

1. *Tom Hervey.* Dissipated, quarrelsome, and generally reputed mad; but a brother of Johnson's benefactor, "Harry Hervey."

2. *Charles the Second.* "Charles the Second by his affability and politeness made himself the idol of the nation, which he betrayed and sold. William the Third was, for his insolence and brutality, hated by that people which he protected and enriched; had the best part of these two characters been united in one prince, the house of Bourbon had fallen before him." *Johnson in the Gentleman's Magazine, 1742.*

3. *Another king.* George the Second, said to have destroyed his father's will so as to cheat his sister, the Queen of Prussia, of her legacies.

4. *George the First.* "An honest, dull German gentleman, as unwilling as unfit to act the part of a king." *Lord Chesterfield.* See also Thackeray's *Four Georges.*

5. *Told of him.* Told without basis of fact, as it happens.

restore the crown to its hereditary successor." He roared
with prodigious violence against George the Second.[1] When
he ceased, Moody interjected, in an Irish tone, and with a
comic look, "Ah! poor George the Second."

We got into an argument whether the judges who went to
India[2] might with propriety engage in trade. Johnson warmly
maintained that they might, "For why," he urged, "should not
judges get riches, as well as those who deserve them less?" I
said they should have sufficient salaries, and have nothing
to take off their attention from the affairs of the public.
JOHNSON. "No judge, sir, can give his whole attention to his
office; and it is very proper that he should employ what time
he has to himself, to his own advantage, in the most profitable
manner." "Then, sir," said Davies, who enlivened the dispute by making it somewhat dramatic, "he may become an
insurer; and when he is going to the bench, he may be stopped—
'Your Lordship cannot go yet; here is a bunch of invoices;
several ships are about to sail.'" JOHNSON. "Sir, you may as
well say a judge should not have a house; for they may come
and tell him, 'Your Lordship's house is on fire'; and so, instead of minding the business of his court, he is to be occupied
in getting the engine with the greatest speed. There is no
end of this. No, sir, there is no profession to which a man
gives a very great proportion of his time. The best employed
lawyer has his mind at work for but a small proportion of his
time; a great deal of his occupation is merely mechanical.
I once wrote for a magazine; I made a calculation that if I
should write but a page a day, at the same rate, I should in
ten years write nine volumes in folio, of an ordinary size and
print." BOSWELL. "Such as Carte's History?" JOHNSON.
"Yes, sir. When a man writes from his own mind, he writes
very rapidly. The greatest part of a writer's time is spent in

---

1. *George the Second.* "His first natural movements were always
on the side of justice and truth; but they were often warped by min-
isterial influence or the secret twitches of avarice. He had rather an
unfeeling than a bad heart." *Lord Chesterfield.*

2. *To India.* The ethics of the English in India had within the last
few years become a subject of intense public interest.

reading, in order to write; a man will turn over half a library to make one book."

While the dispute went on, Moody once tried to say something on our side. Tom Davies clapped him on the back, to encourage him. Beauclerk, to whom I mentioned this circumstance, said that he "could not conceive a more humiliating situation than to be clapped on the back by Tom Davies."

Patriotism having become one of our topics, Johnson suddenly uttered, in a strong, determined tone, an apothegm, at which many will start: "Patriotism is the last refuge of a scoundrel." But let it be considered that he did not mean a real and generous love of our country, but that pretended patriotism which so many, in all ages and countries, have made a cloak for self-interest.

Mrs. Pritchard being mentioned, he said, "Her playing was quite mechanical. It is wonderful how little mind she had. Sir, she had never read the tragedy of Macbeth all through. She no more thought of the play out of which her part was taken than a shoemaker thinks of the skin out of which the piece of leather, of which he is making a pair of shoes, is cut."

On Saturday, April 8, I dined with him at Mr. Thrale's. Johnson had supped the night before at Mrs. Abington's, with some fashionable people whom he named; and he seemed much pleased with having made one in so elegant a circle. Nor did he omit to pique his mistress a little with the jealousy of her housewifery; for he said, with a smile, "Mrs. Abington's jelly, my dear lady, was better than yours."

Mrs. Thrale, who frequently practiced a coarse mode of flattery, by repeating his *bon mots* in his hearing, told us that he had said a certain celebrated actor[1] was just fit to stand at the door of an auction room with a long pole, and cry "Pray, gentlemen, walk in"; and that a certain author,[2] upon hearing this, had said that another still more celebrated actor was fit

---

1. *Celebrated actor.* Spranger Barry, more noted for his voice, grace, and stage presence than for any intellectual gifts.
2. *Certain author.* Arthur Murphy, the dramatist who felt that thrifty David Garrick had underpaid him for a play. Dr. Johnson utterly fails to catch the point of Murphy's joke.

for nothing better than that, and would pick your pocket after
you came out. JOHNSON. "Nay, my dear lady, there is no
wit in what our friend added; there is only abuse. You may
as well say of any man that he will pick a pocket. Besides,
the man who is stationed at the door does not pick people's
pockets; that is done within, by the auctioneer." Mrs. Thrale
told us that Tom Davies repeated, in a very bald manner, the
story of Dr. Johnson's first repartee to me which I have related
exactly. He made me say, "I *was* born in Scotland," instead of
"I *come from* Scotland"; so that Johnson's saying, "That, sir,
is what a great many of your countrymen cannot help," had
no point, or even meaning; and that upon this being mentioned
to Mr. Fitzherbert,[1] he observed, "It is not every man that
can *carry a bon mot.*"

On Monday, April 10, I dined with him at General Oglethorpe's. Mr. Scott of Amwell's Elegies were lying in the
room. Dr. Johnson observed, "They are very well, but such
as twenty people might write." Upon this I took occasion to
controvert Horace's maxim,

$$\text{------} mediocribus \quad esse \quad poetis$$
$$Non \; Di, \; non \; homines, \; non \; concessêre \; columnæ,$$

"for here," I observed, "was a very middle-rate poet, who
pleased many readers, and therefore poetry of a middle sort
was entitled to some esteem; nor could I see why poetry should
not, like everything else, have different gradations of excellence,
and consequently of value." Johnson repeated the common
remark, that "as there is no necessity for our having poetry
at all, it being merely a luxury, an instrument of pleasure, it
can have no value unless when exquisite in its kind." I declared myself not satisfied. "Why, then, sir," said he, "Horace
and you must settle it." He was not much in the humor of
talking.

---

1. *Fitzherbert.* "F-tzh-b-t was a gay, good-humored fellow, generous of his money and of his meat, and desirous of nothing but cheerful society among people, distinguished in *some* way, in *any way,* I
think." *Dr. Johnson, quoted by Mrs. Piozzi.* Again characterized by
Johnson on page 303.

No more of his conversation for some days appears in my journal, except that when a gentleman told him he had bought a suit of lace for his lady, he said, "Well, sir, you have done a good thing and a wise thing." "I have done a good thing," said the gentleman, "but I do not know that I have done a wise thing." JOHNSON. "Yes, sir; no money is better spent than what is laid out for domestic satisfaction. A man is pleased that his wife is dressed as well as other people; and a wife is pleased that she is dressed."

On Friday, April 14, being Good Friday, I repaired to him in the morning, according to my usual custom on that day, and breakfasted with him. I observed that he fasted so very strictly that he did not even taste bread, and took no milk with his tea; I suppose because it is a kind of animal food.

He entered upon the state of the nation, and thus discoursed: "Sir, the great misfortune now is that government has too little power. All that it has to bestow must of necessity be given to support itself; so that it cannot reward merit. No man, for instance, can now be made a bishop for his learning and piety; his only chance for promotion is his being connected with somebody who has parliamentary interest: Our several ministries in this reign have outbid each other in concessions to the people. Lord Bute, though a very honorable man— a man who meant well—was a theoretical statesman—a book minister. Then, sir, he gave up a great deal. He advised the King to agree that the judges should hold their places for life, instead of losing them at the accession of a new king. Lord Bute, I suppose, thought to make the King popular by this concession; but the people never minded it; and it was a most impolitic measure. There is no reason why a judge should hold his office for life, more than any other person in public trust. A judge may be partial otherwise than to the Crown. We have seen judges partial to the populace. A judge may become corrupt, and yet there may not be legal evidence against him. A judge may become froward from age, a judge may grow unfit for his office in many ways. It was desirable that there should be a possibility of being delivered from him by a new king."

After the evening service he said, "Come, you shall go home with me, and sit just an hour." But he was better than his word; for after we had drunk tea[1] with Mrs. Williams, he asked me to go up to his study with him, where we sat a long while together in a serene, undisturbed frame of mind, sometimes in silence, and sometimes conversing, as we felt inclined.

He was pleased to say, "If you come to settle here, we will have one day in the week on which we will meet by ourselves. That is the happiest conversation where there is no competition, no vanity, but a calm, quiet interchange of sentiments." In his private register this evening is thus marked, "Boswell sat with me till night; we had some serious talk." It also appears from the same record that after I left him he was occupied in religious duties, in "giving Francis, his servant, some directions for preparation to communicate; in reviewing his life, and resolving on better conduct." No saint, however, in the course of his religious warfare, was more sensible of the unhappy failure of pious resolves than Johnson. He said one day, talking to an acquaintance on this subject, "Sir, hell is paved with good intentions."

On Sunday, April 16, being Easter day, after having attended the solemn service at St. Paul's, I dined with Dr. Johnson and Mrs. Williams. I maintained that Horace was wrong in placing happiness in *Nil admirari*, for that I thought admiration[2] one of the most agreeable of all our feelings; and I regretted that I had lost much of my disposition to admire, which people generally do as they advance in life. JOHNSON. "Sir, as a man advances in life, he gets what is better than admiration— judgment to estimate things at their true value." I still insisted that admiration was more pleasing than judgment, as love is more pleasing than friendship. The feeling of friend-

---

1. *Drunk tea.* "Boswell and I went to church, but came very late. We then took tea, by Boswell's desire, and I ate one bun, I think, that I might not seem to fast ostentatiously." *Johnson: Prayers and Meditations.*

2. *Admiration.* Probably used here with the Latin meaning of *admirare* in mind: to wonder. "Wonder," says Johnson in the *Rambler*, "is a pause in reason."

ship is like that of being comfortably filled with roast beef; love, like being enlivened with champagne. JOHNSON. "No, sir; admiration and love are like being intoxicated with champagne; judgment and friendship like being enlivened. Waller[1] has hit upon the same thought with you, but I don't believe you have borrowed from Waller. I wish you would enable yourself to borrow more."

He then took occasion to enlarge on the advantages of reading, and combated the idle, superficial notion that knowledge enough may be acquired in conversation. "The foundation," said he, "must be laid by reading. General principles must be had from books, which, however, must be brought to the test of real life.[2] In conversation you never get a system. What is said upon a subject is to be gathered from a hundred people. The parts of a truth which a man gets thus are at such a distance from each other that he never attains to a full view."

On Tuesday, April 18, he and I were engaged to go with Sir Joshua Reynolds to dine with Mr. Cambridge,[3] at his beautiful villa on the banks of the Thames, near Twickenham. Dr. Johnson's tardiness was such that Sir Joshua, who had an

---

1. *Waller*. A seventeenth century poet, noted for the ingenuity and fashionable air with which he set off his thoughts. He was long over-rated by those who set the style in literature. "His thoughts are such as a liberal conversation and large acquaintance with life would easily supply." *Johnson: Life of Waller.*

2. *Test of real life.* "Last Sunday an old acquaintance found me out; not, I think, a school-fellow, but one with whom I played perhaps before I went to school. I had not seen him for forty years, but was glad to find him alive. He has had, as he phrased it, a *matter of four wives,* for which neither you nor I like him much the better; but after all his marriages he is poor, and has now, at sixty-six, two very young children. Such, madam, are the strange things of which we that travel come to the knowledge. We see *mores hominum multorum.* You that waste your lives over a book at home must take life upon trust." *Johnson to Mrs. Thrale, 1771.*

3. *Cambridge.* "A country gentleman whose tastes lay rather in letters and landscape gardening than farming and field sports." *Dictionary of National Biography.* According to Horace Walpole, he "had a rage" for knowing everybody. He lived nine or ten miles from London.

appointment at Richmond early in the day, was obliged to go
by himself on horseback, leaving his coach to Johnson and me.

Johnson was in such good spirits that everything seemed
to please him as we drove along. JOHNSON. "It is wonderful,
sir, how rare a quality good humor is in life. We meet with
very few good-humored men." I mentioned four of our friends,
none of whom he would allow to be good-humored. One was
acid, another was *muddy*, and to the others he had objections
which have escaped me. Then, shaking his head and stretching
himself at ease in the coach, and smiling with much complacency, he turned to me and said, "I look upon *myself* as a
good-humored fellow." The epithet *fellow*, applied to the
great lexicographer, the stately moralist, the masterly critic,
as if he had been *Sam* Johnson, a mere pleasant companion,
was highly diverting; and this light notion of himself struck
me with wonder. I answered, also smiling, "No, no, sir; that
will *not* do. You are good-natured, but not good-humored;
you are irascible. You have not patience with folly and absurdity. I believe you would pardon them, if there were time
to deprecate your vengeance; but punishment follows so quick
after sentence that they cannot escape."

He defended his remark upon the general insufficiency of
education in Scotland, and confirmed to me the authenticity
of his witty saying on the learning of the Scotch: "Their learning is like bread in a besieged town; every man gets a little,
but no man gets a full meal."

He talked of Izaak Walton's *Lives*,[1] which was one of his
most favorite books. Dr. Donne's Life, he said, was the
most perfect of them. He observed that "it was wonderful
that Walton, who was in a very low situation in life, should
have been familiarly received by so many great men, and
added that "he was a great panegyrist." BOSWELL. "No
quality will get a man more friends than a disposition to admire
the qualities of others. I do not mean flattery, but a sincere

---

1. *Walton's Lives*. Five brief biographies, very deferential in tone,
by the retired shopkeeper and life-long angler, Izaak Walton, of the
seventeenth century. Four of them were of clergymen (three bishops)
and three of the five were anglers.

admiration." JOHNSON. "Nay, sir, flattery pleases very generally. In the first place, the flatterer may think what he says to be true; but, in the second place, whether he thinks so or not, he certainly thinks those whom he flatters of consequence enough to be flattered."

No sooner had we made our bow to Mr. Cambridge, in his library, than Johnson ran eagerly to one side of the room intent on poring over the backs of the books. Sir Joshua observed (aside), "He runs to the books as I do to the pictures; but I have the advantage. I can see much more of the pictures than he can of the books." Mr. Cambridge, upon this, politely said, "Dr. Johnson, I am going, with your pardon, to accuse myself, for I have the same custom which I perceive you have. But it seems odd that one should have such a desire to look at the backs of books." Johnson, ever ready for contest, instantly started from his reverie, wheeled about, and answered, "Sir, the reason is very plain. Knowledge is of two kinds. We know a subject ourselves, or we know where we can find information upon it. When we inquire into any subject, the first thing we have to do is to know what books have treated of it. This leads us to look at catalogues and the backs of books in libraries." Sir Joshua observed to me the extraordinary promptitude with which Johnson flew upon an argument. "Yes," said I, "he has no formal preparation, no flourishing with his sword; he is through your body in an instant."

The Beggar's Opera,[1] and the common question, whether it

---

1. *Beggar's Opera*. A musical comedy, by John Gay, which found sources of great joy in the absurdities of Italian opera, and the scandals of English political life. Its hero was a highwayman with ambidextrous affections. The following quotations will give a taste of its wit.

"For on the rope that hangs my Dear
Depends poor Polly's life."

"How happy could I be with either,
Were t'other dear charmer away."

The play, first produced in 1728, had an extraordinary run and has been frequently revived. In 1772 the celebrated magistrate, Sir John

was pernicious in its effects, having been introduced: JOHNSON. "I do not believe that any man was ever made a rogue by being present at its representation. At the same time I do not deny that it may have some influence, by making the character of a rogue familiar, and in some degree pleasing." Then collecting himself, as it were, to give a heavy stroke: "There is in it such a *labefactation* of all principles as may be injurious to morality."

While he pronounced this response, we sat in a comical sort of restraint, smothering a laugh, which we were afraid might burst out. In his life of Gay, he has been still more decisive as to the inefficiency of *The Beggar's Opera* in corrupting society. But I have ever thought somewhat differently; for, indeed, not only are the gayety and heroism of a highwayman very captivating to a youthful imagination, but the arguments for adventurous depredation are so plausible, the allusions so lively, and the contrasts with the ordinary and more painful modes of acquiring the property are so artfully displayed that it requires a cool and strong judgment to resist so imposing an aggregate; yet, I own, I should be very sorry to have *The Beggar's Opera* suppressed; for there is in it so much of real London life, so much brilliant wit, and such a variety of airs, which, from early association of ideas, engage, soothe, and enliven the mind that no performance which the theater exhibits delights me more.

We talked of a young gentleman's[1] marriage with an eminent singer, and his determination that she should no longer sing in public, though his father was very earnest she should, because her talents would be liberally rewarded, so as to make her a good fortune. It was questioned whether the young gentleman, who had not a shilling in the world, but was blessed with very uncommon talents, was not foolishly delicate, or

---

Fielding, wrote to the theater manager, David Garrick, protesting that the play was never presented "without creating an additional number of real thieves."

1. *A young gentleman.* Richard Brinsley Sheridan, twenty-two when he married. Two years later he produced *The Rivals;* four years later, *The School for Scandal.*

foolishly proud, and his father truly rational without being mean. Johnson, with all the high spirit of a Roman senator, exclaimed, "He resolved wisely and nobly, to be sure. He is a brave man. Would not a gentleman be disgraced by having his wife singing publicly for hire? No, sir, there can be no doubt here. I know not if I should not *prepare myself* for a public singer as readily as let my wife be one."

"There is in *Hudibras*[1] [said Johnson] a great deal of bullion which will always last. But the brightest strokes of his wit owed their force to the impression of the characters, which was upon men's minds at the time; to their knowing them at table and in the street; in short, being familiar with them; and above all, to his satire being directed against those whom a little while before they had hated and feared. If Charles the Second had bent all his mind to it, had made it his sole object, he might have been as absolute as Louis the Fourteenth." A gentleman observed he would have done no harm if he had. JOHNSON. "Why, sir, absolute princes seldom do any harm. But they who are governed by them are governed by chance. There is no security for good government." CAMBRIDGE. "There have been many sad victims to absolute government." JOHNSON. "So, sir, have there been to popular factions." BOSWELL. "The question is, which is worst, one wild beast or many?"

Somebody found fault with writing verses in a dead language, maintaining that they were merely arrangements of so many words, and laughed at the Universities of Oxford and Cambridge for sending forth collections of them not only in Greek

---

1. *Hudibras.* A jeering, doggerel poem by Samuel Butler, who had very unwillingly served as a clerk to several Puritan magistrates, and at the Restoration caricatured the species as those who

> "Call fire and sword and desolation
>   A godly, thorough, Reformation,
>
>   .   .   .
>
>   Quarrel with minced pies, and disparage
>   Their best and dearest friend, plum porridge;
>   Fat pig and goose itself oppose,
>   And blaspheme custard through the nose."

and Latin, but even in Syriac, Arabic, and other more unknown tongues. JOHNSON. "I would have as many of these as possible; I would have verses in every language that there are the means of acquiring. Nobody imagines that a University is to have at once two hundred poets; but it should be able to show two hundred scholars. I would have the world to be told, 'Here is a school where everything may be learned.'"

On Monday, May 8, we visited the mansions of Bedlam. I accompanied him home, and dined, and drank tea with him. Talking of an acquaintance of ours, distinguished for knowing an uncommon variety of miscellaneous articles both in antiquities and polite literature, he observed, "You know, sir, he runs about with little weight upon his mind." And talking of another very ingenious gentleman, who from the warmth of his temper was at variance with many of his acquaintance, and wished to avoid them, he said, "Sir, he leads the life of an outlaw."

On Friday, May 12, as he had been so good as to assign me a room in his house, where I might sleep occasionally when I happened to sit with him to a late hour, I took possession of it this night, found everything in excellent order, and was attended by honest Francis with a most civil assiduity. I asked Johnson whether I might go to a consultation with another lawyer upon Sunday, as that appeared to me to be doing work as much in my way as if an artisan should work on the day appropriated for religious rest. JOHNSON. "Why, sir, when you are of consequence enough to oppose the practice of consulting upon Sunday, you should do it; but you may go now. It is not criminal, though it is not what one should do who is anxious for the preservation and increase of piety."

On Saturday, May 13, I breakfasted with him by invitation, accompanied by Mr. Andrew Crosbie and the Hon. Colonel (now General) Edward Stopford. His tea and rolls and butter and whole breakfast apparatus were all in such decorum, and his behavior was so courteous, that Colonel Stopford was quite surprised, and wondered at his having heard so much said of Johnson's slovenliness and roughness.

It being asked whether it was reasonable for a man to be

angry at another whom a woman had preferred to him:
JOHNSON: "I do not see, sir, that it is reasonable for a man
to be angry at another whom a woman has preferred to him,
but angry he is, no doubt; and he is loath to be angry at
himself."

Before setting out for Scotland on the 23d, I was frequently
in his company at different places. I passed many hours
with him on the 17th, of which I find all my memorial is
"much laughing." It should seem he had that day been in
a humor for jocularity and merriment, and upon such occasions I never knew a man laugh more heartily. Johnson's
laugh was a kind of good-humored growl. Tom Davies described it drolly enough, "He laughs like a rhinoceros."

"To Bennet Langton, Esq.

"DEAR SIR: I have an old amanuensis[1] in great distress.
I have given what I think I can give, and begged till I cannot
tell where to beg again. I put into his hands this morning
four guineas. If you could collect three guineas more, it
would clear him from his present difficulty.

                    "I am, sir,
                         "Your most humble servant,
                              "SAM. JOHNSON."

"To James Boswell, Esq.

"DEAR SIR: I am returned from the annual ramble[2] into
the middle counties. Having seen nothing I had not seen

---

1. *Old amanuensis.* Peyton. A year later, Johnson writes to
Mrs. Piozzi: "Poor Peyton expired this morning. He, probably, during
many years for which he sat starving by the bed of a wife, not only
useless but almost motionless, condemned by poverty to personal
attendance, and by the necessity of such attendance chained down to
poverty—he probably thought often how lightly he should tread the
path of life without his burthen. His wife died at last, and before she
was buried, he was seized by a fever, and is now going to the grave
Tears have been shed for the sufferings and wonder excited by the
fortitude of those who neither did nor suffered more than Peyton." He
was one of the five who had worked on the *Dictionary.*

2. *Ramble.* He had left the latter part of May; he writes the latter
part of August.

before, I have nothing to relate. Time has left that part of the island few antiquities; and commerce has left the people no singularities. I was glad to go abroad,* and, perhaps, glad to come home; which is, in other words, I was (I am afraid) weary of being at home and weary of being abroad. Is not this the state of life? But if we confess this weariness, let us not lament it, for all the wise and all the good say that we may cure it. For the black fumes which rise in your mind, I can prescribe nothing but that you disperse them by honest business or innocent pleasure, and by reading, sometimes easy and sometimes serious. Change of place is useful, and I hope that your residence at Auchinleck will have many good effects.

> "Your affectionate, humble servant,
> "SAM. JOHNSON.

"London, Aug. 27, 1775."

To the Same.

"MY DEAR SIR: I now write to you lest in some of your freaks and humors you should fancy yourself neglected. Such fancies I must entreat you never to admit, at least never to indulge, for my regard for you is so radicated and fixed that it is become a part of my mind and cannot be effaced but by some cause uncommonly violent; therefore, whether I write or not, set your thoughts at rest. I now write to tell you that I shall not very soon write again, for I am to set out tomorrow on another journey.

> "I am, sir, etc.,
> "SAM. JOHNSON.

"Sept. 14, 1775."

What he mentions in such light terms as "I am to set out tomorrow on another journey," I soon discovered was no less than a tour to France with Mr. and Mrs. Thrale. This was the only time in his life that he went upon the Continent.

It happened that Foote was at Paris at the same time with Dr. Johnson, and his description of my friend while there was abundantly ludicrous. He told me that the French were quite astonished at his figure and manner, and at his dress,[1] which he obstinately continued exactly as in London—his brown clothes, black stockings, and plain shirt.

Here let me not forget a curious anecdote, as related to me by Mr. Beauclerk, which I shall endeavor to exhibit as well as I can in that gentleman's lively manner; and in justice to him it is proper to add that Dr. Johnson told me I might rely both on the correctness of his memory, and the fidelity of his narrative. "When Madame de Boufflers was first in England," said Beauclerk, "she was desirous to see Johnson. I accordingly went with her to his chambers in the Temple, where she was entertained with his conversation for some time. When our visit was over, she and I left him, and were got into Inner Temple Lane, when all at once I heard a noise like thunder. This was occasioned by Johnson, who, it seems, upon a little recollection, had taken it into his head that he ought to have done the honors of his literary residence to a foreign lady of quality, and, eager to show himself a man of gallantry, was hurrying down the staircase in violent agitation. He overtook us before we reached the Temple gate, and brushing in between me and Madame de Boufflers, seized her hand, and conducted her to her coach. His dress was a rusty brown morning suit, a pair of old shoes by way of slippers, a little shriveled wig sticking on the top of his head, and the sleeves of his shirt and the knees of his breeches hanging loose. A considerable crowd of people gathered round, and were not a little struck by this singular appearance."

In the course of this year Dr. Burney informs me that he very frequently met Dr. Johnson at Mr. Thrale's, at Streatham, where they "had many long conversations, often sitting up as long as the fire and candles lasted, and much longer than the patience of the servants subsisted."

---

1. *His dress.* "By a note in his diary it appears that he laid out near thirty pounds in clothes for this journey." *Sir John Hawkins, quoted by Birkbeck Hill.* "Foote is quite impartial, for he tells lies of everybody." *Johnson, 1776.* Abroad, Johnson pieced out his French with Latin, pronounced by the English, not the continental system.

A few of Johnson's sayings which that gentleman recollects shall here be inserted.

"More is learned in public* than in private schools, from emulation; there is the collision of mind with mind, or the radiation of many minds pointing to one center."

"Too much is expected from precocity,[1] and too little performed. Miss —— was an instance of early cultivation, but in what did it terminate? In marrying a little Presbyterian parson, who keeps an infant boarding-school, so that all her employment now is

> To suckle fools, and chronicle small-beer."

He had come down one morning to the breakfast room, and been a considerable time by himself before anybody appeared. When on a subsequent day he was twitted by Mrs. Thrale for being very late, which he generally was, he defended himself by alluding to the extraordinary morning when he had been too early. "Madam, I do not like to come down to *vacuity*."

Dr. Burney having remarked that Mr. Garrick was beginning to look old, he said, "Why, sir, you are not to wonder at that; no man's face has had more wear and tear."

[1776]. At this time was in agitation a matter of great consequence to me and my family, which I should not obtrude upon the world, were it not that the part which Dr. Johnson's friendship for me made him take in it was the occasion of an exertion of his abilities which it would be injustice to conceal. That what he wrote upon the subject may be understood, it is necessary to give a state of the question, which I shall do as briefly as I can.

---

1. *Precocity.* "The trick which most parents play with their children, of showing off their newly acquired accomplishments, disgusted Mr. Johnson beyond expression; he had been treated so himself, he said, till he absolutely loathed his father's caresses, because he knew they were sure to precede some unpleasing display of his early abilities." *Mrs. Piozzi: Anecdotes of Johnson.* "Mr. Johnson was himself exceedingly disposed to the general indulgence of children, and was even scrupulously and ceremoniously attentive not to offend them." *The same.*

In the year 1504 the barony, or manor,* of Auchinleck[1] (pronounced *Affléck*), in Ayrshire, having fallen to the Crown by forfeiture, James the Fourth, King of Scotland, granted it to Thomas Boswell, a branch of an ancient family in the county of Fife. Thomas Boswell was slain in battle, fighting along with his Sovereign, at the fatal field of Flodden, in 1513.

From this very honorable founder of our family, the estate was transmitted in a direct series of heirs male to David Boswell, my father's great grand uncle, who had no sons, but four daughters, who were all respectably married.

David Boswell, being resolute in the military feudal principle of continuing the male succession, passed by his daughters, and settled the estate on his nephew by his next brother, who approved of the deed, and renounced any pretenses which he might possibly have in preference to his son. But the estate having been burthened with large portions to the daughters, and other debts, it was necessary for the nephew to sell a considerable part of it, and what remained was still much encumbered.

The frugality of the nephew preserved and, in some degree, relieved the estate. His son, my grandfather, an eminent lawyer, not only repurchased a great part of what had been sold, but acquired other lands; and my father, who was one of the judges of Scotland, and added considerably to the estate, now signified his inclination to secure it to his family in perpetuity by an entail,[2] which could not be done without my consent.

---

1. *Auchinleck.* "As I wandered with my reverend friend [Dr. Johnson] in the groves of Auchinleck, I told him that if I survived him, it was my intention to erect a monument to him here, among scenes which, in my mind, were all classical. . . . He turned off the subject, saying: 'Sir, I hope to see your grandchildren.' " *Boswell: Journal of a Tour to the Hebrides.*

2. *Entail.* Such a determination by law of a man's heir in real estate as precluded the man's choice in the matter or any possible claims upon the property by his creditors. Entails were fixed for at least two generations, generally for many more, and often in perpetuity. When such a settlement was made, it could be broken in succeeding generations only by special act of parliament.

In the plan of entailing the estate, I heartily concurred with him, though I was the first to be restrained by it; but we unhappily differed as to the series of heirs which should be established. My father had declared a predilection for heirs general, that is, males and females indiscriminately. He was willing, however, that all males descending from his grandfather should be preferred to females; but would not extend that privilege to males deriving their descent from a higher source. I, on the other hand, had a zealous partiality for heirs male, however remote, which I maintained by arguments which appeared to me to have considerable weight.[1] And in the particular case of our family, I apprehended that we were under an implied obligation in honor and good faith to transmit the estate by the same tenure [by] which we held it, which was as heirs male, excluding nearer females. I therefore, as I thought conscientiously, objected to my father's scheme.

My opposition was very displeasing to my father, who was entitled to great respect and deference; and I had reason to apprehend disagreeable consequences from my non-compliance with his wishes. After much perplexity and uneasiness, I wrote to Dr. Johnson, stating the case, with all its difficulties, and earnestly requesting that he would consider it at leisure, and favor me with his friendly opinion and advice.

"To James Boswell, Esq.

"DEAR SIR: I am going to write upon a question which requires more knowledge of local law and more acquaintance with the general rules of inheritance than I can claim, but I write because you request it.

"Land is, like any other possession, by natural right wholly in the power of its present owner and may be sold, given, or bequeathed, absolutely or conditionally, as judgment shall direct, or passion incite.

---

1. *Considerable weight.* Boswell here appends a note which begins: "As first, the opinion of some distinguished naturalists that our species is transmitted through males only, the female being all along no more than a *nidus*, or nurse, as Mother Earth is to plants of every sort."

"But natural right would avail little without the protection of law; and the primary notion of law is restraint in the exercise of natural right. A man is, therefore, in society, not fully master of what he calls his own, but he still retains all the power which the law does not take from him.

"Of the estate which we are now considering, your father still retains such possession that he can sell it and do with the money what he will, without any legal impediment. But when he extends his power beyond his own life, by settling the order of succession, the law makes your consent necessary.

"Let us suppose that he sells the land to risk the money in some specious adventure, and in that adventure loses the whole; his posterity would be disappointed, but they could not think themselves injured or robbed. If he spent it upon vice or pleasure, his successors could only call him vicious and voluptuous; they could not say that he was injurious or unjust.

"He that may do more may do less. He that, by selling or squandering, may disinherit a whole family, may certainly disinherit part, by a partial settlement.

"Laws are formed by the manners and exigencies of particular times, and it is but accidental that they last longer than their causes; the limitation of feudal succession to the male arose from the obligation of the tenant to attend his chief in war.

"As times and opinions are always changing, I know not whether it be not usurpation to prescribe rules to posterity, by presuming to judge of what we cannot know; and I know not whether I fully approve either your design or your father's, to limit that succession which descended to you unlimited.

"Suppose at one time a law that allowed only males to inherit, and during the continuance of this law many estates to have descended, passing by the females, to remoter heirs. Suppose afterwards the law repealed in correspondence with a change of manners, and women made capable of inheritance. Could the women have no benefit from a law made in their favor? Must they be passed by upon moral principles forever, because they were once excluded by a legal prohibition? Or may that which passed only to males by one law pass likewise to females by another?

"As your whole difficulty arises from the act of your ancestor, who diverted the succession from the females, you inquire, very properly, what was his intention; for you certainly are not bound by his act more than he intended to bind you, nor hold your land on harder or stricter terms than those on which it was granted.

"Intentions must be gathered from acts. When he left the estate to his nephew, by excluding his daughters, was it, or was it not, in his power to have perpetuated the succession to the males? If he could have done it, he seems to have shown, by omitting it, that he did not desire it to be done, and, upon your own principles, you will not easily prove your right to destroy that capacity of succession which your ancestors have left.

"If your ancestor had not the power of making a perpetual settlement, yet, you observe, he set no example of rigorous adherence to the line of succession. He that overlooked a brother would not wonder that little regard is shown to remote relations.

"These, dear sir, are my thoughts, unmethodical and deliberative, but perhaps you may find in them some glimmering of evidence.

"Make my compliments to Mrs. Boswell, though she does not love me.

"I am, sir,

"Your affectionate servant,

"SAM. JOHNSON.

"Feb. 3, 1776."

Having arrived in London late on Friday, the 15th of March, I hastened next morning to wait on Dr. Johnson, at his house; but found he was removed from Johnson's Court, No. 7, to Bolt Court,[1] No. 8, still keeping to his favorite Fleet Street. My reflection at the time upon this change, as marked in my *Journal*, is as follows: "I felt a foolish regret that he had left

---

1. *Bolt Court.* "Behind the house was a garden which [Johnson] took delight in watering; a room on the ground floor was assigned to Mrs. Williams, and the whole of the two pair of stairs floor was made a repository for his books; one of the rooms thereon being his study." *Sir John Hawkins, quoted by Birkbeck Hill.*

a court which bore his name; but it was not foolish to be affected with some tenderness of regard for a place which had often appeared to my imagination while I trod its pavement, in the solemn darkness of the night, to be sacred to wisdom and piety." Being informed that he was at Mr. Thrale's in the Borough,[1] I hastened thither, and found Mrs. Thrale and him at breakfast. I was kindly welcomed. In a moment he was in a full glow of conversation, and I felt myself elevated as if brought into another state of being. Mrs. Thrale and I looked to each other while he talked, and our looks expressed our congenial admiration and affection for him. I exclaimed to her, "I am now intellectually, *Hermippus redivivus;*[2] I am quite restored by him, by transfusion of mind." "There are many," she replied, "who admire and respect Mr. Johnson; but you and I *love* him."

He seemed very happy in the near prospect of going to Italy with Mr. and Mrs. Thrale. "But," said he, "before leaving England I am to take a jaunt to Oxford, Birmingham, Lichfield, and my old friend, Dr. Taylor's, at Ashbourne, in Derbyshire. I shall go in a few days, and you, Boswell, shall go with me." I was ready to accompany him; being willing even to leave London to have the pleasure of his conversation.

I mentioned with much regret the extravagance of the representative of a great family in Scotland, by which there was danger of its being ruined; and as Johnson respected it for its antiquity, he joined with me in thinking it would be happy if this person should die. Mrs. Thrale seemed shocked at this, as feudal barbarity, and said, "I do not understand this preference of the estate to its owner; of the land to the man who walks upon that land." JOHNSON. "Nay, madam, it is not a

---

1. *Borough.* The crowded region of London in which the Thrale town house was situated.

2. *Hermippus redivivus.* Hermippus revived; the title of the English translation of a German book, written with such mock seriousness that it caught the unsuspecting. "[Its] notion of the art of prolonging life by inhaling the breath of young women was eagerly credited. I have a copy with manuscript notes by a learned physician." *D'Israeli: Curiosities of Literature.*

preference of the land to its owner; it is the preference of a family to an individual. Here is an establishment in a country, which is of importance for ages, not only to the chief, but to his people; an establishment which extends upwards and downwards; that this should be destroyed by one idle fellow is a sad thing."

He said, "Entails are good, because it is good to preserve in a country serieses of men to whom the people are accustomed to look up as to their leaders. But I am for leaving a quantity of land in commerce; for if no land were to be bought in the country, there would be no encouragement to acquire wealth, because a family could not be founded there."

I expressed the opinion that the power of entailing should be limited thus: That there should be one-third, or, perhaps, one-half of the land of a country kept free for commerce; that the proportion allowed to be entailed should be parceled out so that no family could entail above a certain quantity. JOHNSON. "Why, sir, mankind will be better able to regulate the system of entails when the evil of too much land being locked up by them is felt than we can do at present when it is not felt."[1]

I suggested a doubt of the justice of the general opinion that it is improper in a lawyer to solicit employment; for why, I urged, should it not be equally allowable to solicit that as it is to solicit votes to be elected a member of parliament? JOHNSON. "Sir, it is wrong to stir up lawsuits, but when once it is certain that a lawsuit is to go on, there is nothing wrong in a lawyer's endeavoring that he shall have the benefit rather than another." BOSWELL. "You would not solicit employment, sir, if you were a lawyer." JOHNSON. "No, sir, but not because I should think it wrong, but because I should disdain it." This was a good distinction, which will be felt by men of just pride. He proceeded: "However, I would not have the lawyer to be wanting to himself in using

---

1. *When it is not felt.* The celebrated Scotch judge, Lord Cockburn, once stated that three-fourths of all the land in Scotland was at this time tied up in entails.

fair means. I would have him to inject a little hint now and then, to prevent his being overlooked."

We got into a boat to cross over to Blackfriars; and as we moved along the Thames, I talked to him of a little volume, which, altogether unknown to him, was advertised to be published in a few days, under the title of *"Johnsoniana, or Bon Mots of Dr. Johnson."* JOHNSON. "Sir, it is a mighty impudent thing." BOSWELL. "Pray, sir, could you have no redress if you were to prosecute a publisher for ascribing to you dull, stupid nonsense, or making you swear profanely, as many ignorant relaters of your *bon mots* do?" JOHNSON. "No, sir; there will always be some truth mixed with the falsehood, and how can it be ascertained how much is true and how much is false? Besides, sir, what damages would a jury give me for having been represented as swearing?" BOSWELL. "I think, sir, you should at least disavow such a publication, because the world and posterity might say, 'Here is a volume which came out in Dr. Johnson's own time, and, by his silence, was admitted by him to be genuine.'" JOHNSON. "I shall give myself no trouble about the matter."

We landed at the Temple Stairs, where we parted.

I found him in the evening in Mrs. Williams's room. We talked of religious orders. He said, "It is as unreasonable for a man to go into a Carthusian convent for fear of being immoral, as for a man to cut off his hands for fear he should steal. Though it is out of his power to steal, yet he may all his life be a thief in his heart. Their silence, too, is absurd. We read in the Gospel of the apostles being sent to preach, but not to hold their tongues. I said to the Lady Abbess of a convent, 'Madam, you are here, not for the love of virtue, but the fear of vice.'" I thought it hard to give her this view of her situation, when she could not help it; and, indeed, I wondered at the whole of what he now said, because both in his *Rambler* and *Idler* he treats religious austerities[1] with much solemnity of respect.

---

1. *Religious austerities.* "As we walked in the cloisters, there was a solemn echo, while he [Dr. Johnson] talked loudly of a proper retirement from the world. JOHNSON. 'Those who are exceedingly scru-

Finding him still persevering in his abstinence from wine, I ventured to speak to him of it. JOHNSON. "Sir, I have no objection to a man's drinking wine, if he can do it in moderation. Every man is to judge for himself, according to the effects which he experiences. One of the fathers tells us he found fasting made him so peevish that he did not practice it."

Though he often enlarged upon the evil of intoxication, he was by no means harsh to those who indulged in occasional excess in wine. One of his friends, I well remember, too plainly discovered* that he had drunk too much[1] at dinner. When one who loved mischief asked Johnson, a few days afterwards, "Well, sir, what did your friend say to you, as an apology for being in such a situation?" Johnson answered, "Sir, he said all that a man *should* say; he said he was sorry for it."

I again visited him on Monday. He took occasion to enlarge, as he often did, upon the wretchedness of a sea life. "There is, in a jail, better air, better company; and a ship has the additional disadvantage of being in danger. When men come to like a sea life, they are not fit to live on land." "Then," said I, "it would be cruel in a father to breed his son to the sea." JOHNSON. "It would be cruel in a father who thinks as I do. Men go to sea before they know the unhappiness of that way of life; and when they have come to know it, they cannot escape from it."

---

pulous (which I do not approve, for I am no friend to scruples), and find their scrupulosity invincible so that they are quite in the dark, and know not what they shall do—or those who cannot resist temptations and find they make themselves worse by being in the world, without making it better, may retire. I never read of a hermit, but in imagination I kiss his feet; never of a monastery, but I could fall on my knees and kiss the pavement. But I think putting young people there, who know nothing of life, nothing of retirement, is dangerous and wicked.' " *Boswell's Journal of a Tour to the Hebrides.*

1. *He had drunk too much.* No doubt, Boswell himself. "To confess to you at once, Temple, I have, since my last coming to town, been as wild as ever." *Boswell to Temple, April 16, 1768.* "My warm imagination looks forward with great complacency on the sobriety, the healthfulness, and the worth of my future life." *Boswell to Temple, April 26, 1768.*

On Tuesday, March 19, which was fixed for our proposed jaunt, we met in the morning at the Somerset coffee-house in the Strand, where we were taken up by the Oxford coach. He was accompanied by Mr. Gwyn, the architect; and a gentleman of Merton College, whom he did not know, had the fourth seat. We soon got into conversation; for it was very remarkable of Johnson that the presence of a stranger had no restraint upon his talk. I observed that Garrick, who was about to quit the stage, would soon have an easier life. JOHNSON. "I doubt that, sir." BOSWELL. "Why, sir, he will be Atlas with the burthen off his back." JOHNSON. "But I know not, sir, if he will be so steady without his load."

Johnson expressed his disapprobation of ornamental architecture, such as magnificent columns supporting a portico or expensive pilasters supporting merely their own capitals "because it consumes labor, disproportionate to its utility." For the same reason he satirized statuary. "Painting," said he, "consumes labor not disproportionate to its effect; but a fellow will hack half a year at a block of marble to make something in stone that hardly resembles a man. The value of statuary is owing to its difficulty. You would not value the finest head cut upon a carrot."

Gwyn was a fine, lively, rattling, fellow. Dr. Johnson kept him in subjection, but with a kindly authority.[1] The spirit of the artist, however, rose against what he thought a Gothic[2] attack, and he made a brisk defense. "What, sir, you will allow no value to beauty in architecture or in statuary? Why should we allow it then in writing? Why do you take the trouble to give us so many fine allusions, and bright images, and elegant phrases? You might convey all your instruction

---

1. *Kindly authority.* Dr. Johnson had written a dedication for one of his books or pamphlets and had helped him "correct and improve" another. And later, when Gwyn got into difficulties not altogether creditable to his business reputation, Johnson did what he could to rescue him. Some time later in writing to Johnson, Boswell recalls this stage coach journey as the "one when you made so much sport with Gwyn the architect."

2. Barbarian; in hostility to classicism.

without these ornaments." Johnson smiled with complacency, but said, "Why, sir, all these ornaments are useful, because they obtain an easier reception for truth; but a building is not at all more convenient for being decorated with superfluous carved work."

Upon our arrival at Oxford, Dr. Johnson and I went directly to University College, but were disappointed on finding that one of the fellows, his friend, Mr. Scott,[1] who accompanied him from Newcastle to Edinburgh,[2] was gone to the country. We put up at the Angel inn, and passed the evening by ourselves in easy and familiar conversation. Talking of constitutional melancholy, he observed, "A man so afflicted, sir, must divert distressing thoughts, and not combat with them." BOSWELL. "May not he think them down, sir?" JOHNSON. "No, sir. To attempt to *think them down* is madness. He should have a lamp constantly burning in his bed chamber during the night, and if wakefully disturbed, take a book, and read, and compose himself to rest. To have the management of the mind is a great art, and it may be attained in a considerable degree by experience and habitual exercise." BOSWELL. "Should not he provide amusements for himself? Would it not, for instance, be right for him to take a course of chemistry?" JOHNSON. "Let him take a course of chemistry, or a course of rope-dancing, or a course of anything to which he is inclined at the time. Let him contrive to have as many retreats for his mind as he can, as many things to which it can fly from itself. Burton's *Anatomy of Melancholy*[3] is a valuable work. It is, perhaps,

---

1. *Mr. Scott.* Later, the eminent judge, Lord Stowell. One of the few able teachers at Oxford. Called by Boswell, a two-bottle man; like Johnson, slovenly in his dress but like him, also, welcome at many tables for his wit and mental ability. In 1778 elected a member of the Club.

2. *From Newcastle to Edinburgh.* When Johnson was on his way to the Hebrides in 1773.

3. *Anatomy of Melancholy.* "I writ of melancholy by being busy to avoid melancholy. There is no greater cause of melancholy than idleness, no better cure than busy-ness." *Burton: Anatomy of Melancholy.* A charming essay by the famous physician, Dr. Osler, points out some of Burton's good counsel.

overloaded with quotation. But there is a great spirit and great power in what Burton says, when he writes from his own mind."

Next morning we visited Dr. Wetherell, Master of University College, with whom Dr. Johnson conferred on the most advantageous mode of disposing of the books printed at the Clarendon press.[1] I often had occasion to remark Johnson loved business, loved to have his wisdom actually operate on real life. Dr. Wetherell and I talked of him without reserve in his own presence. WETHERELL. "I would have given him a hundred guineas if he would have written a preface to his *Political Tracts*, by way of a Discourse on the British Constitution." BOSWELL. "Dr. Johnson, though in his writings, and upon all occasions, a great friend to the constitution both in church and state, has never written expressly in support of either. There is really a claim upon him for both. He should erect a fort on the confines of each." I could perceive that he was displeased with this dialogue. He burst out, "Why should I be always writing?"

We then went to Pembroke College and waited on his old friend Dr. Adams,[2] the master of it, whom I found to be a most polite, pleasing, communicative man. Dr. Adams had distinguished himself by an able answer to David Hume's *Essay on Miracles*. He told me that he had once dined with Hume in London, that Hume shook hands with him and said, "You have treated me much better than I deserve"; and that they exchanged visits. I took the liberty to object to treating an infidel writer with smooth civility:[3] "If a man firmly believes that religion is an invaluable treasure,[4] he will consider a writer who endeavors

1. *Clarendon Press.* The official press of the University.
2. *Dr. Adams.* "Dr. Adams said to me at Oxford in 1776, 'I was his nominal tutor; but he was above my mark.' When I repeated it to Johnson, his eyes flashed with grateful satisfaction, and he exclaimed, 'That was liberal and noble.' " *Boswell.*
3. *Civility.* "Mr. Johnson and General Oglethorpe one day, . . . and David Hume and some more literati another, dine with me next week. I give admirable dinners and good claret." *Boswell to Temple, 1768.*
4. *Invaluable treasure.* "Belief is favorable to the human mind, were it for nothing else but to furnish it entertainment. An infidel, I should think, must frequently suffer from ennui." *Boswell: Corsica.*

to deprive mankind of it as a *robber;* he will look upon him as *odious,* though the infidel might think himself in the right. I do declare, however, that I am exceedingly unwilling to be provoked to anger, and could I be persuaded that truth would not suffer from a cool moderation in its defenders, I should wish to preserve good humor, at least, in every controversy; nor, indeed, do I see why a man should lose his temper while he does all he can to refute an opponent. I think ridicule may be fairly used against an infidel; for instance, if he be an ugly fellow[1] and yet absurdly vain of his person, we may contrast his appearance with Cicero's beautiful image of virtue, could she be seen." Johnson coincided with me and said, "When a man voluntarily engages in an important controversy, he is to do all he can to lessen his antagonist." ADAMS. "You would not jostle a chimney-sweeper." JOHNSON. "Yes, sir, if it were necessary to jostle him *down.*"

Dr. Adams told us that in some of the Colleges at Oxford the fellows had excluded the students from social intercourse with them in the common room. JOHNSON. "They are in the right, sir; there can be no real conversation, no fair exertion of mind amongst them, if the young men are by; for a man who has a character does not choose to stake it in their presence." BOSWELL. "But, sir, may there not be very good conversation without a contest for superiority?" JOHNSON. "No animated conversation,[2] sir, for it cannot be but one or other will come off superior. His superiority of parts and knowledge will necessarily appear; and he to whom he thus shows himself superior is lessened in the eyes of the young men."

We then went to Trinity College, where he introduced me to

---

1. *Ugly fellow.* Birkbeck Hill suggests that Boswell may have had in mind the skeptic Gibbon, the historian of the *Decline and Fall of the Roman Empire,* "who," says Boswell elsewhere, "is an ugly, affected, disgusting fellow, and poisons our literary club to me." There can be no doubt of Gibbon's vanity.

2. *No animated conversation.* Gibbon, who was admitted to the society of the fellows in 1752, speaks of their dull and deep potations, and asserts that "their conversation stagnated in a round of college business, Tory politics, personal anecdotes, and private scandal," and this when most undergraduates were already excluded from the common room, or public parlor.

Mr. Thomas Warton,[1] with whom we passed a part of the evening. We talked of biography.[2] JOHNSON. "They only who live with a man can write his life with any genuine exactness and discrimination; and few people who have lived with a man know what to remark about him." Biography led us to speak of Dr. John Campbell. Johnson was of opinion that there was not so much in his great work, *A Political Survey[3] of Great Britain* as the world had been taught to expect. He observed of it, "That work was his death." Mr. Warton answered, "I believe so; from the great attention he bestowed on it." JOHNSON. "Nay, sir, he died of want of attention, if he died at all by that book."

Mr. Warton, being engaged, could not sup with us at our inn; we had, therefore, another evening by ourselves. I asked Johnson whether a man's being forward to make himself known to eminent people, and seeing as much of life, and getting as much

---

1. *Warton, Thomas* (1728–1790). The distinguished author of a *History of English Poetry*, in which he reviews somewhat apologetically but very sympathetically the more romantic elements in earlier English verse. He spent many of his leisure hours in trying to save the monuments and relics of the past or in wandering among old churches and ruined castles. It was while accompanying him on one of these excursions in 1754 that Johnson "viewed" the ruined abbeys of Oseney and Rewley "with indignation."

Apparently, Dr. Johnson admired Warton's character and scholarship but not his attempts at romantic verse. "I love the fellow dearly," he once said, "for all I laugh at him," and more than once he apologized over the temporary coolness that a little ridicule had caused between them. In 1778, Warton was elected to the Club, of which two of his former pupils, Beauclerk and Langton, had long been members. It is said that he always delighted in burly society and in shocking the fastidious with his old pipe and rough clothes.

2. *Biography.* Warton wrote biographies of at least two men, dead and gone before he was born. Of one of these books, Sir Horace Walpole writes, "Certainly nothing is ever lost, as you may find in Mr. Warton's *Life of Sir Thomas Pope*, which has resuscitated more nothings and more nobodies than Burch's *Life of Tillotson* or Lowth's *William of Wykeham.*"

3. *A Political Survey of Great Britain.* By the popular preacher mentioned a few pages back. "It teems with projects for the construction of harbors, the opening up of new communications by road and canal, and the introduction of new industries." *Dictionary of National Biography.*

information as he could in every way was not yet lessening himself by his forwardness. JOHNSON. "No, sir, a man always makes himself greater as he increases his knowledge."

Next morning, Thursday, March 21, we set out in a post-chaise to pursue our ramble. We dined at an excellent inn at Chapel House, where [Johnson] expatiated on the felicity of England in its taverns and inns. "There is no private house," said he, "in which people can enjoy themselves so well as at a capital tavern. Let there be ever so much grandeur, ever so much elegance, in the nature of the case it cannot be; there must always be some degree of care and anxiety. The master of the house is anxious to entertain his guests; the guests are anxious to be agreeable to him; and no man, but a very impudent dog, indeed, can as freely command what is in another man's house as if it were his own. Whereas, at a tavern you are sure you are welcome and the more noise you make, the more trouble you give, the more good things you call for, the welcomer you are. No servants will attend you with the alacrity which waiters do, who are incited by the prospect of an immediate reward in proportion as they please. No, sir, there is nothing which has yet been contrived by man by which so much happiness is produced as by a good tavern or inn." He then repeated, with great emotion, Shenstone's lines:

> Whoe'er has traveled life's dull round,
> Where'er his stages may have been,
> May sigh to think he still has found
> The warmest welcome at an inn.

In the afternoon, as we were driven rapidly along in the post-chaise, he said to me, "Life has not many things better than this." We stopped at Stratford-upon-Avon, and drank tea and coffee; and it pleased me to be with him upon the classic ground of Shakespeare's native place.

He mentioned to me the singular history of an ingenious acquaintance. "He had practiced physic in various situations with no great emolument. A West India gentleman, whom he delighted by his conversation, gave him a bond for a handsome annuity during his life, on the condition of his accompanying him to the West Indies, and living with him there for two years. He accordingly embarked with the gentleman; but upon the voyage fell in love with a young woman who happened to be one of the passengers, and married the wench. From the imprudence of his disposition he quarreled with the gentleman, and declared he would have no connection with him. So he forfeited the annuity. He settled as a physician in one of the Leeward Islands. A man was sent out to him merely to compound his medicines. This fellow set up as a rival to him in his practice of physic, and got so much the better of him in the opinion of the people of the island that he carried away all the business, upon which he returned to England, and soon after died."

On Friday, March 22, we arrived at Birmingham about nine o'clock and, after breakfast, went to call on his old school-fellow Mr. Hector.[1] A very stupid maid, who opened the door, told us that her master was gone out; he was gone to the country; she could not tell when he would return. In short, she gave us a miserable reception. Johnson said to her, "My name is Johnson; tell him I called. Will you remember the name?" She answered with rustic simplicity, in the Warwickshire pronunciation, "I don't understand you, sir." "Blockhead," said he, "I'll write." I never heard the word *blockhead* applied to a woman before, though I do not see why it should not, when there is evident occasion for it. He, however, made another attempt to make her understand him, and roared loud in her ear, "*Johnson*," and then she catched the sound.

We next called on Mr. Lloyd, one of the people called Quakers. He too was not at home, but Mrs. Lloyd was, and received us courteously, and asked us to dinner. Johnson said to me, "After the uncertainty of all human things at Hector's, this invitation came very well." We walked about the town, and he was pleased to see it increasing.

Mr. Lloyd joined us in the street; and in a little while we

---

1. *Mr. Hector.* A Birmingham surgeon. "The only companion of my childhood that passed through the school with me." *Johnson.* Sometime after this visit Johnson wrote him, "You and I should now cling to one another; we have outlived most of those who could pretend to rival us in each other's kindness."

met *Friend Hector*, as Mr. Lloyd called him. It gave me pleasure to observe the joy which Johnson and he expressed on seeing each other again. Mr. Lloyd and I left them together, while he obligingly showed me some of the manufactures of this very curious assemblage of artificers. We all met at dinner at Mr. Lloyd's, where we were entertained with great hospitality. Mr. and Mrs. Lloyd had been married the same year with their Majesties, and like them had been blessed with a numerous family of fine children, their numbers being exactly the same. Johnson said, "Marriage is the best state for a man in general; and every man is a worse man in proportion as he is unfit for the married state."

Mr. Hector was so good as to accompany me to see the great works of Mr. Bolton, about two miles from Birmingham. I shall never forget Mr. Bolton's expression to me, "I sell here, sir, what all the world desires to have—POWER." He had about seven hundred people at work. I contemplated him as an *iron chieftain*, and he seemed to be a father to his tribe. One of them came to him, complaining grievously of his landlord for having distrained his goods. "Your landlord is in the right, Smith," said Bolton. "But I'll tell you what: find you a friend who will lay down one-half of your rent, and I'll lay down the other half; and you shall have your goods again."

Dr. Johnson said to me in the morning, "You will see, sir, at Mr. Hector's, his sister, Mrs. Careless, a clergyman's widow. She was the first woman with whom I was in love. It dropped out of my head imperceptibly; but she and I shall always have a kindness for each other." He laughed at the notion that a man can never be really in love but once, and considered it as a mere romantic fancy.

On our return from Mr. Bolton's, Mr. Hector took me to his house, where we found Johnson sitting placidly at tea with his *first love*,[1] who though now advanced in years, was a genteel woman, very agreeable and well bred.

---

1. *With his first love.* In 1781 Johnson writes to Mrs. Thrale: "On Thursday, I went to Birmingham and was told by Hector that I should not be well so soon as I expected. Mrs. Careless took me under her care and told me when I had tea enough."

Johnson lamented to Mr. Hector the state of one of their schoolfellows, Mr. Charles Congreve,[1] a clergyman, which he thus described: "He obtained, I believe, considerable preferment in Ireland, but now lives in London, quite as a valetudinarian, afraid to go into any house but his own. He takes a short airing in his post-chaise every day. He has an elderly woman, whom he calls cousin, who lives with him, and jogs his elbow when his glass has stood too long empty, and encourages him in drinking, in which he is very willing to be encouraged; not that he gets drunk, for he is a very pious man, but he is always muddy. When at my last visit I asked him what o'clock it was, he sprung up to look at his watch, like a greyhound bounding at a hare." When Johnson took leave of Mr. Hector, he said, "Don't grow like Congreve; nor let me grow like him, when you are near me."

When he again talked of Mrs. Careless tonight, he seemed to have had his affection revived; for he said, "If I had married her, it might have been as happy for me." BOSWELL. "Pray, sir, do you not suppose that there are fifty women in the world with any one of whom a man may be as happy as with any one woman in particular?" JOHNSON. "Aye, sir, fifty thousand." BOSWELL. "Then, sir, you are not of opinion with some who imagine that certain men and certain women are made for each other; and that they cannot be happy if they miss their counterparts." JOHNSON. "To be sure not, sir. I believe marriages would in general be as happy, and often more so, if they were all made by the Lord Chancellor, upon a due consideration of the characters and circumstances, without the parties having any choice in the matter."

I wished to have stayed at Birmingham tonight, to have talked more with Mr. Hector; but my friend was impatient to reach his native city; so we drove on that stage in the dark, and were long pensive and silent. When we came within the

---

1. *Mr. Charles Congreve.* "He has the appearance of a man wholly sunk into that sordid self-indulgence which disease, real or imaginary, is apt to dictate. He told me he had forgot whether I was bred at Oxford or at Cambridge. The mind that leaves things so fast behind it ought to have gone forward at no common rate." *Johnson, 1774.*

focus of the Lichfield lamps, "Now," said he, "we are getting out of a state of death." We put up at the Three Crowns, not one of the great inns, but a good old-fashioned one, which was kept by Mr. Wilkins, and was the very next house to that in which Johnson was born and brought up, and which was still his own property. We had a comfortable supper, and got into high spirits. I felt all my Toryism glow in this old capital of Staffordshire. I could have offered incense *genio loci;* and I indulged in libations of that ale which Boniface, in "The Beaux Stratagem,"[1] recommends with such an eloquent jollity.

Next morning he introduced me to Mrs.[2] Lucy Porter, his stepdaughter. She was now an old maid, with much simplicity of manner. She had never been in London. Her brother, a Captain in the navy, had left her a fortune of ten thousand pounds, about a third of which she had laid out in building a stately house and making a handsome garden, in an elevated situation in Lichfield. Johnson, when here by himself, used to live at her house. She reverenced him, and he had a parental tenderness for her.

We then visited Mr. Peter Garrick, who had that morning received a letter from his brother David, announcing our coming to Lichfield. The family likeness of the Garricks was very striking. "Sir," said [Johnson], "I don't know but if Peter had cultivated all the arts of gayety as much as David has done, he might have been as brisk and lively. Depend upon it, sir, vivacity is much an art, and depends greatly on habit." I believe there is a good deal of truth in this, notwithstanding a ludicrous story told me by a lady abroad, of a heavy German baron who had lived much with the young

---

1. *The Beaux Stratagem.* The scene of this play is laid in Lichfield. Boniface—a cant name for an inn-keeper—says of his ale: " 'Tis smooth as oil, sweet as milk, clear as amber, and strong as brandy; and will be just fourteen year old the fifth day of next March, old style."

2. *Mrs.* In the eighteenth century often used with unmarried women of respectable age. "This was to have been my last letter from this place, but Lucy says I must not go this week. Fits of tenderness with Mrs. Lucy are not common, but she seems now to have a little paroxysm, and I was not willing to counteract it." *Johnson to Mrs. Thrale, 1775.*

English at Geneva, and was ambitious to be as lively as they; with which view, he, with assiduous exertion, was jumping over the tables and chairs in his lodgings; and when the people of the house ran in and asked, with surprise, what was the matter, answered, "*Sh' apprens t'etre fif.*"

We dined at our inn, and had with us a Mr. Jackson,[1] one of Johnson's schoolfellows, whom he treated with much kindness, though he seemed to be dull and untaught. He had a coarse gray coat, black waistcoat, greasy leather breeches, and a yellow, uncurled wig; and his countenance had the ruddiness which betokens one who is in no haste to "leave his can." He drank only ale. He had tried to be a cutler at Birmingham, but had not succeeded; and now he lived poorly at home, and had some scheme of dressing leather in a better manner than common; to his indistinct account of which Dr. Johnson listened with patient attention, that he might assist him with his advice.

I saw here, for the first time, *oat ale;* and oat cakes, not hard as in Scotland, but soft like a Yorkshire cake, were served at breakfast. It was pleasant to me to find that "*oats,*"[2] the "*food of horses,*" were so much used as the *food of the people* in Dr. Johnson's own town. He expatiated in praise of Lichfield and its inhabitants, who, he said, were "the most sober, decent people in England, the genteelest in proportion to their wealth, and spoke the purest English." I doubted as to the last article of this eulogy, for they had several provincial sounds; as *there,* pronounced like *fear,* instead of like *fair; once,* pronounced *woonse,* instead of *wunse* or *wonse.* Johnson himself never got entirely free of those provincial accents. Garrick sometimes used to take him off, squeezing a lemon into

---

1. *A Mr. Jackson.* A few weeks before this visit, Johnson had written to Mr. Hector: "I had the other day a letter from Harry Jackson, who says nothing, and yet seems to have something which he wishes to say. He is very poor. I wish something could be done for him."

2. *Oats.* An allusion to Johnson's definition of the term in his dictionary: "A grain which, in England, is generally given to horses, but in Scotland supports the people."

a punch-bowl, with uncouth gesticulations, looking round the company, and calling out, "Who's for *poonsh?*"

Very little business appeared to be going forward in Lichfield. I found, however, two strange manufactures for so inland a place, sail-cloth and streamers for ships; and I observed them making some saddle-cloths, and dressing sheepskins; but upon the whole the busy hand of industry seemed to be quite slackened. "Surely, sir," said I, "you are an idle set of people." "Sir," said Johnson, "we are a city of philosophers; we work with our heads, and make the boobies of Birmingham work for us with their hands."

There was at this time a company of players performing at Lichfield. The manager, Mr. Stanton, sent his compliments, and begged leave to wait on Dr. Johnson. Johnson received him very courteously, and he drank a glass of wine with us. He was a plain, decent, well-behaved man, and expressed his gratitude to Dr. Johnson for having once got him permission from Dr. Taylor at Ashbourne to play there upon moderate terms. Garrick's name was soon introduced. JOHNSON. "Garrick's conversation is gay and grotesque. It is a dish of all sorts, but all good things. There is no solid meat in it; there is a want of sentiment in it." When we were by ourselves, he told me, "Forty years ago, sir, I was in love with an actress here, Mrs. Emmet, who acted Flora, in *Hob in the Well.*" What merit this lady had as an actress, or what was her figure or her manner, I have not been informed; but, if we may believe Mr. Garrick, his old master's taste in theatrical merit was by no means refined; he was not an *elegans formarum spectator.* Garrick used to tell that Johnson said of an actor who played Sir Harry Wildair at Lichfield, "There is a courtly vivacity about the fellow"; when, according to Garrick's account, "he was the most vulgar ruffian that ever went upon *boards.*"

We went and viewed the museum of Mr. Richard Green, apothecary here, who told me he was proud of being a relation of Dr. Johnson's. It was truly a wonderful collection, both of antiquities and natural curiosities, and ingenious works of art. He had all the articles accurately arranged, with their

names upon labels, printed at his own little press; and on
the staircase leading to it was a board, with the names of contributors marked in gold letters. A printed catalogue of the
collection was to be had at a bookseller's. Mr. Green's obliging
alacrity in showing it was very pleasing. His engraved portrait, with which he has favored me, has a motto truly characteristical of his disposition, "*Nemo sibi vivat.*"

A physician being mentioned who had lost his practice
because his whimsically changing his religion had made people
distrustful of him, I maintained that this was unreasonable, as
religion is unconnected with medical skill. JOHNSON. "Sir,
it is not unreasonable, for when people see a man absurd in
what they understand, they may conclude the same of him in
what they do not understand. If a physician were to take to
eating of horse-flesh, nobody would employ him; though one
may eat horse-flesh, and be a very skillful physician. If a man
were educated in an absurd religion, his continuing to profess
it would not hurt him, though his changing to it would."

On Sunday, March 24, we breakfasted with Mrs. Cobb, a
widow lady. She and her niece, Miss Adey, were great admirers of Dr. Johnson; and he behaved to them with a kindness and easy pleasantry, such as we see between old and
intimate acquaintances. We dined at Mr. Peter Garrick's,
who was in a very lively humor. He was today quite a London
narrator, telling us a variety of anecdotes with that earnestness
and attempt at mimicry which we usually find in the wits of
the metropolis. Dr. Johnson went with me to the cathedral
in the afternoon.

I returned to tea and coffee at Mr. Peter Garrick's, and
then found Dr. Johnson at the Reverend Mr. Seward's,[1] Canon
Residentiary, who inhabited the Bishop's palace. Mr. Seward
had, with ecclesiastical hospitality and politeness, asked me
in the morning, merely as a stranger, to dine with him; and

1, *Reverend Mr. Seward.* Forever busy in nursing his imaginary
ailments and buttonholing the great; father of the affected poet, Anna
Seward. Both are good illustrations, or, perhaps, caricatures, of intellectual and esthetic snobs in a provincial town.

in the afternoon, when I was introduced to him, he asked Dr. Johnson and me to spend the evening and sup with him. He was a genteel, well-bred, dignified clergyman and had lived much in the great world.

Mr. Seward mentioned to us the observations which he had made upon the strata of the earth in volcanos, from which it appeared that they were so very different in depth at different periods that no calculation whatever could be made as to the time required for their formation. This fully refuted the anti-mosaical remark introduced into Captain Brydone's entertaining tour,[1] I hope heedlessly, from a kind of vanity which is too common in those who have not sufficiently studied the most important of all subjects. Dr. Johnson, indeed, had said before, independent of this observation, "Shall all the

---

1. *Captain Brydone's entertaining tour.   Tour through Sicily and Malta in a Series of Letters.* Two witty volumes by one interested in manners, customs, and the progress of science. Roman Catholics might take offense at his calling the "blessed Virgin" the "universal legatee and executrix to all the ancient goddesses, celestial, terrestrial, and infernal," but there is only one passage which could give umbrage to such protestants as Johnson: "Near to a vault, which is now thirty feet below ground, and has probably been a burial place, there is a draw-well, where there are several strata of lavas, with earth to a considerable thickness over the surface of each stratum. Recupero has made use of this as an argument to prove the great antiquity of the eruption of his mountain. For if it requires two thousand years or upwards to form but a scanty soil on the surface of a lava, there must have been more than that space of time betwixt each of the eruptions which have formed these strata. But what shall we say of a pit they sunk near to Jaci, of a great depth? They pierced through seven distinct lavas, one under the other, most of them covered with a thick bed of rich earth. 'Now,' says he, 'the eruption which formed the lowest of these lavas, if we may be allowed to reason from analogy, must have flowed from the mountain at least 14,000 years ago.'

"Recupero tells me that Moses hangs like a dead weight upon him, and blunts all his zeal for inquiry; for that really he has not the conscience to make his mountain so young as that prophet makes his world. The bishop, who is strenuously orthodox—for it is an excellent See—has already warned him to be on his guard, and not to pretend to be a better natural historian than Moses; Adieu."

"If Brydone were more attentive to his Bible, he would be a good traveler." *Johnson.*

accumulated evidence of the history of the world—shall the authority of what is unquestionably the most ancient writing, be overturned by an uncertain remark like this?"

On Monday, March 25, we breakfasted at Mrs. Lucy Porter's. While we sat at breakfast, Dr. Johnson received a letter by the post, which seemed to agitate him very much. When he had read it, he exclaimed, "One of the most dreadful things that has happened in my time." The phrase *my time*, like the word *age*, is usually understood to refer to an event of a public or general nature. I imagined something like an assassination of the King—like a gunpowder plot carried into execution—or like another fire of London. When asked, "What is it, sir?" he answered, "Mr. Thrale has lost his only son!"[1] This was, no doubt, a very great affliction to Mr. and Mrs. Thrale; but from the manner in which the intelligence of it was communicated by Johnson, it appeared for the moment to be comparatively small. I, however, soon felt a sincere concern, and was curious to observe how Dr. Johnson would be affected. He said, "This

---

1. *Only son.* Aged ten. He died suddenly before his father's door, who, it is said, never recovered from the blow. In his letters of consolation of March 25th and 30th to Mrs. Thrale, Dr. Johnson wrote: "I have known you, madam, too long to think that you want [lack] any arguments for submission to the Supreme Will; nor can my consolation have any effect but that of showing that I wish to comfort you. What can be done, you must do for yourself. You have brought into the world a rational being, have seen him happy during the little life that has been granted him; and can have no doubt but that his happiness is now permanent and immutable.

"When you have obtained by prayer such tranquillity as nature will admit, force your attention as you can upon your accustomed duties and accustomed entertainments. Only by degrees can the pain of an affliction like yours be abated. But Providence always gives us something to do. Do not indulge your sorrow; try to drive it away by either pleasure or pain; for opposed to what you are feeling, many pains will become pleasures. Remember the great precept, *Be not solitary, be not idle.* That I feel what friendship can feel, I hope I need not tell you. I loved him as I never expect to love any other little boy; but I could not love him as a parent. I know that such a loss is a laceration to the mind. I know that a whole system of hopes, and designs, and expectations, is swept away at once, and nothing left but bottomless vacuity. What you feel I have felt, and hope that your disquiet will be shorter than mine."

is a total extinction to their family, as much as if they were sold into captivity." Upon my mentioning that Mr. Thrale had daughters, who might inherit his wealth: "Daughters," said Johnson, warmly, "he'll no more value his daughters than—" I was going to speak.—"Sir," said he, "don't you know how you yourself think? Sir, he wishes to propagate his name." In short, I saw male succession strong in his mind, even where there was no name, no family of any long standing. I said it was lucky he was not present when this misfortune happened. JOHNSON. "It is lucky for *me*. People in distress never think that you feel enough." BOSWELL. "And, sir, they will have the hope of seeing you, which will be a relief in the meantime; and when you get to them, the pain will be so far abated that they will be capable of being consoled by you, which, in the first violence of it, I believe, would not be the case." JOHNSON. "No, sir; violent pain of mind, like violent pain of body, *must* be severely felt." BOSWELL. "I own, sir, I have not so much feeling for the distress of others as some people have, or pretend to have; but I know this, that I would do all in my power to relieve them." JOHNSON. "Sir, it is affectation to pretend to feel the distress of others as much as they do themselves. It is equally so, as if one should pretend to feel as much pain while a friend's leg is cutting off as he does. No, sir; you have expressed the rational and just nature of sympathy. I would have gone to the extremity of the earth to have preserved this boy." He was soon quite calm. The letter was from Mr. Thrale's clerk, and concluded, "I need not say how much they wish to see you." He said, "We shall hasten back from Taylor's."

Mrs. Aston,[1] whom I had seen the preceding night, and her

---

1. *Mrs. Aston.* A spinster, now 65 years of age, of ancient family, daughter of Sir Thomas Aston. "When she is at home, she lives on the top of Stow Hill and I commonly climb to see her once a day." *Johnson to Mrs. Thrale, 1770.* In 1777, she suffered a stroke of paralysis. Johnson wrote her: "Nothing is, in my opinion, of more mischievous tendency in a state of body like yours than deep meditation or perplexing solitude. Gayety is a duty when health requires it. But while I exhort you, my dearest lady, to merriment, I am very serious myself. If at this distance I can be of any use by consulting physicians or for any other purpose, I hope you will employ me."

sister, Mrs. Gastrel,[1] a widow lady, had each a house and garden and pleasure ground, prettily situated upon Stowhill, a gentle eminence, adjoining to Lichfield. Johnson walked away to dinner there, leaving me by myself, without any apology; I wondered at this want of that facility of manners from which a man has no difficulty in carrying a friend to a house where he is intimate; I felt it very unpleasant to be thus left in solitude in a country town where I was an entire stranger, and began to think myself unkindly deserted; but I was soon convinced that my friend, instead of being deficient in delicacy, had conducted the matter with perfect propriety, for I received the following note in his handwriting: "Mrs. Gastrel, at the lower house on Stowhill, desires Mr. Boswell's company to dinner at two." I was not informed, till afterwards, that Mrs. Gastrel's husband was the clergyman who, while he lived at Stratford-upon-Avon, where he was proprietor of Shakespeare's garden, with Gothic barbarity cut down[2] his mulberry tree, and, as Dr. Johnson told me, did it to vex his neighbors. His lady, I have reason to believe, on the same authority, participated in the guilt of what the enthusiasts of our immortal bard deem almost a species of sacrilege.

---

1. *Mrs. Gastrel.* "A dear good lady." *Johnson.* Dr. Johnson cherished a somewhat romantic memory of their sister, Mrs. Brodie or "Molly Aston," as he called her: "When Mr. Thrale once asked him which had been the happiest period of his past life, he replied, it was that year in which he spent one whole evening with M—y As—n. 'That indeed,' said he, 'was not happiness, it was rapture.' I must add that the evening was not passed *tête-à-tête*, but in a select company . . . 'Molly,' says Dr. Johnson, 'was a beauty, and a scholar, and a wit, and a Whig; and she talked all in praise of liberty; and so I made this epigram upon her. She was the loveliest creature I ever saw!!!

> *Liber ut esse velim, suasisti pulchra Maria,*
> *Ut maneam liber—pulchra Maria Vale!'*

'Will it do this way in English,' said I?

> 'Persuasions to freedom fall oddly from you;
> If freedom we seek—fair Maria, adieu.' " *Mrs. Thrale.*

2. *Cut down.* In 1756, to avoid being plagued by sight-seers. In 1759, during a heated quarrel over taxes with the town authorities, he tore down the house in which Shakespeare had died. His memory is therefore not savory in Stratford.

After dinner Dr. Johnson wrote a letter to Mrs. Thrale, on the death of her son. I said it would be very distressing to Thrale, but she would soon forget it, as she had so many things to think of. JOHNSON. "No, sir, Thrale will forget it first. *She* has many things that she *may* think of. *He* has many things that he *must* think of."

In the evening we went to the Town Hall, which was converted into a temporary theater, and saw *Theodosius*, with "The Stratford Jubilee." I was happy to see Dr. Johnson sitting in a conspicuous part of the pit, and receiving affectionate homage from all his acquaintance. We were quite gay and merry. I afterwards mentioned to him that I condemned myself for being so, when poor Mr. and Mrs. Thrale were in such distress. JOHNSON. "You are wrong, sir; twenty years hence Mr. and Mrs. Thrale will not suffer much pain from the death of their son. Now, sir, you are to consider that distance of place, as well as distance of time, operates upon the human feelings. I would not have you be gay in the presence of the distressed because it would shock them, but you may be gay at a distance. Pain for the loss of a friend, or of a relation whom we love, is occasioned by the want which we feel. In time the vacuity is filled with something else; or sometimes the vacuity closes up of itself."

On Tuesday, March 26, there came for us Dr. Taylor's[1] large,

---

1. *Dr. Taylor.* In 1763, Dr. Taylor's disagreements with his wife had been so acute as to call for the following sympathetic comments from Dr. Johnson:

"Your low spirits have given you bad counsel. You shall not give your wife, nor your wife's friends, the triumph of driving you out of life. If you betray yourself who can support you?"

"Do not let this vexation take possession of your thoughts, or sink too deeply into your heart. The happiness of conjugal life cannot be secured either by sense or by virtue, and therefore its miseries may be numbered among those evils which we cannot prevent and must only labor to endure with patience and palliate with judgment. You inquire what the fugitive Lady has in her power. She has, I think, nothing in her power but to return home and mend her behavior. Nature has given women so much power that the law has very wisely given them little. Your first care must be to procure to yourself such diversions as may preserve you from melancholy and depression of mind, which is a greater evil than a disobedient wife."

roomy post-chaise, drawn by four stout, plump horses, and driven by two steady, jolly postillions, which conveyed us to Ashbourne, where I found my friend's schoolfellow living upon an establishment perfectly corresponding with his substantial creditable equipage; his house, garden, pleasure grounds, table, in short everything good, and no scantiness appearing. Dr. Taylor had a good estate of his own, and good preferment in the church. He was a diligent justice of the peace, and presided over the town of Ashbourne, to the inhabitants of which I was told he was very liberal; he had the preceding winter distributed two hundred pounds among such of them as stood in need of his assistance. He had consequently a considerable political interest in the county of Derby, which he employed to support the Devonshire family; for though the schoolfellow and friend of Johnson, he was a Whig. I could not perceive in his character much congeniality of any sort with that of Johnson, who, however, said to me, "Sir, he has a very strong understanding." His size, and figure, and countenance, and manner were that of a hearty English squire, with the parson superinduced; and I took particular notice of his upper-servant, Mr. Peters, a decent, grave man, in purple clothes, and a large white wig, like the butler or *major domo* of a bishop.

Dr. Johnson and Dr. Taylor met with great cordiality; and Johnson soon gave him the same sad account of their schoolfellow, Congreve, that he had given to Mr. Hector, adding: "There is nothing against which an old man should be so much upon his guard as putting himself to nurse." Innumerable have been the melancholy instances of men once distinguished for firmness, resolution, and spirit, who in their latter days have been governed like children, by interested female artifice.

Dr. Taylor commended a physician who was known to him and Dr. Johnson, and said, "I fight many battles for him, as many people in the country dislike him." JOHNSON. "But you should consider, sir, that by every one of your victories he is a loser; for every man of whom you get the better will be very angry, and resolve not to employ him; whereas if people get the better of you in argument about him, they'll think 'We'll send for Dr —— nevertheless.'"

Next day, as Dr. Johnson had acquainted Dr. Taylor of the reason for his returning speedily to London, it was resolved that we should set out after dinner. A few of Dr. Taylor's neighbors were his guests that day.

Dr. Johnson talked with approbation of one who had attained to the state of the philosophical wise man, that is, to have no want of anything. "Then, sir," said I, "the savage is a wise man." "Sir," said he, "I do not mean simply being without —but not having a want." I maintained, against this proposition, that it was better to have fine clothes, for instance, than not to feel the want of them. JOHNSON. "No, sir; fine clothes are good only as they supply the want of other means of procuring respect. Was Charles the Twelfth, think you, less respected for his coarse blue coat and black stock? And you find the King of Prussia dresses plain because the dignity of his character is sufficient." I here brought myself into a scrape, for I heedlessly said, "Would not *you*, sir, be the better for velvet and embroidery?" JOHNSON. "Sir, you put an end to all argument when you introduce your opponent himself. Have you no better manners? There is *your want*." I apologized by saying I had mentioned him as an instance of one who wanted as little as any man in the world, and yet, perhaps, might receive some additional luster from dress.

Having left Ashbourne in the evening, we stopped to change horses at Derby, and availed ourselves of a moment to enjoy the conversation of my countryman, Dr. Butter,[1] then physician there. He was in great indignation because Lord Mountstuart's[2] bill for a Scotch militia had been lost. Dr. Johnson was as violent against it. "I am glad," said he, "that Parliament has had the spirit to throw it out. You wanted to take advantage

---

1. *Dr. Butter*. Dr. Johnson spent a "placid" day with him in 1781. He was one of the four physicians who attended Dr. Johnson, without fee, in his last illness.

2. *Lord Mountstuart*. The eldest son of Lord Bute, whose brief term of office as prime-minister in the early sixties had aroused an intense prejudice against himself, his king, and his Scotch countrymen. Lord Mountstuart's bill was a plan for supporting a Scotch militia out of the general British land tax, most of which fell on England, instead of by special Scotch taxation.

of the timidity of our scoundrels"; (meaning, I suppose, the ministry). It may be observed that he used the epithet scoundrel very commonly, not quite in the sense in which it is generally understood, but as a strong term of disapprobation; as when he abruptly answered Mrs. Thrale, who had asked him how he did, "Ready to become a scoundrel, madam; with a little more spoiling you will, I think, make me a complete rascal";—he meant, easy to become a capricious and self-indulgent valetudinarian, a character for which I have heard him express great disgust. We lay this night at Loughborough.

On Thursday, March 28, we pursued our journey. I mentioned that old Mr. Sheridan[1] complained of the ingratitude of Mr. Wedderburne,[2] and General Fraser,[3] who had been much obliged to him when they were young Scotchmen entering upon life in England. JOHNSON. "Why, sir, a man is very apt to complain of the ingratitude of those who have risen far above him. A man when he gets into a higher sphere, into other habits of life, cannot keep up all his former connections. Then, sir, those who knew him formerly upon a level with themselves may think they ought still to be treated as on a level, which cannot be; and an acquaintance in a former situation may bring out things which it would be very disagreeable to have mentioned before higher company, though perhaps, everybody knows of them."

I mentioned a common remark, that a man may be, upon the

---

1. *Old Mr. Sheridan.* The actor, author, and elocutionist whom Boswell has already mentioned (see the year 1763). There is some reason for believing that his abilities were not properly appreciated, which may account for the undoubted fact that he became a peevish and unreasonable man. His merits, Dr. Johnson says, were obscured by "vanity and Quixotism."

2. *Mr. Wedderburne*, Lord Loughborough. The notorious turncoat already mentioned in relation to Johnson's pension. Sheridan, it is reported, had helped him rid his speech of its Scotticisms, and no doubt, was paid for it.

3. *General Fraser.* Son of the famous Highlander, the twelfth Lord Lovat, who was executed in 1747 for engaging in a Jacobite conspiracy and rebellion. Fraser's character has been described as "hard and rapacious, under a polished exterior." Sheridan may have supplied the polish, at the usual rates.

whole, richer by marrying a woman with a very small portion, because a woman of fortune will be proportionally expensive. JOHNSON. "Depend upon it, sir, this is not true. A woman of fortune being used to the handling of money spends it judiciously, but a woman who gets the command of money for the first time upon her marriage has such a gust in spending it that she throws it away with great profusion."

He praised the ladies of the present age, insisting that they were more virtuous in every respect than in former times, because their understandings were better cultivated. It was an undoubted proof of his good sense and good disposition that he was never querulous,[1] never prone to inveigh against the present times, as is so common when superficial minds are on the fret. On the contrary, he was willing to speak favorably of his own age; and, indeed, maintained its superiority in every respect, except in its reverence for government.

Having lain at St. Alban's, on Thursday, March 28, we breakfasted the next morning at Barnet. I expressed to him a weakness of mind which I could not help; an uneasy apprehension that my wife and children, who were at a great distance from me, might, perhaps, be ill. "Sir," said he, "consider how foolish[2] you would think it in *them* to be apprehensive that *you* are ill." This sudden turn relieved me for the moment; but I afterwards perceived it to be an ingenious fallacy.

I enjoyed the luxury of our approach to London, that metropolis which we both loved so much for the high and varied intellectual pleasure which it furnishes. I experienced immediate happiness while whirled along with such a companion, and said to him, "Sir, you observed one day at General Oglethorpe's that a man is never happy for the present, but when he is drunk. Will you not add—or when driving rapidly in a post-chaise?" JOHNSON. "No, sir, you are driving rapidly *from* something, or *to* something."

We stopped at Messieurs Dillys, booksellers in the Poultry;

---

1. *Never querulous.* But see page 466.
2. *How foolish.* "Yet it is strange I hear nothing from you; I hope you are not angry or sick." *Johnson to Mrs. Thrale, May 16, 1776.*

from whence he hurried away, in a hackney coach, to Mr. Thrale's in the Borough. I called at his house in the evening, having promised to acquaint Mrs. Williams of his safe return; when, to my surprise, I found him sitting with her at tea, and, as I thought, not in a very good humor; for, it seems, when he had got to Mr. Thrale's, he found the coach was at the door waiting to carry Mrs. and Miss Thrale and Signor Baretti, their Italian master, to Bath. This was not showing the attention which might have been expected to the "Guide, Philosopher, and Friend," who had hastened from the country to console a distressed mother, who he understood was very anxious for his return. They had, I found, without ceremony, proceeded on their intended journey.

On Monday, March 31, I called on him, and showed him, as a curiosity which I had discovered, his *Translation of Lobo's Account of Abyssinia*, which Sir John Pringle had lent me, it being then little known as one of his works. He said, "Take no notice of it," or "Don't talk of it." He seemed to think it beneath him, though done at six-and-twenty. I said to him, "Your style, sir, is much improved since you translated this." He answered with a sort of triumphant smile, "Sir, I hope it is."

On Wednesday, April 3, in the morning I found him very busy putting his books in order, and as they were generally very old ones, clouds of dust were flying around him. He had on a pair of large gloves such as hedgers use. His present appearance put me in mind of my uncle, Dr. Boswell's description of him, "A robust genius, born to grapple with whole libraries."

I gave him an account of a conversation which had passed between me and Captain Cook,[1] the day before, at dinner at Sir John Pringle's;[2] and he was much pleased with the conscientious accuracy of that celebrated circumnavigator, who set me right as to many of the exaggerated accounts given by Dr. Hawkes-

---

1. *Captain Cook.* Who had surveyed the St. Lawrence, the coast of Newfoundland and Nova Scotia, had charted New Zealand, and the East Coast of Australia, crossed the Antarctic Circle, and explored the Pacific. The interest excited by his discoveries greatly increased the romantic notions of the time about the South Seas.

2. *Sir John Pringle.* President of the leading scientific body in Great Britain, the Royal Society.

worth[1] of his voyages. I told him that while I was with the Captain I catched the enthusiasm of curiosity and adventure, and felt a strong inclination to go with him on his next voyage. JOHNSON. "Why, sir, a man *does* feel so, till he considers how very little he can learn from such voyages." BOSWELL. "But one is carried away with the general grand and indistinct notion of A VOYAGE ROUND THE WORLD." JOHNSON. "Yes, sir, but a man is to guard himself against taking a thing in general." I said I was certain that a great part of what we are told by the travelers to the South Sea must be conjecture, because they had not enough of the language of those countries to understand so much as they have related. Objects falling under the observation of the senses might be clearly known; but everything intellectual, everything abstract—politics, morals, and religion, must be darkly guessed. Dr. Johnson was of the same opinion. He upon another occasion, when a friend mentioned to him several extraordinary facts, as communicated to him by the circumnavigators, slyly observed, "Sir, I never before knew how much I was respected by these gentlemen; they told *me* none of these things."[2]

---

1. *Hawkesworth.* A hack-writer, accused of being vain and inconsequential. Known to Johnson at least since 1752. The disapproval which greeted his three-volume compilation of other men's "Voyages" was due in part to his courageous refusal to attribute "critical escapes from danger" to the "particular interposition of providence."

2. *They told me none of these things.* "[Johnson] is not contented with believing the Bible, but he fairly resolves, I think, to believe nothing but the Bible." *Hogarth, quoted by Mrs. Piozzi.*

"We were shown in a corner of this vault, a hole into which Col said greater criminals used to be put. It was now filled up with rubbish of different kinds. He said it was of a great depth. 'Aye,' said Dr. Johnson, smiling, all such places, that *are filled up,* were of a *great depth.*'" *Boswell: Journal of a Tour to the Hebrides.*

"The traditions of an ignorant and savage people have been for ages negligently heard and unskillfully related. Distant events must have been mingled together, and the actions of one man given to another. These, however, are deficiencies in story for which no man is now to be censured. It were enough if what there is yet opportunity of examining were accurately inspected and justly represented; but such is the laxity of Highland conversation that the inquirer is kept in continual suspense, and, by a kind of intellectual retrogradation, knows less as he hears more." *Johnson: A Journey to the Western Islands of Scotland.*

We agreed to dine today at the Mitre tavern. I brought with me Mr. Murray, Solicitor-General of Scotland. Mr. Murray praised the ancient philosophers for the candor[1] and good humor with which those of different sects disputed with each other. JOHNSON. "Sir, they disputed with good humor because they were not in earnest as to religion. Had the ancients been serious in their belief, we should not have had their gods exhibited in the manner we find them represented in the poets. The people would not have suffered it. They disputed with good humor upon their fanciful theories because they were not interested in the truth of them; when a man has nothing to lose, he may be in good humor with his opponent. Every man who attacks my belief diminishes in some degree my confidence in it, and therefore makes me uneasy; and I am angry with him who makes me uneasy." MURRAY. "It seems to me that we are not angry at a man for controverting an opinion which we believe and value; we rather pity him." JOHNSON. "Why, sir, if a madman were to come into this room with a stick in his hand, no doubt we should pity the state of his mind, but our primary consideration would be to take care of ourselves. We should knock him down first, and pity him afterwards. No, sir, every man will dispute with great good humor upon a subject in which he is not interested. I will dispute very calmly upon the probability of another man's son being hanged; but if a man zealously enforces the probability that my own son will be hanged, I shall certainly not be in a very good humor with him." MURRAY. "But, sir, truth will always bear an examination." JOHNSON. "Yes, sir, but it is painful to be forced to defend it. Consider, sir, how should you like, though conscious of your innocence, to be tried before a jury for a capital crime once a week."

I mentioned Mr. Maclaurin's uneasiness on account of a degree of ridicule carelessly thrown on his deceased father in Goldsmith's *History of Animated Nature*, in which that celebrated mathematician is represented as being subject to fits of yawning so violent as to render him incapable of proceeding in his lecture; a story altogether unfounded, but for the publication of which

---

1. *Candor.* Amiability.

the law would give no reparation. This led us to agitate the question whether legal redress could be obtained, even when a man's deceased relation was calumniated in a publication. Mr. Murray maintained there should be reparation unless the author could justify himself by proving the fact. JOHNSON. "Sir, it is of so much more consequence that truth should be told[1] than that individuals should not be made uneasy that it is much better that the law does not restrain writing freely concerning the characters of the dead. Damages will be given to a man who is calumniated in his lifetime, because he may be hurt in his worldly interest, or at least hurt in his mind; but the law does not regard that uneasiness which a man feels on having his ancestor calumniated. That is too nice. Let him deny what is said, and let the matter have a fair chance by discussion. But if a man could say nothing against a character but what he can prove, history could not be written; for a great deal is known of men of which proof cannot be brought."

On Thursday, April 4, having called on Dr. Johnson, I said it was a pity that truth was not so firm as to bid defiance to all attacks, so that it might be shot at as much as people chose to attempt, and yet remain unhurt. JOHNSON. "Then, sir, it would not be shot at."

On Friday, April 5, being Good Friday, after having attended the morning service at St. Clement's church, I walked home with Johnson. Mr. Thrale called upon him, and appeared to bear the loss of his son with a manly composure. There was no affectation about him; and he talked, as usual, upon indifferent subjects. He seemed to me to hesitate as to the Italian tour, on which, I flattered myself, he and Mrs. Thrale and Dr. Johnson were soon to set out; and therefore I pressed it as much as I could. JOHNSON. "We must, to be sure, see Rome, Naples, Florence, and Venice, and as much more as we can (speaking with a tone of great animation)."

---

1. *Truth should be told.* "There are many who think it an act of piety to hide the faults or failings of their friends, even when they can no longer suffer by their detection. If we owe regard to the memory of the dead, there is yet more respect to be paid to knowledge, to virtue, and to truth." *Johnson: The Rambler.*

When I expressed an earnest wish for his remarks on Italy, he said, "I do not see that I could make a book upon Italy; yet I should be glad to get two hundred pounds, or five hundred pounds by such a work." This showed that he adhered to that strange opinion which his indolent disposition made him utter: "No man but a blockhead ever wrote, except for money."

"I lately," said he, "received a letter from the East Indies, from a gentleman whom I formerly knew very well; he had returned from that country with a handsome fortune, as it was reckoned before means were found to acquire those immense sums which have been brought from thence of late; he was a scholar and an agreeable man, and lived very prettily in London, till his wife died. After her death he took to dissipation and gaming, and lost all he had. One evening he lost a thousand pounds to a gentleman whose name I am sorry I have forgotten. Next morning he sent the gentleman five hundred pounds, with an apology that it was all he had in the world. The gentleman sent the money back to him, declaring he would not accept of it; and adding that if Mr.—— had occasion for five hundred pounds more, he would lend it to him. He resolved to go out again to the East Indies, and make his fortune anew. He got a considerable appointment, and I had some intention of accompanying him. Had I thought then as I do now, I should have gone."

I have frequently thought that if [Johnson] had made out what the French call *un catalogue raisonné* of all the people who had passed under his observation, it would have afforded a very rich fund of instruction and entertainment. The suddenness with which his accounts of some of them started out in conversation was surprising. I remember he once observed to me, "It is wonderful, sir, what is to be found in London. The most literary conversation I ever enjoyed was at the table of Jack Ellis,[1] a money-scrivener behind the Royal Exchange, with whom

---

1. *Ellis.* Boswell saw him in his ninety-third year and "found his judgment distinct and clear, and his memory, though faded, yet able to serve him very well, after a little recollection. It was agreeable to observe that he was free from the discontent and fretfulness which too often molest old age."

I at one period used to dine generally once a week." Volumes
would be required to contain a list of his numerous and various
acquaintance, none of whom he ever forgot. He was at once
the companion of the brilliant Colonel Forrester[1] of the Guards,
who wrote *The Polite Philosopher*, and of the awkward and
uncouth Robert Levet; of Lord Thurlow,[2] and Mr. Sastres,[3] the
Italian master; and has dined one day with the beautiful, gay,
and fascinating Lady Craven,[4] and the next with good Mrs.
Gardiner, the tallow-chandler, on Snowhill.

On my expressing my wonder at his discovering* so much of
the knowledge peculiar to different professions, he told me, "I
learned what I know of law chiefly from Mr. Ballow,[5] a very

1. *Colonel Forrester.* A fop, so glittering in powder and lace that,
according to one anonymous contemporary, when he ventured to travel
into the country,

> "Each sylvan god, each rival power
> Peeped out to see the raree-show."

His *Polite Philosopher* was a suave little essay, written partly in prose
and partly in verse, to

> ". . . show how easy 'tis to be polite."

2. *Lord Thurlow.* Noted for his subserviency to the Crown, his
bullying support of the National Church, his profanity, his coarseness,
his thorough-going advocacy of illiberal views, and the vigorous interest he sometimes displayed in matters of pure scholarship. "No man
ever was so wise as Lord Thurlow looks." *Charles James Fox.*

3. *Sastres.* He taught the Thrale children Italian. In 1784, Johnson, sick in Lichfield, begs him to write frequent letters: "You may
always have something to tell. You live among the various orders of
mankind, and may make a letter from the exploits, sometimes of the
philosopher and sometimes of the pickpocket."

4. *Lady Craven.* Now, 26 years of age. "There is such an integrity
and frankness in her consciousness of her own beauty and talents that
she speaks of them with a naïveté as if she had no property in them,
but only wore them as the gift of the gods." *Sir Horace Walpole, 1780.*
"She has, I fear, been *infinitamente* indiscreet, but what is that to you or
me; she is very pretty, has parts, and is good natured to the greatest
degree." *Walpole, 1785.* "Lady Craven received the news of her
Lord's death on a Friday, went into weeds on Saturday, and into white
satin and *many* diamonds on Sunday, and in that vestal trim was married
to the Margrave of Anspach by my cousin's chaplain." *Walpole, 1791.*

5. *Ballow.* A lawyer, relieved of practice by a position in the
Exchequer office. Said to be a little deformed man of deep and extensive
learning but of vulgar manners and a splenetic temper. " 'Doctor,'

able man.   I learned some too from Chambers;[1] but was not so teachable then.   One is not willing to be taught by a young man."   When I expressed a wish to know more about Mr. Ballow, Johnson said, "Sir, I have seen him but once these twenty years.   The tide of life has driven us different ways."

"My knowledge of physic," he added, "I learned from Dr. James,[2] whom I helped in writing the proposals for his *Dictionary*, and also a little in the *Dictionary* itself.   I also learned from Dr. Lawrence,[3] but was then grown more stubborn."

said Ballow [to Akenside the physician], 'after all you have said, my opinion of the profession of physic is this: The ancients endeavored to make it a science, and failed; and the moderns to make it a trade, and have succeeded.' "   *Sir John Hawkins.*

1.   *Chambers.* Sir Robert Chambers, twenty-eight years Johnson's junior, whom he first met in 1766.   In 1776, he was drawing eight thousand pounds a year as a judge in India.

2.   *Dr. James.* In 1743 he published a medical dictionary in three volumes folio—a decidedly creditable performance.   Later, he concocted what he called *James's Powders*, which he patented fraudulently and puffed outrageously.   Johnson refused to drop him.

3.   *Dr. Lawrence.* "He was a man of strict piety and profound learning, but little skilled in the knowledge of life or manners, and died without having ever enjoyed the reputation he so justly deserved."   *Mrs. Thrale.* He was Dr. Johnson's physician in all serious cases until his own death in 1783.   "The conversation I saw them hold together in Essex Street one day in 1781 or 1782 was a melancholy one.   Johnson was panting under an asthma and dropsy.   Lawrence had been brought home that very morning struck with the palsy, from which he had two hours before we came, strove to awaken himself by blisters; they were both deaf and scarce able to speak besides.   To give and receive medical counsel, therefore, they fairly sat down on each side a table in the doctor's gloomy apartment and agreed to write Latin billets to each other."   *Mrs. Thrale.*

"This sorry foot, and this sorry Dr. Lawrence, who says it is the gout; but then he thinks everything the gout."   *Johnson, 1775.*   "I found it now time to do something, and went to Dr. Lawrence, and told him I would do what he should order, without reading the prescription."   *Johnson, 1777.*   "Two days ago, Dr. Lawrence ordered a new medicine, which I think to try tonight, but my hopes are not high.   I mean to try, however, and not languish without resistance."   *Johnson, 1778.*   "I have begun to take valerian . . . Dr. Lawrence talked of a decoction, but I say, all or nothing."   *Johnson, 1778.*   "I have done exactly as Dr. Lawrence ordered, and am much better at the expense of about thirty-six ounces of blood.   Nothing in the world!   For a good cause I have six and thirty more."   *Johnson, 1779.*

I mentioned a new gaming-club, of which Mr. Beauclerk had given me an account, where the members played to a desperate extent. JOHNSON. "Depend upon it, sir, this is mere talk. *Who* is ruined by gaming? You will not find six instances in an age. There is a strange rout made about deep play; whereas you have many more people ruined by adventurous trade, and yet we do not hear such an outcry against it." THRALE. "There may be few people absolutely ruined by deep play, but very many are much hurt in their circumstances by it." JOHNSON. "Yes, sir, and so are very many by other kinds of expense." I had heard him talk once before in the same manner, and at Oxford he said he wished he had learned to play at cards. The truth, however, is that he would sometimes in conversation maintain opinions which he was sensible were wrong, but in supporting which, his reasoning and wit would be most conspicuous. He would begin thus: "Why, sir, as to the good or evil of card-playing—"[1] "Now," said Garrick, "he is thinking which side he shall take." Lord Elibank once observed to me, "Whatever opinion Johnson maintains, I will not say that he convinces me; but he never fails to show me that he has good reasons for it." I have heard Johnson pay his Lordship this high compliment:

"I never was in Lord Elibank's company without learning something."

We sat together till it was too late for the afternoon service. Thrale said he had come with intention to go to church with us. We went at seven to evening prayers at St. Clement's church, after having drunk coffee; an indulgence which I un-

---

1. *As to the good or evil of card-playing.* See Introduction. "It is scarcely possible to pass an hour in honest conversation, without being able, when we rise from it, to please ourselves with having given or received some advantages; but a man may shuffle cards or rattle dice, from noon to midnight, without tracing any new idea in his mind or being able to recollect the day by any other token than his gain or loss, and a confused remembrance of agitated passions and clamorous altercations." *Johnson: Rambler, 1750.* "I am sorry I have not learnt to play at cards. It is very useful in life; it generates kindness and consolidates society." *Johnson (1773) in Boswell's Journal of a Tour to the Hebrides.*

derstood Johnson yielded to on this occasion in compliment to Thrale.

On Sunday, April 7, Easter day, after having been at St. Paul's cathedral, I came to Dr. Johnson, according to my usual custom. It seemed to me that there was always something peculiarly mild and placid in his manner upon this holy festival.

Mr. Macbean, author of the *Dictionary of Ancient Geography*, came in. This gentleman, Mrs. Williams, and Mr. Levet dined with us. Dr. Johnson made a remark which both Mr. Macbean and I thought new. It was this: that "the law against usury is for the protection of creditors as well as debtors; for if there were no such check, people would be apt, from the temptation of great interest, to lend to desperate persons, by whom they would lose their money."

Mrs. Williams was very peevish, and I wondered at Johnson's patience with her. The truth is that his consideration of the forlorn and indigent state in which this lady was left by her father induced him to treat her with the utmost tenderness, and even to be desirous of procuring her amusement, so as sometimes to incommode many of his friends, by carrying her with him to their houses, where, from her manner of eating, in consequence of her blindness,[1] she could not but offend the delicacy of persons of nice sensations.

After coffee we went to afternoon service in St. Clement's church. Observing some beggars in the street as we walked along, I said to him, I supposed there was no civilized country in the world where the misery of want in the lowest classes of the people was prevented. JOHNSON. "I believe, sir, there is not; but it is better that some should be unhappy than that none should be happy, which would be the case in a general state of equality."

When the service was ended, I went home with him, and we sat quietly by ourselves. Upon the question whether a man

---

1. *Her blindness.* "Upon remarking one day her facility in moving about the house, searching into drawers, and finding books, without the help of sight, 'Believe me,' said she, 'persons who cannot do these common offices without sight did but little while they enjoyed that blessing.'" *Lady Knight.*

who had been guilty of vicious actions would do well to force himself into solitude and sadness: JOHNSON. "No, sir, unless it prevent him from being vicious again. With some people gloomy penitence is only madness turned upside down. A man may be gloomy, till, in order to be relieved from gloom, he has recourse again to criminal indulgencies."

On Wednesday, April 10, I dined with him at Mr. Thrale's, where were Mr. Murphy and some other company. Before dinner Dr. Johnson and I passed some time by ourselves. I was sorry to find it was now resolved that the proposed journey to Italy[1] should not take place this year. I suggested that going to Italy might have done Mr. and Mrs. Thrale good. JOHNSON. "I rather believe not, sir. While grief is fresh, every attempt to divert only irritates. You must wait till grief be *digested*, and then amusement will dissipate the remains of it."

On Thursday, April 11, I dined with him at General Paoli's, in whose house I now resided, and where I had ever afterwards the honor of being entertained with the kindest attention as his constant guest while I was in London, till I had a house of my own there. I mentioned my having that morning introduced to Mr. Garrick, Count Neni, a Flemish nobleman of great rank and fortune, to whom Garrick talked of Abel Drugger[2] as *a small part;* and related with pleasant vanity that a Frenchman who had seen him in one of his low characters exclaimed, "*Comment! je ne le crois pas. Ce n'est pas Monsieur Garrick, ce Grand Homme!*" Garrick added, with an appearance of grave recollection, "If I were to begin life again, I think I should not play those low characters." Upon which I observed, "Sir, you would be in the wrong; for your great excellence is your variety of playing, your representing so well, characters so very different." JOHNSON. "Garrick, sir, was not in earnest in what he said; for, to be sure, his peculiar excellence is his variety; and, perhaps, there is not any one character which has not been as well acted by somebody else as he could do it." BOSWELL. "Why then, sir, did he talk

---

1. *Italy.* For Johnson's wish to visit it, see also June 28, 1784.

2. *Abel Drugger.* A gullible little tobacconist who plays a very minor part in Ben Jonson's *Alchemist.*

so?" JOHNSON. "Why, sir, to make you answer as you did."
BOSWELL. "I don't know, sir; he seemed to dip deep into his
mind for the reflection." JOHNSON. "He had not far to dip,
sir; he said the same thing, probably, twenty times before."

Of a nobleman raised at a very early period to high office, he
said, "His parts, sir, are pretty well for a lord; but would not
be distinguished in a man who had nothing else but his parts."

A journey to Italy was still in his thoughts. He said, "A man
who has not been in Italy is always conscious of an inferiority,
from his not having seen what it is expected a man should see.
The grand object of traveling is to see the shores of the Mediterranean. All our religion, almost all our law, almost all our
arts, almost all that sets us above savages, has come to us from
the shores of the Mediterranean." The General observed that
" 'The Mediterranean' would be a noble subject for a poem."

"Goldsmith," [Johnson] said, "referred everything to vanity;
his virtues, and his vices too were from that motive. He was
not a social man. He never exchanged mind with you."

We spent the evening at Mr. Hoole's. Mr. Mickle, the excellent translator of *The Lusiad*, was there. I have preserved
little of the conversation of this evening. Dr. Johnson said,
"Thomson had a true poetical genius, the power of viewing
everything in a poetical light. His fault is such a cloud of words
sometimes that the sense can hardly peep through. Shiels,
who compiled *Cibber's Lives of the Poets*,[1] was one day sitting
with me. I took down Thomson, and read aloud a large portion
of him, and then asked, 'Is not this fine?' Shiels having expressed the highest admiration, 'Well, sir,' said I, 'I have omitted
every other line.' "

I related a dispute between Goldsmith and Mr. Robert
Dodsley, one day when they and I were dining at Tom Davies's,
in 1762. Goldsmith asserted that there was no poetry produced
in this age. Dodsley appealed to his own *Collection*,[2] and main-

---

1. *Cibber's Lives of the Poets*. Attributed to the son of Colley Cibber
on the title-page; but claimed by Johnson's old amanuensis Robert
Shiels. The dispute stirred up bitter controversy, which was never
satisfactorily settled.
2. *Collection*. "*Poems by Several Hands in Six Vols.*"

tained that though you could not find a palace like Dryden's "Ode on St. Cecilia's Day," you had villages composed of very pretty houses; and he mentioned particularly "The Spleen." JOHNSON. "I think Dodsley gave up the question. He and Goldsmith said the same thing; only he said it in a softer manner than Goldsmith did, for he acknowledged that there was no poetry, nothing that towered above the common mark. You may find wit and humor in verse, and yet no poetry. 'Hudibras'[1] has a profusion of these, yet it is not to be reckoned a poem. 'The Spleen',[2] in Dodsley's collection, on which you say he chiefly rested, is not poetry." BOSWELL. "Does not Gray's poetry, sir, tower above the common mark?" JOHNSON. "Yes, sir; but we must attend to the difference between what men in general cannot do if they would, and what every man may do if he would. Sixteen-string Jack[3] towered above the common mark." BOSWELL. "Then, sir, what is poetry?" JOHNSON. "Why, sir, it is much easier to say what it is not. We all *know* what light is, but it is not easy to *tell* what it is."

On Friday, April 12, I dined with him at our friend Tom Davies's. Talking of a penurious gentleman of our acquaintance, Johnson said, "Sir, he is narrow, not so much from avarice as from impotence to spend his money. He cannot find in his heart to pour out a bottle of wine, but he would not much care if it should sour."

Johnson and I supped this evening at the Crown and Anchor tavern with Sir Joshua Reynolds, Mr. Langton,

---

1. *Hudibras.* Its author is included in Johnson's *Lives of the Poets.*
2. *The Spleen.* By a droll and pithy clerk in the custom house, Matthew Green (1696-1737).

> "And may my humble dwelling stand
> Upon some chosen spot of land,
> A pond before, full to the brim,
> Where cows may cool and geese may swim,
> Behind, a green, like velvet neat,
> Soft to the eye and to the feet." *The Spleen.*

3. *Sixteen-string Jack.* "A noted highwayman, who amidst other fopperies, wore on the knees of his breeches, a bunch of sixteen strings." *Gilfillan.*

Mr. Nairne,[1] now one of the Scotch Judges, with the title of Lord Dunsinan, and my very worthy friend, Sir William Forbes,[2] of Pitsligo.

We discussed the question whether drinking improved conversation and benevolence. Sir Joshua maintained it did. JOHNSON. "No, sir; before dinner men meet with great inequality of understanding; and those who are conscious of their inferiority have the modesty not to talk. When they have drunk wine, every man feels himself happy and grows impudent and vociferous. But he is not improved; he is only not sensible of his defects." Sir Joshua said the Doctor was talking of the effects of excess in wine; but that a moderate glass enlivened the mind, by giving a proper circulation to the blood. "I am," said he, "in very good spirits when I get up in the morning. By dinner time I am exhausted; wine puts me in the same state as when I got up; and I am sure that moderate drinking makes people talk better." JOHNSON. "No, sir; wine gives not light, gay, ideal hilarity, but tumultuous noisy, clamorous merriment. I have heard none of those drunken—nay, drunken is a coarse word—none of those *vinous* flights." SIR JOSHUA. "Because you have sat by, quite sober, and felt an envy of the happiness of those who were drinking." JOHNSON. "Perhaps, contempt.—And, sir, it is not necessary to be drunk one's self, to relish the wit of drunkenness. Do we not judge of the drunken wit of the dialogue between Iago and

1. *Nairne.* "He was a man of the most scrupulous integrity. When sheriff deputy of Perthshire, he found upon reflection that he had decided a poor man's case erroneously; and, as the only remedy, supplied the litigant privately with money to carry the suit to the supreme court, where his judgment was reversed." *Sir Walter Scott.*

2. *Forbes.* A Scotch banker, apparently gentle and fair-minded. His standards of biography differed from those of Boswell, for in his life of Beattie, he writes: "I have been scrupulous in not admitting anything that I thought would hurt the feelings of others." No doubt the same honest kindness prompted him to praise Boswell's methods as the "most instructive that can possibly be thought of." Hannah More recounts that he was once umpire in a trial between Garrick and Boswell as to which could more nearly imitate Dr. Johnson's manner.

Cassio, the most excellent in its kind, when we are quite sober? Wit is wit, by whatever means it is produced; and, if good, will appear so at all times. I admit that the spirits are raised by drinking, as by the common participation of any pleasure; cock-fighting or bear-baiting* will raise the spirits of a company, as drinking does, though surely they will not improve conversation. I also admit that there are some sluggish men who are improved by drinking; as there are fruits which are not good till they are rotten. There are such men, but they are medlars.[1] I indeed allow that there have been a very few men of talents who were improved by drinking; but I maintain that I am right as to the effects of drinking in general; and let it be considered that there is no position, however false in its universality, which is not true of some particular man." Sir William Forbes said, "Might not a man warmed with wine be like a bottle of beer, which is made brisker by being set before the fire?" "Nay," said Johnson, laughing, "I cannot answer that; that is too much for me."

I observed that wine did some people harm by inflaming, confusing, and irritating their minds; but that the experience of mankind had declared in favor of moderate drinking. JOHNSON. "Sir, I do not say it is wrong to produce self-complacency by drinking; I only deny that it improves the mind. When I drank wine, I scorned to drink it when in company. I have drunk many a bottle by myself; in the first place, because I had need of it to raise my spirits; in the second place, because I would have nobody to witness its effects upon me."

He said that for general improvement a man should read whatever his immediate inclination prompts him to; though to be sure, if a man has a science to learn, he must regularly and resolutely advance. He added, "What we read with inclination makes a much stronger impression. If we read without inclination, half the mind is employed in fixing the attention; so there is but one half to be employed on what we read." He said,

---

1. *Medlars.* "You'll be rotten ere you be half ripe, and that's the right virtue of the medlar." *Touchstone.* "The medlar when fit to be eaten is no more rotten than a ripe peach." *Ellacombe.*

"If a man begins to read in the middle of a book and feels an inclination to go on, let him not quit it to go to the beginning. He may perhaps not feel again the inclination."

Soon after this day he went to Bath with Mr. and Mrs. Thrale. I had never seen that beautiful city, and wished to take the opportunity of visiting it while Johnson was there. Having written to him, I received the following answer.

"Why do you talk of neglect? When did I neglect you? If you will come to Bath, we shall all be glad to see you. Come, therefore, as soon as you can."

On the 26th of April I went to Bath;[1] and on my arrival at the Pelican inn, found lying for me an obliging invitation from Mr. and Mrs. Thrale, by whom I was agreeably entertained almost constantly during my stay. They were gone to the rooms, but there was a kind note from Dr. Johnson that he should sit at home all the evening. I went to him directly, and before Mr. and Mrs. Thrale returned, we had by ourselves some hours of tea-drinking and talk.

I shall group together such of his sayings as I preserved during the few days that I was at Bath.

Of a person who differed from him in politics he said, "In private life he is a very honest gentleman, but I will not allow him to be so in public life. People *may* be honest, though they are doing wrong; that is, between their Maker and them. But *we*, who are suffering by their pernicious conduct, are to destroy them. They who allow their passions to confound the distinctions between right and wrong are criminal. They may be convinced, but they have not come honestly by their conviction."

It having been mentioned, I know not with what truth, that a certain female political writer whose doctrines he disliked had of late become very fond of dress, sat hours together at her toilet, and even put on rouge: JOHNSON. "She is better employed at her toilet than using her pen. It is better she should

---

1. *Bath.* "Upon a stranger's arrival at Bath, he is welcomed by a peal of the Abbey bells." *Goldsmith.*

be reddening her own cheeks than blackening other people's characters."

Of the father of one of our friends[1] he observed, "He never clarified his notions by filtrating them through other minds. He had a canal[2] upon his estate, where at one place the bank was too low.—'I dug the canal deeper,' said he."

A literary lady of large fortune was mentioned as one who did good to many, but by no means "by stealth," and instead of "blushing to find it fame," acted evidently from vanity. JOHNSON. "I have seen no beings who do as much good from benevolence as she does from whatever motive. If there are such under the earth or in the clouds, I wish they would come up or come down. What Soame Jenyns[3] says upon this subject is not to be minded; he is a wit. No, sir; to act from pure benevolence[4] is not possible for finite beings. Human benevolence is mingled with vanity, interest, or some other motive."

He would not allow me to praise a lady then at Bath; observing, "She does not gain upon me, sir; I think her emptyheaded."

A gentleman expressed a wish to go and live three years at Otaheite or New Zealand, in order to obtain a full acquaintance with people so totally different from all we have ever known and be satisfied what pure nature can do for man. JOHNSON.

---

1. *Father of one of our friends.* Old Mr. Langton.

2. *Canal.* Any ornamental sheet of water. According to the story, as others have told it, Mr. Langton proposed to dig deeper only that portion of the canal where the banks were too low.

3. *Soame Jenyns.* Author among other works of a *Free Inquiry into the Nature and Origin of Evil*, which Johnson had reviewed with biting wit some twenty years before this date.

"Though he is far from the contemptible arrogance or the impious licentiousness of Bolingbroke, yet he decides too easily upon questions out of the reach of human determination, and with too little consideration of mortal weakness, and with too much vivacity for the necessary caution." *Johnson.*

4. *Pure benevolence.* "Dr. Johnson used to advise his friends to be upon their guard against romantic virtue, as being founded upon no settled principles. 'A plank,' added he, 'that is tilted up at one end must of course fall down on the other.' " *William Seward.*

"What could you learn, sir? What can savages tell but what they themselves have seen? Of the past, or the invisible they can tell nothing. And what account of their religion can you suppose to be learned from savages? Only consider, sir, our own state: our religion is in a book; we have an order of men whose duty it is to teach it; we have one day in the week set apart for it, and this is in general pretty well observed; yet ask the first ten gross men you meet, and hear what they can tell of their religion."

On Monday, April 29, he and I made an excursion to Bristol,[1] where I was entertained with seeing him inquire upon the spot into the authenticity of *"Rowley's* Poetry,*"* as I had seen him inquire upon the spot into the authenticity of *"Ossian's* Poetry.*"* George Catcot, the pewterer, who was as zealous for *Rowley* as Dr. Hugh Blair was for *Ossian* (I trust my Reverend Friend will excuse the comparison), attended us at our inn, and with a triumphant air of lively simplicity called out, "I'll make Dr. Johnson a convert." Dr. Johnson, at his desire, read aloud some of Chatterton's fabricated verses, while Catcot stood at the back of his chair, moving himself like a pendulum, and beating time with his feet, and now and then looking into Dr. Johnson's face, wondering that he was not yet convinced. We called on Mr. Barret, the surgeon, and saw some of the *originals* as they were called, which were executed very artifi-

---

1. *Bristol*. The birthplace of the gifted young poet, Thomas Chatterton. As a mere child, he was so infatuated with the notion of finding the writings of some old poet among the dry as dust records of the great Church of St. Mary, Redcliff that he invented what he could not discover. Unhappily, he was not as honest as he was imaginative. Not only did he try to palm off his own poems as ancient (the best of them he attributed to an imaginary poet whom he called Rowley), but he practiced other frauds, in the hope of making money from them. Dissipation and poverty drove him to suicide in London before he was out of his teens. His fellow townsmen had been no help to him. The young attorney Barrett used to send for him and differ from him in order to see his eyes strike fire. The merchant Catcot jeered at his poems until they passed into his possession, after which he thriftily insisted that they were genuine. The poets of the next age, moved by his poetic gift, his taint of insanity, and his early suicide, magnified his genius and ignored his dishonesties.

cially; but from a careful inspection of them, and a consideration of the circumstances with which they were attended, we were quite satisfied of the imposture.

Honest Catcot seemed to pay no attention whatever to any objections, but insisted, as an end of all controversy, that we should go with him to the tower of the church of St. Mary, Redcliff, and *view with our own eyes* the ancient chest in which the manuscripts were found. To this Dr. Johnson good-naturedly agreed; and though troubled with a shortness of breathing, labored up a long flight of steps till we came to the place where the wondrous chest stood. *"There,"* said Catcot, with a bouncing, confident credulity, *"there* is the very chest itself." After this *ocular demonstration,* there was no more to be said.

Johnson said of Chatterton: "This is the most extraordinary young man that has encountered my knowledge. It is wonderful how the whelp has written such things."

After Dr. Johnson's return to London, I was several times with him at his house, where I occasionally slept, in the room that had been assigned for me. To avoid a tedious minuteness, I shall group together what I have preserved of his conversation during this period also, without specifying each scene where it passed, except one, which will be found so remarkable as certainly to deserve a very particular relation.

"Where there is no education [he observed] as in savage countries, men will have the upper hand of women. Bodily strength, no doubt, contributes to this; but it would be so, exclusive of that, for it is mind that always governs. When it comes to dry understanding, man has the better."

"There is much talk of the misery which we cause to the brute creation, but they are recompensed by existence."

"Life is a progress from want to want, not from enjoyment to enjoyment."

"Though many men are nominally entrusted with the administration of hospitals and other public institutions, almost all the good is done by one man, by whom the rest are driven on—owing to confidence in him and indolence in them."

Lord Eliot[1] informs me that one day when Johnson and he were at dinner at a gentleman's house in London, upon Lord Chesterfield's *Letters*[2] being mentioned, Johnson surprised the company by this sentence: "Every man of any education would rather be called a rascal than accused of deficiency in *the graces*." Mr. Gibbon,[3] who was present, turned to a lady who knew Johnson well and lived much with him, and in his quaint manner, tapping his box, addressed her thus: "Don't you think, madam (looking toward Johnson), that among *all* your acquaintance you could find *one* exception?" The lady smiled, and seemed to acquiesce.

The uncommon vivacity of General Oglethorpe's mind and variety of knowledge having sometimes made his conversation seem too desultory, Johnson observed, "Oglethorpe, sir, never *completes* what he has to say."

He on the same account made a similar remark on Patrick Lord Elibank: "Sir, there is nothing *conclusive* in his talk."

Being irritated by hearing a gentleman[4] ask Mr. Levet a variety of questions concerning him, when he was sitting by, he broke out, "Sir, you have but two topics, yourself and me. I am sick of both." "A man," said he, "should not talk of himself, nor much of any particular person. He should avoid having any one topic of which people can say, 'We shall hear him upon it.' There was a Dr. Oldfield who was always talking of the Duke of Marlborough. He came into a coffee house one

---

1. *Lord Eliot.* At one time he and Lord Chesterfield's son had traveled on the continent together in charge of the same tutor. On more than one occasion he and Dr. Johnson turned their conversation to the subject here discussed.

2. *Lord Chesterfield's Letters.* Addressed to his son in praise of polish, suavity, diplomacy, and cunning, and published by the son's boorish widow during Lord Chesterfield's lifetime.

3. *Gibbon.* Author of the *Decline and Fall of the Roman Empire.* An unprepossessing man, noted for his florid taste in dress and his clumsy affectation of suavity and of lightness of manner in conversation. His "box" was his snuff-box.

4. *A gentleman.* No doubt, Boswell himself. "Boswell was talking away one evening in St. James's Park with much vanity. Said his friend Temple: 'We have heard of many kinds of hobby horses, but, Boswell, you ride upon yourself.'" *Boswell: Boswelliana.*

day, and told that his Grace had spoken in the House of Lords
for half an hour. 'Did he indeed speak for half an hour?' said
Belchier, the surgeon.—'Yes'.—'And what did he say of Dr.
Oldfield?'—'Nothing.'—'Why then, sir, he was very ungrateful;
for Dr. Oldfield could not have spoken for a quarter of an hour
without saying something of him.'

"Every man is to take existence on the terms on which it is
given to him. To some men it is given on condition of not
taking liberties, which other men may take without much harm."

I am now to record a very curious incident in Dr. Johnson's
life, which fell under my own observation; of which *pars magna
fui*, and which I am persuaded will, with the liberal-minded,
be much to his credit.

My desire of being acquainted with celebrated men[1] of every
description had made me, much about the same time, obtain
an introduction to Dr. Samuel Johnson and to John Wilkes,[2]
Esq. Two men more different could perhaps not be selected
out of all mankind. They had even attacked one another with
some asperity in their writings; yet I lived in habits of friendship with both. I could fully relish the excellence of each, for
I have ever delighted in that intellectual chemistry which can
separate good qualities from evil in the same person.

My booksellers and friends, Messieurs Dilly in the Poultry,
at whose hospitable and well-covered table I have seen a greater
number of literary men than at any other, except that of Sir
Joshua Reynolds, had invited me to meet Mr. Wilkes and some
more gentlemen, on Wednesday, May 15. "Pray," said I,
"let us have Dr. Johnson."—"What, with Mr. Wilkes? not for
the world," said Mr. Edward Dilly; "Dr. Johnson would never
forgive me."—"Come," said I, "if you'll let me negotiate for

---

1. *Celebrated men.* Of his pushing into their society Boswell himself
says: "If a man is praised for seeking knowledge, though mountains
and seas are in his way, may he not be pardoned whose ardor in the
pursuit of the same object leads him to encounter difficulties as great,
though of a different kind?"
2. *Wilkes.* "Wilkes was the ugliest fellow that ever lived and a most
notorious infidel." *Boswell.* "As pleasant a companion as ever lived."
The same. "Lampoon itself would disdain to speak ill of him of
whom no man speaks well." *Johnson.*

you, I will be answerable that all shall go well." DILLY. "Nay, if you will take it upon you, I am sure I shall be very happy to see them both here."

Notwithstanding the high veneration which I entertained for Dr. Johnson, I was sensible that he was sometimes a little actuated by the spirit of contradiction, and by means of that I hoped I should gain my point. I was persuaded that if I had come upon him with a direct proposal, "Sir, will you dine in company with Jack Wilkes?" he would have flown into a passion, and would probably have answered, "Dine with Jack Wilkes, sir! I'd as soon dine with Jack Ketch." I, therefore, while we were sitting quietly by ourselves at his house in an evening, took occasion to open my plan thus: "Mr. Dilly, sir, sends his respectful compliments to you, and would be happy if you would do him the honor to dine with him on Wednesday next along with me, as I must soon go to Scotland." JOHNSON. "Sir, I am obliged to Mr. Dilly. I will wait upon him—" BOSWELL. "Provided, sir, I suppose, that the company which he is to have is agreeable to you." JOHNSON. "What do you mean, sir? What do you take me for? Do you think I am so ignorant of the world as to imagine that I am to prescribe to a gentleman what company he is to have[1] at his table?" BOSWELL. "I beg your pardon, sir, for wishing to prevent you from meeting people whom you might not like. Perhaps he may have some of what he calls his patriotic[2] friends with him." JOHNSON.

1. *What company he is to have.* "I never but once, upon a resolution to employ myself in study, balked an invitation out to dinner and then I stayed at home and did nothing." *Johnson, quoted by Sir John Hawkins.*

2. *Patriotic.* In the days of Robert Walpole, the title of *Patriots* had been assumed by a group of brilliant English politicians who apparently advocated any cause which would embarrass the government. Thus, they demanded a more spirited foreign policy but protested against a competent army. They objected to the methods used for raising revenue but protested against a debt. In 1780, Sir Robert's son, Sir Horace, stigmatized them as "wretches who thought their own want of power a proof that their country was undone." For many years, the term was a current one for demagogic opponents of those in power. "A man may hate his king, yet not love his country. He that has been refused a reasonable or unreasonable request begins soon to talk of natural equality; yet his design in all his declamation is not to benefit his country, but to gratify his malice." *Johnson: The Patriot, 1774.*

After the sketch by Geo. Langton

JAMES BOSWELL

"Well, sir, and what then? What care *I* for his *patriotic friends?* Poh!" Boswell. "I should not be surprised to find Jack Wilkes there." Johnson. "And if Jack Wilkes *should* be there, what is that to *me*, sir? My dear friend, let us have no more of this. I am sorry to be angry with you; but really it is treating me strangely to talk to me as if I could not meet any company whatever, occasionally." Boswell. "Pray, forgive me, sir; I meant well. But you shall meet whoever comes, for me." Thus I secured him, and told Dilly that he would find him well pleased to be one of his guests on the day appointed.

Upon the much expected Wednesday, I called on him about half an hour before dinner, as I often did when we were to dine out together, to see that he was ready in time, and to accompany him. I found him buffeting his books, as upon a former occasion, covered with dust, and making no preparation for going abroad. "How is this, sir?" said I. "Don't you recollect that you are to dine at Mr. Dilly's?" Johnson. "Sir, I did not think of going to Dilly's; it went out of my head. I have ordered dinner at home with Mrs. Williams." Boswell. "But my dear sir, you know you were engaged to Mr. Dilly, and I told him so. He will expect you, and will be much disappointed if you don't come." Johnson. "You must talk to Mrs. Williams about this."

Here was a sad dilemma. I feared that what I was so confident I had secured, would yet be frustrated. He had accustomed himself to show Mrs. Williams such a degree of attention as frequently imposed some restraint upon him; and I knew that if she should be obstinate, he would not stir. I hastened down stairs to the blind lady's room, and told her I was in great uneasiness, for Dr. Johnson had engaged to me to dine this day at Mr. Dilly's, but that he had told me he had forgotten his engagement, and had ordered dinner at home. "Yes, sir," said she, pretty peevishly, "Dr. Johnson is to dine at home."— "Madam," said I, "his respect for you is such that I know he will not leave you unless you absolutely desire it. But as you have so much of his company, I hope you will be good enough to forego it for a day; as Mr. Dilly is a very worthy man, has frequently had agreeable parties at his house for Dr. Johnson, and will be vexed if the Doctor neglects him today. And then, madam, be pleased to consider my situation; I carried the message, and I assured Mr. Dilly that Dr. Johnson was to come; and no doubt he has made a dinner, and invited a company, and boasted of the honor he expected to have. I shall be quite disgraced if the Doctor is not there." She gradually softened to my solicitations, which were certainly as earnest as most entreaties to ladies upon any occasion, and was graciously pleased to empower me to tell Dr. Johnson that, "all things considered, she thought he should certainly go." I flew back to him, still in dust and careless of what should be the event, "indifferent in his choice to go or stay"; but as soon as I had announced to him Mrs. Williams's consent, he roared, "Frank, a clean shirt," and was very soon dressed. When I had him fairly seated in a coach, I exulted as much as a fortune-hunter who has got an heiress into a post-chaise with him to set out for Gretna* Green.

When we entered Mr. Dilly's drawing-room, he found himself in the midst of a company he did not know. I kept myself snug and silent, watching how he would conduct himself. I observed him whispering to Mr. Dilly, "Who is that gentleman sir?"—"Mr. Arthur Lee."[1]—JOHNSON. "Too, too, too" (under his breath), which was one of his habitual mutterings. Mr. Arthur Lee could not but be very obnoxious to Johnson, for he was not only a *patriot*, but an *American*. He was afterwards minister from the United States at the court of Madrid. "And who is the gentleman in lace?"—"Mr. Wilkes, sir." This information confounded him still more; he had some difficulty to restrain himself, and taking up a book sat down upon a window-seat and read, or at least kept his eye upon it intently, till he composed himself. His feelings, I dare say, were awkward enough. But he no doubt recollected his having rated me for supposing that he could be at all disconcerted by any company, and he, therefore, resolutely set himself to behave quite as an easy man of the world who could adapt himself at once to the disposition and manners of those whom he might chance to meet.

---

1. *Lee.* Secret agent for the American Congress before the Revolution. As *Junius Americanus*, he had pamphleteered vigorously for the American cause. His brother, Alderman Lee, is mentioned later.

The cheering sound of "Dinner is upon the table," dissolved his reverie, and we *all* sat down without any symptom of ill humor. There were present, beside Mr. Wilkes and Mr. Arthur Lee, who was an old companion of mine when he studied physic at Edinburgh, Mr. (now Sir John) Miller,[1] Dr. Lettsom,[2] and Mr. Slater, the druggist. Mr. Wilkes placed himself next to Dr. Johnson, and behaved to him with so much attention and politeness that he gained upon him insensibly. No man eat more heartily than Johnson, or loved better what was nice and delicate. Mr. Wilkes was very assiduous in helping him to some fine veal. "Pray give me leave, sir—It is better here— A little of the brown—Some fat, sir—A little of the stuffing— Some gravy—Let me have the pleasure of giving you some butter—Allow me to recommend a squeeze of this orange—or the lemon, perhaps, may have more zest."—"Sir, sir, I am obliged to you, sir," cried Johnson, bowing, and turning his head to him with a look for some time of "surly virtue," but, in a short while, of complacency.

Foote being mentioned, Johnson said, "He is not a good mimic." One of the company added, "A merry Andrew, a buffoon." JOHNSON. "But he has wit, too, and is not deficient in ideas, or in fertility and variety of imagery, and not empty of reading; he has knowledge enough to fill up his part. One species of wit he has in an eminent degree—that of escape. You drive him to a corner with both hands, but he's gone, sir, when you think you have got him—like an animal that jumps over your head. Then he has a great range for wit; he never lets truth[3] stand between him and a jest, and he is some-

---

1. *Miller.* "Who lives near Bath, who is a dilettante man, keeps a weekly day for the literati, and gathereth all the flowers that ladies write." *Rev. Dr. Thomas Campbell.*

2. *Dr. Lettsom.* An odd combination of "volatile creole" and Quaker; opposed to what he called "established system." He says of Johnson: "He had a heavy look; but when he spoke, it was like lightning out of a dark cloud."

3. *Never lets truth.* "A story is a specimen of human manners, and derives its sole value from its truth. When Foote has told me something, I dismiss it from my mind like a passing shadow; when Reynolds tells me something, I consider myself as possessed of an idea the more." *Johnson, quoted by Mrs. Piozzi.*

times mighty coarse. Garrick is under many restraints from which Foote is free." WILKES. "Garrick's wit is more like Lord Chesterfield's." JOHNSON. "The first time I was in company with Foote was at Fitzherbert's.[1] Having no good opinion of the fellow, I was resolved not to be pleased; and it is very difficult to please a man against his will. I went on eating my dinner pretty sullenly, affecting not to mind him. But the dog was so very comical that I was obliged to lay down my knife and fork, throw myself back upon my chair, and fairly laugh it out. No, sir, he was irresistible. He, upon one occasion experienced in an extraordinary degree the efficacy of his powers of entertaining. Amongst the many and various modes which he tried of getting money, he became a partner with a small-beer brewer, and he was to have a share of the profits for procuring customers amongst his numerous acquaintance. Fitzherbert was one who took his small-beer; but it was so bad that the servants resolved not to drink it. They were at some loss how to notify their resolution, being afraid of offending their master, who they knew liked Foote much as a companion. At last they fixed upon a little black boy, who was rather a favorite, to deliver their remonstrance; and having invested him with the whole authority of the kitchen, he was to inform Mr. Fitzherbert, in all their names, upon a certain day, that they would drink Foote's small-beer no longer. On that day Foote happened to dine at Fitzherbert's, and this boy served at table; he was so delighted with Foote's stories and merriment and grimace that when he went downstairs he told them, 'This is the finest man I have ever seen. I will not deliver your message. I will drink his small-beer.'"

Somebody observed that Garrick could not have done this. WILKES. "Garrick would have made the small-beer still smaller. He is now leaving the stage; but he will play Scrub[2]

---

1. *Fitzherbert.* For his wife, see p. 393, note 1.
2. *Scrub.* In Farquhar's *Beaux Stratagem.* "Scrub thus describes his duties: 'Of a Monday, I drive the coach, of a Tuesday, I drive the plow, on Wednesday, I follow the hounds, a Thursday, I dun the tenants, on Friday, I go to market, on Saturday, I draw warrants, and a Sunday I draw beer.'" *Birkbeck Hill.*

all his life." I knew that Johnson would let nobody attack Garrick but himself, as Garrick said to me, and I had heard him praise his liberality; so I said, loudly, "I have heard Garrick is liberal." JOHNSON. "Yes, sir, I know that Garrick has given away more money than any man in England that I am acquainted with, and that not from ostentatious views. Garrick was very poor when he began life; so when he came to have money, he probably was very unskillful in giving away, and saved when he should not. But Garrick began to be liberal as soon as he could; and I am of opinion the reputation of avarice which he has had has been very lucky for him. You despise a man for avarice, but do not hate him. Garrick might have been much better attacked for living with more splendor than is suitable to a player; if they had had the wit to have assaulted him in that quarter, they might have galled him more. But they have kept clamoring about his avarice, which has rescued him from much obloquy and envy."

Talking of the great difficulty of obtaining authentic information for biography, Johnson told us, "When I was a young fellow I wanted to write the Life of Dryden,[1] and in order to get materials, I applied to the only two persons then alive who had seen him; these were old Swinney[2] and old Cibber.[3]

---

1. *Dryden.* Dryden died only eight years before Johnson's birth.

2. *Swinney.* Owen MacSwinney, manager of the Haymarket (theater) 1706-10; of Drury Lane, 1710-11; then again of the Haymarket; he finally went bankrupt and lived abroad twenty years to escape his creditors.

3. *Old Cibber.* In the Revolution of 1688 he was old enough to enlist for William of Orange. He later became actor, author, and the manager of Drury Lane Theater. He played would-be fops with an exquisite precision and wit, wrote one of the best comedies in the language (*The Careless Husband*), composed an autobiography (his "Apology"), the gossiping good humor of which increased rather than diminished the annoyance of his enemies, and died, aged eighty-six, in 1757. Johnson's insistent prejudice against him was perhaps colored by the fact that he was a Whig, had been pilloried by Pope in the *Dunciad*, and was willing to describe himself as "an inconsistent creature . . . . always full of spirits, in some small capacity to do right, but in a more frequent alacrity to do wrong." It is difficult to say whether his worst blunder was writing bad odes or letting the king make him poet laureate for doing so.

Swinney's information was no more than this, That at Will's coffee-house Dryden had a particular chair for himself, which was set by the fire in winter, and was then called his winter-chair; and that it was carried out for him to the balcony in summer, and was then called his summer chair. Cibber could tell no more but that he remembered him 'a decent old man, arbiter of critical disputes at Will's.' You are to consider that Cibber was then at a great distance from Dryden, had perhaps one leg only in the room, and durst not draw in the other." BOSWELL. "Yet Cibber was a man of observation?" JOHNSON. "I think not." BOSWELL. "You will allow his *Apology* to be well done." JOHNSON. "Very well done, to be sure, sir. That book is a striking proof of the justice of Pope's remark:

> Each might his several province well command,
> Would all but stoop to what they understand."

BOSWELL. "And his plays are good." JOHNSON. "Yes; but that was his trade; *l'esprit du corps;* he had been all his life among players and play-writers. I wondered that he had so little to say in conversation, for he had kept the best company, and learned all that can be got by the ear. He abused Pindar to me, and then showed me an ode of his own, with an absurd couplet, making a linnet soar on an eagle's wing. I told him that when the ancients made a simile, they always made it like something real."

Mr. Wilkes remarked that "among all the bold flights of Shakespeare's imagination, the boldest was making Birnam wood march to Dunsinane; creating a wood where there never was a shrub; a wood in Scotland! ha! ha! ha!" And he also observed that "the clannish slavery of the Highlands of Scotland was the single exception to Milton's remark of 'the mountain nymph, sweet Liberty,' being worshiped in all hilly countries."— "When I was at Inverary," said he, "on a visit to my old friend Archibald, Duke of Argyle,[1] his dependents congratulated me on being such a favorite of his Grace. I said, 'It is then,

---

1. *Duke of Argyle.* Of the great Campbell family; head of the Campbell clan.

gentlemen, truly lucky for me; for if I had displeased the Duke, and he had wished it, there is not a Campbell among you but would have been ready to bring John Wilkes's head to him in a charger. It would have been only

Off with his head! So much for Aylesbury.'

I was then member for Aylesbury. "

Mr. Arthur Lee mentioned some Scotch who had taken possession of a barren part of America, and wondered why they should choose it. JOHNSON. "Why, sir, all barrenness is comparative. The *Scotch* would not know it to be barren." BOSWELL. "Come, come, he is flattering the English. You have now been in Scotland, sir, and say if you did not see meat and drink[1] enough there." JOHNSON. "Why yes, sir; meat and drink enough to give the inhabitants sufficient strength to run away from home." All these quick and lively sallies were said sportively, quite in jest, and with a smile, which showed that he meant only wit. When I claimed a superiority for Scotland over England in one respect, that no man can be arrested there for a debt merely because another swears it against him; but there must first be judgment of a court of law ascertaining its justice; and that a seizure of the person before judgment is obtained can take place only if his creditor should swear that he is about to fly from the country: WILKES. "That, I should think, may be safely sworn of all the Scotch nation." JOHNSON (to Mr. Wilkes). "You must know, sir, I lately took my friend Boswell and showed him genuine civilized life in an English provincial town. I turned him loose at Lichfield, my native city, that he might see for once real civility; for you know he lives among savages in Scotland, and among rakes in London."

---

1. *Meat and drink.* "I bought some *speldings*, fish (generally whitings) salted and dried in a particular manner, being dipped in the sea, and dried in the sun, and eaten by the Scots by way of a relish. [Johnson] had never seen them, though they were sold in London. I insisted on *scottifying* his palate; but he was very reluctant. With difficulty I prevailed with him to let a bit of one of them lie in his mouth. He did not like it." *Boswell: Journal of a Tour to the Hebrides.*

"Nobody enjoyed a laugh at the expense of the Scotch more than Boswell, at least when it came from Johnson." *Lettsom.*

WILKES. "Except when he is with grave, sober, decent people, like you and me." JOHNSON (smiling). "And we ashamed of him."

They were quite frank and easy. Johnson told the story of his asking Mrs. Macaulay to allow her footman to sit down with them, to prove the ridiculousness of the arguments for the equality of mankind; and he said to me afterwards, with a nod of satisfaction, "You saw Mr. Wilkes acquiesced." Wilkes talked with all imaginable freedom of the ludicrous title given to the Attorney-General, *Diabolus Regis;* adding, "I have reason to know something about that officer; for I was prosecuted for a libel." Johnson, who many people would have supposed must have been furiously angry at hearing this talked of so lightly, said not a word. He was now, *indeed,* "a good-humored fellow."

After dinner we had an accession of Mrs. Knowles, the Quaker lady, well known for her various talents, and of Mr. Alderman Lee. Amidst some patriotic groans, somebody (I think the Alderman) said, "Poor old England is lost." JOHNSON. "Sir, it is not so much to be lamented that old England is lost, as that the Scotch have found it."[1]

Mr. Wilkes held a candle to show a fine print of a beautiful female figure which hung in the room, and pointed out the elegant contour with the finger of an arch connoisseur. He afterwards in a conversation with me waggishly insisted that all the time Johnson showed visible signs of a fervent admiration of the corresponding charms of the fair Quaker.

This record, though by no means so perfect as I could wish, will serve to give a notion of a very curious interview, which was not only pleasing at the time, but had the agreeable[2] and

1. *Have found it.* Especially since 1762, when the appointment of the Scotchman Lord Bute as chief minister of the Crown led many of his countrymen to try their fortune in London.

2. *Agreeable.* "For my part I begin to settle and keep company with grave aldermen. I dined yesterday in the Poultry with Mr. Alderman Wilkes, and Mr. Alderman Lee, and Counsellor Lee, his brother. There sat you the while, so sober, with your W——'s and your H——'s, and my aunt and her trumpet; and when they are gone, you think by chance on Johnson, what he is doing, what should he be doing? He is breaking jokes with Jack Wilkes upon the Scots. Such, Madam, are the vicissitudes of things." *Johnson to Mrs. Thrale.*

benignant effect of reconciling any animosity, and sweetening any acidity, which, in the various bustle of political contest, had been produced in the minds of two men, who though widely different, had so many things in common—classical learning, modern literature, wit and humor, and ready repartee —that it would have been much to be regretted if they had been forever at a distance from each other.

Mr. Burke gave me much credit for this successful *negotiation;* and pleasantly said that "there was nothing equal to it in the whole history of the *Corps Diplomatique.*"

I attended Dr. Johnson home, and had the satisfaction to hear him tell Mrs. Williams how much he had been pleased with Mr. Wilkes's company, and what an agreeable day he had passed.

On the evening of the next day I took leave of him, being to set out for Scotland.[1] I thanked him with great warmth for all his kindness. "Sir," said he, "you are very welcome. Nobody repays it with more."

It was, I think, after I left London this year that [an epitaph which he wrote for the monument of Dr. Goldsmith in Westminster Abbey] gave occasion to a *Remonstrance* to the MONARCH OF LITERATURE, for an account of which I am indebted to Sir William Forbes of Pitsligo.

Sir William Forbes writes to me thus: "I enclose the *Round Robin.* This *jeu d'esprit* took its rise one day at dinner at our friend Sir Joshua Reynolds's. All the company present, except myself, were friends and acquaintance of Dr. Goldsmith. The epitaph, written for him by Dr. Johnson, became the subject of conversation, and various emendations were suggested, which it was agreed should be submitted to the Doctor's consideration.—But the question was, who should have the courage to propose them to him? At last it was hinted that there could be no way so good as that of a *Round Robin*, as the sailors call it, which they make use of when they enter into a con-

---

1. *To set out for Scotland.* "B—— went away on Thursday night with no great inclination to travel northward; but who can contend with destiny? He carries with him two or three good resolutions; I hope they will not mold upon the road." *Johnson to Mrs. Thrale.*

spiracy, so as not to let it be known who puts his name first or last to the paper. This proposition was instantly assented to; and Dr. Barnard, Dean of Derry, now Bishop of Killaloe, drew up an address to Dr. Johnson on the occasion, replete with wit and humor, but which it was feared the Doctor might think treated the subject with too much levity. Mr. Burke then proposed the address as it stands in the paper in writing, to which I had the honor to officiate as clerk.

"Sir Joshua agreed to carry it to Dr. Johnson, who received it with much good humor, and desired Sir Joshua to tell the gentlemen that he would alter the epitaph in any manner they pleased, as to the sense of it; but *he would never consent to disgrace the walls of Westminster Abbey with an English inscription.*"

My readers are presented with a faithful transcript of a paper, which I doubt not of their being desirous to see:

We, the Circumscribers, having read with great pleasure an intended Epitaph for the monument of Dr. Goldsmith, which considered abstractly, appears to be, for elegant composition and masterly style, in every respect worthy of the pen of its learned Author; are yet of opinion that the Character of the Deceased as a Writer, particularly as a Poet, is perhaps not delineated with all the exactness which Dr. Johnson is capable of giving it. We, therefore, with deference to his superior judgment, humbly request that he would at least take the trouble of revising it; and of making such additions and alterations as he shall think proper, upon a farther perusal. But if we might venture to express our wishes, they would lead us to request that he would write the Epitaph in English rather than in Latin; as we think that the memory of so eminent an English Writer ought to be perpetuated in the language to which his works are likely to be so lasting an ornament, which we also know to have been the opinion of the late Doctor himself."

[1777].   MR. BOSWELL TO DR. JOHNSON.

"Edinburgh, April 4, 1777.

"I think it hard that I should be a whole year without seeing you. May I presume to petition for a meeting with you in the autumn? You have, I believe, seen all the cathedrals in

England except that of Carlisle. If you are to be with Dr. Taylor at Ashbourne, it would not be a great journey to come thither. We may pass a few most agreeable days there by ourselves, and I will accompany you a good part of the way to the southward again. Pray think of this."

MR. BOSWELL TO DR. JOHNSON.

"July 9th, 1777.

"You do not take the least notice of my proposal for our meeting at Carlisle. . . . If you have not a desire to complete your tour of the English cathedrals, I will take a larger share of the road between this place and Ashbourne. So tell me where you will fix for our passing a few days by ourselves. Now don't say 'foolish fellow' or 'idle dog.' Chain your humor and let your kindness play."

"To James Boswell, Esq.

"Dear Sir: I am this day come to Ashbourne, and have only to tell you that Dr. Taylor says you shall be welcome to him, and you know how welcome you will be to me. Make haste to let me know when you may be expected.

"Your most humble servant,

"SAM. JOHNSON.

"August 30, 1777."

On Sunday evening, Sept. 14, I arrived at Ashbourne, and drove directly up to Dr. Taylor's door. Dr. Johnson and he appeared before I had got out of the post-chaise, and welcomed me cordially.

I told them that I had traveled all the preceding night, and gone to bed at Leek, in Staffordshire; and that when I rose to go to church in the afternoon, I was informed there had been an earthquake, of which, it seems, the shock had been felt in some degree at Ashbourne. JOHNSON. "Sir, it will be much exaggerated in public talk; the common people do not accurately adapt their thoughts to the objects, nor do they accurately adapt their words to their thoughts. A great part of their language is proverbial. If anything rocks at all, they say *it rocks like a cradle.*"

The subject of grief for the loss of relations and friends being introduced, Dr. Taylor mentioned a gentleman of the neighborhood as the only instance he had ever known of a person who had endeavored to *retain* grief. He told Dr. Taylor that after his lady's death, which affected him deeply, he *resolved* that the grief, which he cherished with a kind of sacred fondness, should be lasting; but that he found he could not keep it long. JOHNSON. "All grief for what cannot in the course of nature be helped soon wears away unless where there is madness, for all unnecessary grief is unwise. If grief is mingled with remorse of conscience, it should be lasting." BOSWELL. "But, sir, we do not approve of a man who very soon forgets the loss of a wife or a friend." JOHNSON. "Sir, we disapprove of him, not because he soon forgets his grief, for the sooner it is forgotten the better, but because we suppose that if he forgets his wife or his friend soon, he has not had much affection for them."

I was somewhat disappointed in finding that the edition of the *English Poets*, for which he was to write Prefaces and Lives, was not an undertaking directed by him; but that he was to furnish a Preface and Life to any Poet the bookseller pleased. I asked him if he would do this to any dunce's works if they should ask him. JOHNSON. "Yes, sir, and *say* he was a dunce."[1]

[On Monday, September 15], after breakfast, Johnson carried me to see the garden belonging to the school of Ashbourne, which is very prettily formed upon a bank rising gradually behind the house. The Reverend Mr. Langley, the head master, accompanied us.

While we sat basking in the sun upon a seat here, I introduced a common subject of complaint, the very small salaries which many curates have, and I maintained that a clergyman should not be allowed to have a curate unless he gives him a hundred pounds a year; if he cannot do that, let him perform

---

1. *Dunce.* Thus, he called *Sheffield:* "A writer that sometimes glimmers but rarely shines, feebly laborious and at best but pretty." *Granville's* poems he called "trifles written by idleness and published by vanity," and of *Hammond* he said: "It would be hard to find in all his productions three stanzas that deserve to be remembered."

the duty himself. Johnson. "To be sure, sir, it is wrong that any clergyman should be without a reasonable income; but the clergy who have livings cannot afford, in many instances, to give good salaries to curates without leaving themselves too little; and if no curate were to be permitted unless he had a hundred pounds a year, their number would be very small, which would be a disadvantage, as then there would not be such choice in the nursery for the church, curates being candidates for the higher ecclesiastical offices, according to their merit and good behavior."

We had with us at dinner several of Dr. Taylor's neighbors, who seemed to understand Dr. Johnson very well, and not to consider him in the light that a certain person did, who being struck, or rather stunned by his voice and manner, when he was afterwards asked what he thought of him, answered, "He's a tremendous companion."

Johnson told me that "Taylor had such a sort of indolence that if you should put a pebble upon his chimney-piece, you would find it there, in the same state, a year afterwards."

And here is a proper place to give an account of Johnson's interference in behalf of the Reverend Dr. William Dodd, celebrated as a very popular preacher,[1] an encourager of charitable institutions, and author of a variety of works, chiefly theological. Having unhappily contracted expensive habits of living, he forged[2] a bond, flattering himself with hopes that he might be able to repay its amount without being detected. The person whose name he presumed to falsify was the Earl of Chesterfield,[3] to whom he had been tutor, and who, he perhaps flattered himself, would have generously paid the money in case of an alarm being taken, rather than suffer him to fall a victim to the dreadful consequences of violating the law

---

1. *A very popular preacher.* Dr. Alexander Carlyle says of one of his sermons that it "was composed with the least possible delicacy and was fuel for the warm passions of the hypocrites. The fellow was handsome and delivered his discourse remarkably well for a reader. When he had finished, there were unceasing whispers of applause."

2. *Forged.* An offense at this time punishable by death.

3. *Earl of Chesterfield.* Not the celebrated Lord Chesterfield, but his immediate successor.

against forgery, the most dangerous crime in a commercial country; but the unfortunate divine had the mortification to find that he was mistaken. His noble pupil appeared against him, and he was capitally convicted.

Johnson told me that Dr. Dodd was very little acquainted with him, having been but once in his company, many years previous to this period; but in his distress he bethought himself of Johnson's persuasive power of writing, if haply it might avail to obtain for him the Royal Mercy. He did not apply to him directly, but through the late Countess of Harrington, who wrote a letter to Johnson asking him to employ his pen in favor of Dodd. Mr. Allen, the printer, who was Johnson's landlord and next neighbor in Bolt Court, and for whom he had much kindness, was one of Dodd's friends, of whom to the credit of humanity be it recorded that he had many who did not desert him, even after his sentence of death. Mr. Allen told me that he carried Lady Harrington's letter to Johnson, that Johnson read it walking up and down his chamber and seemed much agitated, after which he said, "I will do what I can."

He this evening put into my hands the whole series of his writings upon this melancholy occasion.

Dr. Johnson wrote in the first place, Dr. Dodd's "Speech to the Recorder of London," at the Old Bailey, when sentence of death was about to be pronounced upon him. He wrote also "The Convict's Address to His Unhappy Brethren," a sermon delivered by Dr. Dodd in the chapel of Newgate.

The other pieces are two letters, one to the Lord Chancellor Bathurst and one to Lord Mansfield; A Petition from Dr. Dodd to the King; A Petition from Mrs. Dodd to the Queen; Observations of some length inserted in the newspapers, on occasion of Earl Percy's having presented to his Majesty a petition for mercy to Dodd, signed by twenty thousand people, but all in vain. He told me that he had also written a petition from the city of London; "but," said he, with a significant smile, "they *mended* it."

The last of these articles which Johnson wrote is "Dr. Dodd's Last Solemn Declaration," which he left with the sheriff at the place of execution.

All applications for the Royal Mercy having failed, Dr. Dodd prepared himself for death; and, with a warmth of gratitude, wrote to Dr. Johnson as follows:

"June 25, *Midnight.*

"Accept, thou *great* and *good* heart, my earnest and fervent thanks and prayers for all thy benevolent and kind efforts in my behalf.—Oh! Dr. Johnson! as I sought your knowledge at an early hour in life, would to heaven I had cultivated the love and acquaintance of so excellent a man!—I pray God most sincerely to bless you with the highest transports—the infelt satisfaction of *humane* and benevolent exertions!—And admitted, as I trust I shall be, to the realms of bliss before you, I shall hail *your* arrival there with transports, and rejoice to acknowledge that you was my Comforter,[1] my Advocate, and my *Friend!* God *be ever* with *you!*"

Johnson gave us this evening a portrait of the late Mr. Fitzherbert of Derbyshire. "There was," said he, "no sparkle, no brilliancy in Fitzherbert; but I never knew a man who was so generally acceptable. He made everybody quite easy, overpowered nobody by the superiority of his talents, made no man think worse of himself by being his rival, seemed always to listen, did not oblige you to hear much from him, and did not oppose what you said. Everybody liked him; but he had no friend, as I understand the word, nobody with whom he exchanged intimate thoughts. People were willing to think well of everything about him. A gentleman[2] was making an affected

---

1. *My Comforter.* "He was, I am afraid, long flattered with hopes of life; but I had no part in the dreadful delusion; for as soon as the King had signed his sentence, I obtained from Mr. Chamier [under Secretary of State and a member of the Club] an account of the disposition of the court toward him, with a declaration that there *was no hope even of a respite.* This letter immediately was laid before Dodd; but he believed those whom he wished to be right, as it is thought, till within three days of his end." *Johnson to Boswell, June 28, 1777.*

2. *A gentleman.* John Gilbert Cooper. "The last of the Benevolists, or sentimentalists, who were much in vogue between 1750 and 1760. They were all tenderness in words." *Malone.* "Being told that Gilbert Cooper called him [Johnson] the Caliban of literature: 'Well,' said he, 'I must dub him the Punchinello.'" *Maxwell, quoted by Boswell.*

rant, as many people do, of great feelings about 'his dear son,' who was at school near London; how anxious he was lest he might be ill, and what he would give to see him. 'Can't you,' said Fitzherbert, 'take a post-chaise and go to him?' This, to be sure, *finished* the affected man, but there was not much in it. However, this was circulated as wit for a whole winter, and I believe part of a summer too. He was an instance of the truth of the observation that a man will please more upon the whole by negative qualities than by positive; by never offending, than by giving a great deal of delight. In the first place, men hate more steadily than they love; and if I have said something to hurt a man once, I shall not get the better of this by saying many things to please him."

Tuesday, September 16, Dr. Johnson having mentioned to me the extraordinary size and price of some cattle reared by Dr. Taylor, I rode out with our host, surveyed his farm, and was shown one cow which he had sold for a hundred and twenty guineas, and another for which he had been offered a hundred and thirty. Taylor thus described to me his old school-fellow and friend, Johnson: "He is a man of a very clear head, great power of words, and a very gay imagination; but there is no disputing with him. He will not hear you, and having a louder voice than you, must roar you down."

On Wednesday, September 17, Dr. Butter, physician at Derby, drank tea with us; and it was settled that Dr. Johnson and I should go on Friday and dine with him. Johnson said, "I'm glad of this." He seemed weary[1] of the uniformity of life at Dr. Taylor's.

He had this evening, partly, I suppose, from the spirit of contradiction to his Whig friend, a violent argument with Dr. Taylor as to the inclinations of the people of England at this time toward the Royal Family of Stuart. He grew so outrageous as to say that, "if England were fairly polled, the

---

1. *He seemed weary*. As on a previous occasion. "Having stayed my month with Taylor, I came away on Wednesday, leaving him, I think, in a disposition of mind not very uncommon, at once weary of my stay, and grieved at my departure." *Johnson to Mrs. Thrale, 1771.*

present King would be sent away tonight, and his adherents hanged tomorrow." Taylor, who was as violent a Whig as Johnson was a Tory, was roused by this to a pitch of bellowing. He denied, loudly, what Johnson said; and maintained that there was an abhorrence against the Stuart family, though he admitted that the people were not much attached to the present King. JOHNSON. "Sir, the state of the country is this: the people knowing it to be agreed on all hands that this King has not the hereditary right to the crown, and there being no hope that he who has it can be restored, have grown cold and indifferent upon the subject of loyalty, and have no warm attachment to any king. They would not, therefore, risk any thing to restore the exiled family. They would not give twenty shillings apiece to bring it about. But if a mere vote could do it, there would be twenty to one. For, sir, you are to consider that all those who think a king has a right to his crown, as a man has to his estate, which is the just opinion, would be for restoring the King who certainly has the hereditary right, could he be trusted with it; in which there would be no danger now, when every king will govern by the laws." Dr. Taylor said something of the slight foundation of the hereditary right of the house of Stuart. "Sir," said Johnson, "the house of Stuart succeeded to the full right of both the houses of York and Lancaster, whose common source had the undisputed right. A right to a throne is like a right to anything else. Possession is sufficient, where no better right can be shown. This was the case with the royal family of England, as it is now with the King of France; for as to the first beginning of the right we are in the dark."

Thursday, September 18. [Johnson] observed that a gentleman of eminence in literature had got into a bad style of poetry of late. "He puts," said he, "a very common thing in a strange dress till he does not know it himself, and thinks other people do not know it." BOSWELL. "That is owing to his being so much versant in old English poetry." JOHNSON. "What is that to the purpose, sir? If I say a man is drunk, and you tell me it is owing to his taking much drink, the matter is not mended.

No, sir, ———has taken to an odd mode. For example, he'd write thus:

> Hermit hoar, in solemn cell,
> Wearing out life's evening gray.

Gray evening is common enough but *evening gray* he'd think fine.—Stay,—we'll make out the stanza:

> Hermit hoar, in solemn cell,
> Wearing out life's evening gray;
> Smite thy bosom, sage, and tell
> What is bliss? and which the way?''

Boswell. "But why smite his bosom, sir?" Johnson. "Why, to show he was in earnest (smiling)." He at an after period added the following stanza:

> Thus I spoke; and speaking sighed—
> Scarce repressed the starting tear—
> When the smiling sage replied,
> "Come, my lad, and drink some beer."

I cannot help thinking the first stanza very good solemn poetry, as also the first three lines of the second. Its last line is an excellent burlesque surprise on gloomy sentimental inquirers, and, perhaps, the advice is as good as can be given to a low spirited, dissatisfied being: Don't trouble your head with sickly thinking; take a cup and be merry.

Friday, September 19, after breakfast Dr. Johnson and I set out in Dr. Taylor's chaise to go to Derby. The day was fine, and we resolved to go by Keddlestone, the seat of Lord Scarsdale, that I might see his Lordship's fine house. I was struck with the magnificence of the building; and the extensive park, with the finest verdure, covered with deer and cattle and sheep, delighted me. The number of old oaks, of an immense size, filled me with a sort of respectful admiration; for one of them sixty pounds was offered. The excellent smooth gravel roads; the large piece of water formed by his Lordship from some small brooks, with a handsome barge upon it; the venerable

Gothic church, now the family chapel, just by the house; in short, the grand group of objects agitated and distended my mind in a most agreeable manner. "One should think," said I, "that the proprietor of all this *must* be happy."—"Nay, sir," said Johnson, "all this excludes but one evil—poverty."

In our way, Johnson strongly expressed his love of driving fast in a post-chaise. "If," said he, "I had no duties and no reference to futurity, I would spend my life in driving briskly in a post-chaise with a pretty woman; but she should be one who could understand me, and would add something to the conversation."

I felt a pleasure in walking about Derby, such as I always have in walking about any town to which I am not accustomed. There is an immediate sensation of novelty; and one speculates on the way in which life is passed in it, which, although there is a sameness everywhere upon the whole, is yet minutely diversified. The minute diversities in everything are wonderful. Talking of shaving the other night at Dr. Taylor's, Dr. Johnson said, "Sir, of a thousand shavers, two do not shave so much alike as not to be distinguished." I thought this not possible, till he specified so many of the varieties in shaving —holding the razor more or less perpendicular; drawing long or short strokes; beginning at the upper part of the face or the under; at the right side or the left side. Indeed, when one considers what variety of sounds can be uttered by the wind-pipe in the compass of a very small aperture, we may be convinced how many degrees of difference there may be in the application of a razor.

We dined with Dr. Butter. Johnson and he had a good deal of medical conversation. Johnson said he had somewhere or other given an account of Dr. Nichols's[1] discourse *"De Animâ Medicâ."* He told us that "whatever a man's distemper was, Dr. Nichols would not attend him as a physician, if his mind was not at ease; for he believed that no medicines would have any influence. When Goldsmith was dying, Dr. Turton said to him, 'Your pulse is in greater disorder than it should be

---

1. *Dr. Nichols.* At one time, physician to George III.

from the degree of fever which you have; is your mind at ease?' Goldsmith answered it was not."

After dinner, Mrs. Butter went with me to see the silk-mill which Mr. John Lombe had had a patent for, having brought away the contrivance from Italy. The simplicity of this machine and its multiplied operations struck me with an agreeable surprise. I had learned from Dr. Johnson during this interview not to think with a dejected indifference of the works of art and the pleasures of life because life is uncertain and short; but to consider such indifference as a failure of reason, a morbidness of mind; for happiness should be cultivated as much as we can, and the objects which are instrumental to it should be steadily considered as of importance, with a reference not only to ourselves, but to multitudes in successive ages. Let us guard against imagining that there is an end of felicity upon earth when we ourselves grow old or are unhappy.

Dr. Johnson told us at tea that when some of Dr. Dodd's pious friends were trying to console him by saying that he was going to leave "a wretched world," he had honesty enough not to join in the cant. "No, no," said he, "it has been a very agreeable world to me." Johnson added, "I respect Dodd for thus speaking the truth; for, to be sure, he had for several years enjoyed a life of great voluptuousness."

He told us that Dodd's city* friends stood by him so that a thousand pounds were ready to be given to the jailer if he would let him escape. He added that he knew a friend of Dodd's who walked about Newgate for some time on the evening before the day of his execution, with five hundred pounds in his pocket, ready to be paid to any of the turnkeys who could get him out; but it was too late, for he was watched with much circumspection. He said Dodd's friends had an image of him made of wax, which was to have been left in his place; and he believed it was carried into the prison.

Johnson disapproved of Dr. Dodd's leaving the world persuaded that "The Convict's Address to His Unhappy Brethren" was of his own writing. "But, sir," said I, "you contributed to the deception; for when Mr. Seward expressed a doubt to you that it was not Dodd's own, because it had a great deal more

force of mind in it than anything known to be his, you answered,
'Why should you think so? Depend upon it, sir, when a man
knows he is to be hanged in a fortnight, it concentrates his
mind wonderfully.' " JOHNSON. "Sir, as Dodd got it from
me to pass as his own, while that could do him any good, there
was an *implied promise* that I should not own it. To own it,
therefore, would have been telling a lie, with the addition of
breach of promise, which was worse than simply telling a lie
to make it be believed it was Dodd's. Besides, sir, I did not
directly tell a lie; I left the matter uncertain. Perhaps I thought
that Seward would not believe it the less to be mine for what
I said; but I would not put it in his power to say I had
owned it."

I talked of the difficulty of rising in the morning. Dr.
Johnson told me that "the learned Mrs. Carter, at that period
when she was eager to study, did not awake as early as she
wished, and she therefore had a contrivance, that at a certain
hour her chamber light should burn a string to which a heavy
weight was suspended, which then fell with a strong, sudden
noise; this roused her from sleep, and then she had no difficulty in
getting up." But I said *that* was my difficulty; and wished there
could be some medicine invented which would make me rise without pain, which I never did, unless after lying in bed a very long
time. Perhaps there may be something in the stores of Nature
which would do this. I have thought of a pulley to raise me
gradually; but that would give me pain, as it would counteract
my internal inclination. I would have something that would
dissipate the *vis inertiae* and give elasticity to the muscles.
As I have experienced a state in which rising from bed was not
disagreeable, but easy, nay sometimes agreeable, I suppose
that this state may be produced, if we knew by what. We
can heat the body, we can cool it; we can give it tension or
relaxation; and surely it is possible to bring it into a state
in which rising from bed will not be pain.

Johnson advised me tonight not to *refine* in the education of
my children. "Life," said he, "will not bear refinement; you
must do as other people do."

As we drove back to Ashbourne, Dr. Johnson recommended

to me, as he had often done, to drink water only. I said drinking wine was a pleasure I was unwilling to give up. "Why, sir," said he, "there is no doubt that not to drink wine is a great deduction from life; but it may be necessary." He, however, owned that in his opinion a free use of wine did not shorten life; and said he would not give less for the life of a certain Scotch lord (whom he named), celebrated for hard drinking, than for that of a sober man. "But stay," said he, with his usual intelligence and accuracy of inquiry, "does it take much wine to make him drunk?" I answered, "A great deal either of wine or strong punch." "Then," said he, "that is the worse." I presume to illustrate my friend's observation thus: "A fortress which soon surrenders has its walls less shattered than when a long and obstinate resistance is made."

By the time we returned to Ashbourne, Dr. Taylor was gone to bed. Johnson and I sat up a long time by ourselves.

He was much diverted by an article which I showed him in the *Critical Review* of this year, giving an account of a curious publication, entitled *A Spiritual Diary and Soliloquies*, by John Rutty,[1] M. D. Dr. Rutty was one of the people called Quakers, a physician of some eminence in Dublin, and author of several works. This diary exhibited, in the simplicity of his heart, a minute and honest register of the state of his mind; which, though frequently laughable enough, was not more so than the history of many men would be if recorded with equal fairness. The following specimens were extracted by the Reviewers:

Tenth month, 1753, 23. Indulgence in bed an hour too long.
Ninth month, 28. An overdose of whisky.
29. A dull, cross, choleric day.
First month, 1757, 22. A little swinish at dinner and repast.
31. Dogged on provocation.
Second month, 5. Very dogged or snappish.

---

1. *Rutty.* "I visited that venerable man, Dr. Rutty, just tottering over the grave; but still clear in his understanding, full of faith and love, and patiently waiting till his change should come." *John Wesley.*

14. Snappish on fasting.

26. Cursed snappishness to those under me, on a bodily indisposition.

Third month, 11. On a provocation, exercised a dumb re sentiment for two days, instead of scolding.

22. Scolded too vehemently.

23. Dogged again.

Fourth month, 29. Mechanically and sinfully dogged.

Johnson laughed[1] heartily at this good Quietist's self-condemning minutes. He thought the observations of the Critical Reviewers upon the importance of a man to himself so ingenious and so well expressed that I shall here introduce them:

After observing that "there are few writers who have gained any reputation by recording their own actions," they say:

"We may reduce the egotists to four classes. In the *first* we have Julius Caesar. He relates his own transactions; but he relates them with peculiar grace and dignity, and his narrative is supported by the greatness of his character and achievements. In the *second* class we have Marcus Antoninus.[2] This writer has given us a series of reflections on his own life; but his sentiments are so noble, his morality so sublime, that his meditations are universally admired. In the *third* class we have some others who have given importance to their own private history by an intermixture of literary anecdotes and the occurrences of their own time. In the *fourth* class we have old women and fanatic writers of memoirs and meditations."

On Saturday, September 20, after breakfast, when Taylor was gone out to his farm, Dr. Johnson and I had a serious conversation by ourselves on melancholy and madness, which he was, I always thought, erroneously inclined to confound together. Melancholy like "great wit" may be "near allied to

---

1. *Laughed.* Yet Johnson's own journal records such matters as: "I fasted, though less rigorously than at other times. I by negligence poured milk into the tea, and in the afternoon drank one dish of coffee with Thrale; yet at night, after a fit of drowsiness, I felt much disordered by emptiness, and called for tea with peevish and impatient eagerness."

2. *Marcus Antoninus.* Marcus Aurelius.

madness," but there is, in my opinion, a distinct separation between them.

Johnson said, "A madman loves to be with people whom he fears; not as a dog fears the lash, but of whom he stands in awe." I was struck with the justice of this observation. To be with those of whom a person, whose mind is wavering and dejected, stands in awe, represses and composes an uneasy tumult of spirits, and consoles him with the contemplation of something steady, and at least comparatively great."

He added, "Employment, sir, and hardships prevent melancholy. I suppose in all our army in America there was not one man who went mad."

We entered seriously upon a question of much importance to me, which Johnson was pleased to consider with friendly attention. I had long complained to him that I felt myself discontented in Scotland, as too narrow a sphere, and that I wished to make my chief residence in London, the great scene of ambition, instruction, and amusement; a scene which was to me, comparatively speaking, a heaven upon earth. JOHNSON. "Why, sir, I never knew anyone who had such a *gust* for London as you have; and I cannot blame you for your wish to live there; yet, sir, were I in your father's place, I should not consent to your settling there; for I have the old feudal notions, and I should be afraid that Auchinleck would be deserted, as you would soon find it more desirable to have a country-seat in a better climate."

I told him that one of my ancestors never went from home without being attended by thirty men on horseback. "Pray," said he, "how did your ancestor support his thirty men and thirty horses when he went at a distance from home in an age when there was hardly any money in circulation?" I suggested the same difficulty to a friend who mentioned Douglas's[1] going to the Holy Land with a numerous train of followers. Douglas could, no doubt, maintain followers enough while living upon his own lands, the produce of which supplied them with food; but

---

1. *Douglas*. The famous "Black Douglas," who in 1330 set out to carry the heart of his liege lord, Robert Bruce, to the Holy Land. He was killed on the way.

he could not carry that food to the Holy Land; and as there was no commerce by which he could be supplied with money, how could he maintain them in foreign countries?

I suggested a doubt, that if I were to reside in London, the exquisite zest with which I relished it in occasional visits might go off, and I might grow tired of it. JOHNSON. "Why, sir, you find no man, at all intellectual, who is willing to leave London. No, sir, when a man is tired of London, he is tired of life; for there is in London all that life can afford."

To obviate his apprehension, that by settling in London I might desert the seat of my ancestors, I assured him that I had old feudal principles to a degree of enthusiasm; and that I felt all the *dulcedo* of the *natale solum*. I reminded him that the Laird of Auchinleck had an elegant house, in front of which he could ride ten miles forward upon his own territories, upon which he had upwards of six hundred people attached to him; that the family seat was rich in natural romantic beauties of rock, wood, and water; and that in my "morn of life" I had appropriated the finest descriptions in the ancient Classics to certain scenes there, which were thus associated in my mind; that when all this was considered, I should certainly pass a part of the year at home, and enjoy it the more from bringing with me a share of the intellectual stores of the metropolis. He listened to all this, and kindly "hoped it might be as I now supposed."

As I meditated trying my fortune in Westminster Hall,* our conversation turned upon the profession of the law in England. JOHNSON. "You must not indulge too sanguine hopes, should you be called to our bar. I was told by a very sensible lawyer that a man might pass half a lifetime in the Courts and never have an opportunity of showing his abilities."

We talked of employment being absolutely necessary to preserve the mind from wearying and growing fretful, especially in those who have a tendency to melancholy; and I mentioned to him a saying which somebody had related of an American savage, who, when an European was expatiating on all the advantages of money, put this question: "Will it purchase *occupation?*" JOHNSON. "Depend upon it, sir, this saying is too refined for a savage. And, sir, money *will* purchase occupation; it will purchase variety of company; it will purchase all sorts of entertainment."

I talked to him of Forster's *Voyage to the South Seas*, which pleased me; but I found he did not like it. "Sir," said he, "there is a great affectation of fine writing in it." BOSWELL. "But he carries you along with him." JOHNSON. "No, sir; he does not carry *me* along with him; he leaves me behind him; or rather, indeed, he sets me before him, for he makes me turn over many leaves at a time."

On Sunday, September 12, we went to the church of Ashbourne, which is one of the largest and most luminous that I have seen in any town of the same size. I felt great satisfaction in considering that I was supported in my fondness for solemn public worship by the general concurrence and munificence of mankind.

Johnson and Taylor were so different from each other that I wondered at their preserving an intimacy. Their having been at school and college together might, in some degree, account for this; but Sir Joshua Reynolds has furnished me with a stronger reason; for Johnson mentioned to him that he had been told by Taylor he was to be his heir. Certain it is that Johnson paid great attention to Taylor. He now, however, said to me, "Sir, I love him; but I do not love him more; my regard for him does not increase. As it is said in the Apocrypha, 'his talk is of bullocks.'"

I have no doubt that a good many sermons were composed for Taylor by Johnson. At this time I found, upon his table, a part of one which he had newly begun to write. I, however, would not have it thought that Dr. Taylor, though he could not write like Johnson (as, indeed, who could?), did not sometimes compose sermons as good as those which we generally have from very respectable divines. He showed me one with notes on the margin in Johnson's handwriting; and I was present when he read another to Johnson, that he might have his opinion of it, and Johnson said it was "very well." These, we may be sure, were not Johnson's; for he was above little arts, or tricks of deception.

Johnson was by no means of opinion that every man of a learned profession should consider it as incumbent upon him to appear as an author. When in the ardor of ambition for literary fame, I regretted to him one day that an eminent Judge would leave no perpetual monument of himself to posterity: "Alas, sir," said Johnson, "what a mass of confusion should we have, if every bishop, and every judge, every lawyer, physician, and divine were to write books."

I mentioned to Johnson a respectable person[1] of a very strong mind who had little of that tenderness which is common to human nature; as an instance of which, when I suggested to him that he should invite his son, who had been settled ten years in foreign parts, to come home and pay him a visit, his answer was, "No, no, let him mind his business." JOHNSON. "I do not agree with him, sir, in this. Getting money is not all a man's business; to cultivate kindness is a valuable part of the business of life."

In the evening Johnson being in very good spirits entertained us with several characteristical portraits. "Colley Cibber once consulted me as to one of his birthday odes, a long time before it was wanted. I objected very freely to several passages. Cibber lost patience and would not read his ode to an end. When we had done with criticism, we walked over to Richardson's, the author of *Clarissa*, and I wondered to find Richardson displeased that I did not treat Cibber with more *respect*. Now, sir, to talk of *respect* for a *player* (smiling disdainfully)!" BOSWELL. "There, sir, you are always heretical: you never will allow merit to a player." JOHNSON. "Merit, sir, what merit?"[2] BOSWELL. "As a proof of the merit of great acting, and of the value which mankind set upon it, Garrick has got a hundred thousand pounds." JOHNSON. "Is getting a hundred thousand pounds a proof of excellence? That has been done by a scoundrel commissary."

---

1. *A respectable person.* No doubt, Boswell's father.
2. *What merit?* Yet Johnson wrote of Garrick after his death: "I am disappointed by that stroke of death which has eclipsed the gayety of nations and impoverished the public stock of harmless pleasure."

On Monday, September 22, when at breakfast, I unguardedly said to Dr. Johnson, "I wish I saw you and Mrs. Macaulay together." He grew very angry; and, after a pause, while a cloud gathered on his brow, he burst out, "No, sir; you would not see us quarrel, to make you sport. Don't you know that it is very uncivil to *pit* two people against one another?" Then, checking himself, and wishing to be more gentle, he added, "I do not say you should be hanged or drowned for this; but it *is* very uncivil." Dr. Taylor thought him in the wrong, and spoke to him privately of it; but I afterwards acknowledged to Johnson that I was to blame, for I candidly owned that I meant to express a desire to see a contest between Mrs. Macaulay and him; but then, I knew how the contest would end. JOHNSON. "Sir, you cannot be sure how a contest will end; and no man has a right to engage two people in a dispute by which their passions may be enflamed, and they may part with bitter resentment against each other. I would sooner keep company with a man from whom I must guard my pockets than with a man who contrives to bring me into a dispute with somebody that he may hear it. This is the great fault of ——, endeavoring to introduce a subject upon which he knows two people in the company differ." BOSWELL. "But he told me, sir, he does it for instruction." JOHNSON. "He has no more right to instruct himself at such risk than he has to make two people fight a duel that he may learn how to defend himself."

He thus characterized the Duke of Devonshire, grandfather of the present representative of that family: "He was not a man of superior abilities, but he was a man strictly faithful to his word. If, for instance, he had promised you an acorn, and none had grown that year in his woods, he would not have contented himself with that excuse; he would have sent to Denmark for it."

Talking [in the evening] of the danger of being mortified by rejection when making approaches to the acquaintance of the great, I observed, "I am, however, generally for trying; 'Nothing venture, nothing have.'" JOHNSON. "Very true, sir; but I have always been more afraid of failing than hopeful of success."

And, indeed, though he had all just respect for rank, no man ever less courted the favor of the great.

On Tuesday, September 23, Johnson was remarkably cordial to me. It being necessary for me to return to Scotland soon, I had fixed on the next day for my setting out, and I felt a tender concern at the thought of parting with him.

In the evening [a] gentleman-farmer, and two others, entertained themselves and the company with a great number of tunes on the fiddle. Johnson desired to have "Let ambition fire thy mind," played over again, and appeared to give a patient attention to it; though he owned to me that he was very insensible to the power of music.[1] I told him it affected me to such a degree as often to agitate my nerves painfully, producing in my mind alternate sensations of pathetic dejection, so that I was ready to shed tears; and of daring resolution, so that I was inclined to rush into the thickest part of the battle. "Sir," said he, "I should never hear it, if it made me such a fool."

Much of the effect of music, I am satisfied, is owing to the association of ideas. That air which instantly and irresistibly excites in the Swiss, when in a foreign land, the *maladie du pais* has, I am told, no intrinsic power of sound. And I know from my own experience that Scotch reels, though brisk, make me melancholy, because I used to hear them in my early years at a time when Mr. Pitt called for soldiers "from the mountains of the north," and numbers of brave Highlanders were going abroad, never to return. Whereas the airs in *The Beggar's*

---

1. *Power of music.* In his travels among the peasants of Corsica, Boswell describes one scene which illustrates his own love of music: "I gave them one or two Italian airs, and then some of our beautiful old Scots tunes. The pathetic simplicity and pastoral gayety of the Scots music will always please those who have the genuine feelings of nature.

"My good friends insisted also to have an English song from me. I sung them 'Hearts of oak are our ships, Hearts of oak are our men!' I translated it into Italian for them and never did I see men so delighted with a song as the Corsicans were with 'Hearts of Oak.' 'Cuore di querco,' cried they, 'bravo Inglese.' It was quite a joyous riot. I fancied myself to be a recruiting sea-officer. I fancied all my chorus of Corsicans aboard the British fleet."

Opera, many of which are very soft, never fail to render me gay, because they are associated with the warm sensations and high spirits of London. This evening, while some of the tunes of ordinary composition were played with no great skill, my frame was agitated, and I was conscious of a generous attachment to Dr. Johnson, as my preceptor and friend, mixed with an affectionate regret that he was an old man, whom I should probably lose in a short time. I thought I could defend him at the point of my sword.[1] My reverence and affection for him were in full glow. I said to him, "My dear sir, we must meet every year, if you don't quarrel with me." JOHNSON. "Nay, sir, you are more likely to quarrel with me than I with you. My regard for you is greater almost than I have words to express; but I do not choose to be always repeating it; write it down in the first leaf of your pocket-book, and never doubt of it again."[2]

I talked to him of misery being "the doom of man" in this life, as displayed in his "Vanity of Human Wishes." Yet I observed that things were done upon the supposition of happiness; grand houses were built, fine gardens were made, splendid places of public amusement were contrived, and crowded with company. JOHNSON. "Alas, sir, these are all only struggles for happiness. When I first entered Ranelagh,[3] it gave

---

1. *At the point of my sword.* "It is easy to awaken generous sentiments in privacy; to despise death when there is no danger; to glow with benevolence when there is nothing to be given. While such ideas are formed they are felt, and self-love does not suspect the gleam of virtue to be the meteor of fancy." *Johnson: Life of Pope.*

2. *Never doubt of it again.* "In my 'Tour' [to the Hebrides] from my eagerness to display the readiness of Johnson's wit, I freely showed to the world its dexterity even when I was myself the object of it. I trusted I should be liberally understood, as knowing very well what I was about, and by no means as simply unconscious of the pointed effect of the satire. But it seems I judged too well of the world." *Boswell.*

"Boswell tells me he is printing *anecdotes* of Dr. Johnson. I begged he would mitigate some of his asperities. He said roughly, he would not cut off his claws, nor make a tiger a cat to please anybody." *Hannah More.*

3. *Ranelagh.* "A vast amphitheater [roofed], finely gilt, painted, and illuminated, into which everybody that loves eating, drinking, staring, and crowding is admitted for twelve pence." *Walpole, 1742.*

an expansion and gay sensation to my mind, such as I never experienced anywhere else. But, as Xerxes wept when he viewed his immense army, and considered that not one of that great multitude would be alive a hundred years afterwards, so it went to my heart to consider that there was not one in all the brilliant circle that was not afraid to go home and think; but that the thoughts of each individual there would be distressing when alone."

While Johnson and I stood in calm conference by ourselves in Dr. Taylor's garden at a pretty late hour in a serene autumn night, looking up to the heavens, I directed the discourse to the subject of a future state. My friend was in a placid and most benignant frame of mind. "Sir," said he, "I do not imagine that all things will be made clear to us immediately after death, but that the ways of Providence will be explained to us very gradually." He talked to me upon this awful and delicate question in a gentle tone, and as if afraid to be decisive.

After supper I accompanied him to his apartment, and at my request he dictated to me an argument in favor of the negro who was then claiming his liberty, in an action in the Court of Session in Scotland. He had always been very zealous against slavery in every form, in which I with all deference thought that he discovered* "a zeal without knowledge." Upon one occasion, when in company with some very grave men at Oxford, his toast was, "Here's to the next insurrection of the negroes in the West Indies." His violent prejudice against our West Indian and American settlers appeared whenever there was an opportunity. Toward the conclusion of his "Taxation No Tyranny," he says, "How is it that we hear the loudest *yelps* for liberty among the drivers of negroes?"

The argument dictated by Dr. Johnson was as follows:

"It is impossible not to conceive that men in their original state were equal; and very difficult to imagine how one would be subjected to another but by violent compulsion. An individual may indeed forfeit his liberty by a crime, but he cannot by that crime forfeit the liberty of his children. What is true of a criminal seems true likewise of a captive. A man may accept life from a conquering enemy on condition of perpetual servitude;

but it is very doubtful whether he can entail that servitude on his descendants, for no man can stipulate without commission for another. The condition which he accepts, his son or grandson perhaps would have rejected. He who is now suing for his freedom is certainly subject by no law but that of violence, to his present master; who pretends no claim to his obedience but that he bought him from a merchant of slaves, whose right to sell him never was examined. Whoever is [so] exposed to sale is condemned to slavery without appeal; by whatever fraud or violence he might have been originally brought into the merchant's power. In our own time princes have been sold by wretches to whose care they were entrusted, that they might have an European education; but when once they were brought into a market in the plantations, little would avail either their dignity or their wrongs. The laws of Jamaica afford a negro no redress. His color is considered as a sufficient testimony against him. It is to be lamented that moral right should ever give way to political convenience. But if temptations of interest are sometimes too strong for human virtue, let us at least retain a virtue where there is no temptation to quit it. In the present case there is apparent right on one side and no convenience on the other. Inhabitants of this island can neither gain riches nor power by taking away the liberty of any part of the human species."

I record Dr. Johnson's argument fairly upon this particular case, where, perhaps, he was in the right. But I beg leave to enter my most solemn protest against his general doctrine with respect to the slave trade. For I will resolutely say that his unfavorable notion of it was owing to prejudice, and imperfect or false information. The wild and dangerous attempt which has for some time been persisted in to obtain an act of our Legislature to abolish so very important and necessary a branch of commercial interest, must have been crushed at once, had not the insignificance of the zealots who vainly took the lead in it made the vast body of planters, merchants, and others, whose immense properties are involved in that trade, reasonably enough suppose that there could be no danger. The encouragement which the attempt has received excites my wonder and indignation; and though some men of superior abilities have supported it, whether from love of temporary popularity, when prosperous, or a love of general mischief when desperate, my opinion is unshaken. To abolish a *status*, which in all ages God has sanctioned and man has continued, would not only be *robbery* to an innumerable class of our fellow-subjects, but it would be extreme cruelty to the African savages, a portion of whom it saves from massacre, or intolerable bondage in their own country, and introduces into a much happier state of life; especially now when their passage to the West Indies and their treatment there is humanely regulated. To abolish that trade would be to

——shut the gates of mercy on mankind.

When I said now to Johnson that I was afraid I kept him too late up, "No, sir," said he, "I don't care though I sit all night with you." This was an animated speech from a man in his sixty-ninth year.

Had I been as attentive not to displease him as I ought to have been, I know not but this vigil might have been fulfilled; but I unluckily entered upon the controversy concerning the right of Great Britain to tax America, and attempted to argue in favor of our fellow-subjects on the other side of the Atlantic. I insisted that America might be very well governed, and made to yield sufficient revenue by the means of *influence*,[1] while the people might be pleased with the imagination of their partici- pating of the British constitution. Johnson could not bear my thus opposing his avowed opinion, and the violent agitation into which he was thrown, while answering, or rather reprimanding me, alarmed me so that I heartily repented of my having un- thinkingly introduced the subject. I myself, however, grew warm, and the change was great from the calm state of philo-

---

1. *Influence.* In politics this term gained a special significance in the reign of George III, and often denoted the notorious methods which he used in pushing through legislation agreeable to the Crown. This he did by extending or withholding court favors among those powerful enough to exert a similar social pressure among their hangers-on and dependents. The *influence*, or corruption, which Boswell advocates in this paragraph he decries in the next.

sophical discussion in which we had a little before been pleasingly employed.

I talked of the corruption of the British Parliament, in which I alleged that any question, however unreasonable or unjust, might be carried by a venal majority; and I spoke with high admiration of the Roman Senate, as if composed of men sincerely desirous to resolve what they should think best for their country. My friend would allow no such character to the Roman Senate; and he maintained that the British Parliament was not corrupt, and that there was no occasion to corrupt its members; asserting that there was hardly ever any question of great importance before Parliament, any question in which a man might not very well vote either upon one side or the other. He said there had been none in his time except that respecting America.

We were fatigued by the contest, which was produced by my want of caution; and he was not then in the humor to slide into easy and cheerful talk. It therefore so happened that we were after an hour or two very willing to separate and go to bed.

On Wednesday, September 24, I went into Dr. Johnson's room before he got up, and finding that the storm of the preceding night was quite laid, I sat down upon his bedside, and he talked with as much readiness and good humor as ever.

I spoke with gratitude of Dr. Taylor's hospitality; and as evidence that it was not on account of his good table alone that Johnson visited him often, I mentioned a little anecdote which had escaped my friend's recollection, and at hearing which repeated, he smiled. One evening when I was sitting with him, Frank delivered this message: "Sir, Dr. Taylor sends his compliments to you, and begs you will dine with him to-morrow. He has got a hare."—"My compliments," said Johnson, "and I'll dine with him—hare or rabbit."

After breakfast I departed, and pursued my journey northwards. I took my post-chaise from the Green Man, a very good inn at Ashbourne.

I cannot omit a curious circumstance which occurred at Edensor inn, close by Chatsworth, to survey the magnificence of which I had gone a considerable way out of my road to

Scotland. The inn was then kept by a very jolly landlord, whose name, I think, was Malton. He happened to mention that "the celebrated Dr. Johnson had been in his house." I inquired *who* this Dr. Johnson was, that I might hear mine host's notion of him. "Sir, said he, "Johnson, the great writer; *Oddity*, as they call him. He's the greatest writer in England; he writes for the ministry; he has a correspondence abroad, and lets them know what's going on."

[1778]. On Wednesday, March 18, I arrived in London. On Friday, March 20, I found him at his own house, sitting with Mrs. Williams, and was informed that the room formerly allotted to me was now appropriated to a charitable purpose, Mrs. Desmoulins,[1] and, I think, her daughter, and a Miss Carmichael[2] being all lodged in it. Such was his humanity that Mrs. Desmoulins herself told me he allowed her half a guinea a week. This was above a twelfth part of his pension.

Tom Davies soon after joined us. He had now unfortunately failed in his circumstances and was much indebted to Dr. Johnson's kindness. After he went away, Johnson blamed his folly in quitting the stage by which he and his wife got five hundred pounds a year. I said I believed it was owing to Churchill's attack upon him:

> He mouths a sentence as curs mouth a bone.

JOHNSON. "I believe so, too, sir. But what a man is he who is to be driven from the stage by a line? Another line would have driven him from his shop."

---

1. *Mrs. Desmoulins.* Widow of a writing master. Her father was Johnson's godfather, the physician, Dr. Swinfen, who had betrayed the boy's confidence on the matter of his melancholy (see the early pages of this book). She was encumbered with a peevish temperament and three necessitous children.

2. *Miss Carmichael.* Apparently, a servant too stupid to stay long. Mme. D'Arblay reports the following dialogue concerning her between Mrs. Thrale and Dr. Johnson. MRS. T. "But pray, sir, who is the Poll you talk of? She that you used to abet in her quarrels with Mrs. Williams and call out, '*At her again, Poll! Never flinch, Poll!*'" DR. J. "I had some hopes of her at first; but when I talked to her tightly and closely, I could make nothing of her; she was wiggle-waggle, and I could never persuade her to be categorical." Not much else is known of her.

I told him that I was engaged as counsel at the bar of the House of Commons to oppose a road bill in the county of Stirling, and asked him what mode he would advise me to follow in addressing such an audience. JOHNSON. "Why, sir, you must provide yourself with a good deal of extraneous matter, which you are to produce occasionally, so as to fill up the time. If you begin with the strength of your cause, it may be lost before they begin to listen. When you catch a moment of attention, press the merits of the question upon them." He said, as to one point of the merits, that he thought "it would be a wrong thing to deprive the small landholders of the privilege of assessing themselves for making and repairing the high roads; *it was destroying a certain portion of liberty, without a good reason, which was always a bad thing.*" When I mentioned this observation next day to Mr. Wilkes, he pleasantly said, "What! does *he* talk of liberty? *Liberty* is as ridiculous in *his* mouth as *religion* in *mine.*" Mr. Wilkes's advice as to the best mode of speaking at the bar of the House of Commons was not more respectful toward the senate than that of Dr. Johnson. "Be as impudent as you can, as merry as you can, and say whatever comes uppermost."

In my interview with Dr. Johnson this evening, I was quite easy, quite as his companion; upon which I find in my *Journal* the following reflection: "So ready is my mind to suggest matter for dissatisfaction that I felt a sort of regret that I was so easy. I missed that awful reverence[1] with which I used to contemplate MR. SAMUEL JOHNSON. I have a wonderful superstitious love of *mystery*, when, perhaps, the truth is that it is owing to the cloudy darkness of my own mind."

He returned next day to Streatham, to Mr. Thrale's, where, as Mr. Strahan once complained to me, "he was in a great

---

1. *Awful reverence.* Yet of one episode five years before, Boswell has said: "To hear the grave Dr. Johnson, while sitting solemn in an armchair in the Isle of Skye, talk of his keeping a seraglio and acknowledge that the supposition had often been in his thoughts struck me so forcibly that I could not but laugh immoderately. He retaliated with such a variety of degrading images, of every one of which I was the object, that I would gladly expunge from my mind every trace of this severe retort."

measure absorbed from the society of his old friends." I went to Streatham on Monday, March 30. Before he appeared, Mrs. Thrale made a very characteristical remark: "I do not know for certain what will please Dr. Johnson; but I know for certain that it will displease him to praise anything, even what he likes, extravagantly."

At dinner he laughed at querulous declamations against the age, on account of luxury—increase of London, scarcity of provisions, and other such topics. "Houses," said he, "will be built till rents fall; and corn is more plentiful now than ever it was."

"*Thomas à Kempis*"[1] he observed, "must be a good book, as the world has opened its arms to receive it. It is said to have been printed, in one language or other, as many times as there have been months since it first came out. I always was struck with this sentence in it: 'Be not angry that you cannot make others as you wish them to be, since you cannot make yourself as you wish to be.'"

When we were at tea and coffee, there came in Lord Trimlestown, in whose family was an ancient Irish peerage, but it suffered by taking the generous side in the troubles of the last century. I mentioned that I had in my possession the *Life of Sir Robert Sibbald*, the celebrated Scottish antiquary and founder of the Royal College of Physicians at Edinburgh, in the original manuscript in his own handwriting; and that it was, I believed, the most natural and candid account of himself that ever was given by any man. As an instance, he tells that the Duke of Perth, then Chancellor of Scotland, pressed him very much to come over to the Roman Catholic faith; that he resisted all his Grace's arguments till one day he felt himself, as it were, instantaneously convinced, and with tears in his eyes

---

1. *Thomas à Kempis*. A placid German monk of the fifteenth century. The *Imitatio Christi*, or *Imitation of Christ*, which is commonly attributed to him and universally called after his name, is a volume of devotion in verses like those of the Bible. Sir John Hawkins says that Johnson was "for some time pleased" with it, "but at length laid it aside, saying that the main design of it was to promote monkish piety and ecclesiastical obedience."

ran into the Duke's arms, and embraced the ancient religion; that he continued very steady in it for some time, and accompanied his Grace to London one winter, and lived in his household; that there he found the rigid fasting prescribed by the church very severe upon him; that this disposed him to reconsider the controversy, and having then seen that he was in the wrong, he returned to Protestantism. I talked of some time or other publishing this curious life. MRS. THRALE. "I think you had as well let alone that publication. To discover such weakness exposes a man when he is gone." JOHNSON. "Nay, it is an honest picture[1] of human nature. How often are the primary motives of our greatest actions as small as Sibbald's for his reconversion." MRS. THRALE. "But may they not as well be forgotten?" JOHNSON. "No, madam, a man loves to review his own mind. That is the use of a diary, or journal."

Next morning, while we were at breakfast, Johnson gave a very earnest recommendation of what he himself practiced with the utmost conscientiousness; I mean a strict attention to truth, even in the most minute particulars. Our lively hostess, whose fancy was impatient of the rein, fidgeted at this, and ventured to say, "Nay, this is too much. If Mr. Johnson should forbid me to drink tea,[2] I would comply, as I should feel the restraint only twice a day; but little variations in narrative must happen a thousand times a day, if one is not perpetually watching." JOHNSON. "Well, madam, and you *ought* to be perpetually watching. It is more from carelessness about truth than from intentional lying that there is so much falsehood in the world."

---

1. *Honest picture.* "As you have now little to do, I suppose you are pretty diligent at the Thraliana; and a very curious collection posterity will find it. Do not omit painful casualties, or unpleasing passages; they make the variegation of existence." *Johnson to Mrs. Thrale, Sept. 6, 1777.*

2. *Forbid me to drink tea.* A personal hit. As early as 1757 Johnson had described himself as "a hardened and shameless tea drinker who has for twenty years diluted his meals with only the infusion of this fascinating plant."

"When Sir Joshua Reynolds at my house reminded him that he had drunk eleven cups [of tea], he replied, 'Sir, I did not count your glasses of wine; why should you number up my cups of tea?'" *Richard Cumberland.*

I never knew any person who, upon hearing an extraordinary circumstance told, discovered more of the *incredulus odi*. He would say with a significant look and decisive tone, "It is not so. Do not tell this again." He inculcated upon all his friends the importance of perpetual vigilance against the slightest degrees of falsehood; the effect of which, as Sir Joshua Reynolds observed to me, has been that all who were of his *school* are distinguished for a love of truth and accuracy,[1] which they would not have possessed in the same degree if they had not been acquainted with Johnson.

Talking of ghosts, he said, "It is wonderful that five thousand years have now elapsed since the creation of the world, and still it is undecided whether or not there has ever been an instance of the spirit of any person appearing after death. All argument is against it; but all belief is for it."

He said, "John Wesley's[2] conversation is good, but he is never at leisure. He is always obliged to go at a certain hour. This is very disagreeable to a man who loves to fold his legs and have out his talk, as I do."

On Friday, April 3, I dined with him in London in a company where were present several eminent men whom I shall not name, but distinguish their parts in the conversation by different letters.

F. "I have been looking at this famous antique marble dog of Mr. Jennings, valued at a thousand guineas, said to be Alcibiades's dog." E.[3] "A thousand guineas! The repre-

---

1. *Love of truth and accuracy.* "Sir Joshua Reynolds said one day that nobody wore laced coats now; and that once everybody wore them. 'See now,' says Johnson, 'how absurd that is; as if the bulk of mankind consisted of fine gentlemen that came to him to sit for their pictures. If every man that wears a laced coat (that he can pay for) was extirpated, who would miss them?'" *Mrs. Piozzi: Anecdotes of Johnson.*

2. *John Wesley.* The most famous of English field preachers. Addressing vast and often disorderly masses of people, and hasting on horseback from the outskirts of one town to the outskirts of another kept him hale and self-satisfied till his eighty-ninth year. "When you met him in the street of a crowded city, he attracted notice, not only by his band and cassock and his long hair, white and bright as silver, but by his pace and manner, both indicating that all his minutes were numbered, and that not one was to be lost." *Robert Southey.*

3. *E.* Edmund Burke.

sentation of no animal whatever is worth so much. At this rate a dead dog would indeed be better than a living lion." JOHNSON. "Sir, it is not the worth of the thing, but of the skill in forming it which is so highly estimated. Everything that enlarges the sphere of human powers, that shows man he can do what he thought he could not do, is valuable. The first man who balanced a straw upon his nose; Johnson who rode upon three horses at a time—deserved the applause of mankind, not on account of the use of what they did, but of the dexterity which they exhibited." BOSWELL. "Yet a misapplication of time and assiduity is not to be encouraged. Addison, in one of his *Spectators*, commends the judgment of a king, who, as a suitable reward to a man that by long perseverance had attained to the art of throwing a barley-corn through the eye of a needle, gave him a bushel of barley." JOHNSON. "He must have been a king of Scotland, where barley is scarce."

R. "Mr. E., I don't mean to flatter, but when posterity reads one of your speeches in Parliament, it will be difficult to believe that you took so much pains, knowing with certainty that it could produce no effect, that not one vote would be gained by it." E. "Waiving your compliment to me, I shall say, in general, that it is very well worth while for a man to take pains to speak well in Parliament. If a man speaks well, he gradually establishes a certain reputation, which sooner or later will have its political reward. Besides, though not one vote is gained, a good speech has its effect. Though an act which has been ably opposed passes into a law, yet in its progress it is modeled, it is softened in such a manner that we see plainly the Minister has been told that the members attached to him are so sensible of its injustice or absurdity from what they have heard, that it must be altered." JOHNSON. "And, sir, there is a gratification of pride. Though we cannot out-vote them we will out-argue them. They shall not do wrong without its being shown both to themselves and to the world." E. "The House of Commons is a mixed body. (I except the minority, which I hold to be pure, [smiling] but I take the whole house.) There are many members who generally go with the Minister, who will not go all lengths. There are many honest, well-meaning country gentlemen who are in Parliament only to keep up the consequence of their families. Upon most of these a good speech will have influence." JOHNSON. "We are all more or less governed by interest. But interest will not make us do everything. In a case which admits of doubt, we try to think on the side which is for our interest, and generally bring ourselves to act accordingly. But the subject must admit of diversity of coloring; it must receive a color on that side. In the House of Commons there are members enough who will not vote what is grossly unjust or absurd. No, sir, there must always be right enough, or appearance of right, to keep wrong in countenance." BOSWELL. "There is surely always a majority in Parliament who have places, or who want to have them, and who therefore will be generally ready to support government without requiring any pretext." E. "True, sir; that majority will always follow

> *Quo   clamor vocat et turba faventium."*

BOSWELL. "Well now, let us take the common phrase, Place-hunters. I thought they had hunted without regard to anything, just as their huntsman, the Minister, leads, looking only to the prey." J. "But taking your metaphor, you know that in hunting there are few so desperately keen as to follow without reserve. Some do not choose to leap ditches and hedges and risk their necks, or gallop over steeps, or even to dirty themselves in bogs and mire." BOSWELL. "I am glad there are some good, quiet, moderate political hunters." R. "What would be the consequence, if a minister, sure of a majority in the House of Commons, should resolve that there should be no speaking at all upon his side?" E. "He must soon go out. That has been tried, but it was found it would not do."

E. "From the experience which I have had—and I have had a great deal—I have learned to think *better* of mankind." JOHNSON. "From my experience I have found them worse in commercial dealings, more disposed to cheat than I had any notion of; but more disposed to do one another good than I had conceived." J. "Less just and more beneficent." JOHNSON. "And really it is wonderful, considering how much attention is necessary for men to take care of themselves, and ward off immediate evils which press upon them—it is wonderful how much they do for others. As it is said of the greatest liar that he tells more truth than falsehood, so it may be said of the worst man that he does more good than evil." Boswell. "Perhaps from experience men may be found *happier* than we suppose." Johnson. "No, sir; the more we inquire we shall find men the less happy." P. "Some cunning people will not be satisfied unless they have put men to the test, as they think. There is a very good story told of Sir Godfrey Kneller[1] in his character of a justice of the peace. A gentleman brought his servant before him, upon an accusation of having stolen some money from him; but it having come out that he had laid it purposely in the servant's way, in order to try his honesty, Sir Godfrey sent the master to prison." Johnson. "To resist temptation once is not a sufficient proof of honesty. If a servant, indeed, were to resist the continued temptation of silver lying in a window when he is sure his master does not know how much there is of it, he would give a strong proof of honesty. But this is a proof to which you have no right to put a man. You know, humanly speaking, there is a certain degree of temptation which will overcome any virtue." P. "And, when once overcome, it is easier for him to be got the better of again." Boswell. "I have known a man resolved to put friendship to the test by asking a man to lend him money, when he did not want it." Johnson. "That is very wrong, sir. Your friend may have many good qualities; narrowness may be his only fault."

E. "I understand the hogshead of claret which this society was favored with by our friend the Dean[2] is nearly out; I think

---

1. *Sir Godfrey Kneller.* The famous court painter under Charles II, James II, William and Mary, Queen Anne, and George I. He is said to have been vain and arrogant but of a shrewd, sound judgment.

2. *Dean.* The same civil and polished Dean of Derry (afterwards Bishop of Killaloe) whose address to Johnson in 1776 was too "replete with wit and humor" to be sent him with safety (see page 298). He once ruffled the sexagenarian Johnson by averring that no one improved after forty-five and was harshly told that his own opportunity for improvement was ample. He gracefully avenged himself by a few verses in which he promised to copy Johnson's

"free and easy style,
And from the roughness of his file
Grow like himself—polite."

That no rancor resulted from this encounter the reader will discover for himself when he comes to Boswell's Life of Johnson for the year 1781

he should be written to, to send another of the same kind. Let the request be made with a happy ambiguity of expression, so that we may have the chance of his sending *it* also as a present." JOHNSON. "I am willing to offer my services as secretary on this occasion." P. "As many as are for Dr. Johnson being secretary hold up your hands.—Carried unanimously." BOSWELL. "He will be our Dictator." JOHNSON. "No, the company is to dictate to me. I am no more than humble *scribe*. Were I your Dictator, you should have no wine. Rome was ruined by luxury (smiling)."

On Saturday, April 4, I drank tea with Johnson at Dr. Taylor's, where he had dined. He was very silent this evening, and read in a variety of books, suddenly throwing down one and taking up another.

He talked of going to Streatham that night. TAYLOR. "You'll be robbed, if you do; or you must shoot a highwayman. Now I would rather be robbed than do that; I would not shoot a highwayman." JOHNSON. "But I would rather shoot him in the instant when he is attempting to rob me than afterwards swear against him at the Old Bailey, to take away his life, after he has robbed me. I am surer I am right in the one case than in the other. I may be mistaken as to the man when I swear; I cannot be mistaken if I shoot him in the act. Besides, we feel less reluctance to take away a man's life when we are heated by the injury than to do it at a distance of time by an oath, after we have cooled." BOSWELL. "So, sir, you would rather act from the motive of private passion than that of public advantage." JOHNSON. "Nay, sir, when I shoot the highwayman, I act from both." BOSWELL. "Very well, very well.—There is no catching him." JOHNSON. "At the same time, one does not know what to say. For perhaps one may, a year after, hang himself from uneasiness for having shot a man. Few minds are fit to be trusted with so great a thing." BOSWELL. "Then, sir, you would not shoot him?" JOHNSON. "But I might be vexed afterwards for that too."

On Tuesday, April 7, I breakfasted with him at his house. He said, "nobody was content." I mentioned to him a respectable person in Scotland whom he knew; and I asserted that I really believed he was always content. JOHNSON. "No, sir, he is not content with the present; he has always some new scheme, some new plantation,* something which is future. You know he was not content as a widower, for he married again." BOSWELL. "He seems to amuse himself quite well; to have his attention fixed, and his tranquillity preserved by very small matters. I have tried this; but it would not do with me." JOHNSON (laughing). "No, sir; it must be born with a man to be contented to take up with little things. Women have a great advantage that they may take up with little things, without disgracing themselves; a man cannot, except with fiddling. Had I learnt to fiddle, I should have done nothing else." BOSWELL. "Pray, sir, did you ever play on any musical instrument?" JOHNSON. "No, sir. I once bought me a flageolet, but I never made out a tune. A man would never undertake great things, could he be amused with small." He asked me to go down with him and dine at Mr. Thrale's at Streatham, to which I agreed. I had lent him *An Account of Scotland, in 1702*, written by an English chaplain to a regiment stationed there. JOHNSON. "It is sad stuff, sir, miserably written, as books in general then were. There is now an elegance of style universally diffused. No man now writes so ill as Martin's *Account of the Hebrides* is written. A man could not write so ill if he should try. Set a merchant's clerk now to write, and he'll do better."

He talked to me with serious concern of a certain female friend's[1] "laxity of narration, and inattention to truth."—"I am as much vexed," said he, "at the ease with which she hears it mentioned to her as at the thing itself. I told her, 'Madam, you are contented to hear every day said to you, what the highest of mankind have died for, rather than bear.'—You know, sir, the highest of mankind have died rather than bear to be told they had uttered a falsehood. Do talk to her of it; I am weary."

I told him that I had been present the day before, when Mrs. Montagu, the literary lady, sat to Miss Reynolds for her picture; and that she said she had bound up Mr. Gibbon's *History* without the last two offensive chapters; for that she thought

---

1. *A certain female friend.* No doubt, Mrs. Thrale.

the book so far good, as it gave, in an elegant manner, the substance of the bad writers which the late Lord Lyttelton advised her to read. JOHNSON. "Sir, she has not read them; she shows none of this impetuosity to me; she does not know Greek, and, I fancy, knows little Latin. She is willing you should think she knows them; but she does not say she does."

Talking of drinking wine, he said, "I did not leave off wine because I could not bear it; I have drunk three bottles of port without being the worse for it. University College has witnessed this." BOSWELL. "Why then, sir, did you leave it off?" JOHNSON. "Why, sir, because it is so much better for a man to be sure that he is never to be intoxicated, never to lose the power over himself. I shall not begin to drink wine again till I grow old, and want it." BOSWELL. "I think, sir, you once said to me that not to drink wine was a great deduction from life." JOHNSON. "It is a diminution of pleasure, to be sure; but I do not say a diminution of happiness. There is more happiness in being rational. Philosophers tell you that pleasure is *contrary* to happiness. Gross men prefer animal pleasure. So there are men who have preferred living among savages. Now what a wretch must he be who is content with such conversation as can be had among savages! You may remember an officer at Fort Augustus,[1] who had served in America, told us of a woman whom they were obliged to *bind*, in order to get her back from savage life." BOSWELL. "She must have been an animal, a beast." JOHNSON. "Sir, she was a speaking cat."

I mentioned to him that I had become very weary in a company where I heard not a single intellectual sentence, except that "a man who had been settled ten years in Minorca was become a much inferior man to what he was in London, because a man's mind grows narrow in a narrow place." JOHNSON. "A man's mind grows narrow in a narrow place, whose mind is enlarged only because he has lived in a large place; but what is got by books and thinking is preserved in a narrow place as well as in a large place." BOSWELL. "I don't know, sir; if you had remained ten years in the Isle of Col, you would not have been

---

1. *Fort Augustus.* In the Hebrides.

the man that you now are." JOHNSON. "Yes, sir, if I had been there from fifteen to twenty-five; but not if from twenty-five to thirty-five." BOSWELL. "I own, sir, the spirits which I have in London make me do everything with more readiness and vigor. I can talk twice as much in London as anywhere else."

Of Goldsmith, he said, "He was not an agreeable companion, for he talked always for fame. A man who does so never can be pleasing. The man who talks to unburthen his mind is the man to delight you."

Soon after our arrival at Thrale's, I heard one of the maids calling eagerly on another, to go to Dr. Johnson. I wondered what this could mean. I afterwards learned it was to give her a Bible, which he had brought from London as a present to her.

He was for a considerable time occupied in reading *Mémoires de Fontenelle*,[1] leaning and swinging upon the low gate into the court, without his hat.

I looked into Lord Kames's *Sketches of the History of Man;* and mentioned to Dr. Johnson his censure of Charles the Fifth[2] for celebrating his funeral obsequies in his lifetime, which, I told him, I had been used to think a solemn and affecting act. JOHNSON. "Why, sir, a man may dispose his mind to think so; but if one man out of ten thousand laughs at it, he'll make the other nine thousand nine hundred and ninety-nine laugh too." I could not agree with him in this.

Sir John Pringle[3] had expressed a wish that I would ask Dr.

---

1. *Fontenelle.* A pleasant centenarian. His memoirs were in part edited, in part composed, by the Abbé Trublet.

2. *Charles the Fifth.* Emperor of Spain and Austria. "Kames describes his rehearsal of his funeral as 'an act as wild as any that superstition ever suggested to a distempered brain.'" *Birkbeck Hill.*

3. *Sir John Pringle.* President of the Royal Society. When a Scotch landlord once observed of Johnson, "They say he is the greatest man in England except Lord Mansfield," Johnson was "highly entertained" and remarked, "I like the exception; to have called me the greatest man in England would have been an unmeaning compliment; but the exception marked that the praise was in earnest; and in *Scotland,* the exception must be *Lord Mansfield* or—*Sir John Pringle.*" Johnson and Sir John were equally set on not meeting each other for the radical unitarianism of the one and the orthodoxy and Toryism of the other were too pronounced not to be mutually offensive.

Johnson's opinion what were the best English sermons for style. I took an opportunity today of mentioning several to him— "*Atterbury*"? JOHNSON. "Yes, sir, one of the best." BOSWELL. "I like Ogden's[1] *Sermons on Prayer* very much, both for neatness of style and subtlety of reasoning." JOHNSON. "I should like to read all that Ogden has written." BOSWELL. "What I wish to know is what sermons afford the best specimen of English pulpit eloquence." JOHNSON. "We have no sermons addressed to the passions that are good for anything; if you mean that kind of eloquence." A CLERGYMAN (whose name I do not recollect). "Were not Dodd's sermons addressed to the passions?" JOHNSON. "They were nothing, sir, be they addressed to what they may."

He and I returned to town in the evening. Upon the road I endeavored to maintain, in argument, that a landed gentleman is not under any obligation to reside upon his estate; and that by living in London he does no injury to his country. JOHNSON. "Why, sir, he does no injury to his country in general, because the money which he draws from it gets back again in circulation; but to his particular district, his particular parish, he does an injury. All that he has to give away is not given to those who have the first claim to it. And though I have said that the money circulates back, it is a long time before that happens. Then, sir, a man of family and estate ought to consider himself as having the charge of a district over which he is to diffuse civility* and happiness."

Next day I found him at home in the morning. Talking of a man's resolving to deny himself the use of wine, from moral and religious considerations, he said, "He must not doubt about it. When one doubts as to pleasure, we know what will be the conclusion. I now no more think of drinking wine than a horse does."

---

1. *Ogden.* Twice in Boswell's *Journal of a Tour to the Hebrides*, we find Johnson bored by him: "When we got home, Dr. Johnson desired to see my books. He took down Ogden's *Sermons on Prayer* and retired with them to his room. He did not stay long." "We went to our inn and sat quietly. Ogden he sometimes took up and glanced at; but threw it down again."

On Thursday, April 9, I dined with him at Sir Joshua Reynolds's, with the Bishop of St. Asaph[1] (Dr. Shipley), Mr. Allan Ramsay,[2] Mr. Gibbon, Mr. Cambridge, and Mr. Langton. Mr. Ramsay had lately returned from Italy, and entertained us with his observations upon Horace's Villa,[3] which he had examined with great care. Horace's journey to Brundusium being mentioned, Johnson observed that the brook[4] which he describes is to be seen now, exactly as at that time; and that he had often wondered how it happened that small brooks, such as this, kept the same situation for ages, notwithstanding earthquakes by which even mountains have been changed, and agriculture, which produces such a variation upon the surface of the earth.

The Bishop said it appeared from Horace's writings that he was a cheerful, contented man. JOHNSON. "We have no reason to believe that, my lord. Are we to think Pope was happy, because he says so in his writings? We see in his writings what he wished the state of his mind to appear. Dr. Young,[5] who pined for preferment, talks with contempt of it in his writings, and affects to despise everything that he did not despise."

---

1. *Bishop of St. Asaph.* A very social clergyman; friend of the free-thinker Benjamin Franklin. His giving dinners in Passion Week offended Johnson, who nevertheless attended them rather than seem to rebuke a bishop.

2. *Allan Ramsay.* Son of the famous Scotch poet. Himself a painter and rich enough to be a generous host. He was now 67. After he was 70, he again traveled to Italy.

3. *Horace's Villa.* The supposed site of the Sabine farm which Horace's generous patron, Maecenas, gave him when he was thirty or more years of age. "We turned up a pathway, and crossing a vineyard found ourselves where Horace's Villa is supposed to have stood. A part of a wall rising in the midst of bramble, some mosaic pavements, and the fragments of a column are the only traces which now remain. Its situation is extremely peaceful, placed in a little plain or valley in the windings of Mount Lucretilis." *Eustace, 1814.*

4. *Brook.* As Birkbeck Hill notes, not in Horace's account of his journey to Brundusium, but in his first epistle.

5. *Dr. Young.* Author of the "Night Thoughts," a poem famous for its contemplation of the grave and the Day of Judgment, and its affectation of unworldliness. George Eliot has well called him "a cross between a sycophant and a psalmist."

BISHOP OF ST. ASAPH. "He was like other chaplains looking for vacancies; but that is not peculiar to the clergy. I remember when I was with the army, after the battle of Lafeldt the officers seriously grumbled that no general was killed." CAMBRIDGE. "We may believe Horace more when he says,

Romæ Tibur amem ventosus Tibure Romam,

than when he boasts of his consistency. BOSWELL. "How hard is it that man can never be at rest." RAMSAY. "It is not in his nature to be at rest. When he is at rest, he is in the worst state that he can be in, for he has nothing to agitate him. He is then like the man in the Irish song:

> There lived a young man in Ballinacrazy,
> Who wanted a wife for to make him uneasy."

Goldsmith being mentioned, Johnson observed that it was long before his merit came to be acknowledged, that he once complained to him, in ludicrous terms of distress, "Whenever I write anything, the public *make a point* to know nothing about it"; but that his *Traveller* brought him into high reputation. SIR JOSHUA. "I was glad to hear Charles Fox say it was one of the finest poems in the English language." LANGTON. "Why was you glad? You surely had no doubt of this before." JOHNSON. "No; the merit of *The Traveller* is so well established that Mr. Fox's praise cannot augment it, nor his censure diminish it." SIR JOSHUA. "But his friends may suspect they had too great a partiality for him." JOHNSON. "Nay, sir, the partiality of his friends was always against him. It was with difficulty we could give him a hearing. Goldsmith had no settled notions upon any subject; so he talked always at random. It seemed to be his intention to blurt out whatever was in his mind, and see what would become of it. He was angry too, when catched in an absurdity; but it did not prevent him from falling into another the next minute. I remember Chamier,[1] after talking with him some time, said, 'Well, I do believe he

---

1. *Chamier*, Andrew. A stock broker, with a liberal education.

wrote this poem himself; and, let me tell you, that is believing a great deal.' Chamier once asked him what he meant by *slow*, the last word in the first line of *The Traveller*,

> Remote, unfriended, melancholy, slow.

Did he mean tardiness of locomotion? Goldsmith, who would say something without consideration, answered, 'Yes.' I was sitting by, and said, 'No, sir, you do not mean tardiness of locomotion; you mean that sluggishness of mind which comes upon a man in solitude.' Chamier believed then that I had written the line, as much as if he had seen me write it. Goldsmith, however, was a man who, whatever he wrote, did it better than any other man could do. He deserved a place in Westminster Abbey, and every year he lived would have deserved it better. He had, indeed, been at no pains to fill his mind with knowledge. He transplanted it from one place to another, and it did not settle in his mind; so he could not tell what was in his own books."

We talked of living in the country. JOHNSON. "No wise man will go to live in the country unless he has something to do which can be better done in the country. For instance, if he is to shut himself up for a year to study a science, it is better to look out to the fields than to an opposite wall. Then, if a man walks out in the country, there is nobody to keep him from walking in again; but if a man walks out in London, he is not sure when he shall walk in again. A great city is, to be sure, the school for studying life; and 'The proper study of mankind is man,' as Pope observes." BOSWELL. "I fancy London is the best place for society, though I have heard that the very first society of Paris is still beyond anything that we have here." JOHNSON. "Sir, I question if in Paris such a company as is sitting round this table could be got together in less than half a year. They talk in France of the felicity of men and women living together; the truth is, that there the men are not higher than the women, they know no more than the women do, and they are not held down in their conversation by the presence of women." RAMSAY. "Literature is upon the growth, it is in its spring in France; here it is rather *passée*."

JOHNSON. "Literature was in France long before we had it. Paris was the second city for the revival of letters; Italy had it first, to be sure. Our literature came to us through France. Caxton printed only two books, Chaucer and Gower, that were not translations from the French; and Chaucer, we know, took much from the Italians. No, sir, if literature be in its spring in France, it is a second spring; it is after a winter. We are now before the French in literature, but we had it long after them. In England any man who wears a sword and a powdered wig is ashamed to be illiterate. I believe it is not so in France. Yet there is, probably, a great deal of learning in France, because they have such a number of religious establishments; so, many men who have nothing else to do but study. I do not know this, but I take it upon the common principles of chance. Where there are many shooters, some will hit."

We talked of old age. Johnson (now in his seventieth year) said, "It is a man's own fault, it is from want of use, if his mind grows torpid in old age."[1] The Bishop asked if an old man does not lose faster than he gets. JOHNSON. "I think not, my lord, if he exerts himself." One of the company rashly observed that he thought it was happy for an old man that insensibility comes upon him. JOHNSON (with a noble elevation and disdain). "No, sir, I should never be happy by being less rational." BISHOP OF ST. ASAPH. "Your wish then, Sir, is, γηράσκειν διδασκόμενος." JOHNSON. "Yes, my lord." His Lordship mentioned a charitable establishment in Wales, where people were maintained, and supplied with everything, upon the condition of their contributing the weekly produce of their labor; and he said they grew quite torpid for want of property. JOHNSON. "They have no object for hope. Their condition cannot be better. It is rowing without a port."

This season there was a whimsical fashion in the newspapers of applying Shakespeare's words to describe living persons well known in the world, which was done under the title of "Modern

---

1. *Old age.* "Mr. Tolcher is here; full of life, full of talk, and full of enterprise. To see brisk young fellows of seventy-four is very surprising to those who begin to suspect themselves of growing old." *Johnson, aged 53, to Mrs. Reynolds.*

Characters from Shakespeare," many of which were admirably adapted. Somebody said to Johnson, across the table, that he had not been in those characters. "Yes," said he, "I have. I should have been sorry to be left out." He then repeated what had been applied to him,

"I must borrow GARAGANTUA'S mouth."

Miss Reynolds,[1] not perceiving at once the meaning of this, he was obliged to explain it to her, which had something of an awkward and ludicrous effect. "Why, madam, it has a reference to me, as using big words which require the mouth of a giant to pronounce them. Garagantua is the name of a giant in Rabelais." BOSWELL. "But, sir, there is another amongst them for you:

He would not flatter Neptune for his trident,
Or Jove for his power to thunder."

JOHNSON. "There is nothing marked in that. No, sir, Garagantua is the best." Notwithstanding this ease and good humor, when I, a little while afterwards, repeated his sarcasm on Kenrick,[2] which was received with applause, he asked, "*Who* said that?" and on my suddenly answering—*Garagantua*, he looked serious, which was a sufficient indication that he did not wish it to be kept up.

When we went to the drawing-room, there was a rich assemblage. Besides the company who had been at dinner, there were Mr. Garrick, Mr. Harris,[3] of Salisbury, Dr. Percy, Dr.

---

1. *Miss Reynolds.* Sir Joshua's much bepuzzled sister. "Dr. Johnson tried in vain to cure her of living in an habitual perplexity of mind and irresolution of conduct, which to herself was restlessly tormenting, and to all around her was teasingly wearisome." *Mme. D'Arblay.*

2. *Kenrick.* A hack-writer who supplied the public with anonymous scandal. Johnson had said of him: "Sir, he is one of the many who have made themselves public, without making themselves known."

3. *Harris.* "A sound, sullen scholar, full of misdirected learning." Johnson thought him an intellectual prig, and Boswell once said: "He thinks himself an ancient Greek."

Burney, the Honorable Mrs. Cholmondeley,[1] Miss Hannah More,[2] etc., etc.

After wandering about in a kind of pleasing distraction for some time, I got into a corner, with Johnson, Garrick, and Harris. GARRICK. "Of all the translations that ever were attempted, I think Elphinstone's *Martial* the most extraordinary. He consulted me upon it, who am a little of an epigrammatist myself, you know. I told him freely, 'You don't seem to have that turn.' Why, his translation is more difficult to understand than the original. I thought him a man of some talents, but he seems crazy in this." JOHNSON. "Sir, you have done what I had not courage to do. But he did not ask my advice, and I did not force it upon him, to make him angry with me." GARRICK. "But as a friend, sir—" JOHNSON. "Why, such a friend as I am with him—no." GARRICK. "But if you see a friend going to tumble over a precipice?" JOHNSON. "That is an extravagant case, sir. You are sure a friend will thank you for hindering him from tumbling over a precipice; but, in the other case, I should hurt his vanity, and do him no good. He

---

1. *Mrs. Cholmondeley.* Sister of the actress, Peg Woffington, and, says Johnson, "a very airy lady." Arthur Murphy tells of one dinner party where Johnson "took hold of her hand in the middle of dinner, and held it close to his eye, wondering at the delicacy and the whiteness, till with a smile she asked, 'Will he give it to me again when he has done with it?'"

2. *Hannah More.* Now only forty-three years of age and still affecting a little prudish archness. She lived to be eighty-eight, and as a novelist gratified a later generation by the piety of her death-bed scenes. Johnson abetted her piety, and petted and admonished her with equal affection.

"I alluded rather flippantly, I fear, to some witty passages in *Tom Jones;* he replied, 'I am sorry to hear you have read it, a confession which no modest lady should ever make.'" *Hannah More.*

"He reproved me with pretended sharpness for reading *Les Pensees de Pascal,* alleging that as a good Protestant I ought to abstain from books written by Catholics. I was beginning to stand upon my defense, when he took me with both hands, and with a tear running down his cheeks, 'Child,' said he, with the most affecting earnestness, 'I am heartily glad that you read pious books, by whomsoever they may be written.'" *The same.*

would not take my advice. His brother-in-law, Strahan, sent him a subscription of fifty pounds, and said he would send him fifty more, if he would not publish." GARRICK. "What! eh! is Strahan a good judge of an epigram? Is not he rather an *obtuse* man, eh?" JOHNSON. "Why, sir, he may not be a judge of an epigram, but you see he is a judge of what is *not* an epigram." BOSWELL. "It is easy for you, Mr. Garrick, to talk to an author as you talked to Elphinstone; you, who have been so long the manager of a theater, rejecting the plays of poor authors. You are a practiced surgeon, who have often amputated limbs; and though this may have been for the good of your patients, they cannot like you. Those who have undergone a dreadful operation are not very fond of seeing the operator again." GARRICK. "Yes, I know enough of that. There was a reverend gentleman (Mr. Hawkins),[1] who wrote a tragedy, the *Siege* of something, which I refused." HARRIS. "So, the siege was raised." JOHNSON. "Aye, he came to me and complained; and told me that Garrick said his play was wrong in the *concoction*. Now, what is the concoction of a play?" (Here Garrick started, and twisted himself, and seemed sorely vexed; for Johnson told me he believed the story was true.) GARRICK. "I—I—I—said, *first* concoction." JOHNSON (smiling). "Well, he left out *first*. And Rich,[2] he said, refused him *in false English;* he could show it under his hand." GARRICK. "He wrote to me in violent wrath for having refused his play: 'Sir, this is growing a very serious and terrible affair. I am resolved to publish my play. I will appeal to the world; and how will your judgment appear!' I answered, 'Sir, notwithstanding all the seriousness, and all the terrors, I have no objection to your publishing your play; and as you live at a great distance (Devonshire, I believe), if you will send it to me, I will convey it to the press.' I never heard more of it, ha! ha! ha!"

On Friday, April 10, I found Johnson at home in the morning. We resumed the conversation of yesterday. He put me

---

1. *Hawkins.* At one time Professor of Poetry at Oxford.
2. *Rich.* The manager of Covent Garden Theater.

in mind of some of it which had escaped my memory, and enabled me to record it more perfectly than I otherwise could have done. He was much pleased with my paying so great attention to his recommendation in 1763, the period when our acquaintance began, that I should keep a journal; and I could perceive he was secretly pleased to find so much of the fruit of his mind preserved; and as he had been used to imagine and say that he always labored when he said a good thing, it delighted him, on a review, to find that his conversation teemed with point and imagery.

I said to him, "You were yesterday, sir, in remarkably good humor; but there was nothing to offend you, nothing to produce irritation or violence. There was no bold offender. There was not one capital conviction. It was a maiden assize.* You had on your white gloves."

We dined together with Mr. Scott (now Sir William Scott, his Majesty's Advocate General) at his chambers in the Temple, nobody else there. The company being small, Johnson was not in such spirits as he had been the preceding day, and for a considerable time little was said. At last he burst forth: "Subordination is sadly broken down in this age. No man, now, has the same authority which his father had—except a jailer. No master has it over his servants; it is diminished in our colleges; nay, in our grammar-schools." BOSWELL. "What is the cause of this, sir?" JOHNSON. "Why, the coming in of the Scotch (laughing sarcastically)." BOSWELL. "That is to say, things have been turned topsy-turvy.—But your serious cause." JOHNSON. "Why, sir, there are many causes, the chief of which is, I think, the great increase of money. No man now depends upon the Lord of the Manor, when he can send to another country and fetch provisions. The shoe-black at the entry of my court does not depend on me. I can deprive him but of a penny a day, which he hopes somebody else will bring him. Besides there is a general relaxation of reverence. No son now depends upon his father, as in former times. Paternity used to be considered as of itself a great thing, which had a right to many claims. That is, in general, reduced to very small bounds. My hope is that as anarchy produces tyranny, this extreme relaxation will produce *freni strictio*."

Talking of fame, for which there is so great a desire, I observed how little there is of it in reality, compared with the other objects of human attention. "Let every man recollect, and he will be sensible how small a part of his time is employed in talking of Shakespeare, Voltaire, or any of the most celebrated men that have ever lived, or are now supposed to occupy the attention and admiration of the world. Let this be extracted and compressed; into what a narrow space will it go!" I then slyly introduced Mr. Garrick's fame, and his assuming the airs of a great man. JOHNSON. "Sir, it is wonderful how *little* Garrick assumes. Consider, sir; celebrated men, such as you have mentioned, have had their applause at a distance; but Garrick had it dashed in his face, sounded in his ears, and went home every night with the plaudits of a thousand in his *cranium*. Then, sir, Garrick did not *find*, but *made* his way to the tables, the levees, and almost the bedchambers of the great. Then, sir, Garrick had under him a numerous body of people who from fear of his power, and hopes of his favor, and admiration of his talents, were constantly submissive to him. And here is a man who has advanced the dignity of his profession. Garrick has made a player a higher character." SCOTT. "And he is a very sprightly writer, too." JOHNSON. "Yes, sir; and all this supported by great wealth of his own acquisition. If all this had happened to me, I should have had a couple of fellows with long poles walking before me, to knock down everybody that stood in the way. Consider, if all this had happened to Cibber or Quin,[1] they'd have jumped over the moon.—Yet Garrick speaks to *us* (smiling)." BOSWELL. "And Garrick is a very good man, a charitable man." JOHNSON. "Sir, a liberal man. He has given away more money than any man in England. There may be a little vanity mixed, but he has shown that money is not his first object." BOSWELL. "Yet

---

1. *Quin*, James (1693-1766). "Quin in Falstaff was as excellent as Garrick in Lear." *Walpole.*

Foote used to say of him that he walked out with an intention to do a generous action; but turning the corner of a street, he met with the ghost of a halfpenny, which frightened him." JOHNSON. "Why, sir, that is very true, too; for I never knew a man of whom it could be said with less certainty today what he will do tomorrow than Garrick; it depends so much on his humor at the time." SCOTT. "I am glad to hear of his liberality. He has been represented as very saving." JOHNSON. "With his domestic saving we have nothing to do. I remember drinking tea with him long ago, when Peg Woffington[1] made it, and he grumbled at her for making it too strong. He had then begun to feel money in his purse, and did not know when he should have enough of it."

On the subject of wealth, he observed, "It is wonderful to think how men of very large estates not only spend their yearly incomes, but are often actually in want of money. It is clear they have not value for what they spend. Lord Shelburne told me that a man of high rank, who looks into his own affairs, may have all that he ought to have, all that can be of any use, or appear with any advantage, for five thousand pounds a year. Therefore, a great proportion must go in waste; and, indeed, this is the case with most people, whatever their fortune is." BOSWELL. "I have no doubt, sir, of this. But how is it? What is waste?" JOHNSON. "Why, sir, breaking bottles, and a thousand other things. Waste cannot be accurately told, though we are sensible how destructive it is. Economy on the one hand, by which a certain income is made to maintain a man genteelly, and waste on the other, by which, on the same income, another man lives shabbily, cannot be defined. It is a very nice thing;

---

1. *Peg Woffington.* An immensely popular actress. Her relations with Garrick were open and notorious. She died in 1760. "Davies says she was the handsomest woman that ever appeared on the stage, and that Garrick was at one time in doubt whether he should not marry her. She was the only woman admitted into one of the beefsteak clubs, and is said to have been president of it. These humors, perhaps, though Davies praises her for her feminine manners, frightened Garrick out of his matrimony." *Leigh Hunt.*

as one man wears his coat out much sooner than another, we cannot tell how."

We talked of war. JOHNSON. "Every man thinks meanly of himself for not having been a soldier,[1] or not having been at sea." BOSWELL. "Lord Mansfield[2] does not." JOHNSON. "Sir, if Lord Mansfield were in a company of General Officers and Admirals who have been in service, he would shrink; he'd wish to creep under the table." BOSWELL. "No, he'd think he could *try* them all." JOHNSON. "Yes, if he could catch them; but they'd try him much sooner. No, sir; were Socrates and Charles the Twelfth[3] of Sweden both present in any company, and Socrates to say, 'Follow me, and hear a lecture in

---

1. *Not having been a soldier.* "The life of a modern soldier is ill represented by heroic fiction. War has means of destruction more formidable than the cannon and the sword. Of the thousands and ten thousands that perished in our late contests with France and Spain, a very small part ever felt the stroke of an enemy; the rest languished in tents and ships, amidst damps and putrefaction; pale, torpid, spiritless, and helpless; gasping and groaning, unpitied among men, made obdurate by long continuance of hopeless misery; and were at last whelmed in pits, or heaved into the ocean, without notice and without remembrance. By incommodious encampments and unwholesome stations, where courage is useless and enterprise impracticable, fleets are silently dispeopled and armies sluggishly melted away." *Johnson: Thoughts on the Late Transactions Respecting Falkland's Islands.*

2. *Lord Mansfield.* In 1756, appointed Lord Chief Justice of England. "Sir, you may as well maintain that a carrier, who has driven a packhorse between Edinburgh and Berwick for thirty years does not know the road as that Lord Mansfield does not know the law of England." *Johnson, quoted in Boswell's Journal of A Tour to the Hebrides.*

3. *Charles the Twelfth.* He conducted adventurous, but often foolhardy. campaigns against Russia, Prussia, Poland, and Denmark, suffered imprisonment from his treacherous allies, the Turks, and was killed (probably assassinated) while besieging a Norwegian castle, when he was only thirty-six years of age.

"A frame of adamant, a soul of fire,
No dangers fright him and no labors tire;

.   .   .   .

His fall was destined to a barren strand,
A petty fortress, and a dubious hand;
He left a name at which the world grew pale,
To point a moral, or adorn a tale."
            Johnson: Vanity of Human Wishes.

philosophy'; and Charles, laying his hand on his sword, to say, 'Follow me, and dethrone the Czar', a man would be ashamed to follow Socrates. Sir, the impression is universal; yet it is strange. As to the sailor, when you look down from the quarter-deck to the space below, you see the utmost extremity of human misery; such crowding, such filth, such stench!" BOSWELL. "Yet sailors are happy." JOHNSON. "They are happy as brutes are happy, with a piece of fresh meat—with the grossest sensuality. But, sir, the profession of soldiers and sailors has the dignity of danger. Mankind reverence those who have got over fear, which is so general a weakness." SCOTT. "But is not courage mechanical, and to be acquired?" JOHNSON. "Why yes, sir, in a collective sense. Soldiers consider themselves only as part of a great machine." SCOTT. "We find people fond of being sailors." JOHNSON. "I cannot account for that, any more than I can account for other strange perversions of imagination."

He expressed great indignation at the imposture of the Cock Lane Ghost, and related, with much satisfaction, how he had assisted in detecting the cheat, and had published an account of it in the newspapers. Upon this subject I incautiously offended him by pressing him with too many questions, and he showed his displeasure. I apologized, saying that "I asked questions in order to be instructed and entertained; I repaired eagerly to the fountain; but that the moment he gave me a hint, the moment he put a lock upon the well, I desisted."—"But, sir," said he, "that is forcing one to do a disagreeable thing"; and he continued to rate me. "Nay, sir," said I, "when you have put a lock upon the well, so that I can no longer drink, do not make the fountain of your wit play upon me and wet me."

He sometimes could not bear being teased with questions. I was once present when a gentleman asked so many, as, "What did you do, sir?" "What did you say, sir?" that he at last grew enraged, and said, "I will not be put to the *question*. Don't you consider, sir, that these are not the manners of a gentleman? I will not be baited with *what* and *why*; what is this? what is that? why is a cow's tail long? why is a fox's tail bushy?" The gentleman, who was a good deal out of countenance, said,

"Why, sir, you are so good that I venture to trouble you."
JOHNSON. "Sir, my being so *good* is no reason why you should
be so *ill*."

Talking of the *Justitia* hulk at Woolwich,[1] in which criminals
were punished by being confined to labor, he said, "I do not
see that they are punished by this; they must have worked
equally, had they never been guilty of stealing. They now only
work; so, after all, they have gained; what they stole is clear
gain to them; the confinement is nothing. Every man who
works is confined: the smith to his shop, the tailor to his garret."
BOSWELL. "And Lord Mansfield to his Court." JOHNSON.
"Yes, sir. You know the notion of confinement may be extended, as in the song, 'Every island is a prison.' "[2]

He talked with an uncommon animation of traveling into
distant countries; that the mind was enlarged by it, and that
an acquisition of dignity of character was derived from it. He
expressed a particular enthusiasm with respect to visiting the
wall of China. I catched it for the moment, and said I really
believed I should go and see the wall of China had I not children, of whom it was my duty to take care. "Sir," said he,
"by doing so, you would do what would be of importance in
raising your children to eminence. There would be a luster
reflected upon them from your spirit and curiosity. They
would be at all times regarded as the children of a man who
had gone to visit the wall of China. I am serious, sir."

When we had left Mr. Scott's, he said, "Will you go home
with me?" "Sir," said I, "it is late; but I'll go with you for
three minutes." JOHNSON. "Or *four*." We went to Mrs.
Williams's room, where we found Mr. Allen the printer, who

---

1. *Woolwich.* The site of a great naval dockyard, arsenal, etc., on the
Thames below London. Three hulks lay off Woolwich, the *Warrior*, the
Justitia, and the *Defense*, for the convicts who worked on shore during the
day and returned at night.

2. *Every island is a prison.* In one of the Hebridean islands,
Johnson quotes one stanza to Boswell:

"Every island is a prison,
Strongly guarded by the sea;
Kings and princes, for that reason,
Prisoners are, as well as we."

was the landlord of his house in Bolt Court, a worthy, obliging man, and his very old acquaintance; and what was exceedingly amusing, though he was of a very diminutive size, he used, even in Johnson's presence, to imitate the stately periods and slow and solemn utterance of the great man.—I this evening boasted that although I did not write what is called stenography, or shorthand, in appropriated characters devised for the purpose, I had a method of my own of writing half words, and leaving out some altogether, so as yet to keep the substance and language of any discourse which I had heard so much in view that I could give it very completely soon after I had taken it down. He defied me, as he had once defied an actual shorthand writer; and he made the experiment by reading slowly and distinctly a part of Robertson's *History of America,* while I endeavored to write it in my way of taking notes. It was found that I had it very imperfectly; the conclusion from which was that its excellence was principally owing to a studied arrangement of words, which could not be varied or abridged without an essential injury.

On Sunday, April 12, I found him at home before dinner; Dr. Dodd's poem, entitled "Thoughts in Prison," was lying upon his table. This appearing to me an extraordinary effort by a man who was in Newgate for a capital crime, I was desirous to hear Johnson's opinion of it; to my surprise, he told me he had not read a line of it. I took up the book, and read a passage to him. JOHNSON. "Pretty well, if you are previously disposed to like them." I read another passage, with which he was better pleased. He then took the book into his own hands, and having looked at the prayer at the end of it, he said, "What *evidence* is there that this was composed the night before he suffered? *I* do not believe it." He then read aloud where he prays for the King, etc., and observed, "Sir, do you think that a man, the night before he is to be hanged, cares for the succession of a royal family?—Though, he *may* have composed this prayer then. A man who has been canting all his life may cant to the last.—And yet, a man who has been refused a pardon after so much petitioning would hardly be praying thus fervently for the King."

He and I and Mrs. Williams went to dine with the Reverend
Dr. Percy. Talking of Goldsmith, Johnson said he was very
envious.[1] I defended him, by observing that he owned it frankly
upon all occasions. JOHNSON. "Sir, you are enforcing the
charge. He had so much envy that he could not conceal it.
He was so full of it that he overflowed. He talked of it, to be
sure, often enough. Now, sir, what a man avows, he is not
ashamed to think; though many a man thinks what he is ashamed
to avow. We are all envious naturally; but by checking envy,
we get the better of it. So we are all thieves naturally; a child
always tries to get at what it wants the nearest way; by good
instruction and good habits this is cured, till a man has not even
an inclination to seize what is another's; has no struggle with
himself about it."

And here I shall record a scene of too much heat between
Dr. Johnson and Dr. Percy, which I should have suppressed
were it not that it gave occasion to display the truly tender and
benevolent heart of Johnson, who, as soon as he found a friend
was at all hurt by anything which he had "said in his wrath,"
was not only prompt and desirous to be reconciled, but exerted
himself to make ample reparation.

Books of travels having been mentioned, Johnson praised
Pennant[2] very highly. Dr. Percy knowing himself to be the heir
male of the ancient Perceys, and having the warmest and most
dutiful attachment to the noble House of Northumberland,
could not sit quietly and hear a man praised who had spoken

1. *Very envious.* Goldsmith would sometimes flatter another's
charms by pretending to be envious of them; he was sometimes ill-
humored at the puffery of a worthless book, but his contemporaries'
almost universal testimony as to his envy must be taken with some
allowance. "Mr. Hoole was one day in a coach with Johnson, when
Johnson, who delighted in rapidity of pace and had been speaking of
Goldsmith, put his head out of one of the windows to see they were
going right, and, rubbing his hands with an air of satisfaction, exclaimed:
'This man drives fast and well; were Goldsmith here now he would
tell us he could do better.'" *Birkbeck Hill.*

2. *Pennant.* Thomas Pennant, a distinguished naturalist. His books
of travel in Great Britain are an interminable succession of what Boswell
well calls "curt, frittered fragments," and they are not accurate enough
to justify their dullness.

disrespectfully of Alnwick Castle[1] and the Duke's pleasure
grounds, especially as he thought meanly of his travels. He
therefore opposed Johnson eagerly. JOHNSON. "Pennant, in
what he has said of Alnwick, has done what he intended; he has
made you very angry." PERCY. "He has said the garden is
trim, which is representing it like a citizen's parterre, when the
truth is, there is a very large extent of fine turf and gravel walks."
JOHNSON. "According to your own account, sir, Pennant is
right. It *is* trim. Here is grass cut close, and gravel rolled
smooth. Is not that trim? The extent is nothing against that;
a mile may be as trim as a square yard. Your extent puts me
in mind of the citizen's enlarged dinner, two pieces of roast-
beef and two puddings. There is no variety, no mind exerted
in laying out the ground, no trees." PERCY. "He pretends to
give the natural history of Northumberland, and yet takes no
notice of the immense number of trees planted there of late."
JOHNSON. "That, sir, has nothing to do with the *natural*
history; that is *civil* history. A man who gives the natural
history of the oak is not to tell how many oaks have been
planted in this place or that. A man who gives the natural
history of the cow is not to tell how many cows are milked at
Islington.[2] The animal is the same, whether milked in the Park
or at Islington." PERCY. "Pennant does not describe well;
a carrier who goes along the side of Loch Lomond would describe
it better." JOHNSON. "I think he describes very well."
PERCY. "I traveled after him." JOHNSON. "And *I* traveled
after him." PERCY. "But, my good friend, you are short-
sighted, and do not see so well as I do." I wondered at Dr.
Percy's venturing thus. Dr. Johnson said nothing at the time,
but inflammable particles were collecting for a cloud to burst.
In a little while Dr. Percy said something more in disparage-
ment of Pennant. JOHNSON (pointedly). "This is the resentment of a narrow mind, because he did not find everything in
Northumberland." PERCY (feeling the stroke). "Sir, you may

---

1. *Alnwick Castle.* The famous seat of the Percys, Dukes of Northumberland.
2. *Islington.* A rural suburb two miles from St. Paul's Cathedral.

be as rude as you please." JOHNSON. "Hold, sir! don't talk of rudeness; remember, sir, you told me (puffing hard with passion struggling for a vent) I was short-sighted. We have done with civility. We are to be as rude as we please." PERCY. "Upon my honor, sir, I did not mean to be uncivil." JOHNSON. "I cannot say so, sir; for I *did* mean to be uncivil, thinking *you* had been uncivil." Dr. Percy rose, ran up to him, and taking him by the hand, assured him affectionately that his meaning had been misunderstood; upon which a reconciliation instantly took place. JOHNSON. "My dear sir, I am willing you shall *hang* Pennant." PERCY (resuming the former subject). "Pennant complains that the helmet[1] is not hung out to invite to the hall of hospitality. Now I never heard that it was a custom to hang out a *helmet*." JOHNSON. "Hang him up, hang him up." BOSWELL (humoring the joke). "Hang out his skull instead of a helmet, and you may drink ale out of it in your hall of Odin, as he is your enemy; that will be truly ancient." JOHNSON. "He's a *Whig*, sir; a *sad dog* (smiling at his own violent expressions merely for *political* difference of opinion). But he's the best traveler I ever read; he observes more things than anyone else does."

Having impartially censured Mr. Pennant, as a traveler in Scotland, let me allow him, from authorities much better than mine, his deserved praise as an able zoölogist; and let me also from my own understanding and feelings, acknowledge the merit of his "London," which, though said to be not quite accurate in some particulars, is one of the most pleasing topographical performances that ever appeared in any language. Mr. Pennant, like his countrymen in general, has the true spirit of a *gentleman*. As a proof of it, I shall quote from his "London" the passage in which he speaks of my illustrious friend. "I must by no means omit *Bolt Court*, the long residence of Doc-

---

1. *Helmet.* "You look in vain for the helmet on the tower, the ancient signal of hospitality to the traveler, or for the gray-headed porter to conduct him to the hall of entertainment. Instead of the disinterested usher of the old times, he is attended by a *valet*, eager to receive the fees of admittance." *Pennant.*

tor SAMUEL JOHNSON, a man of the strongest natural abilities, great learning, a most retentive memory, of the deepest and most unaffected piety and morality, mingled with those numerous weaknesses and prejudices which his friends have kindly taken care to draw from their dread abode. I brought on myself his transient anger by observing that in his tour in *Scotland* he once had long and woeful experience of oats being the food of men in *Scotland* as they were of horses in *England*. It was a national reflection unworthy of him, and I shot my bolt. In return he gave me a tender hug."

We had a calm after the storm, stayed the evening and supped, and were pleasant and gay. But Dr. Percy told me he was very uneasy at what had passed; for there was a gentleman there who was acquainted with the Northumberland family, to whom he hoped to have appeared more respectable, by showing how intimate he was with Dr. Johnson, and who might now, on the contrary, go away with an opinion to his disadvantage. He begged I would mention this to Dr. Johnson, which I afterwards did. His observation upon it was, "This comes of *stratagem;* had he told me that he wished to appear to advantage before that gentleman, he should have been at the top of the house all the time." He spoke of Dr. Percy in the handsomest terms. "Then, sir," said I, "may I be allowed to suggest a mode by which you may effectually counteract any unfavorable report of what passed. I will write a letter to you upon the subject of the unlucky contest of that day, and you will be kind enough to put in writing as an answer to that letter, what you have now said, and as Lord Percy is to dine with us at General Paoli's soon, I will take an opportunity to read the correspondence in his Lordship's presence." This friendly scheme was accordingly carried into execution without Dr. Percy's knowledge. Johnson's letter placed Dr. Percy's unquestionable merit in the fairest point of view; and I contrived that Lord Percy should hear the correspondence, by introducing it at General Paoli's as an instance of Dr. Johnson's kind disposition toward one in whom his Lordship was interested. Thus every unfavorable impression was obviated that could possibly have been made on those by whom he wished most to be regarded. I breakfasted the day after with him, and informed him of my scheme and its happy completion, for which he thanked me in the warmest terms, and was highly delighted with Dr. Johnson's letter in his praise, of which I gave him a copy. He said, "I would rather have this than degrees from all the universities in Europe. It will be for me and my children and grandchildren." Dr. Johnson having afterwards asked me if I had given him a copy of it, and being told I had, was offended, and insisted that I should get it back, which I did. As, however, he did not desire me to destroy either the original or the copy, or forbid me to let it be seen, I think myself at liberty to apply to it his general declaration to me concerning his other letters: That he did not choose they should be published in his lifetime; but had no objection to their appearing after his death.

"*To James Boswell, Esq.*
"Sir:
    "The debate between Dr. Percy and me is one of those foolish controversies which begin upon a question of which neither party cares how it is decided, and which is, nevertheless, continued to acrimony, by the vanity with which every man resists confutation. If Percy is really offended, I am sorry; for he is a man whom I never knew to offend anyone. He is a man very willing to learn, and very able to teach; a man out of whose company I never go without having learned something. It is true that he vexes me sometimes, but I am afraid it is by making me feel my own ignorance. So much extension of mind, and so much minute accuracy of inquiry, if you survey your whole circle of acquaintance, you will find so scarce, if you find it at all, that you will value Percy by comparison. Lord Hailes[1] is somewhat like him; but Lord Hailes does not, perhaps, go beyond him in research; and I do not know that he equals him in elegance. Percy's attention to poetry has given grace and splendor

---

1. *Lord Hailes.* Not only a laborious antiquarian, but an eminent judge and a stanch Christian, "whom," said Johnson, "I love better than any man whom I know so little."

▸ his studies of antiquity. A mere antiquarian is a rugged
▸eing.

"Upon the whole, you see that what I might say in sport or pet-
▮ance to him is very consistent with full conviction of his merit.

"I am, dear sir,

"Your most, &c.,

April 23, 1778."   "SAM. JOHNSON.

On Monday, April 13, I dined with Johnson at Mr. Langton's.
▮e was at first in a very silent mood. Before dinner he said
▮othing but "Pretty baby," to one of the children. Langton
▮aid to me afterwards that he could repeat Johnson's conversa-
▮ion before dinner, as Johnson had said that he could repeat a
▮omplete chapter of *The Natural History of Iceland*, from the
▮anish of *Horrebow*, the whole of which was exactly thus:

"CHAP. LXXII. *Concerning Snakes*

"There are no snakes to be met with throughout the whole
▮land."

Mr. Topham Beauclerk came in the evening, and he and
▮r. Johnson and I stayed to supper. It was mentioned that Dr.
▮odd had once wished to be a member of the Literary Club.
▮OHNSON. "I should be sorry if any of our Club were hanged.
▮ will not say but some of them deserve it."[1] BEAUCLERK
▮upposing this to be aimed at persons for whom he had at
▮hat time a wonderful fancy, which, however, did not last long)
▮as irritated, and eagerly said, "You, sir, have a friend[2] (naming
▮im) who deserves to be hanged; for he speaks behind their
▮acks against those with whom he lives on the best terms, and

---

1. *Deserve it.* Possibly intended as a reflection on the charming
▮ord Charlemont, who was too liberal in both his religious and political
▮iews to please Dr. Johnson. "He had," said the Irish agitator Grattan,
"the manners of a court and the principles of a patriot."
2. *You, sir, have a friend.* George Steevens, who exercised extraor-
▮inary ingenuity, sometimes in textual and literary criticism, and
▮ometimes in knavish mischief of the most whimsical perversity. Garrick
▮alled him a pest, and Dr. Parr thought him the most spiteful of men.
▮t was on Johnson's nomination that he had been elected to the club.

attacks them in the newspapers. *He* certainly ought to be *kicked*." JOHNSON. "Sir, we all do this in some degree. To be sure it may be done so much that a man may deserve to be kicked." BEAUCLERK. "He is very malignant." JOHNSON. "No, sir; he is not malignant. He is mischievous, if you will. He would do no man an essential injury; he may, indeed, love to make sport of people by vexing their vanity. I, however, once knew an old gentleman who was absolutely malignant. He really wished evil to others, and rejoiced at it." BOSWELL. "The gentleman, Mr. Beauclerk, against whom you are so violent, is, I know, a man of good principles." BEAUCLERK. "Then he does not wear them out in practice."

On Tuesday, April 14, I dined with him at General Oglethorpe's, with General Paoli and Mr. Langton. General Oglethorpe declaimed against luxury. JOHNSON. "Depend upon it, sir, every state of society is as luxurious as it can be. Men always take the best they can get." OGLETHORPE. "But the best depends much upon ourselves; and if we can be as well satisfied with plain things, we are in the wrong to accustom our palates to what is high-seasoned and expensive. What says Addison in his *Cato*, speaking of the Numidian?

> Coarse are his meals, the fortune of the chase,
> Amid the running stream he slakes his thirst,
> Toils all the day, and at the approach of night,
> On the first friendly bank he throws him down,
> Or rests his head upon a rock till morn;
> And if the following day he chance to find
> A new repast, or an untasted spring,
> Blesses his stars, and thinks it luxury.

Let us have *that* kind of luxury, sir, if you will." JOHNSON. "But hold, sir, a hungry man has not the same pleasure in eating a plain dinner that a hungry man has in eating a luxurious dinner. I suppose the man who decides between the two dinners to be equally a hungry man."

Talking of different governments—JOHNSON. "The more contracted power is, the more easily it is destroyed. A country governed by a despot is an inverted cone. Government there cannot be so firm as when it rests upon a broad basis gradually contracted, as the government of Great Britain, which is founded on the Parliament, then is in the privy council, then in the King." BOSWELL. "Power when contracted into the person of a despot may be easily destroyed, as the prince may be cut off. So Caligula wished that the people of Rome had but one neck, so that he might cut them off at a blow."

On Wednesday, April 15, I dined with Dr. Johnson at Mr. Dilly's, and was in high spirits, for I had been a good part of the morning with Mr. Orme, the able and eloquent historian of Hindustan, who expressed a great admiration of Johnson.

At Mr. Dilly's were Mrs. Knowles,[1] the ingenious Quaker lady, Miss Seward,[2] the poetess of Lichfield, the Reverend Dr. Mayo, and the Rev. Mr. Beresford, tutor to the Duke of Bedford. Before dinner Dr. Johnson seized upon Mr. Charles Sheridan's[3] *Account of the Late Revolution in Sweden*, and seemed to read it ravenously, as if he devoured it, which was to all appearance his method of studying. "He knows how to read better than anyone," said Mrs. Knowles; "he gets at the substance of a book directly; he tears out the heart of it." He kept it wrapped up in the tablecloth in his lap during the time of dinner, from an avidity to have one entertainment in readiness when he should have finished another; resembling a dog who holds a bone in his paws in reserve, while he eats something else which has been thrown to him.

JOHNSON. "Oh, Mr. Dilly—you must know that an English Benedictine monk at Paris has translated the Duke of Berwick's[4]

1. *Mrs. Knowles.* Equally ready to present George III with his portrait done in worsteds, or to comment on the pleasant features of the French Revolution. She used to write up the conversations she had had, so as to bring out her own sweetness of temper and the absurdity of anyone's disagreeing with her.
2. *Miss Seward.* The six volumes of letters she has left are a rich mine of absurdity. Of Mrs. Knowles she says: "She has a portion of metaphysic faith which carries her a great way up the lunar heights of system."
3. *Charles Sheridan.* An eye-witness of the Swedish Revolution of 1772, he published an account of it in the spring of 1778.
4. *Duke of Berwick.* A son of King James II, who shared his exile and fought brilliantly for the French King.

Memoirs from the original French and has sent them to me to sell. I offered them to Strahan, who sent them back with this answer: That the first book he had published was the *Duke of Berwick's Life*, by which he had lost; and he hated the name. Now I honestly tell you that Strahan has refused them; but I also honestly tell you that he did it upon no principle, for he never looked into them." DILLY. "Are they well translated, sir?" JOHNSON. "Why, sir, very well—in a style very current and very clear. They will make two volumes in octavo and I have undertaken to correct every sheet as it comes from the press." Mr. Dilly asked Dr. Johnson if he would write a preface to them. JOHNSON. "No, sir. The Benedictines were very kind to me,[1] and I'll do what I undertook to do; but I will not mingle my name with them. I am to gain nothing by them. I'll turn them loose upon the world, and let them take their chance."

Mrs. Knowles affected to complain that men had much more liberty allowed them than women. JOHNSON. "Why, madam, women have all the liberty they should wish to have. We have all the labor and the danger, and the women all the advantage. We go to sea, we build houses, we do everything, in short, to pay our court to the women." MRS. KNOWLES. "The Doctor reasons very wittily, but not convincingly. Now take the instance of building; the mason's wife, if she is ever seen in liquor, is ruined; the mason may get himself drunk as often as he pleases, with little loss of character; nay, may let his wife and children starve." JOHNSON. "Madam, you must consider, if the mason does get himself drunk, and let his wife and children starve, the parish will oblige him to find security for their maintenance. We have different modes of restraining evil—stocks for the men, a ducking-stool for women, and a pound for beasts. If we require more perfection from women than from ourselves, it is doing them honor. And women have not the same temptations that we have; they may always live in virtuous company; men must live in the world indiscriminately." MRS. KNOWLES. "Still, Doctor, I cannot help thinking it a hardship that more indulgence is allowed to men than to women. It gives a superi-

---

1. *Kind to me.* When he was in Paris, three years before, with the Thrales.

ority to men, to which I do not see how they are entitled."
JOHNSON. "It is plain, madam, one or other must have the
superiority. As Shakespeare says, 'If two men ride on a horse,
one must ride behind.'" MRS. KNOWLES. "Well, I hope that
in another world the sexes will be equal." BOSWELL. "That is
being too ambitious, madam. *We* might as well desire to be
equal with the angels. We shall all, I hope, be happy in a
future state, but we must not expect to be all happy in the same
degree. A worthy carman will get to heaven as well as Sir Isaac
Newton. Yet, though equally good, they will not have the same
degrees of happiness." JOHNSON. "Probably not."

Upon this subject I had once before sounded him, by mentioning the late Reverend Mr. Brown of Utrecht's image; that
a great and small glass, though equally full, did not hold an
equal quantity; which he threw out to refute David Hume's
saying[1] that a little miss, going to dance at a ball, in a fine new
dress, was as happy as a great orator after having made an
eloquent and applauded speech. After some thought, Johnson
said, "I come over to the parson." As an instance of coincidence
of thinking, Mr. Dilly told me that Dr. King, a late dissenting
minister in London, said to him, upon the happiness in a future
state of good men of different capacities, "A pail does not hold
so much as a tub; but, if it be equally full, it has no reason to
complain. Every saint in heaven will have as much happiness
as he can hold." Mr. Dilly thought this a clear, though a
familiar, illustration of the phrase, "One star differeth from
another in brightness."

Dr. Mayo having asked Johnson's opinion of Soame Jenyns's[2]

---

1. *David Hume's saying.* As usual, Boswell has totally misunderstood him.

2. *Soame Jenyns.* "Death opens to us a new prospect, from whence
we shall probably look back upon the diversions and occupations of this
world with the same contempt we do now on our tops and hobbyhorses,
and with the same surprise that they could even so much entertain or
engage us." *Soame Jenyns: A Free Inquiry into the Nature and Origin
of Evil.*

"I assert only that active courage can never be a Christian virtue.
Passive courage is indeed frequently and properly inculcated by this
meek and suffering religion under the titles of patience and resignation."
Soame Jenyns: View of the Internal Evidence of the Christian Religion

View of the Internal Evidence of the Christian Religion: JOHN-
SON. "I think it a pretty book." BOSWELL. "*You* should like
his book, Mrs. Knowles, as it maintains, as you *Friends* do, that
courage is not a Christian virtue." MRS. KNOWLES. "Yes, indeed, I like him there; but I cannot agree with him that friendship is not a Christian virtue." JOHNSON. "Why, madam,
strictly speaking, he is right. All friendship is preferring the
interest of a friend to the neglect, or, perhaps, against the interest of others. Now Christianity recommends universal benevolence—to consider all men as our brethren; which is contrary
to the virtue of friendship, as described by the ancient philosophers. Surely, madam, your sect must approve of this; for
you call all men *friends*." MRS. KNOWLES. "We are commanded to do good to all men, 'but especially to them who are
of the household of Faith.'" JOHNSON. "Well, madam, the
household of Faith is wide enough." MRS. KNOWLES. "But,
Doctor, our Savior had twelve Apostles, yet there was *one* whom
he *loved*. John was called the 'disciple whom JESUS loved.'"
JOHNSON (with eyes sparkling benignantly). "Very well, indeed,
madam. You have said very well." BOSWELL. "A fine application. Pray, sir, had you ever thought of it?" JOHNSON.
"I had not, sir."

From this pleasing subject, he, I know not how or why, made
a sudden transition to one upon which he was a violent aggressor; for he said, "I am willing to love all mankind, *except an
American*"; and his inflammable corruption bursting into
horrid fire, he "breathed out threatenings and slaughter";
calling them "rascals—robbers—pirates"; and exclaiming,
he'd "burn and destroy them." Miss Seward, looking to him
with mild but steady astonishment, said, "Sir, this is an instance
that we are always most violent against those whom we have
injured."—He was irritated still more by this delicate and keen
reproach; and roared out another tremendous volley which
one might fancy could be heard across the Atlantic. During
this tempest I sat in great uneasiness, lamenting his heat of
temper; till, by degrees, I diverted his attention to other
topics.

DR. MAYO (to Dr. Johnson). "Pray, sir, have you read
Edwards, of New England, on Grace?" JOHNSON. "No,

sir." BOSWELL. "It puzzled me so much as to the freedom of the human will, by stating, with wonderful acute ingenuity, our being actuated by a series of motives which we cannot resist, that the only relief I had was to forget it." JOHNSON. "You are surer that you are free than you are of prescience; you are surer that you can lift up your finger or not as you please than you are of any conclusion from a deduction of reasoning. But let us consider a little the objection from prescience. It is certain I am either to go home tonight or not; that does not prevent my freedom." BOSWELL. "That it is certain you are *either* to go home or not, does not prevent your freedom, because the liberty of choice between the two is compatible with that certainty. But if *one* of these events be certain *now*, you have no *future* power of volition. If it be certain you are to go home tonight, you *must* go home." JOHNSON. "If I am well acquainted with a man, I can judge with great probability how he will act in any case, without his being restrained by my judging. God may have this probability increased to certainty." BOSWELL. "When it is increased to *certainty*, freedom ceases, because that cannot be certainly foreknown, which is not certain at the time." JOHNSON. "All theory is against the freedom of the will; all experience for it." I did not push the subject any farther. I was glad to find him so mild in discussing a question of the most abstract nature, involved with theological tenets which he generally would not suffer to be in any degree opposed.

He, as usual, defended luxury: "You cannot spend money in luxury without doing good to the poor. Nay, you do more good to them by spending it in luxury; you make them exert industry; whereas by giving it, you keep them idle. I own, indeed, there may be more virtue in giving it immediately in charity than in spending it in luxury; though there may be a pride in that too." Miss Seward asked if this was not Mandeville's[1] doctrine of "private vices public benefits." JOHNSON. "The fallacy of that book is that Mandeville defines neither

---

1. *Mandeville.* Bernard de Mandeville. (1670–1733). Outspoken, cynical, and in many circles accounted disreputable. The Grand Jury of Middlesex (London) advised that his *Fable of the Bees, or Private Vices Public Benefits*, be subjected to criminal proceedings. "He opened my views into real life very much." *Johnson.*

vices nor benefits. He reckons among vices everything that gives pleasure; and he reckons wealth as a public benefit, which is by no means always true. Pleasure of itself is not a vice. Having a garden, which we all know to be perfectly innocent, is a great pleasure. Mandeville puts the case of a man who gets drunk at an alehouse; and says it is a public benefit, because so much money is got by it to the public. But it must be considered that all the good gained by this, through the gradation of alehouse-keeper, brewer, maltster, and farmer, is overbalanced by the evil caused to the man and his family by his getting drunk. This is the way to try what is vicious, by ascertaining whether more evil than good is produced by it upon the whole, which is the case in all vice. No, it is clear that the happiness of society depends on virtue. In Sparta, theft was allowed by general consent; theft, therefore, was *there* not a crime, but then there was no security; and what a life must they have had when there was no security! Without truth there must be a dissolution of society. As it is, there is so little truth that we are almost afraid to trust our ears; but how should we be if falsehood were multiplied ten times! Society is held together by communication and information; and I remember this remark of Sir Thomas Browne's,[1] 'Do the devils lie? No; for then hell could not subsist.' "

Talking of Miss ———,[2] a literary lady, he said, "I was obliged to speak to Miss Reynolds to let her know that I desired she would not flatter me so much." Somebody now observed, "She flatters Garrick." JOHNSON. "She is in the right to flatter Garrick. She is in the right for two reasons: first, because she has the world with her, who have been praising Garrick these thirty years; and secondly, because she is rewarded for it by Garrick. Why should she flatter *me*? I can do nothing for

---

1. *Sir Thomas Browne.* If he ever made this remark, others have not discovered it.

2. *Miss* ———. Hannah More, to whom he once said: "Dearest lady, consider with yourself what your flattery is worth before you bestow it so freely." His own praise of her not extraordinary verse was certainly as lavish: "Hush, hush, it is dangerous to say a word of poetry before her; it is talking of the art of war before Hannibal."

her. Let her carry her praise to a better market." Then, turning to Mrs. Knowles, "You, madam, have been flattering me all the evening; I wish you would give Boswell a little now. If you knew his merit as well as I do, you would say a great deal; he is the best traveling companion in the world."

I expressed a horror at the thought of death.[1] MRS. KNOWLES. "Nay, thou should'st not have a horror for what is the gate of life." JOHNSON (standing upon the hearth, rolling about, with a serious, solemn, and somewhat gloomy air). "No rational man can die without uneasy apprehension." MRS. KNOWLES. "The Scriptures tell us, 'The righteous shall have *hope* in his death.'" JOHNSON. "Yes, madam; that is, he shall not have despair. But, consider, his hope of salvation must be founded on obedience; and where obedience has failed, repentance. But what man can say that his obedience has been such as he would approve of in another, or even in himself upon close examination, or that his repentance has not been such as to require being repented of? No man can be sure[2] that his obedience and repentance will obtain salvation." MRS. KNOWLES. "But divine intimation of acceptance may be made to the soul." JOHNSON. "Madam, it may; but I should not think the better of a man who should tell me on his deathbed he was sure of salvation." MISS SEWARD. "There is one mode of the fear of death which is certainly absurd; and that is the

---

1. *Thought of death.* "It is worthy the observing that there is no passion in the mind of man so weak but it mates and masters the fear of death." *Sir Francis Bacon.* "If one was to think constantly of death, the business of life would stand still." *Johnson.* "All fear is in itself painful, and, when it conduces not to safety, is painful without use. Every consideration, therefore, by which groundless terrors may be removed, adds something to human happiness." *Johnson: Rambler.*

2. *No man can be sure.* "It is better to have no opinion of God at all than such an opinion as is unworthy of Him; for the one is unbelief, the other is contumely. And certainly superstition is the reproach of the Deity. Plutarch saith well to the purpose. 'Surely,' saith he, 'I had rather a great deal men should say there was no such man at all as Plutarch than that they should say that there was one Plutarch that would eat his children as soon as they were born, as the poets speak of Saturn.'" *Sir Francis Bacon: Of Superstition, 1625.*

dread of annihilation, which is only a pleasing sleep without a dream." JOHNSON. "It is neither pleasing nor sleep; it is nothing. Now, mere existence is so much better than nothing that one would rather exist even in pain than not exist."

Of John Wesley, he said, "He can talk well on any subject." BOSWELL. "Pray, sir, what has he made of his story of a ghost?" JOHNSON. "Why, sir, he believes it; but not on sufficient authority. It was at Newcastle, where the ghost was said to have appeared to a young woman several times, mentioning something about the right to an old house, advising application to be made to an attorney, which was done; and, at the same time, saying the attorney would do nothing, which proved to be the fact. 'This,' said John, 'is a proof that a ghost knows our thoughts.' Now it is not necessary to know our thoughts to tell that an attorney will sometimes do nothing. Charles Wesley does not believe the story. I am sorry that John did not take more pains to inquire into the evidence for it." MISS SEWARD (with an incredulous smile). "What, sir, about a ghost?" JOHNSON (with solemn vehemence). "Yes, madam, this is a question which after five thousand years is yet undecided; one of the most important that can come before the human understanding."

Mrs. Knowles mentioned, as a proselyte to Quakerism, Miss ——, a young lady well known to Dr. Johnson, for whom he had shown much affection; while she ever had, and still retained, a great respect for him. Mrs. Knowles at the same time took an opportunity of letting him know that "the amiable young creature was sorry at finding that he was offended at her leaving the Church of England, and embracing a simpler faith"; and, in the gentlest and most persuasive manner, solicited his kind indulgence[1] for what was sincerely a matter of conscience.[2] JOHNSON (frowning very angrily). "Madam, she is an odious wench. She knew no more of the church which she left, and that which she embraced, than she did of the difference between

---

1. *Solicited his kind indulgence.* "I once told you that ladies were timorous and yet not cautious." *Johnson in 1763 to Miss Reynolds.*

2. *A matter of conscience.* Johnson once remarked to Boswell that he liked individuals among the Quakers, but not the "sect."

the Copernican and Ptolemaic systems." MRS. KNOWLES. "She had the New Testament before her." JOHNSON. "Madam, she could not understand the New Testament, the most difficult book in the world, for which the study of a life is required." MRS. KNOWLES. "It is clear as to essentials." JOHNSON. "But not as to controversial points. The heathens were easily converted, because they had nothing to give up; but we ought not, without very strong conviction indeed, to desert the religion in which we have been educated. That is the religion given you, the religion in which it may be said Providence has placed you. If you live conscientiously in that religion, you may be safe." MRS. KNOWLES. "Must we then go by implicit faith?" JOHNSON. "Why, madam, the greatest part of our knowledge is implicit faith; and as to religion, have we heard all that a disciple of Confucius, all that a Mahometan, can say for himself?" He then rose again into passion, and attacked the young proselyte in the severest terms of reproach, so that both ladies seemed to be much shocked.

We remained together till it was pretty late. Notwithstanding occasional explosions of violence, we were all delighted upon the whole with Johnson. I compared him at this time to a warm West Indian climate, where you have a bright sun, quick vegetation, luxuriant foliage, luscious fruits; but where the same heat sometimes produces thunder, lightning, and earthquakes, in a terrible degree.

April 17, being Good Friday, I waited on Johnson, as usual. I observed at breakfast that although it was a part of his abstemious discipline on this most solemn fast to take no milk in his tea, yet when Mrs. Desmoulins inadvertently poured it in, he did not reject it. I talked of the strange indecision of mind and imbecility in the common occurrences of life, which we may observe in some people. JOHNSON. "Why, sir, I am in the habit of getting others to do things for me." BOSWELL. "What, sir! have you that weakness?" JOHNSON. "Yes, sir. But I always think afterwards I should have done better for myself."

I told him that at a gentleman's house where there was thought to be such extravagance or bad management that he was living much beyond his income, his lady had objected to the cutting of a pickled mango, and that I had taken an opportunity to ask the price of it, and found it was only two shillings; so here was a very poor saving. JOHNSON. "Sir, that is the blundering economy of a narrow understanding. It is stopping one hole in a sieve."

It was a delightful day; as we walked to St. Clement's church, I again remarked that Fleet Street was the most cheerful scene in the world. "Fleet Street," said I, "is in my mind more delightful than Tempé." JOHNSON. "Aye, sir; but let it be compared with Mull."[1]

There was a very numerous congregation today at St. Clement's church, which Dr. Johnson said he observed with pleasure.

And now I am to give a pretty full account of one of the most curious incidents in Johnson's life, of which he himself has made the following minute on this day: "In my return from church, I was accosted by Edwards, an old fellow-collegian, who had not seen me since 1729. He knew me, and asked if I remembered one Edwards; I did not at first recollect the name, but gradually as we walked along, recovered it, and told him a conversation that had passed at an alehouse between us. My purpose is to continue our acquaintance."

It was in Butcher Row that this meeting happened. Mr. Edwards, who was a decent-looking elderly man in gray clothes, and a wig of many curls, accosted Johnson with familiar confidence, knowing who he was, while Johnson returned his salutation with a courteous formality, as to a stranger. But as soon as Edwards had brought to his recollection their having been at Pembroke College together nine and forty years ago, he seemed much pleased, asked where he lived, and said he should be glad

---

1. *Mull.* One of the Hebridean Islands which depressed Johnson with its desolation. "Sir Allan, anxious for the honor of Mull, was still talking of its woods, and pointing them out to Dr. Johnson, as appearing at a distance on the skirts of that island, as we sailed along. *Johnson.* 'Sir, I saw at Tobermorie what they called a wood, which I unluckily took for *heath.* If you show me what I shall take for *furze,* it will be something.'" *Boswell: Journal of a Tour to the Hebrides.*

to see him in Bolt Court. EDWARDS. "Ah, sir! we are old men now." JOHNSON (who never liked to think of being old). "Don't let us discourage one another." EDWARDS. "Why, Doctor, you look stout and hearty. I am happy to see you so; for the newspapers told us you were very ill." JOHNSON. "Aye, sir, they are always telling lies of *us old fellows*."

Wishing to be present at more of so singular a conversation as that between two fellow-collegians who had lived forty years in London without ever having chanced to meet, I whispered to Mr. Edwards that Dr. Johnson was going home, and that he had better accompany him now. So Edwards walked along with us, I eagerly assisting to keep up the conversation. Mr. Edwards informed Dr. Johnson that he had practiced long as a solicitor in Chancery,* but that he now lived in the country upon a little farm, about sixty acres, just by Stevenage in Hertfordshire, and that he came to London (to Barnard's Inn,[1] No. 6) generally twice a week. Johnson appearing to be in a reverie, Mr. Edwards addressed himself to me, and expatiated on the pleasure of living in the country. BOSWELL. "I have no notion of this, sir. What you have to entertain you is, I think, exhausted in half an hour." EDWARDS. "What? Don't you love to have hope realized? I see my grass, and my corn, and my trees growing. Now, for instance, I am curious to see if this frost has not nipped my fruit trees." JOHNSON (who we did not imagine was attending). "You find, sir, you have fears as well as hopes."

When we got to Dr. Johnson's house, and were seated in his library, the dialogue went on admirably. EDWARDS. "Sir, I remember you would not let us say *prodigious* at college. For even then, sir," turning to me, "he was delicate in language, and we all feared him." JOHNSON (to Edwards). "From your having practiced the law long, sir, I presume you must be rich." EDWARDS. "No, sir; I got a good deal of money, but I had a number of poor relations to whom I gave a great part of it." JOHNSON. "Sir, you have been rich in the most valuable sense

1. *Barnard's Inn.* The smallest of the Inns of Court (see Glossary: Lincoln's Inn); being a little red brick structure, only thirty feet by twenty-two.

of the word." EDWARDS. "But I shall not die rich." JOHNSON. "Nay, sure, sir, it is better to *live* rich than to *die* rich." EDWARDS. "I wish I had continued at college." JOHNSON. "Why do you wish that, sir?" EDWARDS. "Because I think I should have had a much easier life than mine has been. I should have been a parson, and had a good living, like Bloxham and several others, and lived comfortably." JOHNSON. "Sir, the life of a parson, of a conscientious clergyman, is not easy. I have always considered a clergyman as the father of a larger family than he is able to maintain. I would rather have Chancery suits upon my hands than the cure of souls. No, sir, I do not envy a clergyman's life as an easy life, nor do I envy the clergyman who makes it an easy life."—Here taking himself up all of a sudden, he exclaimed, "Oh! Mr. Edwards! I'll convince you that I recollect you. Do you remember our drinking together at an alehouse near Pembroke gate? At that time you told me of the Eton boy who, when verses on our Savior's turning water into wine were prescribed as an exercise, brought up a single line, which was highly admired:

Vidit[1] et erubuit lympha pudica DEUM,

and I told you of another fine line in Camden's* *Remains,* an eulogy upon one of our kings, who was succeeded by his son, a prince of equal merit:

Mira cano, Sol occubuit, nox nulla secuta est.

EDWARDS. "You are a philosopher, Dr. Johnson. I have tried too in my time to be a philosopher; but, I don't know how, cheerfulness was always breaking in."—Mr. Burke, Sir Joshua Reynolds, Mr. Courtenay,[2] Mr. Malone,[3] and, indeed,

1. *Vidit,* etc. In reality, a famous Latin line of the seventeenth century poet Richard Crashaw, only slightly changed. Dryden had already translated it as "The conscious water saw its God and blushed."

2. *Courtenay.* John Courtenay, a suave gentleman. It was hard to tell when he was adulatory and when ironical. In either case, he was capable of offending the taste of his fellow members of Parliament by over-emphasis.

3. *Malone,* Edmund. A painstaking and neat scholar, amiable in his manners and somewhat set in his opinions. In his regard for Johnson, he was, says Boswell, *Johnsonianissimus.*

all the eminent men to whom I have mentioned this have thought it an exquisite trait of character. The truth is that philosophy, like religion, is too generally supposed to be hard and severe, at least so grave as to exclude all gayety.

EDWARDS. "I have been twice married, Doctor. You, I suppose, have never known what it was to have a wife." JOHNSON. "Sir, I have known what it was to have a wife, and (in a solemn, tender, faltering tone) I have known what it was to *lose a wife.*—It had almost broke my heart."

EDWARDS. "How do you live, sir? For my part, I must have my regular meals, and a glass of good wine. I find I require it." JOHNSON. "I now drink no wine, sir. Early in life I drank wine; for many years I drank none. I then for some years drank a great deal." EDWARDS. "Some hogsheads, I warrant you." JOHNSON. "I then had a severe illness, and left it off, and I have never begun it again. I never felt any difference upon myself from eating one thing rather than another, nor from one kind of weather rather than another. There are people, I believe, who feel a difference; but I am not one of them. And as to regular meals, I have fasted from the Sunday's dinner to the Tuesday's dinner, without any inconvenience. I believe it is best to eat just as one is hungry; but a man who is in business, or a man who has a family, must have stated meals. I am a straggler. I may leave this town and go to Grand Cairo without being missed here or observed there." EDWARDS. "Don't you eat supper,[1] sir?" JOHNSON. "No, sir." EDWARDS. "For my part, now, I consider supper as a turnpike[2] through which one must pass in order to get to bed."

JOHNSON. "You are a lawyer, Mr. Edwards. Lawyers know life practically. A bookish man should always have them to converse with. They have what he wants."* EDWARDS. "I am grown old; I am sixty-five." JOHNSON. "I shall be sixty-eight next birthday. Come, sir, drink water, and put in for a hundred."

Mr. Edwards mentioned a gentleman who had left his whole

---

1. *Supper.* A late evening meal.
2. *Turnpike.* "I am not absolutely sure but this was my own suggestion, though it is truly in the character of Edwards." *Boswell.*

fortune to Pembroke College. JOHNSON. "Whether to leave one's whole fortune to a college be right must depend upon circumstances. I would leave the interest of the fortune I bequeathed to a college to my relations or my friends, for their lives. It is the same thing to a college, which is a permanent society, whether it gets the money now or twenty years hence; and I would wish to make my relations or friends feel the benefit of it."

Mr. Edwards, when going away, again recurred to his consciousness of senility, and looking full in Johnson's face, said to him, "You'll find in Dr. Young,

O my coevals! remnants of yourselves."

Johnson did not relish this at all, but shook his head with impatience. When he was gone, I said to Johnson I thought him but a weak man. JOHNSON. "Why, yes, sir. Here is a man who has passed through life without experience; yet I would rather have him with me than a more sensible man who will not talk readily. This man is always willing to say what he has to say." Yet Dr. Johnson had himself by no means that willingness which he praised so much, and I think so justly. [He] once observed to me, "Tom Tyers[1] described me the best; 'Sir,' said he, 'you are like a ghost; you never speak till you are spoken to.'"

The gentleman whom he thus familiarly mentioned was Mr. Thomas Tyers, son of Mr. Jonathan Tyers, the founder of that excellent place of public amusement, Vauxhall Gardens, which is peculiarly adapted to the taste of the English nation; there being a mixture of curious show, gay exhibition, music, vocal and instrumental, not too refined for the general ear; for all which only a shilling is paid; and, though last, not least, good eating and drinking for those who choose to purchase that regale. Mr. Thomas Tyers was bred to the law; but having a handsome fortune, vivacity of temper, and eccentricity of mind, he could not confine himself to the regularity of practice. He

---

1. *Tom Tyers.* Under the name of *Tom Restless*, Johnson has described him in the *Idler* as creeping every morning into a coffee-house to overhear conversation which, "when it is strained through Tom's head, is so near nothing that what it once was cannot be discovered."

therefore ran about the world with a pleasant carelessness, amusing everybody by his desultory conversation.

Mr. Edwards had said to me aside that Dr. Johnson should have been of a profession. I repeated the remark to Johnson. JOHNSON. "Sir, it *would* have been better that I had been of a profession. I ought to have been a lawyer." Sir William Scott informs me that upon the death of the late Lord Lichfield, who was Chancellor of the University of Oxford, he said to Johnson, "What a pity it is, sir, that you did not follow the profession of the law. You might have been Lord Chancellor of Great Britain, and attained to the dignity of the peerage; and now that the title of Lichfield, your native city, is extinct, you might have had it." In an angry tone [Johnson] exclaimed, "Why will you vex me by suggesting this, when it is too late?"

Yet no man has a higher notion of the dignity of literature than Johnson, or was more determined in maintaining the respect which he justly considered as due to it. Of this, besides the general tenor of his conduct in society, some characteristical instances may be mentioned.

He told Sir Joshua Reynolds that once when he dined in a numerous company of booksellers where, the room being small, the head of the table at which he sat was almost close to the fire, he persevered in suffering a great deal of inconvenience from the heat, rather than quit his place and let one of them sit above him.

Goldsmith, in his diverting simplicity, complained one day in a mixed company, of Lord Camden.[1] "I met him," said he, "at Lord Clare's house in the country, and he took no more notice of me than if I had been an ordinary man." The company having laughed heartily, Johnson stood forth in defense of his friend. "Nay, gentlemen," said he, "Dr. Goldsmith is

---

1. *Lord Camden.* "An able chief justice who objected to the increase of the royal prerogative, defended the right of juries to pass upon the law as well as the facts, denounced the stamp act, called taxation without representation grievous robbery, and in the main supported John Wilkes in his struggles with George III and the political coterie of the court. He was a small lawyer only in the sense of being of small stature. He was one of Garrick's pall-bearers."

in the right. A nobleman ought to have made up to such a man as Goldsmith."

I told him that one morning when I went to breakfast with Garrick, who was very vain of his intimacy with Lord Camden, he accosted me thus, "Pray now, did you—did you meet a little lawyer turning the corner, eh?"—"No, sir," said I. "Pray what do you mean by the question?"—"Why," replied Garrick, with an affected indifference, yet as if standing on tiptoe, "Lord Camden has this moment left me. We have had a long walk together." JOHNSON. "Well, sir, Garrick talked very properly. Lord Camden *was a little lawyer* to be associating so familiarly with a player."

Sir Joshua Reynolds observed, with great truth, that Johnson considered Garrick to be, as it were, his *property*. He would allow no man either to blame or to praise Garrick in his presence without contradicting him.

We went to St. Clement's church again in the afternoon, and then returned and drank tea and coffee in Mrs. Williams's room, Mrs. Desmoulins doing the honors of the tea table. I observed that he would not even look at the proof-sheet of his *Life of Waller* on Good Friday.

Mr. Allen, the printer, brought a book on agriculture,[1] which was printed, and was soon to be published. It was a very strange performance, the author having mixed in it his own thoughts upon various topics, along with his remarks on plowing, sowing, and other farming operations. Dr. Johnson permitted me to read some passages aloud. One was that he resolved to work on Sunday, and did work, but he owned he felt *some* weak compunction; and he had this very curious reflection, "I was born in the wilds of Christianity, and the briers

---

1. *Book on agriculture.* By William Marshall, an international authority on the subject. "The author of the ensuing pages was born a farmer, bred to traffic, and returned to the plow. He had long been convinced of the imbecility of books. He resolved, therefore, to be a farmer from his own experience." *William Marshall: Minutes of Agriculture.* "Generally the writer hopes not to be judged by men of narrow minds but by men who dare to think in defiance of custom, by men who know that the universe itself is *minutiæ* systematized." *The same.*

and thorns still hang about me." Dr. Johnson could not help laughing at this ridiculous image, yet was very angry at the fellow's impiety.

On Saturday [April 18] I drank tea with him. The gentleman who had dined with us at Dr. Percy's came in. Johnson attacked the Americans with intemperate vehemence of abuse. I said something in their favor, and added that I was always sorry when he talked on that subject. This, it seems, exasperated him; though he said nothing at the time. The cloud was charged with sulphureous vapor, which was afterwards to burst in thunder.—We talked of a gentleman[1] who was running out his fortune in London; and I said, "We must get him out of it. All his friends must quarrel with him, and that will soon drive him away." JOHNSON. "Nay, sir, we'll send *you* to him. If your company does not drive a man out of his house, nothing will." This was a horrible shock, for which there was no visible cause. I afterwards asked him why he had said so harsh a thing. JOHNSON. "Because, sir, you made me angry about the Americans." BOSWELL. "But why did you not take your revenge directly?" JOHNSON (smiling). "Because, sir, I had nothing ready. A man cannot strike till he has his weapons." This was a candid and pleasant confession.

He showed me tonight his drawing-room, very genteelly fitted up; and said, "Mrs. Thrale sneered when I talked of my having asked you and your lady to live at my house. I was obliged to tell her that you would be in as respectable a situation in my house as in hers. Sir, the insolence of wealth will creep out." BOSWELL. "She has a little both of the insolence of wealth and the conceit of parts."* JOHNSON. "The insolence of wealth is a wretched thing, but the conceit of parts has some foundation. To be sure, it should not be. But who is without it?" BOSWELL. "Yourself, sir." JOHNSON. "Why, I play no tricks; I lay no traps."

We talked of the numbers of people that sometimes have composed the households of great families. I mentioned that

---

1. *A gentleman.* No doubt Langton, as also two or three paragraphs farther on.

there were a hundred in the family of the present Earl of Eglintoune's father. Dr. Johnson seeming to doubt it, I began to
enumerate. "Let us see: my Lord and my Lady, two." JOHN-
SON. "Nay, sir, if you are to count by two's you may be long
enough." BOSWELL. "Well, but now I add two sons and
seven daughters, and a servant for each; that will make twenty;
so we have the fifth part already." JOHNSON. "Very true.
You get at twenty pretty readily, but you will not so easily get
further on. We grow to five feet pretty readily, but it is not so
easy to grow to seven."

On Sunday, April 19, being Easter day, after the solemnities
of the festival in St. Paul's Church, I visited him, but could not
stay to dinner. I expressed a wish to have the arguments for
Christianity always in readiness, that my religious faith might
be as firm and clear as any proposition whatsoever, so that I need
not be under the least uneasiness when it should be attacked.
JOHNSON. "Sir, you cannot answer all objections. You have
demonstration for a First Cause; you see he must be good as
well as powerful, because there is nothing to make him otherwise, and goodness of itself is preferable. Yet you have against
this, what is very certain, the unhappiness of human life. This,
however, gives us reason to hope for a future state of compensa-
tion, that there may be a perfect system. But of that we were
not sure, till we had a positive revelation." I told him that
his *Rasselas* had often made me unhappy; for it represented
the misery of human life so well, and so convincingly to a thinking mind, that if at any time the impression wore off, and I
felt myself easy, I began to suspect some delusion.

On Monday, April 20, I found him at home in the morning.
We talked of a gentleman who we apprehended was gradually
involving his circumstances by bad management. JOHNSON.
"Wasting a fortune is evaporation by a thousand imperceptible
means. If it were a stream, they'd stop it. He does not spend
fast enough to have pleasure from it. He has the crime of
prodigality, and the wretchedness of parsimony. If a man is
killed in a duel, he is killed as many a one has been killed; but
it is a sad thing for a man to lie down and die; to bleed to death,
because he has not fortitude enough to sear the wound, or even

to stitch it up." I cannot but pause a moment to admire the fecundity of fancy, and choice of language, which in this instance, and, indeed, on almost all occasions, he displayed. It was well observed by Dr. Percy, now Bishop of Dromore, "The conversation of Johnson is strong and clear, and may be compared to an antique statue, where every vein and muscle is distinct and bold. Ordinary conversation resembles an inferior cast."

On Saturday, April 25, I dined with him at Sir Joshua Reynolds's, with the learned Dr. Musgrave, Counselor Leland of Ireland, son to the historian, Mrs. Cholmondeley, and some more ladies. "The Project," a new poem, was read to the company by Dr. Musgrave.

We talked of a lady's verses on Ireland. MISS REYNOLDS. "Have you seen them, sir?" JOHNSON. "No, madam, I have seen a translation from Horace, by one of her daughters. She showed it me." MISS REYNOLDS. "And how was it, sir?" "Why, very well for a young Miss's verses—that is to say, compared with excellence, nothing. I am vexed at being shown verses in that manner. Nobody has a right to put another under such a difficulty that he must either hurt the person by telling the truth, or hurt himself by telling what is not true." BOSWELL. "A man often shows his writings to people of eminence, to obtain from them, either from their good nature or from their not being able to tell the truth firmly, a commendation, of which he may afterwards avail himself." JOHNSON. "Very true, sir. Therefore, the man who is asked by an author what he thinks of his work is put to the torture, and is not obliged to speak the truth, so that what he says is not considered as his opinion; yet he has said it, and cannot retract it; and this author, when mankind are hunting him with a canister at his tail, can say, 'I would not have published had not Johnson, or Reynolds, or Musgrave, or some other good judge commended the work.' Yet I consider it as a very difficult question in conscience whether one should advise a man not to publish a work, if profit be his object; for the man may say, 'Had it not been for you, I should have had the money.' Now you cannot be sure; for you have only your own opinion, and the public may think very differently." SIR JOSHUA REYNOLDS. "You must

upon such an occasion have two judgments: one as to the real
value of the work, the other as to what may please the general
taste at the time." JOHNSON. "But you can be *sure* of neither.
Both Goldsmith's comedies were once refused; his first by Garrick, his second by Colman, who was prevailed on at last by
much solicitation, nay, a kind of force, to bring it on. His
Vicar of Wakefield I myself did not think would have had
much success."

He observed, "A man cannot with propriety speak of himself,
except he relates simple facts. He is sure he has been at Richmond; he is sure he is six feet high. But he cannot be sure he
is wise, or that he has any other excellence. Then, all censure
of a man's self is oblique praise. It is in order to show how much
he can spare. It has all the invidiousness of self-praise, and all
the reproach of falsehood." BOSWELL. "Sometimes it may
proceed from a man's strong consciousness of his faults being
observed. He knows that others would throw him down, and
therefore he had better lie down softly of his own accord."

On Tuesday, April 28, he was engaged to dine at General
Paoli's, where, as I have already observed, I was still entertained in elegant hospitality and with all the ease and comfort
of a home. I called on him, and accompanied him in a hack-
ney-coach. We stopped first at the bottom of Hedge Lane,
into which he went to leave a letter, "with good news for a
poor man in distress,"[1] as he told me. I did not question him
particularly as to this. He himself often resembled Lady
Bolingbroke's lively description of Pope; that "he was *un
politique aux choux et aux raves.*" He would say, "I dine today in Grosvenor Square"; this might be with a Duke; or, perhaps, "I dine today at the other end of the town"; or, "A gentleman of great eminence called on me yesterday."—He loved
thus to keep things floating in conjecture: *Omne ignotum pro
magnifico est.* I believe I ventured to dissipate the cloud, to
unveil the mystery, more freely and frequently than any of
his friends.

---

1. *Poor man in distress.* "Mauritius Lowe, the painter, lived at No. 3
Hedge Lane in a state of extreme distress." *Croker.* Dr. Johnson's kindness to him at the expense of the public appears later in this book.

At General Paoli's were Sir Joshua Reynolds, Mr. Langton, Marchese Gherardi of Lombardy, and Mr. John Spottiswoode the younger, of Spottiswoode, the solicitor. At this time fears of an invasion[1] were circulated; to obviate which, Mr. Spottiswoode observed that Mr. Fraser, the engineer, who had lately come from Dunkirk, said that the French had the same fears of us. JOHNSON. "It is thus that mutual cowardice keeps us in peace. Were one-half of mankind brave, and one-half cowards, the brave would be always beating the cowards. Were all brave, they would lead a very uneasy life; all would be continually fighting; but being all cowards, we go on very well."

We talked of drinking wine. JOHNSON. "I require wine only when I am alone. I have then often wished for it, and often taken it." SPOTTISWOODE. "What, by way of a companion, sir?" JOHNSON. "To get rid of myself, to send myself away. Wine makes a man better pleased with himself. I do not say that it makes him more pleasing to others. Sometimes it does. But the danger is that while a man grows better pleased with himself, he may be growing less pleasing to others. Wine gives a man nothing. It neither gives him knowledge nor wit; it only animates a man, and enables him to bring out what a dread of the company has repressed. It only puts in motion what has been locked up in frost. But this may be good, or it may be bad." SPOTTISWOODE. "So, sir, wine is a key which opens a box, but this box may be either full or empty?" JOHNSON. "Nay, sir, conversation is the key; wine is a pick-lock, which forces open the box and injures it. A man should cultivate his mind so as to have that confidence and readiness without wine, which wine gives." BOSWELL. "The great difficulty of resisting wine is from benevolence. For instance, a good worthy man asks you to taste his wine, which he has had twenty

---

1. *Invasion.* France had been at war with England since February 6. "Public affairs continue to go on without much mending, and there are those still who either fright themselves or would fright others with an invasion; but my opinion is that the French neither have nor had in any part of the summer a number of ships on the coast equal to the transportation of twenty or of ten thousand men. *Johnson to Dr. Taylor, Oct. 19, 1779.*

years in his cellar." JOHNSON. "Sir, all this notion about benevolence arises from a man's imagining himself to be of more importance to others than he really is. They don't care a farthing whether he drinks wine or not." SIR JOSHUA REYNOLDS. "Yes, they do for the time." JOHNSON. "For the time!—If they care this minute, they forget it the next. And as for the good, worthy man; how do you know he is good and worthy? No good and worthy man will insist upon another man's drinking wine. As to the wine twenty years in the cellar— of ten men, three say this merely because they must say something; three are telling a lie when they say they have had the wine twenty years; three would rather save the wine; one, perhaps, cares. I allow it is something to please one's company, and people are always pleased with those who partake pleasure with them. But after a man has brought himself to relinquish the great personal pleasure which arises from drinking wine, any other consideration is a trifle. To please others by drinking wine is something only if there be nothing against it. I should, however, be sorry to offend worthy men:

> Curst be the verse, how well soe'er it flow,
> That tends to make one worthy man my foe."

BOSWELL. "Curst be the *spring*, the *water*." JOHNSON. "But let us consider what a sad thing it would be if we were obliged to drink or do anything else that may happen to be agreeable to the company where we are." LANGTON. "By the same rule you must join with a gang of cut-purses." JOHNSON. "Yes, sir; but yet we must do justice to wine; we must allow it the power it possesses. To make a man pleased with himself, let me tell you, is doing a very great thing."

I was at this time myself a water-drinker, upon trial, by Johnson's recommendation. JOHNSON. "Boswell is a bolder combatant than Sir Joshua; he argues for wine without the help of wine, but Sir Joshua with it." SIR JOSHUA REYNOLDS. "But to please one's company is a strong motive." JOHNSON (who, from drinking only water, supposed everybody who drank wine to be elevated). "I won't argue any more with you, sir. You are too far gone." SIR JOSHUA. "I should have thought so indeed, sir, had I made such a speech as you have now done." JOHNSON (drawing himself in and, I really thought, blushing). "Nay, don't be angry. I did not mean to offend you." SIR JOSHUA. "At first the taste of wine was disagreeable to me; but I brought myself to drink it, that I might be like other people. The pleasure of drinking wine is so connected with pleasing your company that altogether there is something of social goodness in it." JOHNSON. "Sir, this is only saying the same thing over again." SIR JOSHUA. "No, this is new." JOHNSON. "You put it in new words, but it is an old thought. This is one of the disadvantages of wine: it makes a man mistake words for thoughts." BOSWELL. "I think it is a new thought; at least, it is in a new *attitude.*" JOHNSON. "Nay, sir, it is only in a new coat; or an old coat with a new facing. (Then laughing heartily.) It is the old dog in a new doublet." BOSWELL. "But, sir, you and I should not have been so well received in the Highlands and Hebrides if I had not drunk with our worthy friends. Had I drunk water only, as you did, they would not have been so cordial." JOHNSON. "Sir William Temple mentions that in his travels through the Netherlands he had two or three gentlemen with him, and when a bumper was necessary he put it on them. Were I to travel again through the islands I would have Sir Joshua with me to take the bumpers." BOSWELL. "But, sir, let me put a case. Suppose Sir Joshua should take a jaunt into Scotland; he does me the honor to pay me a visit at my house in the country. I am overjoyed at seeing him; we are quite by ourselves; shall I unsociably and churlishly let him sit drinking by himself? No, no, my dear Sir Joshua, you shall not be treated so, I *will* take a bottle with you."

On Wednesday, April 29, I dined with him at Mr. Allan Ramsay's, where were Lord Binning,[1] Dr. Robertson the historian, Sir Joshua Reynolds, and the Honorable Mrs. Boscawen, widow of the Admiral, and mother of the present Viscount Falmouth. Before Johnson came we talked a good deal of him. I said I worshiped him. ROBERTSON. "But some

---

1. *Lord Binning.* Langton's brother-in-law.

of you spoil him; you should not worship him; you should worship no man." BOSWELL. "I cannot help worshiping him; he is so much superior to other men." ROBERTSON. "In criticism, and in wit and conversation, he is no doubt very excellent; but in other respects he is not above other men; he will believe anything, and will strenuously defend the most minute circumstance connected with the Church of England." BOSWELL. "Believe me, Doctor, you are much mistaken as to this; for when you talk with him calmly in private, he is very liberal[1] in his way of thinking." ROBERTSON. "He and I have been always very gracious; the first time I met him was one evening at Strahan's, where he had just had an unlucky altercation with Adam Smith,[2] to whom he had been so rough that Strahan, after Smith was gone, had remonstrated with him, and told him that I was coming soon, and that he was uneasy to think that he might behave in the same manner to me. 'No, no, sir,' said Johnson, 'I warrant you Robertson and I shall do very well.' Accordingly he was gentle and good-humored and courteous with me the whole evening, and he has been so upon every occasion that we have met since. I have often said (laughing) that I have been in a great measure indebted to Smith for my good reception." BOSWELL. "His power of reasoning is very strong, and he has a peculiar art of drawing characters, which is as rare as good portrait painting." SIR JOSHUA REYNOLDS. "He is undoubtedly admirable in this; but, in order to mark the characters which he draws, he over-

---

1. *Very liberal.* "[Johnson] refused to go and hear Principal Robertson preach. 'I will hear him (said he), if he will get up into a tree and preach; but I will not give a sanction, by my presence, to a Presbyterian assembly.'" *Boswell: Journal of a Tour to the Hebrides.*

2. *Adam Smith.* Johnson appears never to have read his treatise on the Wealth of Nations (1776), or to have realized that it established two essentials of all later political economy. Outside of this field Smith was too unappreciative of the contending tastes and passions of men to appeal to one of Johnson's temperament. Boswell thought he had book-making too much in his thoughts, Dr. Alexander Carlyle said his conversation was like lecturing, and Garrick called it flabby. That he was a complacent admirer of one of Johnson's pet antipathies, Hume, no doubt made him the more obnoxious.

charges them, and gives people more than they really have, whether of good or bad."

No sooner did he, of whom we had been thus talking so easily, arrive, than we were all as quiet as a school upon the entrance of the head-master; and were very soon sat down to a table covered with such variety of good things as contributed not a little to dispose him to be pleased.

We talked of antiquarian researches. JOHNSON. "All that is really *known* of the ancient state of Britain is contained in a few pages. We *can* know no more than what the old writers have told us; yet what large books we have upon it, the whole of which, excepting such parts as are taken from those old writers, is all a dream, such as Whitaker's *Manchester*. I have heard Henry's *History of Britain* well spoken of; I am told it is carried on in separate divisions, as the civil, the military, the religious history; I wish much to have one branch well done, and that is the history of manners, of common life."

Dr. Robertson expatiated on the character of a certain noble-man:[1] that he was one of the strongest-minded men that ever lived; that he would sit in company quite sluggish while there was nothing to call forth his intellectual vigor; but the moment that any important subject was started, for instance, how this country is to be defended against a French invasion, he would rouse himself, and show his extraordinary talents with the most powerful ability and animation. JOHNSON. "Yet this man cut his own throat. The true, strong, and sound mind is the man that can embrace equally great things and small. Now I am told the King of Prussia will say to a servant, 'Bring me a bottle of such a wine, which came in such a year; it lies in such a corner of the cellars.' I would have a man great in great things, and elegant in little things." He said to me afterwards, when we were by ourselves, "Robertson was in a mighty ro-

---

1. *Certain nobleman.* Lord Clive; famous for his brilliant services in behalf of the British Empire in India. His enterprise and daring were sometimes interrupted by periods of constitutional depression, much like those of Johnson himself, and in no way connected with the occasional breaches of honor of which he was guilty. He committed suicide in England in 1774.

mantic humor; he talked of one he did not know, but I *downed* him with the King of Prussia."—"Yes, sir," said I, "you threw a *bottle* at his head."

An ingenious gentleman was mentioned, concerning whom both Robertson and Ramsay agreed that he had a constant firmness of mind; for after a laborious day, and amidst a multiplicity of cares and anxieties, he would sit down with his sisters and be quite cheerful and good-humored. Such a disposition, it was observed, was a happy gift of nature. JOHNSON. "I do not think so; a man has from nature a certain portion of mind; the use he makes of it depends upon his own free will. That a man has always the same firmness of mind, I do not say, because every man feels his mind less firm at one time than another; but I think a man's being in a good or bad humor depends upon his will."

Johnson harangued against drinking wine. "A man," said he, "may choose whether he will have abstemiousness and knowledge, or claret and ignorance." Dr. Robertson, who is very companionable, was beginning to dissent as to the proscription of claret. JOHNSON (with a placid smile). "Nay, sir, you shall not differ with me; as I have said that the man is most perfect who takes in the most things, I am for knowledge and claret." ROBERTSON (holding a glass of generous claret in his hand). "Sir, I can only drink your health." JOHNSON. "Sir, I should be sorry if *you* should be ever in such a state as to be able to do nothing more." ROBERTSON. "Dr. Johnson, allow me to say that in one respect I have the advantage of you: when you were in Scotland you would not come to hear any of our preachers, whereas, when I am here, I attend your public worship without scruple, and indeed with great satisfaction." JOHNSON. "Why, sir, that is not so extraordinary; the King of Siam sent ambassadors to Louis the Fourteenth, but Louis the Fourteenth sent none to the King of Siam."

Next day, Thursday, April 30, I found him at home by himself. JOHNSON. "Well, sir, Ramsay gave us a splendid dinner. I love Ramsay. You will not find a man in whose conversation there is more instruction, more information, and more elegance, than in Ramsay's." BOSWELL. "What I

admire in Ramsay is his continuing to be so young." JOHNSON.
"Why, yes, sir; it is to be admired. I value myself upon this,
that there is nothing of the old man in my conversation. I am
now sixty-eight, and I have no more of it than at twenty-eight."
BOSWELL. "But, sir, would not you wish to know old age?
He who is never an old man does not know the whole of human
life; for old age is one of the divisions of it." JOHNSON. "Nay,
sir, what talk is this?" BOSWELL. "I mean, sir, the Sphinx's
description of it—morning, noon, and night. I would know
night, as well as morning and noon." JOHNSON. "What,
sir, would you know what it is to feel the evils of old age? Would
you have the gout? Would you have decrepitude?"[1] Seeing
him heated, I would not argue any farther; but I was confident
that I was in the right. I would, in due time, be a Nestor, an
elder of the people; and there *should* be some difference between
the conversation of twenty-eight and sixty-eight. A grave picture should not be gay. There is a serene, solemn, placid old
age. JOHNSON. "Mrs. Thrale's mother[2] said of me what
flattered me much. A clergyman was complaining of want of
society in the country where he lived; and said, 'They talk of
runts'; (that is, young cows). 'Sir,' said Mrs. Salusbury,
'Mr. Johnson would learn to talk of runts.'" He added, "I
think myself a very polite man."

On Saturday, May 2, I dined with him at Sir Joshua Reynolds's, where there was a very large company, and a great
deal of conversation; but owing to some circumstance which I
cannot now recollect, I have no record of any part of it, except
that there were several people there by no means of the Johnsonian school; so that less attention was paid to him than
usual, which put him out of humor; and upon some imaginary

---

1. *Decrepitude.* "They whose endeavor is mental excellence will
learn, perhaps too late, how much it is endangered by diseases of the
body, and find that knowledge may easily be lost in the starts of melancholy, the flights of impatience, and the peevishness of decrepitude."
Johnson: The Rambler.

2. *Mrs. Thrale's mother.* Mrs. Salusbury, who used to fret Dr.
Johnson by being habitually fretted herself, on which he sometimes
would plague her. They grew more kindly toward each other before
her death.

offense from me he attacked me with such rudeness that I was vexed and angry, because it gave those persons an opportunity of enlarging upon his supposed ferocity, and ill-treatment of his best friends. I was so much hurt, and had my pride so much aroused that I kept away from him for a week; and perhaps might have kept away much longer, nay, gone to Scotland without seeing him again, had not we fortunately met and been reconciled. To such unhappy chances are human friendships liable.

On Friday, May 8, I dined with him at Mr. Langton's. I was reserved and silent, which I suppose he perceived, and might recollect the cause. After dinner, when Mr. Langton was called out of the room, and we were by ourselves, he drew his chair near to mine, and said in a tone of conciliating courtesy, "Well, how have you done?" BOSWELL. "Sir, you have made me very uneasy by your behavior to me when we last were at Sir Joshua Reynolds's. You know, my dear sir, no man has a greater respect and affection for you, or would sooner go to the end of the world to serve you. Now to treat me so—" He insisted that I had interrupted him, which I assured him was not the case; and proceeded—"But why treat me so before people who neither love you nor me?" JOHNSON. "Well, I am sorry for it. I'll make it up to you twenty different ways, as you please." BOSWELL. "I said today to Sir Joshua, when he observed that you *tossed* me sometimes—I don't care how often, or how high he tosses me when only friends are present, for then I fall upon soft ground; but I do not like falling on stones, which is the case when enemies are present.—I think this a pretty good image, sir." JOHNSON. "Sir, it is one of the happiest I have ever heard."

The truth is, there was no venom in the wounds which he inflicted at any time, unless they were irritated by some malignant infusion by other hands. We were instantly as cordial again as ever, and joined in hearty laugh at some ludicrous but innocent peculiarities of one of our friends. BOSWELL. "Do you think, sir, it is always culpable to laugh at a man to his face?" JOHNSON. "Why, sir, that depends upon the man and the thing. If it is a slight man, and a slight thing, you may; for you take nothing valuable from him."

When Mr. Langton returned to us, the "flow of talk" went on. An eminent author being mentioned: JOHNSON. "He is not a pleasant man. His conversation is neither instructive nor brilliant. He does not talk as if impelled by any fullness of knowledge or vivacity of imagination. His conversation is like that of any other sensible man. He talks with no wish either to inform or to hear, but only because he thinks it does not become —— —— to sit in a company and say nothing."

Mr. Langton having repeated the anecdote of Addison having distinguished between his powers[1] in conversation and in writing, by saying "I have only nine-pence in my pocket; but I can draw for a thousand pounds": JOHNSON. "He had not that retort ready, sir; he had prepared it beforehand." LANGTON (turning to me). "A fine surmise. Set a thief to catch a thief."

Johnson called the East Indians barbarians. BOSWELL. "You will except the Chinese, sir?" JOHNSON. "No, sir." BOSWELL. "Have they not arts?" JOHNSON. "They have pottery." BOSWELL. "What do you say to the written characters of their language?" JOHNSON. "Sir, they have not an alphabet. They have not been able to form what all other nations have formed." BOSWELL. "There is more learning in their language than in any other, from the immense number of their characters." JOHNSON. "It is only more difficult from its rudeness; as there is more labor in hewing down a tree with a stone than with an ax."

He said, "I have been reading Lord Kames's *Sketches of the History of Man*. In treating of severity of punishment he mentions that of Madame Lapouchin in Russia, but he does not give it fairly; for I have looked at Chappe D'Auteroche, from whom he has taken it. He stops where it is said that the spectators thought her innocent, and leaves out what follows, that she nevertheless was guilty. Now this is being as culpable as

---

1. *His powers.* "[Addison] thinks justly, but he thinks faintly." *Johnson: Life of Addison.*

one can conceive, to misrepresent fact in a book, and for what motive?" BOSWELL. "He was only giving a picture of the lady in her sufferings." JOHNSON. "Nay, don't endeavor to palliate this. Guilt is the principal feature in the picture."

On Tuesday, May 12, I waited on the Earl of Marchmont,[1] to know if his Lordship would favor Dr. Johnson with information concerning Pope, whose Life he was about to write. Johnson had said to me, when I mentioned Lord Marchmont as one who could tell him a great deal about Pope, "Sir, he will tell *me* nothing." I had the honor of being known to his Lordship, and applied to him of myself without being commissioned by Johnson. His Lordship promised to tell all he recollected about Pope, and was so very courteous as to say, "Tell Dr. Johnson I have a great respect for him, and am ready to show it in any way I can. I am to be in the city* tomorrow, and will call at his house as I return." His Lordship, however, asked, "Will he write the Lives of the Poets impartially? He was the first that brought Whig and Tory into a dictionary. And what do you think of his definition of Excise? Do you know the history of his aversion to the word *transpire?*" Then taking down the folio *Dictionary*, he showed it with this censure on its secondary sense: "To escape from secrecy to notice; a sense lately innovated from France, without necessity." The truth was, Lord Bolingbroke, who left the Jacobites, first used it; therefore, it was to be condemned.

I proposed to Lord Marchmont that he should revise Johnson's Life of Pope. "So," said his Lordship, "you would put me in a dangerous situation. You know he knocked down Osborne, the bookseller."

Elated with the success of my spontaneous exertion to procure material and respectable aid to Johnson, I hastened down to Mr. Thrale's at Streatham, where he now was, that I might insure his being at home next day; and after dinner, when I thought he would receive the good news in the best humor, I

---

1. *Earl of Marchmont.* A friend of Lord Chesterfield and of Lord Bolingbroke; one of Pope's four executors; when in active politics, he was public-spirited, disinterested, and liberal in his views; when "shelved," he turned to husbandry, forestry, and gardening.

announced it eagerly: "I have been at work for you today, sir. I have been with Lord Marchmont. He bade me tell you he has a great respect for you, and will call on you tomorrow, at one o'clock, and communicate all he knows about Pope." Here I paused, in full expectation that he would be pleased with this intelligence, would praise my active merit, and would be alert to embrace such an offer from a nobleman. But whether I had shown an over-exultation, which provoked his spleen, or whether he was seized with a suspicion that I had obtruded him on Lord Marchmont, and humbled him too much; or whether there was anything more than an unlucky fit of ill-humor, I know not; but to my surprise, the result was: JOHNSON. "I shall not be in town tomorrow. I don't care to know[1] about Pope." MRS. THRALE (surprised, as I was, and a little angry). "I suppose, sir, Mr. Boswell thought that as you are to write Pope's Life, you would wish to know about him." JOHNSON. "Wish! why, yes. If it rained knowledge, I'd hold out my hand; but I would not give myself the trouble to go in quest of it." There was no arguing with him at the moment. Some time afterwards he said, "Lord Marchmont will call on me, and then I shall call on Lord Marchmont." Mr. Thrale was uneasy at his unaccountable caprice; and told me that if I did not take care to bring about a meeting between Lord Marchmont and him, it would never take place, which would be a great pity. I sent a card to his Lordship, to be left at Johnson's house, acquainting him that Dr. Johnson could not be in town next day, but would do himself the honor of waiting on him at another time. I give this account fairly, as a specimen of that unhappy temper with which this great and good man had occasionally to struggle, from something morbid in his constitution. Let the most censorious of my readers suppose himself to have a violent fit of the toothache, or to have received a severe stroke on the shin-bone, and when in such a state to be asked a question; and if he has any candor, he will not be surprised at the answers which Johnson sometimes gave in moments of irritation. But it must not

---

1.   *I don't care to know.*   Boswell quotes Lord Hailes as saying that Johnson "expressed no curiosity to see the room where Charles I was born. 'I know that he was born,' said he; 'no matter where.'"

be erroneously supposed that he was generally thus peevish. It will be seen that in the following year he had a very agreeable interview with Lord Marchmont, at his Lordship's house; and this very afternoon he soon forgot any fretfulness and fell into conversation as usual.

On Saturday, May 16, I dined with him at Mr. Beauclerk's, with Mr. Langton and some others.

He said, "Dr. Mead lived more in the broad sunshine[1] of life than almost any man."

The disaster of General Burgoyne's army was then the common topic of conversation. It was asked why piling their arms was insisted upon as a matter of such consequence, when it seemed to be a circumstance so inconsiderable in itself. JOHNSON. "Why, sir, a French author says, '*Il y a beaucoup de puérilités dans la guerre.*' All distinctions are trifles, because great things can seldom occur, and those distinctions are settled by custom. A savage would as willingly have his meat sent to him in the kitchen as eat it at the table here; as men become civilized, various modes of denoting honorable preference are invented."

On Tuesday, May 19, I was to set out for Scotland in the evening. He was engaged to dine with me at Mr. Dilly's; I waited upon him to remind him of his appointment and attend him thither; he gave me some salutary counsel and recommended vigorous resolution against any deviation from moral duty. BOSWELL. "But you would not have me to bind myself by a solemn obligation?" JOHNSON (much agitated). "What! a vow?—Oh, no, sir, a vow is a horrible thing; it is a snare for sin. The man who cannot go to heaven without a vow—may go—" Here, standing erect in the middle of his library, and rolling grand, his pause was truly a curious compound of the solemn and the ludicrous; he half-whistled in his usual way, when

---

1. *Sunshine.* Namely, great ability, the best foreign medical training, learned, wealthy, and royal patients, a coach and six, the most notable library in the kingdom, and the friendship of wits and scholars. Yet, for years he technically had no right to practice, because he declined to subscribe to the doctrines of the Church of England, as was required by law of all physicians in his day.

pleasant, and he paused, as if checked by religious awe. Methought he would have added—to hell—but was restrained.

[1779]. On the 22d of January I wrote to him on several topics, and mentioned that as he had been so good as to permit me to have the proof sheets of his *Lives of the Poets*, I had written to his servant, Francis, to take care of them for me.

On the 23rd of February I wrote again, complaining of his silence, as I had heard he was ill and had written to Mr. Thrale for information concerning him; and I announced my intention of soon being again in London.

"*To James Boswell, Esq.*

"DEAR SIR: Why should you take such delight to make a bustle, to write to Mr. Thrale that I am negligent, and to Francis to do what is so very unnecessary? Thrale, you may be sure, cared not about it; and I shall spare Francis the trouble by ordering a set both of the Lives and Poets to dear Mrs. Boswell, in acknowledgment of her marmalade. Persuade her to accept them, and accept them kindly. Mrs. Thrale waits in the coach.
"I am, dear sir, &c.,
"SAM. JOHNSON.
"March 13, 1779."

This letter crossed me on the road to London, where I arrived on Monday, March 15, and next morning at a late hour found Dr. Johnson sitting over his tea, attended by Mrs. Desmoulins, Mr. Levet, and a clergyman who had come to submit some poetical pieces to his revision.[1] The subject under immediate

---

1. *His revision.* A Mrs. Brooke repeatedly importuned Dr. Johnson to read her new play before it was acted. He constantly evaded doing so. At last she pressed him so closely that he actually refused, and told her that on carefully rereading it, she could see if there was anything amiss in it as well as he. "But, sir," said she, "I have no time, I have already so many irons in the fire." "Why then, madam," said he (quite out of patience), "the best thing I can advise you to do is to put your tragedy along with your irons." *Paraphrased from Hannah More.* "Henderson asked the Doctor's opinion of *Dido* and its author. 'Sir,' said Johnson, 'I never did the man an injury; yet he would read his tragedy to me.'" *John Nichols.*

discussion was a translation, yet in manuscript, of the *Carmen Seculare* of Horace, which had this year been set to music, and performed as a public entertainment in London. When Johnson had done reading, the author asked him bluntly if it was a good translation. Johnson seemed to be puzzled for a moment what answer to make. He evaded the question thus: "Sir, I do not say that it may not be made a very good translation." A printed *Ode to the Warlike Genius of Britain* came next in review; the bard was a lank, bony figure, with short, black hair; he was writhing himself in agitation while Johnson read, and showing his teeth in a grin of earnestness, exclaimed in broken sentences, and in a keen sharp tone, "Is that poetry, sir?—Is it Pindar?"[1] JOHNSON. "Why, sir, there is here a great deal of what is called poetry." Then, turning to me, the poet cried, "My muse has not been long upon the town, and (pointing to the Ode) it trembles under the hand of the great critic." Johnson, in a tone of displeasure, asked him, "Why do you praise Anson?" I did not trouble him by asking his reason for this question. He proceeded, "Here is an error, sir; you have made Genius feminine."—"Palpable, sir," cried the enthusiast; "I know it. But (in a lower tone) it was to pay a compliment to the Duchess of Devonshire,[2] with which her Grace was pleased. She is walking across Coxheath in the military uniform, and I suppose her to be the Genius of Britain." JOHNSON. "Sir, you are giving a reason for it, but that will not

1. *Pindar.* Eight and sixty years before this interview, Addison had characterized the ancient Pindar as "a great genius hurried on by a natural fire and impetuosity to vast conceptions of things." In his modern imitators, the same critic found only "the distortion, grimace, and outward figure, but nothing of that divine impulse which raises the mind above itself." A few months before the call Boswell refers to, Johnson, in his *Life of Cowley*, had displayed his impatience with the whole fashion and had boasted that "at last it had died away."
2. *Duchess of Devonshire.* A reigning beauty of twenty-two, married to the "first match" of the kingdom; and immortalized by both Reynolds and Gainsborough; so eager a Whig that she is said to have bartered kisses for votes for Fox.
"I have seen the Duchess of Devonshire, then in the first bloom of youth, hanging on the sentences that fell from Johnson's lips and contending for the nearest place to his chair." *Wraxall.*

make it right. You may have a reason why two and two should make five, but they will still make but four."

Although I was several times with him in the course of the following days, I have preserved no memorial of his conversation till Friday, March 26, when I visited him. He said he expected to be attacked on account of his *Lives of the Poets.* "However," said he, "I would rather be attacked than unnoticed. For the worst thing you can do to an author is to be silent as to his works. An assault upon a town is a bad thing, but starving it is still worse; an assault may be unsuccessful, but if you starve the town, you are sure of victory."

Talking of a friend of ours associating with persons of very discordant principles and characters: I said he was a very universal man, quite a man of the world. JOHNSON. "Yes, sir; but one may be so much a man of the world as to be nothing in the world. I remember a passage in Goldsmith's *Vicar of Wakefield,* which he was afterwards fool enough to expunge: 'I do not love a man who is zealous for nothing.'" BOSWELL. "That was a fine passage." JOHNSON. "Yes, sir; there was another fine passage too, which he struck out: 'When I was a young man, being anxious to distinguish myself, I was perpetually starting new propositions. But I soon gave this over; for I found that generally what was new was false.'"

I said I did not like to sit with people of whom I had not a good opinion. JOHNSON. "But you must not indulge your delicacy too much, or you will be a *tête-à-tête* man all your life."

During my stay in London this spring I was unaccountably negligent in preserving Johnson's sayings, more so than at any time when I was happy enough to have an opportunity of hearing his wisdom and wit. There is no help for it now. I must content myself with presenting such scraps as I have.

Talking of the wonderful concealment of the author of the celebrated letters signed *Junius,*[1] he said, "I should have be-

---

1. *Junius.* "*Junius* fought in the dark; he saw his enemy and had his full blow, while he himself remained safe in obscurity. 'But let us not,' said Johnson, 'mistake the venom of the shaft for the vigor of the bow.'" *Arthur Murphy, 1792.*

lieved Burke[1] to be Junius, because I know no man but Burke who is capable of writing these letters, but Burke spontaneously denied it to me. The case would have been different had I asked him if he was the author; a man so questioned as to an anonymous publication may think he has a right to deny it."

At Streatham, on Monday, March 29, at breakfast, he maintained that a father had no right to control the inclinations of his daughters in marriage.

On Wednesday, March 31, when I visited him and confessed an excess of which I had very seldom been guilty—that I had spent a whole night in playing at cards, and that I could not look back on it with satisfaction—instead of a harsh animadversion, he mildly said, "Alas, sir, on how few things can we look back with satisfaction."

On Thursday, April 1, he commended one of the Dukes of Devonshire for a "dogged veracity." He said, too, "London is nothing to some people; but to a man whose pleasure is intellectual, London is the place. And there is no place where economy can be so well practiced as in London. You cannot play tricks with your fortune in a small place; you must make an uniform appearance. Here a lady may have well-furnished apartments, and elegant dress, without any meat in her kitchen."

I was amused by considering with how much ease and coolness he could write or talk to a friend, exhorting him not to suppose that happiness was not to be found as well in other places as in London; when he himself was at all times sensible of its being, comparatively speaking, a heaven upon earth. The freedom from remark and petty censure, with which life may be passed there, is a circumstance which a man who knows the teasing restraint of a narrow circle must relish highly. Mr. Burke,[2] whose orderly and amiable domestic habits might make

---

1. *Burke.* Sir Philip Francis, who professed to be Burke's friend, used to suggest that Burke was Junius. It is now generally supposed that Sir Philip himself was Junius, which perhaps accounts for the suggestion. Burke himself, it is well to remember, has been characterized as "chivalrous," "noble," "unaffected," and "unreserved."

2. *Burke.* "His expenditure, like his rhetoric, was in the grand style. He belongs to Charles Lamb's great race, 'the men who borrow.'" *Augustine Birrell.*

the eye of observation less irksome to him than to most men, said once very pleasantly, in my hearing, "Though I have the honor to represent Bristol, I should not like to live there; I should be obliged to be so much *upon my good behavior*." In London, a man may live in splendid society at one time, and in frugal retirement at another, without animadversion. There, and there alone, a man's own house is truly his *castle*, in which he can be in perfect safety from intrusion whenever he pleases. I never shall forget how well this was expressed to me one day by Mr. Meynell:[1] "The chief advantage of London," said he, "is that a man is always *so near his burrow*."

He said of one of his old acquaintances: "He is very fit for a traveling governor. He knows French very well. He is a man of good principles; and there would be no danger that a young gentleman should catch his manner, for it is so very bad that it must be avoided."

A gentleman has informed me that Johnson said of the same person, "Sir, he has the most *inverted* understanding of any man whom I have ever known."

On Friday, April 2, being Good Friday, I visited him in the morning as usual; and finding that we insensibly fell into a train of ridicule upon the foibles of one of our friends, a very worthy man, I, by way of a check, quoted some good admonition from *The Government of the Tongue*,[2] that very pious book. It happened also remarkably enough that the subject of the sermon preached to us today by Dr. Burrows,[3] the rector of

---

1. *Meynell*. Old Meynell of Bradley who thought all foreigners fools (see later). His daughter "had the best understanding Johnson ever met with in any human being." She was married to the comfortable Mr. Fitzherbert. "Her first care was to preserve her husband's soul from corruption; her second to keep his estate entire for their children." At her death, her husband "felt at once afflicted and released." So at least, says Johnson.

2. *The Government of the Tongue*. About this time given by Langton (who was no doubt the "very worthy man") to Boswell as a gentle admonition. The whole episode illustrates Boswell's characteristic love of little stratagems and sly ironies and also probably casts a light on why he so often led Dr. Johnson into criticizing the worthy Langton's inability to mind his own business.

3. *Dr. Burrows*. "His matter is cold; his manner hot; his voice weak, and his action affected." *Thomas Campbell*.

St. Clement Danes, was the certainty that at the last day we must give an account of "the deeds done in the body"; and amongst various acts of culpability he mentioned evil-speaking. As we were moving slowly along in the crowd from church, Johnson jogged my elbow and said, "Did you attend to the sermon?" "Yes, sir," said I, "it was very applicable to *us*." He, however, stood upon the defensive. "Why, sir, the sense of ridicule is given us,[1] and may be lawfully used. The author of *The Government of the Tongue* would have us treat all men alike."

On Saturday, April 3, I visited him at night, and found him sitting in Mrs. Williams's room. The table had a singular appearance, being covered with a heterogeneous assemblage of oysters and porter for his company, and tea for himself. I mentioned my having heard an eminent physician, who was himself a Christian, argue in favor of universal toleration, and maintain that no man could be hurt by another man's differing from him in opinion. JOHNSON. "Sir, you are to a certain degree hurt[2] by knowing that even one man does not believe."

On Wednesday, April 7, I dined with him at Sir Joshua Reynolds's. I have not marked what company was there. Johnson harangued upon the qualities of different liquors; and spoke with great contempt of claret, as so weak that "a man

---

1. *The sense of ridicule is given us.* It *was* to Johnson. " 'That woman,' cries Johnson, 'is like sour small beer; she never could have been a good thing, and even that bad thing is spoiled.' This was in the same vein of asperity that he observed of a Scotch lady that she resembled a dead nettle; 'Were she alive,' said he, 'she would sting.' " *Mrs. Piozzi: Anecdotes of Johnson.*

2. *To a certain degree hurt.* "I, having a letter to write, left my fellow-traveler [Johnson] with Messieurs Foulis. . . . They had that unsettled, speculative mode of conversation which is offensive to a man regularly taught at an English school and university. I found that they had teased him with questions and doubtful disputations. He came in a flutter to me, and desired I might come back again, for he could not bear these men. 'O ho! sir,' said I, 'you are flying to me for refuge.' He answered with a quick vivacity, 'It is of two evils choosing the least.' I was delighted with this flash bursting from the cloud which hung upon his mind, closed my letter directly, and joined the company." *Boswell: Journal of a Tour to the Hebrides.*

would be drowned by it before it made him drunk." He was persuaded to drink one glass of it, that he might judge, not from recollection, which might be dim, but from immediate sensation. He shook his head and said, "Poor stuff! No, sir, claret is the liquor for boys, port for men; but he who aspires to be a hero (smiling) must drink brandy. In the first place, the flavor of brandy is most grateful to the palate; and then, brandy will do soonest for a man what drinking *can* do for him.[1] There are, indeed, few who are able to drink brandy. That is a power rather to be wished for than attained. And yet," proceeded he, "as in all pleasure hope is a considerable part, I know not but fruition comes too quick by brandy. Florence wine I think the worst; it is wine only to the eye; it is wine neither while you are drinking it nor after you have drunk it; it neither pleases the taste nor exhilarates the spirits." I reminded him how heartily he and I used to drink wine together when we were first acquainted, and how I used to have a headache after sitting up with him. He did not like to have this recalled, or, perhaps, thinking that I boasted improperly, resolved to have a witty stroke at me: "Nay, sir, it was not the *wine* that made your head ache, but the *sense* that I put into it." BOSWELL. "What, sir! will sense make the head ache?" JOHNSON. "Yes, sir (with a smile), when it is not used to it." No man who has a true relish of pleasantry could be offended at this; especially if Johnson in a long intimacy had given him repeated proofs of his regard and good estimation. I used to say that as he had given me a thousand pounds in praise, he had a good right now and then to take a guinea from me.

On Thursday, April 8, I dined with him at Mr. Allan Ramsay's, with Lord Graham[2] and some other company. We talked

---

1. *What drinking can do for him.* "To be forced to drink himself into pains of the body in order to get rid of the pains of the mind is a misery." *Shenstone (1741), quoted by Johnson.*

"He who makes a beast of himself gets rid of the pain of being a man." *Johnson, quoted by Stockdale in 1770.*

2. *Lord Graham.* Afterwards third Duke of Montrose; popularly known as Goose Graham.

of Shakespeare's witches. JOHNSON. "They are beings of his own creation; they are a compound of malignity and meanness, without any abilities; and are quite different from the Italian magician. King James says in his *Demonology,* 'Magicians command the devils; witches are their servants.' The Italian magicians are elegant beings." RAMSAY. "Opera witches, not Drury Lane witches." Johnson observed that abilities might be employed in a narrow sphere, as in getting money, which he said he believed no man could do without vigorous parts, though concentrated to a point. RAMSAY. "Yes, like a strong horse in a mill; he pulls better."

Lord Graham, while he praised the beauty of Loch Lomond, on the banks of which is his family seat, complained of the climate, and said he could not bear it. JOHNSON. "Nay, my Lord, don't talk so; you may bear it well enough. Your ancestors have borne it more years than I can tell." This was a handsome compliment to the antiquity of the House of Montrose. His Lordship told me afterwards that he had only affected to complain of the climate lest, if he had spoken as favorably of his country as he really thought, Dr. Johnson might have attacked it. Johnson was very courteous to Lady Margaret Macdonald. "Madam," said he, "when I was in the Isle of Sky,[1] I heard of the people running to take the stones off the road lest Lady Margaret's[2] horse should stumble."

Lord Graham commended Dr. Drummond at Naples as a man of extraordinary talents, and added that he had a great

---

1. *Isle of Sky.* "The greatest island or the greatest but one among the Hebrides." . . . "A walk upon plowed ground in England is a dance upon carpets compared to the toilsome drudgery of wandering in Sky." . . . "Sky is almost equally divided between the two great families of Macdonald and Macleod. The two great lords do not know within twenty square miles the contents of their own territories." *Johnson.*

2. *Lady Margaret.* Apparently as thoroughly "adored" as her harsh and rackrenting husband, Sir Alexander Macdonald, was detested. In 1746, she had aided in the ingenious devices by which Flora Macdonald had secured the escape of the young Pretender from Scotland, after his defeat at Culloden. The hearing of these services while in the Hebrides had warmed the cockles of Johnson's heart.

love of liberty. JOHNSON. "He is *young*, my Lord; all *boys* love liberty,[1] till experience convinces them they are not so fit to govern themselves as they imagined. We are all agreed as to our own liberty; we would have as much of it as we can get, but we are not agreed as to the liberty of others; for in proportion as we take, others must lose. I believe we hardly wish that the mob should have liberty to govern us. When that was the case some time ago, no man was at liberty not to have candles in his windows."[2] RAMSAY. "The result is that order is better than confusion." JOHNSON. "The result is that order cannot be had but by subordination."

On Friday, April 16, I had been present at the trial of the unfortunate Mr. Hackman,[3] who, in a fit of frantic jealous love, had shot Miss Ray, the favorite of a nobleman. Johnson, in whose company I dined today with some other friends, was much interested by my account of what passed, and particularly with his prayer for the mercy of heaven. He said, in a solemn, fervid tone, "I hope he *shall* find mercy."

This day a violent altercation arose between Johnson and Beauclerk,[4] which, having made much noise at the time, I think it proper, in order to prevent any future misrepresentation, to give a minute account of it.

In talking of Hackman, Johnson argued, as Judge Blackstone had done, that his being furnished with two pistols was a proof that he meant to shoot two persons. Mr. Beauclerk said, "No; for that every wise man who intended to shoot himself took

---

1. *All boys love liberty.* See Appendix I, page 552.

2. *Candles in his windows.* An allusion to the angry London mob of May, 1768, which for several days terrorized London because they found that their favorite John Wilkes, recently elected to Parliament by the County of Middlesex (London), was not released from prison and allowed to take his seat.

3. *Hackman.* A clergyman and ex-army man. The nobleman was the dissolute Earl of Sandwich, First Lord of the Admiralty. On Monday, April 19, "Boswell was present at Hackman's execution, riding to Tyburn with him in a mourning coach." *Birkbeck Hill.*

4. *Beauclerk.* "Topham Beauclerk died in 1780. The close of his life had been clouded by disease, and in his last years he was a morose and tyrannical invalid." *Austin Dobson.*

two pistols, that he might be sure of doing it at once. Lord ——'s cook shot himself with one pistol, and lived ten days in great agony. Mr. ——, who loved buttered muffins, but durst not eat them because they disagreed with his stomach, resolved to shoot himself; and then he eat three buttered muffins for breakfast, before shooting himself, knowing that he should not be troubled with indigestion. *He* had two charged pistols; one was found lying charged upon the table by him, after he had shot himself with the other."—"Well," said Johnson, with an air of triumph, "you see here one pistol was sufficient." Beauclerk replied smartly, "Because it happened to kill him." And either then or a very little afterwards, being piqued at Johnson's triumphant remark, added, "This is what you don't know, and I do." There was then a cessation of the dispute; and some minutes intervened, during which dinner and the glass went on cheerfully; when Johnson suddenly and abruptly exclaimed, "Mr. Beauclerk, how came you to talk so petulantly to me, as 'This is what you don't know, but what I know?' One thing *I* know, which *you* don't seem to know: that you are very uncivil." Beauclerk. "Because *you* began by being uncivil, (which you always are)." The words in parenthesis were, I believe, not heard by Dr. Johnson. Here again there was a cessation of arms. Johnson told me that the reason why he waited at first some time without taking any notice of what Mr. Beauclerk said was because he was thinking whether he should resent it. But when he considered that there were present a young Lord and an eminent traveler, two men of the world with whom he had never dined before, he was apprehensive that they might think they had a right to take such liberties with him as Beauclerk did, and therefore resolved he would not let it pass, adding that "he would not appear a coward." A little while after this the conversation turned on the violence of Hackman's temper. Johnson then said, "It was his business to *command* his temper, as my friend Mr. Beauclerk should have done some time ago." Beauclerk. "I should learn of *you*, sir." Johnson. "Sir, you have given *me* opportunities enough of learning, when I have been in *your* company. No man loves to be treated with contempt." BEAU-CLERK (with a polite inclination toward Johnson). "Sir, you have known me twenty years, and however I may have treated others, you may be sure I could never treat you with contempt." JOHNSON. "Sir, you have said more than was necessary." Thus it ended; and Beauclerk's coach not having come for him till very late, Dr. Johnson and another gentleman sat with him a long time after the rest of the company were gone; and he and I dined at Beauclerk's on the Saturday se'ennight* following.

After this tempest had subsided, I recollect the following particulars of his conversation:

"Mallet, I believe, never wrote a single line of his projected life of the Duke of Marlborough. He groped for materials; and thought of it till he had exhausted his mind. Thus it sometimes happens that men entangle themselves in their own schemes."

"To be contradicted in order to force you to talk is mighty unpleasing. You *shine*, indeed; but it is by being *ground*."

Of a gentleman who made some figure among the *Literati* of his time (Mr. Fitzherbert), he said, "What eminence he had was by a felicity of manner; he had no more learning than what he could not help."

On Saturday, April 24, I dined with him at Mr. Beauclerk's. I mentioned that Mr. Wilkes had attacked Garrick to me as a man who had no friend. "I believe he is right, sir. He had friends, but no friend.¹ Garrick was so diffused that he had no man to whom he wished to unbosom himself. He found people always ready to applaud him, and that always for the same thing; so he saw life with great uniformity." One of the company mentioned Lord Chesterfield as a man who had no friend. JOHNSON. "There were more materials to make friendship in Garrick, had he not been so diffused." BOSWELL. "Garrick was pure gold, but beat out to thin leaf. Lord Chesterfield was tinsel." JOHNSON. "Garrick was a very good man, the cheer-

---

1. *No friend.* "I saw old Samuel Johnson standing beside Garrick's grave, at the foot of Shakespeare's monument, and bathed in tears." *Richard Cumberland: Memoirs.*

fullest man of the age. He began the world with a great hunger for money; the son of a half-pay officer, bred in a family whose study was to make four pence do as much as others make four pence half penny do. But when he had got money he was very liberal."

A celebrated wit being mentioned, he said, "One may say of him as was said of a French wit, '*Il n'a de l'esprit que contre Dieu.*' His trade is wit. It would be as wild in him to come into company without merriment as for a highwayman to take the road without his pistols."

Talking of the effects of drinking, he said, "Drinking may be practiced with great prudence; a man who exposes himself when he is intoxicated has not the art of getting drunk; a sober man who happens occasionally to get drunk, readily enough goes into new company, which a man who has been drinking should never do. I used to slink home when I had drunk too much. A man accustomed to self-examination will be conscious when he is drunk, though an habitual drunkard will not be conscious of it. I knew a physician who for twenty years was not sober; yet in a pamphlet which he wrote upon fevers he appealed to Garrick and me for his vindication from a charge of drunkenness. A bookseller (naming him) who got a large fortune by trade was so habitually and equally drunk that his most intimate friends never perceived that he was more sober at one time than another."

Talking of celebrated and successful irregular practicers in physic,* he said, "Taylor[1] was the most ignorant man I ever knew, but sprightly." BEAUCLERK. "I remember, sir, you said that Taylor was an instance of how far impudence could carry ignorance."

Mr. Beauclerk was very entertaining this day, and told us a number of short stories in a lively, elegant manner, and with that air of *the world* which has I know not what impressive effect, as if there were something more than is expressed, or than per-

---

1. *Taylor.* An illiterate quack oculist who styled himself "The Chevalier Taylor, Ophthalmiator, Pontifical, Imperial, and Royal." He was allowed to practice on several of the royal family.

haps we could perfectly understand. As Johnson and I accompanied Sir Joshua Reynolds in his coach, Johnson said, "There is in Beauclerk a predominance over his company[1] that one does not like. But he is a man who has lived so much in the world that he has a short story on every occasion; he is always ready to talk, and is never exhausted."

Johnson and I passed the evening at Miss Reynolds's, Sir Joshua's sister. I mentioned that an eminent friend of ours, talking of the common remark that affection descends, said that "this was wisely contrived for the preservation of mankind; for which it was not so necessary that there should be affection from children to parents, as from parents to children; nay, there would be no harm in that view though children should at a certain age eat their parents." JOHNSON. "But, sir, if this were known generally to be the case, parents would not have affection for children." BOSWELL. "True, sir, for it is in expectation of a return that parents are so attentive to their children; and I know a very pretty instance of a little girl of whom her father was very fond, who once when he was in a melancholy fit, and had gone to bed, persuaded him to rise in good humor by saying, 'My dear papa, please to get up and let me help you on with your clothes, that I may learn to do it when you are an old man.'"

Johnson, being now better disposed to obtain information concerning Pope than he was last year, sent by me to my Lord Marchmont a present of those volumes of his *Lives of the Poets* which were at this time published, with a request to have permission to wait on him; and his Lordship, who had called on him twice, obligingly appointed Saturday, the first of May, for receiving us.

On that morning Johnson came to me from Streatham and after drinking chocolate at General Paoli's, in South Audley Street, we proceeded to Lord Marchmont's in Curzon Street. His Lordship met us at the door of his library. When we came

---

1. *Predominance over his company*. Elsewhere Johnson said of Beauclerk: "Everything comes from Beauclerk so easily. It appears to me that I labor when I say a good thing."

out I said to Johnson that, considering his Lordship's civility, I should have been vexed if he had again failed to come. "Sir," said he, "I would rather have given twenty pounds than not have come." I accompanied him to Streatham, where we dined, and returned to town in the evening.

On Monday, May 3, I dined with him at Mr. Dilly's. This evening I set out for Scotland.[1] I did not write to Johnson, as usual, upon my return to my family, but tried how he would be affected by my silence.

"To James Boswell, Esq.

"DEAR SIR: What can possibly have happened that keeps us two such strangers to each other? I expected to have heard from you when you came home; I expected afterwards. I went into the country[2] and returned; and yet there is no letter from Mr. Boswell. No ill, I hope, has happened; and if ill has happened, why should it be concealed from him who loves you? Is it a fit of humor that has disposed you to try who can hold out longest without writing? If it be, you have the victory. But I am afraid of something bad; set me free from my suspicions.

"My thoughts are at present employed in guessing the reason of your silence; you must not expect that I should tell you anything, if I had anything to tell. Write, pray write to me, and let me know what is or what has been the cause of this long interruption.

"I am, dear sir,

"Your most affectionate, humble servant,

"SAM. JOHNSON.

"July 13, 1779."

---

1. *Set out for Scotland.* "I got into the fly at Buckden, and had a very good journey. An agreeable young widow nursed me, and supported my lame foot on her knee. *Am I not fortunate in having something about me that interests most people at first sight in my favor?"* Boswell.

2. *Into the country.* For about a month, in which he visited Lichfield and his friend Dr. Taylor in Ashbourne. His pleasure was marred by the news of Mr. Thrale's serious illness.

"Edinburgh, July 17, 1779.

"To Dr. Samuel Johnson.

"MY DEAR SIR: What may justly be denominated a supine indolence of mind has been my state of existence since I last returned to Scotland. In a livelier state I had often suffered severely from long intervals of silence on your part; and I had even been chid by you for expressing my uneasiness. I was willing to take advantage of my insensibility, and while I could bear the experiment, to try whether your affection for me would, after an unusual silence on my part, make you write first. This afternoon I have had very high satisfaction by receiving your kind letter of inquiry, for which I most gratefully thank you. I am doubtful if it was right to make the experiment, though I have gained by it. I was beginning to grow tender and to upbraid myself, especially after having dreamt two nights ago that I was with you. I, and my wife, and my four children are all well. I would not delay one post to answer your letter, but as it is late I have not time to do more. You shall soon hear from me upon many and various particulars, and I shall never again put you to any test. I am, with veneration, my dear sir,

"Your much obliged and faithful, humble servant,

"JAMES BOSWELL."

His next to me was as follows:

"To James Boswell, Esq.

"MY DEAR SIR: Are you playing the same trick again, and trying who can keep silence longest? Remember that all tricks are either knavish or childish.

"What can be the cause of this second fit of silence I cannot conjecture; but after one trick, I will not be cheated by another, nor will harass my thoughts with conjectures about the motives of a man who probably acts only by caprice. I therefore suppose you are well, and that Mrs. Boswell is well too; and that the fine summer has restored Lord Auchinleck. I am much better than you left me; I think I am better than when I was in Scotland.

"Your humble servant,

"Streatham, Sept. 9, 1779."   "SAM. JOHNSON.

My friend, Colonel James Stuart, second son of the Earl of Bute, who had distinguished himself as a good officer of the Bedfordshire militia, having been in Scotland recently, obligingly asked me to accompany him to Leeds, then the headquarters of his corps; from thence to London for a short time, and afterwards to other places to which the regiment might be ordered. Such an offer, at a time of year when I had full leisure, was very pleasing; especially as I was to accompany a man of sterling good sense, information, discernment, and conviviality; and was to have a second crop in one year of London and Johnson.

On Monday, October 4, I called at his house before he was up. He sent for me to his bedside, and expressed his satisfaction at this incidental meeting, with as much vivacity as if he had been in the gayety of youth. He called briskly, "Frank, go get coffee, and let us breakfast *in splendor*."

During this visit to London I had several interviews with him, which it is unnecessary to distinguish particularly. I consulted him as to the appointment of guardians to my children, in case of my death. "Sir," said he, "do not appoint a number of guardians. When there are many, they trust one to another, and the business is neglected. I would advise you to choose only one; let him be a man of respectable character, who, for his own credit, will do what is right; let him be a rich man, so that he may be under no temptation to take advantage; and let him be a man of business, who is used to conduct affairs with ability and expertness, to whom, therefore, the execution of the trust will not be burdensome."

On Sunday, October 10, we dined together at Mr. Strahan's. We left Mr. Strahan's at seven, as Johnson had said he intended to go to evening prayers. As we walked along, he complained of a little gout in his toe, and said, "I shan't go to prayers tonight; I shall go tomorrow. Whenever I miss church on a Sunday, I resolve to go another day. But I do not always do it." This was a fair exhibition of that vibration between pious resolutions and indolence which many of us have too often experienced.

I went home with him, and we had a long, quiet conversation. BOSWELL. "Why, sir, do people play this trick which I observe now when I look at your grate—putting the shovel against it to make the fire burn?" JOHNSON. "They play the trick, but it does not make the fire burn. *There* is a better (setting the poker perpendicularly up at right angles with the grate). In days of superstition they thought, as it made a cross with the bars, it would drive away the witch."

He said, "Dodsley first mentioned to me the scheme of an English Dictionary, but I had long thought of it." BOSWELL. "You did not know what you were undertaking." JOHNSON. "Yes, sir, I knew very well what I was undertaking—and very well how to do it,[1] and have done it very well." BOSWELL. "An excellent climax! and it *has* availed you. In your Preface you say, 'What would it avail me in this gloom of solitude?' You have been agreeably mistaken."

On Tuesday, October 12, I dined with him at Mr. Ramsay's, with Lord Newhaven[2] and some other company, none of whom I recollect but a beautiful Miss Graham, a relation of his Lordship's, who asked Dr. Johnson to hob or nob with her. He was flattered by such pleasing attention, and politely told her he never drank wine; but if she would drink a glass of water, he was much at her service. "Oho, sir!" said Lord Newhaven, "you are caught." JOHNSON. "I don't see *how* I am *caught*; but if I am caught, I don't want to be free again. If I am caught, I hope to be kept."

Lord Newhaven and Johnson carried on an argument for some time concerning the Middlesex election.[3] Johnson said, "As it is clear that the House of Commons may expel, and expel, and expel again and again, why not allow of the power to incapacitate for that parliament rather than have a perpetual contest

---

1. *Very well how to do it.* "When Stockdale expressed his surprise that Johnson 'in his easy circumstances should think of preparing a new edition of a tedious scientific dictionary,' 'Sir,' said he, 'I like that muddling work.'" *Birkbeck Hill.*

2. *Lord Newhaven.* "One of a creation of eighteen Irish peers in 1776. 'It was a mob of nobility,' wrote Horace Walpole. 'The King in private laughed much at the eagerness for such insignificant honors.'" *Birkbeck Hill.*

3. *Middlesex election.* In reality, the series of four elections, 1768-69, over John Wilkes as an issue.

kept up between parliament and the people." Lord Newhaven took the opposite side, but respectfully said, "I speak with great deference to you, Dr. Johnson. I speak to be instructed." [Johnson] bowed his head almost as low as the table, and called out, "My Lord, my Lord, I do not desire all this ceremony; let us tell our minds to one another quietly." After the debate was over, he said, "I have got lights on the subject today, which I had not before." He observed, "The House of Commons was originally not a privilege of the people, but a check for the Crown on the House of Lords. I remember Henry the Eighth wanted them to do something; they hesitated in the morning, but did it in the afternoon. He told them, 'It is well you did, or half your heads should have been upon Temple Bar.'¹ But the House of Commons is now no longer under the power of the Crown, and therefore must be bribed." He added, "I have no delight in talking of public affairs."

Of his fellow-collegian, the celebrated Mr. George Whitefield,² he said, "Whitefield never drew as much attention as a mountebank does; he did not draw attention by doing better than others, but by doing what was strange. Were Astley³ to preach a sermon standing upon his head on a horse's back, he would collect a multitude to hear him; but no wise man would say he had made a better sermon for that. I never treated Whitefield's ministry with contempt; I believe he did good. He had devoted himself to the lower classes of mankind, and among them he was of use. But when familiarity and noise claim the praise due to knowledge, art, and elegance, we must beat down such pretensions."

What I have preserved of his conversation during the re-

---

1. *Temple Bar.* Not used for this purpose until William III's reign.
2. *Whitefield.* Like John Wesley, a field preacher of most positive convictions. "[Whitefield] told me he and I preached two different gospels; and therefore he was resolved publicly to preach against me and my brother wheresoever he preached at all." *John Wesley.* Johnson said his mind was "like a hammer."
3. *Astley,* Philip. An ex-cavalryman, and the best horse-tamer and acrobatic rider of his time. He built in all nineteen amphitheaters for his exhibitions.

mainder of my stay in London at this time is only what follows:
I told him that when I objected to keeping company with a
notorious infidel, a celebrated friend of ours said to me, "I do
not think that men who live laxly in the world, as you and I do,
can with propriety assume such an authority. Dr. Johnson
may, who is uniformly exemplary in his conduct. But it is
not very consistent to shun an infidel today, and get drunk
tomorrow." JOHNSON. "Nay, sir, this is sad reasoning. Because a man cannot be right in all things, is he to be right in
nothing? Because a man sometimes gets drunk, is he therefore
to steal? This doctrine would very soon bring a man to the
gallows."

He, I know not why, showed upon all occasions an aversion
to go to Ireland, where I proposed to him that we should make
a tour. JOHNSON. "It is the last place where I should wish
to travel." BOSWELL. "Should you not like to see Dublin,
sir?" JOHNSON. "No, sir; Dublin is only a worse capital."
BOSWELL. "Is not the Giants' Causeway worth seeing?"
JOHNSON. "Worth seeing? yes; but not worth going to see."

Yet he had a kindness for the Irish nation, and thus generously expressed himself to a gentleman from that country
on the subject of an union[1] which artful politicians have often
had in view—"Do not make an union with us, sir. We should
unite with you only to rob you. We should have robbed the
Scotch if they had had anything of which we could have robbed
them."

Of an acquaintance of ours, whose manners and everything
about him, though expensive, were coarse, he said, "Sir, you
see in him vulgar prosperity."

A foreign minister of no very high talents, who had been in
his company for a considerable time quite overlooked, happened
luckily to mention that he had read some of his *Rambler* in
Italian, and admired it much. This pleased him greatly; and

---

1. *Union.* Under one parliament. In 1707 such a union had been
formed between England and Scotland. Ireland had a separate parliament, though it had to submit all its legislation to the English Privy
Council for approval. This requirement was not abrogated until
1782; the separate parliament was abolished in 1801.

finding that this minister gave such a proof of his taste, he was all attention to him, and on the first remark which he made, however simple, exclaimed, "The Ambassador says well—His Excellency observes—" And then he expanded and enriched the little that had been said, in so strong a manner that it appeared something of consequence. This was exceedingly entertaining to the company who were present, and many a time afterwards it furnished a pleasant topic of merriment. *"The Ambassador says well,"* became a laughable term of applause when no mighty matter had been expressed.

I left London on Monday, October 18, and accompanied Colonel Stuart to Chester,[1] where his regiment was to lie for some time.

MR. BOSWELL TO DR. JOHNSON

"Chester, October 22, 1779.

"My DEAR SIR: If you do not write directly, so as to catch me here, I shall be disappointed. Two lines from you will keep my lamp burning bright."

"To James Boswell, Esq.

"DEAR SIR: Why should you importune me so earnestly to write? Of what importance can it be to hear of distant friends, to a man who finds himself welcome wherever he goes, and makes new friends faster than he can want them? If to the delight of such universal kindness of reception, anything can be added by knowing that you retain my good-will, you may indulge yourself in the full enjoyment of that small addition.

"In the place where you now are there is much to be observed, . . . But what will you do to keep away the black dog at home? . . . The great direction which Burton has left to men disordered like you is this, *'Be not solitary; be not idle';* which I

---

1. *Chester.* "[At Chester] I passed [a] fortnight in mortal felicity. At the mess of Colonel Stuart's regiment I was quite the *great man*, as we used to say; and I was at the same time all joyous and gay. The young ladies there were delightful, and many of them with capital fortunes. Had I been a bachelor, I should have certainly paid my addresses to a Chester lady." *Boswell to Temple, 1780.*

1779] BOSWELL'S MELANCHOLY 409

would thus modify—'If you are idle, be not solitary; if you are solitary, be not idle.'

"*There* is a letter for you, from

"Your humble servant,

"SAM. JOHNSON."

"*To James Boswell, Esq.*

"DEAR SIR: Your last letter was not only kind but fond. But I wish you to get rid of all intellectual excesses, and neither to exalt your pleasures nor aggravate your vexations beyond their real and natural state. Why should you not be as happy at Edinburgh as at Chester? *In culpa est animus, qui se non effugit usquam.* Please yourself with your wife and children, and studies, and practice.

"Let me know what reception you have from your father, and the state of his health. Please him as much as you can, and add no pain to his last years.

"At Bolt Court there is much malignity,[1] but of late little open hostility. I have had a cold, but it is gone.

"Make my compliments to Mrs. Boswell, &c.,

"I am, sir,

"Your humble servant,

"SAM. JOHNSON.

"London, Nov. 13, 1779."

[1780]. His friend Dr. Lawrence having now suffered the greatest affliction to which a man is liable, and which Johnson

---

1. *Much malignity.* "We have tolerable concord at home, but no love. Williams hates everybody. Levet hates Desmoulins, and does not love Williams. Desmoulins hates them both. Poll loves none of them." *Johnson, 1778.* "He really was oftentimes afraid of going home, because he was so sure to be met at the door with numberless complaints; and he used to lament pathetically to me that they made his life miserable from the impossibility he found of making theirs happy, when every favor he bestowed on one was wormwood to the rest. If, however, I ventured to blame their ingratitude, and condemn their conduct, he would instantly set about softening the one and justifying the other; and finished commonly by telling me that I knew not how to make allowance for situations I never experienced." *Mrs. Piozzi: Anecdotes of Johnson.*

himself had felt in the most severe manner, Johnson wrote to him in an admirable strain of sympathy and pious consolation.

"To Dr. Lawrence.

"The loss, dear sir, which you have lately suffered, I felt many years ago, and know therefore how much has been taken from you, and how little help can be had from consolation. He that outlives a wife whom he has long loved sees himself disjoined from the only mind that has the same hopes, and fears, and interest; from the only companion with whom he has shared much good or evil; and with whom he could set his mind at liberty, to retrace the past or anticipate the future. The continuity of being is lacerated; the settled course of sentiment and action is stopped; and life stands suspended and motionless, till it is driven by external causes into a new channel. But the time of suspense is dreadful.

"Our first recourse in this distressed solitude is, perhaps for want of habitual piety, to a gloomy acquiesence in necessity. Of two mortal beings, one must lose the other; but surely there is a higher and better comfort to be drawn from the consideration of that Providence which watches over all, and a belief that the living and the dead are equally in the hands of God, who will reunite those whom he has separated; or who sees that it is best not to reunite.

"I am, dear sir,

"Your most affectionate,

"And most humble servant,

"SAM. JOHNSON.

"January 20, 1780."

"To James Boswell, Esq.

"DEAR SIR: Well, I had resolved to send you the Chesterfield letter, but I will write once again without it. Never impose tasks upon mortals. Poor dear Beauclerk.[1] His wit and his folly, his acuteness and maliciousness, his merriment and reasoning, are now over. Such another will not often be found among

---

1. *Beauclerk.* He had died four weeks before, aged forty.

mankind. He directed himself to be buried by the side of his mother, an instance of tenderness which I hardly expected.

"Poor Mr. Thrale has been in extreme danger from an apoplectical disorder, and recovered, beyond the expectation of his physicians; he is now at Bath, that his mind may be quiet, and Mrs. Thrale and Miss[1] are with him.

"Having told you what has happened to your friends, let me say something to you of yourself. You are always complaining of melancholy,[2] and I conclude from those complaints that you are fond of it. No man talks of that which he is desirous to conceal, and every man desires to conceal that of which he is ashamed. Do not pretend to deny it; *manifestum habemus furem;* make it an invariable and obligatory law to yourself never to mention your own mental diseases; if you are never to speak of them you will think on them but little, and if you think little of them, they will molest you rarely. When you talk of them, it is plain that you want either praise or pity; for praise there is no room, and pity will do you no good; therefore, from this hour speak no more, think no more, about them."

MRS. THRALE TO DR. JOHNSON.

"Yesterday's evening was passed at Mrs. Montagu's; there was Mr. Melmoth.[3] I do not like him, *though,* nor he me. It was expected we should have pleased each other; he is, however, just Tory enough to abhor the Bishop of Peterborough[4] for Whiggism, and Whig enough to abhor you for Toryism.

---

1. *Miss.* Mrs. Thrale's unsympathetic eldest daughter, "Queeney," aged sixteen.

2. *Complaining of melancholy.* "I own I am not so much on my guard against fits of passion or gloom as I ought to be. I ought not to indulge in such fits; it is like a child that lets itself fall purposely to have the pleasure of being tenderly raised up again by those who are fond of it." *Boswell to Temple,* 1770.

3. *Melmoth,* William. Author of the once highly popular *Fitzosborne Letters,* amiable little essays designed to encourage a pretense to enthusiasm. "The worst that can be said of her," he asserts, "is that she is a kind deceiver and an obliging flatterer."

4. *Bishop of Peterborough.* His "liberal views" in part consisted in advocating a conciliatory attitude toward public opinion, even when it was persecutory and bigoted.

"You live in a fine whirl indeed; if I did not write regularly you would half forget me, and that would be very wrong, for I *felt* my regard for you in my *face* last night, when the criticisms were going on.

"[My master] looks well enough, but I have no notion of health for a man whose mouth cannot be sewed up. Burney[1] and I and Queeney tease him every meal he eats, but what *can* one do? He will eat, I think, and if he does eat, I know he will not live; it makes me very unhappy, but I must bear it. Let me always have your friendship. I am, most sincerely, dear sir,

"Your faithful servant,

"H. L. T.

"Bath, Friday, April 28."

DR. JOHNSON TO MRS. THRALE.

"DEAREST MADAM: Mr. Thrale will never live abstinently till he can persuade himself to live by rule.

"Nothing is more common than mutual dislike where mutual approbation is particularly expected. There is often on both sides a vigilance not over benevolent; and as attention is strongly excited, so that nothing drops unheeded, any difference in taste or opinion (and some difference where there is no restraint will commonly appear) immediately generates dislike.

"Never let criticisms operate on your face or your mind; it is very rarely that an author is hurt by his critics. The blaze of reputation cannot be blown out, but it often dies in the socket; a very few names may be considered as perpetual lamps that shine unconsumed. From the author of *Fitzosborne's*

---

1. *Burney.* Dr. Charles Burney's daughter, Frances, a blissful protégée of the Thrales, all eyes and ears for the praises of her first novel, *Evelina*, then just out. After Mr. Thrale's death, she joined in the general outcry against Mrs. Thrale's second marriage, which deprived her of the comforts of Streatham. She later became a lady of the Queen's household, and still later the wife of M. D'Arblay. "Miss Burney was much admired at Bath; the puppymen said, 'She had such a drooping air' and such 'a timid intelligence,' or 'a timid air,' I think it was, and 'a drooping intelligence.'" *Mrs. Thrale, 1780.*

Letters I cannot think myself in much danger. I met him only once about thirty years ago, and in some small dispute reduced him to whistle; having not seen him since, that is the last impression.

"London, May 1, 1780."

While Johnson was preparing a delightful entertainment for the world [*The Lives of the English Poets*], the tranquillity of the metropolis was unexpectedly disturbed. A relaxation of some of the severe penal provisions[1] against our fellow subjects of the Catholic communion had been granted by the legislature with an opposition so inconsiderable that the mildness of Christianity seemed to have become general in this island. But a spirit of persecution soon showed itself in a petition for a repeal of the statute. The petition was brought forward by a mob and was rejected. Of this tumult Dr. Johnson has given the following account in his "Letters to Mrs. Thrale":[2]

[London, June 9, 1780].

"On Friday [June 2], the good Protestants met in St. George's Fields at the summons of Lord George Gordon, and marching to Westminster insulted the Lords and Commons, who all bore it with great tameness. At night the outrages began by the demolition of the mass-house* by Lincoln's Inn.*

---

1. *Severe penal provisions.* Such as depriving Catholic heirs who had studied abroad of their rights of inheritance, prohibiting Catholic schools, if conducted by priests, and withholding from Catholics the power of obtaining real estate by purchase. In 1778 Parliament repealed these provisions for those who took a rigorous oath of allegiance. In 1779 the report that the same relief might be extended to Scotland excited riots in that country. The disorder spread to England, enlisting in its course criminals, labor agitators, and those in panic over the French and American wars. Other towns suffered as well as London. Rumor at one time had it that half of Bath was destroyed. The leader of the mob, Lord George Gordon, was finally captured, tried for treason, acquitted on the ground of insanity, and died insane while still in prison. Some of the destruction, such as the partial burning of Newgate, was within a few minutes' walk of Dr. Johnson's house.

2. *Letters to Mrs. Thrale.* In Boswell's selection of these letters, I have incorporated more passages from the same material. *Editor.*

"On Wednesday I walked with Dr. Scott to look at Newgate, and found it in ruins, with the fire yet glowing. As I went by, the Protestants were plundering the Sessions House at the Old* Bailey. They were not I believe a hundred; but they did their work at leisure, in full security, without sentinels, without trepidation, as men lawfully employed in full day. Such is the cowardice of a commercial place.

"At night they set fire to the Fleet, and to the King's * Bench, and I know not how many other places; and one might see the glare of conflagration fill the sky from many parts. Mr. Strahan[1] advised me to take care of myself. Such a time of terror you have been happy in not seeing.

"The King said in council that the magistrates had not done their duty, but that he would do his own; and a proclamation was published, directing us to keep our servants within doors, as the peace was now to be preserved by force. The soldiers were sent out to different parts, and the town is now at quiet.

"What has happened at your house[2] you will know; the harm is only a few butts of beer, and I think you may be sure that the danger is over. Pray tell Mr. Thrale that I live here and have no fruit, and if he does not interpose am not likely to have much; but I think he might as well give me a little as give all to the gardener."

"June 10, 1780.

"DEAR MADAM: You have ere now heard and read enough to convince you that we have had something to suffer and something to fear, and therefore I think it necessary to quiet the solicitude which you undoubtedly feel by telling you that our calamities and terrors are now at an end. The soldiers are stationed so as to be everywhere within call, and the individuals are

---

1. *Mr. Strahan.* "[He] got a garrison into his house and maintained them a fortnight; he was so frighted that he removed part of his goods." *Johnson to Boswell.*

2. *At your house.* "Some infamous villain has put it into the paper here [Bath] that Mr. Thrale is a papist." *Mme. D'Arblay.* "Everybody here [Bath] is terrified to death. We have intelligence that Mr. Thrale's house in town is filled with soldiers and threatened by a mob with destruction." *Mme. D'Arblay.*

hunted to their holes and led to prison.   Lord George was last night sent to the Tower.   Mr. John Wilkes[1] was this day in my neighborhood to seize the publisher of a seditious paper.   Everybody walks, and eats, and sleeps in security.   Several chapels have been destroyed, and several inoffensive Papists have been plundered, but the high sport was to burn the jails. . . .   The debtors and the criminals were all set at liberty; but of the criminals, as has always happened, many are already retaken; and two pirates have surrendered themselves, and it is expected that they will be pardoned.

"Government now acts again[2] with its proper force, and we are all under the protection of the King and the law.   I thought that it would be agreeable to you and my master to have my testimony to the public security; and that you would sleep more quietly when I told you that you are safe."

"London, June 12, 1780.

"DEAR MADAM: All is well and is likely to continue well. This is a true answer to the first inquiry which obtrudes itself upon your tongue at the reception of a letter from London. The public has escaped a very heavy calamity.   The rioters attempted the Bank[3] on Wednesday night, but in no great number; and like other thieves, with no great resolution.   Jack Wilkes headed the party that drove them away.   It is agreed that if they had seized the Bank on Tuesday, at the height of the panic, when no resistance had been prepared, they might have carried irrecoverably away whatever they had found. Jack, who was always zealous for order and decency, declares

---

1. *Wilkes.* "He had lately been elected City Chamberlain." *Birkbeck Hill.* "I think I see him at this moment, walking through the crowded streets of the city, as Chamberlain, on his way to Guildhall, in a scarlet coat, military boots, and a bag-wig." *Samuel Rogers.*

2. *Government now acts again.* "The Cabinet Council, on Thursday, authorized Lord North to prepare the civil officers to keep the peace, and he *forgot it* till two o'clock at noon, some hours after the procession had begun to march." *Horace Walpole.*

3. *Bank.* Founded in 1694 to further the military and commercial plans of William III. It soon became the supreme financial institution of England and has always been closely related to the government.

that if he be trusted with power, he will not leave a rioter alive. There is, however, now no longer any need of heroism or bloodshed; no blue ribband[1] is any longer worn. ——called on Friday at Mrs. Gardiner's,[2] to see how she escaped or what she suffered; and told her that she had herself too much affliction within doors, to take much notice of the disturbances without."

"London, June 14, 1780.

"DEAR MADAM: Everything here is safe and quiet. This is the first thing to be told; and this I told in my last letter directed to Brighthelmstone. There has, indeed, been an universal panic, from which the King was the first that recovered. Without the concurrence of his ministers or the assistance of the civil magistrates, he put the soldiers in motion and saved the town from calamities such as a rabble's government must naturally produce. No sooner was the danger over than the people of the Borough[3] found out how foolish it was to be afraid, and formed themselves into four bodies for the defense of the place; through which they now march morning and evening in a martial manner."

Upon this occasion, from the timidity and negligence of magistracy on the one hand, and the almost incredible exertions of the mob on the other, the first prison of this great country was laid open, and the prisoners set free; but that Mr. Akerman, whose house was burnt, would have prevented all this had proper aid been sent him in due time, there can be no doubt.

Many years ago a fire broke out in the brick part which was built as an addition to the old jail of Newgate. The prisoners

---

1. *Blue ribband.* Lord George Gordon's followers wore blue ribbons or cockades in their hats and tried to force them on all passers-by. Blue was the chosen color of the Scotch Presbyterians of the seventeenth century in their struggle with the King and the Episcopacy. It was also popular among Tories and among the lower orders.

2. *Mrs. Gardiner.* A charitable soul; wife of a tallow chandler; for some thirty years a friend of Dr. Johnson's.

3. *The Borough.* A short name for the Borough of Southwark, a crowded miscellaneous region just across the Thames from the heart of London. Here the Thrales had their London residence. Here, too, were several of the prisons.

were in consternation and tumult, calling out, "We shall be burnt—we shall be burnt! Down with the gate!—down with the gate!" Mr. Akerman hastened to them, showed himself at the gate, and having, after some confused vociferation of "Hear him!—hear him!" obtained a silent attention, he then calmly told them that the gate must not go down; that they were under his care, and that they should not be permitted to escape; but that he could assure them they need not be afraid of being burnt, for that the fire was not in the prison, properly so called, which was strongly built with stone; and if they would engage to be quiet, he himself would come in to them, and conduct them to the further end of the building, and would not go out till they gave him leave. To this proposal they agreed; upon which Mr. Akerman, having first made them fall back from the gate, went in, and with a determined resolution ordered the outer turnkey upon no account to open the gate, even though the prisoners (though he trusted they would not) should break their word, and by force bring himself to order it. "Never mind me," said he, "should that happen." The prisoners peaceably followed him, while he conducted them through passages of which he had the keys, to the extremity of the jail, which was most distant from the fire. Having by this very judicious conduct fully satisfied them that there was no immediate risk, if any at all, he then addressed them thus: "Gentlemen, you are now convinced that I told you true. I have no doubt that the engines will soon extinguish this fire; if they should not, a sufficient guard will come, and you shall be all taken out and lodged in the Compters. I assure you, upon my word and honor, that I have not a farthing insured. I have left my house that I might take care of you. I will keep my promise, and stay with you if you insist upon it; but if you will allow me to go out and look after my family and property, I shall be obliged to you." Struck with his behavior, they called out, "Master Akerman, you have done bravely; it was very kind in you; by all means go and take care of your own concerns." He did so accordingly, while they remained and were all preserved.

Johnson, speaking of Mr. Akerman's kindness to his prisoners, pronounced this eulogy upon his character: "He who has long had constantly in his view the worst of mankind, and is yet eminent for the humanity of his disposition, must have had it originally in a great degree, and continued to cultivate it very carefully."

This year he wrote to a young clergyman in the country the following letter which contains valuable advice to divines in general:

"DEAR SIR: Not many days ago Dr. Lawrence showed me a letter in which you make mention of me. I hope, therefore, you will not be displeased that I endeavor to preserve your good will by some observations which your letter suggested to me.

"You are afraid of falling into some improprieties in the daily service by reading to an audience that requires no exactness. Your fear, I hope, secures you from danger. They who contract absurd habits are such as have no fear. It is impossible to do the same thing very often without some peculiarity of manner; but that manner may be good or bad, and a little care will at least preserve it from being bad; to make it good, there must, I think, be something of natural or casual felicity, which cannot be taught. My advice is that you attempt, from time to time, an original sermon;[1] and in the labor of composition, do not burthen your mind with too much at once. Set down diligently your thoughts as they rise, in the first words that occur; and when you have matter, you will easily give it form; nor, perhaps, will this method be always necessary, for by habit your thoughts and diction will flow together.

"The composition of sermons is not very difficult; the divisions not only help the memory of the hearer, but direct the judgment of the writer; they supply sources of invention, and keep every part in its proper place.

"What I like least in your letter is your account of the manners of your parish; from which I gather that it has been long neg-

---

1. *Original sermon.* Instead of someone else's, either already printed, or especially written for him, as was then not unusual.

lected by the parson. Such a congregation as yours stands in need of much reformation; and I would not have you think it impossible to reform them. Talk to your people as much as you can; and you will find that the more frequently you converse to them upon religious subjects, the more willingly they will attend, and the more submissively they will learn. A clergyman's diligence always makes him venerable. I think I have now only to say that in the momentous work you have undertaken, I pray God to bless you.

"I am, sir,

"Your most humble servant,

"SAM. JOHNSON.

"Bolt Court, Aug. 30, 1780."

Being disappointed in my hopes of meeting Johnson this year, so that I could hear none of his sayings, I shall compensate for this want by inserting a collection of them, for which I am indebted to my worthy friend, Mr. Langton. Very few articles of this collection were committed to writing by himself, he not having had that habit; which he regrets. I, however, found, in conversations with him that a good store of *Johnsoniana* was treasured in his mind; and I compared it to Herculaneum,[1] or some old Roman field, which when dug fully rewards the labor employed. The authenticity of every article is unquestionable. For the expression, I, who wrote them down in his presence, am partly answerable.

"It is an unhappy circumstance that one might give away five hundred pounds in a year to those that importune in the streets, and not do any good."[2]

"There is nothing more likely to betray a man into absurdity than *condescension;* when he seems to suppose his understanding too powerful for his company."

---

1. *Herculaneum.* Rediscovered beneath the ashes of Vesuvius in 1719, it aroused immense curiosity among the scholars of the eighteenth century.

2. *Do any good.* "Dr. Johnson, being asked by a lady why he so constantly gave money to beggars, replied with great feeling, 'Madam, to enable them to beg on.' " *William Cooke.*

"Having asked Mr. Langton if his father and mother had sat for their pictures, which he thought it right for each generation of a family to do, and being told they had opposed it, he said, 'Sir, among the anfractuosities of the human mind, I know not if it may not be one that there is a superstitious reluctance to sit for a picture.' "

"John Gilbert Cooper related that soon after the publication of his *Dictionary*, Garrick, being asked by Johnson what people said of it, told him that among other animadversions it was objected that he cited authorities which were beneath the dignity of such a work, and mentioned Richardson.[1] 'Nay,' said Johnson, 'I have done worse than that; I have cited *thee*, David.' "

"Talking of expense, he observed with what munificence a great merchant will spend his money, both from his having it at command, and from his enlarged views by calculation of a good effect upon the whole. 'Whereas,' said he, 'you will hardly ever find a country gentleman who is not a good deal disconcerted at an unexpected occasion for his being obliged to lay out ten pounds.' "

"When one was reading his tragedy of *Irene* to a company at a house in the country, he left the room; and somebody having asked him the reason of this, he replied, 'Sir, I thought it had been better.' "

"Talking of a point of delicate scrupulosity of moral conduct, he said to Mr. Langton, 'Men of harder minds than ours will do many things from which you and I would shrink; yet, sir, they will perhaps do more good in life than we. But let us try to help one another. If there be a wrong twist, it may be set right. It is not probable that two people can be wrong the same way.' "

"Once he asked Tom Davies, whom he saw dressed in a fine

---

1. *Richardson.* Samuel, the novelist. "I believe this author should confine his pen to the amours of housemaids and the conversation of the stewards' table, where I imagine he has sometimes intruded, though oftener in the servants' hall." *Lady Mary Wortley Montagu*, 1755.

suit of clothes, 'And what art thou tonight?' Tom answered, 'The Thane of Ross' (which it will be recollected is a very inconsiderable character). 'O brave!' said Johnson."

"Dr. Goldsmith, upon occasion of Mrs. Lennox's[1] bringing out a play, said to Dr. Johnson at the Club that a person had advised him to go and hiss it because she had attacked Shakespeare in her book called *Shakespeare Illustrated*. JOHNSON. 'And did not you tell him he was a rascal?' GOLDSMITH. 'No, sir, I did not. Perhaps he might not mean what he said.' JOHNSON. 'Nay, sir, if he lied, it is a different thing.' Colman[2] slyly said (but it is believed Dr. Johnson did not hear him), 'Then the proper expression should have been, "Sir, if you don't lie, you're a rascal." ' "

"His affection for Topham Beauclerk was so great that when Beauclerk was laboring under that severe illness which at last occasioned his death, Johnson said, with a voice faltering with emotion, 'Sir, I would walk to the extent of the diameter of the earth to save Beauclerk.' "

"Talking on the subject of toleration, one day when some friends were with him in his study, he made his usual remark that the State has a right to regulate the religion of the people, who are the children of the State. A clergyman having readily acquiesced in this, Johnson, who loved discussion, observed, 'But, sir, you must go round to other States than our own. You do not know what a Brahmin has to say for himself. In short, sir, I have got no further than this: Every man has a right to utter what he thinks truth, and every other man has a right to knock him down for it. Martyrdom is the test.' "

"Talking of a court-martial that was sitting upon a very

---

1. *Mrs. Lennox.* The lady whom Johnson once crowned with laurel. Her *Shakespeare Illustrated* was an attempt to compare Shakespeare's works with the sources from which he drew his plots. It had no animus, but to criticize Shakespeare at all was to run counter to that blind idolatry of him which was rapidly spreading in the latter part of the eighteenth century.

2. *Colman*, George. The stage manager who brought out Goldsmith's *Good-Natured Man* and *She Stoops to Conquer*. He had a distinct turn for facetiousness.

momentous public occasion, he expressed much doubt of an enlightened decision; and said that perhaps there was not a member of it who, in the whole course of his life, had ever spent an hour by himself in balancing probabilities."

"Goldsmith one day brought to the Club a printed ode which he, with others, had been hearing read by its author in a public room at the rate of five shillings each for admission. One of the company having read it aloud, Dr. Johnson said, 'Bolder words and more timorous meaning, I think, never were brought together.'"

"Talking of Gray's Odes,[1] he said, 'They are forced plants, raised in a hotbed, and they are poor plants; they are but cucumbers after all.' A gentleman present who had been running down ode-writing in general, as a bad species of poetry, unluckily said, 'Had they been literally cucumbers, they had been better things than odes.'—'Yes, sir,' said Johnson, 'for a hog.'"

"It is very remarkable that he retained in his memory very slight and trivial, as well as important, things. As an instance of this, it seems that an inferior domestic of the Duke of Leeds[2] had attempted to celebrate his Grace's marriage in such homely rimes as he could make; and this curious composition having been sung to Dr. Johnson, he got it by heart, and used to repeat it in a very pleasant manner. Two of the stanzas were these:

> When the Duke of Leeds shall married be
> To a fine young lady of high quality,
> How happy will that gentlewoman be
> In his Grace of Leeds's good company.

> She shall have all that's fine and fair,
> And the best of silk and satin shall wear,
> And ride in a coach to take the air,
> And have a house in St. James's Square.

---

1. *Gray's Odes.* "In 1757 he published *The Progress of Poetry* and *The Bard*, two compositions at which the readers of poetry were at first content to gaze in mute amazement." *Johnson: Life of Gray, 1780.*

2. *Duke of Leeds.* Married November 29, 1773; divorced May 31, 1779.

To hear a man of the weight and dignity of Johnson repeating such humble attempts at poetry had a very amusing effect. He, however, seriously observed of the last stanza repeated by him that it nearly comprised all the advantages that wealth can give.''

"An eminent foreigner when he was shown the British Museum was very troublesome with many absurd inquiries. 'Now there, sir,' said he, 'is the difference between an Englishman and a Frenchman. A Frenchman must be always talking, whether he knows anything of the matter or not; an Englishman is content to say nothing when he has nothing to say.' ''

"His unjust contempt for foreigners was, indeed, extreme. One evening at Old Slaughter's Coffee-house,[1] when a number of them were talking loud about little matters, he said, 'Does not this confirm old Meynell's observation—*For anything I see, foreigners are fools?*' ''

"He said that once when he had a violent toothache a Frenchman accosted him thus: '*Ah, Monsieur, vous étudiez trop.*' ''

"Having spent an evening at Mr. Langton's with the Reverend Dr. Parr,[2] he was much pleased with the conversation of that learned gentleman; and, after he was gone, said to Mr. Langton, 'Sir, I am obliged to you for having asked me this evening. Parr is a fair man. I do not know when I have had an occasion of such free controversy.' ''

"I don't know [said he] whether it might not be true of Lord ———, that from a too great eagerness of praise and popularity, and a politeness carried to a ridiculous excess, he was likely, after asserting a thing in general, to give it up again in parts. For instance, if he had said Reynolds was the first of painters,

---

1. *Old Slaughter's Coffee-house.* Apparently a resort of Frenchmen. Dr. Johnson is said to have gone there frequently in his early days, in order to get French by ear.

2. *Dr. Parr.* Clergyman, scholar, and schoolmaster, picturesque for his clouds of tobacco smoke and his assumption of prodigious learning. He was sometimes called the Whig Dr. Johnson. "Parr, to use his accustomed formula, had Johnson's pomposity without his force of mind, Johnson's love of antithesis without his logical acuteness, Johnson's roughness without his humor." *Dictionary of National Biography.*

he was capable enough of giving up, as objections might happen to be severally made, first, his outline, then the grace in form, then the coloring, and lastly, to have owned that he was such a mannerist that the disposition of his pictures was all alike."

"He used frequently to observe that men might be very eminent in a profession without our perceiving any particular power of mind in them in conversation. 'It seems strange,' said he, 'that a man should see so far to the right who sees so short a way to the left.'"

" 'Snatches of reading,' said he, 'will not make a Bentley[1] or a Clarke.[2] They are, however, in a certain degree advantageous. I would put a child into a library where no unfit books are and let him read at his choice. A child should not be discouraged from reading anything that he takes a liking to, from a notion that it is above his reach. If that be the case, the child will soon find it out and desist; if not, he of course gains the instruction; which is so much the more likely to come, from the inclination with which he takes up the study.'"

"Though he used to censure carelessness with great vehe-

---

1. *Bentley*, Richard (1662-1742). A scholar of profound erudition and masculine sense, who nevertheless was ready to appeal to self-interest when he could not appeal to truth, and bullied where he could not convince. Yet of him, Johnson said in 1742: "May the shade, at least of one great English critic, rest without disturbance; and may no man presume to insult his memory who wants [lacks] his learning, his reason, or his wit."

2. *Clarke*, Dr. Samuel (1675-1729). A liberal-minded controversialist on subtle points of philosophy and theology. His genial desire to make his positions as acceptable as possible sometimes disconcerted and exasperated his opponents, who preferred an antagonist who would stand up and be counted. Johnson would not quote him in his *Dictionary* because "he was a condemned heretic on the Trinity"; later he called Clarke's sermons the best in the English language, "bating a little heresy." On his death-bed he recommended them "because he is fullest on the propitiatory sacrifice." Goldsmith says that once when Clarke was in the midst of mirth and laughter with some of his most learned friends, he saw the chariot of a popular director of fashions stop at his door. "Boys, boys," cried the philosopher, "let us now be wise, for here is a fool coming."

mence, he owned that he once, to avoid the trouble of locking up five guineas, hid them, he forgot where, so that he could not find them.''

"A gentleman who introduced his brother to Dr. Johnson was earnest to recommend him to the Doctor's notice, which he did by saying, 'When we have sat together some time, you'll find my brother grow very entertaining.'—'Sir,' said Johnson, 'I can wait.' ''

"In the latter part of his life, in order to satisfy himself whether his mental faculties were impaired, he resolved that he would try to learn a new language, and fixed upon the Low Dutch for that purpose, and this he continued till he had read about one half of *Thomas à Kempis;* and finding that there appeared no abatement of his power of acquisition, he then desisted, as thinking the experiment had been duly tried. Mr. Burke justly observed that this was not the most vigorous trial, Low Dutch being a language so near to our own; had it been one of the languages entirely different, he might not have been very soon satisfied.''

"Mr. Langton and he having gone to see a Freemason's funeral procession, when they were at Rochester, and some solemn music being played on French horns, he said, 'This is the first time that I have ever been affected by musical sounds'; adding that 'the impression made upon him was of a melancholy kind.' Mr. Langton saying that this effect was a fine one: JOHNSON. 'Yes, if it softens the mind so as to prepare it for the reception of salutary feelings, it may be good; but inasmuch as it is melancholy *per se*, it is bad.' ''

"Goldsmith had long a visionary project that some time or other when his circumstances should be easier, he would go to Aleppo, in order to acquire a knowledge, as far as might be, of any arts peculiar to the East, and introduce them into Britain. When this was talked of in Dr. Johnson's company, he said, 'Sir, he would bring home a grinding-barrow, which you see in every street in London, and think that he had furnished a wonderful improvement.' ''

"Drinking tea one day at Garrick's with Mr. Langton, he

was questioned if he was not somewhat of a heretic[1] as to Shakespeare; said Garrick, 'I doubt he is a little of an infidel.'—'Sir,'
said Johnson, 'I will stand by the lines I have written on Shakespeare in my *Prologue* at the opening of your Theater.'   Mr.
Langton suggested that in the line

> And panting Time toiled after him in vain,

Johnson might have had in his eye the passage in *The Tempest*
where Prospero says of Miranda,

> ——She will outstrip all praise,
> And make it halt behind her.

Johnson said nothing.   Garrick then ventured to observe, 'I
do not think that the happiest line in the praise of Shakespeare.'
Johnson exclaimed (smiling), 'Prosaical rogues!   Next time I
write, I'll make both time and space pant.' "

"Mr. Langton recollects having passed an evening when Mr.
Burke repeatedly entered upon topics which it was evident he
would have illustrated with extensive knowledge and richness of
expression; but Johnson always seized upon the conversation,
in which, however, he acquitted himself in a masterly manner.
As Mr. Burke and Mr. Langton were walking home, Mr. Burke

---

1. *Heretic.*   Johnson's Preface to his edition of Shakespeare was
styled by Dr. Adam Smith "the most manly piece of criticism that
was ever published in any language."   But it was criticized in some
quarters for maintaining Shakespeare's right to break "rules, which no
literary dictator had authority to enact," and in other quarters for
such comments on Shakespeare's taste as: "A quibble is to Shakespeare
what luminous vapors are to the traveler; he follows it at all adventures;
it is sure to lead him out of his way, and sure to engulf him in the mire."
The lines written in the *Prologue* are as follows:

> "When Learning's triumph o'er her barb'rous foes
> First reared the stage, immortal Shakespeare rose;
> Each change of many-colored life he drew,
> Exhausted worlds and then imagined new:
> Existence saw him spurn her bounded reign,
> And panting Time toiled after him in vain.
> His powerful strokes presiding Truth impressed,
> And unresisted Passion stormed the breast."

observed that Johnson had been very great that night; Mr. Langton joined in this, but added he could have wished to hear more from another person (plainly intimating that he meant Mr. Burke). 'Oh, no,' said Mr. Burke, 'it is enough for me to have rung the bell to him.' "

"He had an abhorrence of affectation. Talking of old Mr. Langton, of whom he said, 'Sir, you will seldom see such a gentleman, such are his stores of literature, such his knowledge in divinity, and such his exemplary life'; he added, 'and, sir, he has no grimace, no gesticulation, no bursts of admiration on trivial occasions; he never embraces you with an overacted cordiality.' "

"Being in company with a gentleman who thought fit to maintain Dr. Berkeley's ingenious philosophy, that nothing exists but as perceived by some mind—when the gentleman was going away, Johnson said to him, 'Pray, sir, don't leave us; for we may perhaps forget to think of you, and then you will cease to exist.' "

"When Mr. Vesey[1] was proposed as a member of the Literary Club, Mr. Burke began by saying that he was a man of gentle manners. 'Sir,' said Johnson, 'you need say no more. When you have said a man of gentle manners, you have said enough.' "

"The late Mr. Fitzherbert told Mr. Langton that Johnson said to him, 'Sir, a man has no more right to *say* an uncivil thing than to *act* one; no more right to say a rude thing to another than to knock him down.' "

" 'My dear friend Dr. Bathurst,' said he with a warmth of approbation, 'declared he was glad that his father, who was a West Indian planter, had left his affairs in total ruin because, having no estate, he was not under the temptation of having slaves.' "

"Richardson[2] had little conversation, except about his own

---

1. *Mr. Vesey.* His taste was said to be "Grecian." His wife was the fantastic blue-stocking, Elizabeth Vesey, and certainly outshone him.

2. *Richardson.* "That fellow died merely for want of change among his flatterers; he perished for want of *more*, like a man obliged to breathe the same air till it is exhausted." *Johnson, quoted by Mrs. Piozzi.*

works, of which Sir Joshua Reynolds said he was always willing to talk, and glad to have them introduced. Johnson, when he carried Mr. Langton to see him, professed that he could bring him out into conversation, and used this allusive expression, 'Sir, I can make him *rear*.' But he failed, for in that interview Richardson said little else than that there lay in the room a translation of his *Clarissa* into German.''

"Once when somebody produced a newspaper in which there was a letter of stupid abuse of Sir Joshua Reynolds, of which Johnson himself came in for a share—'Pray,' said he, 'let us have it read aloud from beginning to end'; which being done, he with a ludicrous earnestness, and not directing his look to any particular person, called out, 'Are we alive after all this satire!' ''[1]

"Of a certain noble Lord, he said, 'Respect him you could not, for he had no mind of his own. Love him you could not, for that which you could do with him, everyone else could.' ''

"Of Dr. Goldsmith he said, 'No man was more foolish when he had not a pen in his hand, or more wise when he had.' ''

"He told in his lively manner the following literary anecdote: 'Green and Guthrie, an Irishman and a Scotchman, undertook a translation of Duhalde's *History of China*. Green said of Guthrie that he knew no English, and Guthrie of Green that he knew no French; and these two undertook to translate Duhalde's *History of China*. In this translation there was found, "the twenty-sixth day of the new moon." Now, as the whole age of the moon is but twenty-eight days, the moon, instead of being new, was nearly as old as it could be. The blunder arose from their mistaking the word *neuvième*, ninth, for *nouvelle* or *neuve*, new.' ''

" 'No man' [said Johnson] 'speaks concerning another, even suppose it be in his praise, if he thinks he does not hear him, exactly as he would if he thought he was within hearing.' ''

---

1. *Satire*. "It was said to old Bentley, upon the attacks against him, 'Why, they'll write you down.' 'No, sir,' he replied, 'depend upon it, no man was ever written down but by himself.' '' *Johnson, quoted in Boswell's Journal of a Tour to the Hebrides.*

" 'The applause of a single human being is of great consequence.' This he said to me with great earnestness of manner, very near the time of his decease, on occasion of having desired me to read a letter addressed to him from some person in the north of England; which when I had done, and he asked me what the contents were, as I thought being particular upon it might fatigue him, it being of great length, I only told him in general that it was highly in his praise; and then he expressed himself as above."

"He observed once, at Sir Joshua Reynolds's, that a beggar in the street will more readily ask alms from a *man*, though there should be no marks of wealth in his appearance, than from even a well-dressed *woman;* which he accounted for from the great degree of carefulness as to money that is to be found in women; saying farther that the opportunities that they possess of improving their condition are much fewer than men have; and adding as he looked round the company, which consisted of men only, 'there is not one of us who does not think he might be richer if he would use his endeavor.' "

"He thus characterized an ingenious writer of his acquaintance: 'Sir, he is an enthusiast by rule.' "

In 1781 Johnson at last completed his *Lives of the Poets*, of which he gives this account: "Some time in March I finished the *Lives of the Poets*, which I wrote in my usual way, dilatorily and hastily, unwilling to work, and working with vigor and haste." In a memorandum previous to this he says of them: "Written, I hope, in such a manner as may tend to the promotion of piety." The subject swelled in such a manner that instead of prefaces to each poet, of no more than a few pages, as he had originally intended, he produced an ample, rich, and most entertaining view of them in every respect. The booksellers, sensible of the great additional value of the copyright, presented him[1] with another hundred pounds over and above

---

1. *Presented him.* "On this occasion, Dr. Johnson observed to me, 'Sir, I always said the booksellers were a generous set of men. The fact is not that they have paid me too little but that I have written too much.' " *Nichols: Literary Anecdotes, quoted by Birkbeck Hill.*

two hundred, for which his agreement was to furnish such prefaces[1] as he thought fit.

Against his *Life of Milton* the hounds of Whiggism have opened in full cry. But of Milton's great excellence as a poet, where shall we find such a blazon as by the hand of Johnson? I shall select only the following passage concerning *Paradise Lost.*

Fancy can hardly forbear to conjecture with what temper Milton surveyed the silent progress of his work, and marked his reputation stealing its way in a kind of subterraneous current, through fear and silence. I cannot but conceive him calm and confident, little disappointed, not at all dejected, relying on his own merit with steady consciousness, and waiting without impatience the vicissitudes of opinion, and the impartiality of a future generation.

Indeed, even Dr. Towers, who may be considered as one of the warmest zealots of the Revolution Society[2] itself, allows that "Johnson has spoken in the highest terms of the abilities of that great poet, and has bestowed on his principal poetical compositions the most honorable encomiums."

That a man who venerated the church and monarchy as Johnson did should speak with a just abhorrence of Milton as a politician, or rather as a daring foe to good polity, was surely to be expected; and to those who censure him I would recommend his commentary on Milton's celebrated complaint of his situation when by the lenity of Charles the Second, a lenity of which, as Johnson well observes, the world has had perhaps no

---

1. *Such prefaces.* "In Mr. Morrison's *Collection of Autographs* is Johnson's receipt for £100 from the proprietors of the *Lives of the Poets.* . . . Underneath in Johnson's autograph are these words: 'It is great impudence to put *Johnson's Poets* on the back of books which Johnson neither recommended nor revised. He recommended only Blackmore on Creation and Watts. How then are they Johnson's? This is indecent.' " *Birkbeck Hill.*

2. *Revolution Society.* A club which met annually to celebrate the "glorious revolution" by which William III, the Protestant, was seated on the English throne. Before Boswell finished his *Life of Johnson*, it had the opportunity of welcoming the French Revolution and took advantage of the fact.

other example, he, who had written in justification of the murder of his sovereign, was safe under an *Act of Oblivion:*

No sooner is he safe than he finds himself in danger, *fallen on evil days and evil tongues* [and] *with darkness and with danger compassed round.* This darkness, had his eyes been better employed, had undoubtedly deserved compassion; but to add the mention of danger was ungrateful and unjust. He was fallen, indeed, *on evil days;* the time was come in which regicides could no longer boast their wickedness. But of *evil tongues* for Milton to complain, required impudence at least equal to his other powers; Milton, whose warmest advocates must allow that he never spared any asperity of reproach, or brutality of insolence.

I have indeed often wondered how Milton, "an acrimonious and surly republican,"[1] a man who in his domestic relations was so severe and arbitrary, and whose head was filled with the hardest and most dismal tenets of Calvinism, should have been such a poet; should not only have written with sublimity, but with beauty, and even gayety; should have exquisitely painted the sweetest sensations of which our nature is capable; imaged the delicate raptures of connubial love; nay, seemed to be animated with all the spirit of revelry. It is a proof that in the human mind the departments of judgment and imagination, perception and temper, may sometimes be divided by strong partitions; and that the light and shade in the same character may be kept so distinct as never to be blended.

In drawing Dryden's character, Johnson has given, though, I suppose, unintentionally, some touches of his own. Thus: "The power that predominated in his intellectual operations was rather strong reason than quick sensibility. Upon all occasions

---

1. *Republican.* "Milton's republicanism was, I am afraid, founded in an envious hatred of greatness, and a sullen desire of independence; in petulance, impatient of control, and pride, disdainful of superiority. He hated monarchs in the state and prelates in the church; for he hated all whom he was required to obey. It has been observed that they who most loudly clamor for liberty do not most liberally grant it. What we know of Milton's character in domestic relations is that he was severe and arbitrary. He thought woman made only for obedience, and man only for rebellion." *Johnson: Life of Milton.*

that were presented he studied rather than felt. He is therefore, with all his variety of excellence, not often pathetic; and had so little sensibility of the power of effusions purely natural that he did not esteem them in others." It may indeed be observed that in all the numerous writings of Johnson, whether in prose or verse, there is not a single passage that ever drew a tear.

It is remarkable that in the *Life of Broome* Johnson takes notice of Dr. Warburton's using a mode of expression which he himself used, and that not seldom, to the great offense of those who did not know him. He says, "Dr. Warburton told me in his warm language that he thought the relation given in the note *a lie.*" The language is *warm* indeed; and, I must own, cannot be justified in consistency with a decent regard to the established forms of speech. Johnson had accustomed himself to use the word *lie*, to express a mistake or an error in relation; in short, when the *thing was not so as told*, though the relater did not *mean* to deceive. When he thought there was intentional falsehood in the relater, his expression was, "He *lies*, and he *knows* he *lies*."

While the world in general was filled with admiration of Johnson's *Lives of the Poets*, there were narrow circles in which prejudice and resentment were fostered, and from which attacks of different sorts issued against him. By some violent Whigs he was arraigned of injustice to Milton; by some Cambridge men of depreciating Gray; and his expressing with a dignified freedom what he really thought of George, Lord Lyttelton,[1] gave offense to some of the friends of that nobleman. These minute inconveniences gave not the least disturbance to Johnson. He nobly said, when I talked to him of the feeble, though shrill, outcry which had been raised, "Sir, I considered myself as entrusted with a certain portion of truth. I have given my opinion sincerely; let them show where they think me wrong."

---

1. *Lyttelton.* "The verses [of Lyttelton] cant of shepherds and flocks, and crooks dressed with flowers; and the Letters have something of that indistinct and headstrong ardor for liberty which a man of genius always catches when he enters the world, and always suffers to cool as he passes forward." *Johnson: Life of Lyttelton.*

I wrote to him in February, complaining of having been troubled by a recurrence of the perplexing question of Liberty * and Necessity—and mentioning that I hoped soon to meet him again in London. ·

"To James Boswell, Esq.

"DEAR SIR: I hoped you had got rid of all this hypocrisy of misery. What have you to do with Liberty and Necessity? Or what more than to hold your tongue about it? Do not doubt but I shall be most heartily glad to see you here again, for I love every part about you but your affectation of distress.

"I have at last finished my *Lives,* and have laid up for you a load of copy, all out of order, so that it will amuse you a long time to set it right. Come to me, my dear Bozzy, and let us be as happy as we can. We will go again to the Mitre, and talk old times over.

"I am, dear sir,

"Yours affectionately,

"SAM. JOHNSON.

"March 14, 1781."

On Monday, March 19, I arrived in London, and on Tuesday, the 20th, met him in Fleet Street, walking, or rather indeed moving along; for his peculiar march[1] is thus described in a very just and picturesque manner, in a short Life of him published very soon after his death: "When he walked the streets, what with the constant roll of his head, and the concomitant motion of his body, he appeared to make his way by that motion, independent of his feet." That he was often much stared at while he advanced in this manner, may easily be believed; but it was not safe to make sport of one so robust as he was. Mr. Langton saw him one day, in a fit of absence, by a sudden start, drive the load off a porter's back, and walk forward briskly, without being conscious of what he had done.

---

1. *His peculiar march.* Of a passage in the *Journal of a Tour to the Hebrides,* Boswell has written: "It is remarkable that Dr. Johnson should have read this account of his own peculiar habits without saying anything on the subject."

The porter was very angry, but stood still, and eyed the huge figure with much earnestness, till he was satisfied that his wisest course was to be quiet, and take up his burthen again.

Our accidental meeting in the street after a long separation was a pleasing surprise to us both. He stepped aside with me into Falcon Court and made kind inquiries about my family, and as we were in a hurry going different ways, I promised to call on him next day; he said he was engaged to go out in the morning. "Early, sir?" said I. JOHNSON. "Why, sir, a London morning[1] does not go with the sun."

I found on visiting his friend, Mr. Thrale, that he was now very ill, and had removed, I suppose by the solicitation of Mrs. Thrale,[2] to a house in Grosvenor Square. I was sorry to see him sadly changed in his appearance.

He told me I might now have the pleasure to see Dr. Johnson drink wine again, for he had lately returned to it. When I mentioned this to Johnson, he said, "I drink it now sometimes, but not socially." The first evening that I was with him at Thrale's, I observed he poured a large quantity of it into a glass, and swallowed it greedily. Everything about his character and manners was forcible and violent; there never was any moderation; many a day did he fast, many a year did he refrain from wine; but when he did eat, it was voraciously; when he did drink wine, it was copiously. He could practice abstinence, but not temperance.

He said, "Mrs. Montagu has dropped me. Now, sir, there are people whom one should like very well to drop, but would not wish to be dropped by."

On Sunday, April 1, I dined with him at Mr. Thrale's.

1. *A London morning.* "The other day, looking over old papers, I perceived a resolution to rise early always occurring. I think I was ashamed, or grieved, to find how long and how often I had resolved." *Johnson: Prayers and Meditations, July 22, 1773.*

2. *By the solicitation of Mrs. Thrale.* Mrs. Thrale "has written opposite this passage in her copy of Boswell: 'Spiteful again! He went by direction of his physicians where they could easiest attend to him.' " *Birkbeck Hill.* Grosvenor Square was far more fashionable than the Borough, which the Thrales had just left.

Mrs. Thrale gave high praise to Mr. Dudley Long (now North). JOHNSON. "Nay, my dear lady, don't talk so. Mr. Long's character is very *short*. It is nothing. He fills a chair. He is a man of genteel appearance, and that is all. I know nobody who blasts by praise as you do; for whenever there is exaggerated praise, everybody is set against a character. They are provoked to attack it. Now there is Pepys; you praised that man with such disproportion that I was incited to lessen him, perhaps more than he deserves. His blood is upon your head. By the same principle your malice defeats itself, for your censure is too violent."

Mrs. Thrale mentioned a gentleman who had acquired a fortune of four thousand a year in trade, but was absolutely miserable because he could not talk in company; so miserable that he was impelled to lament his situation in the street to ———, whom he hates, and who he knows despises him. JOHNSON. "Man commonly cannot be successful in different ways. This gentleman has spent, in getting four thousand pounds a year, the time in which he might have learned to talk; and now he cannot talk." Mr. Perkins[1] made a droll remark: "If he had got his four thousand a year as a mountebank, he might have learned to talk at the same time that he was getting his fortune."

Mr. Thrale appeared very lethargic today. I saw him again on Monday evening, at which time he was not thought to be in immediate danger; but early in the morning of Wednesday the 4th, he expired. Mr. Thrale's death was a very essential loss to Johnson, who, although he did not foresee all that afterwards happened, was sufficiently convinced that the comforts which Mr. Thrale's family afforded him would now in a great measure cease. He, however, took upon him the office of one of his executors, the importance of which seemed greater than usual to him, from his circumstances having been always such that he had scarcely any share in the real business of life. His friends of the Club were in hopes that Mr. Thrale might have made a liberal provision for him for his life, which, as Mr. Thrale

---

[1]. *Mr. Perkins.* Superintendent of the Thrale brewery.

left no son, and a very large fortune, it would have been highly to his honor to have done; and, considering Dr. Johnson's age, could not have been of long duration; but he bequeathed him only two hundred pounds, which was the legacy given to each of his executors. I could not but be somewhat diverted by hearing Johnson talk in a pompous manner of his new office, and particularly of the concerns of the brewery, which it was at last resolved should be sold. Lord Lucan tells a very good story, which, if not precisely exact, is certainly characteristical: that when the sale of Thrale's brewery was going forward, Johnson appeared bustling about, with an ink-horn and pen in his buttonhole, like an excise-man; and on being asked what he really considered to be the value of the property which was to be disposed of, answered, "We are not here to sell a parcel of boilers and vats, but the potentiality of growing rich beyond the dreams of avarice."

On Friday, April 6, he carried me to dine at a club, which, at his desire, had been lately formed at the Queen's Arms, in St. Paul's* churchyard. He told Mr. Hoole that he wished to have a *City Club*, and asked him to collect one; but, said he, "Don't let them be *patriots*."* The company were today very sensible, well-behaved men. I have preserved only two particulars of his conversation. He said he was glad Lord George Gordon had escaped, rather than that a precedent should be established for hanging a man for *constructive treason*;[1] which, in consistency with his true, manly, constitutional Toryism, he considered would be a dangerous engine of arbitrary power. And upon its being mentioned that an opulent and very indolent Scotch nobleman, who totally resigned the management of his affairs to a man of knowledge and abilities, had claimed some merit by saying, "The next best thing to managing a man's own affairs well is being sensible of incapacity and not

---

1. *Constructive treason.* In the trial of the "anti-popery" rioters, the judge, when charging the jury said: "Insurrections in order to throw down all inclosures, to alter the established law or to change religion, to enhance the price of labor, or to open *all* prisons—all risings, in order to effect these innovations, of a public and a general armed force are, in *construction of law*, high treason."

attempting it, but having full confidence in one who can do it."
JOHNSON. "Nay, sir, this is paltry. There is a middle course.
Let a man give application; and depend upon it he will soon
get above a despicable state of helplessness, and attain the
power of acting for himself."

On Saturday, April 7, I dined with him at Mr. Hoole's with
Governor Bouchier and Captain Orme, both of whom had been
long in the East Indies. Johnson defended the oriental regula-
tion of different castes of men, which was objected to as totally
destructive of the hopes of rising in society by personal merit.
He showed that there was a *principle* in it sufficiently plausible
by analogy. "We see," said he, "in metals that there are different species; and so likewise in animals, as in the species of dogs
—the cur, the spaniel, the mastiff. The Brahmins are the
mastiffs of mankind."

On Thursday, April 12, I dined with him at a bishop's,
where were Sir Joshua Reynolds, Mr. Berrenger, and some more
company. He had dined the day before at another bishop's.
I have unfortunately recorded none of his conversation[1] at the
bishop's where we dined together; but I have preserved his
ingenious defense of his dining twice abroad in Passion week:
"Why, sir, a bishop's calling company together in this week
is, to use the vulgar phrase, not *the thing*. But preciseness is
also a bad thing; and your general character* may be more
hurt by preciseness than by dining with a bishop in Passion
week. It might be said, 'He refuses to dine with a bishop in
Passion week, but was three Sundays absent from church.'"
BOSWELL. "Very true, sir. But suppose a man to be uniformly
of good conduct?" JOHNSON. "Why, sir, you are to consider
whether you might not do more harm by lessening the influence
of a bishop's character by your disapprobation in refusing him,
than by going to him."

On Friday, April 13, being Good Friday, I went to St.
Clement's church with him as usual. There I saw again his
old fellow collegian, Edwards.

---

1. *Recorded none of his conversation.* Of this dinner, Hannah More
writes: "I was heartily disgusted with Mr. Boswell, who came upstairs
after dinner much disordered with wine."

Dr. Johnson told me that there was very little communication between Edwards and him after their unexpected renewal of acquaintance. "But," said he, smiling, "he met me once, and said, 'I am told you have written a very pretty book called *The Rambler*.' I was unwilling that he should leave the world in total darkness, and sent him a set."

Mr. Berrenger[1] visited him today, and was very pleasing. We talked of an evening society for conversation at a house in town, of which we were all members, but of which Johnson said, "It will never do, sir. There is nothing served about there, neither tea nor coffee, nor lemonade, nor anything whatever; and, depend upon it, sir, a man does not love to go to a place from whence he comes out exactly as he went in." I endeavored, for argument's sake, to maintain that men of learning and talents might have very good intellectual society without the aid of any little gratifications of the senses. Berrenger joined with Johnson and would have all the slight refreshments: "Nay it would not be amiss to have some cold meat and a bottle of wine upon a sideboard." "Sir," said Johnson to me, with an air of triumph, "Mr. Berrenger knows the world."

On Sunday, April 15, being Easter Day, after solemn worship in St. Paul's church, I found him alone; Dr. Scott of the Commons came in. He talked of its having been said that Addison wrote some of his best papers in *The Spectator*, when warm with wine. Dr. Johnson did not seem willing to admit this.

I told him that in a company where I had lately been, a desire was expressed to know his authority for the shocking story of Addison's sending an execution[2] into Steele's house. "Sir," said he, "it is generally known; it is known to all who

---

1. *Berrenger*. Gentleman of the horse to George III, and accused by some of his contemporaries of being more suitable to the stable than the court.
2. *Execution*. A legal document to insure the payment of a debt; if necessary, by the sale of the debtor's property. "Steele, whose imprudence of generosity or vanity of profusion kept him always incurably necessitous, upon some pressing exigence in an evil hour borrowed a hundred pounds of his friend, probably without much purpose of repayment; but Addison, who seems to have had other notions of a

are acquainted with the literary history of that period; it is as well known as that he wrote *Cato*." Mr. Thomas Sheridan once defended Addison to me, by alleging that he did it in order to cover Steele's goods from other creditors, who were going to seize them.

Dr. Scott left us, and soon afterwards we went to dinner. Our company consisted of Mrs. Williams, Mrs. Desmoulins, Mr. Levet, Mr. Allen the printer, and Mrs. Hall, sister of the Reverend Mr. John Wesley, and resembling him, as I thought, both in figure and manner. I mentioned a kind of religious Robin Hood Society, which met every Sunday evening at Coachmaker's Hall[1] for free debate; and that the subject for this night was the text: "And the graves were opened, and many bodies of the saints which slept arose, and came out of the graves after his resurrection, and went into the holy city, and appeared unto many." Mrs. Hall said it was a very curious subject, and she should like to hear it discussed. JOHNSON (somewhat warmly). "One should not go to such a place to hear it." "But, sir," said she, "I should like to hear *you* discuss it." He seemed reluctant[2] to engage in it.

---

hundred pounds, grew impatient of delay and reclaimed his loan by an execution. Steele felt with great sensibility the obduracy of his creditor; but with emotions of sorrow rather than of anger." *Johnson's Life of Addison.*

1. *Coachmaker's Hall.* Successively, an auction room, dancing academy, and place of meetings. Here assembled the Protestant Association under the leadership of Lord George Gordon when they planned their "anti-popery" intimidation of London. Birkbeck Hill quotes the painter Romilly as saying this same spring that several of these Sunday religious debating societies had been established. "The auditors," he was assured, "were mostly weak, well-meaning people, who were inclined to Methodism," but among the speakers were "some designing villains, and a few coxcombs, with more wit than understanding." Parliament passed a bill to suppress them.

2. *Reluctant.* Of apparitions after death, Edmund Malone says: "The reader may be led erroneously to suppose that Dr. Johnson was so fond of such discussions as frequently to introduce them. But the truth is, that [Boswell] delighted in talking concerning ghosts and what he has frequently denominated *the mysterious;* and therefore took every opportunity of *leading* Johnson to converse on such subjects."

He mentioned a thing as not infrequent, of which I had
never heard before—being *called*, that is, hearing one's name
pronounced by the voice of a known person at a great distance,
far beyond the possibility of being reached by any sound uttered
by human organs. [He] said that one day at Oxford as he
was turning the key of his chamber, he heard his mother distinctly call *Sam*. She was then at Lichfield; but nothing
ensued.

Some time after this, upon his making a remark which escaped my attention, Mrs. Williams and Mrs. Hall were both
together striving to answer him. He grew angry and called
out loudly, "Nay, when you both speak at once, it is intolerable."
But checking himself, and softening, he said, "This one may
say, though you are ladies." Then he brightened into gay
humor, and addressed them in the words of one of the songs
in *The Beggar's Opera*,

"But two at a time, there's no mortal can bear."

"What, sir," said I, "are you going to turn Captain* Macheath?"
There was something as pleasantly ludicrous in this scene as
can be imagined. The contrast between Macheath, Polly, and
Lucy, and Dr. Samuel Johnson, blind, peevish Mrs. Williams,
and lean, lank, preaching Mrs. Hall was exquisite.

I stole away to Coachmaker's Hall and heard the text of
which we had talked discussed by several speakers. There
was a difference of opinion as to the appearance of ghosts
in modern times, though the arguments for it preponder-
ated.

On Friday, April 20, I spent with him one of the happiest
days that I remember to have enjoyed in the whole course of
my life. Mrs. Garrick, whose grief for the loss of her husband
was, I believe, as sincere as wounded affection and admiration
could produce, had this day, for the first time since his death,
a select party of his friends to dine with her. We found ourselves very elegantly entertained. She looked well, talked of
her husband with complacency, and while she cast her eyes on
his portrait, which hung over the chimney-piece, said that

"death was now the most agreeable object to her." The very semblance of David Garrick was cheering. Mr. Beauclerk, with happy propriety, [had] inscribed under that fine portrait of him, which by Lady Diana's kindness is now the property of my friend Mr. Langton, the following passage from his beloved Shakespeare:

—————A merrier man,
Within the limit of becoming mirth,
I never spent an hour's talk withal.
His eye begets occasion for his wit;
For every object that the one doth catch
The other turns to a mirth-moving jest;
Which his fair tongue (Conceit's expositor)
Delivers in such apt and gracious words
That aged ears play truant at his tales,
And younger hearings are quite ravishéd;
So sweet and voluble is his discourse.

We were all in fine spirits; and I whispered to Mrs. Boscawen, "I believe this is as much as can be made of life." In addition to a splendid entertainment, we were regaled with Lichfield[1] ale, which had a peculiar appropriated value. Sir Joshua and Dr. Burney and I drank cordially of it to Dr. Johnson's health; and though he would not join us, he as cordially answered, "Gentlemen, I wish you all as well as you do me."

The general effect of this day dwells upon my mind in fond remembrance, but I do not find much conversation recorded. What I have preserved shall be faithfully given.

One of the company mentioned Mr. Thomas Hollis, the strenuous Whig, who used to send over Europe presents of democratical books with their boards stamped with daggers and caps of liberty. Mrs. Carter said, "He was a bad man; he used to talk uncharitably." JOHNSON. "Poh! poh! madam; who is the worse for being talked of uncharitably? Besides, he was a dull, poor creature as ever lived; and I believe he would not have done harm to a man whom he knew to be of

---

1. *Lichfield.* Famous for its ale.

very opposite principles to his own. I remember once at the Society of Arts when an advertisement was to be drawn up, he pointed me out as the man who could do it best. This, you will observe, was kindness to me. I, however, slipped away and escaped it."

Mrs. Carter having said of the same person, "I doubt* he was an atheist."[1] JOHNSON. "I don't know that. He might perhaps have become one if he had had time to ripen (smiling). He might have *exuberated* into an atheist."

Talking of a very respectable author, he told us a curious circumstance in his life, which was that he had married a printer's devil. REYNOLDS. "A printer's devil, sir! Why, I thought a printer's devil was a creature with a black face and in rags." JOHNSON. "Yes, sir. But I suppose he had her face washed, and put clean clothes on her." Then, looking very serious and very earnest: "And she did not disgrace him; the woman had a bottom of good sense." The word *bottom* thus introduced was so ludicrous when contrasted with his gravity that most of us could not forbear tittering and laughing; though I recollect that the Bishop of Killaloe kept his countenance with perfect steadiness, while Miss Hannah More slyly hid her face behind a lady's back who sat on the same settee with her. His pride could not bear that any expression of his should excite ridicule, when he did not intend it; he therefore resolved to assume and exercise despotic power, glanced sternly around, and called out in a strong tone, "Where's the merriment?" Then collecting himself, and looking awful, to make us feel how he could impose restraint, and, as it were, searching his mind for a still more ludicrous word, he slowly pronounced, "I say the *woman* was *fundamentally* sensible"; as if he had said, "Hear this now, and laugh if you dare." We all sat composed as at a funeral.

He and I walked away together; we stopped a little while

---

1. *Atheist.* Yet Horace Walpole notes with disgust that in his diary "there are thanks to God for reaching every birthday, and thanks to Heaven for her Majesty's being delivered of a third or fourth prince and *God send he may prove a good man.*"

by the rails of the Adelphi,[1] and I said to him with some emotion that I was now thinking of two friends we had lost, who once lived in the buildings behind us, Beauclerk and Garrick. "Aye, sir," said he tenderly, "and two such friends as cannot be supplied."

On Tuesday, May 8, I had the pleasure of again dining with him and Mr. Wilkes, at Mr. Dilly's. No *negotiation* was now required to bring them together; for Johnson was so well satisfied with the former interview that he was very glad[2] to meet Wilkes again, who was this day seated between Dr. Beattie and Dr. Johnson (between *Truth* and *Reason*, as General Paoli said, when I told him of it).

The company gradually dropped away. Mr. Dilly himself was called downstairs upon business; I left the room for some time; when I returned, I was struck with observing Dr. Samuel Johnson and John Wilkes, Esq., literally *tête-à-tête*; for they were reclined upon their chairs, with their heads leaning almost close to each other, and talking earnestly, in a kind of confidential whisper, of the personal quarrel between George the Second and the King of Prussia.[3] Such a scene of perfectly easy sociality between two such opponents in the war of political controversy, as that which I now beheld, would have been an excellent subject for a picture. It presented to my mind the happy days which are foretold in Scripture when the lion shall lie down with the kid.

About this time it was much the fashion for several ladies to have evening assemblies, where the fair sex might participate in conversation with literary and ingenious men, animated by a desire to please. These societies were denominated *Bluestocking Clubs*. Johnson was prevailed with to come sometimes

---

1. *The Adelphi.* A large mass of residential buildings, recently erected along the banks of the Thames. Mrs. Garrick still lived in one of them.

2. *Very glad.* "I really think [Dr. Johnson] grows gayer and gayer daily, and more *ductile* and pleasant." *Mme. D'Arblay, May, 1781.*

3. *King of Prussia.* Frederick the Great, nephew of George II. The latter was accused of destroying his father's will and so cheating Frederick's mother out of her rightful legacies.

into these circles, and did not think himself too grave even for the lively Miss Monckton[1] (now Countess of Cork). Her vivacity enchanted the Sage, and they used to talk together with all imaginable ease. A singular instance happened one evening when she insisted that some of Sterne's[2] writings were very pathetic. Johnson bluntly denied it. "I am sure," said she, "they have affected *me*."—"Why," said Johnson, smiling, and rolling himself about, "that is, because, dearest, you're a dunce." When she sometimes afterwards mentioned this to him, he said with equal truth and politeness: "Madam, if I had thought so, I certainly should not have said it."

Another evening, Johnson's kind indulgence toward me had a pretty difficult trial. I had dined at the Duke of Montrose's with a very agreeable party, and his grace, according to his usual custom, had circulated the bottle very freely. Lord Graham and I went together to Miss Monckton's, where I certainly was in extraordinary spirits, and above all fear or awe. In the midst of a great number of persons of the first rank, amongst whom I recollect with confusion a noble lady of the most stately decorum, I placed myself next to Johnson, and thinking myself now fully his match, talked to him in a loud and boisterous manner, desirous to let the company know how I could contend with *Ajax*. I particularly remember pressing him upon the value of the pleasures of the imagination, and as an illustration of my argument, asking him, "What, sir, supposing I were to fancy that the —— (naming the most

---

1. *Miss Monckton.* "She is between thirty and forty, very short, very fat, but handsome; splendidly and fantastically dressed, rouged not unbecomingly, yet evidently, and palpably desirous of gaining notice and admiration." *Mme. D'Arblay, 1782.*

"Tonight I go to Miss Monckton's. Thus I scramble when you do not quite shut me up; but I am miserably under petticoat government, and yet am not very weary nor much ashamed." *Johnson to Mrs. Thrale, May 7, 1780.*

2. *Sterne.* Rev. Laurence Sterne (1713-1768). "Have you read his sermons, with his own comic figure at the head of them? They are in the style I think most proper for the pulpit, and show a very strong imagination and a sensible [sympathetic] heart; but you see him often tottering on the verge of laughter and ready to throw his periwig in the face of his audience." *Thomas Gray, 1760.*

charming Duchess in his Majesty's dominions) were in love
with me, should I not be very happy?"   My friend with much
address evaded my interrogatories, and kept me as quiet as
possible· but it may easily be conceived how he must have felt.
However, when a few days afterwards I waited upon him
and made an apology, he behaved with the most friendly
gentleness.

While I remained in London this year, Johnson and I dined
together at several places.   I recollect a placid day at Dr.
Butter's, who had now removed from Derby to Lower Grosvenor Street, London; but of his conversation on that and
other occasions during this period, I neglected to keep any
regular record, and shall therefore insert here some miscellaneous articles which I find in my Johnsonian notes.

His disorderly habits when "making provision for the day
that was passing over him" appear from the following anecdote
communicated to me by Mr. John Nichols:[1] "In the year
1763, a young bookseller, who was an apprentice to Mr.
Whiston,[2] waited on him with a subscription to his *Shakespeare;*
and observing that the Doctor made no entry in any book
of the subscriber's name, ventured diffidently to ask whether
he would please to have the gentleman's address, that it might
be properly inserted in the printed list of subscribers.—"*I shall
print no List of Subscribers,*" said Johnson, with great abruptness; but almost immediately recollecting himself, added,
very complacently, 'Sir, I have two very cogent reasons for
not printing any list of subscribers: one, that I have lost all
the names; the other, that I have spent all the money.' "

Johnson could not brook appearing to be worsted in argument, even when he had taken the wrong side to show the
force and dexterity of his talents.   When, therefore, he perceived that his opponent gained ground, he had recourse to
some sudden mode of robust sophistry.   Once when I was
pressing upon him with visible advantage, he stopped me thus:

---

1. *John Nichols.* One of the printers of Johnson's *Lives of the
Poets.* Mr. Nichols was a devoted friend of Johnson's, and a painstaking
anecdotist.

2. *Mr. Whiston.* A bookseller.

"My dear Boswell, let's have no more of this; you'll make nothing of it. I'd rather have you whistle a Scotch tune."

Care, however, must be taken to distinguish between Johnson when he "talked for victory," and Johnson when he had no desire but to inform and illustrate. "One of Johnson's principal talents," says an eminent friend of his, "was shown in maintaining the wrong side of an argument, and in a splendid perversion of the truth. If you could contrive to have his fair opinion on a subject, and without any bias from personal prejudice, or from a wish to be victorious in argument, it was wisdom itself, not only convincing, but overpowering."

He had, however, all his life habituated himself to consider conversation as a trial of intellectual vigor and skill; and to this, I think, we may venture to ascribe that unexampled richness and brilliancy which appeared in his own. As a proof at once of his eagerness for colloquial distinction, and his high notion of this eminent friend, he once addressed him thus: "——, we now have been several hours together; and you have said but one thing for which I envied you."

He disliked much all speculative, desponding considerations, which tended to discourage men from diligence and exertion. He was in this like Dr. Shaw, the great traveler, who, Mr. Daines Barrington told me, used to say, "I hate a *cui bono* man." Upon being asked by a friend what he should think of a man who was apt to say *non est tanti:* "That he's a stupid fellow, sir," answered Johnson. "What would these *tanti* men be doing the while?" When I, in a low-spirited fit, was talking to him with indifference of the pursuits which generally engage us in a course of action, and inquiring a *reason* for taking so much trouble: "Sir," said he, in an animated tone, "it is driving on the system of life."

Johnson had called twice on the Bishop of Killaloe before his Lordship set out for Ireland, having missed him the first time. He said, "It would have hung heavy on my heart if I had not seen him. No man ever paid more attention to another than he has done to me; and I have neglected him, not willfully, but from being otherwise occupied. Always, sir, set a high

value on spontaneous kindness. He whose inclination prompts
him to cultivate your friendship of his own accord will love
you more than one whom you have been at pains to attach
to you."

Johnson told me that he was once much pleased to find that
a carpenter who lived near him was very ready to show him
some things in his business which he wished to see:[1] "It was
paying," said he, "respect to literature."

On Saturday, June 2, I set out for Scotland, and had promised to pay a visit, in my way, as I sometimes did, at Southill,
in Bedfordshire, at the hospitable mansion of Squire Dilly,[2] the
elder brother of the booksellers in the Poultry. Dr. Johnson
agreed to be of the party this year, with Mr. Charles Dilly
and me. He talked little to us in the carriage, being chiefly
occupied in reading Dr. Watson's second volume of *Chemical
Essays*, which he liked very well, and his own *Prince of
Abyssinia*, on which he seemed to be intently fixed; having
told us that he had not looked at it since it was first published.
I happened to take it out of my pocket this day, and he seized
upon it with avidity. He pointed out to me the following
remarkable passage: "By what means," said the prince, "are
the Europeans thus powerful; or why, since they can so easily
visit Asia and Africa for trade or conquests, cannot the Asiatics
and Africans invade their coasts, plant colonies in their ports,
and give laws to their natural princes? The same wind that
carried them back would bring us thither."—"They are more
powerful, sir, than we," answered Imlac, "because they are
wiser. Knowledge will always predominate over ignorance,
as man governs the other animals. But why their knowledge
is more than ours, I know not what reason can be given, but

---

1. *Wished to see.* A somewhat snobbish writer in the *Monthly
Review*, who had known Johnson, says: "He always preferred conversation to reading, though it were with the lowest mechanics; and he
constantly listened to professional men with respect. His disputes
were chiefly with those pretenders to that knowledge and science of
which he was himself at least equally qualified to judge."

2. *Squire Dilly.* "The family of Dilly have been land proprietors
in the county for two hundred years." *Boswell.*

the unsearchable will of the Supreme Being." He [Johnson] said, "This, sir, no man can explain otherwise."

We stopped at Welwyn, where I wished much to see, in company with Johnson, the residence of the author of *Night Thoughts*,[1] which was then possessed by his son, Mr. Young. Here some address was requisite, for I was not acquainted with Mr. Young, and had I proposed to Dr. Johnson that we should send to him, he would have checked my wish, and perhaps been offended. I therefore concerted with Mr. Dilly that I should steal away from Dr. Johnson and him, and try what reception I could procure from Mr. Young; if unfavorable, nothing was to be said; but if agreeable, I should return and notify it to them. I hastened to Mr. Young's, found he was at home, sent in word that a gentleman desired to wait upon him, and was shown into a parlor, where he and a young lady, his daughter, were sitting. He appeared to be a plain, civil country gentleman; and when I begged pardon for presuming to trouble him, but that I wished much to see his place, if he would give me leave, he behaved very courteously, and answered, "By all means, sir; we are just going to drink tea; will you sit down?" I thanked him, but said that Dr. Johnson had come with me from London, and I must return to the inn and drink tea with him; that my name was Boswell; I had traveled with him in the Hebrides. "Sir," said he, "I should think it a great honor to see Dr. Johnson here. Will you allow me to send for him?" Availing myself of this opening, I said that I would go myself and bring him, when he had drunk tea; he knew nothing of my calling here. Having been thus successful, I hastened back to the inn, and informed Dr. Johnson that Mr. Young, son of Dr. Young, the author of *Night Thoughts*, whom I had just left, desired to have the honor of seeing him at the house where his father lived. Dr. Johnson luckily made no inquiry how this invitation had arisen, but agreed to go, and when we entered Mr. Young's parlor, he

---

1. *Author of Night Thoughts.* Edward Young (1683-1765). "Young froths and foams and bubbles, sometimes very vigorously; but we must not compare the noise made by your teakettle with the roaring of the ocean." *Johnson, quoted by Mrs. Piozzi.*

addressed him with a very polite bow, "Sir, I had a curiosity to come and see this place. I had the honor to know that great man, your father." We went into the garden, where we found a gravel walk on each side of which was a row of trees planted by Dr. Young, which formed a handsome Gothic arch; Dr. Johnson called it a fine grove. I beheld it with reverence.

He found himself very happy at Squire Dilly's, where there is always abundance of excellent fare, and hearty welcome.

On Sunday, June 3, we all went to Southill church, which is very near to Mr. Dilly's house. It being the first Sunday of the month, the holy sacrament was administered, and I stayed to partake of it. When I came afterwards into Dr. Johnson's room, he said, "You did right to stay and receive the communion; I had not thought of it." This seemed to imply that he did not choose to approach the altar without a previous preparation, as to which good men entertain different opinions, some holding that it is irreverent to partake of that ordinance without considerable premeditation; others, that whoever is a sincere Christian, and in proper frame of mind to discharge any other ritual duty of our religion, may, without scruple, discharge this most solemn one.

Being in a frame of mind which I hope, for the felicity of human nature, many experience—in fine weather—at the country-house of a friend—consoled and elevated by pious exercises—I expressed myself with an unrestrained fervor to my "Guide, Philosopher, and Friend": "My dear sir, I would fain be a good man; and I am very good now. I fear God, and honor the King; I wish to do no ill, and to be benevolent to all mankind." He looked at me with a benignant indulgence; but took occasion to give me wise and salutary caution. "Do not, sir, accustom yourself to trust to *impressions*. There is a middle state of mind between conviction and hypocrisy, of which many are unconscious. By trusting to impressions, a man may gradually come to yield to them, and at length be subject to them, so as not to be a free agent, or what is the same thing in effect, to *suppose* that he is not a free agent. A man who is in that state should not be suffered to live; if he declares he cannot help acting in a particular way, and is irresistibly impelled, there can be no confidence in him, no more than in a tiger. But, sir, no man believes himself to be impelled irresistibly; we know that he who says he believes it, lies. Favorable impressions at particular moments, as to the state of our souls, may be deceitful and dangerous."

Although upon most occasions I never heard a more strenuous advocate for the advantages of wealth than Dr. Johnson, he this day, I know not from what caprice, took the other side. "I have not observed," said he, "that men of very large fortunes enjoy anything extraordinary that makes happiness. What has the Duke of Bedford? What has the Duke of Devonshire? The only great instance that I have ever known of the enjoyment of wealth was that of Jamaica Dawkins, who, going to visit Palmyra, and hearing that the way was infested by robbers, hired a troop of Turkish horse to guard him."

When I observed that a housebreaker was in general very timorous: JOHNSON. "No wonder, sir; he is afraid of being shot getting *into* a house, or hanged when he has got *out* of it."

On Tuesday, June 5, Johnson was to return to London. At Shefford I had an affectionate parting from my revered friend, who was taken up by the Bedford coach and carried to the metropolis. I went with Messrs. Dilly to see some friends at Bedford, dined with the officers of the militia of the county, and next day proceeded on my journey.

[1782]. In one of Johnson's registers of this year there occurs the following curious passage: "Jan. 20. The Ministry is dissolved. I prayed with Francis, and gave thanks." It has been the subject of discussion whether there are two distinct particulars mentioned here, or that we are to understand the giving of thanks to be in consequence of the dissolution of the Ministry. In support of the last of these conjectures may be urged his mean opinion of that Ministry, which has frequently appeared in the course of this work; and it is strongly confirmed by what he said on the subject to Mr. Seward: "I am glad the Ministry is removed. Such a bunch of imbecility never disgraced a country. If they sent a messenger into the City to take up a printer, the messenger was taken up instead of the printer, and committed by the sitting Alderman. If they sent one army to the relief of another, the first army was defeated and taken before the second arrived. I will not say that what they did was always wrong; but it was always done at a wrong time."

"To Bennet Langton, Esq.

"DEAR SIR: "Mr. Levet, to whom, as he used to tell me, I owe your acquaintance, died a few weeks ago, suddenly, in his bed; there passed not, I believe, a minute between health and death. At night, as at Mrs. Thrale's I was musing in my chamber, I thought with uncommon earnestness that however I might alter my mode of life, or whithersoever I might remove,[1] I would endeavor to retain Levet about me; in the morning my servant brought me word that Levet was called to another state, a state for which, I think, he was not unprepared, for he was very useful to the poor. How much soever I valued him, I now wish I had valued him more.

"I am, dear sir,
"Your humble servant,
"SAM. JOHNSON.

"Bolt Court, Fleet Street,
"March 20, 1782."

The following letters require no extracts from mine to introduce them.

"To James Boswell, Esq.

"DEAR SIR: Whatever might have been your pleasure or mine, I know not how I could have honestly advised you to come hither with borrowed money. Do not accustom yourself to consider debt only as an inconvenience; you will find it a calamity. Poverty[2] takes away so many means of doing good,

---

1. *I might remove.* If Mrs. Thrale should leave her comfortable house at Streatham, as Johnson was already suspecting she might.
2. *Poverty.* "The prospect of penury in age is so gloomy and terrifying that every man who looks before him must resolve to avoid it, and it must be avoided generally by the science of sparing." *Johnson: The Rambler.*

and produces so much inability to resist evil, both natural and moral, that it is by all virtuous means to be avoided. Consider a man whose fortune is very narrow; whatever be his rank by birth, or whatever his reputation by intellectual excellence, what can he do, or what evil can he prevent? That he cannot help the needy is evident; he has nothing to spare. But perhaps his advice or admonition may be useful. His poverty will destroy his influence: many more can find that he is poor than that he is wise; and few will reverence the understanding that is of so little advantage to its owner. I say nothing of the personal wretchedness of a debtor, which, however, has passed into a proverb. Of riches it is not necessary to write the praise. Let it, however, be remembered that he who has money to spare has it always in his power to benefit others; and of such power a good man must always be desirous."

"To Mr. Perkins.[1]

"DEAR SIR: I am much pleased that you are going a very long journey, which may by proper conduct restore your health and prolong your life.

"Observe these rules:

"1. Turn all care out of your head as soon as you mount the chaise.

"2. Do not think about frugality; your health is worth more than it can cost.

"3. Do not continue any day's journey to fatigue.

"4. Take now and then a day's rest.

"5. Get a smart sea sickness, if you can.

"6. Cast away all anxiety, and keep your mind easy.

"This last direction is the principal; with an unquiet mind, neither exercise, nor diet, nor physic can be of much use.

"I wish you, dear sir, a prosperous journey, and a happy recovery. I am, dear sir,

"Your most affectionate, humble servant,

"July 28, 1782."   "SAM. JOHNSON.

---

1. *Mr. Perkins.* Formerly the superintendent of the Thrale brewery, but for a year past one of its proprietors. Mr. Perkins kept a picture of Johnson in his counting room to have "one wise man there."

On the 30th of August I informed him that my honored father had died that morning; a complaint under which he had long labored having suddenly come to a crisis while I was upon a visit at the seat of Sir Charles Preston, from whence I had hastened the day before, upon receiving a letter by express.*

"To James Boswell, Esq.

"DEAR SIR: Your father's death had every circumstance that could enable you to bear it; it was at a mature age, and it was expected; and as his general life had been pious, his thoughts had doubtless for many years been turned upon eternity. That you did not find him sensible must doubtless grieve you; his disposition toward you was doubtless that of a kind, though not of a fond, father. Kindness, at least actual, is in our power, but fondness is not; and if by negligence or imprudence you had extinguished his fondness, he could not at will rekindle it. Nothing then remained between you but mutual forgiveness of each other's faults, and mutual desire of each other's happiness.

"I shall long to know the final disposition of his fortune.

"You, dear sir, have now a new station, and have therefore new cares and new employments. Life, as Cowley seems to say, ought to resemble a well-ordered poem of which one rule generally received is that the exordium should be simple, and should promise little. Begin your new course of life with the least show and the least expense possible; you may at pleasure increase both, but you cannot easily diminish them. Do not think your estate your own while any man can call upon you for money which you cannot pay; therefore begin with timorous parsimony. Let it be your first care not to be in any man's debt.

"When the thoughts are extended to a future state, the present life seems hardly worthy of all those principles of conduct and maxims of prudence which one generation of men has transmitted to another; but upon a closer view, when it is perceived how much evil is produced, and how much good is impeded by embarrassment and distress, and how little room the expedients of poverty leave for the exercise of virtue, it grows manifest that the boundless importance of the next life enforces some attention to the interests of this.

"Be kind to the old servants, and secure the kindness of the agents and factors;* do not disgust them by asperity, or unwelcome gayety, or apparent suspicion. From them you must learn the real state of your affairs, the characters of your tenants, and the value of your lands.

"I received your letters only this morning. I am, dear sir,
> "Yours, &c.,

"London, Sept. 7, 1782."   "SAM. JOHNSON.

"To James Boswell, Esq.

"DEAR SIR: Having passed almost this whole year in a succession of disorders, I went in October to Brighthelmstone,[1] whither I came in a state of so much weakness that I rested four times in walking between the inn and the lodging. By physic and abstinence I grew better, and am now reasonably easy, though at a great distance from health. I am afraid, however, that health begins, after seventy, and long before, to have a meaning different from that which it had at thirty. But it is culpable to murmur at the established order of the creation, as it is vain to oppose it. He that lives must grow old; and he that would rather grow old than die has God to thank for the infirmities of old age.

> "Your affectionate, humble servant,
>   "SAM. JOHNSON.

"London, Dec. 7, 1782."

---

1. *Brighthelmstone.* As Mrs. Thrale's guest. She had let Streatham; and Johnson and the other guests, once entertained there, were resentful. "That house," said Dr. Johnson tremulously to Mme. D'Arblay, "is lost to me forever." Mrs. Thrale apparently was thinking of marrying a Signor Piozzi. "Mme. D'Arblay records that some day in the autumn of this year she called on Dr. Johnson. As she sat with him, a sudden change from kind tranquillity to strong austerity took place in his countenance. Then see-sawing violently in his chair, as usual when he was big with any powerful emotion, whether of pleasure or pain, he seemed deeply moved; but without looking at her or speaking, he intently fixed his eyes upon the fire. Then suddenly turning to her with an air of mingled wrath and woe he hoarsely ejaculated 'Piozzi.' At length, and with great agitation, he broke forth with 'She cares for no one.' " *Birkbeck Hill.*

[1783]. On Friday, March 21, having arrived in London the night before, I was glad to find him at Mrs. Thrale's house, in Argyle Street, appearances of friendship between them being still kept up. I was shown into his room, and after the first salutation he said, "I am glad you are come; I am very ill." He looked pale, and was distressed with a difficulty of breathing; but after the common inquiries he assumed his usual strong, animated style of conversation. Seeing me now for the first time as a *Laird*, or proprietor of land, he began thus: "Sir, the superiority of a country gentleman over the people upon his estate is very agreeable; and he who says he does not feel it to be agreeable, lies; for it must be agreeable to have a casual superiority over those who are by nature equal with us.

"It is better to have five per cent out of land than out of money, because it is more secure; but the readiness of transfer, and promptness of interest, make many people rather choose the funds. Nay, there is another disadvantage belonging to land, compared with money. A man is not so much afraid of being a hard creditor as of being a hard landlord." BOSWELL. "Because there is a sort of kindly connection between a landlord and his tenants." JOHNSON. "No, sir, many landlords with us never see their tenants. It is because if a landlord drives away his tenants, he may not get others; whereas the demand for money is so great it may always be lent."

He sent a message to acquaint Mrs. Thrale that I was arrived. I had not seen her since her husband's death. She soon appeared, and favored me with an invitation to stay to dinner, which I accepted. She said she was very glad I was come, for she was going to Bath, and should have been sorry to leave Dr. Johnson before I came. This seemed to be attentive and kind; and I, who had not been informed of any change, imagined all to be as well as formerly.

Talking of conversation, he said, "There must, in the first place, be knowledge, there must be materials; in the second place, there must be a command of words; in the third place, there must be imagination, to place things in such views as they are not commonly seen in; and in the fourth place, there must be presence of mind, and a resolution that is not to be overcome by failures. This last is an essential requisite; for want of it may people do not excel in conversation. Now *I* want it; I throw up the game upon losing a trick.

"Fox[1] never talks in private company; not from any determination not to talk, but because he has not the first* motion. A man who is used to the applause of the House of Commons has no wish for that of a private company. A man accustomed to throw for a thousand pounds, if set down to throw for sixpence, would not be at the pains to count his dice. Burke's talk is the ebullition of his mind; he does not talk from a desire of distinction, but because his mind is full."

He thus curiously characterized one of our old acquaintance: "—— is a good man, sir; but he is a vain man and a liar. He, however, only tells lies of vanity; of victories, for instance, in conversation, which never happened." This alluded to a story which I had repeated from that gentleman, to entertain Johnson with its wild bravado: "This Johnson, sir," said he, "whom you are all afraid of, will shrink if you come close to him in argument and roar as loud as he. He once maintained the paradox that there is no beauty but in utility. 'Sir,' said I, 'what say you to the peacock's tail?' He had recourse to his usual expedient, ridicule, exclaiming, 'A peacock has a tail, and a fox has a tail'; and then he burst out into a laugh. 'Well, sir,' said I, with a strong voice, looking him full in the face, 'you have unkenneled your fox; pursue him if you dare.' He had not a word to say, sir." Johnson told me that this was fiction from beginning to end.

After musing for some time, he said, "I wonder how I should have any enemies; for I do harm to nobody." BOSWELL. "In

---

1. *Fox.* The famous Whig statesman, Charles James Fox. According to his nephew, Lord Holland, he defended Johnson's pension and said it was only to blame in not being large enough.

"Fox," said Johnson, "is a liberal man; he would always be *aut Caesar aut nullus;* whenever I have seen him, he has been *nullus.*"

"In London mixed society, Fox conversed little; but at his own house in the country, with his intimate friends, he would talk on forever, with all the openness and simplicity of a child; he has continued talking to me for half an hour after he had taken up his bedroom candle." *Samuel Rogers.*

the first place, sir, you will be pleased to recollect that you set out with attacking the Scotch; so you got a whole nation for your enemies." JOHNSON. "Why, I own that by my definition of *oats*[1] I meant to vex them." BOSWELL. "Pray, sir, can you trace the cause of your antipathy to the Scotch?" JOHNSON. "I cannot, sir." BOSWELL. "Old Mr. Sheridan says it was because they sold Charles the First."[2] JOHNSON. "Then, sir, old Mr. Sheridan has found out a very good reason."

Next day, Saturday, March 22, I found him still at Mrs. Thrale's, but he told me he was to go to his own house in the afternoon. He was better, but I perceived he was but an unruly patient, for Sir Lucas Pepys,[3] who visited him while I was there, said, "If you were *tractable*, sir, I should prescribe for you."

I found Dr. Johnson in the evening in Mrs. Williams's room, at tea and coffee with her and Mrs. Desmoulins, who were also both ill; it was a sad scene, and he was not in very good humor. He said of a performance that had lately come out, "Sir, if you should search all the madhouses in England, you would not find ten men who would write so and think it sense."

On Sunday, March 23, I breakfasted with Dr. Johnson, who seemed much relieved, having taken opium the night before. He, however, protested against it, as a remedy that should be given only in extreme necessity. Mrs. Desmoulins made tea; and she and I talked before him upon a topic which he had once

---

1. *Oats.* "A grain which in England is generally given to horses, but in Scotland supports the people." *Johnson: Dictionary.* "Stockdale records that he heard a Scotch lady say to Johnson: 'I can assure you that in Scotland we give oats to our horses as you do to yours in England.' He replied: 'I am very glad, madam, to find that you treat your horses as well as you treat yourselves.'" *Birkbeck Hill.*
2. *Sold Charles the First.* In May, 1646, he surrendered to his Scotch foes in hope of combining with them in some compromise against his English ones. After ten months of dickering, they gave him up to the English parliament with its pay in their pockets, ostensibly for their military services against the Crown, and marched back to their own country. Two years later, he was executed.
3. *Sir Lucas Pepys.* Mrs. Thrale's friend and physician, and Physician Extraordinary to the King. "Of great firmness and determination; somewhat dictatorial in his manner." *Dr. Munk.*

borne patiently from me when we were by ourselves—his not complaining of the world because he was not called to some great office, nor had attained to great wealth. He flew into a violent passion, I confess with some justice, and commanded us to have done. "Nobody," said he, "has a right to talk in this manner, to bring before a man his own character, and the events of his life, when he does not choose it should be done. I never have sought the world; the world was not to seek me. It is rather wonderful that so much has been done for me. All the complaints which are made of the world are unjust. I never knew a man of merit neglected; it was generally by his own fault that he failed of success. A man may hide his head in a hole; he may go into the country, and publish a book now and then, which nobody reads, and then complain he is neglected. There is no reason why any person should exert himself for a man who has written a good book; he has not written it for any individual. I may as well make a present to the postman who brings me a letter."

BOSWELL. "But surely, sir, you will allow that there are men of merit at the bar, who never get practice." JOHNSON. "Sir, you are sure that practice is got from an opinion that the person employed deserves it best; so that if a man of merit at the bar does not get practice, it is from error, not from injustice. He is not neglected. A horse that is brought to market may not be bought, though he is a very good horse; but that is from ignorance, not from intention."[1]

On the subject of the right employment of wealth, Johnson observed, "It is in general better to spend money than to give it away; for industry is more promoted by spending money than by giving it away. A man who spends his money is sure he is doing good with it; he is not so sure when he gives it away. A man who spends ten thousand a year will do more good than a man who spends two thousand and gives away eight."

---

1. *Not from intention.*

"See nations, slowly wise and meanly just,
To buried merit raise the tardy dust."

Johnson: Vanity of Human Wishes, 1749.

In the evening I came to him again. He was somewhat fretful[1] from his illness. A gentleman asked him whether he had been abroad* today. "Don't talk so childishly," said he. "You may as well ask if I hanged myself today." I mentioned politics. JOHNSON. "Sir, I'd as soon have a man to break my bones as talk to me of public affairs, internal or external. I have lived to see things all as bad as they can be."

Having mentioned his friend, the second Lord Southwell, he said, "Lord Southwell was the highest-bred man without insolence that I ever was in company with; the most *qualitied* I ever saw. Lord ———[2] is a man of coarse manners, but a man of abilities and information. I don't say he is a man I would set at the head of a nation, though perhaps he may be as good as the next Prime Minister that comes; but he is a man to be at the head of a Club—I don't say *our* CLUB—for there's no such Club."

He said, "Goldsmith's blundering speech to Lord Shelburne, which has been so often mentioned, and which he really did make to him, was only a blunder in emphasis; 'I wonder they should call your Lordship *Malagrida*,[3] for Malagrida was a very good man' meant, 'I wonder they should use *Malagrida* as a term of reproach.' "

On Sunday, March 30, I found him at home in the evening,

---

1. *Fretful.* "If the purpose of lamentation be to excite pity, it is surely superfluous for age and weakness to tell their plaintive stories; for pity presupposes sympathy, and a little attention will show them that those who do not feel pain seldom think that it is felt." *Johnson: The Rambler.*

2. *Lord ———.* The prime minister, Lord Shelburne; fearless in his choice of free-thinking friends; outspoken in his views, in which scorn of the "people" and the championship of their rights against the privileged classes about equally mingled; accused of resorting at times to low cunning to gain his ends; in a word, unpopular. Fox and Burke, both members of the Club, detested him.

3. *Malagrida.* A Jesuit accused of having used the confessional to encourage the assassination of the Portuguese King in 1758. In many circles, his name remained a byword for more than thirty years. Like Malagrida, Lord Shelburne had shaggy eyebrows, but it was his supposed duplicity which gave sharpness to the comparison.

and had the pleasure to meet with Dr. Brocklesby,[1] whose reading, and knowledge of life, and good spirits, supply him with a never-failing source of conversation. He mentioned a respectable gentleman[2] who became extremely penurious near the close of his life. Johnson said there must have been a degree of madness about him. "Not at all, sir," said Dr. Brocklesby, "his judgment was entire." Unluckily, however, he mentioned that although he had a fortune of twenty-seven thousand pounds, he denied himself many comforts from an apprehension that he could not afford them. "Nay, sir," cried Johnson, "when the judgment is so disturbed that a man cannot count, that is pretty well."

I shall here insert a few of Johnson's sayings, without the formality of dates, as they have no reference to any particular time or place.

"Raising the wages of day laborers is wrong; for it does not make them live better, but only makes them idler, and idleness is a very bad thing for human nature."

I praised the accuracy of an account book of a lady whom I mentioned. JOHNSON. "Keeping accounts, sir, is of no use[3] when a man is spending his own money, and has nobody to whom he is to account. You won't eat less beef today because you have written down what it cost yesterday." I maintained

---

1. *Dr. Brocklesby* (1722-97). An able and wide-awake physician. A schoolmate of Burke's and a near neighbor to Johnson, he had for some time "very diligently solicited" Johnson's friendship. Though his nonchalance toward religion sometimes disturbed both Burke and Johnson, he won their confidence by his irrepressible generosity. "Dr. Brocklesby wrote to Burke on July 2, 1788, to make him 'an instant present of £1000, which,' he continues, 'for years past, by will, I had destined as a testimony of my regard on my decease.' Burke, accepting the present, said: 'I shall never be ashamed to have it known that I am obliged to one who never can be capable of converting his kindness into a burthen.'" *Birkbeck Hill.* For a similar offer to Dr. Johnson, see the later pages of this volume.

2. *A respectable gentleman.* The famous anatomist, Dr. William Hunter. He died this same day, leaving behind him a great anatomical collection on which he is said to have spent a hundred thousand pounds.

3. *Of no use.* "On his fifty-fifth birthday [1764] he recorded: 'I resolve to keep a journal, both of employment and of expenses. To keep accounts.'" *Birkbeck Hill.*

that keeping an account has this advantage, that it satisfies a man that his money has not been lost or stolen, which he might sometimes be apt to imagine were there no written state of his expense; and, besides, a calculation of economy so as not to exceed one's income cannot be made without a view of the different articles in figures, that one may see how to retrench in some particulars less necessary than others. This he did not attempt to answer.

Talking of an acquaintance of ours, whose narratives, which abounded in curious and interesting topics, were unhappily found to be very fabulous; I mentioned Lord Mansfield's having said to me, "Suppose we believe one *half* of what he tells." JOHNSON. "Aye; but we don't know *which* half to believe. By his lying we lose not only our reverence for him, but all comfort in his conversation." BOSWELL. "May we not take it as amusing fiction?" JOHNSON. "Sir, the misfortune is that you will insensibly believe as much of it as you incline to believe."

It is remarkable that, notwithstanding their congeniality in politics, he never was acquainted with a late eminent noble judge, whom I have heard speak of him as a writer, with great respect. Johnson, I know not upon what degree of investigation, entertained no exalted opinion of his Lordship's intellectual character. Talking of him to me one day, he said, "It is wonderful, sir, with how little real superiority of mind men can make an eminent figure in public life." He expressed himself to the same purpose concerning another law lord, who, it seems, once took a fancy to associate with the wits of London; but with so little success that Foote said, "What can he mean by coming among us? He is not only dull himself, but the cause of dullness in others." [Johnson] once said to Sir Joshua Reynolds, "This man now has been ten years about town, and has made nothing of it"; meaning as a companion. He said to me, "I never heard anything from him in company that was at all striking; and depend upon it, sir, it is when you come close to a man in conversation that you discover what his real abilities are; to make a speech in a public assembly is a knack. Now I honor Thurlow, sir; Thurlow is a fine fellow; he fairly puts his mind to yours."

I told him I should send him some *Essays* which I had written, which I hoped he would be so good as to read, and pick out the good ones. JOHNSON. "Nay, sir, send me only the good ones; don't make *me* pick them."

As a small proof of his kindliness and delicacy of feeling, the following circumstance may be mentioned: One evening when we were in the street together, and I told him I was going to sup at Mr. Beauclerk's, he said, "I'll go with you." After having walked part of the way, seeming to recollect something, he suddenly stopped and said, "I cannot go—but *I do not love Beauclerk the less.*"

On the frame of his portrait, Mr. Beauclerk had inscribed,

——————Ingenium ingens
Inculto latet hoc sub corpore.

After Mr. Beauclerk's death, when it became Mr. Langton's property, he made the inscription be defaced. Johnson said complacently, "It was kind in you to take it off"; and then after a short pause, added, "and not unkind in him to put it on."

He said, "How few of his friends' houses would a man choose to be at when he is sick!"[1] He mentioned one or two. I recollect only Thrale's.

He observed, "If a young or middle-aged man, when leaving a company, does not recollect where he laid his hat, it is nothing; but if the same inattention is discovered in an old man, people will shrug up their shoulders and say, 'His memory is going.'"

I am very sorry that I did not take a note of an eloquent argument in which he maintained that the situation of Prince of Wales was the happiest of any person's in the kingdom. I recollect only—the enjoyment of hope—the high superiority of rank, without the anxious cares of government—and a great degree of power, both from natural influence widely used, and from the sanguine expectations of those who look forward to the chance of future favor.

---

1. *When he is sick.* Mrs. Piozzi has somewhere said that Dr. Johnson "required less attendance, sick or well, than ever I saw any human creature." Elsewhere she has expressed herself quite differently.

Sir Joshua Reynolds communicated to me the following particulars:

Johnson thought the poems published as translations from Ossian had so little merit that he said, "Sir, a man might write such stuff forever, if he would *abandon* his mind to it."

Dr. Goldsmith once said to Dr. Johnson that he wished for some additional members to the Literary Club, to give it an agreeable variety; "for," said he, "there can now be nothing new among us; we have traveled over one another's minds."[1] Johnson seemed a little angry, and said, "Sir, you have not traveled over *my* mind, I promise you." Sir Joshua, however, thought Goldsmith right; observing that "when people have lived a great deal together, they know what each of them will say on every subject. A new understanding may only furnish the same sense upon a question which would have been furnished by those with whom we are accustomed to live, yet this sense will have a different coloring; and coloring is of much effect in everything else as well as in painting."

Johnson used to say that he made it a constant rule to talk as well as he could, both as to sentiment and expression; by which means, what had been originally effort became familiar and easy. The consequence of this, Sir Joshua observed, was that his common conversation in all companies was such as to secure him universal attention, as something above the usual colloquial style was expected.

Yet, though Johnson had this habit in company, when another mode was necessary, in order to investigate truth, he could descend to a language intelligible to the meanest capacity. An instance of this was witnessed by Sir Joshua Reynolds when they were present at an examination of a little blackguard boy, by Mr. Saunders Welch,[2] the late Westminster Justice.

---

1. *Traveled over one another's minds.* "It is now really a long time that we have been writing and writing, and yet how small a part of our minds have we written! We shall meet, I hope, soon, and talk it out." *Johnson in 1777 to Mrs. Thrale.*

2. *Mr. Saunders Welch.* "Johnson told me that he attended Mr. Welch in his office for a whole winter to hear the examination of the culprits." *Boswell.*

Welch, who imagined that he was exalting himself in Dr. Johnson's eyes by using big words, spoke in a manner that was utterly unintelligible to the boy; Dr. Johnson, perceiving it, changed the pompous phraseology into colloquial language. Sir Joshua Reynolds, who was much amused by this procedure, which seemed a kind of reversing of what might be expected from the two men, took notice of it to Dr. Johnson, as they walked away by themselves. Johnson said that it was continually the case; and that he was always obliged to *translate* the Justice's swelling diction (smiling) so as that his meaning might be understood by the vulgar, from whom information was to be obtained.

Sir Joshua once observed to him that he had talked above the capacity of some people with whom they had been in company together. "No matter, sir," said Johnson; "they consider it as a compliment to be talked to as if they were wiser than they are. So true is this, sir, that Baxter made it a rule in every sermon that he preached to say something that was above the capacity of his audience."[1]

However unfavorable to Scotland, he uniformly gave liberal praise to George Buchanan[2] as a writer. In a conversation concerning the literary merits of the two countries, in which Buchanan was introduced, a Scotchman, imagining that on this

---

1. *Capacity of his audience.* "The justness of this remark is confirmed by the following story, for which I am indebted to Lord Eliot: 'A country parson, who was remarkable for quoting scraps of Latin in his sermons, having died, one of his parishioners was asked how he liked his successor. 'He is a very good preacher,' was his answer, 'but no *Latiner*.' " *Boswell*.

"There is no kind of impertinence more justly censurable than his who is always laboring to level thoughts to intellects higher than his own; who apologizes for every word which his own narrowness of converse inclines him to think unusual; keeps the exuberance of his faculties under visible restraint; is solicitous to anticipate inquiries by needless explanations; and endeavors to shade his own abilities lest weak eyes should be dazzled with their luster." *Johnson: The Rambler*.

2. *George Buchanan* (1506-1582). Notable both for the weight of his classical learning and the massive force of his blows against the vices of the court and the clergy. "At the same time, humane and

ground he should have an undoubted triumph over him, exclaimed, "Ah, Dr. Johnson, what would you have said of Buchanan had he been an Englishman?"—"Why, sir," said Johnson, after a little pause, "I should *not* have said of Buchanan, had he been an *Englishman,* what I will now say of him as a *Scotchman*—that he was the only man of genius his country ever produced."

And this brings to my recollection another instance of the same nature. I once reminded him that when Dr. Adam Smith was expatiating on the beauty of Glasgow, he had cut him short by saying, "Pray, sir, have you ever seen Brentford?"[1] and I took the liberty to add, "My dear sir, surely that was *shocking*."—"Why, then, sir," he replied, "*You* have never seen Brentford."

Though his usual phrase for conversation was *talk*, yet he made a distinction; for when he once told me that he dined the day before at a friend's house, with "a very pretty company," and I asked him if there was good conversation, he answered, "No, sir; we had *talk* enough, but no *conversation;* there was nothing *discussed*."

Mr. Hoole[2] told him he was born in Moorfields, and had

---

vindictive, mirthful and morose, cultured and coarse, fond of truth and full of prejudices." *Dictionary of National Biography.* Dr. Johnson seems always to have spoken of him with great respect and in the sleepless hours of his last illness translated Greek epigrams into Latin verse because the dying Buchanan had done so before him.

1. *Brentford.* A notoriously dirty town about eight miles from London.

> "Even so, through Brentford town, a town of mud,
> An herd of bristly swine is pricked along;
> The filthy beasts that never chew the cud
> Still grunt and squeak and sing their troublous song,
> And oft they plunge themselves the mire among;
> But aye the ruthless drover goads them on."
>
> *James Thomson: Castle of Indolence, 1748.*

2. *Hoole.* A clerk who translated Tasso and Ariosto into English verse at the methodical rate of a hundred lines a day. In 1817, Lady Louisa Stuart describes his plaited cambric ruffles, his snuff-colored suit, and his corresponding sobriety of look.

received part of his early instruction in Grub Street.[1] "Sir,"
said Johnson, smiling, "you have been *regularly* educated."
Having asked who was his instructor, and Mr. Hoole having
answered, "My uncle, sir, who was a tailor," Johnson, recollecting himself, said, "Sir, I knew him; we called him the *meta-
physical tailor*. He was of a club in Old Street, with me and
George Psalmanazar,[2] and some others; but pray, sir, was he
a good tailor?" Mr. Hoole having answered that he believed
he was too mathematical, and used to draw squares and tri-
angles on his shopboard, so that he did not excel in the cut of
a coat—"I am sorry for it," said Johnson, "for I would have
every man to be master of his own business."

He said to Sir William Scott, "The age is running mad after
innovation; and all the business of the world is to be done
in a new way; men are to be hanged in a new way; Tyburn[3]
itself is not safe from the fury of innovation." It having been
argued that this was an improvement—"No, sir," said he,
eagerly, "it is *not* an improvement; they object that the old
method drew together a number of spectators. Sir, executions
are intended to draw spectators. If they do not draw spectators, they don't answer their purpose. The old method was
most satisfactory to all parties; the public was gratified by a
procession; the criminal was supported by it. Why is all this
to be swept away?"

Johnson's attention to precision and clearness in expression
was very remarkable. He disapproved of parentheses; and
I believe in all his voluminous writings not half a dozen of
them will be found. He never used the phrases *the former* and
the latter, having observed that they often occasioned obscurity;
he therefore contrived to construct his sentences so as not to
have occasion for them, and would even rather repeat the
same words, in order to avoid them. Nothing is more common than to mistake surnames, when we hear them carelessly

1. *Grub Street.* "Much inhabited by writers of small histories,
dictionaries, and temporary poems; whence any mean production is
called *Grub Street.*" *Johnson: Dictionary.*

2. *George Psalmanazar.* See page 499.

3. *Tyburn.* A public gallows in London. See Introduction.

uttered for the first time. To prevent this, he used not only to pronounce them slowly and distinctly, but to take the trouble of spelling them; a practice which I have often followed, and which I wish were general.

The heterogeneous composition of human nature was remarkably exemplified in Johnson. His liberality in giving his money to persons in distress was extraordinary. Yet there lurked about him a propensity to paltry saving. One day I owned to him that "I was occasionally troubled with a fit of *narrowness.*" "Why, sir," said he, "so am I. *But I do not tell it.*" He has now and then borrowed a shilling of me; and when I asked him for it again, seemed to be rather out of humor. A droll little circumstance once occurred: As if he meant to reprimand my minute exactness as a creditor, he thus addressed me—"Boswell, *lend* me sixpence—*not to be repaid.*"[1]

Though a stern *true-born Englishman*, and fully prejudiced[2] against all other nations, he had discernment enough to see, and candor enough to censure, the cold reserve too common among Englishmen toward strangers: "Sir," said he, "two men of any other nation who are shown into a room together, at a house where they are both visitors, will immediately find some conversation. But two Englishmen will probably go each to a different window, and remain in obstinate silence. Sir, we as yet do not enough understand the common rights of humanity."

Maurice Morgann, Esq., author of the very ingenious "Essay[3] on the character of Falstaff," had once an opportunity of entertaining Johnson for a day or two at Wickham. Johnson,

---

1. *Repaid.* "A shilling was now wanted for some purpose or other; and none of them happened to have one. I begged that I might lend one. 'Aye, do,' said the Doctor, 'I will borrow of you; authors are like privateers, always fair game for one another.'" *Mme. D'Arblay.*

2. *Fully prejudiced.* "To be prejudiced is always to be weak; yet there are prejudices so near to laudable that they have been often praised, and are always pardoned." *Johnson: Taxation No Tyranny.*

3. *Essay.* To prove that Falstaff's persistent determination to save his own skin under all circumstances of danger has in it the virtue of resoluteness rather than the characteristics of timidity; and that it is this fact which justifies us in enjoying his character. The essay contains many penetrating remarks both on Shakespeare and on literary appreciation in general.

for sport perhaps, or from the spirit of contradiction, eagerly maintained that Derrick[1] had merit as a writer. Mr. Morgann argued with him directly, in vain. At length he had recourse to this device. "Pray, sir," said he, "whether do you reckon Derrick or Smart[2] the best poet?" Johnson at once felt himself roused; and answered, "Sir, there is no settling the point of precedency between a louse and a flea."

Once, when checking my boasting[3] too frequently of myself in company, he said to me, "Boswell, you often vaunt so much as to provoke ridicule. You put me in mind of a man who was standing in the kitchen of an inn with his back to the fire, and thus accosted the person next him, 'Do you know, sir, who I am?' 'No, sir,' said the other, 'I have not that advantage.' 'Sir,' said he, 'I am the *great* TWALMLEY[4] who invented the New Floodgate Iron.'"

He was pleased to say to me one morning when we were left alone in his study, "Boswell, I think I am easier with you than with almost anybody."

He would not allow Mr. David Hume any credit for his political principles, though similar to his own; saying of him, "Sir, he was a Tory by chance."[5]

---

1. *Derrick.* For whom "Johnson had a kindness" (see page 76).

2. *Smart.* Who drank himself mad and had to scrawl his masterpiece on the walls of his cell (see page 82). According to one account, the second writer was *Boyse*, not Smart—a man who repawned his clothes as fast as his friends redeemed them and might "spend his last guinea on truffles and mushrooms."

3. *My boasting.* In his *Boswelliana,* Boswell is his own Johnson. He writes in one passage: "Boswell said that a dull fool was nothing, as he never showed himself. The great thing is to have your fool well furnished with animal spirits and conceit and he'll display you a rich fund of risibility."

4. *Twalmley.* "What the *great* TWALMLEY was so proud of having invented was neither more nor less than a kind of box-iron for smoothing linen." *Boswell.*

5. *By chance.* More of this speech is quoted in Boswell's *Journal of a Tour to the Hebrides.* "Sir, he was a Tory by chance, as being a Scotchman, but not upon a principle of duty; for he has no principle."

"My views of *things* are more conformable to Whig principles; my representations of *persons* to Tory prejudices." *Hume.*

Somewhere Hume advises a young skeptic to continue his profession

His acute observation of human life made him remark, "Sir, there is nothing by which a man exasperates most people more than by displaying a superior ability or brilliancy in conversation. They seem pleased at the time; but their envy makes them curse him at their hearts."

Johnson asked Richard Owen Cambridge,[1] Esq., if he had read the Spanish translation of Sallust, said to be written by a Prince of Spain, with the assistance of his tutor, who is professedly the author of a treatise annexed, on the Phœnician language. Mr. Cambridge said he was disappointed in the purpose for which he borrowed the book; to see whether a Spaniard could be better furnished with inscriptions from monuments, coins, or other antiquities, which he might more probably find on a coast so immediately opposite to Carthage, than the antiquaries of any other countries. JOHNSON. "I am very sorry you were not gratified in your expectations." CAMBRIDGE. "The language would have been of little use, as there is no history existing in that tongue to balance the partial accounts which the Roman writers have left us." JOHNSON. "No, sir. They have not been *partial;* they have told their own story without shame or regard to equitable treatment of their injured enemy; they had no compunction, no feeling for a Carthaginian. Why, sir, they would never have borne Virgil's description of Æneas's treatment of Dido, if she had not been a Carthaginian."

Johnson's love of little children, which he discovered* upon

as a clergyman with the words: "It is putting too great a respect on the vulgar and on their superstitions to pique one's self on sincerity with regard to them. Did ever one make a point of honor to speak truth to children or madmen? The ecclesiastical profession only adds a little more to an innocent dissimulation or rather simulation, without which it is impossible to pass through the world." Yet it is well to note that no one had any doubt as to Hume's skepticism regarding the doctrines of Christianity.

1. *Cambridge.* "I admire him more and more, and think that all that is formal in him wears off upon acquaintance, and all that is pleasant grows more and more conspicuous. But he behaves to me with a kind of deference, as you would listen to Dr. Johnson, and leans forward with an air of respect that, from a man such as him, half petrifies me." *Mme. D'Arblay, 1783.*

all occasions, calling them "pretty dears," and giving them sweetmeats, was an undoubted proof of the real humanity and gentleness of his disposition.

His uncommon kindness to his servants, and serious concern, not only for their comfort in this world, but their happiness in the next, was another unquestionable evidence of what all who were intimately acquainted with him knew to be true.

Nor would it be just, under this head, to omit the fondness which he showed for animals which he had taken under his protection. I never shall forget the indulgence with which he treated Hodge, his cat; for whom he himself used to go out and buy oysters, lest the servants, having that trouble, should take a dislike to the poor creature. I am, unluckily, one of those who have an antipathy to a cat, so that I am uneasy when in the room with one; and I own I frequently suffered a good deal from the presence of this same Hodge. I recollect him one day scrambling up Dr. Johnson's breast, apparently with much satisfaction, while my friend, smiling and half-whistling, rubbed down his back and pulled him by the tail; and when I observed he was a fine cat, saying, "Why, yes, sir, but I have had cats whom I liked better than this"; and then, as if perceiving Hodge to be out of countenance, adding, "but he is a very fine cat, a very fine cat indeed."

This reminds me of the ludicrous account which he gave Mr. Langton, of the despicable state of a young gentleman of good family. "Sir, when I heard of him last, he was running about town shooting cats." And then in a sort of kindly reverie, he bethought himself of his own favorite cat, and said, "But Hodge shan't be shot; no, no, Hodge shall not be shot."

He thought Mr. Beauclerk made a shrewd and judicious remark to Mr. Langton, who, after having been for the first time in company with a well-known wit about town, was warmly admiring and praising him—"See him again," said Beauclerk.

His respect for the Hierarchy, and particularly the Dignitaries of the Church, has been more than once exhibited in the course of this work. Mr. Seward saw him presented to the

Archbishop of York, and described his *bow to an* Archbishop as such a studied elaboration of homage, such an extension of limb, such a flexion of body, as have seldom or ever been equaled.

On Thursday, April 10, I introduced to him at his house in Bolt Court the Honorable and Reverend William Stuart, son of the Earl of Bute. After some compliments on both sides, the tour to the Hebrides was mentioned. JOHNSON. "I got an acquisition of more ideas by it than by anything that I remember. I saw quite a different system of life." BOSWELL. "You would not like to make the same journey again?" JOHNSON. "Why, no, sir, not the same; it is a tale told."

BOSWELL. "This has been a factious reign, owing to the great indulgence of Government." JOHNSON. "*I* think so, sir. What at first was lenity grew timidity. Yet this is reasoning *a posteriori*, and may not be just. Supposing a few had at first been punished, I believe faction would have been crushed; but it might have been said that it was a sanguinary reign. A man cannot tell *a priori* what will be best for Government to do. This reign has been very unfortunate. We have had an unsuccessful war; but that does not prove that we have been ill governed. One side or other must prevail in war, as one or other must win at play. When we beat Louis, we were not better governed; nor were the French better governed when Louis beat us."

On Saturday, April 12, I visited him, in company with Mr. Windham,[1] of Norfolk, whom, though a Whig, he highly valued. One of the best things he ever said was to this gentleman, who, before he set out for Ireland as Secretary to Lord Northington, when Lord Lieutenant, expressed to the Sage some modest and virtuous doubts whether he could bring himself to practice those arts which it is supposed a person in that situation has occasion to employ. "Don't be afraid, sir," said

---

1. *Mr. Windham.* The famous William Windham, a man of strong religious convictions and great integrity of character. Even his violent changes in political views which earned him the nickname of *Weathercock*, did nothing to impair his force of mind or his decisiveness in its expression.

Johnson, with a pleasant smile, "you will soon make a very pretty rascal."[1]

Mr. Lowe, the painter, who was with him, was very much distressed that a large picture[2] which he had painted was refused to be received into the Exhibition of the Royal Academy. He gave Mr. Lowe the following, of which I was diligent enough, with his permission, to take copies at the next coffee-house, while Mr. Windham was so good as to stay by me.

"To Sir Joshua Reynolds.

"SIR: Mr. Lowe considers himself as cut off from all credit and all hope by the rejection of his picture from the Exhibition. Upon this work he has exhausted all his powers, and suspended all his expectations; and, certainly, to be refused an opportunity of taking the opinion of the public is in itself a very great hardship. It is to be condemned without a trial.

"If you could procure the revocation of this incapacitating edict, you would deliver an unhappy man from great affliction.

---

1. *Pretty rascal.* "I have no great timidity in my own disposition, and am no encourager of it in others. Never be afraid to think yourself fit for anything for which your friends think you fit. *You will become an able negotiator—a very pretty rascal." Johnson, as quoted in Windham's Diary.* "He [Johnson] had one piece of advice earnestly to impress upon me, that I would set apart every seventh day for the care of my soul. He then told me that he had a request to make of me: namely, that I would allow his servant Frank to look up to me as his friend, adviser, and protector. Having obtained my assent to this, he proposed that Frank should be called in, and desiring me to take him by the hand in token of the promise, repeated before him the recommendation he had just made of him, and the promise I had given to attend to it." *Windham's diary for Dec. 7, 1783, six days before Johnson's death.*

2. *A large picture.* According to Sir James Northcote the painter, "execrable beyond belief" and therefore placed in a room by itself. The painter was a coarse, brazen fellow. His quarters have been described as "all dirt and filth" and his children as "squalling and wrangling brats." But Dr. Johnson occasionally had him in for a quiet meal, gave him some friendly advice, sometimes begged money or sittings for him, was godfather to one of his daughters, and once, at least, had her repeat the Lord's Prayer while seated on his knee. Some of Lowe's drawings, it is said, though over violent, display genuine power.

The Council has sometimes reversed its own determination; and I hope that by your interposition this luckless picture may be got admitted.

"I am, &c.,

"SAM. JOHNSON.

"April 12, 1783."

"To Mr. Barry.

"SIR: Mr. Lowe's exclusion from the exhibition gives him more trouble than you and the other gentlemen of the Council could imagine or intend. He considers disgrace and ruin as the inevitable consequence of your determination.

"He says that some pictures have been received after rejection; and if there be any such precedent, I earnestly entreat that you will use your interest in his favor. Of his work I can say nothing; I pretend not to judge of painting; and this picture I never saw; but I conceive it extremely hard to shut out any man from the possibility of success; and therefore I repeat my request that you will propose the reconsideration of Mr. Lowe's case; and if there be any among the Council with whom my name can have any weight, be pleased to communicate to them the desire of, sir,

"Your most humble servant,

"SAM. JOHNSON.

"April 12, 1783."

Such intercession was too powerful to be resisted; and Mr. Lowe's performance was admitted at Somerset Place. The subject, as I recollect, was the Deluge, at that point of time when the water was verging to the top of the last uncovered mountain. Near to the spot was seen the last of the antediluvian race exclusive of those who were saved in the ark of Noah. This was one of those giants, then the inhabitants of the earth, who had still strength to swim, and with one of his hands held aloft his infant child. Upon the small remaining dry spot appeared a famished lion, ready to spring at the child and devour it.

On April 18, being Good Friday, I found him at breakfast, in his usual manner upon that day, drinking tea without milk, and eating a cross-bun to prevent faintness; we went to St. Clement's church, as formerly. When we came home from church, he placed himself on one of the stone seats at his garden door, and I took the other, and thus in the open air, and in a placid frame of mind, he talked away very easily. JOHNSON. "Were I a country gentleman, I should not be very hospitable; I should not have crowds in my house." BOSWELL. "Sir Alexander Dick[1] tells me that he remembers having a thousand people in a year to dine at his house; that is, reckoning each person as one, each time that he dined there." JOHNSON. "That, sir, is about three a day." BOSWELL. "How your statement lessens the idea." JOHNSON. "That, sir, is the good of counting. It brings everything to a certainty, which before floated in the mind indefinitely." BOSWELL. "But *Omne ignotum pro magnifico est:* one is sorry to have this diminished." JOHNSON. "Sir, you should not allow yourself to be delighted with error." BOSWELL. "Three a day seem but few." JOHNSON. "Nay, sir, he who entertains three a day does very liberally. And if there is a large family, the poor entertain those three, for they eat what the poor would get; there must be superfluous meat; it must be given to the poor, or thrown out." BOSWELL. "I observe in London that the poor go about and gather bones, which I understand are manufactured." JOHNSON. "Yes, sir, they boil them, and extract a grease from them for greasing wheels and other purposes. Of the best pieces they make a mock ivory, which is used for hafts to knives, and various other things; the coarser pieces they burn, and pound, and sell the ashes." BOSWELL. "For what purpose, sir?" JOHNSON. "Why, sir, for making a furnace for the chymists for melting iron. A paste made of burnt bones will stand a stronger heat than anything else. Consider, sir; if you are to melt iron, you cannot line your pot with brass, because it is softer than iron, and would melt sooner;

---

1. *Sir Alexander Dick.* At his fine country estate, just a mile from Edinburgh, Sir Alexander had entertained Johnson and Boswell in 1771.

nor with iron, for though malleable iron is harder than cast iron, yet it would not do; but a paste of burnt bones will not melt." BOSWELL. "Do you know, sir, I have discovered a manufacture to a great extent, of what you only piddle at—scraping and drying the peel of oranges. At a place in Newgate Street there is a prodigious quantity prepared, which they sell to the distillers." JOHNSON. "Sir, I believe they make a higher thing out of them than a spirit; they make what is called orange-butter, the oil of the orange inspissated, which they mix perhaps with common pomatum, and make it fragrant. The oil does not fly off in the drying."

BOSWELL. "I wish to have a good walled* garden." JOHNSON "I don't think it would be worth the expense to you. We compute[1] in England a park wall at a thousand pounds a mile; now a garden wall must cost at least as much. You intend your trees should grow higher than a deer will leap. Now let us see; for a hundred pounds you could only have forty-four square yards, which is very little; for two hundred pounds, you may have eighty-four square yards, which is very well. But when will you get the value of two hundred pounds of walls, in fruit, in your climate? No, sir, such contention with Nature is not worth while. I would plant an orchard, and have plenty of such fruit as ripen well in your country. My friend, Dr. Madden, of Ireland, said that, 'in an orchard there should be enough to eat, enough to lay up, enough to be stolen, and enough to rot upon the ground.' Cherries are an early fruit; you may have them; and you may have the early apples and pears." BOSWELL. "We cannot have nonpareils." JOHNSON. "Sir, you can no more have nonpareils than you can have grapes." BOSWELL. "We have them, sir; but they are very bad." JOHNSON. "Nay, sir, never try to have a thing merely to show that you *cannot* have it." BOSWELL. "Is not a good garden a very common thing in England, sir?" JOHNSON. "Not so common, sir, as you imagine." BOSWELL. "Has Lang-

---

1. *Compute.* "When Mr. Johnson felt his fancy disordered, his constant recurrence was to arithmetic." *Mrs. Piozzi.* Birkbeck Hill notes an error which must have occurred either in Johnson's calculations regarding this wall or in Boswell's report of them.

ton no orchard?" JOHNSON. "No, sir." BOSWELL. "How
so, sir?" JOHNSON. "Why, sir, from the general negligence
of the county. He has it not, because nobody else has it."

Mr. Walker, the celebrated master of elocution, came in,
and then we went upstairs into the study. Talking of the
origin of language—JOHNSON. "It must have come by inspiration. A thousand, nay, a million of children could not invent
a language. While the organs are pliable, there is not understanding enough to form a language; by the time that there
is understanding enough, the organs are become stiff. We
know that after a certain age we cannot learn to pronounce a
new language. No foreigner who comes to England when
advanced in life ever pronounces English tolerably well; at
least such instances are very rare. When I maintain that
language must have come by inspiration, I do not mean that
inspiration is required for rhetoric, and all the beauties of
language; for when once man has language, we can conceive
that he may gradually form modifications of it. I mean only
that inspiration seems to me to be necessary to give man the
faculty of speech; to inform him that he may have speech;
which I think he could no more find out without inspiration
than cows or hogs would think of such a faculty."

He talked of Dr. Dodd. "A friend of mine," said he, "came
to me and told me that a lady wished to have Dr. Dodd's
picture in a bracelet, and asked me for a motto. I said I
could think of no better than *Currat Lex*. I was very willing
to have him pardoned, that is, to have the sentence changed to
transportation; but, when he was once hanged, I did not
wish he should be made a saint."

Mrs. Burney, wife of his friend Dr. Burney, came in, and he
seemed to be entertained with her conversation.

Garrick's funeral[1] was talked of as extravagantly expensive.
Johnson, from his dislike to exaggeration, would not allow that
it was distinguished by any extraordinary pomp. "Were there

---

1. *Garrick's Funeral.* "A more magnificent funeral was never seen
in London." *Arthur Murphy: Life of Garrick.* "Poor Garrick's funeral
expenses are yet unpaid, though the undertaker is broken [bankrupt]."
Johnson to Mrs. Thrale, 1782.

not six horses to each coach?" said Mrs. Burney. JOHNSON. "Madam, there were no more six horses than six phœnixes."

Mrs. Burney wondered that some very beautiful new buildings should be erected in Moorfields, in so shocking a situation as between Bedlam and St. Luke's Hospital; and said she could not live there. JOHNSON. "Nay, madam, you see nothing there to hurt you. You no more think of madness by having windows that look to Bedlam than you think of death by having windows that look to a churchyard." MRS. BURNEY. "We may look to a churchyard, sir; for it is right that we should be kept in mind of death." JOHNSON. "Nay, madam, if you go to that, it is right that we should be kept in mind of madness, which is occasioned by too much indulgence of imagination. I think a very moral use may be made of these new buildings: I would have those who have heated imaginations live there, and take warning."

Time passed on in conversation till it was too late for the service of the church at three o'clock. I took a walk, and left him alone for some time; then returned, and we had coffee and conversation again by ourselves.

I stated the character of a noble friend of mine, as a curious case for his opinion—"He is the most inexplicable man to me that I ever knew. Can you explain him, sir? He is, I really believe, noble-minded, generous, and princely. But his most intimate friends may be separated from him for years, without his ever asking a question concerning them. He will meet them with a formality, a coldness, a stately indifference; but when they come close to him, and fairly engage him in conversation, they find him as easy, pleasant, and kind as they could wish. One then supposes that what is so agreeable will soon be renewed; but stay away from him for half a year, and he will neither call on you nor send to inquire about you." JOHNSON. "Why, sir, I cannot ascertain his character exactly, as I do not know him; but I should not like to have such a man for my friend. He may love study, and wish not to be interrupted by his friends. He may be a frivolous man, and be so much occupied with petty pursuits that he may not want friends. Or he may have a notion that there is a dignity in appearing indifferent, while he in fact may not be more indifferent at his heart than another." We went to evening prayers at St. Clement's, at seven, and then parted.

On Sunday, April 20, being Easter Day, after attending solemn service at St. Paul's, I came to Dr. Johnson, and found Mr. Lowe the painter sitting with him. Mr. Lowe mentioned the great number of new buildings of late in London, yet that Dr. Johnson had observed that the number of inhabitants was not increased. BOSWELL. "I believe, sir, a great many of the children born in London die early." JOHNSON. "Why, yes, sir." BOSWELL. "But those who do live are as stout and strong people as any; Dr. Price[1] says they must be naturally strong to get through." JOHNSON. "That is system, sir. A great traveler observes that it is said there are no weak or deformed people among the Indians; but he with much sagacity assigns the reason of this, which is that the hardship of their lives as hunters and fishers does not allow weak or diseased children to grow up. Now had I been an Indian, I must have died early; my eyes would not have served me to get food. I must have starved, or they would have knocked me on the head when they saw I could do nothing." BOSWELL. "Perhaps they would have taken care of you; we are told they are fond of oratory—you would have talked to them." JOHNSON. "Nay, sir, I should not have lived long enough to be fit to talk; I should have been dead before I was ten years old. Depend upon it, sir, a savage, when he is hungry, will not carry about with him a looby of nine years old who cannot help himself. They have no affection, sir." BOSWELL. "I believe natural affection, of which we hear so much, is very small." JOHNSON. "Sir, natural affection is nothing; but affection from principle and established duty is sometimes wonderfully strong." BOSWELL. "But some of the Indians have affection." JOHNSON. "Sir, that they help some of their children is plain; for some of them live, which they could not do without being helped."

---

1. *Dr. Price*, Richard (1723-91). A notable Unitarian minister and extreme radical in politics and economics; on these accounts obnoxious to Dr. Johnson.

Having next day gone to Mr. Burke's seat in the country, from whence I was recalled by an express* that a near relation[1] of mine had killed his antagonist in a duel, and was himself dangerously wounded, I saw little of Dr. Johnson till Monday, April 28, when I spent a considerable part of the day with him, and introduced the subject which then chiefly occupied my mind. JOHNSON. "I do not see, sir, that fighting is absolutely forbidden in Scripture; I see revenge forbidden, but not self-defense." BOSWELL. "The Quakers say it is: 'Unto him that smiteth thee on one cheek, offer him also the other.'" JOHNSON. "But stay, sir; the text is meant only to have the effect of moderating passion; it is plain that we are not to take it in a literal sense. We see this from the context, where there are other recommendations, which I warrant you the Quaker will not take literally; as, for instance, 'From him that would borrow of thee, turn thou not away.' Let a man whose credit is bad, come to a Quaker, and say, 'Well, sir, lend me a hundred pounds'; he'll find him as unwilling as any other man. No, sir, a man may shoot the man who invades his character, as he may shoot him who attempts to break into his house.[2] So

---

1. *Near relation.* A third cousin.
2. *Into his house.* "In my *Journal of a Tour to the Hebrides* (Oct. 24) it appears that he made this frank confession: 'Nobody at times talks more laxly than I do,' and (Sept. 19), 'He fairly owned he could not explain the rationality of dueling.' We may therefore infer that he could not think that justifiable which is so inconsistent with the spirit of the Gospel. At the same time it must be confessed that from the prevalent notions of honor, a gentleman who receives a challenge is reduced to a dreadful alternative. A remarkable instance of this is furnished by a clause in the will of the late Colonel Thomas of the Guards, written the night before he fell in a duel, September 3, 1783: 'In the first place I commit my soul to Almighty God, in hopes of his mercy and pardon for the irreligious step I now (in compliance with the unwarrantable customs of this wicked world) put myself under the necessity of taking.'" *Boswell.* Boswell's assumption in this note that dueling is contrary to Scripture, Johnson has just taken pains to deny. Nor is there anything in either Johnson's works or his conversation to make one suppose that he would accept Boswell's other calm assumption that rational conduct is always the finest conduct of which a man is capable.

in 1745,* my friend, Tom Cumming[1] the Quaker, said he would not fight, but he would drive an ammunition cart; and we know that the Quakers have sent flannel waistcoats to our soldiers to enable them to fight better." BOSWELL. "When a man is the aggressor, and by ill-usage forces on a duel in which he is killed, have we not little ground to hope that he is gone into a state of happiness?" JOHNSON. "Sir, we are not to judge determinately of the state in which a man leaves this life. He may in a moment have repented effectually, and it is possible may have been accepted of God. There is in *Camden's Remains* an epitaph upon a very wicked man who was killed by a fall from his horse, in which he is supposed to say

> Between the stirrup and the ground,
> I mercy asked, I mercy found.

We talked of the accusation against a gentleman for supposed delinquencies in India.[2] JOHNSON. "What foundation there is for accusation I know not, but they will not get at him. Where bad actions are committed at so great a distance, a delinquent can obscure the evidence till the scent becomes cold; therefore all distant power is bad. I am clear that the best plan for the government of India is a despotic governor;

---

1. *Tom Cumming.* The African trader and "fighting Quaker," who, under Lord Chatham, engineered a British military expedition against French rival traders and was grievously surprised that any bloodshed ensued. He expected to accomplish his purpose by "bluff."
"There was once a pretty good tavern in Catherine Street in the Strand, where very good company met in an evening and each man called for his own half pint of wine. The house furnished no supper, but a woman attended with mutton pies which anybody might purchase. I was introduced to this company by Cumming the Quaker." *Johnson in Boswell's Journal of a Tour to the Hebrides.*
2. *In India.* Six days before, the reputation of Warren Hastings, Governor of Bengal, had been attacked in Parliament and his recall demanded. His impeachment for corruption and cruelty did not occur until 1788. "I live in a reciprocation of civilities with Mr. H.," Johnson wrote in 1776 to one anxious to discredit Hastings in England, "and therefore cannot properly diffuse a narrative intended to bring upon him the censure of the public."

for if he be a good man, it is evidently the best government; and supposing him to be a bad man, it is better to have one plunderer than many. A governor whose power is checked lets others plunder, that he himself may be allowed to plunder; but if despotic, he sees that the more he lets others plunder, the less there will be for himself, so he restrains them; and though he himself plunders, the country is a gainer, compared with being plundered by numbers."

Upon being told that old Mr. Sheridan, indignant at the neglect of his oratorical plans, had threatened to go to America:[1] JOHNSON. "I hope he will go to America." BOSWELL. "The Americans don't want oratory." JOHNSON. "But we can want Sheridan."

On Tuesday,[2] April 29, I found him at home in the morning, and Mr. Seward with him. Horace having been mentioned: BOSWELL. "There is a great deal of thinking in his works. One finds there almost everything but religion." SEWARD. "He speaks of his returning to it, in his ode[3] *Parcus deorum cultor et infrequens.*" JOHNSON. "Sir, he was not in earnest; this was merely poetical." BOSWELL. "There are, I am afraid, many people who have no religion at all." SEWARD. "And sensible people too." JOHNSON. "Why, sir, not sensible in that respect. There must be either a natural or a moral stupidity, if one lives in a total neglect of so very important a concern." SEWARD. "I wonder that there should be people without religion." JOHNSON. "Sir, you need not wonder at this, when you consider how large a proportion of almost every man's life is passed without thinking of it. I myself was for

---

1. *Go to America.* "I started the subject of emigration. JOHNSON. 'To a man of mere animal life you can urge no argument against going to America but that it will be some time before he will get the earth to produce. But a man of any intellectual enjoyment will not easily go and immerse himself and his posterity for ages in barbarism.'" *Boswell: Journal of a Tour to the Hebrides.*

2. *Tuesday.* In Boswell's original, Monday, which is evidently a slip.

3. *Ode.* "A thunder clap in a clear sky has converted Horace from his youthful belief that the gods 'lie beside their nectar, careless of mankind.' Lessing discusses this ode and sensibly decides that it is the half playful record of a poetical mood." *Shorey and Laing.*

some years totally regardless of religion. It had dropped out of my mind. It was at an early part of my life. Sickness brought it back, and I hope I have never lost it since." BOSWELL. "My dear sir, what a man you must have been without religion! Why you must have gone on drinking and swearing." JOHNSON (with a smile). "I drank enough and swore enough, to be sure." SEWARD. "One should think that sickness, and the view of death, would make more men religious." JOHNSON. "Sir, they do not know how to go about it; they have not the first notion. A man who has never had religion before, no more grows religious when he is sick than a man who has never learnt figures can count when he has need of calculation."

I mentioned Dr. Johnson's excellent distinction between liberty of conscience and liberty of teaching. JOHNSON. "Consider, sir; if you have children whom you wish to educate in the principles of the Church of England, and there comes a Quaker who tries to pervert them to his principles, you would drive away the Quaker. You would not trust to the predomination of right which you believe is in your opinions; you would keep wrong out of their heads. Now the vulgar* are the children of the State. If anyone attempts to teach them doctrines contrary to what the State approves, the magistrate may and ought to restrain him." SEWARD. "Would you restrain private conversation, sir?" JOHNSON. "Why, sir, it is difficult to say where private conversation begins, and where it ends. If we three should discuss even the great question concerning the existence of a Supreme Being by ourselves, we should not be restrained; for that would be to put an end to all improvement. But if we should discuss it in the presence of ten boarding-school girls, and as many boys, I think the magistrate would do well to put us in the stocks, to finish the debate there."

Lord Hailes had sent him a present of a curious little printed poem, on repairing the University of Aberdeen, by David *Malloch*, which he thought would please Johnson, as affording clear evidence that Mallet had appeared even as a literary character by the name of *Malloch;* his changing which to one of softer sound had given Johnson occasion to introduce him into his Dictionary, under the article *Alias*.[1] Johnson having read aloud from the beginning of it, where there were some commonplace assertions as to the superiority of ancient times: "How false," said he, "is all this, to say that in ancient times learning was not a disgrace to a peer, as it is now. In ancient times a peer was as ignorant as anyone else. He would have been angry to have it thought he could write his name. Men in ancient times dared to stand forth with a degree of ignorance with which nobody would dare now to stand forth. I am always angry when I hear ancient times praised at the expense of modern times. There is now a great deal more learning in the world than there was formerly; for it is universally diffused. You have, perhaps, no man who knows as much Greek and Latin as Bentley; no man who knows as much mathematics as Newton; but you have many more men who know Greek and Latin, and who know mathematics."

On Thursday, May 1, I visited him in the evening along with young Mr. Burke. He said, "It is strange that there should be so little reading in the world, and so much writing. People in general do not willingly read, if they can have anything else to amuse them. There must be an external impulse—emulation, or vanity, or avarice. The progress which the understanding makes through a book has more pain than pleasure in it.—It has been said there is pleasure in writing, particularly in writing verses. I allow you may have pleasure from writing, after it is over, if you have written well; but you don't go willingly to it again. I know when I have been writing verses, I have run my finger down the margin to see how many I had made, and how few I had to make."[2]

---

1. *Alias.* "A Latin word signifying otherwise; as, Mallet, *alias* Malloch, that is, *otherwise* Malloch." *Johnson: Dictionary, Abridged Ed., 1756.* Mallet is said to have changed his name for purposes of euphony and, though somewhat shabby morally, was hardly of the sort which can be said to use *aliases.*

2. *I had to make.* "Composition is, for the most part, an effort of slow diligence and steady perseverance, to which the mind is dragged by necessity or resolution, and from which the attention is every moment starting to more delightful amusements." *Johnson, quoted by Birkbeck Hill.*

I have no minute of any interview with Johnson till Thursday, May 15th, when I find what follows: BOSWELL. "I wish much to be in Parliament, sir." JOHNSON. "Why, sir, unless you come resolved to support any administration, you would be the worse for being in Parliament, because you would be obliged to live more expensively." BOSWELL. "Perhaps, sir, I should be the less happy for being in Parliament. I never would sell my vote, and I should be vexed if things went wrong." JOHNSON. "That's cant, sir. It would not vex you more in the house than in the gallery; public affairs vex no man." BOSWELL. "Have not they vexed yourself a little, sir? Have not you been vexed by all the turbulence of this reign, and by that absurd vote of the House of Commons, 'That the influence of the Crown has increased, is increasing, and ought to be diminished?'" JOHNSON. "Sir, I have never slept an hour less nor eat an ounce less meat. I would have knocked the factious dogs on the head, to be sure; but I was not *vexed*." BOSWELL. "I declare, sir, upon my honor, I did imagine I was vexed, and took a pride in it; but it *was*, perhaps, cant; for I own I neither ate less nor slept less." JOHNSON. "My dear friend, clear your *mind* of cant. You may *talk* as other people do; you may say to a man, 'Sir, I am your most humble servant.' You are *not* his most humble servant. You may say, 'These are bad times; it is a melancholy thing to be reserved to such times.' You don't mind the times. You tell a man, 'I am sorry you had such bad weather the last day of your journey, and were so much wet.' You don't care sixpence whether he is wet or dry. You may *talk* in this manner; it is a mode of talking[1] in society; but don't *think* foolishly."

I talked of living in the country. JOHNSON. "Don't set up for what is called hospitality. If your house be like an

---

1. *Mode of talking.* "Part of Dr. Johnson's character for rudeness of manners must be put to the account of his scrupulous adherence to truth. His obstinate silence whilst all the company were in raptures, vying with each other who should pepper highest, was considered as rudeness or ill nature." *Reynolds.* "The shame is to impose words for ideas upon ourselves or others." *Johnson, quoted by Birkbeck Hill.*

inn, nobody cares for you. A man who stays a week with another makes him a slave for a week." BOSWELL. "But there are people, sir, who make their houses a home to their guests, and are themselves quite easy." JOHNSON. "Then, sir, home must be the same to the guests, and they need not come."

On Saturday, May 17, I saw him for a short time. Having mentioned that I had that morning been with old Mr. Sheridan, he remembered their former intimacy with a cordial warmth, and said to me, "Tell Mr. Sheridan I shall be glad to see him, and shake hands with him." BOSWELL. "It is to me very wonderful that resentment should be kept up so long." JOHNSON. "Why, sir, it is not altogether resentment that he does not visit me; it is partly falling out of the habit—partly disgust, such as one has at a drug that has made him sick. Besides, he knows that I laugh at his oratory."[1]

Another day I spoke of one of our friends, of whom he, as well as I, had a very high opinion. He expatiated in his praise; but added, "Sir, he is a cursed Whig, a *bottomless* Whig, as they all are now."

I mentioned my expectations from the interest of an eminent person then in power; adding, "but I have no claim but the claim of friendship; however, some people will go a great way from that motive." JOHNSON. "Sir, they will go all the way from that motive." A gentleman talked of retiring. "Never think of that," said Johnson. The gentleman urged, "I should then do no ill." JOHNSON. "Nor no good either. Sir, it would be a civil suicide."

On Monday, May 26, I found him at tea. I asked whether a man naturally virtuous, or one who has overcome wicked inclinations, is the best. JOHNSON. "I would rather trust my money to a man who has no hands, and so a physical impossibility to steal, than to a man of the most honest principles. There is a witty satirical story of Foote. He had a small bust of Garrick placed upon his bureau. 'You may be sur-

---

1. *I laugh at his oratory.* As when Johnson called his writings "a continual renovation of hope and an unvaried succession of disappointments," or said: "If we should have a bad harvest this year, Mr. Sheridan would say: 'It was owing to the neglect of oratory.'"

prised,' said he, 'that I allow him to be so near my gold—but you will observe, he has no hands.' "

On Friday, May 29, being to set out for Scotland next morning, I passed a part of the day with him in more than usual earnestness; as his health was in a more precarious state than at any time when I had parted from him. He, however, was quick and lively and critical, as usual. I mentioned one who was a very learned man. JOHNSON. "Yes, sir, he has a great deal of learning; but it never lies straight. There is never one idea by the side of another; 'tis all entangled; and then he drives it so awkwardly upon conversation!"

I stated to him an anxious thought, by which a sincere Christian might be disturbed. Suppose a man who has led a good life for seven years commits an act of wickedness, and instantly dies; will his former good life have any effect in his favor? JOHNSON. "Sir, if a man has led a good life for seven years, and then is hurried by passion to do what is wrong, and is suddenly carried off, depend upon it he will have the reward of his seven years' good life; God will not take a catch of him. Upon this principle Richard Baxter[1] believes that a suicide may be saved. 'If,' says he, 'it should be objected that what I maintain may encourage suicide, I answer, I am not to tell a lie to prevent it.' " BOSWELL. "But does not the text say, 'As the tree falls, so it must lie'?" JOHNSON. "Yes, sir, as the tree falls; but (after a little pause) that is meant as to the general state of the tree, not what is the effect of a sudden blast." The common notion, therefore, seems to be erroneous; and Shenstone's witty remark on divines trying to give the tree a jerk upon a death-bed, to make it lie favorably, is not well founded.

He said, "Get as much force of mind as you can. Live within your income. Always have something saved at the end of the year. Let your imports be more than your exports, and you'll never go far wrong."

---

1. *Richard Baxter*. A Puritan divine of the seventeenth century who, though a dissenter, roused Johnson's thorough admiration. When Boswell asked what of Baxter's works he should read, Johnson replied, "They are all good"—all being no less than 20,000 printed pages.

He embraced me, and gave me his blessing, as usual when I was leaving him for any length of time. I walked from his door today with a fearful apprehension of what might happen before I returned.

My anxious apprehensions at parting with him this year proved to be but too well founded; for not long afterwards he had a dreadful stroke of the palsy, of which there are very full and accurate accounts in letters written by himself to show with what composure of mind, and resignation to the Divine Will, his steady piety enabled him to behave.

"To Mr. Edmund Allen.

"DEAR SIR: It has pleased God, this morning, to deprive me of the powers of speech; and as I do not know but that it may be his further good pleasure to deprive me soon of my senses, I request you will, on the receipt of this note, come to me, and act for me, as the exigencies of my case may require.

　　　　　　　　　　　　　　　"I am, sincerely yours,
"June 17, 1783."　　　　　　　　　　　　　　　"SAM. JOHNSON.

Two days after this he wrote[1] to Mrs. Thrale:

　　　　　　　　　　　　　["Bolt Court,[2] Fleet Street,
　　　　　　　　　　　　　　　"June 19, 1783.

"DEAR MADAM: I am sitting down in no cheerful solitude to write a narrative which would once have affected you with tenderness and sorrow, but which you will perhaps pass over now with the careless glance of frigid indifference. For this diminution of regard, however, I know not whether I ought to

---

1. *He wrote.* In his diary for April 5, Johnson, fearing her possible marriage with Signor Piozzi, had written: "I took leave of Mrs. Thrale. I was much moved. I had some expostulations with her. She said she was likewise affected." He wrote her on May 8: "My health in its present humor promises to mend, and I, in my present humor, promise to take care of it, and if we both keep our words, we may yet have a brush at the cobwebs in the sky." On June 5: "Why do you write so seldom?"

2. *Bolt Court.* In this letter, the passages in brackets I have inserted from the full text of the letter as printed by Birkbeck Hill in his edition of Johnson's correspondence. *Editor.*

blame you, who may have reasons which I cannot know, and I do not blame myself, who have for a great part of human life done you what good I could, and have never done you evil.]

"On Monday, the 16th, I sat for my picture, and walked a considerable way with little inconvenience. In the afternoon and evening I felt myself light and easy, and began to plan schemes of life. Thus I went to bed, and in a short time waked and sat up, as has long been my custom, when I felt a confusion and indistinctness in my head, which lasted, I suppose, about half a minute. I was alarmed, and prayed God that however he might afflict my body, he would spare my understanding. This prayer, that I might try the integrity of my faculties, I made in Latin verse. The lines were not very good, but I knew them not to be very good; I made them easily, and concluded myself to be unimpaired in my faculties.

"Soon after, I perceived that I had suffered a paralytic stroke, and that my speech was taken from me. I had no pain, and so little dejection in this dreadful state that I wondered at my own apathy, and considered that perhaps death itself, when it should come, would excite less horror than seems now to attend it.

"In order to rouse the vocal organs, I took two drams. Wine has been celebrated for the production of eloquence. I put myself into violent motion, and I think repeated it; but all was vain. I then went to bed, and strange as it may seem, I think, slept. When I saw light, it was time to contrive what I should do. Though God stopped my speech, he left me my hand; I enjoyed a mercy which was not granted to my dear friend Lawrence,[1] who now perhaps overlooks me as I am writing, and rejoices that I have what he wanted. My first note was necessarily to my servant, who came in talking, and could not immediately comprehend why he should read what I put into his hands.

"I then wrote a card to Mr. Allen, that I might have a

---

1. *Lawrence.* Dr. Lawrence, who had died a few days before. "The palsy had deprived him of the power of writing some time before his death." *Birkbeck Hill.*

discreet friend at hand, to act as occasion should require. In penning this note, I had some difficulty; my hand, I knew not how nor why, made wrong letters. I then wrote to Dr. Taylor to come to me, and bring Dr. Heberden;[1] and I sent to Dr. Brocklesby, who is my neighbor. My physicians are very friendly, and give me great hopes; but you may imagine my situation. I have so far recovered my vocal powers as to repeat the Lord's Prayer with no very imperfect articulation. My memory, I hope, yet remains as it was, but such an attack produces solicitude for the safety of every faculty. [How this will be received by you I know not. I hope you will sympathize with me; but perhaps

> My mistress,[2] gracious, kind, and good,
> Cries, 'Is he dumb? 'Tis time he should.'

"But can this be possible? I hope it cannot. I hope that what, when I could speak, I spoke of you and to you, will be in a sober and serious hour remembered by you; and surely it cannot be remembered but with some degree of kindness. I have loved you with virtuous affection; I have honored you with sincere esteem. Let not all our endearments be forgotten, but let me have in this great distress your pity and your prayers. You see I yet turn to you with my complaints as a settled and unalienable friend; do not, do not drive me from you, for I have not deserved either neglect or hatred. I am almost

---

1. *Dr. Heberden.* A member of Johnson's club in Essex Street. One of England's most eminent, learned, and enlightened physicians. Among other things, he believed in fresh air, good weather, the easing of pain, and a knowledge of the disposition of his patients. He humored William Cowper in his melancholy, gained the confidence of the insane George III, and in the early stages of his illness reassured Dr. Johnson as to his health. "That his opinion is erroneous," says Johnson, "I know with too much certainty; and yet was glad to hear it; he who is by his physician thought well, is at least not thought in immediate danger." Dr. Heberden was versed in classical literature and was a generous benefactor to both literature and learning.

2. *My mistress.* Adapted from some of Dean Swift's biting lines, in which he imagines the indifferent air of his own acquaintance on hearing the news of his death.

ashamed of this querulous[1] letter, but now it is written, let it go.

"I am, &c.,   "SAM. JOHNSON."]

"To Mr. Thomas Davies.

"DEAR SIR: I have had, indeed, a very heavy blow; but God, who yet spares my life, I humbly hope will spare my understanding, and restore my speech. As I am not at all helpless, I want no particular assistance, but am strongly affected by Mrs. Davies's tenderness; and when I think she can do me good, shall be very glad to call upon her. I had ordered friends to be shut out, but one or two have found the way in; and if you come you shall be admitted; for I know not whom I can see that will bring more amusement on his tongue, or more kindness in his heart. I am, &c.,

"June 18, 1783."   "SAM. JOHNSON.

[Johnson] indeed loved Davies cordially, of which I shall give the following little evidence. One day when he had treated him with too much asperity, Tom, who was not without pride and spirit, went off in a passion; but he had hardly reached home, when Frank, who had been sent after him, delivered this note: "Come, come, dear Davies, I am always sorry when we quarrel; send me word that we are friends."

Such was the general vigor of his constitution that he recovered from this alarming attack with wonderful quickness. In August he went[2] as far as the neighborhood of Salisbury.[3]

---

1. *Querulous.* Four days later, Johnson writes to Mrs. Thrale: "Your offer, dear madam, of coming to me is charmingly kind; but I will lay [it] up for future use, and let it not be considered as obsolete; a time of dereliction may come, when I may have hardly any other friend, but in the present exigency I cannot name one who has been deficient in civility or attention. What man can do for man has been done for me. Write to me very often."

2. *Went.* He gives as a reason for going: "It is not easy to grow well in a chamber where one has long been sick, and where everything seen and every person speaking revives and impresses images of pain. Though it be that no man can run away from himself, he may yet escape from many causes of useless uneasiness. That the *mind is its own place* is the boast of a fallen angel that had learned to lie."

3. *Salisbury.* Eighty miles from London. The public coach he took was "high-hung" and "rough" and the time consumed in the journey some fifteen hours.

While he was here he had a letter acquainting him of the death of Mrs. Williams. Though for several years her temper had not been complacent, her departure left a blank[1] in his house.

Chymistry[2] was always an interesting pursuit with Dr. Johnson. While he was in Wiltshire, he attended some experiments that were made by a physician at Salisbury on the new* kinds of air. In the course of the experiments frequent mention being made of Dr. Priestley;[3] Dr. Johnson knit his brows, and in a stern manner inquired, "Why do we hear so much of Dr. Priestley?" He was very properly answered, "Sir, because we are indebted to him for these important discoveries." On this Dr. Johnson appeared well content; and replied, "Well, well, I believe we are; and let every man have the honor he has merited."

A friend was one day, about two years before his death, struck with some instance of Dr. Johnson's great candor.[4] "Well, sir," said he, "I will always say that you are a very candid man." "Will you?" replied the Doctor; "I doubt then you will be very singular. But, indeed, sir," continued he, "I look upon myself to be a man very much misunderstood.[5] I am not an uncandid, nor am I a severe man. I

---

1. *Blank.* "Her curiosity was universal, her knowledge was very extensive, and she sustained forty years of misery with steady fortitude. Thirty years and more she had been my companion, and her death has left me very desolate." *Johnson.*

2. *Chymistry.* Boswell credits this paragraph and the one that follows to one of Johnson's friends, whom he does not name.

3. *Dr. Priestley* (1733–1804). A leading Unitarian minister; and though superficial, admired in radical circles as a profound physicist, chemist, and political and philosophical thinker. He later influenced Lamb, Hazlitt, and Coleridge.

4. *Candor.* Kindness. This sense of the word is now obsolete.

5. *Very much misunderstood.* "One sophism by which men persuade themselves that they have those virtues which they really want [lack] is formed by the substitution of single acts for habits." *Johnson: The Rambler.* "Those faults which we cannot conceal from our own notice are considered, however frequent, not as habitual corruptions, or settled practices, but as casual failures and single lapses." *The Same.* "The tribe is very numerous of those who seem to believe they are not bad while another can be found worse." *The Same.*

sometimes say more than I mean, in jest; and people are apt
to believe me serious; however, I am more candid than I was
when I was younger. As I know more of mankind, I expect
less of them, and am ready now to call a man *a good man*,
upon easier terms than I was formerly."

His fortitude and patience met with severe trials during this
year. The stroke of the palsy has been related circumstantially;
but he was also afflicted with the gout and was besides troubled
with a sarcocele, which Johnson bore with uncommon firmness,
and was not at all frightened while he looked forward to an
amputation. I have before me a letter of the 30th of July of
this year to Mr. Cruikshank,[1] in which he says, "I am going to
put myself into your hands." I have [also] several letters to
Dr. Mudge at Plymouth. I extract such passages as show the
undaunted state of his mind: "My conviction of your skill and
my belief of your friendship determine me to entreat your
opinion and advice. The operation is doubtless painful; but is
it dangerous? The pain I hope to endure with decency; but I
am loath to put life into much hazard. By representing the
gout as an antagonist to the palsy, you have said enough to
make it welcome. Write, dear sir, what you can to inform or
encourage me. The operation is not delayed by any fears or
objections of mine." Happily the complaint abated without his
being put to the torture of amputation.

He this autumn received a visit from the celebrated Mrs.
Siddons.[2] When Mrs. Siddons came into the room, there
happened to be no chair ready for her, which he observing, said
with a smile, "Madam, you, who so often occasion a want of
seats to other people, will the more easily excuse the want of
one yourself."[3]

---

1. *Mr. Cruikshank.* Surgeon; *Mr.* then being the title for surgeons
as distinguished from physicians.
2. *Mrs. Siddons.* The actress. It is said she carried her tragic
manner quite unconsciously into private life; in the kitchen, she "stabbed
the potatoes"; and in shopping awed the clerk whenever she asked,
"Will it wash?"
3. *Want of one yourself.* "It was remarkable in Dr. Johnson that
no external circumstances ever prompted him to make any apology or to
seem even sensible of their existence." *Miss Reynolds.*

I consulted him on two questions of a very different nature: one, whether the unconstitutional influence exercised by the peers of Scotland in the election of the representatives of the Commons, by means of fictitious qualifications, ought not to be resisted; the other, what in propriety and humanity should be done with old horses unable to labor. I gave him some account of my life at Auchinleck; and expressed my satisfaction that the gentlemen of the country had, at two public meetings, elected me their *Præses*, or Chairman.

"To James Boswell, Esq.

"DEAR SIR: Of the exaltations and depressions of your mind[1] you delight to talk, and I hate to hear. Drive all such fancies from you.

"On the day when I received your letter, I think, the foregoing page was written; to which one disease or another has

---

1. *Depressions of your mind.* During the autumn of 1783, Dr. Johnson wrote several letters to the Thrales, from which the following extracts are taken:

To Mrs. Thrale, Oct. 21: "When in your letter of the eleventh, you told me that my two letters had obliged, consoled, and delighted you, I was much elevated, and longed for a larger answer, but when the answer of the nineteenth came, I found that the obliging, consolatory, and delightful paragraphs had made so little impression that you want again to be told what those papers were written to tell you, and of what I can now tell you nothing new."

To Mrs. Thrale, Oct. 27: "If I was a little cross, would it not have made patient Grissel cross to find that you had forgotten the letter that you was answering? But what did I care, if I did not love you?"

"I have a letter signed S. A. Thrale; I take S. A. to be Miss Sophy; but who is bound to recollect initials? A name should be written, if not fully, yet so that it cannot be mistaken."

To Mrs. Thrale, Nov. 13: "Since you have written to me with the attention and tenderness of ancient time, your letters give me a great part of the pleasure which a life of solitude admits. A friendship of twenty years is interwoven with the texture of life. A friend may be often found and lost, but an *old friend* never can be found, and Nature has provided that he cannot easily be lost."

To Miss S. A. Thrale: "Here is a whole week and nothing heard from your house. I live here by my own self, and have had of late very bad nights, but then I have had a pig to dinner, which Mr. Perkins gave me. Thus life is checkered."

hindered me from making any additions. I am now a little better. But sickness and solitude press me very heavily. I could bear sickness better if I were relieved from solitude.

"The present dreadful confusion of the public ought to make you wrap yourself up in your hereditary possessions, which, though less than you may wish, are more than you can want; and in an hour of religious retirement return thanks to God, who has exempted you from any strong temptation to faction,[1] treachery, plunder, and disloyalty.

"As your neighbors distinguish you by such honors as they can bestow, content yourself with your station, without neglecting your profession. Your estate and the courts will find you full employment, and your mind well occupied will be quiet.

"The usurpation of the nobility, for they apparently usurp all the influence they gain by fraud and misrepresentation, I think it certainly lawful, perhaps your duty, to resist. What is not their own, they have only by robbery.

"Your question about the horses gives me more perplexity. I know not well what advice to give you. I can only recommend a rule which you do not want—give as little pain as you can. I suppose that we have a right to their service while their strength lasts; what we can do with them afterwards, I cannot so easily determine. But let us consider. Nobody denies that man has a right first to milk the cow, and to shear the sheep, and then to kill them for his table. May he not, by parity of reason, first work a horse, and then kill him the easiest way, that he may have the means of another horse, or food for cows and sheep? Man is influenced in both cases by different motives of self-interest. He that rejects the one must reject the other.

"I am, &c.,

"Sam. Johnson.

"London, Dec. 24, 1783."

---

1. *Faction.* "The ministry is again broken, and to any man who extends his thoughts to national considerations the times are dismal and gloomy. But to a sick man what is the public?" *Johnson to Mrs. Thrale, Dec. 31.*

I shall here mention what, in strict chronological arrangement, should have appeared in my account of last year, but may more properly be introduced here, the controversy not having been closed till this. The Reverend Mr. Shaw, a native of one of the Hebrides, having entertained doubts of the authenticity of the poems ascribed to Ossian, divested himself of national bigotry; and having traveled in the Highlands and Islands of Scotland, and also in Ireland, in order to furnish himself with materials for a Gaelic Dictionary, which he afterwards compiled, was so fully satisfied that Dr. Johnson was in the right upon the question that he candidly published a pamphlet, stating his conviction, and the proofs and reasons on which it was founded. A person at Edinburgh, of the name of Clark, answered this pamphlet with much zeal and much abuse of its author. Johnson took Mr. Shaw under his protection, and gave him his assistance in writing a reply.

A few paragraphs shall be selected.

"Mr. Clark compares the obstinacy of those who disbelieve the genuineness of Ossian to a blind man who should dispute the reality of colors and deny that the British troops are clothed in red. The blind man's doubt would be rational, if he did not know by experience that others have a power which he himself wants; but what perspicacity has Mr. Clark which Nature has withheld from me or the rest of mankind?

"The true state of the parallel must be this. Suppose a man, with eyes like his neighbors, was told by a boasting corporal that the troops, indeed, wore red clothes for their ordinary dress, but that every soldier had likewise a suit of black velvet, which he puts on when the King reviews them. This he thinks strange, and desires to see the fine clothes, but finds nobody in forty thousand men that can produce either coat or waistcoat. One, indeed, has left them in his chest at Port Mahon; another has always heard that he ought to have velvet clothes somewhere; and a third has heard somebody say that soldiers ought to wear velvet. Can the inquirer be blamed if he goes away believing that a soldier's red coat is all that he has?

"But the most obdurate incredulity may be shamed or silenced by acts. To overpower contradictions, let the soldier show his velvet coat, and the Fingalist the original of Ossian."

"The difference between us and the blind man is this—the blind man is unconvinced, because he cannot see; and we, because, though we can see, we find that nothing can be shown."

Notwithstanding the complications of disorders under which Johnson now labored, he did not resign himself to despondency and discontent. Sir John Hawkins has mentioned the cordiality with which he insisted that such of the members of the old club in Ivy Lane as survived, should meet again and dine together, which they did, twice at a tavern and once at his house; and in order to insure himself society in the evening for three days in the week, he instituted a club at the Essex Head, in Essex Street, then kept by Samuel Greaves, an old servant of Mr. Thrale's.

"To Sir Joshua Reynolds.

"DEAR SIR: It is inconvenient to me to come out; I should else have waited on you with an account of a little evening Club which we are establishing and of which you are desired to be one. The company is numerous, and, as you will see by the list, miscellaneous. The terms are lax, and the expenses light. Mr. Barry[1] was adopted by Dr. Brocklesby, who joined with me in forming the plan. We meet thrice a week, and he who misses forfeits twopence.

"If you are willing to become a member, draw a line under your name. Return the list. We meet for the first time on Monday at eight.

"I am, &c.,
"SAM. JOHNSON.
"Dec. 4, 1783."

---

1. *Barry*, James (1741-1806). A hectoring, grandiose painter, who had often spoken insultingly of Reynolds, and, it is said, had at one time threatened him with clenched fists.

It did not suit Sir Joshua to be one of this Club. Johnson himself, like his namesake, old Ben, composed the rules[1] of his Club.

In the end of this year he was seized with a spasmodic asthma of such violence that he was confined to the house in great pain, being sometimes obliged to sit all night in his chair, a recumbent posture being so hurtful to his respiration that he could not endure lying in bed; and there came upon him at the same time that oppressive and fatal disease, a dropsy. It was a very severe winter, which probably aggravated his complaints, and the solitude in which Mr. Levet and Mrs. Williams had left him rendered his life very gloomy. Mrs. Desmoulins, who still lived, was herself so very ill that she could contribute very little to his relief. He, however, had none of that unsocial shyness which we commonly see in people afflicted with sickness. He did not hide his head from the world, in solitary abstraction; he did not deny himself to the visits of his friends and acquaintances; but at all times, when he was not overcome by sleep, was ready for conversation as in his best days.

[1784]. I wrote to him, March 28, from York, informing him that I was to hasten back to my own county and had some intention of being a candidate to represent [it] in Parliament.

"To James Boswell, Esq.

"DEAR SIR: You are entering upon a transaction which requires much prudence. You must endeavor to oppose without exasperating; to practice temporary hostility without producing enemies for life. This is, perhaps, hard to be done; yet it has been done by many, and seems most likely to be effected by opposing merely upon general principles, without descending to personal or particular censures or objections. One thing I must enjoin you, which is seldom observed in the conduct of elections—I must entreat you to be scrupulous in the use of

---

1. *Rules.* The most significant one was that one penny [a very generous tip as prices ran then] should be left by each member for the waiter.

strong liquors. One night's drunkenness may defeat the labors
of forty days well employed. Be firm, but not clamorous; be
active, but not malicious; and you may form such an interest as
may not only exalt yourself, but dignify your family."

On Wednesday, May 5,[1] I arrived in London, and next morning had the pleasure to find Dr. Johnson greatly recovered. I
but just saw him; for a coach was waiting to carry him to Islington, to the house of his friend the Reverend Mr. Strahan,[2] where
he went sometimes for the benefit of good air, which notwithstanding his having formerly laughed at the general opinion
upon the subject, he now acknowledged was conducive to health.
On Saturday, May 15, I dined with him at Dr. Brocklesby's.
Of these days, and others on which I saw him, I have no memo-
rials, except the general recollection of his appearing to relish society as much as the youngest man. I find only these three small
particulars: When a person was mentioned, who said, "I have
lived fifty-one years in this world, without having had ten minutes of uneasiness," he exclaimed, "The man who says so, lies;
he attempts to impose on human credulity." The Bishop of

1. *Wednesday, May 5*. On April 26, Dr. Johnson wrote to Mrs.
Thrale: "On Saturday, I showed myself again to the living world
at the Exhibition; much and splendid was the company; but like the
Doge of Genoa at Paris, I admired nothing but myself. I went up all
the stairs to the pictures without stopping to rest or to breathe. . . .
Mrs. Davenant called to pay me a guinea, but I gave two for you. Whatever reasons you have for frugality, it is not worth while to save a guinea
a year by withdrawing it from a public charity. . . . Mrs. Davenant
says that you regain your health. That you regain your health is
more than a common recovery, because I infer that you regain your
peace of mind. Settle your thoughts and control your imagination,
and think no more of Hesperian felicity. Gather yourself and your
children into a little system, in which each may promote the ease, the
safety, and the pleasure of the rest."

2. *Reverend Mr. Strahan*. Son of his old bookseller friend, William
Strahan. To him, as a schoolboy, Johnson had written (1763), "You
are not to imagine that my friendship is light enough to be blown away
by the first cross blast. In youth we are apt to suppose that the duties
of life are to be performed with unfailing exactness and regularity; but
in our progress through life we are forced to take friends such as we can
find them, not as we would make them." Mr. Strahan was indefatigable
in his attentions to Johnson in his last illness.

Exeter in vain observed that men were very different. His Lordship's manner was not impressive; and I learnt afterwards that Johnson did not find out that the person who talked to him was a Prelate; if he had, I doubt not that he would have treated him with more respect; for once talking of George Psalmanazar,[1] whom he reverenced for his piety, he said, "I should as soon think of contradicting a Bishop." One of the company[2] provoked him greatly by doing what he could least of all bear, which was quoting something of his own writing against what he then maintained. "What, sir," cried the gentleman, "do you say to

> The busy day, the peaceful night,
> Unfelt, uncounted, glided by?"

Johnson was much offended; his anger burst out in an unjustifiable retort: "Sir, there is one passion I would advise you to command—when you have drunk out that glass, don't drink another." Here was exemplified what Goldsmith said of him, with the aid of a very witty image from one of Cibber's comedies: "There is no arguing with Johnson; for if his pistol misses fire, he knocks you down with the butt end of it."

Another was this: when a gentleman of eminence[3] in the literary world was violently censured for attacking people by anonymous paragraphs in newspapers, he, from the spirit of contradiction, as I thought, took up his defense and said, "Come, come, this is not so terrible a crime; he means only to vex them a little. I do not say that I should do it; but there is a great

---

1. *George Psalmanazar.* The name assumed by an impostor (his real name has never been known) who in the first part of the eighteenth century posed as a Formosan, concocted a Formosan language, and made a great point of worshiping the sun. By 1747, he had acknowledged the fraud; but the sanctimonious confessions which he left to be published after his death reek with new lies. Says Birkbeck Hill of him: "It is indeed very hard, if not altogether impossible, for a man who has passed forty years and more as a lying hypocrite altogether to 'clear his mind of cant.'" Johnson, affected by his airs of humble repentance, used to go and sit with him at an alehouse in the city.

2. *One of the company.* Probably Boswell in his cups. The fact that he has so little to record at this time is suspicious.

3. *A gentleman of eminence.* George Steevens, see page 355, note 2.

difference between him and me; what is fit for Hephæstion[1] is
not fit for Alexander."—Another, when I told him that a young
and handsome countess had said to me, "I should think that to
be praised by Dr. Johnson would make one a fool all one's life";
and that I answered, "Madam, I shall make him a fool today,
by repeating this to him," he said, "I am too old to be made a
fool; but if you say I am made a fool I shall not deny it. I am
much pleased with a compliment, especially from a pretty
woman."

On the evening of Saturday, May 15, he was in fine spirits
at our Essex Head Club. He told us, "I dined yesterday at
Mrs. Garrick's with Mrs. Carter, Miss Hannah More, and
Miss Fanny Burney. Three such women are not to be found.
I know not where I could find a fourth, except Mrs. Lennox,
who is superior to them all." BOSWELL. "Might not Mrs.
Montagu have been a fourth?" JOHNSON. "Sir, Mrs. Montagu
does not make a trade of her wit; but Mrs. Montagu is a very
extraordinary woman; she has a constant stream of conversation, and it is always impregnated; it has always meaning."
BOSWELL. "Mr. Burke has a constant stream of conversation."
JOHNSON. "Yes, sir; if a man were to go by chance at the same
time with Burke under a shed, to shun a shower, he would
say—'This is an extraordinary man.' If Burke should go into
a stable to see his horse dressed, the hostler would say—'We
have had an extraordinary man here.'"

One of the company mentioned his having seen a noble
person driving in his carriage, and looking exceedingly well,
notwithstanding his great age. JOHNSON. "Ah, sir; that is
nothing. Bacon observes that a stout healthy old man is
like a tower undermined."

On Wednesday, May 19, I sat a part of the evening with
him, by ourselves. I observed that the death of our friends
might be a consolation against the fear of our own dissolution
because we might have more friends in the other world than
in this. He perhaps felt this a reflection upon his apprehension as to death; and said, with heat, "How can a man know

---

1. *Hephæstion*. Alexander the Great's candid but sometimes
super-serviceable favorite.

where his departed friends are, or whether they will be his friends in the other world? How many friendships have you known formed upon principles of virtue? Most friendships are formed by caprice or by chance, mere confederacies in vice or leagues in folly."

We talked of our worthy friend Mr. Langton. He said, "I know not who will go to heaven if Langton does not. Sir, I could almost say, *Sit anima mea cum Langtono.*"

He however charged Mr. Langton with what he thought want of judgment upon an interesting occasion. "When I was ill," said he, "I desired he would tell me sincerely in what he thought my life was faulty. Sir, he brought me a sheet of paper, on which he had written down several texts of Scripture, recommending Christian charity. And when I questioned him what occasion I had given for such an animadversion, all that he could say amounted to this—that I sometimes contradicted people in conversation. Now what harm does it do to any man to be contradicted?" BOSWELL. "I suppose he meant the *manner* of doing it: roughly—and harshly." JOHNSON. "And who is the worse for that?" BOSWELL. "It hurts people of weak nerves." JOHNSON. "I know no such weak-nerved people."

Johnson, at the time when the paper was presented to him, though at first pleased with the attention of his friend, whom he thanked in an earnest manner, soon exclaimed in a loud and angry tone, "What is your drift, sir?" Sir Joshua Reynolds pleasantly observed that it was a scene for a comedy,[1] to see a penitent get into a violent passion and belabor his confessor.

---

1. *Scene for a comedy.* "After his decease, I found among his papers an anonymous letter that remarked his propensity to contradiction, his want of deference to the opinion of others, his contention for victory over those with whom he disputed, his local prejudices and aversions, and other of his evil habits in conversation. It was written in a spirit of charity, but contained in it several home truths. In short, it was such a letter as many a one, on receipt of it, would have destroyed. Johnson placed it in his bureau that, whenever he opened that repository of his papers, it might look him in the face." *Hawkins: Life of Johnson.*

I have preserved no more of his conversation during the rest of this month, till Sunday, the 30th of May, when I met him in the evening at Mr. Hoole's. Sir James Johnston happened to say that he paid no regard to the arguments of counsel at the bar of the House of Commons, because they were paid for speaking. JOHNSON. "Nay, sir, argument is argument. If it were testimony, you might disregard it, if you knew that it were purchased. There is a beautiful image in Bacon upon this subject: testimony is like an arrow shot from a long bow; the force of it depends on the strength of the hand that draws it. Argument is like an arrow from a crossbow, which has equal force though shot by a child."

He had now a great desire to go to Oxford,[1] as his first jaunt after his illness; we talked of it for some days, and I had promised to accompany him. He was impatient and fretful tonight, because I did not at once agree to go with him on Thursday. When I considered how ill he had been, and what allowance should be made for the influence of sickness upon his temper, I resolved to indulge him, though with some inconvenience to myself, as I wished to attend the musical meeting in honor of Handel, in Westminster Abbey, on the following Saturday.

In the midst of his own diseases and pains, he was ever compassionate to the distresses of others, and actively earnest in procuring them aid, as appears from a note to Sir Joshua Reynolds, of June, in these words: "I am ashamed to ask for some relief for a poor man, to whom, I hope, I have given what I can be expected to spare. The man importunes me, and the blow goes round. I am going to try another air on Thursday."

On Thursday, June 3, the Oxford post-coach took us up in the morning at Bolt Court. The other two passengers were Mrs. Beresford and her daughter, two very agreeable ladies from America; they were going to Worcestershire, where they then resided. Frank had been sent by his master the day

---

1. *Oxford.* "[A Mrs. Wall] used to narrate that she had seen a double line of people waiting to see Dr. Johnson enter the Cathedral." *Birkbeck Hill.*

before to take places for us; and I found from the way-bill that Dr. Johnson had made our names be put down. Mrs. Beresford, who had read it, whispered me, "Is this the great Dr. Johnson?" I told her it was; so she was then prepared to listen. As she soon happened to mention, in a voice so low that Johnson did not hear it, that her husband had been a member of the American Congress, I cautioned her to beware of introducing that subject, as she must know how very violent Johnson was against the people of that country. He talked a great deal. But I am sorry I have preserved little of the conversation. Miss Beresford was so much charmed that she said to me aside, "How he does talk! Every sentence is an essay." She amused herself in the coach with knotting. "Next to mere idleness," said he, "I think knotting is to be reckoned in the scale of insignificance; though I once attempted to learn knotting. Dempster's sister (looking to me) endeavored to teach me it; but I made no progress."

I was surprised at his talking without reserve in the public post-coach of the state of his affairs: "I have," said he, "about the world I think above a thousand pounds, which I intend shall afford Frank an annuity of seventy pounds a year." Indeed his openness with people at a first interview was remarkable. He said once to Mr. Langton, "I think I am like Squire Richard in 'The Journey to London,' *'I'm never strange in a strange place.'* "

At the inn where we stopped he was exceedingly dissatisfied with some roast mutton which he had for dinner. The ladies, I saw, wondered to see the great philosopher, whose wisdom and wit they had been admiring all the way, get into ill humor from such a cause. He scolded the waiter, saying, "It is as bad as bad can be; it is ill-fed, ill-killed, ill-kept, and ill-dressed."

He bore the journey very well, and seemed to feel himself elevated as he approached Oxford, that magnificent and venerable seat of Learning, Orthodoxy, and Toryism. Frank came in the heavy coach, in readiness to attend him; and we were received with the most polite hospitality at the house of his old friend Dr. Adams, Master of Pembroke College, who had given us a kind invitation.   Before we were set down, I communicated to Johnson my having engaged to return to London directly, for the reason I have mentioned, but that I would hasten back to him again.   He was pleased that I had made this journey merely to keep him company.   He was easy and placid with Dr. Adams, Mrs. and Miss Adams, and Mrs. Kennicot, widow of the learned Hebræan, who was here on a visit.   He soon dispatched the inquiries which were made about his illness and recovery, by a short and distinct narrative; and then assuming a gay air, repeated from Swift,

> Nor think on our approaching ills,
> And talk of spectacles and pills.

Dr. Newton, the Bishop of Bristol, having been mentioned, Johnson, recollecting the manner in which he had been censured by that Prelate,[1] thus retaliated: "Tom knew he should be dead before what he has said of me would appear.   He durst not have printed it while he was alive."   DR. ADAMS. "I believe his *Dissertations on the Prophecies*[2] is his great work." JOHNSON.   "Why, sir, it is *Tom's* great work; but how far it is great, or how much of it is Tom's, are other questions." DR. ADAMS.   "He was a very successful man."   JOHNSON. "I don't think so, sir.   He did not get very high.   He was late in getting what he did get; and he did not get it by the best means.   I believe he was a gross flatterer."

I returned to Oxford on Wednesday, the 9th of June, when I was happy to find myself again in the same agreeable circle at Pembroke College, with the comfortable prospect of making some stay.   Johnson welcomed my return with more than ordinary glee.

Next morning at breakfast Mrs. Kennicot spoke of her brother, the Reverend Mr. Chamberlayne, who had given up great prospects in the Church of England on his conversion

---

1.   *Censured by that Prelate.*   For the "severe reflections," the "spleen," the "ill-humor," and the revival of "old scandal" in his *Lives of the Poets.*

2.   *Dissertations on the Prophecies.*   "Of no great value."   *The Dictionary of National Biography.*

to the Roman Catholic faith. Johnson exclaimed fervently, "God bless him."

On the Roman Catholic religion he said, "If you join the Papists externally, they will not interrogate you strictly as to your belief in their tenets. No reasoning Papist believes every article of their faith. There is one side on which a good man might be persuaded to embrace it. A good man of a timorous disposition, and pretty credulous, might be glad to be of a church where there are so many helps to get to heaven. I would be a Papist[1] if I could. I have fear enough; but an obstinate rationality prevents me. I wonder that women are not all Papists." BOSWELL. "They are not more afraid of death than men are." JOHNSON. "Because they are less wicked." DR. ADAMS. "They are more pious." JOHNSON. "No, hang 'em, they are not more pious. A wicked fellow is the most pious when he takes to it. He'll beat you all at piety."

He argued in defense of some of the peculiar tenets of the Church of Rome. As to the giving the bread only to the laity, he said, "They may think that in what is merely ritual, deviations from the primitive mode may be admitted on the ground of convenience, and I think they are as well warranted to make this alteration as we are to substitute sprinkling in the room of the ancient baptism."

After dinner, when one of us talked of there being a great enmity between Whig and Tory: JOHNSON. "Why not so much, I think, unless when they come into competition with each other. A Tory will marry into a Whig family, and a Whig into a Tory family, without any reluctance. But, indeed, in a matter of much more concern than political tenets, and that is religion, men and women do not concern themselves much about difference of opinion; and ladies set no value on the moral character of men who pay their addresses to them." Our ladies endeavored to defend their sex from this charge; but he roared them down—"No, no, a lady will take Jonathan

---

1. *A Papist.* "It is observed by Lowth that there is less distance than is thought between skepticism and popery; and that a mind wearied with perpetual doubt willingly seeks repose in the bosom of an infallible church." *Johnson: Life of Garth.*

Wild as readily as St. Austin, if he has three-pence more; and, what is worse, her parents will give her to him. Women are less vicious than we, not from choice, but because we restrict them; they are the slaves of order and fashion."

Miss Adams mentioned a gentleman of licentious character and said, "Suppose I had a mind to marry that gentleman, would my parents consent?" JOHNSON. "Yes, they'd consent and you'd go. You'd go though they did not consent." MISS ADAMS. "Perhaps their opposing might make me go." JOHNSON. "Oh, very well; you'd take one whom you think a bad man to have the pleasure of vexing your parents. You put me in mind of Dr. Barrowby, the physician, who was very fond of swine's flesh. One day, when he was eating it, he said, 'I wish I was a Jew.' 'Why so?' said somebody; 'the Jews are not allowed to eat your favorite meat.' 'Because,' said he, 'I should then have the gust of eating it, with the pleasure of sinning.'" Johnson then proceeded in his declamation.

Miss Adams soon afterwards made an observation that I do not recollect, which pleased him much. He said, with a good-humored smile, that there should be so much excellence united with so much *depravity* is strange.

I asked him if it was true, as reported, that he had said lately, "I am for the King against Fox; but I am for Fox against Pitt."[1] JOHNSON. "Yes, sir; the King is my master; but I do not know Pitt; and Fox is my friend." "Fox," added he, "is a most extraordinary man; here is a man who has divided the kingdom with Caesar; so that it was a doubt whether the nation should be ruled by the scepter of George the Third or the tongue of Fox."

On Friday, June 11, we talked at breakfast of forms of prayer. DR. ADAMS (in a very earnest manner). "I wish, sir, you would compose some family prayers." JOHNSON. "I will not compose prayers[2] for you, sir, because you can do it for yourself. But I have thought of getting together all the

---

1. *Pitt.* Prime Minister, with an overwhelming majority behind him. Fox was his most brilliant opponent. Burke, heartsick at the course of events, was, for the time being, pretty much out of the struggle.
2. *Compose prayers.* "It is enough if we have stated seasons of

books of prayers which I could, selecting those which should appear to me the best, adding some prayers of my own, and prefixing a discourse on prayer." We all now gathered about him, and two or three of us at a time joined in pressing him to execute this plan. He seemed to be a little displeased at the manner of our importunity, and in great agitation called out, "Do not talk thus of what is so awful. I know not what time God will allow me in this world. There are many things which I wish to do." Some of us persisted, and Dr. Adams said, "I never was more serious about anything in my life." JOHNSON. "Let me alone, let me alone; I am overpowered." And then he put his hands before his face, and reclined for some time upon the table.

I mentioned Jeremy Taylor's[1] using, in his forms of prayer, "I am the chief of sinners," and other such self-condemning expressions. "Now," said I, "this cannot be said with truth by every man, and therefore is improper for a general printed form. I myself cannot say that I am the worst of men; I *will* not say so." JOHNSON. "Law[2] observes that 'every man knows something worse of himself than he is sure of in others.' You may not have committed such crimes as some men have done; but you do not know against what degree of light they have sinned. Besides, sir, 'the chief of sinners' is a mode of expression for 'I am a great sinner.'" BOSWELL. "But, sir, Taylor founds a conceit upon it. When praying

---

prayer, no matter when. A man may as well pray when he mounts his horse, or a woman when she milks her cow . . . as at meals." *Johnson, quoted in Boswell's Journal of a Tour to the Hebrides.*

"At church, Oct., '65. To avoid all singularity; *Bonaventura.* To come in before service, and compose my mind by meditation or by reading some portions of Scripture. *Tetty.* If I can hear the sermon, to attend it, unless attention be more troublesome than useful. To consider the act of prayer as a reposal of myself upon God, and a resignation of all into his holy hand." *Johnson: Prayers and Meditations.*

1. *Jeremy Taylor* (1616-1667). This great prelate had the good humor of a gentleman, the eloquence of an orator, the fancy of a poet; he had devotion enough for a cloister, and wit enough for a College of Virtuosi." *George Rust: Funeral Sermon, 1667.*

2. *Law*, William (1686-1761). Author of "A Serious Call to a Devout and Holy Life."

for the conversion of sinners, and of himself in particular, he says, 'Lord, thou wilt not leave thy *chief* work undone.'" JOHNSON. "I do not approve of figurative expressions in addressing the Supreme Being; and I never use them. Taylor gives good advice: 'Never lie in your prayers; never confess more than you really believe; never promise more than you mean to perform.' But his example contradicts his precept."

Dr. Johnson and I went in Dr. Adams's coach to dine with Dr. Nowell, Principal of St. Mary's Hall, at his beautiful villa at Iffley, on the banks of the Isis, about two miles from Oxford. While we were upon the road, I had the resolution to ask Johnson whether he thought that the roughness of his manner had been an advantage or not, and if he would not have done more good if he had been more gentle. I proceeded to answer myself thus: "Perhaps it has given weight to what you said. You could not, perhaps, have talked with such authority without it." JOHNSON. "No, sir,[1] I have done more good as I am. Obscenity and impiety have always been repressed in my company." BOSWELL. "Yet, sir, many people who might have been benefited by your conversation have been frightened away. A worthy friend[2] of ours has told me that he has often been afraid to talk to you." JOHNSON. "Sir, he need not have been afraid, if he had anything rational to say. If he had not, it was better he did not talk."

We were well entertained and very happy at Dr. Nowell's, where was a very agreeable company, and we drank "Church and King" after dinner with true Tory cordiality.[3]

---

1. *No, sir.* See fifteen paragraphs further on, page 514.

2. *Worthy friend.* Boswell's usual phrase for Langton.

"I am sure you will honor Mr. Langton when I tell you he is come on purpose to stay with Dr. Johnson, and that during his illness. He has taken a little lodging in Fleet Street in order to be near, to devote himself to him. He has as much goodness as learning, and that is saying a bold thing of one of the first Greek scholars we have." *Hannah More, March 8, 1784, quoted by Birkbeck Hill.*

3. *Tory cordiality.* Twelve years before, Dr. Nowell had suffered a public rebuke from the House of Commons for declaring in a public sermon that the opponents of George III's policies were no better than the rebellious subjects of the "sacred martyr," Charles I, and that the so-called grievances under both monarchs were purely illusory.

We talked of a certain clergyman[1] of extraordinary character, who, by exerting his talents in writing on temporary topics, and displaying uncommon intrepidity, had raised himself to affluence. I maintained that we ought not to be indignant at his success; for merit of every sort was entitled to reward. JOHNSON. "Sir, I will not allow this man to have merit. I will, indeed, allow him courage, and on this account we so far give him credit. We have more respect for a man who robs boldly on the highway than for a fellow who jumps out of a ditch and knocks you down behind your back. Courage is a quality so necessary for maintaining virtue that it is always respected, even when it is associated with vice."

I censured the coarse invectives which were become fashionable in the House of Commons, and said that if members of Parliament must attack each other personally in the heat of debate, it should be done more genteelly. JOHNSON. "No, sir; that would be much worse. The difference between coarse and refined abuse is as the difference between being bruised by a club and wounded by a poisoned arrow."

On Saturday, June 12, there drank tea with us at Dr. Adams's, Mr. John Henderson, student of Pembroke College, celebrated for his acquirements in alchemy, judicial astrology, and other abstruse and curious learning. I have no note of this evening's conversation, except a single fragment. When I mentioned Thomas Lord Lyttelton's[2] vision, the prediction of the time of

---

1. *A certain clergyman.* Probably the dissolute Henry Bate, known as the "Fighting Parson." In 1781, he was sentenced to a year's imprisonment for "an atrocious libel on the Duke of Richmond." Though a clergyman, he had fought more than one duel. He was an intimate friend of Garrick's.

2. *Lord Lyttelton.* Known as the wicked Lord Lyttelton, to distinguish him from his more celebrated father. Though a brilliant man, his nerves were no doubt affected by his dissipated habits; he is said to have suffered from heart disease and to have used drugs freely. "On November 24, 1779, at his home in Berkeley Square, he dreamt that a bird flew in at his window and changed into a woman, who warned him that he had not three days to live. He told the dream, and the story at once became the talk of the town. Though he affected to make light of it, the occurrence weighed on his mind. After passing apparently a placid evening in good health, he died the night of the third day.

his death, and its exact fulfillment: JOHNSON. "It is the most extraordinary thing that has happened in my day. I heard it with my own ears from his uncle, Lord Westcote. I am so glad to have every evidence of the spiritual world that I am willing to believe it." DR. ADAMS. "You have evidence enough; good evidence, which needs not such support." JOHNSON. "I like to have more."

Mr. Henderson, with whom I had sauntered in the venerable walks of Merton College, supped with us. Dr. Johnson surprised him not a little by acknowledging, with a look of horror, that he was much oppressed by the fear of death. The amiable Dr. Adams suggested that God was infinitely good. JOHNSON. "That he is infinitely good, as far as the perfection of his nature will allow, I certainly believe; but it is necessary for good, upon the whole, that individuals should be punished. As to an *individual*, therefore, he is not infinitely good; and as I cannot be *sure* that I have fulfilled the conditions on which salvation is granted, I am afraid I may be one of those who shall be damned (looking dismally)." BOSWELL. "But may not a man attain to such a degree of hope as not to be uneasy from the fear of death?" JOHNSON. "A man may have such a degree of hope as to keep him quiet. You see I am not quiet, from the vehemence with which I talk; but I do not despair." MRS. ADAMS. "You seem, sir, to forget the merits of our Redeemer." JOHNSON. "Madam, I do not forget the merits of my Redeemer; but my Redeemer has said that he will set some on his right hand and some on his left."—He was in gloomy agitation, and said, "I'll have no more on't."—If what has now been stated should be urged by the enemies of Christianity, as if its influence on the mind were not benignant, let it be remembered that Johnson's temperament was melancholy, of which such direful apprehensions of futurity are often a common effect. We shall presently see that when he approached nearer to his awful change, his mind became tranquil, and he exhibited as much fortitude as becomes a thinking man in that situation.

On Sunday, June 13, our philosopher was calm at breakfast.

There was something exceedingly pleasing in our leading a College life, without restraint, and with superior elegance, in consequence of our living in the Master's House, and having the company of ladies.

We talked of the question, whether it was allowable at any time to depart from *Truth*. JOHNSON. "The general rule is that Truth should never be violated, because it is of the utmost importance to the comfort of life that we should have a full security by mutual faith; and occasional inconveniences should be willingly suffered that we may preserve it. There must, however, be some exceptions. If, for instance, a murderer should ask you which way a man is gone, you may tell him what is not true, because you are under a previous obligation not to betray a man to a murderer." BOSWELL. "Supposing the person who wrote *Junius* were asked whether he was the author, might he deny it?" JOHNSON. "I don't know what to say to this. If you were *sure* that he wrote *Junius*, would you, if he denied it, think as well of him afterwards? Yet it may be urged that what a man has no right to ask, you may refuse to communicate; and there is no other effectual mode of preserving a secret and an important secret, the discovery of which may be very hurtful to you, but a flat denial; for if you are silent, or hesitate, or evade, it will be held equivalent to a confession. But stay, sir, here is another case. Supposing the author had told me confidentially that he had written *Junius*, and I were asked if he had, I should hold myself at liberty to deny it, as being under a previous promise, express or implied, to conceal it. Now what I ought to do for the author, may I not do for myself? But I deny the lawfulness of telling a lie to a sick man for fear of alarming him. You have no business with consequences; you are to tell the truth. Besides, you are not sure what effect your telling him he is in danger may have. It may bring his distemper to a crisis, and that may cure him. Of all lying, I have the greatest abhorrence of this, because I believe it has been frequently practiced on myself."

On Monday, June 14, and Tuesday, 15, Dr. Johnson and I

dined, on one of them, I forget which, with Mr. Mickle, translator of the *Lusiad*, at Wheatley, a very pretty country place a
few miles from Oxford; and on the other with Dr. Wetherell,
Master of University College. From Dr. Wetherell's he went
to visit Mr. Sackville Parker, the bookseller; and when he
returned to us, gave the following account of his visit, saying,
"I have been to see my old friend, Sack. Parker; I find he
has married his maid; he has done right. She had lived with
him many years in great confidence, and they had mingled
minds; I do not think he could have found any wife that
would have made him so happy. The woman was very attentive and civil to me; she pressed me to fix a day for dining
with them, and to say what I liked, and she would be sure to
get it for me. Poor Sack.! He is very ill, indeed. We parted
as never to meet again. It has quite broke me down." This
pathetic narrative was strangely diversified with the grave and
earnest defense of a man's having married his maid. I could
not but feel it as in some degree ludicrous.

In the morning of Tuesday, June 15, while we sat at
Dr. Adams's, we talked of a printed letter from the Rev. Herbert
Croft, to a young gentleman who had been his pupil, in which
he advised him to read to the end of whatever books he should
begin to read. JOHNSON. "This is surely a strange advice;
you may as well resolve that whatever men you happen to get
acquainted with, you are to keep to them for life. A book
may be good for nothing; or there may be only one thing in
it worth knowing. These Voyages (pointing to the three large
volumes of *Voyages to the South Sea*, which were just come out),
who will read them through? A man had better work his way
before the mast than read them through; they will be eaten
by rats and mice before they are read through. There can
be little entertainment in such books; one set of savages is like
another." BOSWELL. "I do not think the people of Otaheite
can be reckoned savages." JOHNSON. "Don't cant in defense
of savages." BOSWELL. "They have the art of navigation."
JOHNSON. "A dog or a cat can swim." BOSWELL. "They
carve very ingeniously." JOHNSON. "A cat can scratch, and

a child with a nail can scratch." I perceived this was none of the *mollia tempora fandi;* so desisted.

That he was much satisfied with the respect paid to him at Dr. Adams's is thus attested by himself: "I returned last night from Oxford, after a fortnight's abode with Dr. Adams, who treated me as well as I could expect or wish; and he that contents a sick man,[1] a man whom it is impossible to please, has surely done his part well."

After his return to London from this excursion, I saw him frequently, but have few memorandums; I shall therefore here insert some particulars which I collected at various times.

It having been mentioned to Dr. Johnson that a gentleman who had a son whom he imagined to have an extreme degree of timidity, resolved to send him to a public* school that he might acquire confidence: "Sir," said Johnson, "such a disposition should be cultivated in the shade. Placing him at a public school is forcing an owl upon day."

Johnson having argued for some time with a pertinacious gentleman, his opponent, who had talked in a very puzzling manner, happened to say, "I don't understand you, sir"; upon which Johnson observed, "Sir, I have found you an argument; but I am not obliged to find you an understanding."

He disapproved of Lord Hailes, for having modernized the language of the ever-memorable John Hales[2] of Eton, in an edition which his Lordship published of that writer's works. "An author's language, sir," said he, "is a characteristical part of his composition, and is also characteristical of the age in which he writes. Besides, sir, when the language is changed we are not sure that the sense is the same. No, sir; I am sorry Lord Hailes has done this."

Here it may be observed that his frequent use of the ex-

---

1. *A sick man.* "It is so *very* difficult for a sick man not to be a scoundrel." *Johnson, quoted by Mrs. Piozzi.*

2. *John Hales.* In 1659, three years after his death, his writings were published as *The Golden Remains of the Ever Memorable Mr. John Hales of Eton College.* His fine and generous temper of mind was expended on controversies which have long since lost their interest.

pression, "No, sir," was not always to intimate contradiction, for he would say so when he was about to enforce an affirmative proposition which had not been denied, as in the instance last mentioned. I used to consider it as a kind of flag of defiance; as if he had said, "Any argument you may offer against this is not just. No, sir, it is not." It was like Falstaff's "I deny your Major."

Sir Joshua Reynolds having said that he took the altitude of a man's taste by his stories and his wit, and of his understanding by the remarks which he repeated; being always sure that he must be a weak man who quotes common things with an emphasis as if they were oracles—Johnson agreed with him; and Sir Joshua having also observed that the real character of a man was found out by his amusements—Johnson added: "Yes, sir; no man is a hypocrite in his pleasures."[1]

When I pointed out to him in the newspaper one of Mr. Grattan's animated and glowing speeches in favor of the freedom of Ireland, in which this expression occurred (I know not if accurately taken): "We will persevere till there is not one link of the English chain left to clank upon the rags of the meanest beggar in Ireland"—"Nay, sir," said Johnson, "don't you perceive that *one* link cannot clank?"

When somebody talked of being imposed on in the purchase of tea and sugar, and such articles: "That will not be the case," said he, "if you go to a *stately shop*, as I always do. In such a shop it is not worth their while to take a petty advantage."

The difference, he observed, between a well-bred and an ill-bred man is this: "You love the one till you find reason to hate him; you hate the other till you find reason to love him."

The wife of one of his acquaintance had fraudulently made a purse for herself out of her husband's fortune. Feeling a

---

1. *A hypocrite in his pleasures.* In the *Idler*, Johnson says: "Pleasure is seldom such as it appears to others, nor often such as we represent it to ourselves. Of the ladies that sparkle at a musical performance, a very small number has any quick sensibility of harmonious sounds. But everyone that goes has her pleasure. She has the pleasure of wearing fine clothes."

proper compunction in her last moments, she confessed how much she had secreted; but before she could tell where it was placed, she was seized with a convulsive fit and expired. Her husband said he was more hurt by her want of confidence in him than by the loss of his money. "I told him," said Johnson, "that he should console himself; for *perhaps* the money might be *found*, and he was *sure* that his wife was *gone*."

A foppish physician once reminded Johnson of his having been in company with him on a former occasion. "I do not remember it, sir." The physician still insisted, adding that he that day wore so fine a coat that it must have attracted his notice. "Sir," said Johnson, "had you been dipped in Pactolus,* I should not have noticed you."

He seemed to take a pleasure in speaking in his own style; for when he had carelessly missed it, he would repeat the thought translated into it. Talking of the comedy of *The Rehearsal*, he said, "It has not wit enough to keep it sweet." This was easy; he therefore caught himself, and pronounced a more round sentence: "It has not vitality enough to preserve it from putrefaction."

He censured a writer of entertaining travels for assuming a feigned character, saying (in his sense of the word), "He carries out one lie; we know not how many he brings back." At another time, talking of the same person, he observed, "Sir, your assent to a man whom you have never known to falsify is a debt; but after you have known a man to falsify, your assent to him then is a favor."

No man was more ready to make an apology when he had censured unjustly than Johnson. When a proof sheet of one of his works was brought to him, he found fault with the mode in which a part of it was arranged, refused to read it, and in a passion desired that the compositor might be sent to him. The compositor was Mr. Manning, who had composed[1] about one-half of his *Dictionary*, and a great part of his *Lives of the Poets;* and who (in his seventy-seventh year) composed a

1. *Composed.* Set up in type.

part of the first edition of this work concerning him. By producing the manuscript, he at once satisfied Dr. Johnson that he was not to blame; upon which Johnson candidly and earnestly said to him, "Mr. Compositor, I ask your pardon. Mr. Compositor, I ask your pardon again and again."

His generous humanity to the miserable was almost beyond example. The following instance is well attested: Coming home late one night, he found a poor woman lying in the street, so much exhausted that she could not walk; he took her upon his back, and carried her to his house, where he discovered that she was one of those wretched females who had fallen into the lowest state of vice, poverty, and disease. Instead of harshly upbraiding her, he had her taken care of with all tenderness for a long time, at considerable expense, till she was restored to health, and endeavored to put her into a virtuous way of life.

He once in his life was known to have uttered what is called a *bull:* Sir Joshua Reynolds, when they were riding together in Devonshire, complained that he had a very bad horse, for that even when going down hill he moved slowly step by step. "Aye," said Johnson, "and when he *goes* up hill, he *stands still.*"

He had a great aversion to gesticulating in company. He called once to a gentleman who offended him in that point, "Don't *attitudenize.*" And when another gentleman thought he was giving additional force to what he uttered, by expressive movements of his hands, Johnson fairly seized them, and held them down.

A gentleman having said that a *congé d'elire* has not, per-haps, the force of a command, but may be considered only as a strong recommendation: "Sir," replied Johnson, who over-heard him, "it is such a recommendation, as if I should throw you out of a two-pair-of-stairs window, and recommend to you to fall soft."

The anxiety of his friends to preserve so estimable a life, as long as human means might be supposed to have influence, made them plan for him a retreat from the severity of a British winter, to the mild climate of Italy. This scheme was at last brought to a serious resolution at General Paoli's, where I had

often talked of it. One essential matter, however, I understood was necessary to be previously settled, which was obtaining such an addition to his income as would be sufficient to
enable him to defray the expense in a manner becoming the
first literary character of a great nation. The person to whom
I above all others thought I should apply to negotiate this
business was the Lord Chancellor, because I knew that he
highly valued Johnson, and that Johnson highly valued his
Lordship. I have mentioned what Johnson said of him to
me when he was at the bar; and after his Lordship was advanced
to the seals, he said of him, "I would prepare myself for no
man in England but Lord Thurlow. When I am to meet
with him, I should wish to know a day before." How he
would have prepared himself, I cannot conjecture.

I first consulted with Sir Joshua Reynolds, who perfectly
coincided in opinion with me; and I therefore, though personally very little known to his Lordship, wrote to him. I mentioned that I was obliged to set out for Scotland early in the
following week, so that if his Lordship should have any commands for me as to this negotiation, he would be pleased to
send them before that time; otherwise Sir Joshua Reynolds
would give all attention to it.

This application was made not only without any suggestion
on the part of Johnson himself, but was utterly unknown to
him, nor had he the smallest suspicion of it. Any insinuations,
therefore, which since his death have been thrown out, as if
he had stooped to ask what was superfluous, are without any
foundation. But had he asked it, it would not have been
superfluous; for though the money he had saved proved to
be more than his friends imagined, or I believe than he himself,
in his carelessness concerning worldly matters, knew it to be,
had he traveled upon the Continent, an augmentation of his
income would by no means have been unnecessary.

On Thursday, June 24, I dined with him at Mr. Dilly's.
I recollect nothing that passed this day, except Johnson's
quickness, who, when Dr. Beattie observed, as something remarkable which had happened to him, that he had chanced
to see both No. 1 and No. 1000 of the hackney-coaches, the

first and the last: "Why, sir," said Johnson, "there is an equal chance for one's seeing those two numbers as any other two."

On Sunday, June 27, I found him rather better. I mentioned to him a young man who was going to Jamaica with his wife and children, in expectation of being provided for by two of her brothers settled in that island, one a clergyman, and the other a physician. JOHNSON. "It is a wild scheme, sir, unless he has a positive and deliberate invitation. There was a poor girl, who used to come about me, who had a cousin in Barbadoes, that, in a letter to her, expressed a wish she should come out to that island, and expatiated on the comforts and happiness of her situation. The poor girl went out; her cousin was much surprised, and asked her how she could think of coming. 'Because,' said she, 'you invited me.'—'Not I,' answered the cousin. The letter was then produced. 'I see it is true,' said she, 'that I did invite you; but I did not think you would come.' They lodged her in an outhouse, where she passed her time miserably; and as soon as she had an opportunity she returned to England. In the case which you mention, it is probable the clergyman spends all he gets, and the physician does not know how much he is to get."

We this day dined at Sir Joshua Reynolds's. An addition to our company came after we went up to the drawing-room; Dr. Johnson seemed to rise in spirits as his audience increased. He entered upon a curious discussion of the difference between intuition and sagacity, one being immediate in its effect, the other requiring a circuitous process; one he observed was the *eye* of the mind, the other the *nose* of the mind.

A young gentleman present took up the argument against him and maintained that no man ever thinks of the *nose of the mind*, not adverting that though that figurative sense seems strange to us, it is truly not more forced than Hamlet's "In my *mind's eye*, Horatio." He persisted much too long, and appeared to Johnson as putting himself forward with too much presumption; upon which he called to him in a loud tone, "What is it you are contending for, if you *be* contending?"—And afterwards imagining that the gentleman retorted upon him with a kind of smart drollery, he said, "Mr. —, it does not become you to talk so to me. Besides, ridicule is not your talent; you have *there* neither intuition nor sagacity."—The gentleman protested that he had intended no improper freedom, but had the greatest respect for Dr. Johnson. After a short pause, during which we were somewhat uneasy: JOHNSON. "Give me your hand, sir. You were too tedious, and I was too short." MR. —. "Sir, I am honored by your attention in any way." JOHNSON. "Come, sir, let's have no more of it. We offended one another by our contention; let us not offend the company by our compliments."

He now said he wished much to go to Italy, and that he dreaded passing the winter in England. I said nothing; but enjoyed a secret satisfaction in thinking that I had taken the most effectual measures to make such a scheme practicable.

On Monday, June 28, I had the honor to receive from the Lord Chancellor the following letter:

"To James Boswell, Esq.

"SIR: I should have answered your letter immediately, if (being much engaged when I received it) I had not put it in my pocket, and forgot to open it till this morning.

"I am much obliged to you for the suggestion; and I will adopt and press it as far as I can. The best argument, I am sure, and I hope it is not likely to fail, is Dr. Johnson's merit. But it will be necessary, if I should be so unfortunate as to miss seeing you, to converse with Sir Joshua on the sum it will be proper to ask—in short, upon the means of setting him out. It would be a reflection on us all if such a man should perish for want of the means to take care of his health.

"Yours, &c.,

"THURLOW."

This letter gave me a very high satisfaction; I next day showed it to Sir Joshua Reynolds, who was exceedingly pleased with it. He thought that I should now communicate the negotiation to Dr. Johnson, who might afterwards complain if the attention with which he had been honored should be too long concealed from him. I intended to set out for Scotland next morning, but Sir Joshua cordially insisted that I should stay another day, that Johnson and I might dine with him, and, as Sir Joshua expressed himself, "have it all out." I hastened to Johnson, and was told by him that he was rather better today. Boswell. "I am very anxious about you, sir, and particularly that you should go to Italy for the winter, which I believe is your own wish." Johnson. "It is, sir." Boswell. "You have no objections, I presume, but the money it would require." Johnson. "Why, no, sir." Upon which I gave him a particular account of what had been done, and read to him the Lord Chancellor's letter. He listened with much attention; then warmly said, "This is taking prodigious pains about a man." "Oh, sir," said I, with most sincere affection, "your friends would do everything for you." He paused, grew more and more agitated, till tears started into his eyes, and he exclaimed with fervent emotion, "God bless you all." I was so affected that I also shed tears. After a short silence, he renewed and extended his grateful benediction, "God bless you all, for Jesus Christ's sake." We both remained for some time unable to speak. He rose suddenly and quitted the room, quite melted in tenderness. He stayed but a short time, till he had recovered his firmness; soon after he returned I left him, having first engaged him to dine at Sir Joshua Reynolds's next day. I never was again under that roof which I had so long reverenced.

On Wednesday, June 30, the friendly confidential dinner with Sir Joshua Reynolds took place, no other company being present. Both Sir Joshua and I expatiated with confidence on the liberal provision which we were sure would be made for him, conjecturing whether munificence would be displayed in one large donation, or in an ample increase of his pension. He himself catched so much of our enthusiasm as to allow himself to suppose it not impossible that our hopes might in one way or other be realized. He said that he would rather have his pension doubled than a grant of a thousand pounds; "For," said he, "though probably I may not live to receive as much as a thousand pounds, a man would have the consciousness that he should pass the remainder of his life in splendor, how long soever it might be."

As an instance of extraordinary liberality of friendship, he told us that Dr. Brocklesby had upon this occasion offered him a hundred a year for his life. A grateful tear started into his eye, as he spoke this in a faltering tone.

Sir Joshua and I endeavored to flatter his imagination with prospects of happiness in Italy. "Nay," said he, "when a man goes to Italy merely to feel how he breathes the air, he can enjoy very little."

Our conversation turned upon living in the country, which Johnson, whose melancholy mind required quick successive variety, had habituated himself to consider as a kind of mental imprisonment. "Yet, sir," said I, "there are many people who are content to live in the country." JOHNSON. "Sir, it is in the intellectual world as in the physical world; we are told by natural philosophers that a body is at rest in the place that is fit for it; they who are content to live in the country are *fit* for the country."

Talking of various enjoyments, I argued that a refinement of taste[1] was a disadvantage, as they who have attained to it must be seldomer pleased than those who have no nice discrimination, and are therefore satisfied with everything that comes in their way. JOHNSON. "Nay, sir; that is a paltry notion. Endeavor to be as perfect as you can in every respect."

I accompanied him in Sir Joshua Reynolds's coach to the entry of Bolt Court. He asked me whether I would not go with him to his house; I declined it, from an apprehension that my spirits would sink. We bade adieu to each other affectionately in the carriage. When he had got down upon the foot-pavement, he called out, "Fare you well"; and with-

---

1. *Refinement of taste.* "The nice people found no mercy from Mr. Johnson; such I mean as can dine only at four o'clock, who cannot bear to be waked at an unusual hour, or miss a stated meal without inconvenience. *He* had no such prejudices himself, and with difficulty forgave them in another. 'Delicacy does not surely consist (says he) in impossibility to be pleased, and is false dignity indeed which is content to depend upon others.'" *Mrs. Piozzi: Anecdotes.*

out looking back, sprung away with a kind of pathetic briskness, which seemed to indicate a struggle to conceal uneasiness, and impressed me with a foreboding of our long, long separation.

Soon after this time[1] Dr. Johnson had the mortification of being informed by Mrs. Thrale, that, "what she supposed he never believed," was true; namely, that she was actually going to marry Signor Piozzi, an Italian music-master. He endeavored to prevent it, but in vain. If she would publish the whole of the correspondence that passed between Dr. Johnson and her on the subject, we should have a full view of his real sentiments. As it is, our judgment must be biased by that characteristic specimen which Sir John Hawkins has given us: "Poor Thrale, I thought that either her virtue or her vice would have restrained her from such a marriage. She has now become a subject for her enemies to exult over; and for her friends, if she has any left, to forget or pity."

It must be admitted that Johnson derived a considerable portion of happiness from the comforts and elegancies which he enjoyed in Mr. Thrale's family; but Mrs. Thrale assures us he was indebted for these to her husband alone, who certainly respected him sincerely. Her words are, *"Veneration for his virtue, reverence for his talents,* delight *in his conversation, and* habitual endurance of a yoke my husband first put upon me, *and of which he contentedly bore his share for sixteen or seventeen years, made me go on so long with* Mr. Johnson; *but the perpetual confinement I will own to have been* terrifying *in the first years of our friendship, and* irksome *in the last; nor could I pretend to* support *it without help, when my coadjutor was no more."* Alas! how different is this from the declarations which I have heard Mrs. Thrale make in his lifetime, without a single murmur against any peculiarities, or against any one circumstance which attended their intimacy.

As a sincere friend of the man whose *Life* I am writing, I think it necessary to guard my readers against the mistaken notion of Dr. Johnson's character which this lady's *Anecdotes* of him suggest. The evident tendency of the following is to

---

1. *Soon after this time.*   See Appendix J, page 553.

represent Dr. Johnson as extremely deficient in affection, tenderness, or even common civility:

"*When I one day* lamented *the loss of a first cousin killed in* America—'*Prithee, my dear,*' said he, '*have done with all this canting; how would the world be worse for it, I may ask, if all your relations were at once spitted like larks, and roasted for* Presto's *supper?*' Presto *was the dog that lay under the table while we talked.*"

But let the circumstances fairly appear as told by Mr. Baretti,[1] who was present:

"Mrs. Thrale, while supping very heartily upon larks, laid down her knife and fork, and abruptly exclaimed, 'Oh, my dear Mr. Johnson, do you know what has happened? The last letters from abroad have brought us an account that our poor cousin's head was taken off by a cannon ball.' Johnson, who was shocked both at the fact, and her light, unfeeling manner of mentioning it, replied, 'Madam, it would give *you* very little concern if all your relations were spitted like those larks and dressed for Presto's supper.'"

Having left the *negotiation*, as I called it, in the best hands, I shall here insert what relates to it. Johnson wrote to Sir Joshua Reynolds on July 6, as follows: "I am going, I hope, in a few days, to try the air of Derbyshire, but hope to see you before I go. Let me, however, mention to you what I have much at heart. If the Chancellor should confer with you on the means of relieving my languid state, I am very desirous to avoid the appearance of asking money upon false pretenses. I desire you to represent to his Lordship what, as soon as it is suggested, he will perceive to be reasonable— that, if I grow much worse, I shall be afraid to leave my physicians, to suffer the inconveniences of travel, and pine in the solitude of a foreign country; that, if I grow much better, of

---

1. *Baretti.* Neither of these versions can gain much weight from the character of the teller. Mrs. Piozzi was capable of coloring and enlarging a story. Baretti had become her enemy; and as an enemy he was always brutal and far from scrupulous. The only basis of judgment is the comparative plausibility of the two reports, regardless of their authors.

which indeed there is now little appearance, I shall not wish to leave my friends and my domestic comforts; for I do not travel for pleasure or curiosity; yet if I should recover, curiosity would revive. In my present state, I am desirous to make a struggle for a little longer life, and hope to obtain some help from a softer climate. Do for me what you can." He wrote to me July 26: "I wish your affairs could have permitted a longer exertion of your zeal and kindness. They that have your kindness may want* your ardor. In the meantime I am very feeble, and very dejected."

By a letter from Sir Joshua Reynolds I was informed that the Lord Chancellor had acquainted him that the application had not been successful; but that his Lordship, after speaking highly in praise of Johnson, as a man who was an honor to his country, desired Sir Joshua to let him know that on granting a mortgage of his pension, he should draw on his Lordship to the amount of five or six hundred pounds; and that his Lordship explained the meaning of the mortgage to be that he wished the business to be conducted in such a manner that Dr. Johnson should appear to be under the least possible obligation.

How Johnson was affected upon the occasion will appear from what he wrote to Sir Joshua Reynolds:

Ashbourne, Sept. 9. "Many words I hope are not necessary between you and me, to convince you what gratitude is excited in my heart by the Chancellor's liberality and your kind offices.

"I have inclosed a letter to the Chancellor, which, when you have read it, you will be pleased to seal and convey it to him; had I sent it directly to him, I should have seemed to overlook the favor of your intervention."

"To the Lord High Chancellor.

"MY LORD: After a long and not inattentive observation of mankind, the generosity of your Lordship's offer raises in me not less wonder than gratitude. Bounty, so liberally bestowed, I should gladly receive, if my condition made it necessary; for, to such a mind, who would not be proud to own his obligations?

But it has pleased GOD to restore me to so great a measure of health that if I should now appropriate so much of a fortune destined to do good, I could not escape from myself the charge of advancing a false claim. My journey to the continent, though I once thought it necessary, was never much encouraged by my physicians; and I was very desirous that your Lordship should be told of it by Sir Joshua Reynolds as an event very uncertain; for if I grew much better, I should not be willing, if much worse, not able, to migrate.—Your Lordship was first solicited without my knowledge; but when I was told that you were pleased to honor me with your patronage, I did not expect to hear of a refusal; yet, as I have had no long time to brood hope, and have not rioted in imaginary opulence, this cold reception has been scarce a disappointment; and, from your Lordship's kindness, I have received a benefit, which only men like you are able to bestow. I shall now live *mihi carior*, with a higher opinion of my own merit.

"I am, my Lord,

"Your Lordship's most obliged,

"Most grateful, and

"Most humble servant,

"SAM. JOHNSON.

"September, 1784."

Upon this unexpected failure, I abstain from presuming to make any remarks or to offer any conjectures.

Let us now contemplate Johnson thirty years after the death of his wife, still retaining for her all the tenderness of affection.

"To the Reverend Mr. Bagshaw, at Bromley.

"SIR: Perhaps you may remember that in the year 1753 you committed to the ground my dear wife. I now entreat your permission to lay a stone upon her; and have sent the inscription, that, if you find it proper, you may signify your allowance.

"You will do me a great favor by showing the place where she lies, that the stone may protect her remains.

"Mr. Ryland[1] will wait on you for the inscription, and procure it to be engraved. You will easily believe that I shrink from this mournful office. When it is done, if I have strength remaining, I will visit Bromley once again, and pay you part of the respect to which you have a right from,

"Reverend Sir,

"Your most humble servant,

"July 12, 1784."   "SAM. JOHNSON.

Next day he set out on a jaunt to Staffordshire and Derbyshire, flattering himself that he might be in some degree relieved.

During his absence from London, he kept up a correspondence with several of his friends, from which I shall select what appears to me proper for publication, without attending nicely to chronological order.

To Dr. Brocklesby, he writes:

"Ashbourne, July 20.

"The kind attention you have so long shown to my health and happiness makes it as much a debt of gratitude as a call of interest, to give you an account of what befalls me. The second day brought me to Lichfield without much lassitude; but I am afraid that I could not have borne such violent agitation for many days together. I stayed five days at Lichfield, but being unable to walk, had no great pleasure, and yesterday (19th) I came hither, where I am to try what air and attention can perform. The weather indeed is not benign; but how low is he sunk whose strength depends upon the weather. I am now looking into Floyer,[2] who lived with his asthma to almost his ninetieth year. His book by want of order is obscure and his asthma, I think, not of the same kind. Something, however, I may perhaps learn."

August 19. "I never thought well of Dr. James's compounded medicines; his ingredients appeared to me sometimes inefficacious

---

1. *Mr. Ryland.* Though an Old School Whig and dissenter, Dr. Johnson's lifelong friend.

2. *Floyer.* The Lichfield physician on whose advice Johnson at three years of age was touched by Queen Anne.

and trifling, and sometimes heterogeneous and destructive of each other. This prescription exhibits a composition of about three hundred and thirty grains, in which there are four grains of emetic tartar, and six drops [of] thebaic tincture. He who writes thus surely writes for show."

Sept. 2. "Mr. Windham has been here to see me; he came, I think, forty miles out of his way, and stayed about a day and a half; perhaps I make the time shorter than it was. Such conversation I shall not have again till I come back to the regions of literature."

Sept. 11. "I hope with good help to find means of supporting a winter at home, and to hear and tell at the Club what is doing, and what ought to be doing in the world. I have no company here, and shall naturally come home hungry for conversation."

Lichfield, Sept. 29. "On one day I had three letters about the air balloon;[1] yours was far the best, and has enabled me to impart to my friends in the country an idea of this species of amusement. In amusement, mere amusement, I am afraid, it must end."

October 6. "The fate of the balloon I do not much lament; to make new balloons is to repeat the jest again. We now know a method of mounting into the air, and, I think, are not likely to know more. The vehicles can serve no use till we can guide them; and they can gratify no curiosity till we mount with them to greater heights than we can reach without. We know the state of the air in all its regions, to the top of Teneriffe, and, therefore, learn nothing from those who navigate a balloon below the clouds. The first experiment, however, was bold, and deserved applause and reward. But since it has been performed, and its event is known, I had rather now find a medicine that can ease an asthma."

October 25. "The town is my element; there are my friends, there are my books, to which I have not yet bid farewell, and

---

1. *The air balloon.* "You observe, madam, that the balloon engages all mankind, and, indeed, it is a wonderful and unexpected addition to human knowledge."—*Johnson to Mrs. Thrale, Jan. 12, 1784.*

there are my amusements. Sir Joshua told me long ago that my vocation was to public life, and I hope still to keep my station, till God shall bid me go in peace."

"To Sir Joshua Reynolds.

Sept. 2. "I still continue by God's mercy to mend. My breath is easier, my nights are quieter, and my legs are less in bulk and stronger in use. I have, however, yet a great deal to overcome before I can yet attain even an old man's health.[1] Write, do write to me now and then; we are now old acquaintance, and perhaps few people have lived so much and so long together with less cause of complaint on either side. The retrospection of this is very pleasant, and I hope we shall never think of each other with less kindness."

Sept. 18. "I flattered myself that this week would have given me a letter from you, but none has come. Write to me now and then, but direct your next to Lichfield. I am still in my legs weak, but so much mended that I go to Lichfield in hope of being able to pay my visits on foot, for there are no coaches. I have three letters this day, all about the balloon; I could have been content with one. Do not write about the balloon, whatever else you may think proper to say."

We now behold Johnson for the last time in his native city, which, by a sudden apostrophe, under the word *Lich*, he introduces with reverence into his immortal Work, *The English Dictionary:* *"Salve, magna parens!"* While here, he felt a revival of all the tenderness of filial affection.

To Mr. Henry White, a young clergyman, with whom he now formed an intimacy, so as to talk to him with great freedom, he mentioned that he could not in general accuse himself of

---

1. *An old man's health.* "Dear Sir, Coming down from a very restless night I found your letter, which made me a little angry. You tell me that recovery is in my own power. This, indeed, I should be glad to hear if I could once believe it. But you mean to charge me with neglecting or opposing my own health. Tell me, therefore, what I do that hurts me, and what I neglect that would help me. Tell it as soon as you can. Answer the first part of this letter immediately. Lichfield, October 23, 1784." *Dr. Johnson to Dr. Taylor.*

having been an undutiful son. "Once, indeed," said he, "I was disobedient; I refused to attend my father to Uttoxeter market. Pride was the source of that refusal, and the remembrance of it was painful. A few years ago I desired to atone for this fault. I went to Uttoxeter in very bad weather, and stood for a considerable time bareheaded in the rain, on the spot where my father's stall used to stand. In contrition I stood, and I hope the penance was expiatory."

"I told him," says Miss Seward, "in one of my latest visits to him, of a wonderful learned pig, which I had seen at Nottingham, and which did all that we have observed exhibited by dogs and horses. The subject amused him. 'Then,' said he, 'the pigs are a race unjustly calumniated. We do not allow *time* for his education, we kill him at a year old.' Mr. Henry White, who was present, observed that great torture must have been employed ere the indocility of the animal could have been subdued. 'Certainly,' said the Doctor; 'but (turning to me) how old is your pig?' I told him, three years old. 'Then,' said he, 'the pig has no cause to complain; he would have been killed the first year if he had not been *educated*, and protracted existence is a good recompense for very considerable degrees of torture.'"

Such was his intellectual ardor even at this time that he said to one friend, "Sir, I look upon every day to be lost, in which I do not make a new acquaintance"; and to another, when talking of his illness, "I will be conquered; I will not capitulate." And such was his love of London that he languished when absent from it. Although at Lichfield surrounded with friends who loved and revered him, and for whom he had a very sincere affection, he still found that such conversation as London affords could be found nowhere else. These feelings, joined, probably, to some flattering hopes of aid from the eminent physicians and surgeons who kindly and generously attended him without accepting fees, made him resolve to return to the capital. He arrived in London on the 16th of November.

Having written to him [the previous summer] in bad spirits, a letter filled with dejection and fretfulness, and at the same time expressing anxious apprehensions concerning him, on account of a dream which had disturbed me, his answer was chiefly in terms of reproach, for a supposed charge of "affecting discontent, and indulging the vanity of complaint."

Feeling very soon that the manner in which he had written might hurt me, he two days afterwards, July 28, wrote to me again, giving me an account of his sufferings; after which, he thus proceeds: "Before this letter, you will have had one which I hope you will not take amiss; for it contains only truth, and that truth kindly indeed. *Spartam quam nactus es orna;* make the most and best of your lot, and compare yourself not with the few that are above you, but with the multitudes which are below you. Go steadily forward with lawful business or honest diversions. '*Be,*' as Temple says of the Dutchmen, '*well when you are not ill, and pleased when you are not angry.*' This may seem but an ill return for your tenderness; but I mean it well, for I love you with great ardor and sincerity. Pay my respects to dear Mrs. Boswell, and teach the young ones to love me."

I unfortunately was so much indisposed during a considerable part of the year that it was not, or at least I thought it was not, in my power to write to my illustrious friend as formerly, or without expressing such complaints as offended him. Having conjured him not to do me the injustice of charging me with affectation, I was with much regret long silent. His last letter to me then came, and affected me very tenderly:

"*To James Boswell, Esq.*

"DEAR SIR: I have this summer sometimes amended and sometimes relapsed. In this uncomfortable state your letters used to relieve; what is your reason that I have them no longer? Are you sick or are you sullen? Whatever be the reason, if it be less than necessity, drive it away; and of the short life that we have, make the best use for yourself and for your friends. I am sometimes afraid that your omission to write has some real cause, and shall be glad to know that you are not sick, and that nothing ill has befallen dear Mrs. Boswell, or any of your family.

"I am, sir, yours &c.,
"SAM. JOHNSON.

"Lichfield, Nov. 5, 1784."

Yet it was not a little painful to me to find that in a paragraph of this letter, which I have omitted, he still persevered in arraigning me as before, which was strange in him who had so much experience of what I suffered. I, however, wrote to him two as kind letters as I could; the last of which came too late to be read by him, for his illness increased more rapidly upon him than I had apprehended; but I had the consolation of being informed that he spoke of me on his deathbed with affection, and I look forward with humble hope of renewing our friendship in a better world.

Soon after Johnson's return to the metropolis, both the asthma and dropsy became more violent and distressful. Still his love of literature did not fail. During his sleepless nights he amused himself by translating into Latin verse, from the Greek, many of the epigrams in the *Anthologia*. These translations, with some other poems by him in Latin, he gave to his friend Mr. Langton, who sold them to the booksellers for a small sum to be given to some of Johnson's relations, which was accordingly done; and they are printed in the collection of his works.

Johnson's affection for his departed relations seemed to grow warmer as he approached nearer to the time when he might hope to see them again.

"To Mr. Green, Apothecary, at Lichfield.

"DEAR SIR: I have inclosed the epitaph for my father, mother, and brother, to be all engraved on the large size, and laid in the middle aisle in St. Michael's Church, which I request the clergyman and churchwardens to permit. The first care must be to find the exact place of interment, that the stone may protect the bodies. Then let the stone be deep, massy, and hard; and do not let the difference of ten pounds, or more, defeat our purpose.

"I have inclosed ten pounds, and Mrs. Porter will pay you ten more, which I gave her for the same purpose. What more is wanted shall be sent; and I beg that all possible haste may be made, for I wish to have it done while I am yet alive. Let me know, dear sir, that you receive this. I am, sir,

"Your most humble servant,
"Dec. 2, 1784."   "SAM. JOHNSON.

My readers are now, at last, to behold Samuel Johnson preparing himself for that doom from which the most exalted powers afford no exemption to man. Death had always been to him an object of terror; so that though by no means happy, he still clung to life with an eagerness at which many have wondered. A member of the Eumelian Club informs me that upon one occasion, when he said to him that he saw health returning to his cheek, Johnson seized him by the hand and exclaimed, "Sir, you are one of the kindest friends I ever had."

His own state of his views of futurity will appear truly rational; and may, perhaps, impress the unthinking with seriousness.

"You know," says he, "I never thought confidence with respect to futurity, any part of the character of a brave, a wise, or a good man. Bravery has no place where it can avail nothing; wisdom impresses strongly the consciousness of those faults, of which it is, perhaps, itself an aggravation; and goodness, always wishing to be better, and imputing every deficience to criminal negligence, and every fault to voluntary corruption, never dares to suppose the condition of forgiveness fulfilled, nor what is wanting in the crime supplied by penitence.

"This is the state of the best; but what must be the condition of him whose heart will not suffer him to rank himself among the best, or among the good? Such must be his dread of the approaching trial as will leave him little attention to the opinion of those whom he is leaving forever; and the serenity that is not felt, it can be no virtue to feign."

His great fear of death and the strange dark manner in which Sir John Hawkins imparts the uneasiness which he expressed on account of offenses with which he charged himself may give occasion to injurious suspicions, as if there had been something of more than ordinary criminality weighing upon his conscience. On that account, therefore, as well as from the regard to truth which he inculcated, I am to mention (with all possible respect and delicacy, however) that his conduct, after he came to London and had associated with Savage and others, was not so strictly virtuous as when he was a younger man.

Here let the profane and licentious pause; let them not thoughtlessly say that Johnson was a *hypocrite*, or that his *principles* were not firm, because his *practice* was not uniformly conformable to what he professed. Is a prodigal, for example, a *hypocrite*, when he owns he is satisfied that his extravagance will bring him to ruin and misery? We are *sure* he *believes* it; but immediate inclination, strengthened by indulgence, prevails over that belief in influencing his conduct. Why then shall credit be refused to the *sincerity* of those who acknowledge their persuasion of moral and religious duty, yet sometimes fail of living as it requires? I heard Dr. Johnson once observe, "There is something noble in publishing truth, though it condemns one's self." And one who said in his presence, "he had no notion of people being in earnest in their good professions, whose practice was not suitable to them," was thus reprimanded by him: "Sir, are you so grossly ignorant of human nature as not to know that a man may be very sincere in good principles without having good practice?"

It is not my intention to give a very minute detail of the particulars of Johnson's remaining days, of whom it was now evident that the crisis was fast approaching when he must *"die like men, and fall like one of the Princes."* Yet it will be instructive, as well as gratifying to the curiosity of my readers, to record a few circumstances, on the authenticity of which they may perfectly rely, as I have been at the utmost pains to obtain an accurate account of his last illness, from the best authority.

Dr. Heberden, Dr. Brocklesby, Dr. Warren[1] and Dr. Butter, physicians, generously attended him, without accepting any fees, as did Mr. Cruikshank, surgeon; and all that could be done from professional skill and ability was tried, to prolong a life so truly valuable. He himself, indeed, having, on account of his very bad constitution, been perpetually applying himself to medical inquiries, united his own efforts with those of the gentlemen who attended him; and imagining that the

---

1. *Dr. Warren.* Apparently notable chiefly for his extremely lucrative practice among the wealthy and fashionable.

dropsical collection of water which oppressed him might be drawn off by making incisions in his body, he, with his usual resolute defiance of pain, cut deep,[1] when he thought that his surgeon had done it too tenderly.

About eight or ten days before his death, when Dr. Brocklesby paid him his morning visit, he seemed very low and desponding, and said, "I have been as a dying man all night." He then emphatically broke out in the words of Shakespeare,

> Can'st thou not minister to a mind diseased;
> Pluck from the memory a rooted sorrow;
> Raze out the written troubles of the brain;
> And, with some sweet, oblivious antidote,
> Cleanse the stuffed bosom of that perilous stuff
> Which weighs upon the heart?

To which Dr. Brocklesby readily answered from the same great poet:

> ——therein the patient
> Must minister to himself.

On another day after this, when talking on the subject of prayer, Dr. Brocklesby repeated from Juvenal,

> *Orandum est, ut sit mens sana in corpore sano,*

and so on to the end of the tenth satire; but in running it quickly over, he happened, in the line,

> *Qui spatium vitæ extremum inter munera ponat,*

to pronounce *supremum* for *extremum;* at which Johnson's critical ear instantly took offense, and discoursing vehemently

---

1. *Cut deep.* "When he [Dr. Cruikshank] was lancing the dying man's legs to reduce the dropsy, Johnson called out to him, 'I want life and you are afraid of giving me pain—deeper, deeper.'" *Gentleman's Magazine, 1800.*

on the unmetrical effect of such a lapse, he showed himself as full as ever of the spirit of the grammarian.[1]

Having no near relations, it had been for some time Johnson's intention to make a liberal provision for his faithful servant, Mr. Francis Barber, whom he had all along treated truly as an humble friend. Having asked Dr. Brocklesby what would be a proper annuity to a favorite servant, and being answered that it must depend on the circumstances of the master; and, that in the case of a nobleman, fifty pounds a year was considered an adequate reward for many years' faithful service—"Then" said Johnson, shall I be *nobilissimus*, for I mean to leave Frank seventy pounds a year, and I desire you to tell him so." It is strange, however, to think that Johnson was not free from that general weakness of being averse to execute a will, so that he delayed it from time to time; and had it not been for Sir John Hawkins's repeatedly urging it, I think it is probable that his kind resolution would not have been fulfilled.

The consideration of numerous papers of which he was possessed seems to have struck Johnson's mind with a sudden anxiety, and as they were in great confusion, it is much to be lamented that he had not intrusted some faithful and discreet person with the care and selection of them; instead of which, he in a precipitate manner burnt large masses of them, with little regard, as I apprehend, to discrimination. Two very valuable articles, I am sure, we have lost, which were two quarto volumes, containing a most particular account of his own life, from his earliest recollection. I owned to him that having accidentally seen them, I had read a great deal in them; and apologizing for the liberty I had taken, asked him if I could help it.

---

1. *Of the grammarian.* "I went to sleep in a chair, and when I waked, I found Dr. Brocklesby sitting by me and fell to talking with him in such a manner as made me glad, and, I hope, made me thankful. The Doctor fell to repeating Juvenal's ninth satire; but I let him see that the province was mine." *Dr. Johnson to Mrs. Thrale, June 20, 1783.* "No man forgets his original trade; the rights of nations and of kings sink into questions of grammar, if grammarians discuss them." *Johnson: Life of Milton.*

He placidly answered, "Why, sir, I do not think you could have helped it." I said that it had come into my mind to carry off those two volumes, and never see him more. Upon my inquiring how this would have affected him: "Sir," said he, "I believe I should have gone mad."

During his last illness Johnson experienced the steady and kind attachment of his numerous friends. Nobody was more attentive to him than Mr. Langton, to whom he tenderly said, *Te teneam moriens deficiente manu.* And I think it highly to the honor of Mr. Windham that his important occupations as an active statesman did not prevent him from paying assiduous respect to the Sage whom he revered. Mr.. Langton informs me that one day he found Mr. Burke and four or five more friends sitting with Johnson. Mr. Burke said to him, "I am afraid, sir, such a number of us may be oppressive to you." "No, sir," said Johnson, "it is not so; and I must be in a wretched state, indeed, when your company would not be a delight to me." Mr. Burke, in a tremulous voice, expressive of being very tenderly affected, replied, "My dear sir, you have always been too good to me." Immediately afterwards he went away. This was the last circumstance in the acquaintance of these two eminent men.

The following particulars of his conversation within a few days of his death, I give on the authority of Mr. John Nichols:

"He said that the Parliamentary Debates were the only part of his writings which then gave him any compunction; but that at the time he wrote them he had no conception he was imposing upon the world, though they were frequently written from very slender materials, and often, from none at all—the mere coinage of his own imagination.

"Of his friend Cave, he always spoke with great affection. 'Yet,' said he, 'Cave (who never looked out of his window, but with a view to the *Gentleman's Magazine*) was a penurious paymaster; he would contract for lines by the hundred, and expect the long hundred, but he was a good man, and always delighted to have his friends at his table.'

"He said at another time, three or four days only before his death, speaking of the little fear he had of undergoing a surgical operation, 'I would give one of these legs for a year more of life, I mean of comfortable life, not such as that which I now suffer'; and lamented much his inability to read during his hours of restlessness. 'I used formerly,' he added, 'when sleepless in bed, *to read like a Turk*.'"

Amidst the melancholy clouds which hung over the dying Johnson, his characteristical manner showed itself on different occasions.

When Dr. Warren, in the usual style, hoped that he was better, his answer was, "No, sir; you cannot conceive with what acceleration I advance toward death."

A man whom he had never seen before was employed one night to sit up with him. Being asked next morning how he liked his attendant, his answer was, "Not at all, sir; the fellow's an idiot; he is as awkward as a turnspit when first put into the wheel, and as sleepy as a dormouse."

Mr. Windham having placed a pillow conveniently to support him, he thanked him for his kindness, and said, "That will do —all that a pillow can do."[1]

As he opened a note which his servant brought to him, he said: "An odd thought strikes me: we shall receive no letters in the grave."

He requested three things of Sir Joshua Reynolds: to forgive him thirty pounds[2] which he had borrowed of him; to read the Bible; and never to use his pencil on a Sunday. Sir Joshua readily acquiesced.

Dr. Brocklesby having attended him with the utmost assiduity and kindness as his physician and friend, he was peculiarly desirous that this gentleman should not entertain any loose speculative notions, but be confirmed in the truths of Christianity,

---

1. *All that a pillow can do.* "The cure for the greatest part of human miseries is not radical, but palliative." *Johnson: The Rambler.*

2. *Forgive him thirty pounds.* "In the course of the conversation [on December 7, 1784], he asked whether any of the family of Faden, the printer, were living. Being told that the geographer near Charing Cross was Faden's son, he said, after a short pause: 'I borrowed a guinea of his father near thirty years ago; be so good as to take this, and pay it for me.'" *Murphy: Essay on Johnson's Life and Genius.*

and insisted on his writing down in his presence, as nearly as he could collect it, the import of what passed on the subject; and Dr. Brocklesby having complied with the request, he made him sign the paper, and urged him to keep it in his own custody as long as he lived.

Johnson, with that native fortitude which, amidst all his bodily distress and mental sufferings, never forsook him, asked Dr. Brocklesby, as a man in whom he had confidence, to tell him plainly whether he could recover. "Give me," said he, "a direct answer." The Doctor having first asked him if he could bear the whole truth, which way soever it might lead, and being answered that he could, declared that, in his opinion, he could not recover without a miracle. "Then," said Johnson, "I will take no more physic, not even my opiates; for I have prayed that I may render up my soul to God unclouded." In this resolution he persevered, and, at the same time, used only the weakest kinds of sustenance. Being pressed by Mr. Windham to take somewhat more generous nourishment, lest too low a diet should have the very effect which he dreaded, by debilitating his mind, he said, "I will take anything but inebriating sustenance."

Having, as has been already mentioned, made his will on the 8th and 9th of December,[1] and settled all his worldly affairs, he languished till Monday, the 13th of that month,[2] when he expired, about seven o'clock in the evening, with so little apparent pain that his attendants hardly perceived when his dissolution took place.

Of his last moments, my brother, Thomas David, has furnished me with the following particulars:

"The Doctor, from the time that he was certain his death was near, appeared to be perfectly resigned, was seldom or

---

1. *9th of December.* "He [Johnson] will not, it seems, be talked to—at least, very rarely. At times, indeed, he reanimates, but it is soon over, and he says of himself, 'I am now like Macbeth—question enrages me.'" *Mme. D'Arblay, Dec. 9, 1784.*

2. *13th of that month.* "William Hutton, who left London for Birmingham on the night of December 12, describes how 'our bill of lading being completed, we began to roll over one hundred and twenty miles of snow without any noise but that of the wheels.'" *Birkbeck Hill.*

never fretful or out of temper, and often said to his faithful servant, who gave me this account, 'Attend, Francis, to the salvation of your soul, which is the object of greatest importance'; he also explained to him passages in the Scripture, and seemed to have pleasure in talking upon religious subjects.

"On Monday, the 13th of December, the day on which he died, a Miss Morris, daughter to a particular friend of his, called, and said to Francis that she begged to be permitted to see the Doctor, that she might earnestly request him to give her his blessing. Francis went into his room, followed by the young lady, and delivered the message. The Doctor turned himself in the bed, and said, 'God bless you, my dear!' These were the last words he spoke.—His difficulty of breathing increased till about seven o'clock in the evening, when Mr. Barber and Mrs. Desmoulins, who were sitting in the room, observing that the noise he made in breathing had ceased, went to the bed, and found he was dead."

A few days before his death, he had asked Sir John Hawkins, as one of his executors, where he should be buried; and on being answered, "Doubtless, in Westminster Abbey,"[1] seemed

---

1. *Westminster Abbey.* "The noble ruins of the great cathedral [of Elgin] Johnson examined with a most patient attention, though the rain was falling fast." The lead had been stripped off the roof and shipped to be sold in Holland. "I hope," Johnson says in his *Journey to the Western Isles*, "every reader will rejoice that this cargo of sacrilege was lost at sea. Let us not, however, make too much haste to despise our neighbors. Our own cathedrals are moldering by unregarded dilapidation. It seems to be part of the despicable philosophy of the time to despise monuments of sacred magnificence, and we are in danger of doing that deliberately which the Scots did not do but in the unsettled state of an imperfect constitution." To this Birkbeck Hill adds:

"He had learned, there seems good reason to believe, that the chapter of the cathedral of his own town of Lichfield intended to strip the lead off its roof and cover it instead with slate. As he had first printed his narrative, he had much more closely pointed the attack. It had run as follows: 'There is now, as I have heard, a body of men, not less decent or virtuous than the Scottish council, longing to melt the lead of an English cathedral. What they shall melt it was just that they should swallow.' Before publication, he had the leaf cancelled from the tender recollection that the dean had done him a kindness about forty years before. 'He is now very old and I am not young. Reproach can do him no good and in myself I know not whether it is zeal or wantonness.'"

to feel a satisfaction, very natural to a poet; and indeed in my opinion very natural to every man of any imagination who has no family sepulcher in which he can be laid with his fathers. Accordingly, upon Monday, December 20, his remains were deposited in that noble and renowned edifice; and over his grave was placed a large blue flagstone, with this inscription:[1]

"SAMUEL JOHNSON, LL.D.
Obiit XIII *die Decembris,*
Anno Domini
M.DCC.LXXXIV.
Ætatis suæ LXXV."

I trust I shall not be accused of affectation when I declare that I find myself unable to express all that I felt upon the loss of such a "Guide, Philosopher, and Friend." I shall, therefore, not say one word of my own, but adopt those of an eminent friend, which he uttered with an abrupt felicity, superior to all studied compositions: "He has made a chasm which not only nothing can fill up, but which nothing has a tendency to fill up.—Johnson is dead.—Let us go to the next best:—there is nobody; no man can be said to put you in mind of Johnson."

Many who trembled at his presence were forward in assault when they no longer apprehended danger. When one of his little pragmatical foes was invidiously snarling at his fame, at Sir Joshua Reynolds's table, the Reverend Dr. Parr exclaimed, with his usual bold animation, "Aye, now that the old lion is dead, every ass thinks he may kick at him."

The character of Samuel Johnson has, I trust, been so developed in the course of this work that they who have honored it with a perusal may be considered as well acquainted with him. As, however, it may be expected that I should collect into one

---

1. *Inscription.* "The best subject for epitaphs is private virtue. He that has delivered his country from oppression or freed the world from ignorance and error can excite the emulation of a very small number, but he that has repelled the temptations of poverty and disdained to free himself from distress at the expense of his virtue may animate multitudes by his example to the same firmness of heart and steadiness of resolution." *Johnson: Essay on Epitaphs.*

view the capital and distinguishing features of this extraordinary man, I shall endeavour to acquit myself of that part of my biographical undertaking, however difficult it may be to do that which many of my readers will do better for themselves.

His figure was large and well formed, and his countenance of the cast of an ancient statue; yet his appearance was rendered strange and somewhat uncouth by convulsive cramps, by the scars of that distemper which it was once imagined the royal touch could cure, and by a slovenly mode of dress. He had the use only of one eye; yet so much does mind govern, and even supply the deficiency of organs, that his visual perceptions, as far as they extended, were uncommonly quick and accurate. So morbid was his temperament that he never knew the natural joy of a free and vigorous use of his limbs; when he walked, it was like the struggling gait of one in fetters; when he rode, he had no command or direction of his horse, but was carried as if in a balloon. That with his constitution and habits of life he should have lived seventy-five years is a proof that an inherent *vivida vis* is a powerful preservative of the human frame.

Man is, in general, made up of contradictory qualities; and these will ever show themselves in strange succession, where a consistency in appearance at least, if not reality, has not been attained by long habits of philosophical discipline. In proportion to the native vigor of the mind, the contradictory qualities will be the more prominent, and more difficult to be adjusted; and, therefore, we are not to wonder that Johnson exhibited an eminent example of this remark which I have made upon human nature. At different times he seemed a different man, in some respects; not, however, in any great or essential article, upon which he had fully employed his mind, and settled certain principles of duty, but only in his manners, and in the display of argument and fancy in his talk. He was prone to superstition, but not to credulity. Though his imagination might incline him to a belief of the marvelous and the mysterious, his vigorous reason examined the evidence with jealousy. He was a sincere and zealous Christian, of high Church of England and monarchical principles, which he would not tamely suffer to be questioned; and had, perhaps, at an early period, narrowed his mind somewhat too much, both as to religion and politics. His being impressed with the danger of extreme latitude in either, though he was of a very independent spirit, occasioned his appearing somewhat unfavorable to the prevalence of that noble freedom of sentiment which is the best possession of man. Nor can it be denied that he had many prejudices; which, however, frequently suggested many of his pointed sayings, that rather show a playfulness of fancy than any settled malignity. He was steady and inflexible in maintaining the obligations of religion and morality; both from a regard for the order of society, and from a veneration for the Great Source of all order; correct, nay, stern in his taste; hard to please, and easily offended; impetuous and irritable in his temper, but of a most humane and benevolent heart, which showed itself not only in a most liberal charity, as far as his circumstances would allow, but in a thousand instances of active benevolence. He was afflicted with a bodily disease, which made him often restless and fretful; and with a constitutional melancholy, the clouds of which darkened the brightness of his fancy, and gave a gloomy cast to his whole course of thinking. We, therefore, ought not to wonder at his sallies of impatience and passion at any time; especially when provoked by obtrusive ignorance or presuming petulance; and allowance must be made for his uttering hasty and satirical sallies even against his best friends. And, surely, when it is considered, that, "amidst sickness and sorrow," he exerted his faculties in so many works for the benefit of mankind, and particularly that he achieved the great and admirable *Dictionary* of our language, we must be astonished at his resolution. The solemn text, "of him to whom much is given, much will be required," seems to have been ever present to his mind, in a rigorous sense, and to have made him dissatisfied with his labors and acts of goodness, however comparatively great; so that the unavoidable consciousness of his superiority was, in that respect, a cause of disquiet. He suffered so much from this, and from the gloom which perpetually haunted him, and made solitude frightful, that it may be said of him, "If in this life only he had hope, he was of all men most miserable." He loved praise, when it was brought to him; but was too proud to seek for it. He was somewhat susceptible of flattery. As he was general and unconfined in his studies, he cannot be considered as master of any one particular science; but he had accumulated a vast and various collection of learning and knowledge, which was so arranged in his mind as to be ever in readiness to be brought forth. But his superiority over other learned men consisted chiefly in what may be called the art of thinking, the art of using his mind; a certain continual power of seizing the useful substance of all that he knew, and exhibiting it in a clear and forcible manner; so that knowledge, which we often see to be no better than lumber in men of dull understanding, was, in him, true, evident, and actual wisdom. His moral precepts are practical; for they are drawn from an intimate acquaintance with human nature. His maxims carry conviction; for they are founded on the basis of common sense, and a very attentive and minute survey of real life. His mind was so full of imagery that he might have been perpetually a poet; yet it is remarkable, that, however rich his prose is in this respect, his poetical pieces, in general, have not much of that splendor, but are rather distinguished by strong sentiment and acute observation, conveyed in harmonious and energetic verse, particularly in heroic couplets. Though usually grave, and even awful in his deportment, he possessed uncommon and peculiar powers of wit and humor; he frequently indulged himself in colloquial pleasantry; and the heartiest merriment was often enjoyed in his company; with this great advantage that, as it was entirely free from any poisonous tincture of vice or impiety, it was salutary to those who shared in it. He had accustomed himself to such accuracy in his common conversation that he at all times expressed his thoughts with great force, and an elegant choice of language, the effect of which was aided by his having a loud voice, and a slow, deliberate utterance. In him were united a most logical head with a most fertile imagination, which gave him an extraordinary advantage in arguing; for he could reason close or wide, as he saw best for the moment. Exulting in his intellectual strength and dexterity, he could, when he pleased, be the greatest sophist that ever contended in the lists of declamation; and from a spirit of contradiction and a delight in showing his powers, he would often maintain the wrong side with equal warmth and ingenuity; so that, when there was an audience, his real opinions could seldom be gathered from his talk; though when he was in company with a single friend, he would discuss a subject with genuine fairness; but he was too conscientious to make error permanent and pernicious, by deliberately writing it; and, in all his numerous works, he earnestly inculcated what appeared to him to be the truth; his piety being constant, and the ruling principle of all his conduct.

Such was SAMUEL JOHNSON, a man whose talents, acquirements, and virtues were so extraordinary that the more his character is considered, the more he will be regarded by the present age, and by posterity, with admiration and reverence.[1]

---

1. *Reverence.* "I used to tell [Dr. Johnson] in jest that his morality was easily contented, and when I have said something as if the wickedness of the world gave me concern, he would cry out aloud against canting, and protest that he thought there was very little gross wickedness in the world, and still less of extraordinary virtue. 'Heroic virtues,' said he, 'are the *bon mots* of life; they do not appear often, and when they do appear are too much prized. I think life is made up of little things, and that character is best which does little but repeated acts of beneficence. I hope I have not lost my sensibility of wrong; but I hope likewise that I have lived long enough in the world to prevent me from expecting to find any action of which all the original motives and all the parts were good.'" *Mrs. Piozzi: Anecdotes of Dr. Johnson.*

APPENDIXES

APPENDIX A

RICHARD SAVAGE

Savage, Richard (1697?-1743).   Author of the *Wanderer* (1729) and other works.

"An author whose manufactures had long lain uncalled for in the warehouse, till he happened, very fortunately for his bookseller, to be found guilty of a capital crime."   *Henry Fielding.*

"To the acquisition of extensive acquaintance every circumstance of his life contributed. He excelled in the arts of conversation . . . He was always ready to comply with every invitation, having . . . often no money to provide for himself; and by dining with one company, he never failed of obtaining an introduction into another."

"To supply him with money was a hopeless attempt, for no sooner did he see himself master of a sum sufficient to set him free from care for a day than he became profuse and luxurious."

"If his miseries were sometimes the consequences of his faults, . . . his faults were very often the effect of misfortunes."

"It must be confessed that Mr. Savage's esteem was no very certain possession, and that he would lampoon at one time those whom he had praised at another." . . . "That Mr. Savage was too much elated by any good fortune is generally known . . . . His prosperity was heightened by the force of novelty and made more intoxicating by a sense of the misery in which he had so long languished, and perhaps by the insults he had formerly borne, and which he might now think himself entitled to revenge."   *Johnson: Life of Savage.*

"It is impossible to pass a day or an hour in the confluxes of men without seeing how much indigence is exposed to contumely, neglect, and insult; and in its lowest state to hunger and nakedness; to injuries against which every passion is in arms, and to wants which nature cannot sustain."   *Johnson: The Rambler.*

APPENDIX B

MRS. SAMUEL JOHNSON

Deepest distress.   According to Johnson's friend, Mrs. Williams, who had lived with them both, Mrs. Johnson "had a good understanding and great sensibility, but [was] inclined to be satirical."

"Some cunning men choose fools for their wives, thinking to manage them, but they always fail. . . . And suppose a fool to be made do pretty well, you must have the continual trouble of making her do. Depend upon it, no woman is the worse for sense and knowledge." *Johnson, quoted in Boswell's Journal of a Tour to the Hebrides.*

"Of another lady, more insipid than offensive, I once heard him say, 'she has some softness, indeed, but so has a pillow,' and when one observed in reply that her husband's fidelity and attachment were exemplary . . . 'why, sir,' said the Doctor, 'being married to those sleepy-souled women is just like playing at cards for nothing: no passion is excited, and time is filled up.' " "I asked him if he ever disputed with his wife (I had heard that he loved her passionately). 'Perpetually,' said he; 'my wife had a particular reverence for cleanliness, and desired the praise of neatness in her dress and furniture, as many ladies do, till they become troublesome to their best friends, slaves to their own besoms [brooms], and only sigh for the hour of sweeping their husbands out of the house as dirt and useless lumber. . . .' " "One day . . . I asked him if he ever huffed his wife about his dinner. 'So often,' replied he, 'that at last she called out to me, and said, "Nay, hold, Mr. Johnson, and do not make a farce of thanking God for a dinner which in a few minutes you will protest not eatable." ' " *Mrs. Piozzi.*

"Wives and husbands are, indeed, incessantly complaining of each other; and there would be reason for imagining that almost every house was infested with perverseness or oppression beyond human sufferance, did we not know . . . how naturally every animal revenges his pain upon those who happen to be near, without any nice examination of its cause." *Johnson: The Rambler.*

"Though it must be allowed that he suffers most like a hero that hides his grief in silence, . . . yet it cannot be denied that he who complains acts like a man, like a social being, who looks for help from his fellow-creatures." *The same.*

In 1739, Johnson wrote to his wife: "Dearest Tetty, after hearing that you are in so much danger, as I apprehend from a hurt on a tendon, I shall be very uneasy till I know you are recovered, and beg that you will omit nothing that can contribute to it, nor deny yourself anything that may make confinement less melancholy. You have already suffered more than I can bear to reflect upon, and I hope more than either of us shall suffer again."

In 1778, Johnson wrote to one recently bereaved of his wife: "A loss such as yours lacerates the mind, and breaks the whole system of purposes and hopes. It leaves a dismal vacuity in life, which affords nothing on which the affections can fix, or to which endeavor may be directed. All this I have known, and it is now, in the vicissitude of things, your turn to know it."

APPENDIX C

RASSELAS AND CANDIDE

Wonderfully similar in its plan and conduct. The story of *Rasselas* closes under the shadow of those tombs of ancient kings, the pyramids. " 'Let us return,' said Rasselas, 'from this scene of mortality. Those that lie here stretched before us, the wise and powerful of ancient times, warn us to remember the shortness of our present state; they were, perhaps, snatched away while they were busy, like us, in the *choice of life.*' 'To me,' said the princess, 'the choice of life is become less important; I hope hereafter to think only on the choice of eternity.' "

Candide ends more cynically and more gayly, "In the neighborhood there was a celebrated dervish, who passed for the best philosopher in Turkey.. They went to consult him. Pangloss began by saying: 'Master, we come to beg you to tell us why such an extraordinary animal as man was ever created.' 'Why do you meddle with that question?' said the dervish. 'Is it any of your business?'

" 'I had hoped,' said Pangloss, 'to reason with you a little about causes and effects, the best of possible worlds, the origin of evil, and preëstablished harmony.' The dervish, on hearing this, shut the door in his face.

" 'I presume,' said the Turk, 'that in general, those who meddle in public affairs have perished—sometimes most miserably. I am content to raise fruit and send it to market.' 'You must have,' said Candide to the Turk, 'a vast and magnificent estate.' 'I have only twenty acres,' responded the Turk; 'I cultivate them with the help of my children. The labor saves us from three great evils—boredom, vice, and want.'

"Candide soon learned to follow this excellent example and when anyone attempted to discuss the problems of life with him, responded, 'That is very well put, but I must go now and work in my garden.' "

APPENDIX D

MACPHERSON AND OSSIAN

Macpherson, James (1736-96). A Scotchman who professed to have discovered in the Highlands of Scotland oral traditions and even some Gaelic manuscripts containing fragments of third-century poetry by one *Ossian*, son of the warrior *Fingal*. Macpherson never showed any manuscripts to the general public, but in 1760, 61, and 63 offered what he called translations of them. His works excited interest not only because of the unusualness of their theme and the vagueness and strangeness of their pictures of nature, but also because of the suspicions that quickly gathered about his claims. In 1805, a committee of the Highland Society of Scotland, after a careful investigation, reported (a) that a great legend of Fingal and his son Ossian had from times immemorial existed in Scotland, and that "Ossianic poetry was still found in great abundance in the Highlands"; but (b) that no one poem could be discoverable, quite like Macpherson's publications, and (c) that Macpherson had very freely edited his originals and inserted passages of his own. Macpherson was evidently neither a scrupulously honest man nor a complete impostor; and Dr. Johnson, in some other episodes of his life, credulous to the point of absurdity, was in this too skeptical.

"He [Macpherson] means to publish a collection he has of these specimens of antiquity, if it be antiquity, but what plagues me—I cannot come at any certainty on that head. I was so struck so *extasie* with their infinite beauty that I writ into Scotland to make a thousand inquiries. The letters I have in return are . . . calculated (one would imagine) to deceive one, and yet not cunning enough to do it cleverly. In short, the whole external evidence would make me believe these fragments . . . counterfeit, but the internal is so strong on the other side that I am resolved to believe them genuine, spite of the devil and the Kirk [Church]." *Thomas Gray, 1660.*

"I have the pleasure of being taken every evening to the homes of many of the upper middle class. One of them sings very well. She knows many ancient Scotch airs which charm me by their simplicity. It is a fact that many of the hymns of Ossian still preserve their first settings. She has repeated to me Ossian's apostrophe to the moon. The music is like nothing I have ever heard. . . . It is a soft and gentle music which seems to come from a far distant shore of the sea, and to echo among tombs." *Fontanes to Joubert, 1785.*

"Of the Erse language, as I understand nothing, I cannot say more than I have been told. It is the rude speech of a barbarous people, who had few thoughts to express, and were content, as they conceived grossly, to be grossly understood . . . [Two hundred years ago] the Erse merely floated in the breath of the people. . . . In an unwritten speech, nothing that is not very short is transmitted from one generation to another. Few have opportunities of hearing a long composition often enough to learn it, or have inclination to repeat it so often as is necessary to retain it; and what is once forgotten is lost forever. . . . Yet I hear that the father of Ossian boasts of two chests more of ancient poetry, which he suppresses because they are too good for the English . . .

"To revenge reasonable incredulity by refusing evidence is a degree of insolence with which the world is not yet acquainted and stubborn audacity is the last refuge of guilt . . . He has doubtless inserted names that circulate in popular stories, and may have translated some wandering ballads, if any can be found; and the names, and some of the images, being recollected, make an inaccurate auditor imagine, by the help of Caledonian [Scotch] bigotry, that he has formerly heard the whole." *Johnson: A Journey to the Western Islands of Scotland.*

APPENDIX E

THE STATE OF NATURE

A fashionable topic. Years before Rousseau contributed his tremendous energy to the notion, men who felt themselves over-civilized had begun to debate whether man in his primitive state (the state of nature) was not healthier, happier, and more virtuous than themselves. Few men were more charmed with the notion than Boswell, though he never thought to act on it, and often childishly echoed Dr. Johnson's disapproval of it.

Mr. Dempster. "I have now for the first time in my life passed a winter in the country . . . I used not only to wonder at, but pity, those whose lot condemned them to winter anywhere but in either of the capitals [London or Paris]. But every place has its charm to a cheerful mind." *George Dempster to Boswell, 1775.*

Nothing to a wise man. "*Boswell:* 'The philosophers, when they placed happiness in a cottage, supposed cleanliness and no smoke.' *Johnson:* 'Sir, they did not think about either.'" *Boswell: Journal of a Tour to the Hebrides.*

"The traveler now and then finds a heap of loose stones and a turf in a cavity between rocks, where a being born with all those powers which education expands and culture refines is condemned to shelter itself from the wind and rain. Philosophers there are who try to make themselves believe that this life is happy; but they only believe it while they are saying it. Privation of pleasure can never please, and content is not much to be envied when it has no other principle than ignorance of good." *Johnson from the Hebrides in 1773.*

"Among savage nations, imaginary wants find, indeed, no place; but their strength is exhausted by necessary toils, and their passions agitated, not by contests about superiority, affluence, or precedence, but by perpetual care for the present day, and by fear of perishing for want of food." *Johnson: Life of Drake.*

"Our satisfaction in finding ourselves again in a comfortable carriage was very great. We had a pleasing conviction of the commodiousness of civilization and heartily laughed at the ravings of those absurd visionaries who have attempted to persuade us of the superior advantages of a *state of nature.*" *Boswell: Journal of a Tour to the Hebrides.*

APPENDIX F

BOSWELL AND CORSICA

Returned to London. Boswell had visited the principal countries of Europe, had made pilgrimages to Rousseau and to Voltaire; and had spent many weeks with General Paoli and the Corsicans while they were engaged in their vain struggle for independence against the ambitions of France.

"I shall see Voltaire; I shall also see Switzerland and Rousseau; these two men are to me greater objects than most statues and pictures." *James Boswell to Sir Andrew Mitchell, 1764.*

"Before I was accustomed to the Corsican hospitality I sometimes forgot myself, and, imagining I was in a public house, called for what I wanted, with the tone which one uses in calling to the waiters at a tavern. I did so at Pino, asking for a variety of things at once; when Signora Tomasi, perceiving my mistake, looked in my face and smiled, saying with much calmness and good nature, '*Una cosa dopo un altra, Signore*—One thing after another, Sir." *Boswell: Corsica.*

"One day when I rode out I was mounted on Paoli's own horse, with rich furniture of crimson velvet, with broad gold lace, and had my guard marching along with me. I allowed myself to indulge a momentary pride in this parade, as I was curious to experience what could really be the pleasure of state and distinction with which mankind are so strangely intoxicated.

"When I returned to the Continent after all this greatness, I used to joke with my acquaintance, and tell them that I could not bear to live with them, for they did not treat me with a proper respect.

"My time passed here in the most agreeable manner. I enjoyed a sort of luxury of noble sentiment. . . . " *Boswell: Corsica.*

"I harangued the men of Bastelica with great fluency. I expatiated on the bravery of the Corsicans, by which they had purchased liberty, the most valuable of all possessions, and rendered themselves glorious over all Europe. . . . I bid them remember that they were much happier in their present state than in a state of refinement and vice, and that therefore they should beware of luxury." *Boswell: Corsica.*

"I took leave of Paoli with regret and agitation, not without some hopes of seeing him again. From having known intimately so exalted a character, my sentiments of human nature were raised, while by a sort of contagion, I felt an honest ardor to distinguish myself, and be useful, as far as my situation and abilities would allow; and I was, for the rest of my life, set free from a slavish timidity in the presence of great men, for where shall I find a man greater than Paoli?" *Boswell: Corsica.*

APPENDIX G

THE HEBRIDES

Stay in Scotland. "Whoever had been in the place where I then sat, unprovided with provisions, and ignorant of the country, might, at least before the roads were made, have wandered among the rocks till he had perished with hardship before he could have found either food or shelter. Yet what are these hillocks to the ridges of Taurus, or these spots of wilderness to the deserts of America? . . .

"It is not to be imagined without experience how, in climbing crags and treading bogs, and winding through narrow and obstructed passages, a little bulk will hinder and a little weight will burden; or how often a man that has pleased himself at home with his own resolution, will, in the hour of darkness and fatigue, be content to leave behind him everything but himself. . . .

"The inhabitants were for a long time perhaps not unhappy; but their content was a muddy mixture of pride and ignorance, an indifference for pleasures which they did not know, a blind veneration for their chiefs, and a strong conviction of their own importance." *Johnson: A Journey to the Western Islands of Scotland.*

"Dr. Johnson appeared today very weary of our present confined situation. He said, 'I want to be on the mainland, and go on with existence. This is a waste of life.' " *Boswell: Journal of a Tour to the Hebrides.*

"Such are the things which this journey has given me an opportunity of seeing, and such are the reflections which that sight has raised. Having passed my time almost wholly in cities, I may have been surprised by modes of life and appearances of nature that are familiar to men of wider survey and more varied conversation. Novelty and ignorance must always be reciprocal, and I cannot but be conscious that my thoughts on national manners are the thoughts of one who has seen but little." *Johnson: A Journey to the Western Islands of Scotland.*

APPENDIX H

SECOND SIGHT

"The *Second Sight* is an impression made either by the mind upon the eye or by the eye upon the mind, by which things distant and future are perceived and seen as if they were present. A man on a journey far from home falls from his horse; another, who is perhaps at work about the house, sees him bleeding on the ground, commonly with a landscape of the place where the accident befalls him. Another seer, driving home his cattle, or wandering in idleness, or musing in the sunshine, is suddenly surprised by the appearance of a bridal ceremony or funeral procession, and counts the mourners or attendants, of whom, if he knows them, he relates the names. . . . The impression is sudden and the effect painful. . . . It is the common talk of the Lowland Scots that the notion of the *Second Sight* is wearing away with other superstitions; and that its reality is no longer supposed but by the grossest people. How far its prevalence ever extended, or what ground it has lost I know not. The islanders of all degrees, whether of rank or understanding, universally admit it, except the ministers, who usually deny it. . . . Strong reasons for incredulity will readily occur . . . It is a breach of the common order of things, without any visible reason, or perceptible benefit. It is ascribed only to a people very little enlightened; and among them, for the most part, to the mean and ignorant. To the confidence of these objections it may be replied that by presuming to determine what is fit, and what is beneficial, they presuppose more knowledge of the universal system than man has attained; and therefore depend upon principles too complicated and extensive for our comprehension. . . . There is against it the seeming analogy of things confusedly seen and little understood; and for it, the indistinct cry of national persuasion, which may be perhaps resolved at last into prejudice and tradition. I never could advance my curiosity to conviction; but came away at last only willing to believe." *Johnson: A Journey to the Western Islands of Scotland.*

"He [Johnson] inquired here if there were any remains of the second sight. Mr. M'Pherson, Minister of State, said he was *resolved* not to believe it, because it was founded on no principle. *Johnson:* 'There are many things then which we are sure are true that you will not believe. What principle is there why a loadstone attracts iron, why an egg produces a chicken by heat, why a tree grows upwards when the natural tendency of all things is downwards? Sir, it depends upon the degree of evidence that you have." *Boswell: Journal of a Tour to the Hebrides.*

APPENDIX I

ALL BOYS LOVE LIBERTY

All boys love liberty. "The liberty of the press is a blessing when we are inclined to write against others, and a calamity when we find ourselves overborne by . . . our assailants, as the power of the Crown is always thought too great by those who suffer by its influence and too little by those in whose favor it is exerted; and a standing army is generally accounted necessary by those who command, and dangerous and oppressive by those who support it." *Johnson: Life of Savage.*

"Subordination supposes power on one part and subjection on the other; and if power be in the hands of men, it will sometimes be abused." *Imlac in Johnson's Rasselas.*

"I said I believed mankind were happier in the ancient feudal state of subordination than they are in the modern state of independency. *Johnson.* . . . 'That state from which all escape as soon as they can, and to which none return after they have left it, must be less happy; and this is the case with the state of dependence on a chief or great man.'" *Boswell: Journal of a Tour to the Hebrides.*

"The miseries of the poor are such as cannot easily be borne: such as have already incited them in many parts of the kingdom to an open defiance of government, and produced one of the greatest of political evils—the necessity of ruling by immediate [direct use of] force." *Johnson: Considerations of the Corn Laws,* 1766 (?).

"[Johnson] said, with a smile, that he wondered that the phrase of *unnatural* rebellion should be so much used, for that all rebellion was natural to man." *Boswell: Journal of a Tour to the Hebrides.*

"Every man that crowds our streets is a man of honor, disdainful of obligation, impatient of reproach, and desirous of extending his reputation among those of his own rank; and as courage is in most frequent use, the fame of courage is most eagerly pursued. From this neglect of subordination I do not deny that some inconveniences may from time to time proceed; . . . but good and evil will grow up in this world together; and they who complain in peace of the insolence of the populace must remember that their insolence in peace is bravery in war."—*Johnson, 1758.*

"We live in an age in which there is much talk of independence, of private judgment, of liberty of thought, and liberty of press. Our clamorous praises of liberty sufficiently prove that we enjoy it; and if by liberty nothing else be meant than security from the persecutions of power, it is so fully possessed by us that little more is to be desired except that one should talk of it less and use it better.

"But a social being can scarcely rise to complete independence; he that has any wants which others can supply must study the gratification of them whose assistance he expects; this is equally true whether his wants be wants of nature or of vanity." *Johnson: in The Gentleman's Magazine, October, 1760.*

"The manners of the world are not a regular system planned by philosophers upon settled principles, in which every cause has a congruous effect, and one part has a just reference to another. Of the fashions prevalent in every country, a few have arisen, perhaps, from particular temperatures of the climate; a few more from the constitution of the government; but the greater part have grown up by chance; been started by caprice, been contrived by affectation, or borrowed without any just motives of choice from other countries. . . . Yet by the observation of these trifles it is that the ranks of mankind are kept in order and the address of one to another is regulated, and the general business of the world carried on with facility and method." *Johnson: The Adventurer.*

"Why, sir, a man grows better humored as he grows older. He improves by experience. When young, he thinks himself of great consequence, and everything of importance. As he advances in life, he learns to think himself of no consequence, and little things of little importance; and so he becomes more patient and better pleased. All good humor and complaisance are acquired. Naturally a child seizes directly what it sees, and thinks of pleasing itself only. By degrees it is taught to please others." *Johnson, quoted in Boswell's Journal of a Tour to the Hebrides.*

"The general story of mankind will evince that lawful and settled authority is very seldom resisted when it is well employed." *Johnson: The Rambler.*

APPENDIX J

MRS. THRALE'S SECOND MARRIAGE

Soon after this time. Signor Piozzi was an accomplished Italian tenor of Roman Catholic persuasion. Years after this marriage, Samuel Rogers, an exacting English critic, found him "very handsome, gentlemanly, and amiable" and "a very good husband." But Mrs. Thrale's first husband, a substantial, though somewhat heavy Protestant brewer, had been more to the taste of those who had enjoyed the lavish Thrale hospitality at Streatham.

The Signor's manners were so markedly Italian that even Mrs. Thrale had caricatured him behind his back in a musical gathering only a few months before; she had not dared to be quite candid about the engagement, forgetting that, as Johnson has somewhere said, "the bravest man is not always in the greatest danger"; she was also putting once hospitable Streatham up to rent and taking all her social gifts to a land of Roman Catholics and foreigners. Her own daughters broke with her.

Her little protégée, Fanny Burney, describes the effect of this marriage on an old English lady, whose name she does not mention: "Rage more intemperate I have not often seen, and the shrill voice of feeble old age, screaming with unavailing passion is horrible." And Fanny Burney herself says very smugly: "Following, with this so long dearest friend the simple but unrivaled golden rule, I would only preserve such [of her letters] as evince her conflicts, her misery, and her sufferings, mental and corporeal, to exonerate her from the banal reproach of yielding unresisting to her passions. Her fault and grievous misfortune was, not combating them in their origin; not flying even from their menace."

According to Mrs. Piozzi's records of her own correspondence, perhaps not altogether trustworthy, on June 30, 1784, she wrote with much warmth of sentiment to Dr. Johnson to announce her decision to remarry. The time of the marriage, which was not to occur until July 28, she left in obscurity. Johnson rashly jumped at the conclusion that the ceremony had already occurred and wrote:

"Madam,

"If I interpret your letter right, you are ignominiously married; if it is yet undone, let us once more talk together. If you have abandoned your children and your religion, God forgive your wickedness; if you have forfeited your fame and your country, may your folly do no further mischief. If the last act is yet to do, I who have loved you, esteemed you, reverenced you, and *served* you, I who long thought you the first of womankind, entreat that before your fate is irrevocable I may once more see you. I was, I once was,

"Madam, most truly yours,
"Sam. Johnson.

"July 2, 1784.

"I will come down if you will permit it."

To which Mrs. Thrale replied:

"July 4, 1784.
"Sir,

I have this morning received from you so rough a letter, in reply to one which was both tenderly and respectfully written, that I am forced to desire the conclusion of a correspondence which I can bear to continue no longer. The birth of my second husband is not meaner than that of my first; his sentiments are not meaner; his profession is not meaner, and his superiority in what he professes acknowledged by all mankind. It is want of fortune then that is ignominious; the character of the man I have chosen has no other claim to such an epithet. The religion to which he has always been a zealous adherent will, I hope, teach him to forgive insults that he has not deserved; mine will, I hope, enable me to bear them at once with dignity and patience. To hear that I have forfeited my fame is indeed the greatest insult I ever yet received. My fame is as unsullied as snow, or I should think it unworthy of him who must henceforth protect it. . . .

"Farewell, dear sir, and accept my best wishes. You have always commanded my esteem, and long enjoyed the fruits of a friendship never infringed by one harsh expression on my part during twenty years of familiar talk. Never did I oppose your will, or control your wish; nor can your unmerited severity itself lessen my regard, but till you have changed your opinion of Mr. Piozzi, let us converse no more. God bless you."

To this, Mrs. Thrale *reports* that Dr. Johnson wrote what follows. Only portions of it, however, seem to be in his manner.

"London, July 8, 1784.

"Dear Madam,

"What you have done, however I may lament it, I have no pretense to resent, as it has not been injurious to me; I therefore breathe out one sigh more of tenderness, perhaps useless, but at least sincere.

"I wish that God may grant you every blessing, that you may be happy in this world for its short continuance, and eternally happy in a better state; and whatever I can contribute to your happiness I am very ready to repay for that kindness which soothed twenty years of a life radically wretched. Do not think slightly of the advice which I now present to offer. Prevail upon Mr. Piozzi to settle in England; you may live here with more dignity than in Italy, and with more security; your rank will be higher, and your fortune more under your own eye. I desire not to detail all my reasons, but every argument of prudence and interest is for England, and only some phantoms of imagination seduce you to Italy. . . .

"I am afraid, however, that my counsel is vain, yet I have eased my heart in giving it. . . .

"Your, &c.,

"Sam. Johnson."

"The last time Miss Burney [Mme. D'Arblay] saw Johnson, not three weeks before his death, he told her that the day before he had seen Miss Thrale. 'I then said, "Do you ever, sir, hear from her mother?" "No," cried he, "nor write to her. I drive her quite from my mind. If I meet with one of her letters, I burn it instantly. I have burnt all I can find. I never speak of her, and I desire never to hear of her more. I drive her, as I said, wholly from my mind."' *Birkbeck Hill.*

GLOSSARY

Abroad, out; away from home.

Ah, Monsieur, vous étudiez trop, ah, sir, you study too much.

Après tout c'est un monde passable, after all, this is a passable world.

Assize, session of court.

Aut Cæsar aut nullus, either Cæsar or nobody.

Baubee, the Scotch equivalent of a cent.

Bear-baiting, the setting of fierce dogs on a bear which had been chained to a stake for the purpose; a popular sport in eighteenth century England.

Bedlam, a public insane asylum in London.

Bills, an old-fashioned term for formal notes or letters.

Bow Street, the Bow Street Police Station.

Bulk, "part of a building jutting out." *Johnson: Dictionary.*

Caledonia, a poetic name for Scotland.

Camden's Remains, by William Camden (1551-1623), clergyman, schoolmaster, historian, and antiquarian. "The title complete is *'Remains of a Greater Work concerning Britain, the Inhabitants thereof, their Languages, Names, Surnames, Impresses, Wise Speeches, Poesies, and Epitaphs'*; London, 1605, 4to. The design of this work was to preserve to posterity a great variety of curious things communicated to him while making collections for his *Britannia,* and which he probably thought did not exactly accord with the main object of that more finished work." *George Burnett.*

Captain Macheath, "the principal character in Gay's 'Beggar's Opera'; a gay and dissolute highwayman." *The Century Cyclopedia of Names.*

Chairman, one who carried people in a sedan chair for hire.

Chancery, solicitor in, a lawyer practicing in the Chancery courts—courts originally established to correct the injustices produced by the intricate precedents binding upon all other tribunals. By this time, however, they had become as technical in their rules and as circuitous in their procedure as any judicial body in England.

Character, reputation.

City, the principal business quarter of London. To this the term London was often given in distinction from the resident and pleasure quarters of the town, which were called *Westminster.* Temple Bar was the dividing point between the two.

Civilian, one who studies, teaches, or practices Civil Law.

Civility, civilization.

Closet, private study.

Comment! je ne le crois pas, etc., why, I do not believe it! That is not Mr. Garrick, that great man!

Common law, legal principles, usages, and rules which have grown up without actual acts of the legislative body.

Commoner, one without a fellowship or scholarship.

Commons, a group of law buildings near St. Paul's Cathedral, London. They included apartments for lawyers and courts for the trial of ecclesiastical and admiralty cases.

Conge d'elire, "the king's permission royal to a dean and chapter in time of vacation to choose a bishop." *Johnson: Dictionary.* "The permission to elect is a mere form. The choice is practically made by the Crown." *Bouvier's Law Dictionary.*

Covin, "a deceitful agreement between two or more to the hurt of another." *Johnson: Dictionary.*

Crabs, crab apples.

Cui bono man, one whose acts are based on ultimate personal benefit.

Currat lex, let the law take its course.

De non existentibus et non apparentibus eadem est ratio, reason takes the same attitude toward that for which there is no evidence and that which doesn't exist.

Discover, reveal.

Dissipated, distracted, wasted on a multiplicity of trifles.

Doubt, suspect.

Dulcedo . . . natale solum, charm . . . native soil.

Elegans formarum spectator, "a nice observer of the female form." *Croker.*

Express, a special messenger or his message.

Factor, the manager of one's estate.

Fellow, one privileged to remain at an English college for independent study after receiving his Master of Arts degree; and given a substantial income for his support. The fellowship was usually, if not always, a life appointment, forfeited only by marriage.

Feudal system, the system by which men were obliged to render personal or military service to some superior as a condition of possessing land. The king demanded such service from his great vassals; they of lesser men, and so on down to the humblest possessors of land. This system flourished from the ninth or tenth century until the sixteenth, and has left its mark on later civilization.

Final causes, first causes or origins.

First motion, the motive to begin.

Flambeau, a flaming torch used to light people into and out of the theater.

Forsitan et nostrum, etc., perhaps our names shall be mingled with these. In the second version Goldsmith stresses **istis** ("these").

Frank, until 1840, English postage was ten times what it is today, and was paid by the receiver, not the sender. Members of parliament and high officials by the use of their autographs (or *frank*) could send matter free. This they were often asked to do for the letters of friends.

Freni strictio, drawing in the [horse's] reins.

Gazette, the official organ of the English government.

Γηράσκειν διδασκόμενος, to go on learning through old age.

Gretna Green, a Scotch village near the border, long notorious as the resort of eloping couples who could not comply with the requirements of the English marriage laws.

High-church man, one who lays great stress on the authority of the clergy and on the power and significance of the ceremonies of the Church of England.

Il a bien fait, etc., he has done right, my Prince; you began it.

Il y a beaucoup de puérilités dans la guerre, there are many childish acts in war.

In culpa est animus, qui se non effugit usquam, "but the mind is most in fault, which ne'er leaves self behind." *Horace, trans. by John Conington.*

Incredulus odi, a phrase from Horace, meaning "I am too disgusted to believe."

Ingenium ingens, etc.
"Underneath this rude, uncouth disguise,
A genius of extensive knowledge lies."
Horace, trans. by Francis.

Jacobite, a follower of the House of Stuart, after it was driven from the throne; from the Latin *Jacobus* for *James;* the first Stuart to be exiled being *James II.*

J'ai fait dix mécontents et un ingrat, I have caused ten people to be discontented, and one to be ungrateful.

Jeu d'esprit, witticism.

Kings Bench, a famous prison in the Thrales' quarter of the town.

La théorie des sensations agréables, the theory of agreeable sensations.

Le vainqueur du vainqueur de la terre, the conqueror of the earth's conqueror.

L'homme d'épée, soldier, swordsman.

Liberty and necessity, free-will and predestination.

Lincoln's Inn, one of the famous *Inns of Court*; that is, one of the halls of residence for lawyers and law-students, and invested with certain rights and privileges regarding the admission of lawyers to the bar and the disbarring of unworthy members of the profession.

Living, the income granted by law to an English clergyman who is appointed to a parish or to any ecclesiastical office.

Ma foi, etc., in truth, sir, our happiness depends on the manner in which our blood circulates.

Maladie du pais [pays], homesickness.

Manifestum habemus furem, we have the rascal caught in the act.

Manor, "a tract of land originally granted by the king to a person of rank. . . . Originally, . . . it was not a bare tract of land, but a complex, made up of land and of a great part of the agricultural capital that worked the land, men and beasts, plows and carts, forks and flails." *Bouvier's Law Dictionary.*

Mass House, an ultra-protestant term for a Roman Catholic church.

Mediocribus, etc.,
"But God and man and lettered post denies
That poets ever are of middling size."
Ars Poetica, trans. by Francis.

Mira cano, sol occubuit, nox nulla secuta est, I sing wonders; the sun has set, and yet night has not come.

Mollia tempora fandi, agreeable times to speak.

N. S. New Style, according to the method of reckoning dates adopted by parliament in 1750, by which eleven days were dropped out of the calendar.

Natural philosophy, natural science, and the scientist's mental and moral philosophy connected with it.

Nemo sibi vivat, no one may live unto himself.

New kinds of air, nitrogen and other gases newly discovered.

Nil admirari, an admonition not to wonder.

Non est tanti, it's nothing much.

North Britain, Scotland.

O. S., see N. S.

Old Bailey, a short narrow street in the criminal quarter. On it were Newgate and the *Sessions House* or Central Criminal Court. Near it and near Fleet Street was the prison called The Fleet. The term Old Bailey was also applied to a London prison for minor offenders.

Omne ignotum pro magnifico est, everything that is unknown is considered wonderful.

Orandum est ut sit mens sana in corpore sano, "pray to have a sound mind in a sound body"; or as Johnson has paraphrased it in his *Vanity of Human Wishes*:
"Pour forth thy fervors for a healthy mind,
Obedient passions, and a will resigned."

Ordinary, a table d'hote, or general table.

Os homini sublime, etc.:
"Man looks aloft and with erected eyes,
Beholds his own hereditary skies."
Ovid, trans. by Dryden.

Pactolus, a small river of Asia Minor, celebrated for the gold to be found in its sandy bottom.

Pantheon, a large domed building, consisting of a spacious rotunda for promenading, and fourteen public rooms. It was first opened in 1772 and was used for concerts, masquerades, and other entertainments. The stir it made was great but brief.

Pars magna fuit, he had a great part.

Parts, abilities.

Pass ours, surpass ours.

Patriot, "it is sometimes used for a factious disturber of the government." *Johnson: Dictionary, 4th ed. 1773.*

Physic, medicine.

Plantation, grove of trees.

Pomponius Mela de Situ Orbis, Pomponius Mela's *Concerning the Situation of the Earth.* P. Mela, who lived during the first century A. D., was the earliest Roman geographer.

Public school, any large, heavily endowed school.

Qui spatium vitae extremum inter munera ponat, "who counts the closing period of life as one of [Nature's] gifts.

Quo clamor vocat et turba faventium, "whither calls the loud approving throng." *Horace, trans. by F. W. Newman.*

Reformed, Scotch Presbyterians and others of their general way of thinking.

Romæ Tibur amem, ventosus Tibure Romam:
"Restless as air, from Rome to Tibur fly,
Then O for Rome, dear Rome; at Tibur sigh."
Trans. by Sir Theodore Martin.

Rose, adjourned.

St. Paul's churchyard, the irregular space, lined with unpretending shops and lodgings, which surrounded St. Paul's Cathedral and burial ground. No more than a narrow lane in one place; in another it opened out into a little square. Several of the booksellers had their shops here.

Se'nnight, week.

1745, a year in which the Stuart claimant to the British throne invaded England.

Sh' apprens t'etre fif, I'm learning to be gay.

Sit anima mea cum Langtono, may my soul be with Langton's.

Te teneam moriens deficiente manu, let me in dying hold you by my trembling hand.

Thirty-nine Articles, the principal creed of the Church of England. To it the students of Oxford and Cambridge were obliged to subscribe their assent before they could graduate.

Un gentilhomme est toujours gentilhomme, a gentleman is always a gentleman.

Un politique aux choux et aux raves, a politician in regard to cabbages and turnips.

Usher, assistant teacher in a school.

Vails, tips.

Vis inertiae, force of inertia.

Vulgar, the, ordinary people; the populace.

Walled garden, for fruit trees trained against the wall so as to give them both the heat of the sun and the heat of the reflecting wall.

Want, lack.

Warren, any hunting preserve for small game that was established by special permission of the king.

Westminster, that part of London which contained the fashionable residences, the parks, the law courts, and the theaters; more especially, the seat of Parliament and the law courts.

Westminster Hall, a spacious hall in London in which the law courts met.

Yeomanry, the owners of very small parcels of land. They could serve on juries and perform other functions equally modest in the government of their respective localities.

INDEX